HISTORY of the 47th GEORGIA
VOLUNTEER INFANTRY REGIMENT
CONFEDERATE STATES ARMY

2013 ©William A. Bowers, Jr.

ALL RIGHTS RESERVED

No part of this book may be produced in any form, by photocopying or by any electronic or mechanical means, including information storage or retrieval systems, without permission in writing from both the copyright owner and the publisher of this book, except for the minimum words needed for review.

ISBN: 978-0-9846536-5-2
Library of Congress Control Number: 2013907458
Published by

Swampfox Publishing Company

Edited by Deloris W. Bowers and Barbara Sachs Sloan
Interior Design by KathleenWalls
Cover Design by William A. Bowers, III
Cover photograph of the 47th Georgia Volunteer Infantry flag
Courtesy of the Capital Flag Collection
Georgia Secretary of State

Second Edition, April 2019
Printed in USA for Swampfox Publishing Company

HISTORY
of the
47th GEORGIA
VOLUNTEER INFANTRY REGIMENT

CONFEDERATE STATES ARMY

Compiled by:

WILLIAM A. BOWERS, JR.

ACKNOWLEDGEMENT AND THANKS:

The Compilation of a Regimental History is a long and arduous task. The nearly 20 years taken to bring this work to this point is worth all the toil to make this information available to those interested in this "Storied Regiment." There are so many people who have aided my research and given encouragement to me in this quest. There are too many to name them all.

Most of all I need to thank my wife, Deloris for standing by me in thick and thin, always there when I would bog down in research. She and my son Billy have been in so many Libraries, Cemeteries and on so many Battlefields with me as I attempted to understand facts surrounding the events, locate where my ancestors had been and their part in the battles. As I had a grandfather, some uncles and many cousins in the 47th Regiment so did she. I also want to thank Billy for keeping me up to date with my computer. My membership in the Sons of Confederate Veterans was predicated upon my Second great grandfather who lost an arm while fighting with the 47th.

I wish to thank my fellow members in the Appling Grays Camp #918 Sons of Confederate Veterans for helping me get started and encouraging me along the way. Also I would like to thank the members of the Tattnall Invincibles and the Robert Toombs Camps of the SCV.

My Cousin Derwood Tootle who helped me to locate the Battle Flag of the 47th that was lost and assisted me in eventually getting it returned to the State of Georgia Flag Collection from the State of South Carolina. I owe him many thanks.

Dan Bell of the South Carolina State Parks Service for the help in reconstructing the Battle of Rivers Bridge, South Carolina and all the information and data he shared with me.

My Aunt Mary Ketus Holland and my Uncle Zachry Grantham Holland who researched the Family Genealogies and marked David Rivers

Tuten's grave at Wesley Chapel Church in Bacon County, Georgia.

My debt is great to these and all the others that have assisted at the State Parks and National Parks I have visited and all of the patient librarians and government officials who have put up with my inquiries.

Special thanks to my eighth grade Georgia History Teacher, Mrs. Carolyn McCall, for peaking my interest in the "War For Southern Independence" and for taking our class to Atlanta to expose us more.

Thanks to my cousin, friend and author, E. Randall Floyd, who shared my beginnings of interest in the 2nd grade as we would draw Confederate Soldiers in battle on scraps of paper "way back then."

Last but not least the descendants of the 47th soldiers who have shared information, photos and data with me.

Table of Contents

Introduction	VIII
The Memoirs of Captain Benjamin S. Williams Adjutant 47th Georgia Volunteer Infantry	1
Chronological History of the Forty-seventh Georgia Regiment	264
Field, Staff and Band of the 47th Regt., Ga. Vol. Infantry Company Commanders	333
Roster of Company A, Chatham County	335
Roster of Company B, Randolph County	337
Roster of Company C, Bulloch County	339
Roster of Company D, Screven County	340
Roster of Company E, Bryan, Chatham and Effingham Counties	342
Roster of Company F, Appling County	343
Roster of Company G, Tattnall County	345
Roster of Company H, Glynn County	347
Roster of Company I, Effingham County	349
Roster of Company K, Bulloch County	351
Alphabetical Roster of the Regiment from the National Archives	352
Thanks	b
The Flag Returned	e
Index of Captain Ben Williams' Letters and Articles	g
Bibliography	i

Photographs

The 47th Georgia Regimental flag made in 1862	I
Captain Benjamin S. Williams, Adjutant of the 47th Regiment	X
Captain Benjamin S. Williams with flag	259
Ben Williams and Belle Williams Gautier with the 47th Georgia Flag.	260
Four Generations of Williams	261
The Second 47th Georgia Regimental Flag made by the Ladies of Charleston South Carolina	262
Colonel Gilbert William Martin Williams	263
Surgeon Stiles Kennedy	322
Sergeant David Rivers Tuten Company F	323
Private Samuel Deen Company F	324
Lt. Jeremiah Tootle Company G.	325
Private Jacob Oliver Company G	326
Sergeant Simon Brewton Company G	227
Private Sherrod Willis Company H	228
Private Mathias Quinn Company F	229
Private James A. Williams Company F	230
UCV Reunion at Spring Branch Church, Appling County	231
UCV Reunion at Reidsville, Tattnall County	232
The 47th Georgia Flag returned to the State of Georgia	d

INTRODUCTION

The brave and heroic men that fought, bled and died for the cause of the Confederate States of America were unequaled in the performance of their duty. For four years they held at bay the most powerful and well-equipped army in the world. This under-fed, under-equipped sometimes rag-tag army fought on. They would have followed their leaders still despite privation and starvation and being outnumbered two to one on most occasions. There has been altogether too little of their history preserved for posterity.

When I became interested in retracing the footsteps of my Confederate ancestors, this fact became painfully obvious. As I searched for information on units such as the Forty-seventh Regiment, Georgia Volunteer Infantry, only small bits and pieces emerged. A paragraph here and a page there was the extent of their traces that were available. The more research that was performed the more the story of the regiment began to unfold. I realized what I needed to do was to compile all the small fragments that I had been able to uncover into a comprehensive history so that those who were to follow in the search would have the history of this valiant and much campaigned regiment readily available. It seemed that wherever the thick of the battle was, you would find the Forty-seventh Georgia. This regiment was called upon to perform some very difficult missions and their valor was quite evident. There leaders were courageous and without fear, leading their troops in an exemplary fashion.

To my great-great-grandfather, Sergeant David Rivers Tuten of Company F and my uncles, Privates Phillip Herndon, Daniel Miles, Willis Miles of Company F and all my cousins that were in the regiment I dedicate this work. It is to honor their sacrifice and dedication that this history is submitted.

Captain Ben Williams was a prolific writer in the area newspapers where he lived. The following is his memoirs as transcribed by the author/compiler. The writings have been arranged to give a chronology of the events of the war as he witnessed them. This is not a complete collection of his works that were published as he retold the events that were written earlier in later letters and articles. First are the writings in the Charleston Sunday News and Courier and related papers beginning before the turn of the century until the first decade of 1900. The second set of selections is from the Hampton County Guardian written a decade or so later.

Captain Williams was active in the community where he lived until his death which is reported at the end of the published articles

WILLIAM A. BOWERS, JR.

Benjamin Stuart Williams
June 25, 1843 - May 13, 1931

Benjamin Stuart Williams was born June 25, 1843 in Barnwell County, South Carolina and was a son of Gilbert William Martin Williams who was a Baptist minister and physician. Rev. Williams moved along with his family from Barnwell County, South Carolina to Liberty County, Georgia in 1857 or 1858. G.W.M. Williams was an ardent Secessionist and a signer of the Georgia ordinance of secession. He also organized a company of infantry and was elected colonel of the 47th Georgia Infantry Regiment when it was formed at Camp Davis in Guyton, Georgia. The regiment was the one in which both of his sons would eventually serve, Benjamin as a captain and adjutant, and Abraham as Quarter-master.

When Benjamin was a young boy his health was described as delicate and his physique slender. His parents trained him in out-of-doors activity including and especially horseback riding. He was known for his riding ability in the neighborhood. He was also known for his love of reading, especially history which is obvious in his later writings.

Sergeant Benjamin S. Williams was mustered into the Confederate Army in April 1861 in Savannah as a member of a company of the 25th Georgia Infantry Regiment. After a few months he received orders to report to the 47th Georgia Volunteer Infantry. He was commissioned a lieutenant and was to be the Adjutant of the Regiment. At 18 years of age he joined the 47th, in which he served for the duration of the war was promoted to Captain and was a Brevet Major at the conclusion of the war after the battle at Bentonville. He and some others in the Regiment did not surrender. Nor did they allow their flag to be surrendered. He tucked the 47th Georgia flag under his saddle and rode west to join the Army of Trans-Mississippi.

When the war was over he went into the timber business through the help of a Savannah merchant. In November 1867 he married Miss Josephine Richardson of South Carolina. They resided in the Beaufort District of South Carolina.

Benjamin served as a member of the South Carolina legislature and once ran for the state senate but was defeated. For a time he served as the commander of the Confederate Soldiers' Home in Columbia, South Carolina. During Reconstruction he led a company of "Red Shirts." He was known for his oratory skills and debate skills. When Hampton County was formed, he was appointed its first auditor.

Captain Ben was a prolific writer and his Reminisces of the War Between the States published in several newspapers were very popular in that section of the state. He was active in the Memorial Ceremonies at Rivers Bridge where the 47th had played a prominent role.

His writings compile the best historical information on the 47th Georgia Volunteer Infantry and the actions in which they were participants.

William A. Bowers, Jr.

Captain Benjamin S. Williams, Adjutant, 47th Georgia

Captain Ben S. Williams and The Flag

*D*ear Madam – and as I feel – Kinswoman
Your letter and the Kodak of our old flag reached me safely.

I was sincerely glad to hear from you and derived real pleasure in viewing the excellent picture of the star-studded old battle flag of our old Regiment.

To you I feel I – we, are indebted for the happy thought of portraiture of the old Ensign; A thought, a design conceived in love and executed in patriotic fealty and undying affection. I thank the God of my fathers, the great God of hosts, that the tattered old battle flag of the "47th Ga." has true lovers besides myself, these who, remaining on the world's stage longer than I, will cherish its sacredness in memory and bequeath to sons and daughters the love, the admiration, the pride of and in the "story of the glory" of the men who followed where it waved, in camp, on the march and on the field where beneath its folds as the Standard of their Cause, they struck and sacrificed "all save honor" in defence of their rights and all that was and is nearest, dearest and most sacred on earth.

Representing, now, nothing on God's green earth save sentiment, yet truly – and heartfully – do you conjecture "That there is much written in the – "meshes of its fabric and beneath the braid of its decoration" – its shiverd staff, its stained folds, its riven decoration – Much to many who have forever passed away; much to a few who remain, yet.

As I have before stated my mother made the flag and presented it to the 47th Regt – My father then Colonel commanding. It was received on behalf of the Regt. by a gallant officer and an eloquent orator: John D. Ashton, Captain of Co D - 47th Regt. His speech, in accepting, was truly splendidly eloquent. His home was in, or near Sylvania, Screven County.

My wife and daughters tell me my mother stated that at the time of: the making of the flag she found it impossible to obtain such material as she desired and, consequently, had to resort to the use of two shawls, of different colors. These with some white silk she had, she used. The fringe or cords and tassels, I think, was taken from some pieces of' old furniture – sofas or curtains, and the tinsel she purchased it in Savh. She there, had made – in Savh. – a handsome staff, spear-shaped with gilded point. I think this staff was shivered and lost at Chickamauga Sept. 20th – Sunday – 1863.

When it came time to save the flag, it was tied to a small, peeled oak "sapling". My mother is still alive though living far from me. She is becoming quite feeble. Up to two or three years ago she was quite active and retained – apparently, full possession of all her mental faculties – keen perception, strong mind and retentive memory. She will be 88 years of age in April next, and will soon die with a heart filled with love of the past – our history, record, and tradition, and loyalty to a Cause for and in which she suffered as she and her God, only, know.

I wish I could give you the names of all the members of the Regt. but that, now, is impossible. No one could do that. In order to so do it would be absolutely essential to have – 1st a muster-roll of all the "Field and Staff" Officers. This I could accomplish – 2nd, there would have to be complete Muster rolls of the ten Companies, officers and men, composing the Regiment, in existence for reference. They are not, and can never, by any living man be made up again. I have two or three of these muster-rolls in my possession and forward you one of Co "D" Company made up, principally, I think in Screven Co. I enclose this one for your inspection that you may understand what I mean by a complete Muster-roll of a company. Ten of these – in consolidated form made up the muster roll of the Regiment. Now in sharp and active service in the field we could not make up the rolls, but as it was necessary for the Regimental Commander to be cognizant of his force, the fighting strength of his command a daily "morning report" had to be made by each Co. Commander – if ever so hastily – and handed in to "Regimental Head Quarters" for purpose above stated. I have a number of the hastily made field reports and enclose you that of Co "I," Capt. Wilson. This gives you many of the names of members of the Co. at the time of its rendering. I can't say when as it is not dated though certainly not prior to 1863. Now, as to number and dates of engagements in which the 47th took part I will supply you as nearly as I can from memory and such data as I have. There shall be no errors save, mayhap, those of omissions.

Our first fight was an assault by the Regiment, unsupported, on an overwhelming number of the Federals entrenched and under cover of fire from their "gunboats" on the Stono River, James Island, So. Ca. June 10th, 1862. "Somebody blundered." The advance was ordered by a gallant but inexperienced General, the assault was led by a gallant and impetuous Colonel. The men "did but do and die". A writer, (unknown to me) of late years, writing of this engagement in the Charleston News & Courier speaks of it as "the magnificent charge of Col Williams' Regiment where 60 Georgians go down in twenty minutes." Capt. Williams, Co "C" of Bulloch County was killed here.

Six days later we were again engaged, June 16th, Secessionville, So. Ca. Here we lost a splendid officer Lieutenant Graham of Co. "B". I enclose you copy of old Charleston paper mentioning our first battle June 10th.

History of the 47th Georgia Volunteer Infantry, CSA

During the remainder of 1862 and until April 1863 We did coast guard duty on the coast of N. C., S. C. and Ga. – from Topsoil Sound near Wilmington to Savh. guarding coast, erecting batteries and fortifications, etc. This labor was very hard and demoralizing to the volunteer soldiery. See remarks of mustering officer, on Muster roll as to appearance, etc. April 1863 ordered to Mississippi. Next fighting at Jackson, Miss – 9 days-siege in July 1863. Here our loss was considerable, fighting continuous, starving "ditto!"

Our next "battle was at Chickamauga Sept 20th all of day, Sunday. Then Missionary Ridge, November 24th. In the two last named battles our loss was heavy. Record in my possession shows that at Chickamauga we lost in a charge, Sunday morning, 87 – officers and men. Of the killed was the gallant and splendid lst Lieutenant Carswell Co "D" of Screven County. He was shot and fell close by my side. He fell quickly in front of me and I stepped across his handsome, lifeless form. Some time after battle of Missionary Ridge and Lookout Mountain, Johnston's Army went into winter quarters near Dalton Ga. In spring of 1864 Sherman began his march through Georgia.

Now, I can not enumerate the engagements of our Regt., the 47th, with the enemy or give dates. Often we were engaged in skirmishes with Sherman's troops which did not really amount to what we termed battles. Yet they were warm and hotly contested fights and lost as many lives. (See Barnes: History of U.S.) Our main battles, hardest engagements, were – Resacca, Oostanaula, Kennesaw Mountain, Atlanta. These dates, I have not at hand. After battle of Atlanta the 47th Ga. and 32nd Ga. Regts. were detached from the main Army and hurried to Charleston, S. C. The Federals were massing a heavy force on John's Island for an attack, by land, on Charleston. We reached Charleston and assaulted the enemy's works at 3 o'clock in the morning winning a splendid victory and driving the Federal force from the Island – July 1864. Our next battle was at Honey Hill, S. C. November 1864. At this battle, of the wounded were Major J. G. Cone, and Capt. Dedge, Co. F. Next, in November 1864, at Tulifinny. Here of the killed was Capt. P. C. Sheffield Co. K. of Bulloch County.

This ended our fighting in 1864, and reduced the number of men in Regt to about 250. In Febr'y 1865 we made, a last stand in So. Ca. along the line of the Salkahatchie River. Here, again, the 47th bore the hardest of the fight and lost heavily. Of the severely wounded here was Capt. J. C. Thompson Co "C", a son of the former Editor of the Savannah Morning News. We were pressed back into N. C. and in March were in the battle of Averysboro. Finally, March 21st, 1865, the remnant, the fragment, the remaining few of the 47th Ga. fought, as gallantly and, as desperately as they had ever fought, their last battle at Bentonville N. C.

Oh! Well do I remember that dire day. Many of our gallant leaders and brave men were no more. Scarcely 200 strong the 47th formed in battle lines. With hope dead the dark shadows of despair and ruin, like a funeral pall, enveloping us, freely as ever was flung the old flag and proudly as ever did it wave. As steadily as I ever saw troops move did they advance upon the embattlen point designated for their assault. "Cannon to right of us, Cannon in front of us" volleying and thundering: overwhelming numbers of brave Federal troops opposed to us. Verily, it seemed to me our day of doom. But steadily did those men move forward" and yet floated the flag in clouds of smoke that seemed to issue from the very gates of hell. Men were falling but soon we were at close range and began to deliver our fire, and now the battle "trebly thundering shook the gale". Broken, bleeding old 47th still in the front.

It appeared to me that no man of the Regt could live and come out but that all must go down unless we could dislodge and beat back the serried columns in our front. The 32nd. Ga. Regt. was immediately on our right, in line and fighting despately to hold their advanced position. Brv't Brig. Gen'l Geo P. Harrison commanding our Brigade finding the fight of the 32nd (of which he was formerly commander, as Colonel), losing ground, sent a young officer of his staff to Col. Pruden, commanding, 32nd, with orders to advance his line if it cost him every man in the Regt-. I had been associated with the young officer while serving, myself, on Staff of Harrison. He had shown me some pieces of gold coin and a very handsome watch and asked that if he fell, I, if living, should take coin and watch from his person and send to address of his mother. On his errand to Col. Pruden he passed me and halting for an instant said "My God this is awful". I was at the moment at the center of our Regt, very near the flag. Fearing that the right of the 47th might also yield ground I ran as hastily as I could amid the blinding smoke to that point our right. Before reaching our right I noticed, as I ran, among the dead, directly in my way, the lifeless body of the young and gallant staff officer. I could not, for a moment, pause. I knew that faltering and confusion there, meant annihilation, extermination, and I resolved in my mind and heart to go forward to victory or down to death then with the remaining few with whom I had fought in every engagement in which our flag had floated save Missionary Ridge and Johns' Island, from first to last.

This was our last battle. On that field it floated in victory over the remaining few. Soon after, it was furled.
You know the rest. (words torn off) imperfect sketch. It is probably the last I shall ever write.

I send you likeness of my Mother (as you request) also my father. I thought you would like to see the organizer and first Commander of the Regiment. I know is dear to you. I send you a few old papers in which I wrote of the 47th.
Sometimes by request, sometimes just because the "spirit moved me". You

can return same with likenesses.

Now as to other matters mentioned in your letter "Nil desperaudum." You shall have a copy of "The Annals of Newberry" by Judge O'Neal. And I shall aid you in your genealogical research. So surely as the sun shines (and it is a beautiful day of bright sunshine). No, don't advertise. I have been slow, but did you only know the man. Many things I've had to do: business, work – but this for you is pleasure. I shall perform my promise.

I regret to learn of your Mother's feebleness. Trust that she is better and that you are feeling better. Hope old Ensign Wakefield is well. My regards to the Doctor and family. With best wishes

Very truly

Ben S. Williams

Since writing in searching for other data.

I "came across" my reports of casualties in 47th Regt. in battles of Chickamauga and Oostanaula. These were published, I see, in Savh Morning News of date, Sept. 26th 1863 and May 16th 1864. I find reported 23 killed and 64 wounded some mortally – Sunday Sept 20th/63, and 6 killed and 26 wounded some mortally, May 15, /64. I can, from this report give you casualties in Co. I feel that same would be interesting to you all.

"List of Casualties in CO "I", 47th Ga. Capt. S A. Wilson,"

Chickamauga, Sunday Sept 20th 1863
Killed – Private D. A. Metzger.
Mortally wounded – Privates F. Usher and W B Nungazer.

Severely wounded – Sergt B B Dasher and Privates G Arnsdorff , F, S. Mercer, C C Bebee, S C Elkins, D W Edward, W H Morgan. W. J. Crosby. Color Corporal E S Sewell wounded and missing

Oostanaula, May 5th 1864
Lieut. T E Bourquin wounded in knee,
Private D W Edwards mortally wounded and left on field.
W. W. Gnann, seriously in shoulder.
R W Tullis, severely in thigh
These "reports" were copied from reports of (torn off) to Adjutant:
By Adjt, consolidated and (words torn off).

The Charleston Sunday News and Courier, Charleston, South Carolina, August 31, 1913

A CONFEDERATE SOLDIER'S MEMOIRS
(By Captain Ben S. Williams, Brunson, S. C.)

The dawning of the morning of the 15th of August 1864 marked the beginning of my 60 days absence from my command and stay in hospital and on post duty in Macon, Ga. The latter part of that period was a single and only oasis in the strenuous active service of my four years of army life, an epoch in my experience never by me to be forgotten.

Stepping out of school a slender, delicate boy into the ranks of the mustering squadrons – nebulae of the splendid armies of the Southern Confederacy at the beginning of the war, composed of the ready, anxious volunteers – about six months of hard, active training in different branches of the service on the field and in forts, under the strain and stress of which I came oftener than once collapsing, then to the front and two and a half years of marching and suffering in heat and cold, starving and fighting "in season and out of season" participating in every engagement, skirmish and battle in which my command took part with never a day's furlough save leave of absence tendered me by Major Gen John C. Breckinridge in 1863, to accompany and to return to the front the military escort detailed by him to escort my father's remains to our home for burial.

I had been tenderly nursed and cared for by the blessed "women of the war" in Macon after weeks of racking pains and fever with days and nights alike made miserable by suffering came gentle convalescence and hours peaceful rest. Up and on light post duty in the city, my environment was rendered most pleasing and delightful by reason of care in my behalf on the part of an hitherto unknown splendid and wealthy kinswoman, who had discovered me in the hospital, claimed me as her kinsman and acted not alone the part of the good Samaritan, but the part of a tender, loving mother. By reason of her interest and influence the delights of my life and surroundings were made sufficiently pleasing to warrant that conception on my part that I had suddenly passed from an extended period of baneful existence in war and what Gen Sherman said war was into enjoyment for a season, brief though it be, of exquisite delights of a blissful, beautiful paradise of social joys and festive pastime.

I was really enjoying much of the pleasure pictured forcefully in the imagination of the Mohammedan warrior who goes gladly in from the battlefield to the Elysian gardens where are fountains and music and moonlight and roses where sylvan dells and sequestered bowers sport rosy slyphs and sweet houris in all their charming and feminine loveliness. The main point of difference was in my favor, in that in order to realize the Turk must first be in battle slain while I was realizing and living to fight again.

Occasionally in memory I return to these scenes in the parterre of my life's plane, but when I would gather the withered roses for a garland for memory's tablet I am pricked by the thorns of which we must ever beware when roses are plucked, as I remember the dear friends I have seen around me fall "like leaves in wintry weather." When I remember the eyes that shone in tenderness and truth and trust, now dimmed and gone, when I remember the hearts that were warm and true and faithful, now sad and broken. I turn me sadly from the scene away and reminded that "smiles and tears, the song and the dirge still follow each other like surge upon surge."

Leaves for Active Service

About 11 o'clock at night the 15th day of August, Col Wyley and I sat at opposite sides of a table in the centre of our wall tent home, a candle burning and giving us its flickering light, between us. We had discussed the latest published news and existing conditions generally so far as our information enabled us so to do, when I surprised and displeased my good, close friend and superior officer by suddenly saying:

"Wyley, I am going to join my command without delay."

He started and looking hard at me replied. "The devil, you are! What's the matter? Have you received an almost mortal wound from the stunning kick of an idolized sweetheart?"

"No," I said, "no jesting or anything of that sort. I am feeling almost well again and am sufficiently active and strong to take my place with my command. I greatly, regret to part, with you. Our intimate association here, for the past thirty days has been as ever before, very pleasant to me. I am indebted to you for many kindnesses in danger of stress I would stand by you with all my might, until my latest breath, but after days of deliberation I have concluded that I should not remain longer away when every soldier of our army is needed in the field. I am an officer and though my commission was awarded for service in the field, as you are aware. I feel that if able I should stand again in the ranks in sorest day of our country's need."

Wyley listened restlessly, then said: "See here, we are off duty by ourselves in our own privacy and in all friendliness I say to you that you in this matter are going to act the damned fool."

I replied quickly, "I prefer being called, by my friend, a 'damned fool' to being branded by my conscience a 'damned coward.'"

Col Wyley was an eloquent and astute lawyer. He pleaded eloquently with me to "pause, reflect and stay." "You have done hard, rough, dangerous field service enough," he said, "you have given three years of your life, you have given of your blood, your gallant father gave his life, your widowed mother hopes and prays for your safety as her shield and stay. You are comfortably ensconced here under official assignment to honorable and important duty to our country's cause. Think of the awful carnage through which you have passed time and again, your recent pitiful condition and now your partial recovery; in the name of God and common sense do you purpose to sacrifice all your honorable advantages, cast them to the winds and in a spirit of overwrought patriotism, amounting to fanaticism, again rush in."

"I am deeply grateful, my friend," I said, "for your friendship from which springs your interest and appreciate the same more than you can know, I have fully made up my mind, Col Wyley, I ask to be relieved from further duty to-night that I may tomorrow arrange for my transportation and to bid my friends good-bye."

Rising hastily he replied, "All right, if you've set your head all hell can't turn you. Go ahead, but I suggest that you part with your friends to-morrow with no "au revoirs" but rather with "forever farewell.""

I rose, bowed and said, "Thanks for the suggestion," and without further word retired to our respective couches on our narrow army cots and slept near each other for the last time ever.

Prepares to Start

The day following I carried out my programme. Some of my friends were as surprised at my speedy going as was Col Wyley and his pleading was not the most touching to which I listened on that subject. Declining all invitations for the evening I returned early to my late camp home, that I might spend my last evening alone with my friend and comrade.

I packed my few "belongings" into my saddle roll and got all ready for the early start next morning.

It was getting late and I was alone, Col Wyley being absent. At a late hour I "turned in" for rest and sleep, but could not rest on account of horrid dreams. In the "wee small" hours I dozed off but soon I heard the boom of cannon and crash of rifle fire. I was again back at Chickamauga. I saw Adams' Louisiana brigade again being cut to pieces on our right at the very mouths of the cannon. Again did I see my own gallant regiment stayed in their charge in the face of a blasting, withering fire for the broken North Carolina regiment on our left to rally. I see again my dear friend Carswell, commanding the left color company, drop dead at my feet and the color bearer within reach of my touch go down on my right. Again do I snatch up the colors as we charge again and feel the shaft shattered to splinters above my hands and feel myself going down, down – when I awake with a start and feel my heart beats keeping time in the crashing sound of revelle on base and kettle drums just back of our tent.

Rising and hastily lighting our candle, I looked over at Col Wyley's unoccupied and unrumpled cot-bed. Instantly I felt a quick dash of temper as "discourtesy" flashed through my mind, and I murmured between my teeth, "Wyley is making an ass of himself and may go to ____." I was soon ready to "fall in in full dress," even to a plume, sash and spurs. Taking a hasty glance at myself in Col Wyley's tent mirror, in my boyish vanity, I slapped my hands together and exclaimed, "Richard is himself again."

Taking a hasty, last look at the canvas walls, I threw back the flap of the tent, stepped out and through the grey mist of the morning took my way to the railroad depot. Arriving, I found my train about ready to pull out, while quite a number were going aboard, civilians and a few soldiers. As I neared the steps of the car I felt a hand laid heavily on my shoulder from the rear. Quickly turning, I confronted my quondam friend, Col Wyley. Quick as a man he grasped my right hand and said, "I am due you an apology and am here to render it. I am ashamed of my conduct. I was all out of sorts last evening and feeling as blue as indigo. I shut myself in my room at the Lanier Hotel, but could not sleep, as I was haunted by the most infernal dreams. Forgive me and remember me kindly, for you know not how I love you and esteem you. You are right, but what a pity for you to become food for powder and ball. Your grit is fine, but you are showing damned poor judgment."

The bell rang and the wheels began to move. Throwing left arm around my neck, and placing his face near mine, he murmured, "Good-bye and may God shield and bless you." Springing on to the platform of the moving car, I turned and saluted the gifted, proud, handsome officer who, returning the salute, quickly faced about and I saw him no more during our awful struggle in the closing scenes of the war.

Joins His Command

Arriving at my station of command, I found myself on somewhat familiar ground. They were encamped at Secessionville, James Island, just across from Charleston. Here, on June 16, 1862, occurred the battle of Secessionville, in which very nearly all the troops on the island engaged. In this fight one of the most accomplished officers of my regiment was killed, First Lieut. Graham, of Company B.

Six days before, June 10, my regiment alone, 1,000 strong, fresh, jubilant and eager, but inexperienced, first "dimmed their armor's shine in glorious battle fray," and sealed their fealty in their country's cause by a free libation of blood of some of the best in the regiment, but alas, a fateful day for the strong and proud command with sad result.

We were ordered to proceed through a dense forest bordering the Stono River – in which lay the enemy's gunboats – to find and feel the enemy, landed and intrencehed, and if possible assault. We moved with great difficulty and in battle line, preserving as nearly as possible proper alignment. We did not advance a line of skirmishers in front as we well learned to do later, nor did the enemy have any advance lines in their front, but suddenly we were within short range of their full fire and volley after volley from their light batteries and small arms were poured into our ranks.

The colonel commanding desperately rallied the companies into line, delivered a volley, ordered "Fix bayonets, ready to charge." It was a smoke-choked field, but the men had delivered their fire, were fixing bayonets, heard their leader's voice and saw his sword flash in front; another half a minute and nothing but death would have staved their onslaught, but there came ringing down the line, repeated from company to company commander, "About face – fall back – retreat."

In another minute the two companies were retracing their way through the dense wood, followed by whizzing balls from the field artillery and bursting shells overhead from the overarching fire from the gunboats. The colonel was very loath to leave the field and when surrounded by several officers and almost a dozen men, two of whom quickly fell dead, and entreated to escape, he looked around upon the dead and on seeing the upturned face of Capt. Williams. Williams, Company C and with such anguish as I have seldom witnessed, cried out, "My God, would that I had fallen for these are my men!"

I was with him and urged him to hasten. He was my father! I told him that we would soon all be killed or captured, and stated that I had seen several men leave the right flank of our enemy and move into the woods on our right. We started back at a quick walk. The colonel ordered the eight or ten men around him to hurry forward and join their command, and directed the several officers to move forward as rapidly as possible and aid in reforming the regiment on the edge of the wood.

All obeyed except Capt. Frazier and Capt. Latimer, who kept close beside him, and a young soldier of Capt. Williams Company, C, who reloaded his musket as we went and walked close beside me, we preceding the officers.

"Shoots a "Yankee"

And there in those woods I took my first point blank shot at a Yankee. We had not gone far when we emerged from the woods and tough undergrowth into an open space, a kind of glade not more than perhaps, 50 feet in width and extending about 30 or 40 paces to our right. I was sharply on the lookout for the men who had circled out on our right. As we stepped out into the opening described, three men in blue sprang out from behind trees and one, a sergeant, I saw by his bright red chevrons on sleeve, instead of firing, threw up his arm and called out "Surrender." At the first glimpse of them I snatched the musket from the hands of the young soldier on my left and as the soldier in blue threw up his hand I fired. The poor fellow staggered backward and fell; the other two fired wildly and fled.

We crossed the open space, as several other shots were fired in our direction from the trees on our right. I have often hoped, and do yet sincerely hope, that I wounded and did not kill the sergeant, for he was a brave fellow, as evidenced by the fact that he did not sneakingly fire on us, but attempted our capture.

The gallant Capt. Williams who fell in the fight was not a relative of mine. The Charleston papers published his fall, the Savannah papers copied and stated that it was I, and for a time was placed upon me the unenviable notoriety of being dead. Capt. Williams was not instantly killed: he was taken aboard one of the nearby gunboats, his wounds properly bandaged and he partly restored and there lived about an hour. He requested an officer on the boat to furnish him with a sheet of writing paper, pen and a glass or cup. Paper, pen and glass were brought and he caught some of the blood flowing from a wound not entirely staunched, and dipping his pen in this, wrote a short letter to his wife, only a few lines:

"My Own Dear Wife: I was wounded, captured and am now a prisoner of enemies. Grieve not. I shall very soon be free. This is written with my life's ebbing blood, which I freely shed for my country. God bless you: Good-bye." The letter is probably still in possession of some of the descendants of Capt. Williams.

We were met, placed in position for an expected attack and so held until dark, when we returned to our quarters. Our loss was about 70 men.

A writer, unknown to me, in The News and Courier several years ago, writing of this engagement, said, "Ninety Georgians fell in twenty minutes." Our loss did not exceed 75. I have often wondered what would have been the result had that order for retreat not been sounded. It was given by the Lieutenant colonel of the regiment. For this he was Court-martialed and suspended from rank and pay for twelve months. We were not supported and were sacrificed. (See Gen Johnston Haygood's Memoirs as to gallantry of our attack.)

I think this was the first fight on land around Charleston and the greatest loss of any one regiment in South Carolina.

The above in June 1862. Since, the regiment had been in the front in all the bloody battles of the campaign under Bragg and Johnston in the Army of the West. Our dead rested in the soil of every field from near Vicksburg to Kennesaw, but, "Deo gratias", we escaped Knoxville, Franklin and Nashville, helped save Charleston from Gen Hatch and now August 1864, the remnant of the one thousand – about 250, rank and file – was camped on James Island, ready to fight again, which we soon had to do.

The Sunday News, Charleston, South Carolina – October 15, 1911

MEMOIRS OF A SOLDIER IN WAR BETWEEN STATES

Funeral Rites Over Brave Soldier in Savannah – Encounter with Black Soldiers Wearing Blue Uniforms – When Gen Braxton Bragg "Forced the Issue"

(By Captain B. S. Williams, Brunson, S. C.)

In September 1863, just four months from the time my command marched through the city of Savannah Ga. en route to Jackson, Miss., I was in Savannah again, but apart from my command which was then in Tennessee. The troops garrisoning the city marched with "arms reversed" to the slow steady measure and sad, weird strains of the "dead march" beaten on muffled drums, following a flag-draped, and varnished casket, in which reposed, in full Confederate army uniform, the late colonel of the 47th Georgia Infantry – my father. He who, just four months before, rode as gallantly along those streets at the head of his splendid regiment on his lead to the battlefields of the Army of the West. As sounded Coronach o'er bler of Highland Scottish chief, so was voiced the grief and gloom of the 47th in the language of the fallen colonel's kinsman and comrade Lieut Col Wm P. Ashley:

> "Our chief has fallen; the icy hand of death
> Hath chilled forever the patriot's breath.
> Silent that voice that once midst war's alarms
> Was wont to call his comrades to their arms.
> Unstrung that arm that drew the trusty blade
> When Northern foemen dared our rights invade.
> Oh, would to God that he had lived to see
> His beautiful Southland for which he struck
> So valiantly, redeemed, triumphant, free."

Our division commander, that knightly soldier and chivalrous prince of gentlemen, Major Gen John C. Breckinridge, had given to me leave and passport unlimited and a detail of four men under a non-commissioned officer as escort for his fallen regimental commander to his last resting place in the soil of his "loved Southland."

Witnessing the last sad rites, I with my escort guard, turned my face toward the front, leaving Savannah to return there, not again until after the passage of more than two years. Oh, the changes time wrought in those two years. Merciful is He, our omnipotent Commander, who plans campaigns and would lead us on all life's march; who holds between our present, in which we exist and must act, and our future which we can neither avert, delay or alter, an impenetrable veil through which we cannot peer and beyond which we may not even get "Such glimpse as prophets eye gains on thy depths futurity."

When circumstances again necessitated my going into that city in 1865, I found it thronged with Federal troops, white and black soldiers in blue. My costume on that occasion was my black felt hat with plumes removed, my high army boots, spurs off, my old grey suit with bars and lace ripped from collar and sleeves – my only and entire wardrobe. As I passed and was passed by groups of these white and black "blue soldiers" I could see from the corner of my eye that many of them looked at me most malignantly, though not one white soldier showed any disrespect. As I was passing a building used as an arsenal a young, black negro soldier was on guard at the front on the street. As I neared him, he placed himself squarely at the center of the pavement, causing me to walk past him on the outer edge of the pavement; several other negro soldiers passed the sentinel at about the same time and just then he struck up in bitter tone – "We'll hang Jeff Davis on a sour apple tree." And amid the guffaws that followed another chimed in – same tone and measure – "Yes and every other G__ d___ rebel in the gang." I felt only contempt for the trained and uniformed black brutes who were evidently Southern negros (whose coney pensions I am now helping to pay) but the memories of the recent past come surging to my mind, the tears, sacrifices, supplications and prayers of those at home; the suffering, endurance, blood-shed and death of those in front, there came from my lips, wrung from the very depths of my tortured soul. "My God, our God, why dids't thou forsake us."

At the time of returning to my regiment at the front in 1863, our banners were waving proudly, our armies were invincible. Strong was our faith in the justness of our cause, abiding was our trust in the God of battles and that the noon-tide of our hope, confident were we of ultimate success, which meant to us, not conquest and acquisition, but salvation, freedom, independence, power, national glory and happiness.

> "On the future battle heath
> No eye beheld the ranks of death."

I went forward sanguinely, to aid in weaving the pattern of our army's fair and glowing annals for record in our country's pregnant history. Learning that my regiment was in the vicinity of Resaca, Ga., I made for that point. Arriving there I learned that the 47th was at Lafayette, a small town about 30 miles west. I could get no transportation and had to "foot it." The road led over a rocky mountainous section, skirting the ridge of mountains known as Taylor's Ridge, the distance of about 12 miles, then crossing the Ridge. It was a hard road to travel but the scenery along the route was lovely. Early in the morning of the third day, after leaving Resaca, I reached my command. Our cavalry were skirmishing briskly with the enemy in front. Breckinridge's division was in line of battle. Strong hands grasped mine and words of gladness and welcome welled up from warm hearts to lips of some who were, alas, so soon to lie on battlefields with hearts cold and lips forever sealed. I took my accustomed place and we awaited the expected attack from Federal forces in front.

The day, Friday, September 18, passed without an attack on our lines. Late that evening a circular order from Gen Braxton Bragg, commanding, was read to our troops. This said; "We have twice offered the enemy battle and both times he has refused. Now, trusting in God and the justness of our cause and relying on the bravery of the gallant troops under my command for the result I will force the issue."

Well did we know the import of the closing sentence of that order. Our main line was now considerably advanced, skirmishers deployed and posted in our front, pickets posted in their front and me bivouacked for the night. I noticed that we had moved in the direction of Chattanooga. Early Saturday morning, the 19, we were up, and after eating our last morsel of ration, fell into line and took up our march. Soon we could hear the distant boom of cannon ahead, louder and louder, as tired and hungry, we pushed on. In the early afternoon we began to catch sound of small arms and at 4 o'clock this rattle deepened into continuous rolling volleys, and we knew that Gen Bragg had begun to "force the issue."

The Sunday News, Charleston, South Carolina – October 1, 1911

MEMOIRS OF A SOLDIER IN WAR BETWEEN STATES

From Picket Duty at Savannah to Reinforcing Johnston's Army at Jackson Mississippi – Then on to Vicksburg and Story of Sharp Encounter with the Enemy

(By Captain. B. S. Williams, Brunson, S. C.)

In the early spring of 1863 my regiment was sent to Savannah, Ga., from Topsail Sound, near Wilmington, N. C., for picket and outpost duty around Savannah. This service was very heavy and trying to the health and spirits of the men. Headquarters of the regiment was very near to Forsyth Park, and where now stand the monument to the Confederate dead that part of the regiment off duty held daily our evening dress parade. Hundreds of people came each evening to witness our manoeuvers and hear the martial music of our fine band of negro musicians.

    Of the ten companies of about 100 men each, five companies were on duty at the time; these relieved about every week or ten days by other companies. At each point to be guarded, a company was stationed. Some of these outposts were far advanced in marshy, muddy regions. The spring weather was very warm, sandflies and mosquitoes vastly innumerable, aggressive and very annoying, the water was brackish and warm and the "sick list" consequently large. The companies would go out to those posts more sullenly and reluctantly than to any duty or into danger I ever saw them go. Jim McFall said that "shot for desertion from Proctor's Point" wouldn't a d___ bit of disgrace on any man's head board." Seab Lawrence said " I can't possibly imagine why the H___ anybody wants to keep the Yankees away from there, there is only one single place I ever heard of I would rather help land them." Company D of my regiment was commanded by Capt. Jno. R. Ashton, a brilliant lawyer, eloquent orator and one of the most chivalric gentlemen I ever knew; besides he was a splendid specimen of fine, physical manhood. Company D had been left on one of those dreadful, dreary outposts a little longer than usual on account of some inevitable occurrence. The sun was growing hotter, the water worse and the insectile population more aggressive and savage. By courier who passed daily to and fro between headquarters on the mainland and the picket outposts, Capt. Ashton sent a letter to his colonel (letter now among my war papers.) in which he pleads "for God's sake, my dear colonel, relieve us, leave us not here to die miserably, to perish ingloriously. You know my brave men love you and rely on you. We would rather, at your command, charge the battlement of hell to-day than be tortured here longer than to-morrow."

Ordered to Johnston's Army

About the first of May there came suddenly in the night, like a meteoric flash, from our war department the following order: "Col Williams, commanding the 47th Regiment, Georgia Infantry, Savannah, Ga.:

"You will see that the men of your command are immediately provided with sixty rounds of ammunition to each man and three days' cooked rations. You will report with all possible dispatch with your command, including quartermaster and commissary departments, ordinance and medical stores, to Gen Johnston, commanding, at Jackson, Miss."

The beat of the alarming drum roused up the Camp. Then "there was hurrying to and fro" and mounting in hot haste of couriers to summon the absent companies. In the early morning tents were struck, wagons were loaded and soon all was ready to "fall in." The color guard with the flag of the regiment, double quicked to its accustomed position in our dress parade ground, the ten companies quickly formed on right and left of colors in regimental formation for the last time even on the ground where he had so often formed before – if after a little more than two years from that time the war was over, they the victors, the position theirs – I faced about from a line of blue holding their dress parade on the same ground, while the tears trickled down my cheeks. I am not yet ashamed of those tears.

It was a bright, beautiful spring day in the Forest City. The early morning air was laden with the fragrance of violets and jasmine, and roses bloomed in the snowy whiteness and crimson. Keeping measure with the inspiring strains of the "Bonnie Blue Flag" and "Dixie", rendered by the regimental band, the 47th Georgia Infantry, 800 rifles, marched through the city, past crowded porches and thronged balconies along the streets leading to the Central Railroad depot. Swinging gait, easy regular stride and even dress. Proudly at the head of the command rode the gallant colonel commanding, with his staff officers near. Gaily above the line floated the "Starry Cross." On reaching the depot we found our train of cars ready. Halting, fronting, dressing on the colors and ordering arms, we faced, it appeared to me, the entire population of the city of Savannah, who had come to see us off and who looked for the last time on the "Gallant 47th" as the command had been named. We were soon "entrained" and amid smiles and tears and waving handkerchiefs another of Georgia's splendid commands went forward to "Illustrate Georgia."

"Fre long to be trodden like the grass,
Which now beneath them, but above shall grow.
In its next verdure, when this firey mass
Of living valor, rolling on the foe,
And being with high hope, shall moulder cold and low

Gen Breckinridge

After a wearisome journey prolonged by tedious delays, we reached the capital city of Mississippi. While stores were being unloaded and the regiment getting ready for formation, I was ordered to report our arrival to Gen Johnston and inform him that the colonel would very soon call and report officially. I was directed by the provost marshal to Gen Johnston's headquarters. I rode rapidly there, dismounted and passing a sentinel at the gate, who presented arms, was met on the plaza by a pert, young officer with insignia of rank of Lieutenant. With most pompous manner and haughty tone he asked, "What is your pleasure?" I said, "To see Gen Johnston." He said, "Gen Johnston is out of the city and Gen John C. Breckinridge is in command here." "Then", I said, "I wish to see Gen Breckinridge." "For what purpose," he asked. "To report to him," I replied. "Report what?" he demanded. Angered by his rude conduct, I replied, "That which I am ordered only to the general commanding without any reference to you." As he turned from me abruptly, Gen Breckinridge came to the door. I saluted and made my report to him. Returning my salute, he replied: "I am pleased to learn of the arrival your command. We have been on the lookout for you for the past 48 hours." Gen Breckinridge detained me for some time with questions as to fighting strength, kind of arms, length and nature of former service, engagements, etc. and finally dismissed me with the message, "Tell the colonel he may proceed directly to camp, pitch tents, rest his men and prepare for inspection tomorrow."

Moving Toward Vicksburg

A courier was sent with me and pointed out our place for encampment in a wood just outside the city and near the Pearl River. Here we remained throughout May and June and labored on the fortifications around the city. Troops were constantly arriving from various points and July 1 Johnston's force was estimated from fifteen to twenty thousand. About the first of July this force moved in the direction of Vicksburg. Gen Johnston's object was to cross the Big Black River and attack Grant's army in the rear. Grant, with a large force, was then besieging Vicksburg. Reaching the river about dark, we camped upon the bank. During the night we learned of Pemberton's surrender and of Grant's movement in our direction toward Jackson. Our troops were aroused, faced about and, as

"The King of France, with forty thousand men,
Marched up the hill, then marched down again"

We began a hurried forced march back to Jackson. That march was awful. The weather was intensely hot, the roads very dry and the clouds of dust along the line of march suffocating. There were few wells, springs or streams of water on our way. The citizens were using cisterns. Some of these were drained by the famishing troops.

I rode a short way off the line of march to where a large and fierce looking woman stood guard over her cistern, and offered her $10 to fill my canteen with water. She took the bill, looked at it, rolled it up and deliberately put it in her pocket saying: "I've a durned good mind to keep the money to pay for what you fellers drunk 'tother day." I assured her I hadn't drunk any. "Yes but" she said "you are an officer, and if you can't influence your men from taking things, you ain't worth a cuss, and oughtn't to be no officer." Bowing low, I told her she was right, and that no lady could express it stronger, whereupon she filled my canteen and offered me a drink extra. Many a poor fellow on this march fell by the wayside and died or was captured by the pursuing Federals. I began my help to the men of my command by taking an exhausted soldier up behind me on my horse until he was rested enough to walk some: then I would dismount and put two men on my horse and I would walk, and so helped quite a number to hold out to reach Jackson. It was pitiable to see some poor fellows fall and hear their sobs and moans because of their utter helplessness.

Grant's Warm Reception

On reaching Jackson, the fortifications were hastily mounted and scarcely had we prepared for Grant's warm reception when the shells from his guns were hurtling over our heads. For eight days and nights the city was en siege. Their artillery fire was continuous and scarcely a day passed without an assault, gallant and determined, on some part of our works without success. Our rations were cooked miles in our rear and hauled to us in army wagons, only after dark, as our line of defence could not be approached from rear, at our point, without coming in view and range of the Federal batteries. Sharp shooters with long range rifles took position in tree tops far to our front, which necessitated extreme caution on our part and a lying low and close to our breast works.

Sunday morning, July 12, I think I was sitting close in the shade of our breast works listening to the monotonous boom of the enemy's cannon. Our batteries were replying with an occasional shot, only merely apparently in defiance. I was thinking of home, of loved ones there, of the "distant church bells chime." I longed to exchange the crashing boom of those guns and the whir of their deadly missiles for the soft music of sweet voices in the church choir. I longed for the coolness, the quiet, the sacred stillness, in peace, of the Sabbaths of the past and the presence of loved ones far away. And then I wondered if ever again I would listen to such music, if ever again I should see those absent loved ones, I should be spared to see the dawn of peace, at the close of the war, if I should ever see another Sabbath day, if I should see the close of this Sabbath, when a quick, sudden, crashing "fire by battery" from the guns of our brigade battery immediately on our right shook the earth around me.

Springing up instantly I looked and saw emerging from their works in a wood in front, a brigade of blue infantry advancing a double-quick across the wide, open space between our lines. Above the center of their well-closed line floated the Stars and Stripes and on either side at some distance were borne banners of blue silk. On they came, steadily and gallantly. "To arms and to your places. Fall in, make ready, and hold your fire until I command you to fire." Rang out in clarion tone from one colonel as he drew his sword and sprang recklessly onto the works in front of his men.

A Deadly Encounter

On came the advancing line and all was silent on our side. The five guns of Cobb's battery were being double-shotted with grape and canister. The hoarse "Hurrah! Hurrah!" sounded up and down their line as they came gallantly on. They near our line and Cobb's guns belch their double charges into the closed columns of the advancing infantry. Whole platoons go down, they close up, moving rapidly forward all the while, still shouting their hurrahs until within close pistol shot of our line. The order "fire" is given and our regiments of infantry mow down their ranks. Their colors are down and only a few shattered remnants of companies remain standing. These crowd together in groups as if to come on while some seek safety in backward flight. Our colonel (I think in mercy to the defeated, confused and defenceless remnant) leaps over the works and waves his sword to his men who pour out and onto the field after him and accept the surrender of the gallant few who have thrown down their arms and stand at our mercy.

Near Baxley, Appling County, Georgia, there lives one Jack Williams, unless he has passed away within the past year, whose share of the trophy was five stalwart soldiers of an Ohio regiment, with their beautiful blue silken banner with number and name of regiment in large gilt letters. These Jack presented to the colonel with "compliments Colonel, and here's hoping." I don't know which was the prouder, Jack of his trophy or the Colonel of Jack. I learned from a captive lieutenant, I think of an Illinois regiment, that their commander in that reckless charge was Brevet Brig-Gen Pugh. He was called "Fighting Sick" by his troops. The Lieutenant assured me that if Pugh had not been killed he would have led every living man onto our works. The enemy's cannonade was fierce in our front the remainder of that Sabbath day. There were many dead men very close our line and we were compelled to bury them hastily the next morning which we did under flag of truce.

Not longer than 48 hours, I think, after this we evacuated the city quietly, in the still of the night, imagining and speculating as to their surprise and rejoicing on the morrow.

The Sunday News, Charleston, South Carolina – October 29, 1911

MEMOIRS OF A SOLDIER IN WAR BETWEEN STATES

At Chickamauga Breckinridge's Division Met Crushing Defeat at Hands of Rosecran's Army – The Gallant Charge of the Old Forty-seventh – Gen Adams at Head of Brigade Made Great Fight and Lost

(By Captain B. S. Williams, Brunson, S. C.)

At the close of the day, Saturday, September 19, 1863, Breckinridge's division, weary, worn and hungry, was on the edge of the battlefield of Chickamauga. Close in our front on the ground fought over during the day were many dead men and artillery horses. Lying dead very near each other in one place, I noticed six large gray horses, and close around were many dead blue artillerymen. I learned afterward that the fire from a Federal battery posted there was very annoying and destructive to W. H. T. Walker's division while forming into line of battle, shelling his columns as they came up into line. Walker ordered a battery into position and opened fire on the Federal guns; after a short but very hot artillery duel, the Federals quickly changed position and harassed Walker from a new point. Gen Walker then sent a select detail of sharpshooters at double quick through a wood to a point where they could reach the Federal battery, with orders, not as was customary, to "pick off the gunners," but to kill the horses harnessed to the caissons of the battery. This proved excellent tactics, as in the hurried effort to move their guns after the killing of their horses they lost many of their men, their caissons and two of their field pieces, which fell into our hands. Many of our wounded passed us in ambulances on their way to the field hospitals in the rear. Longstreet's corps had been sent hurriedly from Virginia to reinforce Bragg in Tennessee; many of the wounded were newly arrived soldiers of the Virginia army.

A wounded officer gave me very discouraging news of the day's fight; he said; "You can't break their lines; they dispute and fight over every inch of ground and don't mind the bayonet; you'll catch h__l when you strike them tomorrow." Cold comfort for us.

A Sunday Morning Fight

Gen Breckinridge was ordered by Bragg to move to the right and farther front. In this movement we passed over many dead Confederates and a few Federals.

We rested under orders to sleep in lines "on arms." Very early

Sunday morning we were up and awaiting orders. We were very hungry. Very near our line, where we had slept, at regular intervals of space on the ground were small quantities of shelled corn, evidently where artillery horses had been fed and moved before they had eaten all their feed. This corn was hastily raked up and small fires kindled in which the corn was parched and greedily eaten by the men of my command. Just as orders came to fall in, Lieut. Jas Cheshire, Company H. (now an aged citizen of Putnam County, Fla.) ran up to the line and gave me a double handful of this, then, delicious and heartily relished breakfast food.

Into line, we were ordered to advance in line of battle 300 or 400 yards. We emerged from this wooded tract into open meadow-like ground. As we reached this glade we encountered a hot fire from a line of skirmishers in the wood beyond. They retired hastily before our advance and the Federal batteries in their rear opened fire with solid shot and shell, firing high above their advanced lines, their shot cutting and crashing through the tree tops above us, many limbs large and small falling around. We were in the wood, through which the blue skirmishers retreated. Here we were halted and allowed to rest in line, while some of Longstreet's brigades moved to our left that we might take a position on the right and open the battle by an attack on the heavily-massed columns of the Federal left wing. Those passing brigades of Longstreet's corps had suffered severely and met with repulse the evening before. The raillery almost insuppressible, between commands in the field not yet actually engaged, began. "O, yes." said a Longstreet man, "you are a fine set when Uncle Bob has got to send Longstreet from Virginny to advance Bragg's picket lines." "Yes" said a "wire-grass" man of the 47th, "you played hell advancing them yesterday evening, didn't you? And I say, sonny, before sundown this evening, you'll strike the durndest picket line you ever hit. You ain't a fighting Dutch and 'Downeasters' such as you all have been used to up in Virginny."

"Into the Gates of Hell"

Hushed was the friendly gibe and stifled the rising jest, for "Attention" rang out down our line and we knew that our time had come that, like "the six-hundred" at Balaklava, we were to move "into the jaws of death, into the gates of hell." That some of us would soon have fought our last battle and ere the morrow sleep our last sleep somewhere on the field before us. We moved to the right and forward into another opening, apparently a corn field. Here we must have surprised completely a line of Federal skirmishers as without firing they rose up, apparently panic-stricken, some fleeing percipitately to their rear, while others, throwing down their guns, ran up to us arms thrown up, begging for mercy. We were holding our fire and hurt not one of them who surrendered, though I had considerable difficulty in preventing gigantic Lieut. Cheshire from sabring a poor fellow, who, too frightened to drop his gun, ran toward us with it in his hands.

Their commanding officer, captain, Company B, 42nd regiment, Indiana infantry, handed me his sword, saying he was completely cut off from their army. I gave his sword to our regimental commander who ordered a detail of two men to conduct the prisoners to the rear. Beyond the field through which we were passing, directly in front of the 47th, was a heavily timbered wood; on reaching this we were ordered to advance cautiously, as the Federal battle lines were thought to be on an elevation just beyond this wood. Company E. Capt. DeWitt Bruyn, was deployed as skirmishers at intervals to cover front of regiment and ordered to feel the way in advance of the regiment. The right of the regiment rested near a public road, our skirmishers right of line moved along and near this road in the edge of the woods. When near the field in front, a Federal officer mounted upon a fine cream-colored horse, was seen riding along the road approaching our skirmish line, apparently carefully reconnoitering, instantly a shot rang out from the right of our skirmish line. The Federal officer, throwing up his arms wildly, fell from his horse, "Oh, what a pity." Said the brave but tender-hearted Capt. Bruyn, commanding the line. "Yes." Said the skirmisher, "I hated it, Cap'n but we got to do that way to keep from being done that way."

Capt. DeWitt Bruyn

(DeWitt Bruyn, Captain Company E., 47th Georgia, was born and reared in the state of New York, made Savannah his home in early manhood, and took up arms for the South. His parents appealed to him by letter to return North and enlist, if he would, under the "Stars and Stripes." He replied that he had made his home here, admired the people, loved the South and deemed our cause just. He was anathematized a rebel, denounced as a traitor and ostracized by his entire family. Cultured and refined, he was as modest as a virtuous woman, true as steel of Damascus blade, brave and gallant as Noy or Murat. He was my messmate in camp, my close companion on the march and side by side we fought in battle. About five years ago he became an inmate of the Home for Confederate veterans in Atlanta, Ga. Two years ago he crossed over the river and I pray that his pure and noble soul is at rest with our God.)

Breckinridge's division formed the right wing of our army. Adams's Louisiana brigade was on the extreme right of our division, the 47th, next to the left of Adams's brigade. At the farther edge of the wood, our skirmishers met with a galling fire from the enemy's skirmishers in front of their main line and their batteries opened fire on us in the wood.

A Field of Carnage

Moving into the open field, we were close and in full view of the parked batteries and massed columns of Rosecrans's left wing. The order was given to charge after our first volley and with fixed bayonets we swept on into the field. Under the terrible fire of grape, a regiment on the immediate left of the 47th, gave way and fell back into the woods; this caused some confusion in our brigade and for a short time 47th was halted in the open field under the terrible fusillade of shot and shell from the batteries and rapid fire from the lines of supporting infantry. The brigade of Louisianians, unaware of this break on their left, swept on and up to the guns in their front. Seeing that the regiment on our left did not rally and come into line and that Adams's brigade unsupported was being cut to pieces on our right, our regimental commander ordered the 47th to charge in support of Adams. Into the blaze and crash and smoke the 47th dashed, but too late; troops could not live in such a fire. The large bay horse of Gen Adams dashed back through the lines, riderless. Adams was down and his gallant men strewed the ground.

The gallant Louisiana brigade was almost annihilated. The remnant of that splendid command and the 47th were hurried back, broken and bleeding, and Breckenridge's whole division, defeated and crushed, fell back in disorder. Twice on the first assault the flag of the 47th went down and two color-bearers lay upon the field. Our flagstaff was cut in two and our colors riddled, but a young officer of our command caught up the flag, bore it safely to the rear, where a temporary staff replaced the old and polished one and around it the 47th again rallied, but the field was lost and strewing it over were some of the flower of the command. To this first charge, on Sunday morning, the 47th lost in killed and wounded, two officers and 74 noncommissioned officers and privates. The whole division sustained heavy loss. In my possession to-day is the same tattered old flag that waved on that day on that field, recalling vividly to my memory the scenes of those days.

William A. Bowers, Jr.

The Sunday News, Charleston, South Carolina – November 12, 1911
MEMOIRS OF A SOLDIER IN WAR BETWEEN STATES

Battle of Chickamauga, Stubbornly fought, with Fearful Fatalities, Great Charge that Routed Rosecran's Army – Mention of Several Officers Figuring in Encounter

(By Captain B. S. Williams, Brunson, S. C.)

"As where the rude Trosachs dread defile. Opens on Katrine's lake and Isle,"

"Clan Alpines best were backward borne," fighting without their chief; so fighting for the first time without their trusted chief, Sunday, September 20, 1863, the 47th Georgia was backward borne in the tangled wood and dank defiles close by the dark tide of the River of Death, deep sluggish Chickamauga.

During some time of our unsuccessful assault before referred to I was only a few minutes, I think, "hors de combat" and utterly unconscious of all surroundings. When the color-bearer, Jack Newberne, fell clutching to his brave, broad bosom the flag and I caught it up, the Federal batteries were firing at very short range, grape, shrapnel and shell, the shells exploding in front, above and around us. One of these exploded so close my front that I was thrown forward and shocked into insensibility by the force of the concussion. A fragment of the shell cut and shattered the flagstaff in two just above my hand-hold. When I recovered consciousness I was lying face downward on the field. My first sensation upon awakening into semi-consciousness was that I was dead, as thousands of tinkling, tiny bells seemed ringing in my ears and I felt neither weariness nor hunger then. I felt that I had dreamed but was sinking and lapsing back into sweet, peaceful, dreamless sleep again; then it seemed that someone tenderly raised my head off the ground and I heard someone say "the adjutant is killed," so I must be dead. I thought of my lately widowed mother and wondered if I would soon meet my father, the late colonel of the 47th. I wondered where I was. I caught, as if in echo, a low-sounding "thud," reverberating continuously and seemingly growing clearer, louder and more and more distinct until I recognized the familiar booming of cannon. Then I seemed to be falling and struggled to rise. On my hands and knees I looked around me and saw dead and wounded men wherever I looked. I then thought of our flag, then I remembered the charge. I remembered that Adams's brigade was being cut to pieces. I remembered our charge to the rescue. I remembered the confusion, because of a break in the line on our left, the wavering of my regiment and then – nothing more. Again I looked, and close beside me, within arms reach, lay the handsome form of one of the finest officers of my regiment and although my senior by many years, my fast, firm friend – First Lieut. Wm. A. Carswell, commanding Company D, 47th Georgia. I looked close in his face and saw that he was dead. I crawled to him and called his name and took his hand, it was yet warm. I remembered then that I had seen him fall close by my side. I must have gone down the instant after.

A Bitter Hatred

Carswell was only 35 years of age, but his hair and mustache were white, He was tall, erect and handsome, cool brave and courteous in manner, but in speech was terse and curt without being rude. He was esteemed and admired as an efficient officer, but had few friends in the regiment. He had a near kinsman in the Cabinet at Richmond and was influential at headquarters. Proud and of inflexible honesty, as a friend he was true as steel, as an enemy he was unbending, vindictive and aggressive. Officers of the army, even of the same command, were not always friends. Quite often a spirit of rivalry made them antagonistic and often bitter enemies. Lieut. Carswell died with his heart filled with hatred – bitter as gall – of the Captain of his company, J. Lawton Singleton. Capt. Singleton was a smooth, resourceful, brilliant lawyer; keen deviser, plausible, expounder, ambitious, daring adventurer. He loved his curt, independent, defiant Lieutenant about as his Satanic Majesty is reputed to love, "holey water" and there was "no love lost" between them. Upon an occasion while off duty, and Singleton and Carswell met, by chance, in my tent, it was only by the quick exercise of all the tact and coolness I possessed that I averted a clash between them, after reference by one to "presumptuous, important subalterns" and by the other arrogant, asinine superiors."

The high-spirited, sensitive, proud Major Gen W. H. T. Walker fell dead from his horse in battle at Atlanta, Ga., with this declaration scarcely off his lips, that his superior officer, Gen Hardee, should account to him personally, for language used by him, (Hardee,) in an order to Walker to move his division to a designated point, after a sane and earnest protest by Walker. Capt. Singleton remarked to me, as we started from Savannah, Ga., to join the Western army; "Now, adjutant, by God, sir, for me a yollow sash or the graveyard." Officers below the rank of brigadier general wore red sashes, a yellow sash was insignia of rank of general. Capt. Singleton never attained the rank higher than Captain and continued to wear his red sash so long as he remained in the service, but Carswell, the Christian gentleman and gallant soldier, had fought his last battle and Singleton had need no more to dread his Lieutenant, in whom he knew an alert, unyielding rival and dangerous influential enemy.

In substantiation of my belief that there is an undefinable, unimaginable occult source from which, through some inconceivable, mystical, medium of transmission are on occasion conveyed to brain and mind of man, inspiratary impression, presentment a momentary, vague insight or glimpse of futurity, is the fact that brave, practical, unwavering, irony Carswell confided to me before the beginning of the battle of Chickamauga his firm conviction that he would soon fall in battle, never to rise, and in our strictly private interview expressed severe regret that his early fall would end his aid in his country's defence and his opportunity to crush Singleton.

A Trying Experience

Where I had fallen in front of those smoke-enveloped Federal guns and lay for some time among the dead and wounded was comparatively safe, for the gun muzzles were elevated and shot and shell were going far above us into the woods beyond, where our lines were reforming. Sitting up, I noticed my coat front and one sleeve were very much blood-stained and I began to question if I had been hit and if so where, as I felt no pain, except in my head. Reaching my hand to my head I felt no wound, but discovered that I was bare-headed. My hat and sword lay close to me; these I at once secured. Then I rose and tried to stand up, but fell forward again on my hands and knees. I sat down and tried to locate myself. A dense smoke was over the field and men were lying around in all attitudes and I could not tell whether I had fallen with my head or my "feet to the foe." I could hear cannon in front of me and cannon in the rear of me. I quickly concluded that those nearest smoke-veiled, quick-firing guns must be the Federal batteries so I began to crawl in an opposite direction and toward the noise now in front. Going thus some distance I stopped to rest and instinctively crawled to and laid down behind a little stump near which were two dead men. Resting a few moments I got onto my feet and walked, falling several times to my hands and knees as my right side and limb seemed partially paralyzed or benumbed.

Reaching the wood, I saw our troops coming into battle line. Shot and shell were hurling around and above, and our batteries to left of us were replying hotly. Officers were giving their commands for formation in loud tones and rallying their shattered commands in excited manner. Rejoining my command, I found my regiment apparently more demoralized than I had ever seen it. This gave me great concern and mortification, and I determined to remain with them as I could stand, though I was by this time suffering severely with racking pains in my head. Our regimental line was about one company shorter than an hour before. Somebody had blundered. We should not have made that charge unless strongly supported and I wondered why we attacked then as we did. I learned afterward that our premature advance was because of persistent request by Brig Gen Adams, of the Louisiana brigade, to be allowed to charge and capture the batteries in our front, which were so furiously cannonading us. "Ours not to reason why." Ours but to charge and die. Many very brave and gallant officers and men were sacrificed in that desperate encounter.

Vain Glory Cost Many Lives

There was too frequent exercise of vain-glorious recklessness on the part of officers in our army at the cost of precious blood and life. Col C. J. Colcock, colonel of the 3rd regiment, South Carolina cavalry, recited to me an instance of a dashing young brigadier of cavalry forcing, unnecessarily and unreasonably, with every tactical advantage on the enemy's side, an engagement between part of his command and far superior Federal force, near Savannah, Ga., losing several men and meeting defeat. The only apparent reason for his action, in the opinion of every officer cognizant of the affair, was to get a "puff" in the Savannah newspapers, citing his chivalric daring, intrepid gallantry, etc., and the same to be read by a very handsome and wealthy young widow in Savannah, to whom he had been paying court (and who, by the way, married, after the war, a gentleman from South Carolina, whose estate lay between Savannah and Charleston).

Rallying and reforming, we were ordered to rest in line, while other troops were coming up. The battle was raging on our left and centre. While lying on the ground and big, athletic Lieut. James S Patterson, Company F, and tall broad-shouldered Sergt Major John R. Miniss (Scotch and Irish) were telling me how they raised me up to bring me off the field in front when Miniss cried out, "No use, the adjutant is dead." And both proceeded to get themselves off, for a large shell struck and exploded in the earth very near us, leaving a longitudinal opening. Jack Williams, private in Company F, by rolling over about twice, dropped into the fissure and appeared quite pleased. "Jack," I asked, "why do you tumble in that hole that way?" "Why, Adjutant," he replied, "a damned bomb shell is like lightning; it never strikes twice in the same place." I did not argue with Jack, his philosophy was generally as incredible and irrefutable as "What is to be will be." We were held idle in those woods for fully two hours, while the battle in front "trebly thundering shook the gale." It is a severe strain on troops to keep them on the edge of a battlefield, within hearing of the fray and range of fire. Illustrative of this fact was the exclamation of Lieut. Doyle, of Company A; "Adjutant, why the divil do they hould us here to be hit without even being shot at?" There were two Lieutenants Doyle in my regiments, both Irish. This one was known as "Red" Doyle. He was more than six feet tall, powerfully built, with red hair, red beard, and red skin – ferocious as a tiger. He "went through the war" and was post bellum sheriff of a county in upper Georgia. Heavens! What a sheriff "Red," I imagine.

William A. Bowers, Jr.

Battle of Chickamauga

At about 4 P. M. came the order "fall in" and "be ready" to move quickly to left. As we stood in line, awaiting the passage of some batteries moving to the left, where the battle seemed to be terrific and into which I knew we were going, and incident, slight, unimportant in our proceeding scarcely, heeded at the time, occurred, which always appears in my memory-picture of the battle of Chickamauga. A battery of Tennessee artillery halted, for a moment in front of our line. At the halt, the driver on the rear horse of the first gun was not more than eight feet front of me and about two feet on the right from a straight line. He was a fine, handsome fellow and sat on his horse so "a la chevalier" as to attract my attention and excite my admiration. I thought "what a superb cavalryman he would be." At that instant, a small conical shell from the enemy whizzed across, and just above the back of the horse on his right, struck the young soldier squarely in the side and completely disemboweling him, passed on the distance of about 30 feet, struck a large tree and exploded. He was not jolted in his saddle, and as I observed him closely his eyes closed as gently as if he were falling asleep, his arms dropped by his side and he began to sink forward. Before I could step to his side, two of the gunners of the battery sprang from the gun chest and caught him in their arms as he swayed slowly forward. Laying him on the ground, almost at my feet, one sprang into the saddle, the other back on the chest, and the battery moved quickly forward as the bugle was sounding "forward."

The artillery out of the way we began to move, at quick time, to the left. Instead of moving "right oblique," thus nearing our line of action, we swept around almost at right angle, nearing the Chickamauga River; halted, fronted and double-quicked forward through a wood bordering a stream into the edge of a large opening, which extended far in our front. Here we formed a line of our batteries, guns unlimbered, loaded, pointed and gunners standing with fuse inserted and lanyard in hand, ready to fire. Close in rear of this line of field pieces was a line of infantry with fixed bayonets. Through those lines we passed and halted about ten paces in front of the artillery, fixed bayonets and laid down in closed rank in line-front line as seemed ever our forte. Our line of battle engaged in front was suffering severely and being pressed slowly backward, by overwhelming numbers, but they were stubbornly fighting over every inch of ground, giving way only as they were pressed and borne backward. They were Cleburne's regiments, than which no better ever marshaled on any field of earth. In the momentary lulls that occurred and always occur in battle, we could hear the cheering of the men engaged and knew by experience how the battle went. Now the fierce yell of the Confederates told of their onslaught as aggressors; the horse sounding hurrahs of the federals told of their forward movement, but all coming nearer, steadily, told that we were gradually giving ground. We were to hold our fire until our engaged line had fallen back, under orders, and was safe in our rear, then at the first cannon broadside, we were to deliver our fire and charge everything in our front with bayonet.

The Critical Moment

Never throughout my four years of service did I experience such suspense, subdued excitement, intense anxiety, fearful anticipation and powerful hope as in those fifteen minutes of waiting. I knew that victory was trembling in the balance, and upon us then and there devolved a great responsibility of turning the mighty tide of battle, deciding the issue that was perhaps to shape our destiny. For two whole days the battle had lasted, fought with skill, valor, desperation and ferocity and now the critical moment had come which was to decide for the one victory, the other defeat. Generals of division and brigades rode back and forth in front of their phalanxed lines waving on high their swords and exhorting their men "for God's sake to stand firmly and at the word of command to charge and let nothing between Heaven and earth stay them and that victory was theirs." A general officer on immediate right of my command rode at full speed up and down his line with plumed hat held high on point of sword inciting his command to greatest enthusiasm. The troops caught the spirit of their leaders and panted in almost breathless suspense for the movement of action; in fact, it was difficult to restrain and prevent them from singing out their "rebel yell" and dashing pell-mell into the smoke-enshrouded fray in front.

Our regimental commander of the morning had been wounded in the morning's fight and the senior Captain had succeeded to the command. No braver man than he wore sword and bars in Breckinridge's division, but he was unpopular and very much disliked by the men. I feared his leading on this account. He appealed to me to sustain him in the coming ordeal. Personally, we were unfriendly, and had his reputation alone been at stake, I, as did a famous warrior at the siege of Troy, might have "sulked in my tent," but cherishing fondly in my heart the reputation of my command and dear to me as was our cause, I was willing and ready to sacrifice all, even life, for victory in this hour. Passing down the line of the 47th, I said to the company commanders; "We are well supported and victory is within our reach this hour. I will never come off this field alive if every man in the regiment falls back. I appeal to you, officers and men, we will shout in victory, or sleep in death on the field in front of us." "Living or dead, adjutant, we will stay with you. We will go and stay with you, so help me God. We'll bite the dust before we'll turn our backs." "G_d d____d the Yankee hoard, we will rout them now and pay them for this morning's work, lead us now, adjutant," and other like responses came thick and fast to me. I said to the Captain commanding; "The regiment is all right, do your duty."

I had scarcely regained my place in line when our advanced and struggling line came falling back under orders to fall in our rear. They came in perfect order and more defiantly than I ever saw troops fall back, for they would face about, fire, yell and load again. Seeing our supporting line they wanted to rally and charge again, but the men were exhausted. As we let them through our ranks many of them would fall, pitching forward like wounded or dead. Others would fall to a sitting posture and then sway backward, in collapse, to the earth. Then could be heard the cheery and loud hurrah from thousands of throats rising and swelling like the mighty roar of a tempest-tossed sea, and out from under the battle smoke clouds and beyond the smoke-line of the ensanguined field came the serried, lines of blue like the mighty waves of ocean sweeping in all their power and majesty toward a crag-bound shore. Officers, on rearing steeds, waved their swords gallantly and cheered their columns on. On our side was a deathly stillness – silent as the soundless crags.

A Magnificent Charge

Into the open, suddenly, they are confronted by our lines, their cheering dies upon their lips or in their throats and for an instant they halt in startled surprise. In that instant there rings out the command "fire," and as if a thousand thunder bolts from Heaven, our cannon crash and our rifles ring, then from ten thousand throats rang out the "rebel yell. "As all the fiends from Heaven that fell, had pealed the banner cry of hell" and our double line of grey dashed forward with the bayonet. The blue columns wavered an instant, delivered a straggling fire, then broke and fell back in confusion and disorder, a few surrendering, but far the greater number fleeing to their rear, many of them throwing down their arms and stripping off their accoutrements. Some of their officers acted magnificently and displayed great gallantry in their efforts to rally their shattered, routed and fleeing columns. Our line swept forward not waiting to load and fire, and the rout became general. Far on our right and left we could hear the victorious shouts of our troops. Rosecrans' splendid army, all save Thomas's division, was beaten, routed and in full retreat at sundown of that fateful Sabbath day. We were in full possession of the field and of the thousands of dead and wounded. Such a sight as I witnessed in the flight of those shattered lines and broken columns of thousands of the finest soldiers of the Federal army – grand, glorious, and magnificent to me then – is seldom seen in life. I pray God that it may never again be seen in this nation by posterity.

When we halted at about twilight on the farther edge of the field, next to Chattanooga, we were on the ground on which the 47th had fought in the morning and that night we slept after the day's separation, with our comrades, the victorious living with the immortal dead of the regiment.

The whole field, of broad extent, was strewn with the dead and wounded – thousands – of blue and grey, and the men of my regiment broke their long fast with food from the haversacks of some of the dead. When I had, after dark, opportunity to rest I was too hungry to sleep, so started out to "hunt rations." I felt, in the dark, many a dead man's haversack before I found one containing anything. Finding one at last on a Federal Corporal with a small piece of meat and a few "hardtack." I cut the strap so as to pull it from around him without disturbance of the dead body. Haversacks of food and canteens of water was all and everything that I ever took from the person of a dead soldier and that only when I was actually suffering. We were up early in the morning of the first, Monday. Heavy details of men were made from each regiment to bury the dead. As soon as possible I hastened to look after my old friend, Carswell. He was lying as I had last seen him, at full length on his back, but his sash sword and belt were gone, also his hat and costly new shoes. The eagle staff buttons had been cut and taken from his coat and his pockets rifled of everything they contained, among which was a very handsome, valuable watch.

Major London Butler

The orderly sergeant of Company D was a nephew of the dead officer. To this young sergeant I gave a special detail to bury his uncle and my friend. We marked the grave and not long after, the body was taken from the narrow, rocky grave at Chickamauga and now rests among his loved ones and living ones in Screven County, Georgia.

After viewing Carswell's dead body in the early morning, as I turned toward the road opposite, a group of officers of the 47th was standing in the road where Adams's brigade had fought on our right in the morning. Several of these officers were of South Carolina stock; Aiken, Singleton, Hazzard, Kennedy, Cone. Capt. Singleton beckoned to me and as I approached the group he said, pointing to a dead man lying in the road: "Adjutant, there lies a scion of a noble stock of your and our old Palmetto State." I saw at a glance that the dead man was an officer, that he was young, of medium size, finely formed, of dark complexion- evidently in life a very handsome man. He had been robbed as had been Carswell, but I saw on his collar the imprint of a single star. I said, "He was a major; of what name and command?" Singleton replied, "Major London Butler, commanding the 14th Louisiana, Adams's brigade, and you well know that; he led his command on this field gallantly as did ever his noble ancestor lead his on the fields of Mexico."

The litter corps and burial detail were hard at work; surgeons and nurses were busy on the field and in the improvised hospital under the tent-flies and trees; bugles were sounding and drums beating; the call "to arms" was ringing out from right to left. We, who heard, took our places in line, turning our backs on and marching away from those, who, on the yesterday morning, had fallen in and fought beside us. We left them with only "Glory to guard the bivouac of our dead."

The Sunday News, Charleston, South Carolina – December 10, 1911
MEMOIRS OF A SOLDIER IN WAR BETWEEN STATES
Tales, Both Merry and Sad, of the Sixty Days Siege Around Chattanooga, Following Great Battle of Chickamauga An Irish Captain and an Irate Surgeon.
(By Captain B. S. Williams, Brunson, S. C.)

Turning from the awful and harrowing scenes of the Chickamauga battlefield Monday morning, September 21, 1863, our Army of the West turned toward Chattanooga, Tenn., nine miles distant. Late in the afternoon of that day we were in sight of the city, then thoroughly garrisoned by the Federal army, which had gone in during the night before on their retreat from Chickamauga. My command had marched in front and now took position in battle line on right. Regiments, brigades and divisions moved up and deployed in lines on our left and rear. Our ever watchful foe in front began service of notice on us of knowledge of our presence by messengers from the heaviest of their artillery behind their outer fortifications.

The order came "in place rest," and the men laid down, their arms close beside them. Infantry thus resting usually sat down, slipped their knapsacks on their shoulders upward, reclined upon their backs with knapsacks pillowing their head, canteen and haversack at their sides. Thus resting they could eat and drink providing there was anything in haversack. Our march had been slowly made (too slowly I thought and too long delayed) yet was fatiguing and the men, tired and hungry, were as soon as allowed, resting and eating, as our commissarist had "issued rations" in the early morning.

Dismounting and leaning to rest against my saddle, I thought sorrowfully of the sad record of the day before, and as I looked down along the line, much shorter than of forty-eight hours ago, of those resting grey-clad, gallant men, some of them eating, some of them resting quietly, others chatting and laughing gaily, I, knowing that assault on the fortifications meant death to thousands, wondered what of to-day would be the record of the morrow. We were already within range of their guns. I was standing about ten feet to right of the first file on right of my regiment. Several officers had come up and standing in group we were estimating the distance to be traversed before we could reach the works in front, commenting, on fact that, as usual, we were in front line again, wondering what had become of our artillery etc., etc. In reply to question by Capt. Joe Thompson, Company C, I gave as my opinion that in the absence of all obstacles in our front, such as abattis or chevaux de frise we could not possibly reach the fortifications in a charge in less time than fifteen minutes and preserve our order of alignment.

Figuring on a Charge

"Fifteen minutes of hell and carnage and then twice fifteen minutes to count the dead," commented Capt. J. Lawton Singleton, Company D, "and adjutant," he continued, "yesterday we counted but, by G__, sir, to-day you and I may be counted." I had just time to reply "yes and by God, sir, you and I may be again shielded though we may not deserve it," when that peculiar and demoralizing, whizzing, whirring sound produced by the passage of a shell through air, coming apparently directly toward you and rapidly nearer and nearer, familiar to all soldiers of field service, startled our group into instant silence. In another instant every officer of the group had dropped to knees on earth for in that instant a crashing, deafening report from the explosion of a shell seemingly in our very midst blinded us. A large fragment of shell struck the earth at our feet, throwing earth and leaves around on us. We were thus warned that we were well within reach of our friends in front and that with those friends there were clear glasses and good ammunition, good guns and a good gunner.

Springing quickly to our feet, Capt. Dan Kennedy, Company G, ever ready with wit and repartee, quickly called out; "Singleton, you can yet count – count us." The shell had exploded just as it struck earth, directly between our group and the right of the regiment. Looking quickly, I saw the man who was on the extreme right flank, in front rank, Private Summerlin – one of six brothers who had enlisted for the war – apparently in the throes of death. A small fragment of shell glancing by his head had knocked his cap several feet away, cutting through the scalp and fracturing the skull; he was struggling for breath while cornbread crumbs and frothy blood gurgled from his mouth; his body quivered in convulsion from head to feet. Several men near him had jumped to their feet and were over and around him. I called to two men in rear with a litter and had him borne back to our surgeon. Summerlin was a brave and excellent soldier. I saw him only once afterward. He was in hospital in Atlanta, Ga., convalescing, and the surgeon in charge enlightened me somewhat as to the art of trepanning the skull.

Surgical Methods

Summerlin said to me, lying on his hospital bunk: "Adjutant, I was looking right at you, talking to Capt. Singleton, when that infernal thing hit me, and I saw from your looks that we were likely to catch a whole lot of hell pretty soon, but had no idea that I was to get my share right then, and I swear that I thought you were the first man I saw when I opened my eyes, but it was old Dr. Matthews (our surgeon) tinkering with my head." The hospital surgeon hearing this, treated me to quite a scientific dissertation on the brain, connected thought and vision effect of instantaneous pressure and sudden relief on the film of brain, etc. etc. etc., the greater part of which I did not understand, but presumed applied to Summerlin's case. Several years after the war I learned that Summerlin, the only one of his six brothers spared, was living with his family in Screven County, Ga. The aforesaid shell had dispersed our group and we awaited orders "at rest in place."

While thus and then resting in front of Chattanooga, I think I realized more clearly or was more impressed with the fact of the absolute loss of individuality, the complete sinking of self into automatac, or exchange of self into alter ego on the part of our volunteer citizen soldiery. There were numbers of talented, educated, intelligent men; strong in intellect, authoritative, dictatorial and assertive in their own former spheres; confident in their own powers of judgment and independent in thought and action; brooking no opposition or counter-contending influences; strong and grand in all the elements that make a man, standing, sitting or lying down, awaiting orders to rise, fall in, go forward or rearward, either fast or slow; shorn of authority; without privilege of consultation, advise or suggestion; compelled by peremptory orders to implicit obedience, prompt action and continuous effort, regardless of their judgment, opinion or desire. "Theirs but to do and die." The only palliative reflection in this chafery was confidence in the ability of our leaders, firm belief in the justice of our cause, knowledge of necessity of obedience and consequent concert of action and determination to performance of duty, all capped with the golden crown of sanguine hope of glorious success.

Siege Instituted

Gen Braxton Bragg, commanding, after counsel with his Lieutenants, Longstreet, Breckenridge, Cleburne, Walker and Cheatham, decided not to attack but to occupy with his army the Heights – Lookout Mountain and Missionary Ridge – in front of and near to the city and cut off all its communications. We retired but a short distance and went into camp, my command at the foot of the Ridge, so near to the Federal lines that the "Star Spangled Banner," "Hail Columbia," and "Yankee Doodle," and cheering hurrahs were plainly audible to us, as were our "Bonnie Blue Flag," "Dixie" and cheering "yells" to them, ringing out from our bands respectively on every clear, still night, while sounding notes of our respective reveilles mingling in echo, died out together on the surrounding hillsides or reverberating and wasting slowly and gently dissolved in the soft, crisp breezes of those beautiful autumnal, early mornings.

Our line extended from the top of Missionary Ridge on right across the Chattanooga Valley to crest of Lookout Mountain on left. Here we stayed and did little else than intrench and fortify during the following sixty days. While at times, many times, most of times, our soldiers' "lot was not a happy one," during periods of rest in bivouac or camp, they had their fun, their merriment, their jests and practical jokes, officers and men found pleasure in social intercourse and converse, song and story. Rests on these cases was as nourishing food to the hungry, cooling drink to the thirsty, sweet rest to the weary and soothing music to the "savage beast." Beneath my recently pitched tent fly on Missionary Ridge, I was lying on my blanket on the ground, for I had not fully recovered from the effects of my shock in the charge of Sunday morning. Several officers of my command were sitting around me; we were discussing and commenting on our repulse Sunday morning and our retrieving charge in the afternoon.

Capt. Bryan Connor

Capt. Bryan Connor, commanding Company A, (a purely Irish company) one of the finest drill officers I ever knew, was always dignified, always full of Irish wit and humor, always jovial and often dramatic in speech, tone and manner. He was fond of repeating Shakespeare and had it "by heart," as he had Hardee's Tactics, (by which we drilled). His rendition of Shakespeare in basso tone of his splendid voice was very fine.

At a point in our talk when reference was made to my apparent anxiety and fear of repulse Sunday evening just before our final charge and my appeal to the company commanders – as related in a former writing – Capt. Connor exclaimed dramatically, "but now is the winter of our discontent made glorious summer by sun of York." All recognized – the "compliment by implication."

Just then Capt. Connor's first Lieutenant, Putrell, entered. Putrell was a fine scholar and polished gentleman, but a poor officer. He was fond of and apt at mimicry, and when off duty and "on fun and pleasure bent," as we then were delighted in saying, delicately of course, his Capt. Connor. As Putrell entered I said to him; "Lieutenant, I regret exceedingly that I cannot welcome you to a seat in the audience on either sofa, chair or divan." Quickly pointing upward he exclaimed, a la Connor; "The sun is my father, the earth is my mother and on her bosom will I recline," and he reclined, his anatomy occupying considerable space on his mother's bosom. With slight pause he continued; "I was just in time to catch and enjoy my Captain's poetic and eloquent exclamation, which is, I presume relative to our recent fall from grace and rehabilitation (again al la Connor), on dark Chickamauga's bloody plain. Ours was a glorious victory, but when the adjutant is sufficiently recovered I may suggest to him the propriety of formulating charges and specifications against my honored and gallant Captain, specifying conduct prejudicial to military glory and language calculated to cause a retreat to the rear, instead of an advance."

Connor's Lurid Language

I am witness to said language of my captain in response to the adjutant's appeal, and here it is, ver batim and imitating Connor's bass voice and rolling "r's", he repeated: "Company A, the field is in our front, and that d___ yelling crowd of blue bellies soon will be; the Chickamauga River is close on our rear, but divil a bit of crossing there, for every bridge is burned. We have either to charge through hell, if needs be, in front, or sleep on the bank of the river, be Jazez." Putrell proved by me that he quoted Connor accurately and exactly, then assured all present that if there was a single man of Company A who would prefer going into hell than to sleep "by Jazus" that he hailed not from the Emerald Isle and was too big a fool to be a true son of the soil of the shamrock. The laugh was on Connor, for, really, he, in the intense excitement of the moment, did make that speech, which meant to go forward and kill Yankees rather than be caught between the river and the Yankees and there be killed by them.

My good old friend, Surgeon Matthews, had given me orders to keep out of the cold, rainy weather, then beginning. At the time of this conversation I was expecting him, though I had little faith in, and expected to refuse to take the usual prescription, (the best we could then do) "an opium pill now and one at 12 o'clock," but the old doctor was late in coming by two hours of his appointment. He was a large, corpulent, gruff, matter of fact, high-tempered, splendid surgeon. Our assistant surgeon, Denson, of Talladega, Ala., was a stout and very handsome man, the opposite of his superior in every characteristic. They worked together in perfect accord, ate and slept together, and were the best of friends and chums, notwithstanding the fact that Denson was constantly playing some prank, trick or practical joke on stern, fat, old Dr. Matthews, "Pap", Denson called him when "behind his back."

A Surgeon's Wrath

On Surgeon Matthews's entrance we were astounded at his appearance – red, almost purple in the face, his eyes swollen and he apparently ready to explode or be exploded by pent-up wrath. None dared question him, and one by one those gallant officers, who feared not to face death on the field, began slipping away in silent retreat; then the old surgeon exploded. He was a good old church-man, as nearly as I could judge, about one-half Baptist and the other half Presbyterian, but – well, he was mad, sure mad. He was going to prop me up within the next few days, and then I should prefer charges against Denson. He had hunted Denson for the past hour, but failed to come up with him, but would have him hunted down, arrested and Court-martialed. He left me – well, it was pretty near "cussing" Denson. Denson spent the next twenty-four hours, he afterward laughingly told me, "at the quarters of a brother medico of an Alabama regiment in another division. The casus belli was that to their large wall living tent they had their Negro man servant, "Harclas," to build a little chimney of rocks and clay, both surgeons superintending and aiding. The chimney finished to the top by Harclas standing on a barrel, oak and chestnut wood was brought in and Harclas was sent off to attend to the horses. Denson proposed that they start a rousing fire in the fireplace, that Dr Matthews should kindle and start the fire, and that he (Denson) would stand outside to see how the chimney "drew."

All was ready and "Pap" got down on his knees to kindle the fire. Denson left the tent and was to call out if the smoke came out freely. On leaving the tent he quickly and stealthily tied in hard, fast knots the strong strings of the tent tightly drawn around the tent pole on the outside. Passing to rear of the tent about the time the fire began burning, he mounted the barrel and took the wide-blade shovel Harclas had used and slapped it down closely on the wet clay over the chimney top, completely stopping every avenue of escape of smoke. Dr. Matthews soon began to call out between his fits of coughing and strangling. "What's the matter, Denson? The smoke is all coming back into the tent. I am about to stifle," "Stick it out a little longer," called Denson, "there's not much smoke coming yet, but may be it will soon began to draw." Almost suffocating and blinded the old doctor started on a run for the door and butted against the tightly drawn canvas of the tent front. He began calling to Denson and trying to untie the tent fastenings, struggling and suffocating in the strong smoke pouring down the chimney into the tightly closed tent. A passing soldier heard the noise inside, saw that something was wrong, quickly untied the tent strings and the old surgeon staggered out, blinded and strangling.

Denson's Practical Joke

After twenty-four hours of "absence without leave" Denson sent Harclas to "Pap" with a good, fat chicken and a haversack full of potatoes, (of which the old doctor was very fond) as a propitiatory offering. Denson assured me he had ridden ten miles back into the country to buy this peace offering for "Pap."

Memory often, often "brings the light of those other days around be," and in its effulgent glow I see the forms and faces and in imagination hear the voices and I move again among those men of that day and time; awakening from the illusion I cannot suppress the exclamation. Oh, for one touch of those vanished hands, for one word of greeting from those voices forever stilled.

October has passed and we were in the month of November. The esprit de corps of our army was fine and we were ready and felt anxious to again whip Rosecrans's army in the open field. Suddenly there was cast a gloom over our army as our force was divided, one part going toward Knoxville, Tenn., the remaining number stretched out in thin line to defend our position. This movement proved to be bad generalship on the part of someone, as in the disasters following, our splendid Army of the West, divided as it was, and the parts pitted against overwhelming numbers in secure fortifications at Nashville and Franklin, was that part of our army almost entirely annihilated, while we but half of our former force, were at the mercy of Rosecran's entire former force, strengthened by reinforcements.

The Sunday News, Charleston, South Carolina – January 28, 1912

MEMOIRS OF A SOLDIER IN WAR BETWEEN STATES

Defeat of the Mighty Hosts of the Southland at Missionary Ridge and Lookout Mountain – Some Sidelights On these Bloody Affrays

(By Captain B. S. Williams, Brunson, S. C.)

The Confederate States Army of the West investing the city of Chattanooga, Tenn., in the autumn of 1863, was a splendid martial host. On the field of Chickamauga, on the 19th and 20th of September 1863, in fair, open battle these troops had met, fought and defeated an army superior in numbers, superior in armament and equipment, with equal advantages of position, and composed of the very best material of the armies of the United States, North, South, East, or West; splendid regiments of New York, Pennsylvania, Illinois, Indiana, Ohio, Missouri, Kentucky and Tennessee troops. In the fierce battle at Chickamauga for victory and a mighty struggle for conquest the Confederate demonstrated their fealty and consecration to their cause and illustrated their patriotism, their sterling manhood and the splendid fighting qualities of the chivalric Southern citizen soldiery.

While besieging Chattanooga and anxious again to meet our mighty and gallant foe on the field, I saw only once, in October, the troops of our army marshaled for general review. On that occasion, as I looked up and down the phalanxed lines of grey-clad warriors and noted the star-spangled crosses of our blue and crimson battle flags glittering and glimmering in the sunlight, as the standard of each regiment, battery and battalion was proudly upheld and waved, as altar pieces, above the heads and hearts of the thousands of officers and men who were willing to sacrifice their lives and their all on the blood-crimsoned altar of their loved native land, my heart beat fast as I felt an elution of pride and power and glory in our grandeur and might, and in my boyish fancy and youthful ardor I repeated in soliloquy, the declaration of Marmion, who bent on peace, viewing Scotland's mustering clans of the army of King James Stuart, just before his defeat and utter rout on the fatal field of Flodden:

> "By St. George, were that host mine,
> No power infernal or divine,
> Should once to peace my soul incline,
> Till I dimmed their armor's shine
> In glorious battle fray."

Then I recalled in mind, the "glorious battle fray" of just a month past and noted the shortened line of my own command: Thought of the cold forms and pale faces wrapt in their soldier-blanket shrouds in the narrow confines of their shallow, rocky graves on Chickamauga's field – some of our proudest and bravest and best. I thought of the thousands of fond, true hearts at home, sad and broken – this on both sides – then glancing down the serried ranks I thought – and knew – "the end is not yet."

The Fate Awaiting

At that time, far from me was the thought, and never did I dream, nor could I have conceived that the dreadful fate of these proud Scottish chiefs and knights and kilted clans – the pride and power of Scotland – at Flodden, pictured the fate of the gallant officers and brave, intrepid men, of those splendid regiments before me, sanguine, defiant, and invincible.

Scotland's bard and historian wrote of Scotland's glittering hosts, after the fight at Flodden:

"When day dawned on the mountain side,
There, Scotland, lay thy bravest pride,
Chiefs, knights and nobles – many a one."

As the thought flashed, for an instant, in my mind I saw in myself, "There'll be many a torn and trampled banner, many a broken line, many a shattered column and many a blood-drenched field, and the air of the North as well of the South will be filled with the wails of the widowed ere this force is crushed.

The Great Slaughter

Yet, of that marshaled array, that "army in grey" afterwards disjointed and divided, and contending against overwhelming odds at Missionary Ridge. November 23, 24 and 26, and again at Ringold, November 27, and the campaign through Georgia of seventy-four days of almost incessant marching and fighting, losing in the campaign (according to report of Gen Hood) 22,750 men; and when the remnant, hurled by Hood, against the entire Federal force at Atlanta, losing 5,427, a total of 27,997 – great God of hosts; it is written in history, of the remnant at Nashville; "The Confederate forces were driven from their intrenchments into headlong fight. The Union cavalry thundered upon their heels with remorseless energy. The infantry followed close behind. The entire Confederate army, except the rear guard, which fought bravely to the last, was dissolved into a rabble of demoralized fugitives who made their escape across Tennessee."

While history is a methodical record of important continuous events and should be plain, unwarped and true, yet in "history" are garnishment and embellishment of facts and omission of details, minutiae. These minutiae are the nebulae of history, and not one thousandth part of the nebulae of the history of our States war will ever be written. In these memoirs I am only gleaning in history's fields. Most of the sheaves have been garnered, but there are many missing, left over, wisps and many scattered grains. As to embellished history we need not go from our position on Missionary Ridge, near Chattanooga, to see and point it out. Some of our histories say that the army of Rosecrans in Chattanooga was "barefoot and starving and freezing for want of food and clothing." Their flight, after defeat, into the fortified city of Chattanooga was in the night of September 20, all day on the field I saw thousands of those troops, living and dead, and I have no recollection of seeing one Federal soldier, dead or alive, in ragged uniform, and the only bare feet Federals I saw were the dead whose shoes had been "appropriated "by the Confederate living." About the middle of October a young Lieutenant and four men of an Ohio or Indiana regiment, while reconnoitering a little too far in their front, were captured by our pickets. I had them in charge to send to the rear as prisoners of war. I conversed at length with the intelligent young officer. I treated him with all courtesy and he, of course, disclosed nothing to me of conditions within their lines; but these men were well clad and had no appearance of starving or even hungry men.

At Chattanooga

October 23, following, Gen Grant reached Chattanooga with reinforcements and bountiful supplies of food, clothing and ammunition. I said to the young officer; "Lieutenant, why are you here with an invading army, with sword and cannon, to kill Southern men on Southern soil, around their own homes? Is it for the purpose of abolishing slavery? Of freeing the negro slaves of the South?" "No Sir," he replied; "damn the negroes of the South. If I were, this moment, not a prisoner, and were I armed and at equal advantage with yourself, so help me God, since your kind and courteous treatment to me and my comrades. I would not shoot you down to free every negro in Dixie." "Then why," I asked.

Pointing to our battle flags planted along our earthworks in front, he said; "Put in place of that flag the Stars and Stripes and I pledge you my word there are thousands of men within the fortifications of Chattanooga, who fought you at Chickamauga and will again soon fight you, who would throw down their arms, as I would have sheathed my sword and refuse to fire on you or advance against you." Lieut. Doyle, of Company A, 47th Georgia, being present fairly hissed out, in his Irish brogue; "To hell with your shpotted and shtriped flag; we will tread on it again and again, as we did at Chickamauga, and had I my way I would burn ivery flag and shoot ivery damned prisoner captured. I think that would aid in putting an end to the whole damned bloody business." I quickly interrupted with, "Lieut. Doyle, you are a brave man, but remember you are speaking to an officer of equal rank with yourself, but who is captive and powerless. Let us hold our temper and fire until we meet his comrades, who are not prisoners, on the field." "Right, sir," said Doyle, "I am anxious for the meeting: I would not insult a prisoner: I only advocate a black flag with no quarter asked or given, so long as they invade our soil and desecrate our homes." I regretted to see the gallant young fellow, but little older than myself, go to the rear. On leaving he extended his hand in parting, he in blue and I in grey, and I grasped it warmly, in sympathy and well wishing, as I would have grasped his throat had we met in combat the day before or the day after on the field.

Lookout Mountain

Of the skirmish on Lookout Mountain historians wrote "The far-famed battle above the clouds." In truth, our line on Lookout Mountain was little more than a picket line. Major Gen Stevenson, commanding a part of said line, spoke in his official report of the "serious weakness of force, there not being a man for yards on some parts of the line." This thin line, up and down the mountain sides, could only "fire and fall back" at the approaching overwhelming Federal forces, or remain and be captured. In this firing they were guided by the fire of the approaching Federal lines, as the mountain was, at the time, enveloped in a dense fog, except for about one hour from about 10:30 to 11:30 A. M. during the day. Of our three brigades extended, drawn out, and in action there, Moore's, Wathall's and Pettus's, the casualties were, killed, Moore's brigade 4, Wathall's 8, Pettus's 9. This does not include the wounded and missing, but shows the immensity and sanguineness of the "far-famed battle above the clouds." Also in some of our school histories which have come under my notice there are accounts of the battle of Missionary Ridge, in which it appears that the capture of that position from Bragg's depleted army by Grant, who was then in command of the largely reinforced federal force, was a kind of frolic or picnic for the Federals. That the Federal forces mustered as if for review and then just came on and on, smoothly and beautifully, almost without hindrance, until they possessed themselves easily of our works and guns and many of our troops.

In truth, when Longstreet's corps and other of our forces were sent on to Knoxville in November, and our remaining force stretched out and extended into such thin line that "there was not one man for yards on some parts of the line," the able Gen Grant, Sherman and others, pent up in Chattanooga, saw their opportunity and thought, evidently, with their army of 80,000 men, our weakened line could be easily swept away at any and every point, and they did move to assault fiercely, coolly and apparently very confidently. Their force that struck our right consisted of the divisions of Major Gen Jeff C. Davis, three divisions brought by Sherman from Vicksburg, and Howard's (11th) corps of the army of the Potomac, all under command of Gen Sherman. These were met by Cleburne's and Walker's divisions of our side and repulsed again and again with heavy loss. Our loss also was heavy. As an instance, Sweet's battery, of Govan's brigade, went into action under command of Lieut. Shannon. Shannon was soon wounded and the only remaining commissioned officer, Lieut. Ashton, took command. In a few minutes Ashton was mortally wounded and the non-commissioned officers were killed and disabled until in a short time the command of the battery devolved on a corporal, Corpl. F. M. Williams, and a detail of men from an Infantry regiment had to be made to work the guns. The assaults and charges of the Federals were spirited, gallant and desperate. The hillsides and valleys in our front were thickly strewn with their dead and wounded. One major general and three brigadier generals fell in Cleburne's front. As soon as the enemy was repulsed and driven back on our right Cleburne was ordered to "reinforce our centre with all possible haste." He said, "I pushed forward, but before I had gone far a dispatch from Gen Hardee reached me with the appalling news that the enemy had pierced our centre and were on Missionary Ridge."

Retreat

Our troops now fell back across the Chickamauga. Many prisoners were captured from us at Missionary Ridge and Lookout Mountain who could have avoided capture, but as Gen Cleburne afterward said, "They lingered here and there in the shadow of the trees, for the purpose of being captured; faint-hearted patriots, succumbing to the hardships of war and the imagined hopelessness of the hour." "Hopelessness!" That was the cause. When our army was reduced and weakened greatly, while the enemy was being strongly reinforced, our troops were dispirited, discouraged. Hope dried out, confidence waned and I could clearly perceive a spirit of care, dissatisfaction, disappointment and "hopelessness." We were, divided, too weak to withstand an assault from the heavily reinforced enemy, yet we must stand and oppose him. It could result only in death and defeat, nevertheless we must risk the death and suffer the defeat. Many "succumbed in the imagined hopelessness of the hour." Some at the close of the fight and the beginning of the retreat "lingered under the shadow of the trees for the purpose of being captured." On our right, eight stands of colors of the Federal commands fell into the hands of Cleburne and Walker. Among them the flags of the 27th Pennsylvania regiment and the 93rd Illinois regiment, with about 500 prisoners. Not much of a jubilee or picnic on that part of the field. Had our troops been unaware of the serious depletion of our strength and the heavy reinforcement of the enemy the fight would have been fiercer and longer and there would have been fewer prisoners and many more dead men.

Gen Cleburne

As to the nebula of history – all of which cannot – and perhaps should not – be gathered and chronicled. The fall of the gallant Major Gen Cleburne at the head of his splendid division on the field at Franklin is historical data; but there are minor relative details, which are not on record and will never be in history. Cleburne loved his splendid regiments. His officers and men honored, admired and confided in and relied on him. No danger or risk too great to be undertaken or incurred if Cleburne said "Forward." I regarded Major Gen Cleburne as one of the most effective fighters in the Confederacy. I regarded his division as I saw it march in review at Dalton, 28 regiments, 10 Arkansas, 8 Texas, 3 Tennessee, 3 Alabama, 2 Mississippi, 5th and 3rd Confederate regiments, as the best division of troops I ever saw on either side. In the Tennessee campaign, under Gen Hood, on an occasion Cleburne was ordered to assault with his division. He, as did Major Gen W. H. T. Walker, just before he was shot and fell from his horse dead at the battle of Atlanta, Ga., protested and pointed out that it would be sheer murder of his troops to assault as ordered. Emphatically ordered to advance, he asked to be supported. Without support he charged, was overwhelmed, and after desperate fighting, was repulsed with terrible slaughter of his men. He declared privately to one or two of his officers and personal friends that if ever again he was compelled to sacrifice his command he would remain on the field, to which he led them, with his dead. Very soon after, at Franklin, he performed his solemn vow. Again his division had to advance, unsupported, through abattis, on the enemy's most strongly fortified and comparatively inaccessible position. Cleburne led his men through and over every obstacle to the works. Gen Hood, commanding, in his official report said, speaking of the same: "The troops moved on most gallantly to the attack. Here the engagement was of the fiercest possible character. Our men possessed themselves of the exterior of the works while the enemy held the interior. Many of our men were killed entirely inside the works. The struggle lasted until midnight, when the enemy abandoned the works."

During the fierce and terrible fighting in front of the works Cleburne rode back and forth, along and through his battle lines, recklessly lingering at the muzzle of the enemy's belching guns and seeming for a time shielded from death by strange oracular power. But when morning dawned there almost on the embankment of the fortifications, lay Cleburne and his horse among the hundreds of his "sacrificed" dead and wounded. Brig Gen S. R. Gist, of South Carolina, lay dead close to him. Chivalrous, indomitable Pat Cleburne! Gallant leader of an invincible host of splendid troops as I ever saw marshaled. His place in the Army of the West could no more have been filled than could that of Stonewall Jackson have been filled in the Army of Northern Virginia.

William A. Bowers, Jr.

Jeff Davis's Visit

History registers the visit of the President of the Southern Confederacy to Bragg's army encamped before Chattanooga in October 1863. The review of the Army mentioned in the beginning of this writing was on the occasion of President Davis's visit, in honor of his presence and for his inspection. This same is historical data. A gleaning of nuclear history is that of our army was mustered into line, in "close order," with colors in centre of line of each command, regiment, battalion and battery. President Davis, splendidly mounted and splendidly riding, escorted by Gen Bragg and staff, started at right and rode near in front along line in left. The troops stood at "parade rest." As the President and party approached the right of a regiment, or rather command, the commanding officer of same would order "Attention!" "Shoulder arms!" As the President reached a point opposite the colors he would wheel his horse to left, facing the colors. At order "Present arms," officers would come to "Present," with swords, guns were held at "present," and the colors would be dipped low in "salute." The President would raise his hat and bow low in acknowledgment of salute. At this the regiment would give a lusty, ringing, yelling cheer. The President would wheel to right and proceed down along the line. These formalities were strictly, heartily and joyously adhered to, without break or intermission, until the regiment was passed.

Troops Refuse to Cheer

On our immediate left were two Florida regiments. When the President and escort reached the first of these the forming of military salute was, of course, strictly observed and carried out. The President faced the command and clearly and distinctly rang out the order, "Present arms!" The colors sank low in salute, the President saluted, but instead of yelling the cheer, silence, deep and profound as midnight now in a national cemetery reigned. I saw the President turn quickly and say something to Gen Bragg. His hat went on and his wheeling to right was done a little more quickly than formally. All of same was repeated at the next stop in front of the other Florida command. These regiments passed the cheering rang out again and again along down the line. On inquiry I learned that the refusal to cheer was intended to rebuke, in resentment, the failure on the part of the Government to protect or defend some point or port of Florida: some denial or neglect of that State's rights and dues.

Thus did I witness, in surprise and regret, the silent but unmistakable censure and rebuke, publicly and pointedly, of the illustrious President of the Southern Confederacy, the Commander and Chief of the Confederate armies and navy, by a section of his troops in the field on review.

Bad Policy

I now question in my mind if such conduct as on that occasion on the part of those troops, composed of the volunteer citizen soldiery of the southernmost State of our Confederacy, was not suggestive and somewhat illustrative of the fiery, resentful and revolutionary spirit with which our Government – had we succeeded – would have had to contend and against the eruptive manifestations of which to provide, and which it would have been necessary to subdue in the maintenance of supremacy of power and preservation of Confederate States.

I opine that from the Palmetto State, long ere this date, there would have issued – prompted by some Cromwell-like statesman of her soil – a flaming manifestation to charging infringement and violation of certain inalienable rights guaranteed her, and whereas now fully convinced of the wisdom of the policy of imperium in imperio, and trusting in the justice of our adoption of said policy, our vast and ample resources, our indomitable strength and absolute security by reason of our sea-girt shore and mountain ranges on east, north and south, lined with our invulnerable forts and batteries and our line of boundary and defense west, along the intrenched and fortified banks of the broad and torpedo-minded – our side of the Savannah River – owing to and because of all aforesaid and same we hereby bid defiance to the civilized and all other quarters of the world, and do declare the sovereign State an independent and incomparable republic, with design and intent of ultimate transformation into exclusive and celestial empire, our motto and slogan, Divide et impera.

Jest and flippancy aside. In my opinion that a spirit of egotism, insubordinate independence of properly constituted authority, desire for self-promotion, aggrandizement and glorification, prompting disobedience of orders and failure in the prompt and hearty discharge of duty on the part of many officers of rank in our army, losing us bloody battles, costing us precious victims, contributing to the causes of our downfall and hastening final defeat. I am supported by instances and instances and facts abundant.

After Defeat

Overwhelmed at Missionary Ridge and Lookout Mountain we fell back across the Chickamauga River, the enemy closely pursuing. At Ringold, about twenty miles southeast of Chattanooga, Gen Cleburbne received orders, "Take strong position in the gorge of the mountain and attempt to check pursuit of enemy. He must be punished until our trains and the rear of our troops get well advanced." Cleburne with his usual celerity, took position and checked the advance of the enemy until about 1 o'clock P. M. when he received orders to retire. The enemy showed no disposition to pursue or again attack. We now proceeded leisurely to Dalton, Ga., where about December 1 we went into winter quarters. Here we spent our Christmas. On the 27th of December Gen Joseph E. Johnston assumed command of the Western army.

Of our winters stay and life at Dalton I have written in a former article. We had for several dreary winter months a peaceful, quiet time only guarding our lines of communication, transportation and defense. Hushed was the cannon's roar and the ringing, crashing fire of carbine and rifle, stilled the din of battle. But it was as the stillness that precedes and presages the approaching blasting, withering, devastating storm. We soon felt its lightning blasts and thundered bolts at Resacca, New Hope Church, Kennesaw Mountain, Cassville, Atlanta, Franklin and Nashville, realizing in harrowing, awful experience the depth and truth and intensity of Gen Sherman's terse declaration that "War is Hell."

The Sunday News, Charleston, South Carolina – March 16, 1912

MEMOIRS OF A SOLDIER IN WAR BETWEEN STATES

The Beginning of the Campaign of 1864 in Georgia, when the Thinned Ranks of Johnston's Army were Making a Last Stand – Negroes in Confederate Army

(By Captain B. S. Williams, Brunson, S. C.)

When the Confederate Army of the West, forty-four thousand strong, of all arms, under command of Gen. Joseph E. Johnston, filed out from winter quarters at Dalton at the beginning of the campaign of 1864 my regiment had been a component part of that army in active service in the field just one year. I have written a former chapter on the dreary winter's stay in camp near Dalton, our departure therefrom and our clash with Sherman's splendid Federal columns on the field of Resaca.

While standing at "attention" in line of battle, awaiting orders for action in the edge of the field at Resaca, I looked closely down our regimental line. From right to left and marked the well closed files and even "dress" of the ranks. I noted the shell-torn and bullet-riven "Starry Cross" in the centre of the line, as it draped the rough improvised staff which had replaced the polished, gilded staff shattered into pieces at Chickamauga. In that moment I was backward borne in memory through time's flight of two years, and again I witnessed the ceremonial and soul-inspiring presentation of that flag – the fresh handwork of my mother – to the one thousand gallant men formed in "hollow square" to receive and adopt it. Again I saw father's sword flash beneath its virgin folds as he led in the charge. Again I saw the regiment – eight hundred rifles – in closed files, with broad, firm tread and martial men, marching through the streets of Jackson, Miss., to take their place in the vanguard of the army of which they were to be a constituent part and parcel – the bulwark of flesh and blood to be reared between homes and the invading hosts. Then in quick reversion, there floated in my mind that donor and mother in her widow's weeds, a refugee from her home, and that father sleeping in his uniform in the "bivouac of the dead."

The pounding, ponderous sound of artillery horses' hoof-beats as several batteries neared our position, passing down on our left at full speed, brought me back to the present, and again glancing down that line of grim and silent men; I realized that we could not muster more than 400 rank and file. Where were the missing ones? A few were at home convalescing and recovering from wounds; a few were in hospitals, a few were in Northern prisons, but by far the greater number of the missing had gone down in battle in the eight days and nights, fighting around the city of Jackson and on the field of Chickamauga, Lookout Mountain and Missionary Ridge.

The thought then occurred to me, one year's service and suffering in duty done, scores of precious lives paid, homes saddened and wrecked, hundreds of innocent hearts wrung in anguish and steeped in despair, and then the question not "for what" but "what for these? The consequence, the result?" We had staggered under the shock of the surrender of Vicksburg and its garrison; we had marched sadly in the evacuation of Jackson; we had suffered regret in the bareness, of materially beneficial results, of the glorious victory of Chickamauga; we suffered in disappointment and humiliation when overwhelmed and defeated at Missionary Ridge and in the abandonment of Chattanooga, and now we were taking our stand in the State of Georgia, confronting an army of more than double our numerical strength. As I recalled these saddening and indisputable facts hope did not die entirely in my heart, but then and there grew exceedingly grey.

In a preceding article I wrote of the battle of Resaca and our movement to the rear. At the close of that day's action we went into camp with plenty of time for sleep during the night for those who could sleep. Greatly fatigued, quite unwell and sad of heart because of the loss of twenty odd men of my regiment in the day's action, I spread my blanket on the ground near the fire at our regimental headquarters and with my saddle for a pillow, tried to sleep. I could hear the hum of the voices of the men around the company camp-fires down the line. Occasionally I could hear laughter and once or twice snatches of a camp song. I could not sleep. Again and again the sad fact forced itself to my mind that we had lost and given ground. I thought of what Col. Ashley, my kinsman and closest personal friend, had told me some time before breaking camp at Dalton. He imparted to me in strict confidence the information that at a council of general officers, in which our status and general conditions relative to our "Cause" were thoroughly reviewed and measures for future action suggested and discussed, an officer in the council, of very high rank, submitted the proposition of enlisting, arming and putting in our army one hundred thousand negro men, in commands separate from white troops, officered by army white officers. His proposition he earnestly advocated and proposed to superintend, personally, the immediate organization of twenty regiments. The proposed measure met strenuous urged in deep desperation, as a dernier reported by a vote of a large majority of the officers in council.

I had discussed with Col. Ashley, privately, the merits of the proposition of enlistment of negro men in our army. The idea was repulsive to as being contra to all my ideas of the true principals of chivalric warfare. I remembered then that to all of my sophistical arguments Ashley, chivalric, proud spirited, and aristocratic in every fibre if his being, replied; "The project was conceived in wisdom, suggested in patriotic devotion, urged in deep desperation, as a dernier resort, and rejected in a spirit of false pride and inflated egoism damning to our chances in this unequal warfare and blighting to our every hope of ultimate success. As all these thoughts and memories revolved in my fevered brain as I looked up with sleepless eyes through the clear atmosphere to the gleaming stars my heart was wrung with the contemplation. Great God, have we reached an era, when under necessity, we are grasping at hitherto undreamed of means and ways – of doubtful honor and questionable propriety – as a last resort, a "dernier resort?"

The camp-fires had burned low; the troops were silent, many of them sleeping to wake at reveille on the morrow for the last time on earth. The only sound to be heard was the champing and occasional hoof-stamps of our horses around our quarters. Drawing my hat down over my face, and in my heart beseeching God to grant us favorable opportunity on the morrow for a general engagement with the enemy, in which I knew thousands would fall, but in which I hoped for victory, I slept. At the same time, at army headquarters, the corps and division commanders were assembled. Planning – in view of the ascertained plain fact that the enemy had secured and occupied position from which he could advantageously attack us at daylight with a full force equal to our whole and entire strength and with a detached force of forty thousand troops strike our line of communication – with maps before them, for another movement to the rear, another fall-back by best "ways" and surest "means," to Adairsville or Cassville.

The plans were put into operation and were admirably and expeditiously executed by the awakened troops while the dew was gently descending on the field of growing young wheat along the road-sides, and white "in the infinite meadow of heaven" still "blossomed the beautiful stars" – the "forget-me-nots of the angels" though pity "twould have been for the angels" to have heard some of the remarks made on that occasion by reason of the recurrent incident.

The Sunday News, Charleston, South Carolina – April 14, 1912

MEMOIRS OF A SOLDIER IN WAR BETWEEN STATES

Dispiriting Retreat Through Georgia when Soldiers, Hopeful of Battle, Were Deceived by Fatal Policy Pursued by Gen Johnston. Deception and Dissension Among Officers – Some Sidelights

(By Captain B. S. Williams, Brunson, S. C.)

When the troops of the Confederate Army of the West, under the command of Gen Joseph E. Johnston, first made their stand in battle line, in the opening of the campaign of 1864 on Georgia soil, we had given up, practically, Arkansas, East Tennessee, Mississippi, Louisiana and Texas. The strength of the Southern Confederacy lay in the armies on the field; of Lee in Virginia and Johnston in Georgia. On the manufactories, foundries of mills of upper Georgia the armies of the South were entirely dependent for clothing, wagons, harness, powder, balls, and cannon. In fact it was known that Georgia, at that time, was the "workshop, storehouse, granary and arsenal of the Confederacy." When then, the order came to fall back from Resaca (as I have written) we knew that we were again being forced back and were to give up more of our circumvallated and steadily diminishing territory, and that in Georgia.

As we wearily marched on – to the rear – I could not resist and overcome the imagination and impression that the wall of darkness of the night in which we were moving, surrounding and enveloping us was but typical of the dark, funeral-like pall of disaster lowering, enveloping all that earth held dear to us.

But, Oh, how kind in divine ordination is the merciful and munificent provision that hope shall spring "eternal in the human breast," and that because of the perennial budding of hope of man never he is "alway to be blest."

Relative to the first retreating of which I ever heard or read, the falling back before the flaming sword at Eden, someone has written – somewhat ambiguously – "All, all forsook the guilty mind but hope; that charmer lingered still behind."

We arriving near Adairsville and bivouacking for rest, our commanding general received dispatches from Richmond, Va., our capital, telling of glorious successes of our Army of Virginia of battles fought and victories won by Lee and Jackson, in which the enemy's loss was very great. These glad tidings were duly heralded to our troops and bright gleams of hope dispelled our despondency as the glowing rays of early morn had scattered the darkness of the gloomy night. Alas, we learned that, in view of these recently occurring events at the other end of our collapsing Confederacy and other lights apparent to our leaders, but invisible to the faithful "rank and file," Gen Johnston had declared, "The Confederacy is as fixed an institution as England or France." Coming from that exhalted source and venerate authority, the declaration was an inciting prophecy and inspiratory as if proclaimed by an Isaiah or a Daniel. Hope sprang up and budded into flower in the "human breasts," of forty thousand warriors. We had not of late been but now at last were to be "blest."

Hoping for Battle

Weary were our troops of labor by day, constructing temporary fortification and "breastworks," and their fatiguing and prostrating marches at night to the rear. Sad at heart were they because of failure and refusal on the part of those in authority to marshal them in a decisive test of their strength and valor against the invading Federal hosts. But now there was cheer and animation in revived hope, and an earnest, eager desire for a fair, square, immediate meeting in battle of Sherman's splendid pressing divisions was very manifest and seemed to pervade our entire army, officers and men. We knew we would be greatly outnumbered, but the troops feared not defeat. They might have been enveloped and overwhelmed by superior numbers, but those forty thousand men could not, then have been whipped from any field in Georgia, by any army on earth, and were eager to test fate in a life and death grapple, in a general engagement, for victory or annihilation.

Moving through Adamsville and reaching a favorable position near Cassville, we faced "about," westward, and formed into battle lines. Here we learned we were to await the approach of the pursuing enemy and if not at once attacked we would attack and force the issue.

The corps of Hardee, Hood and Polk were in line and ready for action by early afternoon. My regiment, of Hardee's corps, was in position in front line, our right resting on the main road from Adairsville. A "battle order" by Gen Johnston was read to the troops in line. Our General thanked the troops for their patience and patriotic devotion and assured them they would "now be led against the enemy." Copies of this convincing and welcomed manifesto were read to each of the companies and all along down the lines, infantry, cavalry, and artillery, could be heard the glad, fierce, ringing cheers of the troops at prospect of the hoped-for, longed-for closing in deadly and decisive strife. In my opinion not one hundred men in those massed and compact lines of thousands would have voted to fall back one step from the vastly superior force in front in preference to fighting to a finish right there and then.

Skirmishes Begin

Soon a brisk artillery fire began not far in our front and I knew our cavalry was skirmishing with the vanguard of the Federals. The firing came nearer, steadily, and our cavalry came in and took position on our flanks. The Federal advance columns soon struck our strong infantry skirmish line in our front, and the fighting there was spirited and fierce, neither side gaining ground. The columns of the infantry were coming up and cautiously deploying into battle lines and began feeling our main lines with their foremost batteries and artillery. The position of my regiment was on a slightly elevated open ground on the eastern edge of an open level glade about 150 yards in width. On the western (enemy's) side was quite a large and dense wood.

Realizing the great disadvantage of our position, we worked hard and rapidly piling rails from a nearby old fence into line and loosening with sword and bayonet earth and rocks and piling against the rails, soon had a slight "breastwork." We were now ready and anxiously awaited the coming of the blue-coated columns in our front. Their shells were exploding around us. Just as I took my place in line a small fragment of shell whizzed unpleasantly near my face and, missing me, struck Lieut. Mallard, of the 24th S. C. Infantry, about five paces to my rear, as he was moving rapidly with his regiment to take position on our left. The Lieutenant was badly wounded.

It would be impossible for me to describe my feelings and emotions as I stood, in place, looking constantly across that level glade, expecting momentarily, to see our skirmishers coming across, followed by the massed columns of blue infantry with fixed bayonets and floating Star Spangled Banners. Realizing that defeat meant dire disaster and destruction, but that in victory was glorious redemption and salvation; feeling keenly our necessities and fully cognizant of our precarious status; weary of procrastination, retreat and avoidance tactics and believing confidently in the invincibleness, then of our troops, I longed as never in all my service for the closing in and clash and crush of battle, and determined, so help me God, to incite my regiment to win victory or go down in death in what I believed would be the fiercest encounter and most sanguinary battle in all the annals of warfare.

The skirmishers fire in our front continued until dark and we rested in line, "on arms," to prevent surprise in attack, confident of beginning on the impending battle at the break of day.

Order to Retreat

About 1 o'clock A. M. orders came to take up line of march hurriedly to rear. The remainder of the night and the day following we marched with scarcely a halt for rest. Weary and worn we halted just at dark for the night. The troops were compelled to rest in line, as the Federal cavalry was hanging close to our rear. Rain had fallen throughout the entire afternoon and was continuing. The night was very dark. My command occupied, in the line, for rest – our entire length of line – ground in an abandoned old field, level and low. Our wagon trains and artillery, in our front, had trampled and cut the low rain-soaked earth in slosh and mire, and the still falling rain was greatly adding to the sloppiness. The tired, worn-out men had to rest and sleep. Many of them dropped on their knees and bending forward rested their faces on their folded arms in front, their guns resting against their arms or shoulders, and slept. Others sat in groups of three or four and leaning against each other, slept. Some went to a fence, a hundred yards away, and brought rails. Two rails a short distance apart served to keep the heads and bodies of five of six men out of the mud. I enjoyed the luxury of two rails all to myself, on which, resting lengthwise, I slept. The rain ceased in a violent wind storm just before daylight, and on the dry wooded hill, just beyond our own wallowing place in the mire, gallant, handsome Lieut. Frank Bourquin, of the 25th Georgia Infantry was crushed to death by a falling tree, and higher on the hill the beautiful, cream-colored mare of Gen Jackson's young, dashing courier met, close by the side of her fond master, the fate of gallant Bourquin. No tree fell on us. Many of the men, now dispirited and worn out, dropped down. There were hundreds of barefooted men. Hundreds of completely broken down men were sent to the rear on sick tickets. The night retreat after the issue and publication of the battle order and our completed formation and wall created, surprise and disappointment; greatly inspired confidence and again blasted hope.

  Gen Johnston, in view of the great numerical superiority of the Federal army, deemed it expedient to risk battle only when position of some blunder on the part of the enemy might give us counterbalancing advantages. He said; "I determined to fall back slowly until circumstances should put the chances of battle in our favor; keeping so near the U. S. army as to prevent it sending reinforcements to Grant and hoping by taking advantage of position to reduce, by partial engagements, the disadvantages against us." In pursuance of these tactics Gen Johnston labored under difficulties and serious disadvantages. Had he shot one or two of his lying courier scouts who brought him sensational and misleading reports, and cashiered one or two of his self-assertive and antagonistic general officers, in my opinion, he and his army would have gained by their loss.

False Reports and Hesitation

  As a sample, this item of relative historic data; "Feeling in army. One Lieutenant general talks about attack and not giving ground publicly, and quietly urges retreat." On one occasion, and a very important one, Gen Hood reported to Gen Johnston a heavy Federal force in line of battle near his (Hood's) position on the Camden road. This report caused Gen

Johnston to change his lines, formed for battle, and move to the rear, as the federal force on his (Johnston's) flank was unexpected and very surprising. In reference to same, Gen Mackall, reporting to Gen Johnston, said;" I saw no troops as reported and do not believe there were any there." The reason for abandonment of position at Cassville after issuing the battle orders and formation for battle is given by Gen Johnston. He said; "The fire of the enemy's artillery commenced soon after the troops were formed and continued until after dark. Soon after dark Lieut. Gens Polk and Hood together expressed to me decidedly, the opinion, formed upon the observation of the afternoon, that Federal artillery would render their positions untenable the next day, and urged me to abandon the ground immediately and cross the Etowah (river.) Lieut. Gen Hardee, whose position I thought was weakest, was confident that he could hold it. The other two officers were so earnest, however, and so unwilling to depend on the ability of their corps to defend that ground, that I yielded and the army crossed the Etowah, a step which I have regretted ever since."

Also, there were many disloyal citizens in that section, and in my opinion, Gen Sherman's ability to locate our position before battle and perform some of his flank movements by devious ways was by reason of information gained from Unionist and deserters from our army who were spying on Johnston's movements, and who were familiar with the topography of the country and knew every pass and ford of Mountain and streams. But for Sherman's knowledge of our position and battle formation he would doubtless have attacked us immediately at Cassville. In which case either Sherman's marching through Georgia "to the sea," or "Hood's campaign in Tennessee," would not now be on record in history.

We continued to fall back. When near New Hope Church we again faced about and confronted our pursuing, exultant, but extremely discrete and cautious foe. Whenever we turned and went into shape for action the enemy would halt, intrench, skirmish and flank. My regiment rested in a grove near to the church, and the men were lying down in line, about noon, while other troops were forming on our left and rear, as we, as usual, were in the front line in our formation. I was lying down near a small oak tree just in rear of our line, my horse standing near. I was very hungry and had nothing to eat. I had given away the half pound ration of fat, rancid bacon and eaten a few "hard tack," crackers dry. Gen Walthall's Mississippi regiments were forming close in our rear from right to left.

Wife and Children

As the formation was rapidly completed by the regiment directly in rear of my regiment, their men stacked arms and hurriedly broke ranks, and began eating. A group of three moved toward me until they came within a few paces of where I was lying, seemingly wanting to separate from the others of their command, or to get into a shady spot. They were, all of them, privates and fine looking fellows. As they neared me I noticed the strong resemblance of a tall, erect, black-bearded one of the group to Capt. Steve Wilson, Company I, of my regiment. Hurriedly seating themselves, they opened their haversacks and piled up between them some really nice looking victuals, apparently home-cooked and were soon eating and talking spiritedly and rapidly. As they sat in triangular order the tall, bearded man was directly facing me. As I looked, I violated one of the holy commands. I did "covet" some of that dinner of my neighbors. I was close to them. I was about to rise, approach them and ask to join in, just for a bite, but hesitated; first, I was an officer, then they were strange troops. Had I acted on impulse and risen, there might have been short shrift and brief opportunity for me to repent or atone for the aforesaid violation as to coveting. In reply to a remark of one the tall, bearded man exclaimed, with apparent feeling, "I wouldn't mind fighting 'em for the next six months if I could only hear from my wife and children." In that instant there came crashing from a Federal battery, which had been quickly and very stealthily moved into a screen of woods in our front, a shot which, passing directly over my prostrate self at a height of not more than three feet, and between two of the trio of diners, struck square in the upper part of the face of the handsome, bearded soldier, crushing his head into atoms as if it had been an eggshell. As I sprang quickly to my feet the two living men grasped and quietly raised their fallen comrade, but lowered him instantly, as there remained little of the fine, manly face other than the flowing black beard.

We were quickly into line and ready, but skirmishing and cannonading continued in front until an hour before sunset, when Hooker's corps moved in heavy force and great gallantry against us and were met and driven back with heavy loss by Stewart's corps, after two hours of hard fighting. Constant skirmishing was kept up along the whole line for two days following. At 5:30 P. M. of the second day Howard's corps finally assaulted our line in their front, were met by Cleburne's division and repulsed about dark with great slaughter. Cleburne lost, in killed and wounded, 450. The enemy's dead in Cleburne's front, except those borne from the field, counted 600. Desultory skirmish firing continued for the next few days. Gen Sherman was accommodating Gen Johnston in his wish for "partial engagements."

The enemy was intrenching in our front, parking their artillery and massing their columns. We were waiting, watching and conforming our movements to their apparent preparations for attack.

Out Foraging

During this temporary lull I decided to ride out to rear and hunt something that I could eat. Mounting and leaving the main highway, I rode about six miles to the rear, southeast, when I came to quite a nice and comfortable "settlement." I had my canteen along and was after milk, buttermilk, clabber and something else than my daily fare. Dismounting at the front gate, I approached the front steps of the neat looking log house. I noticed a neat looking elderly woman and two young women, one of whom I instantly perceived was very pretty, sitting in homemade chairs on the plaza, while near them, on the outer edge of the floor, with feet swinging just above the ground, sat two fine looking young soldiers. While I raised my hat and bowed low to the ladies the young grey-jackets stood and saluted. I noticed that each of these had two canteens slung around him. I could see that the canteens were not empty and at once realized that somebody else was "out foraging," and using the tactics of Gen Bedford Forrest, had "got thar first," but I did not realize then how fully and entirely such was the case. While stating to the eldest lady my wants and my hunger, I was feasting my eyes on the loveliness of the beautiful girl with black hair and blue eyes, not more than 19 years of age. I conversed with the young folks a few minutes until invited by the elderly woman into the dining room and kitchen of the family in the back yard, she had prepared me a lunch. Hungry and famished as I was, upon my word, I rode and left the plaza reluctantly. While I ate and enjoyed the beef and biscuit and bowl of clabber with sugar on top, the good motherly soul filled my canteen with clabber. I offered her a Confederate bill, but she would not have pay. "No'" she said, "my poor boy, Joe, has been and may be again starving and beggarly for vittles, and I can't pray to God to be good to Joe unless I am good to others." I slipped a $5 bill under the turned down plate at the end of the table and hurried back to the front plaza. The young men were some thirty or forty paces away at the side gate of the yard, looking at a mare and colt. I seated myself near the beautiful girl, and as I looked I thought of "flowers born to blush unseen," etc. and wondered why the duce I had not found this one several days sooner; and (I plead guilty) I determined, quickly, to get up in the shortest time possible the fastest, finest, and fondest flirtation imaginable. I expressed my gratitude for kindness, my pleasure in the visit, and meeting, and my earnest wish for another meeting at the earliest possible moment on the morrow; I assured her that a thirty minute ride would bring me there again the following evening unless something serious happened at the front to prevent (and I thought unless it was mighty serious it would not prevent.) She was assuring me that they would surely save me a canteen of milk and I was flattering myself on my splendid progress when the young soldiers in the yard returning, seated themselves on the front steps. Very near them was a door opening into a "shed room," at the end of the plaza.

"A Little "Sojer"

A moment later there issued from the shed room the shrill, loud squall of a baby, and the elder and taller of the young soldiers sprang up and on to the plaza as a minie ball or bombshell had struck at his feet, darted into the room and the next moment came out hugging to him a bouncing half-year old baby, holding it so awkwardly that my charming young vis-a-vis, calling out, "Joe, don't let him fall," sprang up and gathered the youngster in her own arms. "Joe" said, "Well I must be getting back to camp. Spank him, Annie, if he hollers." "No," said "Annie, he won't hollar. He is leetle sojer, and tell popper you will soon be big enough to take his place and let him stay home wid mummer." The other young soldier and the other young lady were walking in the yard, slowly, toward the gate. The elder mother was standing in the doorway, Joe not far from her. Annie was near me with the "leetle sojer" in her arms. I – well had been completely surprised, utterly defeated and was anxious to fall back. I rallied, however, as quickly as possible and said, "Joe, if I had as pretty wife and as fine a boy as you have I think I could whip twenty Yankees here in Georgia. To which command do you belong?" I asked. He replied, "The 5th Georgia, Jackson's brigade; I have seen you many a time with the 47th." "Then," I replied, "we are in the same brigade and will fight close by each other for mother, Annie and the boy; and God grant that we may soon have opportunity to make those who do not bite the dust turn their backs in flight from our home." "Captain, I wish to God they were a hundred miles." "Say a thousand, Joe," I said. "No," said he, "I don't mean the Yanks I mean mother, Annie and the baby." Brave, strong man that he was, he could not have uttered another word, for "baby" his last word was scarcely audible as it came from his twitching and quivering lips, while in his steel-grey eyes there blazed a light as dangerous as dynamite.

When Hope was Gone

I glanced toward the mother, her hands covered her face. Turning toward the beautiful young wife, I marked that her cheeks and lips were deathly pale, her lithe form quivered with suppressed emotion, while from her deep, dark blue eyes there shown a shrinking, frightened look. I knew what they apprehended. I knew the danger was not to them only, and my very soul was wrung in anguish. I could only say, "Cheer up, God keeping us, we will strike low the cursed horde who would overrun us." Saying good-bye, I mounted and rode rapidly back into camp.

Never again did I see either one of that party. The following day Walker's division was hotly engaged and Jackson's brigade lost many men. In ten days' time that entire vicinity was in the scope of our abandoned and the enemy's invaded territory. Often have I thought of "mother" and "Joe" and "Annie" and the "leetle sojer," and sometimes I wished that, standing in their home, before too late, I had said to "Joe" what my heart felt, prompted, but which my ideas of honor as a soldier and my duty as an officer of the army forbade and precluded. Often I wished I could have informed the wife of that splendid, black-bearded soldier, killed while eating, that the last words spoken in the instant of his death were, "My wife and children."

Another incident, occurring only a few days later, is still fresh on my mind, and my conduct, or failure to act as I now could, is somewhat a "thorn in my Pillow."

The Sunday News, Charleston, South Carolina – October 12, 1913

A Confederate Soldier's Memoirs
(By Captain B. S. Williams, Brunson, S. C.)

During the months of September and October, 1864, humdrum camp life, desultory picket duty and continuously reinforcing Fort Sumter at night while we were on James Island, while comparatively restful at first, and preferable to the marching and countermarching, skirmished and battles, days and nights in front of Sherman's forces in Upper Georgia, was becoming by the first of November exceedingly monotonous to us. We should have been thankful for the opportunity and spell of rest, quiet and comparative safety from shot, shell and bayonet charge to which we had been so accustomed, by almost daily contact, for more than the year past, but is man ever satisfied?

We had escaped the fighting and defeats of our Army of the West, under the new commander, Gen Hood, in his engagements with Gen Sherman, around Atlanta, where fell the gallant Gen Walker, in whose division we had fought before detachment from the army at Kennesaw.

My regiment had served in the divisions of Gen John C. Breckinridge, of Kentucky, Cheatham, of Tennessee, and Walker, of Georgia, respectively. I was under deepest obligation to Gen Breckinridge and still today reserve his memory for personal kindness to me. Through his influence I was enabled to visit our army headquarters and confer with our commanding general, Joseph E. Johnston, and in person make application to him, which was in violation to all custom, and secure from Gen Johnston special favors, in the instance, which were under prohibition in our army by general orders. Gen Breckinridge was one of the most majestic, imperial appearing men I ever saw and true, noble dignity was personified in his deportment.

Gen Cheatham I knew as a rough and ready fighter, at all times and in any way, from a personal fisticuff with an obstreperous teamster to a bayonet charge, by division against Federal breastworks and booming cannon, but in my boyish fancy the slender, erect, impulsive, gallant Gen W. H. T. Walker, of Georgia, was my ideal of a knightly soldier. I think he is the only man I ever saw who seemed to really delight in the prospect of a fight, to glory in the opportunity. Whenever visiting the city of Augusta, I never fail to halt on my way and for a few moments look steadily at the very life like marble image of this proud and gallant soldier standing on one of the corners of the pedestal of the handsome monument on Broad Street.

Augusta's Tribute to Heroes.

This beautiful monument is an honor to the "Empire State" of the South, upon whose soil was poured the lifeblood of her illustrious son, the gallant Walker. Oh, had we had, in the hour of need, at the head of each and every division of our Army of the West such earnest, unselfish, true and indomitable leaders as Walker and Cleburne, brighter to-day would be the glow of our prestige and sweeter the lay of the lore of our glory.

The reversed order of conditions and our position on James Island contributed very considerably to the restlessness of the men of my regiment. We were not now, as formerly, with our backs to our homes and our front to the foe; our homes were between the enemy and us. Atlanta had fallen and was occupied by the enemy and was now his pivotal point; his objective position was Savannah, which was held by Gen Hardee with a force entirely inadequate for a successful defence. Hood had started on his ill-fated march into Tennessee and the way open to Sherman to march without opposition to Savannah. The intervening territory to be traversed in the march embraced the homes of three-fourths of the men of my regiment.

These facts were well known to those at home and the piteous appeals of frenzied, defenceless wives, mothers, daughters and sisters, to husbands, fathers, brothers and sons, for counsel, advice and protection wrung the hearts and tortured the souls of the bravest, truest men in the ranks. No wonder that in several instances men failed to withstand the agonizing fear and dread and returned, to wife or mother to secure her safety from the invading hordes as we had so often faced in battle. And yet few deserted! I was spared this torture and test, as my mother had refugeed to far South Georgia, yet I was not without friends who were correspondents, from whom I received letters, several of which have been treasured until now and are within my reach as I write.

"The Homespun Dress"

The talented young poetess of Georgia, Miss Carrie Belle Sinclair, then in Savannah, wrote me and enclosed a copy of her composition, "The Homespun Dress," which was sung in bivouac and camp, at home and hearth and fireside from the Potomac to the Rio Grande. It was in same metre and sung to the tune of "The Bonnie Blue Flag." Many Federal soldiers had copies, as there was an occasional exchange of literature on battlefields, but receipt and possession of same in every instance vested in the party or parties last on the field and first in the pillage.

Miss Sinclair was the gifted daughter of a minister of the Methodist Church. "The Homespun Dress" was the most popular of her compositions. Before offering the verses for publication she submitted them for inspection and criticism, to Alexander H. Stephens, of Georgia, the Vice President of the Confederacy and one of the most eloquent orators of America, who was a friend, adviser and admirer – in a fatherly way – of the gifted girl. She was not robust and physically strong, and died in 1883.

I read with sadness of the death of the talented, romantic, true-hearted writer of several letters to me, treasured still in my possession. Of the communications received by me was one which caused me to remain awake many nights after "taps" had sounded and awake before the call of "reveille" and think. The writer was a schoolmate, but three or four years my senior. At the age of about 24, when I saw him last, he was a very handsome officer in uniform with rank of first Lieutenant. He was quite tall, broad of shoulder, full chest, thin flank, straight as an arrow and lithe and active as an Indian. Fight? One look into those steely, blue-grey eyes close beside the thin Roman nose, one glance at the thin, compressed lips below the drooping, auburn mustache and above the firm, square chin, and you read the answer. What a splendid fighter in the field he would have made, and yet he never fought a battle in the ranks on any field. I withhold his name and number of command. He was first Lieutenant M__, of the __th Georgia volunteer infantry.

Move Resented

Either in the very last part of the year in 1862 or very early in 1863 several Georgia regiments of infantry were stationed at Savannah, Ga., mobilized to reinforce Johnston's small army, at that time in Mississippi. At this time an order issued from our war department in Richmond, authorizing the selecting and detaching, by a selected board of officers, not of the regiments from which the men were to be taken, to be known as "The 1st Battalion of Georgia Sharpshooters." This order was like a bombshell thrown into the camp of each regiment to be so partially emasculated, and there was "trouble in the camp" amounting to insubordination and almost mutiny and concerted open rebellion. Finally there was forced acquiescence, as reflection convinced that when the official powers, combined, "imposes, man must needs abide." This drastic measure caused the desertion of eight or ten good men from my regiment, and even greater numbers from other commands.

When the __th regiment was ordered to form for inspection and the detaching of the contingent from that regiment, my friend, Lieut. M____, temporarily in command of his company refused to form the company and take his place in line. Second Lieutenant R___ was ordered to form the company and he, too, flatly refused. (R___ was a fine officer, too.) Both were immediately placed under arrest. Before charges were preferred both forwarded to Richmond, their commissions and resignations, sheathed their swords and returned to their homes. Desertion from the army by numbers of their company followed.

The communication referred to as causing me such serious consideration was from my friend, Ex-Lieut. M__, and in part was as follows.

Lieutenant M_____'s Letters

"I left the army, not as a deserter, but as a dissenter from radical views, and a resenter of gross injustice; free, after a tender of my commission, I had committed no crime and my offense was one of omission – a refusal to act and become particeps criminis to a most damnable injustice to the members of my company who had mustered into service to serve with me as their officer along with their comrades and guarantee that as volunteers they should have and exercise the right to select their commands in which to serve and elect their own officers under whom to serve. They were willing, anxious, to fight as organized, but despite their earnest protests they were dragged from the ranks of their command and consolidated with fractions of twenty other commands and officered by a set of pompous, bombastic strangers without command of their own but, who were evidently pets of somebody at the head of our war department. If these filibustering freebooters are native Georgians, why the devil didn't they do as you and I and others, enlisted with the men of their section and win rank, either by election or promotion? What right had they to prey upon organized volunteer commands for office and command so far as they are concerned? If the practice of such nepotism, despotism and like damned 'isms' is the policy upon which our Confederate Government is based and to be founded, then to hell with the Government for which you are fighting, and the quicker the better. I shall not re-enter the service, regularly, and I defy all the conscript officers that can be sent for making arrests and forcing service.

"I am here on the banks of the broad Altamaha River; the swamp is broad and long and within the dark morass are 'safe and silent islands.' I can muster fifty in two hours' time, as brave and gallant as are in your ranks, some of them are from your ranks and have fought with you in several battles. With them at my back this community might become exceedingly unwholesome for any ordinary force that insisted on butting in on us."

"But here is what I want to say to you: I want to do some good for this, my section of country, and here is my proposition:"

"Atlanta has fallen: the broad way is open to Sherman to reach Savannah. He is coming, and what the devil will old Hardee be able to do with 15,000 or 18,000 troops, good, poor and indifferent, against Sherman's army? Very soon Savannah, Darien and Brunswick, with all the coast along, will be in the hands of the Yankees. They will establish military posts along the coast, from which they will sally and ravage this section of country, if not opposed. Where the A. and G. Railway crosses the Altamaha, (Doctortown,) is with 20 miles of where I am and I expect a military post to be established there. Our armies are depleted and dispirited; Hood is, in my opinion, acting the fool in giving up all of Georgia and going back into Tennessee. I keep pretty well posted and it looks to me very much so, as if we are now rapidly nearing the breakers. In such case I think it well to look after 'home and mother.'"

Urged to Come

"Now, forward your resignation and come home at once. I will tender you, on arrival, if you give me one week's notice, 50 men well mounted and armed and will pledge myself and them to follow you to and over the brink of hades, if you lead. I will take second place in command and make Williams – no kin to you, but a devil in a fight – third in command. There is plenty of provision in this section of country; this and other property we can save and take some valuable prizes by capturing raiding parties and small garrison posts. Besides we can and will – like Lochinvar, do you remember? – swim the Savannah River, 'where ford there is none,' and can range widely into your section of your State. You can easily increase the force to 100 men. Come, you will see some familiar faces. I have conferred with them and all say 'come.' We will organize and pledge you command and leadership; firm, true, fealty and implicit obedience. Come."

I thought seriously, weighed well the suggestion and realized that in Lieut. M_____ and the force with him was an element that might be wielded with benefit to our cause or be converted into a formidable, menacing, ever-impending danger. I wanted to go in answer to the call, if I could do so honorably, without tarnishing my record and name. I made known the status to only two or three close friends. Col Ashby said:

"I don't want you to leave us, but by Heaven, were your youth and opportunity mine, when Sherman reaches this part of the country and these regular troops go from here to – God knows where – I would pale Mosby's deeds by comparison." (Mosby was a famous chief of a guerilla clan in Virginia.)

My friend, the surgeon of the regiment, the handsome, gifted, rollicking, dare-devil Denson, from Talladega, Ala, discussing the matter with me in my tent one night declared:

"I like your suggestion, to apply for authority to muster and fight that force as an independent organization but as an appendix to the regular army, do that, and I shall go with you. With our mounts, we can easily reach the designated post in six days."

Then knitting his brow and stroking his long, black beard for a moment, he reached across the table and, taking up a pencil and piece of paper, scribbled rapidly for a few minutes and handed me over his "production," which was as follows;

"Were your chance, mine,
So sure as yonder moon doth shine,
At their desire, at their request,
Their mettle and their steel I'd rest,
Of camp in forest, dale and dell,
History, in years long hence, should tell,
And of midnight raid, of victories won,
Whene'er you mount, with that I go,
You, leader, I your Medico."

Too Late

Thus urged I thought and brooded and dreamed: I could not comprehend why Ex-Lieut. M____ competent, fitted, my senior, and my superior, by far, physically, should so urge me to supplant him and I brooded on. But the tide in our affairs was turning and events interesting were floating around us. (I wish to state just here that I did not go and take command of that set of desperate men at home, but when Johnston's army surrendered in North Carolina, April, 1865, there was pending in our war department an application by me for assignment to duty of mustering in and using those men as I at first suggested. I was reliably informed that my application met very favorable consideration, but on account of chaotic conditions, action was delayed until too late.)

As I feared, there was danger in that element at home. Ex-Lieut. M___ and Williams – no kin to me – with their followers, became a terror to friend as well as foe. Living now in the county of Appling, near the town of Baxley, Ga., is a man by the name of Isaac Higgs – 83 years of age, of sound mind and body and excellent memory. In July last he was in this neighborhood on a visit to relatives and was inquiring after me. I went for him, captured him and brought him to my home, keeping him all day and listened again to the familiar but ever interesting story of how Ex-Lieut. Williams, with their band, one dark night, captured a steamer on the Altamaha River loaded with Confederate Government supplies and compelled Higgs (the engineer) and pilot to steam down the Altamaha past Darien to Savannah, where they sold steamer and cargo to Federal officials for $9,000 in gold, silver and "greenbacks." Old man Higgs gets fighting mad before he finishes his relation and pulls out his pocket knife to show how he did when firs hailed in the "dead hour" of that night by Ex-Lieut. M___. Thinking there might be only one or two he proposed using his knife on them in protection of his boat. Then he shuts up his knife to illustrate his action on seeing himself surrounded by a "mighty host all around," and finally ends by "cussing out" Williams and Ex-Lieut. M____.

On return of the regulars from the army at the close of the war, there were settlements of scores in which blood flowed freely in that community.

But coming as a tidal wave of wonder onto a hitherto dreary shore was the unique event to which I referred in a former article. Just before the twilight of the day of October 30 there appeared suddenly, much to the surprise to the men of the regiment, quite a long line of blue-coated Federal soldiers in the very midst of the camp, moving briskly toward headquarters of the regiment. They were marching in double file, right in front, and as they neared our tent the order was given them, "On right, by files into line" and they swung into line, halted and dressed, facing headquarters with the alacrity and precision of trained troops. They were without arms and by the time the order "parade rest" was given, the blue line was encompassed by a solid wall of grey. Perfect silence prevailed and it was amusing to witness the wide-open-eyed stares exchanged by the Blue and the Grey.

The Sunday News, Charleston, South Carolina – September 17, 1911

Memoirs of a Soldier in War Between the States

Personal Recollections of Stirring Times Encountered by Regiment that Began Service on James Island and Later Joined Forces with Johnston's Army --- A Great Battle

(By Benj S. Williams, Brunson, S. C.)

During my military service in the Confederate States army, beginning early in the year 1861 and continuing to the seacoasts of North Carolina, South Carolina and Georgia, from Topsail Sound to Darien, until May 1863, when my command became a part of Johnston's Army of the West, to the end in April 1865, I engaged in many skirmishes and quite a number of battles, some of these the hardest fought and most sanguinary of our woeful war.

The recollection of my feelings just before, at the beginning and throughout many of the battles is clear and discriminative, more so than as to the occurrences of ten or fifteen years only ago. My hypothesis or theory of accounting for this fact is that at the age of 17 I threw down my books at school to enter the army; not until I was past 21 did I leave the army, those four intervening years between 17 and 21 constituted the formative state and most impressible and susceptive period of my life. Into some of those battle frays I would dash – some times mounted, at other times afoot – gladly, impetuously exultantly, glorying in the ring and clash and shock of battle, defiantly and recklessly defending our standard amid falling friends or reveling and rejoicing in the shouts of victory over fleeing and fallen foes. On other like occasions I would advance cautiously, timorously, reluctantly, no esprit de corps, chafing under and within myself almost ashamed of an irresistible feeling of timidity and effect of my speculative view of the shadows of quickly coming events. On occasion I could have been checked or stayed home from the fight by only high or stern authority, and for victory would have sacrificed my life; on other occasions I would gladly have avoided the contest and shielded myself from danger could I have done so and preserved my honor. Why such was the case I could not then truly understand, nor can I now satisfactorily explain. It may be that confidence of ability of leadership at the time and doubt at another time were causes for the varying emotional effect. In conversation with a very gallant officer of the Northern army in Savannah, Ga., years ago, swapping experiences and relation of incidents of battles in which we both had fought, on opposite sides, of course, he said to me, "I caught myself on more than one occasion framing in my mind a plausible pretext for avoidance of the fury of the storm of impending battle. At such times I would inwardly chide myself with cowardice and thus spur on my failing confidence."

From James Island to Bentonville

In my memory of almost every engagement in which I took part, from James Island, S. C., June 10, 1862, to the last desperate struggle at Bentonville, N. C., March, 1865, where the tattered standard of the remnant of my regiment waved in victory and the remaining few around it shouted in triumph for the last time on battlefield, there stands forth prominently as a part and parcel of the event, the day's doings, some happening or spectacle, a mere unimportant incident in the awful drama, pre-eminent and paramount to other greater and more important occurrences. Recalling to my mind the picture of any one of those scenes of long ago, indelibly stamped on my memory's tablet, there may be in base relief or glowing and looming above much more serious and important transactions, some trivial circumstantial incident, comparatively insignificant and void of material effect at the time of happening, yet ineffaceable throughout the grind and passage of decades of time and the occurrence of legions of varying events; time when the "days of danger and nights of waking" had given place to "weary nights on which dawned wearier days;" throughout the shifting scenes of almost half a century, until this time when "the hills grow dark and on the purple peaks a deeper shade descending" warns that soon not one who was a soldier of the cause that was lost "a wandering which note of the distant spell may record; that soon taps, then silent all."

In our first engagement – our baptism of fire – James Island, June 10, 1862, the conflict was short but spirited and bloody. Among the killed was the gallant Capt. Williams, commanding Company C. Well do I remember our gallant advance, (I am speaking of our command) our complete surprise, our impetuous, reckless charge, our crushing defeat by overwhelming numbers intrenched and waiting to receive us, reinforced by the heavy artillery of their gunboats lying in the Stono River, our sullen retreat, our grief over fallen comrades, and yet that which appears as vivid in my memory as any other sight or sound of that engagement is the fantastic antics and voluble profanity of a brave Irish Lieutenant while trying in the confusion of retreat to rally his company for another charge, a forlorn hope.

At Secessionville

Six days after June 16, at Secessionville, we lost one of the finest young officers of the regiment, First Lieutenant Graeme, Company B. Relative to this engagement was abundant food for thought and ample picture material for memory. From a position on our right, where we were supporting our artillery, I watched the 4th Louisiana battalion, under Lieut. Col McHenry, go beautifully into the fight at double-quick, double file, right in front until reaching the pivotal point, then rapidly "on the right, into line." Riding over the field after the battle, in company with the colonel of our regiment, I noticed among the dead Federals a large man with enormously large feet lying on his back with arms extended on the earth and his face carefully covered, apparently, with a large colored silk pocket handkerchief, placed there, I presume, by some departing comrade. The movement into the action by that single battalion and that kerchiefed, dead Yankee soldier are prominent features in my mind's picture of the fight at Secessionville. Of every battle in which I took part I have a picture in my mental storehouse; Jackson, Chickamauga, Lookout Mountain, Missionary Ridge, Dalton, Resaca, Oustanaula, New Hope Church, Kennesaw Mountain, Atlanta, Johns Island, Honey Hill, Rivers's Bridge, Averysboro, and Bentonville. For Instance in my memory picture of the field and fight at Resaca there are magnificent phalanxed battalions after battalions of blue; splendid regiments, brigades and divisions of grey. Thousands of officers and men on each side – the power of both armies in the West. Looming prominently in the fore-ground of the picture is a rather slender, blue-eyed, lithe, active man, rather below medium height, erect and quick in movement, about 30 years of age –"only a private." Private B. Summerlin, Company D, 47th Georgia infantry. I feel it due him from me to record somewhat of his action in his last battle.

  The battles of Resaca and Dalton opened the campaign of 1864 in Georgia, which resulted so disastrously to our cause.

  After a hard campaign in 1863, marching, countermarching, fighting and starving, 1863-64, Johnston's Army of the West went into winter quarters just over the line of Tennessee, near to the town of Dalton, in upper Georgia, to keep from freezing during a part of the winter of 1863-64.

A Severe Winter

  The winter's weather was very severe, tents were scarce and rations very slim, and although we were not very comfortable, the temporary cessation of hostilities afforded a welcome "rest for the weary" and our troops made the best of this little opportunity for rest, recreation and enjoyment, yes enjoyment. Poor fellows! Their clothes were worn thin and tattered, their shoes ragged and holey; they had to "double up" in pairs to have a blanket between them and earth and one between them and sky, yet they were in good spirits and there was never a day or night, and hour or minute that they were not willing and ready to fight "at the drop of a hat."

  Fatigue duty was made light, drills were shortened and the cutting and carrying of wood and building of fires occupied much of the time. Rain, sleet and snow, day and night. One day, when the snow to the depth of several inches covered the ground, wood, hillside and valley, the clouds rolled temporarily away and the sunshine, bright, warm and genial, burst in beauty and brilliancy on our camp, kissing everyone into warmth and animation.

From tent and cover, on right and left, on hill and glen, there seemed to spring suddenly into life forty thousand men in grey. Some just beyond my quarters began snowballing each other, others rushed into the mimic fight, whole companies joined in, then regiments and brigades. Dignity, for the nonce, was aside and rank ignored. Generals surrendered to privates, colonels fought valiantly for victory, desperately in self-defence or sought safety in retreat, covered decidedly more with snow than glory.

I had sometime before witnessed "the battle above the clouds," Lookout Mountain. I witnessed here a battle amidst clouds formed by flying snowballs. A few sunlit hours, then more clouds and rain and snow. It was with considerable difficulty that our teams could haul our rations of stale meal and poor beef over the boggy, ravined road from Dalton to commissary headquarters. Washouts on the railroad, too were frequent, cutting off our mail and communications with the outside world.

Mail, Male and Meal

One night, sitting around our camp-fire, Col Ashley, of the 47th Georgia, was complaining bitterly on account of receiving no mail from home. "D___d the railroads! They ought to get the mails through, day after day and no mail!" John Barrett, a broad-shouldered six-footer, typical son of the Emerald Isle, knelt at the fire carefully attending to three slices of frying meat which, with three pieces of corn cake and three "hard-tacks" and three tin cups of parched meal "coffee," were soon to serve for supper for three of us. "Was it male that you were after, Colonel, when you and the adjutant rode to town this evening?" asked Barrett. "Yes," said Col. Ashley, "Why Colonel, a plenty of male (meal) there is right here in the commissary." There was a quick flash from the Colonel's hazel-colored eyes, but in another instant he was joining in my hearty laugh. Barrett, with a merry twinkle in his deep blue Irish eyes, disappeared within the adjacent fly tent, from where he soon called out. "Gintlemen, the avening male is ready."

In 1894 I saw Barrett for a minute near his home, in Liberty County, Georgia. His tall erect form was bent, his broad shoulders stooping, his former raven locks as white as the snow flakes of Dalton. He is now resting in that bivouac "under the shade of the trees beyond the river."

Our lines had been shortened considerably in the past season's campaign. Thousands and thousands of brave men in grey and blue were sleeping in freshly made narrow graves in the soil of the States of Mississippi, Tennessee and Georgia – the sleep that knows no waking at drum-beat or bugle call – "their warfare o'er." Our enrolling officers were

busy at the rear hunting up recruits for our decimated ranks. The Federal army was being heavily reinforced. Of the many songs sung in our camps there was a popular ard, frequently sung parody of "Annie of the Vale." The refrain of which was –
"Come, come, come, rain, come; Come to the tops of my boots;
Oh, come and I'll thank ye, to keep back the Yankee
Only till our ranks are filled out with recruits."

The rain certainly came, came, came, but the recruits did not, for then in our ranks stood the slender youth of 16 beside the gray-haired sire of 50.

Private B. Summerlin

Here during our rest, the orders of freemasons and Odd Fellows held their meetings in secluded and guarded dells, and chaplains of the army labored faithfully to advance in the lull of earthy war, the banner of their captain, the Commander and King of all hosts. Among the many in the camps who embraced religion and donned new robes (only spirituously) of righteousness was the aforesaid Private B. Summerlin, of Company B, 47th Georgia infantry. Berry had been horribly wicked and awfully profane, though never vulgar. He was a queer character, a rare avis. Without advantages of money or education, he was veritably an aristocrat. He was fond of poetry and song. He was valorous and modest, reticent and courageous, aspiring and sensitive, exclusive and independent, dictatorial and proud, and quick as a flash to fight. He had been for some time detached from his company, "detailed for special duty" at the adjutant's quarters. With great pride and pains, as soon as we had gone into winter quarters, he constructed a neat little hut of hewn and split logs of oak and chestnut, chinked the cracks with clay and stretched my large tent fly (my only shelter) over this cabin, and then built a chimney, at one end, of rocks, clay and green short poles. Going to a nearby old field, he gathered and brought in bundles of clean broom straw and strewed fully six inches deep as a floor. When finished he truly pronounced it the "coziest, d_____, ___est" quarters in the regiment. My domicile was a camp palace and the rendezvous of friends. Many a song was sung, many a joke was told and many a pipe smoked there after roll call (I have an excellent picture of these quarters near me as I write, sketched by a camp artist. Berry sits outside on a stump, with pipe in mouth and hands in pockets.) Poor fellow! The winter wore away, the clouds rolled by. The rains ceased and no longer "kept back the Yankees." Arms were burnished, ammunition distributed, letters written home and last messages to loved ones sent. Baggage wagons were taking on their light loads of supplies. Drums were beating, bugles were sounding, lines of grey infantry were moving out to the front; closely following were batteries of field artillery, while squadrons of cavalry fringed our front and flanks. Johnston, with 44,000 men, all told, was moving out to confront Sherman at the head of 100,000 men, the flower of the Federal army.

When about ready to move Berry approached me and said, "Adjutant, I am just longing to go into battle; I want to ask you when the very next fight comes on to let me go in?" I said, 'What's wrong, Berry, our inactivity has made you restless. You know I am the fighting part of the household. I have to fight, at present, you do not. You should be satisfied. Besides, you have a loving, waiting wife and little children at home, and on their account you should take no needless risk. True we need every good man in our ranks, for God alone knows what is going to be the outcome of this campaign, but you are very useful in your present place." For the first time ever, I saw tears come into his eyes as he replied in a scarcely audible tone "you are right, Adjutant, but I don't know what ails me. I feel like I must take one more bresh" (brush.)

Clash with Sherman

One of our divisions struck the vanguard of Sherman's Army near Resaca. Our (W. H. T. Walker's) division was ordered up to the support of our attacking column. Nearing the field, we were halted and from my position on an eminence I had quite a fine view of part of the battle around, but a dense cloud of smoke covered all, and even with the aid of my field glasses I could see but little. The fire of artillery was very heavy, but I judged from the glimpses I had of position that it was on the Federal side. This was soon made clear, as a stiff breeze lifted the sheet of smoke. There were columns and columns of blue and above them floated the Stars and Stripes, while their artillery pealed forth shot and shell and canister. And there are the lines of grey and above the Starry Cross. The line of grey is firmly advancing, but I see no line of support; gaps and gaps are cut in their well dressed ranks; there from the rear and right comes Cleburn's division a double-quick, and God have mercy now on those in front. They sweep down in a whirlwind charge and the lines of blue are broken, but blue and grey are falling like the leaves of the forest in the late wintry blasts. I see fresh lines of blue double-quicking to the support, the rescue of their broken lines, and now close to our grey lines swings into position Cobb's Kentucky battery – our best brigade battery – well do I know them, only five guns; and now the crash and roar and ring as only Cobb's death-dealing guns can crash. Woe, woe to the foe in front! And now the battle is on. Heavens! We can't stand here. Why are we not ordered in? We must soon move. In my excitement – I turn suddenly to mount and stand face to face with Private Berry Summerlin, with accoutrements on and gun in hand. "Adjutant," he says, "I just could not stand it. I want to take a hand in this one fight and I will not ask to go in again. I will fall in and fight with my old Company D. (Drur __ __k) Mock has your papers to take care of. Take care of yourself, Adjutant, God help us!" "Attention!" rings out down our line. Our brigade moves briskly by the left flank. "Close up!"

"double-quick." We oblique to the right and enter a strip of low pine woods bordering a field of young growing wheat. We halt, front, dress and stand at parade rest. "Ready for a charge, Colonel," and the aid dashes on down the line with the order. "Attention!" "Fix bayonets!" "Shoulder arms!" "Close men!" "Steady!" "Dress on the colors!" "Forward March!" Out of the low pine woods, into the field of wheat we go. All line of grey, there is your work ahead.

Death of a Brave Man

There, on the crest of the hill, in front among those trees, rocks and rails piled waist high down their line of breastworks. See their waving colors. See those glittering field pieces – a line of smoke puffs from them, a deafening crash and our ranks are torn with shot and shell. "Charge," and forward to the living and down upon the green growing wheat, now stained with red, sink the wounded with the dead. The living press forward, we near the woods, the artillery fire ceases and now can be heard the ring of the "Rebel yell." But the infantry fire staggers our line; it reels and is broken. So we press on up to the works and the struggle is fierce, deadly at close quarters. As I attempt to go on to the breastworks an officer of artillery leaps in front of me. I see his florid face, his flashing blue eyes and blond mustache. He shouts out something, I could not hear what, I think it was "surrender." I had emptied every chamber of my Colt's army pistol. He held his sabre drawn high above his head. I quickly turned my pistol and grasped the barrel to hurl it with all my might full in his face before I could draw my sword. As I threw my left foot forward and before I could act he staggered backward, his gilt-braided red cap fell off, his sabre point described a wide circle from front to rear, and he sank down among the wounded and dead on his side. Their guns were silenced and their lines broken and pressed back, but before we could enter their works and turn their guns on them, heavy reinforcements poured in and down on us, and we were swept from the field in disorder back to our starting point in the pine wood. Rallying hastily there we moved rapidly to the left again to check a flank movement. Late in the evening, on our first stop and rest, I passed down our line shorter far than it was in the morning – there were missing forms and faces. Reaching Company D., 47th Georgia, I missed Berry Summerlin. Of the orderly sergeant I asked, "Where is Berry?" "We left him on the field, Adjutant," he replied, "he fell in the very last of the fight. He and I were right behind you when you went on to the works and was met by that Yank officer. I had fired my gun but Berry fired then, and I saw the officer fall and we turned for everything was giving way in the rear, and as Berry turned I saw him fall forward."

In my next morning report, under the head of "killed and missing" was "Private B. Summerlin, Company D, 47th Georgia."

We again moved southward as Sherman had begun his "march to the sea."

The Sunday News, Charleston, South Carolina – May 12, 1912

MEMOIRS OF A SOLDIER IN WAR BETWEEN STATES

When Gen Joseph E. Johnston's Army Among the Mountains of North Georgia in June, 1864, when All Hope was Gone and but Little Life Remained --- The Pathetic Death of a Brave Soldier.

(By Captain B. S. Williams, Brunson, S. C.)

The springtime of A. D. 1864 had come and had departed and we, the troops of the Army of the West, were in the month of June, among the mountains of Georgia. Slightly had we noted the loveliness of the passing springtime in that beautiful section of the "Empire State of the South."

Occasionally when bivouacking on the edge or in the midst of a woodland on some mountain side, if the welkin was not ringing with the boom of cannon and the ring of rifle, we would hear the softer sounds of sweet music of happy song birds' trilling notes. Occasionally on the march, sometimes while double-quicking into battle line, we would pass close to a yard or garden of beautiful flowers in bloom and by "eyes right" or "eyes left" enjoy a hasty glimpse of the floral beauties and the while inhale, perchance, a breath of their delightful fragrance wafted toward us – as if in coquetry – on the fickle, passing summer breeze. The strains and sounds with which we were more familiar were the whirr and buzz and burst of the deadly shell and hissing song of minie ball. The odor to which we were more accustomed and by which oftenest greeted was the pungent perfume of smoke of burning gunpowder.

Sherman's legions were pressing mightily forward toward Savannah and the sea, while, yet in firm array, the decimated ranks of grey, under Gen Joseph E. Johnston, sternly interposed, and frequently was the sky with battle smoke overcast, the air with shout and din of conflict rent and the soil ensanguined because of "partial engagements" of part of the forces of the contending unequal armies.

Only partial engagements, but fraught with direful results. To wit, an instance; May 27, near New Hope Church, Howard's corps, Federal, 18,000 to 20,000 strong, advance in five battle lines against position held by Cleburne's division, Confederate, 8,000 to 12,000 strong. Two hours hard, fierce fighting; Federals beaten back; 700 dead left on field by Howard; 400 dead in Cleburne's line. More than 1,000 fresh graves at that spot. Result of only a partial engagement of two hours that evening; yet a thousand hearts, a thousand forms of a thousand braves bidden and lost in those narrow, shallow graves. Fierce in the conflict, fearing not to die, The Grey and the Blue in the dust together lie.

Johnston and Sherman, trained army officers, skillful commanders both, incessantly manoeuvering for advantage, eager for opportunity to strike effectually; the advantage of defense Johnston's; advantage of superior numbers – "the heaviest battalions" – Sherman's; mighty strategists and movers in a great and desperate game of human lives and precious blood, the wager victory, the ultimatum inevitable doom and destiny of nations.

We had abandoned much of our estimably valuable territory in Georgia, but were still in a section of country where ranges of mountains and hills and deep streams of water afforded us positions, positions from which an army properly posted and well commanded can be scarcely driven.

Such position as was wisely chosen and hastily and dexterously seized by the Federal commanders at Gettysburg which Gen Lee and his able Lieutenants – stayed as by providential somnambulism – allowed, and which by the most gallant and desperate fighting of Lee's splendid battalions they failed to secure. Gen Lee said, "We met the enemy and he gave way on all sides and was driven through Gettysburg with great loss." Speaking of the day following, Gen Lee said: "He occupied a strong position with his right upon two commanding elevations adjacent to each other, one known as Cemetery Hill." From this position one of the heaviest and most prolonged, continuous cannonades of modern warfare and the charge of Pickett's division, as furious and gallant as the charge of "the 600" at Balaklava, failed to dislodge them.

We had withdrawn from our position near New Hope Church and were carefully marching and counter-marching in counteraction of the enemy's very cautious manoeuvering in his advance toward Marietta. We were attacking and driving him at one point, staying his advance at another point, causing him to halt, entrench and flank, sometimes in wide detours.

Halted near the roadside, to permit the passage of troops down on our left, my commander was resting when the 25th Georgia Infantry filed steadily by us. Recognizing the regiment as it approached I mounted my horse and joined Col Winn, commanding the 25th, and Adj. Lester, old friends. Their regiment halted, fronted and stacked arms for rest just beyond us. Riding back down the line I dismounted when I came to Company F, of the 25th, and shook hands with the men of the company in which I first enlisted and with whom I was mustered into service as a private. The ranks had been greatly thinned since I bade them good-bye one year before, at Sansavilla, to take my place, under orders, in another command. In this company, when I left them, were three excellent young men, first cousins, John H. Smith and John W. McGowan, of the same neighborhood, and John M. Smith, of another and distant section. McGowan was only 19 but sturdy, strong and manly; John H., 20, slender, graceful and gallant. Both of these were eldest sons of widowed mothers. John M. was 23, exceptionally handsome in form, features and presence. He left at home a beautiful young wife. He was urbane to friends and associates, but reserved and haughty in his general demeanor. Their Uncle, Capt. Madison Smith, was captain of their company, "The Altamaha Scouts." All these men were close friends of mine while I was with them in the 25th Georgia, but especially fond of me, apparently, was the proud and spirited "John M." At this my first meeting with the company since my transfer from it I quickly noticed that McGowan and John H were among those I missed. John H. informed me that both had been killed in battle. He was as handsome and proud in his bearing as ever, but I at once noticed a change in expression, in his piercing black eyes never seen by me before now. Bidding all good-bye I moved toward my horse, near and John M. walked with me.

Preparing to mount I extended my hand; he clasped it closely in both his hands and said, "Not good-bye, but au revoir, as soon as I can get permission I will walk over there and see you. I have something to impart."

"All right," I said, "then au revoir; but hasten your visit as we will remain here not much longer than one hour." He soon came to where I was lying resting in rear of our line. I well remember his haughty, but courteous bearing; his proud and elastic step. Reclining near me in the shade he confided in me his distress. He began; "I have for some time past been looking, watching and almost praying to meet you, knowing your regiment was here and had been placed in our division. Outside my company I know no one in the army and did not wish to confide in Uncle Madison (his captain.) I know you and love and trust you and feel assured that you would not let your rank of office bar my approach to our former friendly intercourse and confidence." "No," I said, "Speak freely, John M, I am your friend and your trust is safe in my keeping. My rank makes no difference. 'A man's a man for a' that.'"

He continued; "Since the falling in battle of the two boys we knew so well, John H. and John W., I have been lonely and restless and at times felt very much like following them into the beyond. In fact, in our fight on the 27th I tried to get hit, but afterward, remembering my dear wife at home, I felt ashamed of my foolhardy conduct. But for the past few days I have lived and moved in what seems to me a supernatural sphere, and God alone knows how I suffer. In bivouac of camp, however worn or fatigued, I cannot sleep. As I close my eyes to sleep invariably there appears, standing before me, beckoning to me, clearly and plainly outlines as I saw her, my wife all white robed and deathly pale. Sometimes I drop quickly to sleep only to be awakened by the same strange vision and repeatedly the last few nights I have waked to find myself sitting up, my eyes straining into the darkness and my arms outstretched in an effort to clasp her – not as in a loving embrace, but to grasp, support and shield what so plainly appears to me her trembling, quivering form. Great God; I cannot much longer stand the strain. I must end it, if in death." And he sprang quickly to his feet.

"Sit down, John M," I said, "and calm yourself. When did you last hear from home?"

"More than two months ago," he replied, "and I believe my wife is dead."

"What do you intend doing?" I asked.

"Why I so wished to see you," he replied, "was to advise me. I must see my wife, in life or death. I could quit and go home, as many are doing, but I would rather die than desert. Tell me what to do, my dear and trusted friend, and I will abide by your decision and advice, so help me, God. I realize my present unfitness to judge as to what is best to do, even had I the privilege of acting in accordance with my judgment. I could easily reach home, but I will stay and sacrifice myself, my life, as I believe we are all now doing in a hopeless cause, before I would cowardly sneak away, if you say so – I will start within this hour; hasten home, spend that one day only and return with all dispatch and report immediately to you and then to my own company. To you I pledge my word as a friend and my sacred honor."

Reaching across and taking his arm in mine I said to him, "No, my dear friend. I sympathize with you in the depths of my heart and would risk my life in your relief, but I, too, must preserve my honor. I cannot tell you to go. I will, as soon as possible, see your captain and Col. Winn and try and get you off duty for a few days, when you can honorably carry out your programme and fulfill your sacred promise to me."

As he grasped my hand, his eyes filling with tears, I heard, far down on the left, a bugle call of "Forward:" then nearer the roll of a drum and another and another. We both rose. Standing for a moment with hands clasped, he pointed with his left and said; "See, the 25th is falling in to move. I go. Good-bye, Ben, and God bless you," and dashed rapidly back to take his place in line.

The following day there was hot and continuous skirmishing along our entire division front. At times the ringing cheers and yells and rolling volleys of fire denoted fierce, close fighting. The day after was comparatively quiet and my command was withdrawn from the front and moved farther right, where we expected to "catch h___ and a whole lot of it in the morning," as Jack Williams expressed it. (Jack generally prophesied truly.) Late that evening I rode to Stevens's brigade and found the 25th Georgia in line, but not engaged. Reaching Company F, Capt. Madison Smith met me grasping my hand tightly, but in perfect silence. I glanced hastily down his company line and missed several men I had seen in the ranks two days before. I did not see John M, and asked of the captain, "Where is John M Smith?" The great, broad-shouldered, deep-chested, bearded, stern warrior-captain for some moments did not, could not, reply. Still grasping my hand, he said in broken, halting voice; "Poor fellow; the last one of my three brave and gallant nephews. He was killed yesterday."

"Where and how?" I asked.

"We were whipping the Yankees out of the woods; he was in front of the fight; a mini ball."

"Where was he struck, Captain?" I inquired.

Placing his forefinger in the centre of his forehead, he replied. "Just as plumb and centrally there as you could have placed your finger. He never knew he was hit."

With no other word I turned and rode sadly back to my own command. It was night and the troops were soon resting and sleeping. All was comparatively quiet, and as I rested with my back on the earth I looked long up at the silent stars in the heavens and wondered was the gallant, chivalrous, spirited young soldier now with his loved young wife. He could not see her "in life" without sacrifice of honor, truth and manhood. He "would rather die than desert." Was he, after the sacrifice of life, with her "in death?" He had said, "I must see her, in life or death."

A soft refreshing air wafting down the mountain was cool and pleasing. The deep-vaulted canopy of the clouds was clear and azure. The stars in their soft light glimmered, but darkly hung the impenetrable veil that completely enshrouds and entirely hides from us forever the mysteries and secrets of the future in the great and near beyond.

Oh, that I had detained my friend, that I had kept him by some means out of that last fight. In this gloomy channel ran my thoughts until I was relieved by "death's deep counterfeit silent sleep."

We were now nearly approaching the great crisis in our "storm-cradled," hope-cherished, way.

The Sunday News, Charleston, South Carolina – June 9, 1912

MEMOIRS OF A SOLDIER IN WAR BETWEEN STATES

Skirmishes in Neighborhood of Marietta, Ga.---Personal Experiences Following Stroke of Paralysis, Caused by wound at Chickamauga---In Hospital at Marietta

(By Captain B. S. Williams, Brunson, S. C.)

On the 14th of June, 1864, the troops of the Western Army, under Gen Joseph E. Johnston, were in battle formation and occupied a position in hastily constructed breastworks on a line several miles in length near Pine Lost and Kennesaw mountains, close to the city of Marietta, Ga.

Our line was confronted in its entire length by the heavily massed columns of Sherman's army.

Several thousand "State Troops" – militia – had been sent to Gen Johnston by Governor Joseph E. Brown, Georgia's "War Governor," and by official reports Johnston's army numbered 112,800. My command in Walkers Division, at this time, was on the left near Pine Mountain.

During the morning of the 14th, while little firing was going on, I noticed upon our right, a group of mounted officers slowly riding down along our line. They halted as if for consultation or reconnaissance and instantly from a Federal battery in front, there came a rapid fire of several rounds and the explosion of one or two shells very near the group of officers. At the third shot from the battery I noticed a commotion, hasty dismounting and a closer gathering of the group, and in a few moments there came word down the line, passed from man to man and company to company – like the wafting of sound on the billows of air – that Gen Polk, one of our army corps commanders, had been struck and instantly killed. He and Gen Johnston, accompanied by a few staff officers, were inspecting our lines and the ground in front, apparently regardless or forgetful of the alert, ever watchful and ever ready enemy.

Great sorrow was felt throughout our army because of the death of the Bishop-General, but consolation was felt in the thought of how worse it might have been if Gen Johnston, so near, had been struck.

The remainder of the day passed in comparative quiet, with only desultory cannonading along the line, on the right chiefly.

I had been constantly with my command, in long engagement – occurring almost daily from the opening of the campaign at Dalton, May 1. Many battles had been fought in "partial engagements" of parts of two armies. Many fields on Georgia soil had been ensanguined and many lives sacrificed in those clashes of manoeuvering for advantage to strike or close promise and prospect of victory in decisive, general engagement. I had longed for the day when the two numerically equal armies, in their entire strength, would close for decisive conflict and in the inevitably deadly strife prove the final result – the finale of the awful drama in which we were so earnestly interested and faithfully engaged. My hope and desire to witness an engagement in the culmination of the extraordinary campaign were – in the mercy of God, it may be – to be blighted and denied.

In the afternoon of that 14th of June, in the lessening heat of the sloping sun and lengthening shades and shadows of those hills and mountains, there came to me no thought that my service there was ended. That never again would I see those Phalanxed lines of Hood; that never again would I see the gallant Cleburne leading his invincible regiments into the very "gates of hell;" that never again would I, under the leadership of my division commander, the proud, intrepid, spirited Walker, hear amid the smoke clouds of battle the ringing cheers of victory or defiance, around me all his gallant brigades. I had suffered all the day with high fever-racking pains in my head and slight paralysis of my right side, but had remained on the firing line. My old friend, Brigade Surgeon Matthews, visited me at the close of the day and insisted on my going at once to the rear, saying that the pains in my head and partial paralysis of limbs on my right side was the effect of my old Chickamauga hurt. I didn't believe him. (Dr. Matthews was one of the faculty of the Baltimore, Md., Medical College, and when Maryland did not secede the old M. D. did and brought a dozen young medical students with him and joined the Confederate army. My father, at the time, commanded the regiment at Savannah, Ga., and appointed Dr. Matthews his regimental surgeon. He afterwards advanced in rank to brigade surgeon.)

I practically refused to go to the rear and be sent off to a hospital, as he suggested. I told him I had never been in a hospital as a patient and earnestly hope never to be. My gruff, old friend was somewhat angered with me and gave me some physic to swallow right then and left me, after murmuring that he would put me in a hospital or someone else would put me in a hole in the ground, and that pretty soon. I told him if allowed to rest I would be better in the morning. He must have dosed me on some strong narcotic, for I soon became stupid and slept heavily, not awaking until about 4 o'clock in the morning, when I found myself lying on my back and absolutely unable to turn myself over to either side. Awakening a younger brother sleeping near me, he aided me in turning on my left side for rest, and as I refused to let him call the surgeon he nestled close by me and slept. Very early the next morning my old Esculapian friend, Matthews, visited me and provoked me to some wrath by his "Aha; I told you so, Mr. Hothead, Self Will,' and when he again mentioned "hospital or hole in the ground" I said to him, "I am willing to go to the rear, as I am helpless and useless here, and into a field hospital, but I'll be D__d if

I go into a city hospital." "All right, all right." he said and induced me to swallow another concocted decoctions and ordered me to remain quiet and perfectly still until his return, "in about half an hour." I don't believe he returned in half an hour's time, but I cannot positively say; nor can I record anything that occurred on the line or any part of the field that day. In the early afternoon I was aroused by feeling an arm under my aching head, which was swathed in bandages, and feeling a spoon between my teeth from which trickled some liquid into my throat and I swallowed. I opened my eyes and it appeared to me that I was looking right into a strange female face close above me but I was not sure. I looked and tried to "wake up" and comprehend, but felt my eyes again closing. Again looking I saw nothing but a white plaster ceiling above. I thought "that must be the sky and the face a baseless fabric of a dream," but hearing a slight noise I turned my head and saw a table and a woman standing near it shaking a bottle containing a liquid. I closed my eyes and tried hard to remember. I got to where Dr. Matthews said, "until my return in half an hour." I then addressed the woman, saying, "Madam, where am I?" She came quickly and softly to the bed and, sitting on its edge, removed the bandages from my head and returned them moistened and cooler before speaking. "There, now," she said "you are in a hospital in Marietta." "When and how did I get here?" I inquired. "Oh, you were brought here in an ambulance from the front this morning, as dozens are each day and night, only a field surgeon came with you and helped bring you upstairs and put you in bed in this little room, in which, you see, you are the only patient. Now that was real nice, wasn't it? But our chief surgeon said he would see you when you roused up, so I will go and call him now. I am your nurse, you see." "One moment, madam, please," I said. "How looked the field surgeon who brought me here?" "Oh he was a stout, bearded man of middle age. Our surgeon knows him and can tell you his name." "Thank you," I said to the nurse, and to myself I said, "old Matthews got me." The lady nurse soon returned and said, "Both your doctor and ours are coming to see you." They entered and Dr. Matthews introduced me to the hospital surgeon and then, placing both hands on the bed and leaning over me, laughed until his huge fat sides and ample abdominal proportions shook and shook. "O ho, my young friend, hot spur; you would be d__d if you ever went into a city hospital, eh? Instead of being that you will be saved from the hole in the ground to which you were heading." I only said to him "you doped me." At which all three, doctors and nurse, laughed heartily.

Under the kindest treatment there I suffered intensely for several days. The wounded were coming in such numbers from the front that my doctor concluded to ship me farther to the rear and I was sent to Macon. Soon after my arrival there I suffered a relapse and was very ill for several weeks. There were many sick and wounded in all the hospitals in Macon. I was placed in a large room in the second story of a commodious brick building, the State Asylum for the blind, with four other officers; A captain of Georgia infantry, a captain of Virginia artillery – both wounded – and two Lieutenants of infantry, sick.

Such kindness, attention and tender ministration to the sick and wounded soldiers there by the ladies of Macon I have never seen equaled save in my own home, by my own family to myself. Sitting weak and emaciated, but convalescing, one afternoon chatting with the wounded captain of artillery, with my feet upon the window sill and seated in a very comfortable rocker sent up to me by a wealthy elderly widow lady, Mrs. Lockett, who had taken almost entire charge of me because, as she said, her maiden name was Williams, that her family was of Newberry County, South Carolina; that I closely resembled her folks and that I was her kinsman, (all of which was very fortunate for me.) She insisted on removing me to her splendid home, but I gratefully protested. A detailed soldier nurse of our room handed me a note. At first glance I recognized the peculiar chirography as that of a friend I had left at the front, Lieut. Col William H. Wyley, of the 25th Georgia infantry, brilliant young lawyer, a wild, reckless, extravagant man, a very handsome and gallant officer. He informed me he had been in Macon about three weeks on sick leave; had left the hospital and was then occupying a suite of rooms in a private residence in the city. He had learned of my extreme illness, of my recovery and convalescence and wanted me to "come at once" to see him. The nurse informed me that an old negro man waited at the door for an answer. I very quickly wrote Col Wyley that under presumption if he were able to move he could have visited me in my illness, and now in view of the fact that he had seen fit not to do so, and wishing now to see me, I would most respectfully suggest for his consideration that, in my opinion, the distance from my quarters to his rooms was about the same as vice versa. Telling the nurse to send the negro courier in. I was not surprised to see old Anthony, the Colonel's polite but garrulous old body servant, enter. He bowed low, right and left, to the officers in the room until he faced me, when raising his hands above his head, he exclaimed; "Good Lord. Capn, you young mossa, you astonishes me unspeakable. You must hab been close on to de border of de spirit land." In answer to my inquires as to his master, the Colonel, he assured me, "Mas Bill-Henry is mighty poorly, boss; he won't go nowhere to see nobody and pears not to want anybody but doctor to come to see him, 'cept you, for he says you an' him is ole friends, same as I know; but he says you is a man of sebunction and sabilities after his own heart and must come let him know how soon you cin cum." I tore up my note to Wyley and told Anthony to say to the Colonel that I would go to see him the next morning. Often afterward my roommates would allude to each other in jovial conversation as a "gentleman of sebunction and sabilities." The day following I hobbled along about three city blocks to Wyley's place of abode, was met by Anthony, who appeared to be on guard, and conducted through a beautiful flower yard to the rooms on the flank of a handsome residence, occupied by the young Colonel. He met me in full dress uniform, a handsome new suit of finest grey, with all the stars, lace, buttons and trimmings to which the rank of Lieutenant colonel in the army entitled him. Of fine form, splendid physique, handsome features and the picture of strong, healthy young manhood as he rose to receive me, it would have been difficult to select from the thousands of officers of the two armies in front a finer specimen of physical manhood or a handsomer officer of any rank. My poor appearance must have "stonished him unspeakable" as Anthony had expressed himself in the hospital, for without salutation the Colonel caught hold of my arms and, half lifting and half pushing, seated me in an easy chair, then turning quickly to a table poured some wine into a glass, held it to my lips, saying, "Drink! Drink! You are weak and exhausted." "Pardon me," he said "for causing you the fatigue of your walk; you are unable and could not have gone much farther. You are in bad shape;" then laughingly, "Your complexion is about that of a brunette ghost; your avoirdupois that of a depleted skeleton, and – well, the only natural appearing parts about you are your hat and boots. By heavens! You are a wreck!" "Thank you," I replied, "and if you have finished your flattering diagnosis in my case permit me to say that there is no appearance of ghost, skeleton or wreck about you. I never saw you look heartier and stronger and in such shape. I would like to know what the devil you are doing here and what are you up to?"

Throwing back his head in laughter, as was his habit, he said: "Well, my inexperienced young friend – you know I have the advantage of you in eight or ten years and the experience thereof – the answer to your terse and curtly put question, containing only two clauses, would, if truly and fully made out, contain several lengthy and pregnant paragraphs. Briefly stated, in nutshell form, my answer might be, in part, that I am doing just what you should have done ere this, rest up; and I am doing it to keep out of the fix you are in or even one worse, to wit, a hole in some of these mountain sides or valleys. As to what am I 'up to,' among other things I am up to serving my country and our cause more effectively than I could at the front with my regiment, as second in command of the same, under Wynn, who is in full command. If the regiment reaps victory at the cannon's mouth the glory is Wynn's, even if my head were shot off in the charge, as came near to being your fate at Chickamauga. So I have simply, for the time being, changed my base and modus operandi." "But," I said, "I thought you were, and are still, here on sick leave." "Of course, I am; but hold on," he interrupted, "suppose that where you felt you had stayed and had been buried on the field of Chickamauga, as many of your regiment and mine were, who outside your own family and kindred and other than your closest comrade-friends would think of you now? You would be mouldering there, not especially honored and considerable unsung. The same as to myself. Why, if you or I, as officers, die at this military post and were given complimentary funeral rites, according to military rule and custom after the 'dead march,' beaten on draped and muffled drum, to our grave and three volleys fired over our entombed remains, the orders to the escorting platoon would be 'about face; forward march,' and they would step off the lively tune of 'to the devil and shake yourself and then come back and behave yourself' as you well know. Fairly illustrative of the soldier's career and meed are those ceremonies. You and I entered the army about the same date; two years of marching, starving and fighting suffice for me. From the same in future excuse me, please." While he was speaking I thought of how old Anthony had lied to me as to "Mass Bill Henry is mighty poorly." I thought I could see why the Colonel "didn't want anybody but de doctor to come to see him" and then I wondered how the duce it was that any surgeon would continue that prototype of strong, healthy, manly vigor on "sick leave." (The whole matter was divulged to me later by my friend in strict confidence, which even at this time I would not betray.) "Wyley," I said, "you have reaped me in part of your meed. You were captain of your company of Irish 'Telfair Greys' when I first knew you; now you are a lieutenant colonel of a fine regiment of infantry. What do you intend to do, resign? Throw up your commission and leave the army? Cease your bushwhacking skirmish fire. Come from your ambuscade, squarely, on the firing line proper and tell me. What do you do here and toward what end or object are you manoeuvering." "Well," said he, "in this hot weather I, usually en dishabille, lounge, read, smoke, eat, drink and sleep. Occasionally I consume a whole day pouring out my soul in a letter to my beloved fiancee – of whom you know. Then, as Major Thraugmorton, our past quartermaster, has kindly placed at my service his handsome dappled gray and buggy, in dewy evening's soft and silent gloaming, dressed in my best, I ride out beyond this dusty city's farthermost limit until, amid the beauties of God's natural adornments of earth, in the light of the twinkling stars, I bask in the softer light of lustrous orbs of my esteemed hostess's beautiful daughter, the handsomest woman in the city of Macon, and speak not thou this Goth nor whisper in it Askalon; but in the aforesaid light of the aforesaid orbs I read that she thinks me as handsome as I know her to be." I did not try to repress the exclamation. "Vanity, vanity, Wyley, it is a d___d shame, I did hope that, under the influence of that beautiful, intellectual, virtuous, Christian woman, your promised wife, you would, like the stained web that whitens the sun, grow purely being purely shone upon; but here you are at your deviltry again. Pouring out your soul to that loving, praying, waiting woman: there, and flirting – and I know how you flirt with this trusting, unsuspecting woman here. I believe you are the same Bill Wyley." And he replied, "Essentially the same." "But how," I asked, "dare you claim, ensconced here, with your side arms hanging on that wall, to serve our country and our trembling cause, smoking, drinking, writing and flirting." "A truce to that," he quickly replied. "We are now at close quarters. My regiment at the front is under its proper commander. Were I with it I would not fire a gun, for I carry neither carbine, musket or rifle. I might not be able within the next month's time to kill or wound one Yankee or save from death or wound one Confederate; therefore being of little help to our cause or hurt to the enemy. Should Col Winn fall or be removed in any way, I, as second in rank, am ready in an instant to take command and lead my regiment."

"Here I think I can help and do good. Now for my object and 'end toward which I manoeuvred' as you put it. I had a plan and consummated same, and now I want your aid and co-operation – not for the first time, as we both remember. Attention! Every available building in Macon has been converted into a hospital. You are quartered at the State Asylum for the Blind. Every one of our hospitals here is crowded to its utmost capacity with our wounded and sick. They continue to pour in from the front, and the very serious question, what shall we do in the premises, has for weeks confronted and baffled the surgeons and commandant of this post. Many of our men convalescing, but unfit for duty, are allowed to go home, are of necessity given leave of absence and go far to the rear, whereas a great majority of them should be kept as near the front as possible, to be returned to duty at the earliest possible opportunity. Well, I conceived a plan for the establishment of a convalescent camp right here in the outskirts of the city, where scores of convalescing wounded and sick will be provided with shelter, care, rations and medical attention and kept in order under strict discipline and thereby make room for scores of the severely wounded and sick in the regular hospitals. Do you endorse my plan, or are you ready with criticism and objection?" "I mark and admire your shrewd ingenuity and I endorse your scheme," I replied. "Well," he continued, "our chief surgeon, who is in full accord with me, and I this morning selected the site for the camp. We had seen the commandant of the post and obtained orders for the establishment of the camp, also for commissary and quartermaster supplies, including tents, utensils, etc." Reaching back to a table he handed me several official documents, saying, "There are the orders, read them." I read and handed them back. Taking another from his pocket, he said, "This is a special order; read that." That was an order directing me to leave the hospital the following day and "report to Lieut. Col William H. Wyley at the convalescent camp, for duty until relieved from same by Col Wyley, as assistant and second in command of said camp to Col Wyley," etc. etc. Wyley, throwing back his head, laughed long and heartily. "There you are," he said; "you dare not disobey nor can you get off until relieved by me, as the order states – which relief, you well know, you can secure if you wish to go home, tomorrow, or next week or at any time." "No, Wyley." I said, "I thank you and appreciate your kindness to me, but I have no home save that on the field or in the camp where my command is, to which I am unable, as yet, to go."

After discussing thoroughly arrangements for the establishment of our camp, the Colonel aided me in climbing into Quartermaster Thraugmorton's buggy and Anthony drove me to the door of my hospital home – the first buggy ride I had taken in many a day. The next day, with my saddle roll containing my very limited wardrobe, and with my sword, sash and pistol in hand I repaired to and took up quarters in a large wall tent pitched beneath the branches of a large oak at the head of a large group of trees forming the convalescent camp at Macon, Ga.

(As I may never have occasion to again refer to my erratic but brilliant, brave and big-hearted friend, Lieut. Col Wyley, in my memoirs, I will say that after the war he married the splendid woman to whom "he poured out his soul" in letters – some of which his, not hers – he would read to me, and for about five years preached, a minister of the Methodist Church. His wife died, he abandoned the pulpit and the Church and resumed the practice of law in Savannah, Ga. A few years after, I was in Beaufort, S. C., awaiting the arrival of the train, on which I was compelled to leave, due in five minutes. Court was in session in Beaufort. A fine looking man approached me and I looked straight into the face of Lieut. Col, the Rev William H. Wyley, Esq. – our first meeting since the war. Informing him of my short time there we talked rapidly. He was there engaged in the trial of a murder case. He spoke gravely of his marriage, feelingly of his wife's death and laughingly of his ministry, saying, "You know I have had some good times, but that was the d___nest biggest time of my life." My train was up. Clasping our hands, I said, "Wyley, I believe you are yet the same Bill Wyley," and as I turned to jump aboard he answered, "Essentially the same." He died a few months later.

William A. Bowers, Jr.

The Sunday News, Charleston, South Carolina – August 17, 1913

MEN OF THE CLOTH WHO FOUGHT FOR THE SOUTH

Bishop, Priest and Prelate Gave their Services and Lives to a Cause they Believed Just---Date and Manner of Death of Bishop---General Polk. South's Star Began to Sink at Chancellorsville – How Two Georgia Regiments Saved Charleston

(By Captain B. S. Williams, Brunson, S. C.)

(About two years ago the *Sunday News* published, under the caption, "Memoirs of a Soldier, In the War Between the States," a series of articles written by Capt. Ben S. Williams, the well-known Confederate Veteran of Brunson, S. C. These articles were widely read and excited great interest in this and other Southern States. They, however, did not cover the entire range of Capt. Williams' war experiences, so he has consented to resume the writing of his memoirs, and *The Sunday News* takes pleasure in presenting to its readers to-day the article of the new series. Others will follow from time to time, and those who preserve them will find themselves in possession of accurate information regarding some of the most stirring incidents of the war,)

In the great struggle and sanguinous strife in the '60s, for right and salvation and might and supremacy between the South and the North, proof, in part, that we of the South were right and truly deemed our quarrel just and believed our "cause" based on principles of truth, justice and righteousness, is the fact that throughout the ranks of the army of the Southern Confederacy were men behind the guns in fort and field, who had preached – for years, many of them – from sacred precincts of holy church altars, in earnestness and faith the gospel of love and charity of "peace on earth good will." They, with reverence for, and in obedience to the dictates of, their consciences, with Christian ideal of true chivalry, stood to the front and struck to maintain the right, to redress human wrongs, to defend the weak against the stronger, the oppressed against the oppressor: in protection of altars and homes from merciless ravage of ruthless invaders.

Gallant cavaliers, too, were some of these same, as I can truly attest, knightly and Lancelot and as true to the cause of their espousal as was Galahad in quest of the Holy Grail. In memory, I clearly recall many.

At first sight a captain of one of the companies of the splendid 6th Georgia cavalry, the Rev McCall, a Baptist minister, attracted my attention and excited my admiration as I marked his fine, graceful figure, knightly bearing and easy, splendid horsemanship, as I aided in the inspection and review of Anderson's brigade of troops of Georgia's fine cavalry.

A colonel and commander of one of the best regiments of volunteer infantry the State of Georgia ever sent to the field was a minister of the gospel and a thunderbolt in the battle's storm. He commanded until his death. He offered up his life upon his country's altar, in his country's service – my father.

Father Ryan, the blessed "poet-priest of the South," with clarion-note lyric and beauteous, burning epic verse, in song thrilled and inspired thousands of hearts and souls to be brave, to suffer and endure and nerved thousands of arms to more bravely and more fiercely strike. Afterwards, in story, he told of chivalry and valor in defeat of "a banner furled and glory, but wreathed with glory."

At the first sounding of the tocsin of per war, Leonidas Polk, of Louisiana, was an eminent prelate, a bishop of the Episcopal Church. Doffing the surplice of white, he donned the "suit of grey' and exchanged the rarified atmosphere of ecclesiastical purity and peacefulness for the powder-smoke of the field and the din and carnage of battle. He cast his lot in his country's cause and rose rapidly in rank and distinction in our army of the West.

Death of General Polk

On the morning of the 14th of June, 1864, Johnston's army was in battle-line at Pine Mountain, near Marietta, Ga., with Sherman's lines close facing us in front. The artillery fire at intervals along the lines was hot and rapid, at short range. About 10 o'clock my attention was attracted to a group of mounted officers riding leisurely along down our line, close in rear. They halted on a slight elevation as if to make observation in front, when almost instantly from a Federal battery came in very rapid order four or five shots. At the first shot I saw the fire was trained at the group of mounted men, in the next moment I saw the hasty dismounting and rushing together of the members and word passed quickly down the line to us that "Bishop-Gen" Polk was killed.

Gen Joseph E. Johnston, accompanied by Lieut. Gen Polk and a few members of their respective staffs, were on a tour of inspection of our position and lines, expecting and awaiting of Sherman's massed blue columns. The third shot fired by the ever alert and ready enemy struck Gen Polk in his left side, killing him instantly. Shrouded in his coat of grey with stars and wreath on collar, the dead "Bishop-General" was quickly conveyed to Marietta.

Bishop, priest and prelate, of their own volition, fought for our cause and seeking divine guidance besought God for victory. Many of them heard our shouts of triumph on fields of battle, but few of them lived to see our banner furled in defeat, when "broken was its staff and shattered."

"For their hands that once had grasped it,
And their hearts that firmly clasped it,
Cold and dead were lying low."

Apropos of the death of Gen Polk, recently I noticed the want of correct data relative to events of the time of which I write. In a published account of the proceedings of the Diocesan Convention of the Episcopal Church of Georgia, held recently in the city of Augusta, in a panegyric by a member of the convention on Gen Polk, the eloquent speaker stated that the "Bishop-General" was killed at the battle of Chickamauga. Gen Polk's corps, Gen Polk commanding, was engaged at the battle of Chickamauga, which was fought Saturday and Sunday, September 19 and 20, 1863. Gen Polk was killed at Pine Mountain, Ga., June 14, 1864.

The day following, June 15, I was hauled off the firing line and lodged in one of the military hospitals of Marietta. I was soon forwarded on to Macon, when during my early convalescence, I was assigned to light "post duty" as second in command of a large convalescent camp just within the city limits. Lieut. Col Wyley, of the 25th Georgia infantry, was my superior in command. I had served a few months in 1861-62 in the same regiment with Wyley. He then commanded a company mustered in service under the name of "The Telfair Irish Greys." There were some awful characters in the company and they were soon dubbed by the regiments the "Irish Hell-fired Greys." Wyley and I after two years active field campaigning, in separate commands, were again camped together.

Beginning of the End

At this time, June, 1864, the crisis in the heroic struggle for existence by our "storm-cradled," hope-cherished, war nurtured nation had been passed. Fierce and gallant fighting by the two depleted armies of Lee, in Virginia, and Johnston, in the West, occasional victory on the ensanguined field over the mighty invading hosts of the North availed us not. Prayer, faith and sacrifice availed not. Precept of our inevitable destiny was plainly written on the unchangeable scroll of coming events and the gruesome document sealed by the mailed hand of unrelenting fate.

The shadows were falling around. Within the past year Vicksburg, with 31,600 men, had surrendered. Port Hudson, our last fortification on the Mississippi River, had been taken from us. The great victory at Chickamauga, won at such fearful costs of blood and lives of thousands of gallant men, had been annulled by defeat and loss at Lookout Mountain and Missionary Ridge.

Johnston's army had been forced back over broad expanse of the most valuable territory, to the Confederacy, down as far as Marietta, Ga., and there stood confronted by overwhelming numbers. This is the status in the West.

In Virginia, while Lee had checked and driven back the splendid Federal armies at Fredericksburg and Chancellorsville, the great genius, the hope, the stay and shield of Lee's army had fallen at Chancellorsville, and Lee, deprived of his right arm, as he termed Stonewall Jackson, had met defeat at Gettysburg, with loss of 21,000 troops and many valuable officers of high rank.

We were without resources of strength or power from which to draw, or even to look, for aid. Surely the handwriting of our doom was plain and unmistakable. And yet, as we looked forward and upward in our beclouded horizon, in illusion we saw a fair bow of promise and from its rose-tinted arch was reflected in our sanguine hearts a spirit of courage and hope, of faith and confidence. Hugging to our hearts the sweet delusion, we dared disaster, defied fate and fought on.

The aurora of the Southern Confederacy did not begin to pale and fade at Gettysburg; it did before, at Chancellorsville. Under destiny, the lustre of the star of the South was dimmed and began its descent when Gen Stonewall Jackson fell.

Jackson was the Napoleon of the armies of Virginia. His heart and soul were in the cause, and every faculty of mind and body were bent, to the uttermost for success. His ends were purely public. He was self-denying and self-postponing. He sacrificed every-thing to his sole object and aim – troops, officers and himself. Victory to him was precious, and meant a door to greater victory.

No Jackson to Come

Bonaparte said: "There shall be no Alps." Jackson said then shall be no obstacles between the enemy and me, as fighting is the mode adopted for settlement of our national difference and is that upon which our national life depends. He was never reckless. He quickly decided what was to be done and then did that with all his might and strength and knew no impediment to his will. Keenly comprehending that "on a moment more or less depends glory or shame," he moved like a cloud and struck like the thunderbolt. At Gettysburg there was no Jackson, no victory, no hope of Jackson's coming – as of yore – and the Star of the South sank lower.

In Macon, July 9, I received letters from several officers of my regiment at the front, informing me that two regiments the 32d and the 47th Georgia infantry, had been hastily detached from the main army of Johnston to go with all possible dispatch to the defence of Charleston, S. C., as a large force of the enemy had landed on John's Island, too strong to be met by the slender forces within reach of the city. I was surprised and very anxious, as I knew the danger to Charleston was great and the need of help imperative to cause the detachment of those two regiments from Johnston's greatly inferior force in front of Sherman.

The many engagements in which those two old regiments had actively participated in the two years' campaigning in the West had reduced the numbers to about 300 men in each. But sure did I feel – for well did I know – that "many a man" in blue would bite the dust ere Charleston's gates were entered, by any kind of a force, passing over those 600 rifles and the men behind them, and I longed to be with my command again in the field, for never before had they gone into battle – and never after – in which I did not take part. A few days later I received from one in the regiment a letter mailed in Charleston saying;

"'Veni-vici' without much of the 'vici' for we came in a hurry back into your old State, thrashed a motley crowd of damned Yankees and niggers off John's Island, but didn't see much of them, as it was about 3 o'clock in the morning when we struck them. They fought hard, but, Lord, not like those fellows from Ohio, Indiana etc., at the front with Sherman. We killed a goodly number of them – took but few prisoners in the dark – and many of our men have shoes, blankets, hats, canteens etc., who were pretty well minus of same on arrival here. Wish you had been along. How are you getting on? And some of the folks back home used to say, "When yer comin?'"

Account of Engagement

Of the engagement alluded to history says: "The Federal force, under Brig Gen Hatch, consisted of 5,000 infantry, 100 cavalry and two sections of artillery."

In that excellent book, "The Defence of Charleston Harbor," by the Rev John Johnson, an eminent clergy-man of the Episcopal Church of Charleston, formerly major of engineers of the Confederate army – a copy of which is before me at this writing with inscription on blank leaf; "Presented with the regards of the author and W. A. Courtenay," Capt. Courtenay formerly quartermaster in the army, later Mayor of Charleston, both my good friends, now at rest. May God keep them close to Him eternally. It is recorded: "From their position, dangerously menacing, the invaders were driven. The finishing blow had been given to their campaign. In this assault, while all did well, the artillery under Lieut. Col Del Kemper, the cavalry under Major John Jenkins, it was the brigade of infantry, the 32d and the 47th regiments and Bonaud's battalion under command of Col. Geo P. Harrison, of the 32d Georgia, that won for itself special commendation for the dash and thoroughness of its work.

That gallant soldier and gentleman, Major John Jenkins, said in his official report: "We advanced under severe and rapid fire, with loss, which we could not return, but before we reached Col Harrison that gallant officer and his splendid troops under him had swept the enemy's lines and his skirmishers had swept beyond."

The enemy hastily burned their stores brought on to the Island, and embarked on their gunboats for glory in other fields. So, ingloriously ended the campaign so beautifully laid and so "previously" counted on, but so illy hatched by Gen Hatch to flank Fort Sumter and take Charleston via her islands, adjacent. Whipped and driven off then and there, we had them to whip again between Charleston and Savannah.

The Sunday News, Charleston, South Carolina – July 14, 1912
MEMOIRS OF A SOLDIER IN WAR BETWEEN STATES
(By Captain B. S. Williams, Brunson, S. C.)

Succeeding my transportation, about the middle of June, 1864, from the ranks of the Army of the West in the field, then near Kennesaw Mountain, and my egress from the hospital convalescent from my severe illness, my six weeks' service on "post duty" in Macon, Ga., under assignment, was about the only oasis in the arid, hard and oft times very hot period of my four years of active service in the field as a soldier of the Confederate States army.

At the convalescent camp, to which I had been assigned as second in command, my superior being my friend, Col Wyley, of the 25th Georgia infantry, who had conceived, devised and consummated the plan of its establishment, my duties were light, actually requiring not more than half of my time, though I was frequently in full and sole charge.

Headquarters of the camp were a large wall tent with cloth curtains across the centre, two cots, two chairs, a washstand and centre table. On left, adjoining this, was a smaller tent with table and camp stools. This was our dining department, in which our meals were served from a nearby restaurant. On right of large tent was a wall tent with desk, chairs and table. This was our business and reception room. We received quite a number of visitors. Groups of ladies would often come, attracted by the arrangement and camp life.

The wounded and sick sent back from the front kept the hospitals filled and we were heartily congratulated by the surgeons and commandant of post for advantage and recourse, to our annexed resource, in the emergency, and our camp tenantry was of a heterogeneous body, composed of every arm of the service; infantry, cavalry and artillery. Army regulations and military discipline were strictly maintained with little difficulty, as every inmate of the camp had learned discipline in service in the field. Soldiers are made of men, men are men, in army were "many men of many kind," and, of course, occasionally we found a rather tough customer in camp; but discipline enforced with tact and tempered with reasonable leniency overcame all difficulty and secured the desired results.

One of our most troublesome cases, for a time, was a young athletic, really fine Texas cavalryman. I readily recall to mind his picture. Tall, lean, muscular, and suave in manner, fair skin, light-colored hair, blue eyes with a light of the very devil in them on occasion. Haughty, but of graceful bearing, with swinging step of the trained cavalryman. In his grey cavalry jacket open, in camp, showing a dark, wine colored flannel shirt of soft and fine texture, with wide rolling collar over black silk tie, buff stripes on pants seams, wide belt at waist with heavy nickel-plate clasp with C. S. A. in raised letters, long, well fitting boots and soft felt hat, with rim on right held to crown by a brazen spread-eagle pin with letters of "__ th Mich. Cav." on scroll in eagle's mouth – taken from hat of a slain officer of the Federal cavalry, he looked the very cavalier that he was. A wounded captain of cavalry who knew him well informed me that "the devilish young fellow is of some of the best stock of Texas, but wild, dissipated and unmanageable; respectful in deportment to superiors in rank but defiant, utterly regardless of threat or punishment, dangerous and most skillful swordsman, reckless rider and daredevil fighter in the regiment."

A folded cloth bandage around his neck and hanging in front supported his wounded bridle arm. I cannot recall his name, as I habitually addressed him as Texas and so remember him.

Our rule required all inmates of camp to answer roll calls and to remain in camp at night. "Texas" persisted in "running the blockade," as the soldiers termed absenting themselves without leave every night. Col Wyley placed him in arrest one morning and ordered him to remain within his tent for forty-eight hours, and assured him that if he continued to violate orders he would be ironed down in his tent until forwarded to the front. In the afternoon of the day of his confinement I received a note from him – Col Wyley being away – asking to be allowed to come to headquarters and speak to me. I sent him word to come. I invited him to be seated and he began:

"Captain, I have availed myself of your charge to explain to you. While I am your senior in age, we are much nearer together than Col. Wyley and I. I am just 23. Beside, with due respect to military rank, I do not like Col Wyley. I dislike him." "Well, Texas." I interrupted, "in your case Col. Wyley is only endeavoring to enforce proper discipline. You know, having been in service long enough, that to do so is essential to desirable results." "Yes," he said, "I have been in the cavalry just two years and I have no good opinion of Col Wyley's manner and mode of command and control." "Remember the trite aphorism," I said: "'no rouge e'er felt the halter draw, with good opinion for the law.'"

"Granted," he said. "I am exceeding sorry that I offended Col Wyley, but a durned sight more exceedingly so that he caught up with me, but more exceedingly do I regret his ban upon my exit from camp: that plays Cain with my arrangements. Captain, hear me for my cause. So you remember meeting me on Mulberry street last evening?" "Yes," I said, "and a very pretty little woman was clinging to you with her arm entwined in and supporting that crippled bridle arm of yours." "Well, sir," said he, "that is my wife. By George, she is pretty. Damned if I don't believe she is the prettiest woman I ever married." "Your wife! Prettiest woman you ever married! Now, see here, Texas, no hocus-pocus plea, or false statement will secure to you immunity from punishment for defiance of authority and violation of orders." Quick as a flash he was on his feet, erect and tense and a dangerous light in his eyes. Very deliberately, but with a quaver of voice, he said, "Sir, outside of military rank I am the peer of any man in my command, or in Macon. I am but a private soldier in the army and may be charged, duly, with faults and acts, branded by society as degrading and even criminal, but no man dare charge me with falsehood. He who with advantage of official rank does so places me at disadvantage and blasts my confidence:" and saluting, as if mechanically, he strode quickly back to his tent.

I was possessed of no sluggish temper and at mention of "advantage of official rank" felt for an instant hot blood course through my veins, but in a moment's thought and reflection was born a feeling of regret, and I sent for Texas to report at headquarters. He soon stood before me, haughtily, but as if expecting reprimand. I said to him: "I regret that a few minutes ago I was misunderstood and you mistaken. I disclaim all intention of insult or charging you with falsehood. I only wanted to warn you of the popular but beaten and worn-out way of pleading wife, wife and children, in plea for sympathy and excuse for misdemeanor. I was surprised at your declaration of marriage and astounding following remark. Sit down and let me hear you for your cause and my gratification and curiosity."

He sat down, placed his hat on the ground near his camp stool, crossed his long boots, took his wounded arm carefully from the folded cloth sling and extended it on his knee, then looking at me and smiling as gently and softly as a diffident, modest woman said: "Captain, I thank you." Continuing after a moment's pause, he said, "A web-foot" (the infantrymen were thus denominated by the cavalry) "here in camp, who says he knows you, says you are a South Carolinian. My mother and father were bred and married in South Carolina. They have told me the first light that guided my infant eyes was from the sun ray beaming off the soil of the old Palmetto State. For two years I have lived a hell and heaven of a life. Under this right boot leg, about midway between ankle and knee, is a long, deep trench of a wound. Got that at Perryville, Ky, about a year and a half ago. We were having it hand to hand and my partner was a strapping young Yankee, who handled his sword splendidly. Luck favored me and I got in a fairly good front cut above his guard, and he fell forward almost under my horse's feet. He was on his knees and I would not cut again, as God knows, I would not strike a fallen man, his sabre gone; but from that position he fired at me twice, rapidly. The second shot had hardly ceased plowing up my leg when, by a swinging right to rear downward sweep, I put him out of business forever. Then I was in the hospital sixty days." He continued, "Not quite a year ago, near Chickamauga, we rode right into a squadron of Kilpatrick's men and they were good ones. We were soon all mixed up and I found myself somewhat separated from the main body and a huge Dutchman on my left hacking at me with his heavy sabre about as skillfully as you would use a pole killing a snake. I parried several of his heavy cuts and was keenly watching to bury my sabre point in his bulky body when there dashed up close on my right a slender young sergeant, splendidly mounted. Had he passed and cut to right and rear he would have got me unless I had uncovered in front to the Dutchman, who yelled out, "Keel 'em, got damn," but the sergeant, checking his spirited horse, suddenly caused him to rear, and his well aimed stroke barely grazed my saddle pommel. The Dutchman, at the same instant throwing his sabre high for a master stroke, received a left thrust with all my might my sabre point in his globby throat and went to earth backward as if a shell had hit him. I had paid the Dutchman too much attention. The young sergeant had closed in and as I recovered my guard and before I could thrust or cut felt his keen sword point enter here" unbuttoning his shirt front and pushing it back, he pointed to a broad, ugly scar on his right breast very near the armpit. "My quick cut to right was partially foiled by his thrust, but my sabre rang against his cap and, glancing downward, made a fearful scalp wound on the right side of his head, and the gallant young fellow, clutching wildly at his saddle, reeled and pitched forward."

"There was great din and loud yelling as the Yanks were falling back, but fighting like devils, and our boys crowding them. I started forward to join the melee again, but felt blood running down my side and beginning to feel weak, halted and, loosening my jacket front, stuffed my handkerchief as well as I could into the bleeding cut and held it there, and, drinking some of the water from my full canteen, turned and rode to the rear, knowing I would soon need help. Reaching, with a short space, my very recent battle arena, I saw my Dutchman friend gurgling unconscious, the young sergeant drenched in his blood, was on his back and was moaning piteously. He saw me and called out, quite strong, 'Water, water, for God's sake, water!' I dismounted and as I stood I felt weak and faint, but, kneeling down, I raised his head and held my canteen to his mouth and he drank as if famishing. As I lowered softly his gashed and bleeding head he looked straight into my eyes, and then at my bare, gashed and bleeding breast. Taking my arm from beneath his head, I said to him, 'Sergeant, I am very sorry.' 'Oh, my God,' said he, 'you couldn't help it. Look at your breast. Oh, God, forgive me and bless you for that water." So help me, Heaven, Captain, I remember nothing more, neither sound nor light, until I rouse up from high fever in the field hospital near Missionary Ridge a week after, another sixty days in the hospital."

"Now this last hurt." pointing to his wounded arm, "I got up near Kennesaw in a kind of a pell-mell fight. I don't know from whence or whom came the ball that cracked in two one of the bones in this forearm. How this hodge-podge medley with which I have afflicted your ears is but part and parcel of my hell-tuned experience. But, mind you, no whine from me, for you may expect Hell in war."

"But now for Heaven; the silver lining, the roses among the thorns along the stony pathway, the Eve in the barren Eden. For each severe wound received in battle I have secured unto myself a pretty little wife and one better. One in Mississippi, one in Kentucky, one in Tennessee and one, so far, in Georgia. You have seen No. 4, Georgia. I make this statement to you in strict confidence, for the sake of sweet No. 4. She is my wedded wife of one week."

"But you have been here only three weeks, and was married a week ago? How do you manoeuvre to accomplish so much so expeditiously?" I inquired. "Oh, well," he replied, "my tactics in love are about the same as yours in war. My object in front, I advance along a line, in skirmish, of careful action and cautious, but pressing, language. If met with a bombshell, I fall back, gracefully as possible, under courteous apology and the engagement is off. But if my love, the enemy, skirmishes with me the action becomes fast, if not furious. I advance and charge gallantly, for 'faint heart ne'er won fair lady.' Capitulation follows, the victory is mine and to the victor belongs the captive."

"But for the captives?" I asked, "Have you no mercy, no thought of the future, their future." "All mercy, care and affection, for the time being, our dwelling together," said he, "As to the future, no man knoweth, nor may he provide in destiny, for by destiny are our ends shaped, 'rough hew them as we may.' Our wedlock is honorable and without fraud on their part. Each and all are ignorant of their error and what you deem my perfidy. Here ignorance is bliss. Should they weep because of my absence and danger, they weep only as thousands weep and there's no tears of shame; and what is life but joy and grief, sunshine and clouds ,smiles and tears, with fragrant flowers strewing biers of blighted hope? Should two of them ever in future meet and converse in condolement to the one, the last or fallen, I would be departed A, to the other the departed B."

"Then, Texas," I replied, "in your campaigns de amour do you resort to lying?' "No," he replied, laughingly, "you might say deception, but that is a misnomer, it is strategy, and here our tactics parallel again, for strategy is fair and always employed to some extent in love and war."

"You will leave soon for the front," I suggested. "Yes, see here," and he raised and moved about his arm, clasped and unclasped his fingers. "I could almost use this arm for my bridle now. About one week more and I am ready to share again in the hell that's broke loose in Georgia."

"On leaving?" I asked, "Well, I will fondly kiss the tears from the smooth, sweet cheeks of my sweetheart and hie me to the front; for in these days 'men must fight and women must weep' and God only knows to-day what will happen by the morrow's morning. If again sent to hospital of stationed long in one locality, I will seek to find another pretty wife."

"Do you propose to continue that wicked, awful practice?" I asked. "Indefinitely, as long as I may survive during this war."

"And after?" I asked. "There will be no after for me. I have so written to mother and begged her not to expect me home."

For the first time I saw a shadow of sadness in his face and a moisture in his eyes and noted that he swallowed hard, as if choking back emotion.

"Texas," I exclaimed – but just then there came running up to him a little boy 10 or 11 years of age, bouncing and catching in front of him, a rubber ball, without halting. Holding the ball in one hand the little fellow fished out of his pocket with the other hand a note neatly folded and handed it to Texas and dashed off again to join some other little fellows calling him at the camp line.

"That," said Texas "is my unceremonious, juvenile brother-in-law. Excuse me one moment please, Captain," and he opened, read and handed me the note, saying, "Your reading will be no breach of Propria quae maribus on my part." I read:

"Dear Jack: Can't you come soon and let's go take tea with Mrs. _____. Please, for I have promised. Come just as soon as you can.

Your own wifey."

Texas," I said, "you ought to be shot." "Thank you, Captain," he broke in. "I expect to be now soon if I escape sabreing." "No," I said. "I mean in punishment, by Court-martial."

"Now, thanks to the army regulations," he said, "we only shoot spies and deserters."

Glancing at my watch I saw it was past 6 o'clock and said to him: "Texas, you deserve punishment by being locked out from all sympathy, consideration, mercy and kindness; but this note is an open sesame. I shall assume no responsibility for rescinding, temporarily, the order for your confinement and you are excused from camp until 7 tomorrow morning. I caution you against hereafter absenting yourself from this camp without my permission."

He understood, and for the moment, forgetting his military training, this wayward, perverse, unmanageable, wicked young man, bowing low, like a courtier, said: "My friend, indeed, again I thank you. You know not how sincerely: not only for opportunity granted, but for shield from humiliation of confinement in arrest and perhaps serious trouble and embarrassment. If it will afford you any pleasing reflection, rest assured that, after my relation of the occurring events of to-day, one little woman, at least, will on her bended knees to-night beseech the God whom she worships to shield and guide and bless you; and my amen, worthless maybe, but earnest, shall mingle with her fervent, faithful plea."

Then suddenly straightening, the young trained and skillful swordsman, reckless rider and daredevil fighter, saluted, about faced and moved away with proud step and peculiar swinging strode which, even to-day, marks the booted belted cavalier and daredevil cavalryman of the army of the South, in the sixties.

Beside my general routine of light military duty in camp my social enjoyments – quaffed and imbibed by me, a worn, maimed and thirsting young soldier, as droughts of rare nectar and strains of soft music, soothing, invigorating and compensatory, and plucked as sweet roses of peaceful pleasure afar from the sating din of the field in front – were delightful, although not entirely without an occasional slight "rift within the lute" or tiny thorn among fragrant flowers. Introduction by my kind and proud kinswoman, who had so tenderly cared for and nursed me in the hospital, Mrs. Lockett – than whom none in Macon was superior in social status – to her friends and acquaintances afforded me the pleasure and esteemed privilege of an entree into the charming and delightful circle of the elite of the city.

I met refined, graceful, modest and beautiful women and girls and some splendid manly men. By far too many of the latter out of uniform and the service, apparently heedless of the constant daily libation of blood and sacrificial offering of precious lives on the ensanguined altar of country for the salvation of our weakening, expiring, sacred cause. But these dissenters, truants from duty, and shirkers of danger, were not confined to or wholly embraced within the ranks of the ununiformed civilians. There were many army officers in Macon not on duty or in hospitality, whose service, for which they were commissioned and being paid, was sorely needed in the unequal contest at the front waged by the remaining steadfast and true, desperately and gallantly fighting in defense of home and for a cause they were too weak, numerically, to save.

The "airs' and bombast of some of these gaily uniformed, strutting "Carpet Knights," who were dodging duty and danger, were wonderful. For them only disgust and contempt were felt by those who knew what and where their duty was, the sore need of their performance of that duty and were cognizant of their shameful malfeasance. But many continued to stay, and shirk and strut.

Fresh in my mind is the recollection of a trio of young officers of the kind whom I saw quite often and, occasionally, casually met.

Col Wyley and I would occasionally dine at the Lanier Hotel, then a hotel in Macon. On these occasions the aforesaid young officers, the trio, were invariably there dining together at a nearby table to ours, specially provided for and occupied only by themselves. Two were of rank of only Lieutenant; the other a staff officer, with rank of captain. They were of about the same age, I judge not over 22 or 23 years, and were really fine looking, handsome young fellows. They were evidently offsprings of wealth, as they were elegantly uniformed and indulged, at their dining, in unstinting use of costly wined and the finest cigars, over which they grew boisterously demonstrative and disgustingly egotistic.

How they managed to keep away from service at the front and remain away from their commands in the city, unassigned to duty and unemployed, I do not know. One of them, of a broad-shouldered, tall, but somewhat ungraceful and bulky figure, was Lieutenant C_____. I noticed that he apparently dominated in their convivial intercourse. I attributed his influence to his prestige as a son of the Governor of the State. On those days governors were "some pumpkins."

While merely saluting and returning salute on meeting either one or the trio, I had conceived an aversion to the vain, dominating Lieut. C_____. I had met him on more than one visit in the parlors of the palatial residence of Mr. F____, whose younger daughter was a recent graduate of school, debutante in society and one of the most beautiful and popular of Macon's belles and, by the way, daughter of a deceased ex-governor of Georgia. To this girl, my relative, Mrs. L_____, at my earnest request, introduced me, after the humorous, mock earnest, private admonition:

"My cousin, I tremble at the thought of your danger. Beware, oh, beware. She is charming and fascinating; but she is the most consummate coquette in Macon. During her short reign her victims have been numerous. She possesses the art, skill, power, witchery, or what you please to term it, to swiftly elevate her admirers to almost heavenly heights and then drop them, oh, so suddenly, back to earth again. She saw you yesterday in church with me, where you saw her. At our meeting this morning she asked me why I did not summon her to help me nurse you and remarked that you looked as if you needed more nursing back to health. I will present you; but, oh, kinsman mine, beware. When she smiles so sweetly trust her not; she's fooling you."

I very soon noted the complete infatuation of Lieut. C____ and was not surprised, but the young lady rose in my estimation for I saw not a spark of the spirit of coquetry in her deportment toward Lieut. C____, her social equal.

He should have seen in her courteous and perfect lady like but cool demeanor toward him that he was not one of the elect. But the young man was vain and was charmed, enchanted and blind.

Accompanying the young lady to an evening religious service in her family's church, we – just she and I – occupied the family pew. In the assembling of the audience Lieut. C____ and his Lieutenant comrade entered and occupied, alone the pew next in our rear. As the singing in the church began Lieut. C____ leaned forward, attracted the attention of the young lady and quickly, rather stealthily, handed her a note. She glanced at the penciled words and dropped the note at my feet. Stooping, I quickly recovered the note and handing it to her asked if she wished to retain it. I noted a flush in her cheek and compression of her pretty lips. Holding the note a few moments between her gloved fingers she handed it to me with a whispered "read."

I read: "Miss F____: If you are not irrevocably entangled with your effete escort of this evening (and several evenings of late, I note) I crave the pleasure of your company to-morrow evening for the opera. Please answer now." Leaning nearer, I whispered; "What is your answer?" "No," she said, and I saw she was agitated. Placing the note against the cover of her hymn book I wrote, on blank side, "Ignore the uncouth fool and forget his boorish insolence." She read and quietly placing the note between the leaves of her book and placing the book on the pew cushion at her side gave her attention to the service, which had begun.

At the close of service some young lady acquaintances in the pew in front immediately faced about end and we engaged in rapid and lively conversation and we were, very soon, laughing and chatting along down the aisle. Glancing rearward I saw Lieut. C___ toss a book upon the seat of the pew just vacated by Miss F___ and myself. He walked by without notice and as we passed out he stood in the outer edge of the circle of light at the door and glared at us as only he can who is possessed of the "green-eyed monster." On our way home my young lady companion was unusually silent. At parting in her home she lingered and in earnest tone said to me, "I am going to request of you two promises e'er we part. Will you make them?" "Name them," I said, "in any number of the whole scale or catalogue." Well, then," said she, "promise we, first, that you will avoid Lieut. C___ to-morrow." "I promise you that I will absolutely ignore Lieut. C___ tomorrow, and ever after, unless he compels my notice." "Oh, please do, and now for promise number two. If we are to go to the opera tomorrow evening call at 7, take tea with us and then we can take our own sweet time in going and getting there. Will you?" "As sincerely as I invoke vigil of guardian angels over you throughout the silent watches of this starlit night, I thank you for your invitation to tea and for the pleasure of fond anticipation guaranteed me by promise of the pleasure of your company then and later. I gladly promise. Au revoir," I said, and sweetly and softly she replied, "Good night, and pleasant dreams."

Preceding campward I bethought me of my excellent, astute kinswoman a warning and laughed as I said to myself, "I am about as heedful as was the Scottish chieftain of the mystical wizard's subtle

"Lochiel, Lochiel, beware of the day.
When the Lowlanders meet in the battle array."

Early the following morning I had scarcely finished my "report," "requisition," "receipt," etc., papers pertaining to the business of our camp when young Mr. F___, brother of the aforesaid Miss F___, stepped in my tent. He was incapacitated for military service by a serious hurt received in early childhood. He appeared worried and seating himself said, right away, "I am just from home and left the folks quite anxious on your account." "Why?" I asked; "What's to pay?" "I was at the Lanier Hotel until quite late last evening and learned that Lieut. C___ is red hot angry with you. You will receive a visit this morning from him or a friend of his. Forewarned, forearmed. I left sister L___ shedding tears of repentance because of her part in the contretemps in the church." "I thank you," I said. "Your sister is absolutely blameless of all that relates to the little foolish 'tempest in a teapot' that Lieut. C___ is kicking up. He is making an ass of himself and needs a toning down. Do me the kindness to present my complements to your mother and sisters and say to Miss L___ for me that I expect to be busily engaged in camp today, but will surely be on hand in time this evening. You have my thanks."

  He left. At 10 o'clock I invited to a seat in my tent the young staff captain, which he politely declined and informed me, courteously, that he represented his friend, Lieut. C___, who felt compelled to require of me written retraction of certain language in writing used last evening, to a young lady in church. Presumed I need not have same repeated if my memory served me. I said to him that I would neither retract or apologize, but would add that as his friend had secured the data upon which he based his complaint by purloining it from the hymn book of a young lady, inadvertently left by her in her family's reserved pew, he had well nigh placed himself outside the pale of claims of gentlemen or notice of gentlemen.

  "That," said he "is fuel for the flame." Glancing at the curtain of cloth across the tent, he said, "May I take the liberty to inquire if you are entirely alone?" "Entirely," I replied, "save for your presence." "Then, sir, may I assume that, notwithstanding your rank, and our army regulations, you will afford Lieut. C___ the opportunity for satisfaction which one gentleman, under certain circumstances may demand of another?" "Yes," I said, "I will afford him an opportunity here in some secluded spot near Macon to deliver himself of some of the valor of which he boasts, but has never displayed on any field in the face of a foe." "Then, sir, I request conference with a friend of your selection at the earliest moment suiting your convenience and pleasure."

  "My friend will meet you at the Lanier Hotel within an hour," I told him. He bowed, faced about and was face to face with Col. Wyley, who was just returning from the post office. Asking the young officer to wait a few moments, I explained the situation briefly, in his presence, to Col. Wyley and watched his cheek twinge with the sporting blood in his Irish-American veins. Turning to the young captain, Wyley said, "This business must be over this evening, as I leave at 4 A. M. to-morrow for Savannah." Then to me, "You will have the choice; pistols I presume?" "Colt's army. Ten paces," I replied. "All right, captain," said Wyley, "I will be necessarily detained here about an hour answering these letters. Meet me at the Lanier promptly at 12:30. Hold, one moment, I think it but due you young men, to say to that, save one, Col. Ashby, Williams is the best pistol shot in the brigade. Promptly at 12:30, please; good morning."

  The young captain bowed haughtily, deliberately and silently and I saw that his metal was pure, true steel. Wyley seated himself opposite me and handed me a cigar and match. Watching me narrowly as I lit my cigar he said: "How is your nerve?" "O. K." I said, "nothing the matter with me but off in flesh and strength." "'Effete,' as the Lieutenant pronounced me to the young lady."

"Good," said Wyley. "By G__, that inflated, conceited ass will be at your mercy and, damn him, shoot the self-sufficiency stuffing out of him. He is no good to the army or country, in any way."

"No," I assured him, "I don't want to kill him if I can avoid it. I do want to tone him down, but don't believe I will have the opportunity of even winging him. He is a blustering braggart, bluffer and coward. I doubt the ability of his friends and chums to make him toe the mark and will bet my boots that he will, in some way wriggle out and fail to face the music."

At 12:30 Wyley and I sat on the veranda at the Lanier. He had arranged for me, in case of necessity, to go in his stead to Savannah on the early morning train for 30 days. At 1:30 we still sat chatting, smoking and wondering. At 2 I moved adjournment to the dining room. At 3, coming back on the veranda, we were met by the young captain of staff, who appeared crestfallen and chagrined. Beckoning us to one side, he said, "Gentlemen, I am due you an explanation and I wish to make an apology. I am just from our rooms. During my absence this morning Lieut. C___ drank heavily of whiskey and continued after my return in spite of my earnest protests. He is now stupidly, helplessly drunk: drunk as a fool. I delayed while we tried to sober him up. I wash my hands of his affairs and of him. I assure you that I sincerely regret all participation in the affair of this morning, in his behalf. And now, gentlemen, as I leave very early tomorrow to take my place at the front I ask the pleasure of your company while you join me in a smoke."

We each took from his proffered handsome gold-mounted case a fine cigar and for the next half hour, apart from the thronging crowd, we smoked and chatted, never once mentioning the affair of the morning.

Rising, we wished each other "good luck," shook hands heartily and parted. Never since have I seen the gallant, chivalrous, disgusted and repentant, young captain.

Returning to quarters about 5 P. M. I found on my desk, directed to me, a sweet little note written by Miss F_____ on delicately perfumed pink-tinted paper, pleading "very severe headache" as reason for suggestion of "postponement of our engagement, for this evening, in toto, for tomorrow evening."

So, in headquarters of camp that night, after supper and roll call, Wyley and I chatted and laughed until bedtime over the day's doings.

The Sunday News, Charleston, South Carolina – August 18, 1912

MEMOIRS OF A SOLDIER IN WAR BETWEEN STATES
(By Captain B. S. Williams, Brunson, S. C.)

During my confinement in hospital, my convalescence and assignment to post duty at Convalescent Camp, in Macon, Ga., July, 1864, old Father Time had halted not; but marching onward, as ever, unceasingly, irresistibly, had wrought his inevitable changes; changes of greater of less import to individual, community, army, and country. As a people of a great, but rent and divided nation, watched, prayed and waited they witnessed with mingled feelings of joy, grief and despair the rapidly shifting scenes of tragical events of that pregnant, eventful era.

The two mighty, antagonistic armies of the West were in close confrontation seeking advantage in opportunity to strike and close in deadly conflict as at Chickamauga; cautiously, carefully manoeuvering as great and mighty tragedians in a world wide stage or mighty foeman stragegiats in a vast arena of war; the one, bent on realization of heart cherished, hope nurtured vision of glory and national power, honor and prestige. The other sternly bent on execution of sworn resolve to dash in earth the hope, destroy the dream, dispel the vision and render impossible the permanent dissolution of the Union of American "United States."

Act after act fraught with blood, carnage and direful results altering aspect, changing condition – conditions essential to success or material in failure – engaged and held the attention and interest of millions here, and held in wrapt attention, surprise and interest the many millions in regions beyond the seas.

Johnston Criticized.

Abandonment of position after position of defense taken by the Confederate army, in the face of numerically superior forces of the Federal army and the consequent relinquishment of large scopes of inestimably valuable territory within the very heart of the Southern Confederacy called forth severe and bitter condemnation of Gen Joseph E. Johnston and his evasive tactics and brought down censure and anathema on President Davis. Gen Johnston was blamed for refusing or failing to force a general and decisive engagement – as Bragg had done at Chickamauga – in the mountain region of Georgia, whose mountains and deep streams afforded advantages in position for defense. President Davis was greatly censured for failure to compel Johnston to fight or place in his stead one who would.

Gen Johnston says in defense of his policy, "Various men, some published in newspapers in such manner as to appear to have official authority, and others circulated orally in Georgia and Alabama and imputed to Gen Bragg. (Gen Bragg had been relieved of command of the Army of the West after losing the battle of Missionary Ridge, and Gen Johnston was appointed to command – in his stead.) "The principal are: That I persistently disregarded the instructions of the President; that I would not fight the enemy; that I refused to communicate with Gen Bragg in relation to the operations of the Army; that I disregarded his entreaties to change my course and attack the enemy, and gross exaggerations of the losses of the army. I had not taken advantage of receiving the President's instructions in relation to the manier of conducting the campaign, but as the conduct of my predecessor (Gen Bragg) in retreating before odds less than those confronting me had apparently been approval, as Gen Lee, in keeping on the defensive and retreating toward Grant's objective point under circumstances like mine was adding to his fame, both in the estimation of the administration and the people, I supposed that my course would not be censured. I believed then, as I do now, that it was the only one at my command that promised success. The great numerical superiority of the enemy made the chances of battle much against us, and even if beaten they had a safe refuge behind the fortified pass of Ringgold and in the fortress of Chattanooga. Our refuge, in case of defeat, was Atlanta, one hundred miles off with three rivers intervening. Therefore, victory for us could not have been decisive, while defeat would have been utterly disastrous." This, in reference to the beginning of the campaign, while the armies were at Dalton, and is an extract from the full report of the operations of the Army of the West written by Gen Johnston at Vineville, Ga., October 20, 1864, embracing the period of his command from December 27, 1863, to July 17, 1864. He proclaims that on more than one occasion he had planned for a general engagement with Sherman's army which would have been decisive, and had carefully formed his forces in well selected positions, with full intention to force the issue, but had been balked and prevented, not by the tactics of the enemy, but by opposition, dilatory movements and failure to carry out orders on the part of his own generals, principal of whom he claimed was Lieut. Gen Hood. After great pressure brought to bear on President Davis, he, on the 18th of July 1864 relieved Johnston and appointed Gen Hood to command. Gen Hood, at once assuming the aggressive, ordered an attack on Gen Thomas, as his corps was crossing a stream, Peachtree Creek, on the 19th of July. Thomas's corps had become detached from the other two corps, McPherson's and Schofield's. Hood says: "My object was to crush Thomas's army before he could fortify himself and then turn upon Schofield and McPherson. The attack was to begin at 1 P. M., but was delayed until 4 P. M." The delay caused failure and loss of victory, and Hood blamed his Lieutenant General, Hardee, for delay and failure to obey orders, thus losing the victory. He again severely censured Hardee for negligence, disobedience and failure. Thus it would seem that the tactics of Hood – in his "vaulting ambition" – toward his superior, Johnston, was adopted by Hardee, in his "vaulting ambition" toward his superior, Hood. And thus it appears "that we but teach bloody instructions, which being taught, return to plague the inventor, this evenhanded justice commends the ingredients of our poisoned chalice to our own lips." Rivalry, amounting to antagonism and strife for supremacy in rank and powering the military, especially in the armies in the field in front of the enemy – where there should be perfect honesty in discharge of duty – trust, honor and fidelity – is destructive of efficiency and desirable results. I am cognizant of such unfortunate conditions existing at times among the officers of high rank in our army during my service. History shows that our army was not the exception and records rivalry, treachery and murder on the part of officers of the armies of ancient Rome and Greece in the days of Romulus, Pompey, Alexander and Caesar. Eumancs, when appointed to the command of the forces of Arminia and Cappadocia, 318 years before Christ, discovered a plot by two of his Lieutenant generals to profit by his great genius in an impending battle and assassinate him immediately after, whereupon he exclaimed to his friends, "I live among a herd of savage beasts." Again while in his army "winter quarters" in Celaena, three of his generals, Alcetus, Poleman and Docimus, contended with him for command of the army. Eumancs said, "This makes good the observation, every one thinks of advancing himself, but no one thinks of the danger that may accrue to the public weal."

History Repeats Itself

How appropriate and applicable are those words, spoken more than 2,000 years ago by the Cardian general, relative to conditions existing at that time in his army, to and how they remind me of some of the unwritten history of the time of armies and officers and war in this educated, civilized, evangelized, Christianized portion of the world during my service in the years A. D. 1861-65. And how pointedly applicable they are to our conduct in politics in the good year A. D. 1912. Human nature is even about the same and "history repeats itself."

I was kept thoroughly posted as to our army's movements by communications of war correspondents at the front published in the Macon newspapers and occasionally letters and messages from comrades in the lines. About the 7th of July I learned that my regiment, the 47th Georgia, and the 32nd Georgia, had just been detached from the main army and hastily forwarded under command of Col George P. Harrison, colonel of the 32nd, to Charleston, S. C. I received this information with mingled surprise, disappointment and pleasure. I had so long looked forward to and hoped for a great battle in upper Georgia, in which I had hoped and expected a crushing defeat of the Federal forces and a turning in the tide of our dangerously drifting affairs. We all anxiously awaited the onset. I would receive word from my comrades: "Make haste and get well and hurry back. We miss you and want you. God grant that you be here with the regiment when the grand fight comes off." I was anxious to return. Not that I wanted to fight "for the love of it." I had had plenty in the past two years to do me a lifetime, long or short. I had seen many fall and dear friends go down to death close by my side, but did want to be with my comrades when the "grand fight" came off; a fight that I knew would be to victory or death. Well did I know that our army, on Georgia soil, with 10,000 Georgia troops in line, would never quit the field in defeat. God knows I loved those old lines and columns of grey – bleeding and torn at times – and I wanted to charge with them, do my part and share the fate. On reflection I felt pleasure in the thought that for a time the remaining only 350 of 1,000 of my worn and depleted regiment would be spared the hard knocks they had been receiving, almost daily, in those partial engagements ever since we had confronted the enemy at Dalton in May. Beside, I know there must be some great danger threatening Charleston: great, indeed, to warrant the detachment of those two veteran infantry regiments from the ranks of the struggling Army of the West in the hour of sore need of more men and strength there. As I thought of old Charleston, Queen City by the Sea, on the shore of my native State, site of conception of "Southern Rights." Birthplace of manhood's assertion of Southern States' right of confederation and cradle of infantry of our scared "cause." I thought of her dismantled batteries, her battered forts, her shot-torn, war-worn but invincible front, and knew that the enemy was threatening her in rear by way of Johns and James Islands, and rejoiced in the knowledge that these two old regiments of trained, tried, seasoned men there "many a banner will be torn and many a knight to earth be borne" ere the enemy passed over those islands and entered Charleston. With all possible haste those troops proceeded to Charleston, and well was the need, for they had scarcely touched ground when they were in the fight.

Before me now is an excellent book, "The Defense of Charleston Harbor," written by the Rev. John Johnson, late of Charleston, S. C. Dr. Johnson was an active, useful civil engineer in our war. (On fly leaf of my copy of said work is written, by Capt. Courtenay. "With regards of the author and Capt. William A. Courtenay, August, 1897." God rest the souls of both my departed noble friends.) On page 156 of the book is a report by Major John Jenkins, 3rd South Carolina cavalry. I quote the extract from same; "At 2 o'clock on the morning of the 9th," says Major Jenkins, "I was ordered by Gen Robertson to direct Col George P. Harrison, of the 32^d Georgia, to advance upon the enemy and carry his lines unless he encountered too severe a fire of artillery, in which event he was to withdraw and not sacrifice his men. Col Harrison at 3:30 A. M. moved forward his line of battle, formed parallel with the enemy's breastworks. His attacking force consisted of seven companies of his own regiment, Bonaud's battalion and the 47th Georgia. His line of battle was preceded by a line of skirmishers in front. Col Harrison then ordered the charge and his lines moved steadily and sternly across the field, drove in the enemy's skirmishers and advanced upon their breastworks. Col Harrison and the splendid troops under him swept the enemy's skirmishers and his lines and pushed beyond. The enemy withdrew to the protection of their gunboats and embarked their forces, burning their commissary stores ashore."

Charleston's Salvation

An account of the affair was published in the newspapers of Macon and as I read my heart warmed in thankfulness to God for Charleston's salvation and glowed in pride and admiration of the gallant soldiers who charged in her defense. I felt like exclaiming, ever so heartily, "Aha, I told you so." I felt myself growing stronger each day and, though pleasantly situated, delightfully surrounded and rendering light service, I began to feel a restlessness and desire to return to my command in the field almost like unto "homesickness." My friend and comrade in camp, Col Wyley, said it was "a fool notion" and I had better get it out of my head unless I was "anxious to get something more solid in my head, something in the shape of a minie ball." If I was "itching for a fight" – I was not, though – it appeared that I might be accommodated. It seemed that about this time "the mountain was coming to Mohammet." Gen Stoneman, of the Federal army, with a picked cavalry of 2,000 cavalry and several batteries of light artillery, made a daring, dashing raid around our flank and down into our territory by Covington and toward Macon. Gen Joe Wheeler detached the commands of Col Iverson and Col Breckenridge and they, with about 800 picked cavalry, started after Stoneman – like falcon after prey. Stoneman was far ahead of his pursuers and his movements at first were cautious and not very rapid. As the vanguard was reported to be moving directly toward Macon the news spread rapidly that "the Yankees are advancing on Macon." Then there was great excitement and the anxious inquiry was "What shall we do?" Col Wyley, my superior in the camp, was away and I was in command. I quickly sounded the sentiment of the men occupying the convalescent camp and almost everyone was willing and ready to fight. I found we could muster 11 army rifles and 9 "Colt's army" pistols. I had more men than arms and ammunition, but by borrowing from houses a few "shot-guns" I could arm about thirty men, but not one strong, well man. I called for volunteers and selected those apparently best able to march a little and fight some. In a short time I had organized, officered and somewhat armed a force of about thirty-five, all weak from sickness or wounds, some wearing bandages, but ready to fight. Leaving with directions to hold themselves in readiness "to move at a moment's notice," I went as quickly as I could to the office of the commandant of the post and reported and asked for orders.

In a Quandary

"Why," said he, "we can't oppose the enemy. Our forces are all to the front. If you could get yourself and your weak and wounded men sufficiently far from the city to meet the raid outside the city, as you propose, you would only sacrifice yourselves. You are not able to march and not able to fight, and what's the use?" "Well, General," I said, "we can do a little fighting. My plan is to get on their route in their front, into selected position. Possibly their vanguard is small, maybe twenty-five or fifty men. The fire from us might check their advance and cause a deflection in their march and save Macon until they are checked by some force of ours, which I feel certain is rapidly bearing down on their rear. I don't feel like sitting down and letting them ride in and all over us without making some resistance." "All right," said he, "You best take care of yourselves in camp. But I give you cart blanche; do your best." As I said "Thank you, General," and was bowing myself out there came double quicking in a courier and hastily delivered a dispatch. I paused until the General, turning to me said; "Too late, Williams, the enemy is reported within eight miles of Macon and moving this way." "In what force, sir?" I asked. "Small force; numbers not given; probably an advanced guard." "All right, General," I replied, "I will meet them if it is outside the city." And I started for camp. The next moment I heard the boom of a small field gun at some five or six miles distance, but plainly heard. This greatly increased the excitement of the citizens and there was "wild hurrying to and fro." Reaching camp I found my force in readiness under their officers and awaiting my return. They, too, had caught to them the familiar sounding boom and though some few were feeling "powerful poorly" and a few others felt "mighty painful twitchings" about their old hurts, I was soon moving along in the street at the head of about thirty infantry, cavalry and artillery all mixed up, but in perfect formation, moving slowly and steadily and keeping dress and step, a pageant of pale and weak but stern and gallant men, ready to fight to the death in defense of the helpless inhabitants of the threatened city. Men in citizens' dress passed me hurriedly, some armed with sporting shotguns, or rifles and some only with pistols, all moving to a point near the city, designated to me by the commandant of post, which the enemy would have to pass before reaching the city on their route. It took me three-quarters of an hour to reach the objective point, about one mile, I think, from the city limit. There, I found forty or fifty citizens collected. They were without order of formation and appeared to be in some confusion, as either dispatches had come in and a few more cannon shot, nearer and amore distinctly heard, had been noted. There was at this place of rendezvous an old wooden frame building at the end of an embankment, of perhaps 100 yards in length. If I mistake not in memory it was an old mill site. The public highway over which the enemy would have to pass in entering the city from that side ran parallel with and not far from this embankment, or dam, and the house at the end of the dam next to the city. The citizen force had halted near the house on the embankment. I passed over, beyond the dam, and took position at right angle across the highway in a skirt of wood, fronted the way of approach of the enemy and had a position very favorable for a fight in defence. My men posted and resting I turned my attention to my citizen friends in the rear, near the house. They were busy organizing into a company proper and had formed into line. I readily recognized at the extreme end of the line nearest to me, in the gentleman in the long black coat and high silk hat, the eminent divine and eloquent minister, pastor of the church I had regularly attended as soon as I was able to go to church. He was a very fine and noble looking man; tall, portly, full-chested, with long, wavy brown hair falling in clusters on his broad shoulders. He was one of the most eloquent pulpit orators I ever heard. Listening to his bursts of patriotic, fiery eloquence and fulsome praise of order, chivalry and deeds of knightly daring, I thought what a leader, what a general, he would be as a leader and commander of troops in the field. What a pity that he should be confined to the pulpit in this time of our need of heroes in the arena of war.

An Amazing Incident

I was called by a citizen friend for a brief consultation. Approaching their poorly framed line I noticed on the handsome face of the minister an expression which I had never before seen there. I noticed also that he seemed not to recognize me as I bowed to him and saluted in passing. He appeared too nervous or excited to stand still in line. Turning to resume my place there came, like a sharp clap of thunder, the report of a field piece of artillery in my front and at a distance of not more than half a mile away. Quickly following this report came the demoralizing, peculiar whirring sound of a shell passing directly over our position, but at considerable height, in the direction of the city. My men in front were on their feet in an instant, steady and firm in place, and you could hear the ready click, click of their arms. Glancing back I saw my citizen friends in considerable disorder. Some were standing firm and ready with their arms, others appeared to have suddenly reached the conclusion that inside the old house was the better place and reached the house about as rapidly as the conclusion. The parson, gun in hand, started for the house, but just as a second shot came over he let fall his gun and fell to his knees; his high top "beaver hat" rolled off and for the moment it seemed that he had suddenly assumed the attitude of worship, but it did not last long enough, for quickly grabbing up his hat and forgetting his gun, he hastily joined those of his companions who had taken position inside the house. I could not help laughing heartily. The enemy's firing ceased and I remarked to Captain W____, a wounded captain of a Virginia battery of artillery; "Captain, our fight is over. A small scouting force, they have either passed us by or have fallen back on their main body." "I agree with you," said the Captain. "That gun was on an elevation and they were merely saluting us and trying to drop one of those little point shells or shot inside Macon for pure cussedness." He was correct; one shot crashed into a house well inside the city limit. In half an hour's time, in a reconnaissance we found that a small body had come up, halted, fired from the top of a hill and returned by way of their approach. We slowly counter-marched back to camp.

Of the dashing raid by those splendid "blue coat" cavalrymen Gen Wheeler reported: "Gen Iverson was successful in his pursuit of Gen Stoneman, whom he met, defeated and captured with 800 of his command some twenty miles from Macon. The remainder of Stoneman's command was much demoralized and scattered. Col Breckinridge pursued and captured the only organized party which attempted escape. Thus ended (the raid) in most ignominious defeat and destruction.

Two days after our fright because "the Yankees are advancing on Macon," I sat in church and again listened, while preached the eloquent minister, whom I admired more as a minister of the Gospel than as a soldier at arms. His sermon was splendidly delivered, but to tell the truth, I did not greatly enjoy it as I had done before the raid.

William A. Bowers, Jr.

The Charleston Sunday News and Courier, Charleston, South Carolina, October 26, 1913

A CONFEDERATE SOLDIER'S MEMOIRS

(By Captain Ben S. Williams, Brunson, S. C.)

On the morning of November 1, 1864, on James Island, S. C., there issued from our regimental headquarters the following order. I copy from my old order book before me now:

"Hd Qrs 47th Regt GA Vols, Secessionville, November 1st, 1864: Company commanders will forward at once to this office complete lists of recruits received in their companies on yesterday, the 31st of Oct. This list will embrace name, rank, company, age and place of nativity."

This order was signed by myself and was an extraordinary issuing; it related to the influx of recruits of the evening before. The number of recruits received was one hundred – about one-third the strength of the wreck and remnant of the old regiment that in June 1862 went into action very near the spot where we were, November 1, 1864, camping one thousand strong,

There was no source throughout the South from which to recruit our reduced ranks and the sudden injection, by enlistment, of 100 men at one time into our command was little short of miraculous. But the newly arrived and enrolled soldiers of the Confederacy were captive Federal soldiers, all in blue United Sates uniform and directly from the Andersonville, Ga., prison. From the depot in Charleston they were marched directly into our camp by Confederate officers and "turned over" to us – the 47th Georgia infantry – to be clad in grey, placed in our ranks and under the "Stars and Bars" fought against their former comrades under the "Stars and Stripes."

Prisoner Furnished Problems

They were volunteers for such enlistment and service in furtherance of an experiment by us, hitherto untried and unique, incongruous and hazardous. But in said prison we had an army of between thirty and forty thousand men, Yankee prisoners, and like the individual who has seized by the horns the bellowing bovine, the question was how to hold onto them or how to let them go. Our own active armies in the field were but half fed; much of our territory upon which we had depended for subsistence was lost to us and yet this inactive and hostile force in our prison had to be "rationed" and cared for.

We had striven sedulously, with the Federal Government to effect an exchange of captured soldiers, but in vain. They, the United States Government officials, were well aware that to release our men was to swell our ranks and strengthen our lines – which we could not possibly otherwise do – and at the same time afford us relief, by exchange, of the heavy burden of sustenance and care of the imprisoned, defenseless host, while by draft, conscription and purchase the United States Government could easily replace their lost men with double the number at short notice. So we ventured the experiment, on a small scale, of fighting the "galvanized" Yankee against the "genuine article."

I have never heard but one such experiment.

Our Yanks were really a fine, soldierly looking set of fellows and though somewhat lean and hungry – as were we – seemed rejoiced at their release from close confinement and ready for business. We apportioned them ten to each company of the regiment. They were a cosmopolitan set and were not pleased with the accessions to their regiments.

Captain's Comments

Connor, captain of Company A, said: "My contingent is a heterogeneous bunch of d__d hoboes, but as we have only twenty-three men left in my company, it is "Hobson's choice." Laurence, captain of Company B, said; "I have for my share two Irishmen, two Germans, one Italian, one Swede, two Michiganders, and two d__d Pennsylvania Dutchmen. Capt. Kennedy, of Company G, said: "Mine are all regular 'blue-bellied' Yanks, but hail from hell to breakfast." – And so on.

These remarks were, of course, made aside to me, and our "galvanized Yanks" were treated by the officers just as the regular members of their commands were and by their comrades in the ranks just as if they had enlisted and stood together instead of having fought in opposing ranks in battle. They touched elbows, kept step in ranks and on drill, parade and inspection, and laughed and jested as they smoked around the camp fires at night. We would not trust them on picket posts, and non-commissioned officers and alert reliable men in the companies were instructed privately keep close, strict watch upon them at all hours, for notwithstanding their implicit obedience to orders, ready conformation to our customs and apparent satisfaction with surroundings we felt that we had enemies within our lines, and had enemies in our camp, As (illegible) Pomeroy put it:

> "We ration them, clothe them
> and them do drill,
> But we know they are Yanks
> and our enemies still."

Sent Back to Prison

When we had them with us a week or two, in order to test them we placed some of them on picket posts. When this had been done several times and they had learned the lay of the land, our lines and the position of their former comrades, the enemy, they proved their treachery and falsehood to our cause and their fealty to their "first Love" by deserting at every opportunity. They were adepts in the art of concealment and trickery of slipping away. Their conduct necessitated an order for the return of all remaining ones to the prison.

The enforcement of this order was fraught with sadness. They begged piteously to be kept and tried, and not be returned to prison for the sins of those who had proven false. But military law was quite inflexible and almost as unchangeable as that formerly, of the Medes and Persians.

On the morning of the 29th of November we received orders to "be ready to march and fight at a moment's notice." The late evening of the same day saw the remaining number of our Yankee "recruits" marching "quick time" across the island toward the depot to be entrained for Andersonville, Ga.

Again on the March

I felt sorry for some of them and bade them good-bye with regret. By sunset, the battered remnant of my command was in line and above us waved our tattered and battle-riven flag and as the breeze from the sea unfurled its folds, in the glinting rays of the setting sun could be plainly seen the grim evidence abundant of its presence on fields where missiles of destruction sped and left their traces where they struck.

Poor old remnant of a once mighty corps; in your thinned ranks others are soon to fall, and yet, by Heaven, as those gallant Veterans gazed upon those scarred folds of their waving battle-flag, a yell went up from every throat and ere its echoes died upon the waters around old Fort Sumter we were moving, in measured tread, away from James Island and Charleston, forever, toward our fate before us.

Arriving after dark at the railroad, where we were to be "entrained," the orders were given "Halt, front, right dress, order arms, parade rest," but on learning that our train was not ready, the order, "Attention, fix bayonets, stack arms, in place rest."

A Surprise

Knowing that we would soon go into action, I embraced the opportunity afforded by this delay to arrange some of my official papers. I borrowed from our quartermaster a piece of "tallow-dip" candle. Lighted it, placed it on the end of a cross-tie apart from the command and seating myself on the earth to windward of my light I hastily finished my work. As I arose with candle in hand, its flickering light revealed to me, not more than five feet in my front, the stalwart form and firm fine Irish features of one of our late "galvanized" Yanks." Holding the light nearer and stepping toward him as he saluted, I said: "Why, Hogan, what the___."

"Adjutant," he whispered, passing his fingers across his lips, "for God's sake don't, don't give me away."

"But how came you here; where are your comrades; how did you escape and what are you up to?" I hastily questioned.

Stepping quickly and so near to me that I instinctively placed my hand on my "Colt's army pistol," he whispered:

"Adjutant, I cast myself on your mercy. In the name of Christ and the Holy Virgin, I beg ye to save me. I have been waiting and watching and praying to God to get the chance to speak to you and me heart went up into my throat when I saw you strike a light and get off to yourself: then I marked the cross upon me heart and crept to you.

Pleads for Another Chance

"Adjutant, I have suffered the torments of purgatory in the last few hours since I slipped out of the ranks on the march in the dusk of the evening and waited for the regiment that I knew was coming, and praying that I might get to you before being captured and sent back into prison. Adjutant, give me a chance. Let me go with the regiment, by me soul, I love it; try me in the battle and be Jazes if there is a 'reb' that will go further to the front in the fight, or fire more rounds while we last than myself; then send me to Andersonville or to hell, which you rather. Save me, Adjutant, I pray you; if you will not, then shoot me dead right now."

A moment's reflection and I said; "Hogan, the regiment will be in battle before the sun sets to-morrow, possibly before it rises. I am going to assume the grave responsibility and give you a chance of arming you and placing you back in our ranks. There is a very sick man in Company C; you shall have his gun and accoutrements; I will give them to you. Keep off here in the dark and when the men are taking the train get in with them. Keep your mouth shut and in the dark you will not be discovered. I will acquaint Capt. Thompson, of Company C, with the facts and on the way will make it all right with the Colonel.

"On landing from the train, fall in line with your company, C. Act the man to-morrow when you go into action. Rest assured I will be near you and shall keep the closest possible watch on you. If I see one symptom of wrong or cussedness in you, I will shoot you dead in the ranks as I would a dog. Do you understand, and do you want to go with us?"

An Irishman's Gratitude

Poor fellow, stalwart and brave and strong; his hands went up before his face and his bosom heaved with insuppressible emotion. Oh, now filled with gratitude and tenderness is an Irishman's heart – when his "stomach" is not filled with whiskey. I sent the sick man over to the hospital in Charleston and saw Hogan belt himself in the dark and grasp the gun I handed him to use on the men in blue whom we were to meet in battle on the morrow.

Hogan had escaped from the prison squad on their march to the train in the dusk of the evening, with guards in front and rear, by falling quickly and quietly to earth, from about the centre of the squad, and rolling over and over rapidly into the high grass and weeds on the roadside until concealed, where he hugged the ground until the rear of the column had passed him. He continued in concealment there, as he knew the regiment – preparing to move when he left – would pass that point on their march. He fell in on the rear and hung close to the regiment on their way to the point of entrainment and ventured up as described.

Hogan Kept His Promise

I will say that we were hotly engaged in battle the following day, November 30, and I kept my eye on Hogan. He acted well his part. We made but one short charge and I was near Company C when we went in and in the weird, shrilling, thrilling, piercing music of the "rebel yell" I noted a discordant sound; it was Hogan's hoarse Yankee battle-field "hurrah," "hurrah."

On the battle field of Bentonville, N. C., where waved our battle-flag for the last time in battle's storm, March 19, 1865, Hogan fell, close beside his comrades in grey – who fell with him to rest,

> "Their warfare o'er, to sleep the sleep
> that knows not breaking,
> To dream of battle-fields no more: days
> Of danger, nights of waking."

Our train of freight box cars was late in reaching us; when it came we were shipped, like cattle, down on the Charleston and Savannah Railway to a point nearly midway between Charleston and Savannah – Grahamville – where we landed, tired and hungry, about daylight on the morning of November 30, and awaited further orders.

Charleston Sunday News and Courier, Charleston, South Carolina – September 21, 1913

A CONFEDERATE SOLDIER'S MEMOIRS
(By Captain Ben S. Williams, Brunson, S. C.)

In writing my memoirs of the war time of the '60s, I do not intend to write history of manoeuvres of the army and battles fought; my object is to record some of the main incidents occurring in my life and service as a soldier of the Confederacy, my own personal experiences and impressions, the nebulae of history, the one-thousandth part of which is not and will never be made known. In so doing I rely not only on my notes and diary and other war papers now in my possession and accessible for reference, but also upon reminiscence. Many, very many, of the scenes and incidents of the four years of my "army life" are so fresh in my memory and as plain to my mind's eye as are occurrences of last year or last month. Ten years ago I drew, at the request of a gentleman of Charleston, engaged in a controversy, a diagram of a battlefield in which my command engaged in the year 1864. My memory was my only aid. Never after the battle did I see the ground until three months ago, June 1913. I could not have then improved as to accuracy in any particular on my diagram from memory. Adverse to falsehood in every phase, I avoid embellishment. The detestable habit of greatly exaggerating and boastfully misrepresenting by some in narrative of what is most aptly yelped "war stories" is contemptible, misleading and disgusting. In the truth there is much glory and honor for the brave and true. For the pearl-lined casket of impartial history, equity and truth are the fairest jewels.

Many who pose as 'twas "I Killed Cock Robbin" did precious little of the shooting of the "arrows." Relators of great, grand and glorious performances – mirable dietu – on their own part were probably not there at all. A boaster is almost always surely a coward, usually more an "accessory after the fact."

He who pictures the soldiers of the armies of the North, all, as vicious cutthroats in the camp and on the march and weak-kneed poltroons on the field is either a fool, an arrant falsitior, or is ignorant of the facts. Thousands of "our friends, the enemy," were men of fibrine like unto that of ourselves. Some of them were our own kith and kin.

The boast and pride and reliance of the Federal army of the West, their "Rock of Chickamauga" and "Sledge of Nashville," was Gen. George H. Thomas, a gallant son of the State of Virginia, and kinsman to chivalrous foemen in his front. He was major of cavalry in the United States Army, with Albert Sidney Johnston, the Lees, R.E. and Fitzhugh, and others from Southern states in the army of the United States. When the States of the

South seceded these men, almost without exception, resigned from the United States army and tendered their services to their States, respectively, as they seceded from the Union. Thomas did not resign, but remained in the United States army. As a division commander he stood as an immovable barrier between us and complete, crushing victory at Chickamauga, and with his overwhelming, phalanxed columns crushed into fragments Hood's depleted and hopeless struggling divisions at Nashville. His wife was a Northern woman of considerable strength of mind and force of character, and to her influence is attributed the course of Gen. Thomas.

Gen. Keyes, of the United States Army, on one occasion, after the war, when asked to what he attributed Gen. Thomas's action in remaining in the United States army, with his well-known strong and warm Southern proclivities jocosely replied; "I guess it was another case of the gray mare being the better horse."

The kinsmen of Gen. Thomas on father's and mother's sides were in the Southern armies. Two of his brothers were Confederate officers. His two sisters in Virginia were ardent advocates and supporters of the Southern cause. These sisters and one brother never spoke to him from the date of his apostasy, in 1861, when he turned his back upon his mother State in her hour of sorest need until his death, which occurred in 1870.

James Island, August 1864

August 20, 1864, I was back in camp with my command at Secessionville, James Island, S. C. I hastily took in the conditions in the regiment. The status of affairs was by no means pleasing or gratifying to me. The companies were considerably reduced in numbers. A few had fallen in the fight on Johns Island immediately on their arrival to save Charleston, as the regimental order book showed record of promotion of several non-commissioned officers "to fill the place of those killed on Johns Island, June 9, 1864." Some were "absent on furlough," visiting their homes passed by on their hurried trip from Kennesaw Mountain, Ga., to Charleston, and a few more were "absent without leave," having left without orders, or overstaying the length of time specified in furloughs. I was surprised to see that about one-half of the commissioned officers were away from their commands. I readily noted the absence of the esprit de corps of the regiment and the several causes to which same was attributed.

Gen Joseph E. Johnston had been relieved of the command of the Army of the West; Hood, succeeding him, had taken the aggressive and had attacked, but after three unsuccessful attacks on Sherman, July 20, 23 and 28, in which our loss was 3,000 men, Hood moved within the fortifications of Atlanta and that city was in siege. The territory embracing the homes of the men of the regiment was now not in our rear and the enemy in our front, as formerly, but was between us and the two contending armies of Hood and Sherman.

The men were anxious, restless and dissatisfied. Of the number of absent officers were the colonel and the lieutenant colonel of the regiment, thus was the regiment placed under the command of Major J. S. Cone. Major Cone was a capable officer, of military education and as brave and gallant as any officer of the command, but was very unpopular because of his rigid discipline and merciless, despotic rule. He was the only officer of the regiment who visited the punishment – pain and indignity – of "bucking" on the men for comparatively slight offenses. "Bucking" consisted of bringing the hands together in front, securely tying the wrists, seating the prisoner on the earth, drawing his knees up high toward his chin, passing the arms over and around the knees and passing an iron ramrod or heavy stick through under the knees and above the arms and turning the absolutely helpless subject over on his side. More than one desertion was caused by this treatment ordered by this same cruel officer. To Cone the words "the bravest are the tenderest" did not apply.

The young major was erect, athletic and impulsive; had very dark complexion with hair black and straight as an Indian's – and he was as crafty and cruel as an Indian.

The major and I did not love each other, yet I knew his mettle and admired his gallantry in the field. His conduct towards the majority of the officers in the regiment was arrogant, dictatorial and discourteous, but to me he was ever courteous, affable and communicative. He had been raising the devil in the regiment, had reduced three or four non-commissioned officers to the ranks, had Court-martialed several privates, some of whom were undergoing punishment and several others confined in arrest awaiting trial. In addition to the latter was Lieut. Purtell, of Company A.

Of those who, having fallen under the displeasure of the major, and undergoing punishment, were two fine young fellows – Crosby and Farmer. The charge against Crosby was that having been discharged from hospital on healing of wound on 13th of July; he had visited his home and remained there a day or two, reporting to his command on the 23d instead of going directly from the hospital to his command. The charge against Farmer was that in a controversy with the ensign of the regiment, begun by the ensign, Farmer had told him to "go to hell," and when threatened, said, "Report and be damned." The sentence imposed on each of them was to "wear a 32-pound ball attached to the leg by a chain two feet long, for the term of fifteen days and forfeit all pay and allowance for that time." The cases of these two fine young fighters appealed to me, as did Lieut. Putrell, personally, to aid him, paying me the extraordinary compliment, "You are the only officer in the regiment either feared or respected by Major Cone." After a somewhat warm and earnest colloquy between my friend, the major and myself, in the privacy of his headquarters, the following order issued from Major Cone, commanding:

Sentences Commuted

"Special Order, No 50, The sentences of Privates Crosby and Farmer, of the 47th Georgia regiment, are commuted to 3 days solitary confinement in the post guard house."

Subsequently, the charges were withdrawn against Lieut. Purtell.

I found the regiment doing hard picket duty on the edge of the marsh and mud of the island. I noted the following order from "Island Headquarters:"

"Special Order, No 52 Major Cone, commanding the 47th Geo. Vols., will detail 100 men, with a suitable number of officers and non-commissioned officers, to report to Major Mangault of Battery No 2, this evening at 7'oclock for picket duty."

That was a very heavy attachment form one depleted regiment, at one time. I perceived, also, that the men were living on very scant rations of poor food, consisting of one pint of poorly cleaned rice and one pint of watery, green looking sorghum syrup, a day, with three pounds of stringy, blue looking beet, each Saturday. This was a burning shame, as our regimental commissary assured me there was, stored up in the nearby city and in control of our military authorities, provisions sufficient for the supply of the forces then around Charleston for two years time, and in this section of South Carolina, at that time there was an abundance of food stuffs; corn, rice, potatoes, hogs, cattle and sheep.

Gen. Sherman declared that he found no difficulty in provisioning his army on the products of the part of the state traversed in his tardy march through, some months later. Wondrous, that with home so near the members of my regiment did not feel sense of duty and patriotism "oozing from their fingertips," and go home to stay; yet very few deserted or failed to return at expiration of leave of absence. I subsisted – barely existed – on this d__d demulcent, diluent, diet of rice and sorghum until the scent of the insipid sorghum would nauseate me and I would go it on dry rice until beef-ration day. Occasionally, like a momentary rift in the clouds, would come a little feasting, then back, with most of us, to the routine famine.

Soon after reaching camp, from Macon, I received, Sunday morning, this following note by courier from my kinsman, Col Ashley:

"Ben, dodge inspection this A. M., and come, dine and spend the day with us. You can return in time for dress parade. No excuse. Come at once."

The courier was Jim Baugn, a waggish fellow and a fine fighter, member of Company C, of my regiment. He had been detailed to drive the regimental quartermaster wagon. The quartermaster was camping and messing with Col Ashley and Baugn was chief cook. Baugn was a glutton and an arrant thief, and, off duty, would take "anything eatable or drinkable, lying around loose," as he would say, but not from his own command; yet would he have fought, quick as a flash, any man accusing him of theft. His plea of avoidance and defense was; "Nearly all damned rascality is fair in war, providing you don't go too far."

I was soon mounted and on my way, to Ashley's quarters. I, of course, enjoyed the real good dinner. Most of all I enjoyed some highly seasoned, and, to me, delicious soup. I don't know whether this was because of the deliciousness of the dish or because it was first served and seasoned by the sauce of keen hunger. But while lingering at the (illegible) but festive board enjoying Ashley's good Charleston cigars, I spoke of the soup and inquired as to the chief ingredients thereof. Baugn, the "chef," was summoned and Col Ashley said to him; "Baugn, your dinner was relished. Of what did you make the soup served?" "Well Colonel, "said Baugn, "the patoory, as my French friend and old messmate Pom-(illegible) dish with me and is made of cowtails. There was four tails in that soup and them tails," – "hold up there, Baugn, halt," said the Colonel, "it is too soon after dinner to be telling us of feeding us on cowtails. You spoil the whole flavor of the dish. Call them caudal appendages."

"Don't know what the hell – beg pardon, Colonel, that is, sir, but tails ain't to be sneezed at, they are held high, them butchers at the commissary pens charge us twenty-five cents a tail, cash money."

"Now, see here, Baugn," said the Colonel, "you haven't drawn a cent of pay in a month past. You promised me to stop gambling when I gave you half a dollar in Charleston the other day to buy tobacco. Where did you get a dollar to pay for these aforesaid articles at 25 cents a piece?"

"Well, a-hem, er, Colonel," said Baugn, "I, er, found them four articles in the back part of my waggin when I reached home from the pens and I suppose some durned thief put 'em there with the intention of stealing 'em and it was just our good luck for me to find 'em for our use and benefit."

"That will do, Baugn," quoth the Colonel, "With all thy faults I believe thy tale, every word of it, but don't relish being made so nearly particeps criminis. Take this cigar, go and smoke, reflect, and damn you, try and sin no more."

"Thank ye, Colonel," said Baugn, saluting, "for the compliment, the advice and the seegar."

The men soon began to receive boxes of victuals from their homes, which greatly relieved and enlivened them, for along with the boxes came letters and little tokens of love and remembrance from "home, sweet, home."

An Anonymous Benefactor

I had no home. Our home was broken up; my mother a refugee in far South Georgia. There was no one from whom to expect presents by me. But somewhere, somewhere there was a ministering angel, somewhere, whose thoughts and care were with and for the young soldier. On my return, one afternoon, from a visit to the picket posts I found in my tent, left by the regimental wagoner, a large, strongly made box with my name, rank and command neatly printed on top. The contents were bewildering and almost convinced me that their source was where winter and clouds of our war were not. After the boiled whole ham, pineapple, cheese, biscuit, crackers, pickles, preserves, etc., etc., was a beautifully iced, large pound cake, a jar of loaf sugar and a jar of parched and ground genuine coffee; and, carefully wrapped, a pure white china cup, that looked like celluloid, to drink from. There was no letter, note or other information as to identity of the donor, and to this day I am entirely and absolutely ignorant as to whom my gratitude is due. I know it was a woman's thought and kindness, and I today, pray God that if she is living, her heart is filled with gladness and happiness; that her pathway be one of peace and joy even down to the portal of the silent tomb beyond which may she dwell, eternally, in the light of the countenance of the God to whom she prayed, while I fought, in the days when she so kindly remembered me.

Affairs of the command were improving and I rejoiced, for I knew that our war was not ended, that of the original one thousand of the regiment there were about two hundred and fifty of us, rank and file, left; that upon us devoted additional duties and the discharge of same the preservation of name and record.

The colonel of the regiment returned to camp and our austere major was deposed from supreme command.

Occasionally the monotony of our picket duty life was disturbed by proceedings in pursuance of orders as follows:

"General Orders, No. 41. In pursuance of General Order No 84. C. S., from departmental headquarters. Privates D. Otts and George Sherwith, Company B, Lucas's battalion, will be shot to death with musketry at or about 12 o'clock on Friday, the 11th inst. Commanding officers of east and west lines and of the light artillery will order two men from each company in their commands, the detachment of each to be in charge of a commissioned officer, who will report at 10:30 A. M. on the day above specified to Major Lucas, of Lucas's battalion, who is in charge of the execution of the preceding paragraphs of this order. By command of Brig Gen Taliaferro, commanding 3d sub district, South Carolina, departments of South Carolina, Georgia and Florida."

The orders were carried out promptly and literally. The crimes for which these two men were executed were desertion and the murder of the two guards in whose charge they were placed for return to camp after capture. These prisoners displayed grit and fearlessness to the very last moment of their lives. One standing facing the firing squad with his rude box coffin and open grave at his feet in front, stood proud and erect. At the command, "Ready," he threw back his head proudly. At the word, "Aim," he defiantly slapped his protruding breast with his right hand; in the next instant after the command "Fire," he fell, lifeless, forward almost into his open coffin. All the troops on the island, off duty, were mustered to witness the execution. That was not my first witnessing of such scenes.

Later we had cause for astonishment and food for thought in the enactment of one of the most un-thought of, surprising and unique proceedings of my whole war experience.

The Sunday News, Charleston, South Carolina – November 9, 1913

A Confederate Soldier's Memoirs

(By Captain B. S. Williams, Brunson, S. C.)

Just as the light of the 30th day of November, 1864, dawned across the sea and lifted night's sable curtain from forest and field of South Carolina's foe-encompassed coastland, a train of freight cars "slowed up" at a little way station on the Charleston and Savannah Railway, nearly midway between the cities of Charleston and Savannah, when, like "yellow-jacket wasps" disturbed in their nests, three hundred grey-jacketed Confederates sprang through the open doors of the cars to earth and in less than five minutes were in phalanxed line of battle on the east side of the railway facing the seacoast, ready for duty whate'er the duty be. The order, "In place rest," was given and the colonel commanding sought authority for action, as we were not met by courier or guide and were without orders as to proceeding.

Now, these men in line were veterans tried and true; tried in many battles and true as steel. They were seasoned veterans, fine fighters and good soldiers, but I cannot write that they were "goody-good" fellows or good Christian churchmen, for when the discipline of silence was waived in the order, "In place rest," and I passed down the line from right to left I heard many expressions of opinion and feeling couched in language not exactly in accord with the prescribed forms of religious worship or embraced in any volume of modern Sunday-school literature.

Fighting Hungry

These men were very hungry and very mad – they were in fine fighting trim. I would never select for a desperate charge or to lead in a "forlorn hope' troops whose stomachs were full of food and whose hearts were filled with contentment, good cheer and the "milk of human kindness."

We had gone without food from noon of the day before – our "ration day." We understood that we were to arrive at night and find rations awaiting us. We arrived at day – dawn and the place was as bare of food as were barren the hearts and swollen heads of some of the conceited and asinine petty officials whose duty it was to see to such matters of sympathy and regard for the comfort and welfare of the "rank and file" of the armies.

In this case it is quite possible that some of these aforesaid valiant carpet knights were at the time comfortably ensconced in the pleasant homes of the hospitable citizens of the little village of Grahamville, about two miles away coastward, very sure of the cavalry between them and the enemy.

This neglect of duty and indifference to results was not confined to the line of petty staff officers; officers of high rank and command, in some instances were negligent and apparently indifferent to very important, grave and serious results.

At the close of the first day's battle at Chickamauga, when the blood of thousands of men drenched the field without great advantage to either side, Gen Bragg, commanding the Confederate Army of the West planned to attack at daylight next morning, Sunday, September 20, the left of the Federal army and crush their columns there before they could be strongly reinforced. Gen Polk was instructed to attack accordingly, Breckinridge's division was a part of Polk's corps and my regiment was a part of Breckinridge's division. Orders were issued and arrangements made for the desperate attack at daylight on the enemy's left. Weary and worn we slept in line upon our arms and were ready at day's first dawning to attack.

Delay Was Fatal

Relative to the planned attack, in his official report Gen Bragg says; "Before the dawn of day myself and staff were ready for the saddle, occupying a position immediately in rear of and accessible to all parts of the line."

"With increasing anxiety and disappointment I waited until after sunrise without hearing a gun and at length dispatched a staff officer to Lieut. Gen Polk to ascertain the cause of the delay and to urge him to a prompt and speedy movement. This officer not finding the General with his troops and learning where he had spent the night, over the Chickamauga and there delivered the message. A reconnaissance made in the front of our extreme right during this delay proved the important fact that this greatly desired position was open to our possession."

The enemy soon learned of our delayed movement, strongly reinforced their extreme left and cut our troops to pieces when assaulted about 10 o'clock A. M.

It was said that when Gen Polk was reached by the messenger from Gen Bragg he was breakfasting at a fine residence a few miles from the field with his gilt-laced staff around him. On receiving the urgent message he replied that he would soon be on the field, as it was the desire of his heart to facilitate the intended engagement.

The sun was riding high in the heavens and his rays had dispelled the mists of the morning, while we waited, wondering what was to happen and if we would ever enjoy another breakfast on earth.

Near 9 o'clock a staff officer of Gen W. Smith, to whom we had been ordered to report when leaving Charleston, rode up with orders for us to proceed at once and report to Gen Smith at the earth works on the road leading to Boyd's Landing. The officer was our guide and we took up our line of march. The men marched slowly and sullenly, for they were weary from loss of sleep, hungry and mad because of their bad treatment.

Colonel Notes Men's Mood

The colonel remarked to me, "I have never seen the regiment so sullen and dispirited as they now appear. They seem weary and somewhat exhausted, but mad and devilish, too. Do you think in their present mood we can depend on them for good work?"

"Never saw them in better trim for a savage fight," I replied, "and if we have not too far to march, woe to the boys in blue with haversacks on when we strike them to-day."

Now, where were we marching to, against whom, or what?

"Ours not to reason why,
Ours but to do-and die."

In the light of the past and of public record we learn that the landing of troops at Boyd's Landing on our coast was "piece and parcel" of Gen Sherman's tactics while marching through Georgia.

Gen Sherman had telegraphed Gen Halleck, on November 11, from Kingston, Ga.: "I would like to have Foster break the Charleston and Savannah Railroad near Pocatalligo about the 1st of December."

Gen Halleck ordered Gen Foster to make the attack, who replied as follows: "Hilton Head, November 5, 1864 – Major Gen Halleck U. S. Army-General: "I have the honor to acknowledge the receipt of your confidential letter. I am preparing to carry out your instructions and shall move on the night of the 28th and make my attack the next day." etc.

In strict obedience to orders and true to the programme, Gen Foster moved with a fleet of five gunboats, carrying a naval brigade composed of 500 sailors, two batteries – B and F, of New York artillery – under command of Lieut. Col William Ames, a detachment of the 4th Massachusetts cavalry and two brigades of infantry, the 56th, 127th, 144th, 157th, New York: the 25th Ohio, and the 32d, 34th and 35th U. S. colored troops, infantry commanded by Gen Potter: the 54th and 55th Massachusetts regiments, and the 26th and 102d regiments U. S. colored troops, commanded by Col A. S. Hartwell. Total: One company cavalry, three batteries of artillery and twelve regiments of infantry, seven white and five negro, about 6,000 troops all told.

Landing of the Enemy

The fleet left Hilton Head before daylight on the morning of the 29th, but on account of delays did not reach Boyd's Landing until about 8 o'clock A. M.; then only two advance naval vessels had arrived. By noon all the craft was up and the place was alive with Federal cavalry, artillery and infantry. Gen Foster appeared and took command at 2 P. M. One hour later Gen Potter appeared and the landing of this little army of 6,000 men, eighteen pieces of artillery, horses, stores etc., began. The entire remainder of the day – the 10th of November – was consumed in completely effecting their landing.

This part of the 3d military district of South Carolina, where the enemy landed, and Honey Hill, where they were met, was under command of Col C. J. Colcock, of the 3d S. C. cavalry.

About 8 o'clock our cavalry vidette reported the approach of the enemy and the news was sent to Grahamville, near the headquarters of Col Colcock. Col Colcock was away at Matthew's Bluff, on the Savannah River, some fifty or sixty miles distant. Major John Jenkins, second in command, was absent in Charleston, Capt. W. B. Peeples, Company K, 3d S. C. cavalry, was at Grahamville, hastily preparing to report with his command to Gen Wheeler, in Georgia in front of Sherman.

Capt. Peeples, being the senior officer present, took command and with about 100 men of his company and slight detachments of other cavalry commands, moved forward gallantly and with all haste to meet the enemy. Major Jenkins arrived from Charleston in the afternoon and relieved Capt. Peeples of command. Col Colcock did not arrive until next morning – the 30th.

Enemy's Advance Delayed

The enemy advanced steadily and cautiously toward Grahamville, between which place and their landing place was Honey Hill, with earthworks constructed by order of Robert E. Lee, who was in command of this department in the early part of the year 1862.

Two cavalry companies, Capt. Peeples, Company K, and Capt. Raysor, Company E, 3d S. C. cavalry, confronted the invading hosts, and by tactful skirmishing delayed their progress and then bivouaced for the night near Bolan Church. It was a night of watchfulness on the part of the few Confederates, who awaited in anxious sleepless suspense, the coming of the morning. Every man was determined to check the enemy's advance, but unless expected reinforcements came up before daylight they would have to contend against fearful odds – more than twenty-five to one. Reinforcements were coming in, assembling at Honey Hill and Grahamville.

There was "mounting in hot haste" for "the despots' heels" – thousands of them – "were on our shore." Every cavalry command, every piece of artillery within reach and available were headed during the night of the 29th for Honey Hill. Several companies and battalions of Georgia militia were sent from Savannah. All these reinforcements had reached Honey Hill where my command, the 47th Georgia infantry, came up and started forward, as above described.

The State: Columbia, S. C., Sunday Morning, September 4, 1921

Relates Story of Honey Hill Battle

Captain Ben S. Williams, Commanding Gallant Forty-seventh Georgia Infantry, Recalls Fighting of Three Hundred Against Far Superior Numbers

To the Editor of The State:

Just as the light of the 30th day of November, 1864, dawned across the sea and lifted night's sable curtain from the forest and field of South Carolina's foe encompassed coastland, a train of freight cars slowed up at a little way station on the Charleston and Savannah railway, midway between the cities of Charleston and Savannah and 300 gray jacketed Confederates sprang through the open doors of the cars.

The bullet riven, shell torn colors of the Stars and Bars of the command quickly marked the centre for formation and in less than five minutes a phalanxed line of battle on the east side of the railway facing toward the coast was ready for action.

The orders, "On the center dress," "Steady," "Order arms," "In place rest," quickly followed and the colonel commanding sought authority for movement and action, as we were not met by courier or guide and were without orders to proceeding.

This gray line of 300 was the remnant of the Forty-Seventh Georgia Volunteer infantry, the command to which I had been assigned, early in 1862, and in April, 1863, marched so bravely, so steadily, so gallantly, through the city of Jackson, Miss., beneath the proudly floating Stars and Bars to the ringing notes of Dixie, 1,000 strong.

These 300 men in line were veterans tried and true; tried in many battles and true as steel. They were seasoned veterans, fine fighters and good soldiers but I can not write they were good Christian churchmen, for when the discipline of silence was waived in the order "In place rest" and I passed down the line from right to left I heard many expressions of opinion and feeling couched in language not exactly in accord with the prescribed forms of religious worship or embraced in any volume of modern Sunday school literature.

In Mood to Fight

These men were very hungry and very mad. They were in fine fighting trim. I would never select for a desperate charge or to lead in a forlorn hope, troops whose stomachs were full of food and whose hearts were filled with contentment, good cheer and the "milk of human kindness." We had gone without food from noon of the day before, our ration day. We understood that we were to arrive at our objective point at 12 o'clock at night and find rations awaiting us. We arrived just at dawn. There was no food, no one to meet us, friend or foe, and no information only that from an old countryman that, "Lots of soldiers from Savannah had gone on to Boyd's Landing." We impatiently awaited orders from somebody, somewhere.

This neglect of duty, regardless of results, was not confined to the line of petty staff officers. Officers of high rank in our army were, in some instances, negligent and apparently indifferent to very important results.

At the close of the first day's battle at Chickamauga, when the blood of thousands of men drenched the field without great advantage to either side, General Bragg, commanding the Confederate army of the West, planned to attack at daylight next morning, Sunday, September 20, the left of the Federal army and crush their columns there before they could be strongly reinforced. General Polk, a West Point graduate, Episcopal bishop and army corps commander, was instructed to attack, accordingly. Breckinridge's division was a part of Polk's corps, and my regiment a part of Breckinridge's division. Orders were issued and arrangements made for the desperate attack at daylight on the enemy's left. Weary and worn we slept in line upon our arms and were ready at day's first dawning to attack.

Relative to the planned attack in his official report, General Bragg says: "Before the dawn of day, myself and staff were ready for the saddle, occupying a position immediately in rear of and accessible to all parts of the line."

Anxious for Orders

With increasing anxiety and disappointment, I waited until after sunrise without hearing a gun and at length dispatched a staff officer to Lieutenant General Polk to ascertain the cause of the delay and to urge him to prompt and speedy movement. This officer, not finding the general with his troops, and learning where he had spent the night, crossed over the Chickamauga, and there delivered the message.

A reconnoissance made in the front of our extreme right during this delay proved the important fact that this greatly desired position was open to our possession.

The enemy soon learned of our delayed movement, strongly reinforced their extreme left and cut our troops to pieces when assaulted about 10 o'clock a.m.

It was said that when General Polk was reached by the messenger from General Bragg he was breakfasting at a fine residence, a few miles from the field, with his gilt laced staff around him. On receiving the urgent message, he replied that he would soon be on the field, as it was the desire of his heart to facilitate the intended engagement.

General Polk was killed near Marietta, Ga., either at Pine or Kennesaw Mountain. I was very near when the shell by which he was killed exploded.

The sun was riding high in the heavens and its rays had dispelled the mists of the morning, while we waited, wondering what was to happen and if we would ever enjoy another breakfast on earth.

Awaiting at Honey Hill

Near 9 o'clock a staff officer of Gen. Gustavus W. Smith, to whom we had been ordered to report when leaving Charleston, rode up with orders for us to proceed at once and report to General Smith at the earthworks on the road leading to Boyd's Landing. The officer was our guide and we took up our line of march. He informed us that a large force of the enemy had landed on the coast. This force he told us, we were to meet at Honey Hill, where others of our troops were in waiting.

The men marched slowly and sullenly, for they were weary from loss of sleep, hungry and mad because of their bad treatment. The colonel remarked to me as we rode at the head of the column, "I have never seen the regiment so sullen and dispirited as they now appear. They seem weary and somewhat exhausted, but mad and devilish, too. Do you think in their present mood we can depend on them for good work?"

"Never saw them in better trim for a savage fight," I replied, "and if we have not too far to march, woe to the boys in blue with haversacks on when we strike them today."

General Foster had moved out from his bivouac at Bolan church on the morning of the 30th in serried columns, steadily and cautiously. A small body of our cavalry under Captain Peeples moved carefully at safe distance in his front and noted his action. When about a mile from his starting point the enemy entered and was passing through a large open space of land, formerly cultivated but abandoned and grown up in thick, luxuriant broom grass or straw.

Fought With Flames

The wind was setting toward the enemy and Captain Peeples hastily dismounted his men and started fire along the edge of this field of straw on our side. The wall of flame sweeping toward the enemy caused confusion in their ranks. There was no manner possible of adoption for fighting the flames. The only tactics to be pursued was to "about face and double quick."

This movement was hastily performed and the consequent delay gave us additional time for preparation for reception. Foster then began to clear his way with his artillery as he advanced. Our forces assembled, awaited his coming within range of our batteries at Honey Hill.

As we moved forward toward the field of action the guns boomed louder and louder. The effect was perceptible in the ranks of the 300 veterans; heads lifted higher, guns held more evenly, rifles drawn closer, step quicker and lighter, "keeping step," indicative of training experience, alertness, steadiness and readiness.

Just after passing the village of Grahamville we were met by a stout gentlemanly looking man with hair and beard snowy white. He was mounted on horseback and across his lap was a large, old double barreled shotgun. The old man reined out to one side, halted and fronted the troops and told in excited manner how he had been close in front of the infernal Yankees and how he had emptied both barrels of buckshot at them, etc.

The men began gently guying that old gentleman. One of them asked "Well, say, mister, did you kill'em all at one shot?" Another, "Well, mister, why the hell didn't you load up agin and kill the last d—d one of the whole bunch?" "Say, old pard, dismount, shoulder arms and fall in with us and we'll show you some fun."

Another, "What the hell did you fall back for? You ain't killed or wounded. Was you liked or just got skeered and run?"

The last I saw of the old gentleman he was replying angrily and gesticulating fiercely.

Hurry Call Sent

When within about a mile of the din of the fight, which was now fairly on, a mounted officer from the direction of the field approached us at full speed and urged that we make all possible haste to reach the front.

The order was given: "Right shoulder shift arms, double quick." We would "double quick," then rest in "quick," until we neared the works behind which our artillery was rapidly firing, when we were halted by General Smith and ordered to move nearer the works, halt and be ready to move at a moment's notice.

When we had taken our place as designated, I rode forward to the breastworks and saw the guns of our batteries being splendidly handled and doing very effective work in front.

Several cavalry companies dismounted were gallantly holding the line of entrenchments to the left of the main works on the road.

I noticed some infantry commands that did not impress me favorably. A few companies appeared well, but other companies composed of young boys and old men, the last call of available material, were not behaving admirably under fire, although behind the works.

After my general reconnaissance, rapidly made, and not without ducking my head a few times, I returned to my command. Colonel Edwards, commanding, asked me, "What of the forces in front? What is our fighting force? Is the enemy gaining any ground?"

I replied, "Our artillery is doing fine work. The dismounted cavalry seems anxious to fight and I believe will do, but about three-fourths of the infantry I have seen are 'milish,' and if the Yanks can ever once get under the muzzle of our field pieces and have any considerable force, these works are gone unless the cavalry force is sufficient to check them, and I think they are untrained troops. Some of the 'milish' are ready right now to break ranks and fall back. There is a creek or swamp 150 yards in front of the works' left and broadening and curving to the right on this side of this road which passes through the breastworks and the creek beyond, the entire force of the enemy is beyond this creek or swamp and in the swamp – there are pine woods beyond."

Doing Little Damage

"The enemy's fire is doing little damage as our batteries are sweeping the road in front and the enemy's fire, on either side of the road, over the tree tops is very slightly damaging. The road crossing the branch is filled with dead bodies of their negro troops, torn by our grape and cannister and shrapnel they have repeatedly charged, gallantly led by a white officer.

As the road crosses at the farther side of the branch of water, they come in sight only as they appear in the branch when they are swept by our guns and break and fall back. Our infantry in the trenches sweep with their fire the woods on both sides of the road. The officer commanding our artillery so informs me and says he is confident that he can keep the front swept clean."

The firing from the enemy's guns became more rapid and effective and I noticed a lull in the cheering of our troops. "By thunder," said Colonel Edwards, "I don't like that! I wonder when and where we go in."

Before I could reply our Major Cone, a gallant officer and fine tactician, who was present said; "Very soon and here on the right. If I mistake not we are halted here for that purpose. Smith is general enough to know that the enemy is not going to waste his force in continuing front attacks and not flank through this swamp. They are showing devilish poor tactics, if they have the force, in not enfilading our lines ere this."

He had scarcely finished the last sentence, when there came a rattling through the swamp to our right oblique in front a volley of what seemed a thousand rifles. The regiment was on foot in an instant and ready for action. It sounded like old times. Rattling volley after volley swept the space between the rifles and our works slightly enfilading our lines on the right. In a minute orders from General Smith came to "move forward, check the enemy's advance on the right and drive them from the woods." We moved rapidly forward, right of column in front, until we reached the bullet raked zone, when we rapidly changed front and into line by our old movement. "On right, by file into line," and once more the old Forty-seventh was under hot fire in battle line with faces to the foe. Only 300 rifles, but they had rung out on fields before and the men behind them had seen death and carnage in their front as well. Amidst the roar of guns on left and in front, the commands "Ready! Aim! Fire!" rang out along our line and from the muzzles of those guns that chimed in the roar and clash of battle at Chichamauga, Lookout Mountain, Missionary Ridge, Resaca, etc., rang out again and again the same death-dealing sound at Honey Hill.

Under Gallant Fire

For a time the battle, strenuous struggle for possession of the wooded field seemed doubtful of results. We were facing overwhelming numbers of splendid troops, New York and Ohio whites. For a time they yielded not one foot of ground and their hoarse "hurrahs" answered our "rebel yell." We were without support. Gun no. 1 of the Beaufort artillery "ceased firing" in order that my regiment might charge in front. The enemy's rifle fire was galling and destructive and I felt sure that if we had been in open ground we could not have survived.

Our colonel was too ill for active duty. Captain Dedge of Company F, one of the strongest companies of the Forty-seventh, was wounded and down. Captain Thompson, Company C, was disabled and out. Major Cone came running down right to left and meeting me informed me that the two companies on the right were without commanders and under very hot fire.

We started rapidly up to the right, shouting encouragement as we were close along the line. I was in advance of the major, and hearing a loud exclamation from him faced about quickly and saw him pale with his hand pressed against his side and reeling to fall. I caught him hastily and eased him down at the root of a large tree and left him there with a minie ball in his side, as I hurried on to the two companies without officers. When I reached them they were giving ground. Amidst the roar of guns and rattling, crashing volleys, the order "Fix bayonets!" Forward!" "Charge bayonets!" was given. Yells rang through the battle smoked wood, as the men sprang to charge. The first man to go down then and there fell close to my side. A fine young soldier, Collins of Company G. His gun fell from his hand as he sank on his knees to earth. Then he pitched forward on his face.

The troops in front gave ground but fought stubbornly and gallantly as we pressed them backward.

Battle Ends With Day

The while we were clearing the woods to the right, the war in front of our works, "trebly thundering, shook the gale." Charge after charge in quick succession was made and repulsed. The day was near its close. Before night our wood was cleared of every live soldier in blue. Twilight, the columns of the enemy, considerably reduced in number, were marching back to their barges at Boyd's Landing.

The field was ours, the victory won and our erstwhile proud and formidable foe was practicing the illustrious example of the "King of France with 40,000 men," who "marched up the hill and down again." So ended the battle of Honey Hill, S. C., and so were foiled the plans of Gen Foster, to break the C & S railroad in obedience to dictate of Gen Sherman. This cost my decimated old regiment, killed and wounded 27 men and three officers. Foster admitted to the loss of 1,000, killed and wounded.

Had not the flank movement of the enemy on the right been checked in 30 minutes time there would have been 1,000 men in the rear of our forces and the field would have been lost to us. When Gen Smith ordered the Forty-seventh on the right he said; "The enemy will never come through that wood and over that line."

Captain Courtenay, former mayor of Charleston, present said: "it is very evident that if that movement on the right by the Forty-seventh Georgia, had not been made the day would have been lost to us."

I wrote, "If the movement on our right had not been made in 20 minutes time the fate of Hal Stuart and his gunners at Honey Hill, would have been that of James Stuart and his Scottish knights, on Flodden Field."

Captain Stuart wrote; "I sanction every word of Adjutant Williams' declaration."

Elated By Yell

In the last conversation I ever had with my friend Colonel Colcock, just before his death, he said; "I did not know that your regiment had come up and been halted by Gen Smith, but realizing the trouble on our right and turning there to meet it, I saw your regiment taking position rapidly, but as if they were performing a maneuver on drill. I knew it was the Forty-seventh Georgia, a veteran command, and when I heard them fire and charge with a yell, I think I felt more elated than ever before in my life."

Sergt. John Richardson, of Georgetown, commanding a gun of the Beaufort artillery, wrote me; "I very well remember being ordered to cease firing to allow the Forty-seventh Georgia to charge through the swamp. Shortly after several of your wounded men were brought out at our gun. I personally assisted in taking one poor fellow to the rear, whose arm appeared to be shot off at the shoulder, and only hanging by a small piece of flesh."

General Foster had blundered. He was met and his forces, though greatly superior numerically, had been fairly whipped.

My regiment came out of the wood on the field near the road and laid down in line to rest, hungry and tired. No rations yet. We awaited orders in silence.

Ben S. Williams

The Charleston Sunday News and Courier, Charleston, South Carolina, September 5, 1897

RECORD OF THE 47TH GEORGIA REGIMENT

On May, 1863, Col G. W. M. Williams 47th Georgia Regiment reported at Jackson, Miss., through Major Gen John C. Breckinridge, to Gen Johnston, 800 rifles. A year's campaigning out West, and the brave Colonel and many of his men were resting under the shade of the trees "across the river." When in July, 1864, the 47th Georgia, detached from the main army and hurried from Atlanta to attack the enemy on Johns Island, we left our gallant dead strewn behind us along the banks of the Big Black River; on the red clay hillsides at Jackson; from the crest of Missionary Ridge; in wood and field at Chickamauga; at Resacca, Kennesaw, and along the flowery banks of the Oostanaula.

When we assaulted the enemy, Johns Island, July 9, 1864, (See "Defense of Charleston Harbor," by Major John Johnson, Page CLVI, Appendix.) we carried about 300 rifles. After, on James Island, we adopted a plan of recruiting, which proved a dismal failure, i e, so far as applies to my own regiment.

It was to put into our ranks Federal soldiers held in our prisons on their oaths to fight for the Confederacy. On 31st of October we received our contingent. I think 90 men was the number sent to the 47th Georgia to be distributed in the ranks of our ten companies. They were assigned to the companies respectively: they were drilled, armed and accoutred. Some of them were fine soldiers.

On November 1 the following unique order issued from regimental headquarters: "Headquarters, 47th Georgia Regiment, Secessionville, November 1, 1864. – Company commanders will forward at once to the headquarters complete lists of all "recruits" received in their companies on yesterday, October 31. This list will embrace name, former rank, age and place of nativity. By command of Col A. C. Edwards. Ben S. Williams, Adjutant."

The report sent in by company commanders was a mélange. Our "recruits" hailed from Londonderry to Limerick; Gramplan Hills to Gretna Green, and from Maine to Missouri.

One of our captains declared that his men "hailed from Dan to Bersheba," another impiously said his "hailed from hell to Boston."
These "recruits" soon tired of our service and began deserting, at first singly, then in squads. It was decided to send the whole remaining number back to prison. On hearing this some of the poor fellows begged piteously to be tried further. Our "galvanized yanks" were marched, under guard to the depot to be returned to Andersonville, only a short time before the

regiment was ordered to Honey Hill.

On the evening of the 29th of November we received orders to march, to depot to take the train on the Charleston and Savannah Railroad for Grahamville. It was after dark when we reached the railroad. While waiting for the train I was a little apart from the troops arranging some papers by the light of a spiral candle made of wax and tallow, with a cotton string wick, then very much in vogue.

A BRAVE GALVANIZED CONFEDERATE

I had just finished when, hearing myself addressed, I arose, and turning found myself face to face, just inside a narrow circle of light, with Private O'Brien, one of our "galvanized Yanks," a splendid specimen of the sons of the Emerald Isle.

He was standing erect and saluted like a regular. "How came you here, sir?" I said, in surprise. "Adjutant," said he, "for God's sake let me speak with you, and then help me." He had escaped after being turned over by our guard, had hidden and starved, determined – not knowing what else to do – to make his way back to the regiment and appeal for mercy; had neared our camp, had seen the men strike tents, followed and joined in the march in the darkness.

"Oh, Adjutant," he pleaded, get the colonel to take me back and try me, and if I am not as good a soldier as you've got in the regiment tie me and cast me back in the prison pen."

The train was coming; there was little time, I said; "O'Brien, fall in with the regiment and stick close. Mark me, you may be tested in battle before another day passes, perhaps before daylight. Act the man; be true to us and I will stand by you and do what I can for you. You will be watched; Prove false or show the slightest treachery, and you will be shot down like a dog."

"God bless you, Adjutant," a salute and he was gone in the darkness.

At Honey Hill the next day we were checking the enemy's flank movement on the right of Stuart's guns. Major Cone of the 47th, was shot down while ordering an advance of the right wing of the regiment. He fell by the writer's side. I quickly extended the order to advance.

As the men sprang forward I noticed for the first time in the fight, O'Brien, our Yank. With a whoop, very unlike our "rebel yell," he advanced, firing as he went. He was with us in our last charge at Bentonville, and no more gallant soldier fought under the starry folds of the flag of the 47th Georgia regiment.

A WORSE FOE THAN FEDERALS

That food was scarce "goes without saying." For weeks at

Secessionville my bill of fare was rice and sorghum syrup. The rice was fairly good; the sorghum was execrable. I detested it, and that cut me down to rice, rice, rice. Occasionally we would get a little beef, usually very poor.

Paragraph 1, of Special Order No 184 reads:

"Headquarters Department South Carolina and Florida, Charleston, S. C., July 21, 1864. – From and after this date the rations of corn to be issued to private and public animals is established at (8) eight pounds for each animal. By command of Major Gen S. Jones.

"P. C. Warwick, A. A. A. Gen."

This meant about four quarts for each animal every twenty-four hours. In consequence our horses were by no means in fine condition.

When ordered to Honey Hill we were out of rations; it was our ration day. We understood we were to receive rations at the depot. Later we were to proceed to Grahamville where rations would be awaiting us. Arriving at Grahamville in the early twilight of morning, November 30, we could hear nothing of rations. It was long after sunrise when we took up our line of march for Honey Hill. The troops were very hungry.

I had eaten my last "hard tack" on the train some time in the night. The regiment was in fine trim for a fight when they reached the enemy, for the men were "fighting mad."

Our engagement lasted throughout the remainder of the day. We went into bivouac on the left and rear of our line of works. We had not tasted food and the supply of water brought in our canteens was exhausted. A creek or branch of water ran along our front, but this was strewn with dead men, many of them, I learned, in the water. We were greatly fatigued, and the hungry, tired men were soon sleeping close their arms. The preparation for and the order of rest at regimental headquarters were the writer's blanket spread upon the earth, the writer, in boots and spurs and with saddle for pillow, stretched upon it; Col Edwards, commanding regiment, likewise clad and pillowed, close beside; his blanket covering both of us. Often did we thus rest, thankful for being on the sod instead of under it.

Col Edwards now sleeps where no bugle call or drum beat wakes him, in a narrower bed in the soil of his native State, under the shade of the trees, not far on the other side of the Savannah River.

When I awoke the stars were shining brightly overhead and a few faint streaks of gray were in the east. I felt weak and sick from hunger. My throat was parched and dry. I determined to have something to eat at all hazards. While clasping my belt, before rising, the Colonel started up, asking if we were to move. I said, "No Colonel, the day is breaking, and I must have something to eat and some water."

"I, too, am awfully hungry and thirsty, but how are we to get anything?"

I told him that I would go over and beyond the works, and try and find someone with rations who did not need them.

"Be very cautious, Adjutant," he advised, "we don't know how near the enemy's picket line may be."

Making my way in the misty twilight I was soon startled by the approach of a party of men in front, coming directly toward the works, and already much nearer to them than the enemy had been able to come the day before. The thought flashed across my mind that this was the advance guard of the enemy in a surprise attack, but they had now come sufficiently near for me to make that they were not marching in any order or formation, and I saw they were without arms – that is guns – their arms were full of haversacks, canteens, hats, overcoats, etc. Some of these men were strangers, others were men of my own command. I saw that the dead along the road were stripped of accoutrements, so turned from the road and entered the wood, obliquely, on the left.

I went but a short distance when I came to two dead Federals solders; the first, a private, who seemed to be lying just as he had fallen.

SOMEBODY'S DARLING

A few paces to the left of him, at the base of a pine tree, the other, a sergeant, by the three chevrons on the sleeve. He was rather under medium size, fair skin, blue eyes and light hair. He appeared as if quietly sleeping. His uniform was neat and new; his clean white haversack well filled, and his cloth-covered canteen filled with water to the chained cork stopper. I unbuckled the canteen strap and, pulling it gently from under him, drank; the draught as sweet to me as was ever dipped from crystal spring or quaffed from "old oaken bucket."

Then I cut the cloth strap of his haversack, and with these trophies started, when I saw a picture case lying near his side and close to his hand. I picked this up, and opening it, saw, on the one side in "ambrotype," a slender, dark-eyed woman, apparently about 30 years of age; on the other, two children; a boy about 8 or 9, a girl, 10 or 11. One glance at the faces of the fair boy and the dead soldier discovered father and son, and equally close was the resemblance between the dark-eyed mother and daughter. There was the story. The widowed waiting woman; the expectant orphaned little ones; the soldier husband and father cold in death – killed at Honey Hill. I took the picture with me, and it is before me now.

I hurried back to the lines. I had not been away longer than twenty minutes, but already the camp fires were kindling. The Colonel and I drank from the captured canteen, after which we ate the best breakfast we had seen in a long time.

"'Tis passing strange" that I have forgotten many matters of import relative to that day at Honey Hill, and yet I remember distinctly and can enumerate every article of food contained in that captured Yankee's haversack. So runneth the memory of man.

Rations came up, the men ate, "talked the battle over," and were "keen for orders" to attack the enemy again at Boyd's Landing.

Gen Foster had not yet given up the Charleston and Savannah Railroad. A few days later, December 8, I think, we were between the railroad and the enemy, driving him coastward, through a dense wood, near Tulifinny. This action was short but sharp; the enemy stubbornly fighting for every foot of ground.

Among the lost of my regiment in this hot skirmish fight was the intrepid soldier, Capt. P. C. Sheffield, commanding Company K. He was shot through the heart. Here, entrenched and reinforced, Col Edwards commanding brigade, we repulsed the enemy again.

GALLANTRY OF THE CITADEL CADETS

Participating in this engagement – our last on this line of road – was the splendid corps of Charleston Citadel Cadets. Had I not made this article already too lengthy, by far, I would tell of the splendid bearing of the cadets under fire. It became my duty to order them into action. Never did they cross their Citadel square on drill or dress parade with firmer tread or prouder bearing than when advancing on the enemy at Tulifinny.

Their youthful appearance and tidy uniforms attracted the notice of the regular troops, as did also their soldierly bearing.

An old 47th Georgia veteran, noting their advance said, "Them youngsters'll fight like hell." Another said of them, after the fight, "D___d if they didn't fight like Texicans."

Soon after Savannah was evacuated, our line on the Charleston and Savannah Railroad abandoned, and the collapsing Confederacy marked its western boundary in South Carolina, along the east bank of the Saltkehatchie River.

Here, at Rivers Bridge, under Major Gen McLaws, my regiment made its last fight in defence of this loved old State. The patriotic people of the community of Rivers Bridge have erected over our dead there a handsome monument. On Memorial Day of each year hundreds of all ages and conditions, assemble there and deck with flowers this soldier's tomb. Words fitting and appropriate are written in the marble. On one side of the draped and wreathed shaft we read:

Soldiers rest, thy warfare o'er
Sleep the sleep that knows no breaking,
Dream of battlefields no more,
Days of danger, nights of waking."
Brunson, September 2, 1897,   B. S. W.

The Battle of Honey Hill

Editor Hampton Guardian;

From time to time there have appeared in the columns of THE GUARDIAN interesting articles from the facile pen of Rev. W. H. Dowling reminiscent of that time that "tried men's souls in" a fiery furnace of blasting withering war; when the fair bosom of our sunny South was drenched and swept by a crimson tide that bore upon its swelling flood – out into the ocean of eternity – the flower of our chivalry and manhood. Oh, in how many homes, even yet, is felt an aching void. And as memory brings the light of those other days around these whose footsteps are brushing the evening dews on the banks of that River whose shore sands will soon be marked by their last footprints how dims the eye the starting tear as sighs on the aching heart, ever and ever. "Oh for one touch of a vanished hand for one sound of a voice forever stilled." Vanished illusion, dreary idea, baseless fabric of a shadowy human hope.

Our father's warriors are no more forever. Between them and us rolls, deep and dark the silent mystical River. We can but honor their dust and treasure fondly in memory their imperishable glory. While it is not meet or becoming that we, living, who fought with those who fell should chant praises, it is well that the literature of to-day embrace the events of the most important epoch of our country's pregnant annals and it is fair and fitting that the matchless deeds of the gallant men of the grandest army ever marshaled on earth should be treasured in heart and memory "like flowers kept fresh in water."

In coming years, when our flags are dust and our good swords rust on history's page and in the poets lay will be learned "The story of the glory of the men who wore the grey."

In the last issue of THE GUARDIAN I note this request "Capt. Ben S. Williams, Adjutant of the 47th Georgia Regiment, which Regiment turned the tide of victory is requested to give the readers of THE GUARDIAN a short sketch of the battle of Honey Hill as he saw it."

To comply with this request – which I do with pleasure – I must look back adown the vista of a third of a century.

When General Hood took command of the army of the West, after making his rash assault on Sherman in Atlanta, he turned westward into Tennessee, while Sherman started his march through Georgia. It was then that the remnant of the 47th Georgia Regiment was detached from Hood's army (thank God) and sent hastily to protect Charleston from a land attack by way of Johns and James Island.

The enemy repulsed we were soon ordered to Grahamville. We made the trip in freight cars at night on C & S R. R., arriving at Grahamville in the twilight of the morning of Nov. 30th, 1864. Thence we were ordered to Honey Hill on which point the Federals were moving in force in order to cut the C & S R. R. and "bottle up" Gen Hardee's force in Savannah for capture by Sherman. As we marched from Grahamville toward Honey Hill – several miles – we heard heavy firing in front and knew the attack was coming. I can see now those gallant fellows as they swung steadily along toward the crashing of cannon.

What reckoned they? Had they not marched toward the same sounds at Vicksburg. Had they not – 800 strong – cut to pieces Pugh's Brigade and seized their silken standard under the very mouths of Grant's guns, at Jackson. Had they not borne in triumph their rent and tattered flag on the blood drenched field of Chichamauga; and at Resacca and Atlanta. Crash on guns at Honey Hill; three hundred of the 800 are in battle array and woe to those who face them on the field.

We were met on the way by an officer of the staff of Gen. Gustavus W. Smith, to whom we had orders to report. We were informed that the Federals were attacking in overwhelming force, that the small force of South Carolina Cavalry of Col Colcock's Regiment, and our artillery supported by some raw troops of Georgia "Reserves," were gallantly defending our line and holding earthworks which extended across the public highway. "Right shoulder shift arms, double quick" rang down the line and the 47th moved at a run toward the flashing of the guns. We were halted by Gen Smith on the edge of the field until it should be seen where we were most needed. The fighting was fierce along our whole line. I rode forward, to reconnoitre, and saw Colcock's Cavalry, dismounted, and fighting gallantly in the trenches on the left, and the artillery supported by the "reserves," was firing rapidly. The battery pointed out to me as the Beaufort Artillery, Capt. Stuart, was doing magnificent work. I had never seen guns more effectively handled on any field of battle. In vain did the blue columns bravely assault in front. Their leading files would go down like grain before the mower's scythe. Their hoarse hurrahs were answered by ringing yells as our grape and canister ripped through their columns and tore to pieces their foremost ranks. I saw that our thin line was gallantly grappling with a force far superior in numbers. I knew the havoc in their advance columns would cause a change in their tactics and hastening to my own command I told them what I had learned and assured them that our time would come and very soon.

As the remainder of my narrative relates, unnecessarily, to the actions of my own command in the engagement, I beg leave to quote a few extracts from what others say.

In an article published in the *Charleston Sunday News* of Dec. 10th, 1899, one writer, Capt. Stuart, says "The Federal forces next attempted an advance and flank movement on the right. The enemy began to overlap and flank the Confederate right and the situation became extremely grave." Capt. Stuart says Col Colcock had just remarked to me, "unless the enemy can be driven back and our line reestablished we will soon be forced to retire and form another line, as our right is being flanked." Just then the 47th Georgia were reported and he immediately ordered them into the right saying, "They will save us."

Maj. John Jenkins says, "Gen Smith ordered the 47th Georgia

forward, at the critical moment, to save the Confederate right." Another writer, Capt. Colcock, says "Such was the important service of the gallant 47th Georgia, the writer has heard Col Colcock say that his feeling of relief was indescribable when he heard this veteran Regiment bravely driving back the foe."

When ordered to check the enemy's advance we double quicked into position and met a galling fire in the front and things soon became lively. The enemy bravely stood their ground until they delivered several volleys and stubbornly resisted until we forced them out of the woods, which they had taken in their flank movement, and drove them back on to their mail column which then began a retreat. The battle of Honey Hill was won. This cost the 47th twenty-two in killed and wounded. The major and one captain of the regiment were among the casualties. Night closed the scene and weary and sore we slept on the hard won field and awaited the dawning of the morning.

Ben S. Williams

The Sunday News and Courier, Charleston, South Carolina, November 23, 1913

A CONFEDERATE SOLDIER'S MEMOIRS

(By Captain Ben S. Williams, Brunson, S. C.)

An epoch in the war-swept period in our country's history of half a century ago is the 30th day of November 1864.

On that fateful day the remnant of the splendid Army of the West, whose serried lines I had seen swept on to victory over legions and phalanxed columns of the finest soldiers in the United States Army, won its last victory on ensanguined field.

It is the day of the battle of Franklin, Tenn. The commanding general, J. B. Hood, in his official report of his Tennessee campaign, says of the battle of Franklin, "Never did troops fight more gallantly and never did any army pay more dearly for victory won."

Among the thousands slain were many of the best generals and bravest men, leaving a crying void impossible to fill, and felt and realized keenly a few days after in the overwhelming, crushing defeat at Nashville.

"Lord, God of hosts, we can't forget."

On this same day, November 30, 1864, early in the morning the little army of 6,000 or 7,000 – "horses, foot and artillery which had landed the evening before on Carolina's coast, at Boyd's Landing, under Gen Foster's command, with intention to seize and "break the Charleston and Savannah Railroad near Pocotaligo, about the first of December," as Gen Sherman had directed, on leaving their bivouac at Bolans Church, three miles from their landing place, reckoned not, I presume, on doing as "the King of France, with forty thousand men, marched up the hill and – then marched down again."

Little reckoned they, I presume, that they would, with their – six thousand men, march about two miles farther to Honey Hill and then skedaddle back to Boyd's Landing again.

But that is what they did, exactly, and just a "wee amu'" particle of the Army of the West, hastily detached near Atlanta, and hurriedly sent to Charleston, and thence to Grahamville, embraced the opportunity and enjoyed the pleasure of aiding in the facilitation of the of the aforesaid skedaddle – my regiment, the 47th Georgia infantry.

I have often wondered why this engagement of considerable importance, and upon the result of which depended issue of much moment, is not recorded in the written history of our times.

About 1896-1897 there appeared in the *Charleston News and Courier* several articles relative to the Honey Hill engagement, and there arose from these, quite a controversy on points material and immaterial.

It was decided then by those interested to write a true, historic account of the affair.

Capt. Wm A Courtenay, who served in the army on our coast, afterward Mayor of Charleston, a gentleman of accomplishment, in finest form, of the task assigned and assayed, after months of time and labor, and money spent in procuring data, quit in disgust, because of apparent lack of appreciation and interest on the part of some who could and should have aided, and a flood-tide of ridiculous misrepresentation, absurd and false statements and contention by some who wanted to figure conspicuously in the picture. He appealed to me for aid in the way of data; I could aid him a little, as my command was at the time of the Honey Hill fight recently from the Western Army and knew but one officer – outside my own regiment – on the field; he was Gen Gustavus W. Smith. The other officers on the field, Col Colcock, Major Jenkins, Capt. Peoples, Raysor, etc., I had never before seen. Besides, I had but a glimpse of the field and forces before going into action.

I deem it now no breach of trust or confidence to say my friend, Capt. Courtenay, wrote me frequently during his work and enclosed me copy of information (?) received, with parenthetic comment of his own.

Gave Up in Disgust

In one letter before me now is – ("Ridiculous stuff,") in another, ("What a liar,") and in another ("Don't believe he was there at all; you and I know the fight lasted until dark.")

In his last letter to me, of date February 1899, he says:

"Dear Captain: Your favor of the 30th is with much thanks, my good friend. If I write a historic account of Honey Hill I will have to state facts * * * There are conditions in South Carolina – facts that are not generally known – and if I make them known I raise a row. Query: Why should I do this work? * * *

God Rest My Good Friend's Soul

A little later an interesting sketch was published by a brilliant young man, whose father, Col Colcock, was prominent in command of the troops at Honey Hill.

So far as it related to my command and our action I can vouch for its accuracy, and for fair reference to and correct quotation of myself I thank him. His work is fit for history.

From among many thistles he plucked some figs. From much chaff of falsehood he sifted grains of truth.

In his movement in accordance with careful programme Gen Foster blundered: had he moved rapidly forward on the evening of the 29th as soon as he landed; he would have had a mere "walk over" to the railroad and their object accomplished by morning perhaps, without loss of a dozen men.

He camped until morning. Ready there to meet him on his way were according to the best careful estimates, 246 cavalry, 415 men and 16 guns, artillery and 860 infantry.

The infantry consisted of detachments from the Georgia militia, Col Willis and Col Wilson, Major Cook and Major Jackson amounting to about 500 men; and the 47th regiment, Georgia infantry – regular army – about 300 men.

As we moved forward toward the field of action the guns boomed louder and louder. The effect was perceptible in the ranks of the 300 veterans; heads lifted higher, guns held more evenly, men closed closer, step quicker and "keeping step," indicative of training, experience, alertness, steadiness and readiness.

Just after passing the village of Grahamville we were met by a stout, old gentlemanly-looking man, with hair and beard snowy white.

He was mounted on horseback and across his lap was a large, old double-barrel shotgun.

The old man reined out to one side, halted and fronted the troops and told in excited manner how he, "had been close in front of the interval Yankees," and how "he had emptied both barrels of buckshot at them." Etc.

The men began gently guying the old gentleman. One of them asked, "Well, say mister, did you kill 'em all at one shot?" Another, "Well, mister, why the hell don't you load up again and kill the last d__d one of the whole bunch?" "Say, old pard, dismount, shoulder arms and fall in with us and we'll show you some fun."

Another, "What the hell did you fall back for? You ain't killed or wounded. Was you licked or just got skeered and run?"

The last I saw of the old gentleman he was replying angrily and jesticulating fiercely.

When within about a mile of the din of the fight, which was now fairly on, a mounted officer from the direction of the field approached us at full speed and urged that "we make" all possible haste to reach the front.

The order was given, "Right shoulder, shift arms, double quick." We would "double quick" then rest in "quick," until we neared the works behind our artillery was rapidly firing, when we were halted by Gen Smith and ordered to move nearer the works, halt, and be ready to move at a moment's notice.

When we had taken our place as designated I rode forward to the breast-works and saw the guns of our batteries being splendidly handled and doing very effective work in front.

Several cavalry companies dismounted, were gallantly holding the line of intrenchments to the left of the main works on the road.

I noticed some infantry commands that did not impress me favorably;

a few companies appeared well, but other companies, composed of young boys and old men, the last call of available material, were not behaving admirably under fire, although behind the works.

After my general reconnaissance – rapidly made – and not without ducking my head a few times – I returned to my command to find that Company H, Capt. Hazard, had been hastily detached and sent to the far right to support a gun of the Beaufort artillery, commanded by Lieut. Rhoads.

Col Edwards, commanding, asked me, "What of the force in front? What is our fighting force? Is the enemy gaining any ground?"

Infantry Mostly "Milish"

I replied, "Our artillery is doing fine work. The dismounted cavalry seem anxious to fight and I believe will do, but almost three-fourths of the infantry I've seen are 'milish,' and if the yanks can ever get under the muzzles of those field pieces and have any considerable force these works are gone unless the cavalry force is sufficient to check them, and I think they are untrained troops."

"Some of the 'milish' are ready right now to break ranks and fall back."

"There is a creek or swamp 150 yards in front of the works paralleling our earth-works to left and broadening and curving to right on this side of this road, which passes through the breastworks and the creek beyond, the entire force of the enemy is beyond the creek or swamp and in the swamp. There are pine woods beyond."

The firing from the enemy's guns became more rapid and effective and I noticed a lull in the cheering of our troops. "By thunder," said Col Edwards, "I don't like that. I wonder when and where we go in."

Before I could reply, Major Cone, present, said; "Very soon, and here on the right if I mistake not, we were halted here for that purpose and Smith is general enough to know that the enemy is not going to waste his force in a continuous front attack and not flank through the swamp. They are showing devilish poor tactics, if they have the force, in not enflading those works before this. They cannot, easily on the left, if the swamp parallels the works, but here on the right the swamp spreads almost up to the works. Devilish poor tactics in not flanking strong here."

He had scarcely finished the last sentence when there came rattling through the swamp to our right-oblique in front a volley of what seemed a thousand rifles.

The regiment was on foot in an instant and ready for action. It sounded like "old times."

Rattling volley after volley swept the space between the rifles and our works, slightly enflading our lines on the right. In a minute orders from Gen Smith came to "move forward, check the enemy's advance on the right and drive them from the woods."

We moved rapidly forward, right of column in front, until we reached the whistling bullet-raked zone, when we rapidly changed front and into line by our old movement, "On right, by file, into line," and once more the old 47th was under hot fire, in battle line with faces to the foe.

Amidst the roar of guns on left and in front, the commands "Ready, aim, fire," rang out along our line and from the muzzles of those guns that chimed in the roar and clash of the battle of Chickamauga, Lookout Mountain, Missionary Ridge, Resaca, etc., rang out again and again the death dealing sound at Honey Hill. Bayonets were on and as the order, "Forward, charge bayonets," sounded the first man to go down in our ranks fell at my feet – young Collins of Company G.

His gun fell from his hands as he sank on his knees to earth, then pitched forward on his face. Others went down, for we encountered a hot galling fire from the Ohio and New York regiments in there. They were unyielding, and we had to get right down to old-time hard fighting to dislodge them, and then they fought hard as they were being forced back.

For a time things looked doubtful. They were too many for us and we had no support.

Gun No 1, of the Beaufort artillery, worked by Sergt Richardson, had to be silenced for us to charge in front of it.

Capt. Dedge, of Company F, one of our best and strongest companies, was wounded and went down; Capt. Thompson, of Company C, hurt and out, and Major Cone came running down to left and meeting me informed me that the two companies on the right were without officers and under very hot fire.

We started rapidly up to right, shouting encouragement as we went close along the line. I was in advance of the major, and hearing a loud exclamation from him, faced about quickly and saw him pale with his hand pressed against his side and reeling to fall. I caught him hastily and eased him down at the root of a large tree and left him there with a mini ball in his side, as I hurried on to the two companies without officers.

We took the ground the major was anxious to retake and the advantage was ours there, which we pressed with rapid telling volleys and forward movements.

Before night we had whipped the last Yank out of the woods and by dark their columns were falling back toward Boyd's Landing.

This cost the depleted old 47th 27 men, killed and wounded.

While we were thus engaged the troops and guns in the works on our left were raking everything in their front with rapid and continuous fire, and the firing along the entire line "Trebly thundering shook the gale."

Had not the flank movement of the enemy on our left been checked, in 30 minutes' time there would have been 1,000 men in the rear of our forces and the field would have been lost to us.

When Gen Smith ordered the 47th in on the right, he said; "The enemy will never come through that wood and over that line."

Saved the Day

Capt. Courtenay said, "It seemed very evident that if the movement on the right by the 47th Georgia had not been made, the day would have been lost to us."

When I wrote; "If the movement on our right had not been made, in 20 minutes' time, the fate of Hal Stuart and his gunners at Honey Hill would have been that of James Stuart and his Scottish knights on Foldden Field." Capt. Stuart wrote; "I sanction every word of Adjt. Williams's declaration."

In the last conversation I ever had with my friend, Col Colcock, just before his death, he said; "I did not know that your regiment had come up and been halted by Gen Smith, but realizing the trouble on our right and turning there to meet it I saw your regiment taking position rapidly, but as if they were performing a manoeuvre on drill, and I knew it was the 47th Georgia's veteran command, and when I heard them fire and charge with a yell I think I felt more elated than ever before in my life."

Sergt John Richardson of Georgetown, commanding a gun of the Beaufort artillery, wrote me; "I very well remember being ordered to cease firing to allow the 47th Georgia to charge through the swamp. Shortly after, several of your wounded men were brought out at our gun. I personally assisted in taking one poor fellow to the rear, whose arm appeared to be shot off at the shoulder and only hanging by a small piece of flesh." etc.

More recently, a gentleman of Dillon, S. C., who was a gallant young trooper in the 3d South Carolina cavalry, written me apropos of the Honey Hill battle; "My company, K, was behind the works watching the fight in which the 16's and 60's were taking an active part. Hearing a yell down the road, we saw what we were told were the Georgia Veteran troops, and I will never forget the object lesson then learned as to recruits and veterans."

Gen Foster had blundered. He was met and his force, though greatly superior numerically, had been fairly whipped. He admitted a loss of 1,000 killed and wounded. At dark his whole force was in full retreat, back to the place of their landing.

Hungry and Tired

My regiment came out of the wood on to the hill near the road and laid down in line to rest, hungry and tired. No rations yet. We awaited orders in silence.

The colonel, Edwards, and I had for some time past been trying to freeze each other, and neither had just cause or offense or warrant for such conduct, but were each filled with a spirit of rivalry and – cussedness.

We had, habitually, around the camp fire, each eaten his own rations and slept on his own single blanket on opposite sides of the fire, with little to say to each other save that which related to our duties.

While resting and awaiting orders I was sitting on a log and several of the company commanders near.

Colonel Edwards came and sat close to me and said; "My God, suppose we had been forced back through that wood; we would all now be either dead or prisoners. Had our right continued to give way when Dedge and Thompson fell out we would have been gone."

"You know my condition. I am really too unwell for duty. Suppose you had not been present when Major Cone was wounded? I saw you recklessly risk your life to retake our ground on the right, and I knew it was to save the regiment and preserve our reputation, and I shall ever ascribe to you the credit."

"Let us now, forever, bury the hatchet. Here is my hand, and by heaven, I am from now your friend, and let us share benefit, hope, promotion and rank in future as we share danger."

I took his offered hand in all sincerity. Only for a very short time did we share either "hope or danger." Ere the hand I pressed was cold in death.

We were soon moved across the road and told to bivouac for the night. Fires were kindled, for the night was cool. We had nothing to eat and nothing to drink, for in the branch of water in front, above and below were many dead men, white and black. Our horses were brought up near the fire. Spreading one blanket on earth, using our saddles for pillows, we covered with the other blanket – the colonel and I – and for the first time rested side by side.

I had ceased to be hungry, but felt more of nausea and weakness. Our thirst was awful, for the throats were dried by the inhalation of powder smoke in the wood.

Edwards had fever and suffered greatly from thirst. We were directed to keep in readiness in our position near the works to resist attack, as the object and movement of the enemy were not known.

Merely unclasping our belts in front we were very soon wrapt in "nature's sweet restorer, balmy sleep."

The next thing I knew I was looking straight up and imagining the glimmering stars above were eyes of guardian angels. I knew it was near day – dawn, and clasping my belt easily, undertook to rise stealthily and not disturb my sleeping comrade, but my spur caught in the blanket and the colonel, clasping his belt hastily and rising to a half-sitting position, quickly inquired; "Is the enemy advancing?"

"No," I replied; "but I am going to advance on the enemy's position and get some water." "For God's sake, adjutant, be careful. You don't know where their pickets may lurk." I pushed him gently back onto his saddle-pillow, tucked the blanket close around his shoulders and said; "Rest."

When crossing over the works I noticed faint streaks of day in the east and moving cautiously, with pistol in hand, I made for the crossing of the creek by the road leading in front of our main earthworks.

I had not gone more than thirty or forty steps when I saw in the dim twilight a number of men approaching.

Instantly, I thought it was a surprise attack and my first impulse was to fire into them as rapidly as possible with my pistol and thus perchance check their assault and arouse our line. But I quickly noted no regularity of formation or movement, no dash, no hurry and no arms as they came closer, besides there was something familiar about the shapes and gait of the dimly-outlined forms.

Speaking to a group of ten or fifteen nearest to me I said; "Who comes there?" Quickly came the reply; "This is us, Adjutant, the 47th."

It was useless for me to ask what they were doing: I well knew and there was abundant evidence present in piles of overcoats, hats, shoes, haversacks, canteens, etc. in possession of "us" the 47th.

My whole regiment was in front of the works. "Boys, how long have you been out here?" I asked. "Off and on ever since about midnight," they said.

Just Wanted Rations

As soon as we rested awhile and found out there were no live Yanks around we hunted rations. Now we are fixing for winter. "Here's a brand new overcoat, adjutant, won't you accept it?" I thanked them, "No, I was just out after something to eat."

"Sorry we can't offer you anything in that line, Adjutant, but ate every d__d scrap we could find, but had a tolerable plenty."

"Very well," I said, "get back over the works, boys, and to your places, for day is breaking broadly."

Soon reaching the creek crossing I found the road strewn with dead men, and it was somewhat difficult to walk without stepping on them.

Many of them were lying in the shallow water in the road. They were white and black, and nearly every one stripped of baggage, clothing, shoes, haversacks and canteens.

Just beyond the crossing was an exploded ammunition chest and several dead horses and more dead men.

Leaving the road of the enemy's route I moved left oblique, into the pine woods, passing other stripped dead men. A little further on I came upon a young man with a good uniform on, dead close beside a small log, but he was without haversack or canteen. Ten paces beyond at the root of a large pine was a dead sergeant. His uniform was new and neat and his shoes had recently been polished. His haversack was white and clean and contained some food. His cloth-covered canteen was entirely filled with water. He was lying on his back, his cap had partly slipped off his head, his blue eyes were wide open, his right arm across his chest and left arm extended close to his side. He was rather under medium size, with light brown hair and mustache. He looked as if he had just lain down to rest and breathed out life peacefully there.

I unbuckled the narrow strap of his canteen and pulling it from beneath him, drank several swallows of water and recorked the canteen. Then with my knife I cut the cloth strip of his haversack and pulled it gently from around him without disturbing his pose. I threw it across my arm and started back, but turned to take a last look at the trim, dead soldier, who a few hours ago was my active, deadly foe.

I Saw "Ohio" on his cap and noticed on the ground, near his right hand across his breast, something I thought was a small book, but picking it up, I saw it was a daguerreotype case; thrusting this into the inner pocket of my coat I walked rapidly back to my command, as it was becoming broad daylight.

On arrival I relieved the thirst of my fevered comrade and we made quite a nice little breakfast off the contents of our captured spoils. (Surprising to me is the fact that I recall every article of food in that haversack and just how it was nicely wrapped and packed.)

Daylight had come, our reveille sounded, our shortened roll called; rations had come in and had been eaten, our arms cleaned, ammunition looked after, and the 47th was again ready for business, and as keen for a fight as I had ever seen them.

They were very anxious to get at the negro troops, in the open.

Gen Smith had returned to Savannah, Ga., and Col Colcock was in command.

After conference with Col Edwards, I approached Col Colcock and asked if attack on the enemy at Boyd's Landing was contemplated.

Col Colcock replied he thought not, that we had better rest on our laurels of yesterday.

Resting and waiting and thinking I remembered the dead sergeant and the thought of the "likeness case" in my pocket. Opening as a book there were likenesses in both inner sides under glass. On the one side was a slender, dark-eyed woman of about 30 years of age, on the other side, a girl and boy; the girl about 10 years, the image of the woman, the boy, about 8 years, the very image of the fair-haired, blue-eyed, dead sergeant, whose blood had stained our soil; whose life had gone out probably while he had been looking for the last time and thinking of his wife and children, widowed and orphaned in his wrecked home in distant Ohio. One minor result of the battle of Honey Hill.

But Foster was not yet done trying to "break the Charleston and Savannah Railroad."

(As I write, said picture is within my reach, and until my home and some of its furniture burned some years ago, the aforesaid canteen, packed away with other war paraphernalia, was fit for service in another war.)

The News and Courier, Monday Morning, July 26, 1897 Charleston, South Carolina

Georgia Troops at Honey Hill

Adjt. Ben S. Williams, of the Forty-seventh Georgia Infantry, Controverts Mr. Wm. C. Davis' Story, which has Occasioned so Much Comment – Adjt. Williams Shows that he Speaks Whereof he Knows

To the editor of the News and Courier. I have read with interest, the article appearing recently in print, descriptive in purport, of the battle of Honey Hill, November 30, 1864. The purpose of these, as I understand, is to furnish and elicit data for a history of that fight now in course of preparation by a gentleman whose object should be, and doubtless is, to sift facts from fiction, separate truth from braggadocio and record the actual events of that engagement fairly and impartially, without bias, warp or prejudice, "favor or affection."

In The News and Courier of the 10th inst there appeared, under the "Battle of Honey Hill," "a report from the adjutant of the 47th Georgia," copied from the Savannah Morning News. The Savannah Morning News says: "Some years ago Adjutant Williams wrote this graphic account of the gallant and effective conduct of the 47th, not 17th, Georgia regiment in the action at Honey Hill, and enclosed it to a soldier friend in South Carolina. From this source the Morning News has received it for publication." The following is the report:

"On the 26th of November 1864, the 47th regiment, Georgia Volunteers, Col G. W M Williams, stationed on James Island at Secessionville, received orders to march to the Charleston and Savannah Railroad depot, where transportation would be furnished to Grahamville on said road. Lieut. Col A. C. Edwards, commanding the regiment, was ordered to report to Gen Gustavus W. Smith at the point designated. A rapid march across the island to the point of embarkation was begun late in the afternoon, and Grahamville was reached on the morning of the 30th.

"A courier met us, with orders to march at once to join forces at Honey Hill, three miles below depot. The troops were hungry and much fatigued, having left James Island without rations, performing a long march to the railroad depot, and had passed the entire night in the cars on the road.

"The march to Honey Hill was made with all possible rapidity. Artillery firing was first heard in our front. A staff officer from Gen Smith joined our command on the road, with instructions to hasten the march. Firing was soon distinctly heard and we knew that the engagement was warm. When within a mile of the field, another staff officer met our command with orders to move with all possible haste, as our troops were being hotly pressed at all points. The fire of artillery and small arms was very rapid. Our instructions were to move in support of the field artillery at the head of the public road. The 47th proceeded now at double quick. Guns had been loaded at Grahamville. We were now almost up, and could see some confusion on the right of our line, as the enemy were about to flank it, and had begun hot enflading fire down our lines. Being ordered to check this flank movement, and dislodge the enemy on our right, the writer (adjutant) galloped forward rapidly, ascertained where right of the line rested, and when our column reached the point indicated the regiment were gallantly in position, with rapid movement on "right by files into line," as soon as fronted: charged the enemy, driving him back, after a stubborn resistance, and forced him through the woods some distance and occupied the ground taken, and they were soon in full retreat.

"Memo – Lieut. Col A. C. Edwards, Commander:
(Col Williams, deceased :) Major J. S. Cone, acting lieutenant colonel; Capt. J. C. Thompson; acting major; Adjt. Ben S. Williams. Major J. C. Cone and Capt. Dedge, Company F, were seriously wounded, I cannot recall other casualties."

In the News and Courier of the 13th inst there appears a communication flatly contradicting the statement contained in the above report.

This demands of me notice and compels reply, which, but for circumstances beyond my control, would have been made earlier.

I was at the time of the battle of Honey Hill "Adjutant" Williams, of the 47th Regiment of Georgia Infantry.

The above report is a brief and true account of the part taken by the 47th Georgia regiment in the action at Honey Hill; and is accurate in every essential particular.

I challenge any intelligent, honorable gentleman who was or was not "an active participant in the battle" to point out a single statement in said "report" which he deems erroneous, and I will furnish indisputable evidence of its absolute authenticity.

Mr. Davis says, "Adjutant Williams may have been referring to the battle of Pocotaligo." "My foot is on my native health." I know Pocotaligo from Honey Hill. Mr. Davis says, "No such charge as he (Adjutant Williams) describes took place at Honey Hill." The movement of my regiment in taking position and attacking is as exactly described as I know how, as an officer in the infantry line of service. Perhaps Mr. Davis, of the Beaufort Artillery, may differently designate such movement.

It certainly took charging, yelling and good shooting to dislodge and drive the enemy back through the swampy wood, which they had penetrated. Beaten in front their flank movement was their dernier resort; to foil this cost my regiment twenty-two officers and men killed and wounded. (Reference to data in my possession.)

As to Mr. Davis assertion, "Nor were the troops on the field ever in danger of being driven back." That is a matter of opinion, and in this I fully agree with Mr. Davis. I do not believe the troops on that field could have been driven back one inch. But my judgment then was, and I believe now, is that had the double-quick movement of troops to the right to check the flanking column had been delayed thirty minutes there would have been a thousand rifles in rear of our batteries and the slender lines supporting them and Honey Hill would have been to Hal Stuart and his splendid gunners what Flodden Field was to James Stuart.

Mr. Davis says "the 11th regiment, Beaufort Artillery, and another artillery company, were in front, and most undoubtedly deserve the credit of this success.

This statement "is so at variance with the facts in the case that it would be a gross injustice to" (some of) "the South Carolina troops, who bore" (some of) "the burden of this battle" (to say nothing of other troops) "to allow such a statement to pass unnoticed."

In justice to the gallant Ransor?? and his company, to Howard and his men, to Capt. Peebles and command – all cavalry.

According to Mr. Davis, of the Beaufort Artillery, the 11th Regiment, the Beaufort Artillery and another artillery company brushed out in less than an hour's time the whole Federal force, estimated at 8,000, at Honey Hill. Pretty good. Beside I protest against the transfer, by Mr. Davis, of the 11th regiment from Virginia to Honey Hill in 1864.

Major Gooding, of the 11th regiment, says in a letter to me under the date of 21st inst: "The 11th Regiment was not in the Honey Hill fight. It was in Virginia in November, 1864. "The 11th Regiment was at Petersburg on the 24th of June, 1864, and remained in Virginia. It was not at Honey Hill. "Very probably there is some confusion" (in the mind of Mr. Davis) between the numbers 11 and 47. Mr. Davis "may have been referring" to the 47th Georgia.

Certainly Mr. Davis "tells of a regiment which no survivor of Honey Hill saw" on that day. "Any active participant in the battle is aware of "this simple fact."

In the most kindly spirit I must protest against the, perhaps, well meant criticism of Mr. Davis. His version of the fight at Honey Hill is inaccurate, because, may be, his memory fails. His statements are "certainly at variance with the facts in the case." His criticism of my report is as unkind and unjust as it is unfounded.

In my published report I fail to discover anything which does injustice to anyone. I emphatically deny any such intention. My report, written years ago, was descriptive only of the part taken by my own command and on our end of the line, with out comment or reference to other troops or parts of the field.

Though an active participant in the battle I have written nothing for publication or for history.

I have little desire for controversy, and less ambition to pose as the "I who killed Cock Robin" at Honey Hill. I am proud of the part acted there by the gallant command to which I had the honor to belong, but the record of that veteran regiment was wrought on broader fields before and after Honey Hill. Our Flag furled forever in the writer's keeping, shows rent and tear and tatter by shot and shell on Chickamauga's hard won field; from Secessionville to where the last shouts of victory rang and where for the last time the Southern Cross, proud and defiant, waved under the pines at Bentonville.

But I felt no more proud of my command at Honey Hill than I did of the other troops, "where all were brave" and fought desperately and gallantly.

Especially did I feel an elation of pride when, rapidly taking position on the right, I was told that the battery doing such splendid work near in front – that which I had never seen better in an experience of more than two years in the field – was the Beaufort Artillery; my brother Carolinians, on the soil of our mother State.

I pointed them to my Georgia comrades, and, "with a heart swelling with pride, said "That is the way South Carolinians fight."

All honor to the gallant men who fought at Honey Hill, of every command, horse, foot and artillery, and damned be he who would pluck a single bud from the laurel wreath of their fame, which is their proud and imperishable heritage.

Ben S. Williams

                         Brunson, Hampton County.

The Sunday News, Charleston, South Carolina – January 25, 1914

Citadel Cadets at Tulifinney

How They Received Their "First Baptism of Fire" in the War of the '60s as Told by One of Them.

The letter printed below, written by Col John C. Sellers, of Sellers S. C. and addressed to Capt. Ben S. Williams, whose "Confederate Soldiers Memoirs" have been appearing in the Sunday News, contains much interest regarding the services rendered the Confederacy by the Citadel cadets. Col Sellers letter follows:

Capt. Ben S. Williams, Brunson, S. C. – My Dear Sir: I have greatly enjoyed reading your memoirs as published in the Sunday News, and especially have I enjoyed the one in the issue of January 11, in which you relate your impressions of the Citadel cadets as they received their first baptism of fire at Tulifinny, as I happen to be one of the "dandy-fine" boys who did "stand square to the rack" when we struck "the Yanks." In the main your account of the fight at Tulifinny is correct, and it is quite complimentary of the two companies which composed the cadet battalion, under the command of Major J. B. White, but in a few instances you are in error, which is not surprising, as it has been forty-nine years since those fights, and human memory is a most treacherous thing.

Aided by a pretty tenacious memory and a rereading of Major White's report, as found in Thomas's "History of the South Carolina Military Academy," on pages 205-6-7-8, I find that Capt. (afterwards Governor) Hugh S Thompson commanded Company A, and Capt. J. P. Thomas, with Lieuts. A. J. Norris and R. O. Sams, commanded Company B, and not "Lieut. Huger," as you suppose; in fact, there was no Lieut. Huger in either company, but a C. huger was a private in Company B. December 6 the train carrying the hospital battalion was stopped just beyond Tulifinny, and against the fighting about three miles off, in the direction of Gregory's Point the noise of the rifle firing could be plainly heard, and we were marched at a double-quick in the direction of the battle, and soon the whistle of the minie balls could be heard, but none of us were hit, and when we arrived at the scene of the fight the Yankees had retired. We then fell back to Tulifinny trestle and slept on our arms at the trestle that night.

I well recollect an incident of that night that furnished considerable amusement to all the cadets, except one. Just before day a train came thundering over trestle and Cadet D. A. Miller, of Company B, waking up suddenly and not knowing what was the matter, plunged into Tulifinny Creek and got thoroughly soaked. It was a very cold night and there was a heavy frost on the ground next morning. The next day, which was December 7, we ere, with the 47th Georgia, marched in the direction of the enemy in order to ascertain his exact position and determine the propriety of attacking him in his intrenched position, about three miles east of the railroad towards the coast. The entire line of skirmishers soon became engaged with those of the enemy, and steadily drove them back on their intrenchments. This skirmish lasted about three hours, Company B relieving Company A (its ammunition having been exhausted and the entire battalion was thus engaged in the skirmish. When the ammunition of Company A became exhausted they retired in good order, and Company B was rushed in to take their places during a brisk fire from the enemy. When the order came for Company B to fall back, having driven in the skirmish line to the intrenchments of the enemy, we had to go through a dense swamp and woods under a heavy fire from the batteries of the enemy, and many of us had forgotten whether we were No 1 or No 2, and there was considerable confusion along the line.

Capt. Thomas, with his sword drawn, rushed in front of us and gave the command, "Halt!" "Fall in," according to height, just as on the parade ground at the Citadel; when in line the command was given, "Front!" "Dress to the right;" "Count off from the right," and then every one double-quicked to his position on the skirmish line and leisurely retired. While all this was going on the bullets, grape and canister were whistling all around us, and it has always been a wonder to me that we were not all killed.

We then fell back to the railroad and slept that night under our arms in an old broom sedge field by the side of the railroad. I remember I slept very soundly that night in that grass, with my gun by my side, and no covering except "the clouded canopy of the heavens," and next morning there was a heavy white frost all over that old field. The next day, which was the 8th, we were engaged in throwing up temporary breastworks on the east side and parallel with the railroad.

The casualties in the skirmish were as follows: Lieut. Amory Coffin, severely wounded in the head; Cadet J. B. Patterson, mortally wounded, afterward died; Cadets Joseph W. Barnwell and E. C. McCarty, severely wounded; Cadets B. F. Hollingsworth, A. J. Green, A. R. Heyward and W. A. Pringle, slightly wounded.

The next morning, which was December 9, the enemy advanced in full force against our position on the railroad. Our position was on the left next to the 47th Georgia, on our right. Major White acted with great coolness and daring that day. He cantered his horse up and down our line admonishing us to remain concealed behind the breastworks and hold our fire until the command to fire was given. As soon as the enemy got through the swamp in our front and emerged into the old field, where they could be seen, Major White, at the head of the battalion, rose in his stirrups and gave the command, just as on the parade ground, "Attention battalion. Ready, aim, fire." At the command "attention battalion," each cadet sprang to his feet and when the command "fire" was given our three hundred rifles belched forth as one gun. The effect was instantaneous. They fell back in great confusion. Leaving their dead and wounded on the field. We continued firing for awhile and when the command, "Cease firing," was given and the smoke lifted, the enemy was nowhere to be seen.

I remember one poor fellow, an officer, was brought out on a litter through our lines, and appeared to be desperately wounded, and I think soon died. It was after this affair at the railroad that the Yankees planted a battery across the swamp in an old field and commenced shelling the passing trains. We were moved into the woods on the west side of the railroad. When not on picket duty, we kept ourselves comfortable by building huge fires, where we cooked our scanty rations. It was while in these woods that W. D. Palmer was struck by a solid shell in the left hand, tearing his hand into shreds. His hand was amputated just above the wrist, but he never left us but stayed with the command till we were disbanded at Greenville. After the war he settled near St. Stephens and successfully engaged in farming. He never married and died last year. He was as gallant a soldier as ever shouldered a gun.

I have no recollection of the North Carolina "reserves" you mention, and am pretty sure the reference is to a militia company from Marion County (then district) commanded by Capt. W. J. Davis. This company was composed of "elderly men" and 16 year old boys and mustered in rank and file about 154 men. They arrived after the fights at Tulifinny and camped in the old field on the right of the railroad, just beyond Tulifinny Creek, and near to the woods, where the cadet battalion was bivouacked. They arrived soon after the Federal battery began shelling the passing trains and knew very little about military tactics and were encumbered with a lot of "pots, ovens, frying pans, bedding, etc.," as you describe. The cadets were detailed every day to drill this disorganized mass of old men and boys, who had not even learned to change step, and when a shell from the Yankee battery would come streaming over the old field it was with difficulty that discipline could be maintained.

With a number of the 16-year-old boys I had gone to school in the old Marion District, and to some of them I was closely related, and I had known a number of the elderly men from my earliest recollection, and they were our most solid and respectable citizens. Five years after, I married the daughter of the fourth sergeant of this company, the late John Mace; and two uncles of my wife, the late Gewood and Elihu Berry, were privates in this same company. In looking over the roll of this militia company from Marion I find –that all the elderly men are long since dead and a majority of the 16-year-old boys have already "crossed over the river." A few, now prominent citizens of Marion, Dillon, and Florence counties, still survive, among them the Hon Jas D. Montgomery, for years county treasurer of Marion County and member of the Constitutional Convention of 1895, and Ex-Sheriff Wm. A. Wall, of Marion; Wm. B. Allen, Neal McInnis and T. C.

Sherwood, of Dillon County; R. J. Rogers, Mullins, and Isham E. Watson, of Florence County.

The Citadel cadets left Tulifinny on Christmas Day, 1864, and went direct to James Island, where they did picket duty twenty-four hours on and twenty-four hours off, till the evacuation of Charleston, February 17, 1865. For a part of the time we were on James Island we had tents, and though the duty was hard and exacting, we greatly enjoyed life, living as we did in open and drinking in the salt water breezes. My messmates on the Island were John C. Tiedeman, an Ex-Alderman of the city, and now a prominent wholesale grocer of Charleston; Lewis Meng, of Union, and J. P. Allen, now holding a Government position in the Custom House at Charleston. Meng's father sent him down a negro man, who was a fine cook. Tiedeman's father, the venerable Otto Tiedeman, kept us supplied with groceries of all kinds, while Allen's father, who was a truck framer near the city, furnished us with vegetables fresh from the fields, and these, with the rations we drew, gave us "plenty and variety." My physical condition soon became such that I was only able to button the top button of my cadet uniform.

On the night of the evacuation I was on picket in the lower part of the island, in the direction of Stono River. That afternoon while on vidette duty I could plainly see the men on the picket line of the enemy and could see transports and gunboats moving around. The Yankees evidently believed that the island was being evacuated, as Sherman was then in our rear at Columbia. About 9 o'clock we were quietly taken off the picket line and marched to the long bridge over the Ashley in pursuit of the main body of the battalion, which had crossed the bridge much earlier. I am pretty sure our pickets were the last to leave the island by way of the long bridge. We caught up with our command early next morning. Marching on to St. Stephens after a few days' delay, we secured transportation to Cheraw, where we got in front of Sherman. At Cheraw our battalion acted as the rear guard of the army and crossed the bridge over the Pee-Dee into Marlboro County in rear of the cavalry. The bridge was fired before the Yankees could cross, but they ran up a battery on the hill near St David's Church and fired at us as long as we were within range. At the crossroads, about one and one-half miles from Cheraw, we were allowed to take the first rest we had had in hours. In a few moments, though bombshells were occasionally bursting around us, I was sound asleep. We were right at a road I had often traveled in my boyhood days, and when the bugle sounded "fall in," I looked longingly down the road towards my home, thirty miles away, and took up the weary tramp, tramp, tramp, to Fayetteville, N.C.

This was the beginning of the great March rain of 1865, known in all this section as the "great Sherman freshets." The rains were incessant, streams greatly swollen and the roads in a terrible condition. Arriving at Fayetteville we crossed the Cape Fear River and proceeded to Raleigh by way of Smithfield. Before reaching Raleigh the battalion was at the request of Governor Magrath, ordered back to South Carolina. At Raleigh we got railroad transportation to Chester, S.C., by way of Greensboro and Charlotte, N.C. From Chester we marched across the country to Shelton, on Broad River, and then by rail to Spartanburg, where we took up quarters in Wofford College. It was while we were in Spartanburg that we first heard, as a rumor, that Lee had surrendered. Late in April we marched to Greenville, S. C., where, on April 29, we were given a twenty days' furlough, and we all got home as best we could.

Besides those wounded at Tulifinny the following cadets died from disease: R. R. Nichols, John Culbreath, G.O. Buck, T. A. Johnson and R. Noble. T. A. Johnson died in the Wofford College building while we were camped there. From the first we received nothing for our services, either from the State or the Confederacy, except the rations we consumed.

After the war Major White removed to Marion, where he lived till his death a few years ago, full of years and honors. For many years he taught the Marion High School, and for several terms was county school superintendent. He also worked as a civil engineer, and was a most painstaking and accurate land surveyor. He owned a small farm near the town and was the pioneer of this section of the great strawberry business. It was at Marion that his first wife died, childless. He afterwards married the daughter of the Rev Hugh A. C. Walker, late of the South Carolina Conference, and reared and educated four noble sons, now first class men. Some of his boys graduated at the Citadel. There never was a nobler man than Major White. Modest as a maiden, he was courageous as a lion; kind and gentle, yet he was a rigid disciplinarian; with a fine sense of humor, he was pure and chaste of speech. It was a delight to visit his home, for he was given to hospitality, and as a guest he was pleasant and entertaining. On the long march through slush and mud from Cheraw to Raleigh I have often seen him with as many guns of the boys as he could hold on the withers of his horse, and often he would dismount and walk for miles in the mud, while two, and sometimes three, worn-out boys were astride the old bay horse. Peace to his ashes! One of the "Dandy-Jim boys" of 1864.

John C. Sellers, Sellers, S. C.

The Sunday News, Charleston, South Carolina – February 1, 1914

PLEASED AT PRAISE OF HIS WARTIME COMRADE

Capt. Williams Glad His "Memoirs" Are Enjoyed by Survivors of the War Between the States, But Differs With Col Sellers Regarding the North Carolina "Reserves" at the Tulifinny Fight.

The following letter from Capt. Ben S. Williams is in reply to the communication of Col John C. Sellers, printed in The Sunday News last Sunday, and addressed to Capt. Williams:

Col John C. Sellers, Sellers, S. C – My Dear Sir: Your letter addressed to me through the columns of the Sunday News of the 25th inst was welcome, and the assurance therein contained that my written "memoirs" were enjoyed by a comrade in arms of the days of long ago afforded me sincere gratification. I am confident that many enjoyed, as I did, the recital in your communication of interesting events which are nebulae of the most direful epoch of the country's unwritten history.

Your data is given with remarkable accuracy as to date and eventuality. The narration of your armed comrade's somnambulistic plunge into the cold waters of the dark Tulifinny, your frosted couch in the broom-grass field, the huge glowing campfires at night, etc, brings back to my memory many scenes and incidents of that bivouac life for weeks on the war storm-swept coast of our State.

In your after statement of occurrences in our march from Cheraw, at which point the cadets again joined us, toward Raleigh, via Smithfield, is data interesting, and to me valuable, as refreshing to my memory; for same I thank you.

I thank you for the correction and information also as to the name of the Captain – Thomas – commanding one of the companies of the battalion of cadets. I must, however, most respectfully resent your suggestion as to the possibility of my mistaking "a militia company from Marion, County (then district) commanded by Capt. W. J. Davis," for the body of North Carolina "reserves" which I so well remember and tried aptly to represent.

Had you merely affirmed your belief that I was mistaken, without further comment and explanation, I might, in view of the fact that "it has been forty-nine years since these fights, and human memory is a most treacherous thing," have yielded to your opinion and acceded correctness to your "tenacious memory." Had you stopped after mentioning that half a dozen of those "old vets" are still living in your section – one of whom is an ex-sheriff – I would have been in considerable doubt as to the advisability of acknowledging that my depicture of the unique command was one of the "militia companies from Marion County' in view of the fact that I may at some time "happen along" up there; but when you state that Mrs. Sellers is the daughter of the 4th sergeant of said "company from Marion County" and that two uncles of the good madame were in that command, I "take my stand at Armageddon" and affirm most positively and reiterate most emphatically that I referred especially and only to a battalion, or company, of North Carolina "reserves" and urgently request that you, in my behalf, refer to Johnson's "Defence of Charleston Harbor," page 239, where you will find the following relative to the fights at Tulifinny occurring "forty-nine years ago;****"The chief engagements being December 7 and 9."****"The Southern troops engaged were from the 5th, the 32d and the 47th Georgia regiments, the 7th North Carolina battalion, the 3d South Carolina cavalry, the battalion of cadets from the South Carolina Military Academy, under Major J. B. White, together with some militia and reserves and a battery of light artillery under Capt. W. R. Bachman." So I stick to the reserves, and thank God for the privilege of this interchange of views – "forty-nine years after the fights" – with one of those "Dandy Jim boys who stood square up to the rack" when they "met the Yanks" and fought like "Hood's Texicans." Ben S. Williams, Brunson, S. C.

P. S. – Let's go to the grand Reunion in Jacksonville, April 29-30.

B. S. W.

The Sunday News, Charleston, South Carolina – December 21, 1913

A Confederate Soldier's Memoirs

(By Captain B. S. Williams, Brunson, S. C.)

On the early morning of the first day of the last month of the year 1864 gloomy was the apparent status of our perishing "Cause" and various were the scenes in our waning collapsing Southern Confederacy.

As the sun, rising on that morning, lit up the scene on the battlefield of Franklin, Tenn., oh, what scenes of woe were uncovered by the lifting of the settled, enshrouding smoke cloud of battle of the day and night before.

It was as if "The angel of death had spread his wings on the blast, and breathed in the face of friend and foe as he passed."

Among the thousands of slain upon the field, distorted and pale, with the icy chill of death and the cold dew of heaven on their pallid faces, were our Gens Cleburne, Gist, Adams, Strahl and Grandbury dead; Brown, Carter, Manigualt, Quarles, Cockrel and Scott wounded.

We were victorious on that glory field, but for the glory of victory the god of battles had imposed an awful toll.

And yet, piercing the powder-smoked air of that early December morning, rang out from fife and bugle, shrilly, our reveille, and with clashing cymbals and rolling drums sounded clearly and defiantly the inspiring soul-stirring strains of "Dixie" – "In Dixie land we have taken our stand, We'll fight to the death in Dixie, away, away, in our loved Southland, our Dixie."

There were no responsive heart-thrills, no thrilling nerves in strengthened arms, no kindling inspirations in sentimental souls, no flashing eyes and answering calls from the pale, still warriors on the field who had advanced so gallantly so recently – "No sound could awake them to glory again" – but those whose ears caught the stirring strains and whose eyes beheld again the waving, Starry Southern Cross responded, "In our own loved land, our Dixie,"

Closed their ranks, grasped more firmly their arms and were ready again.

Hood's order, "On to Nashville!" rang out and the shorn and depleted Army of the West was on the aggressive.

Great "God of Hosts," could such faith and valor count for naught and avail not? Yea, verily, verily. Sixteen days later the spared, gallant few of those lines of grey – in which I had so often stood, which I had so often seen sweep on to victory over valiant foemen, were overwhelmed, crushed and defeated at Nashville.

In Virginia our cause was shrouded in gloom. Our Confederacy was cut to pieces, our railroads destroyed, our resources almost exhausted. A large majority of the chivalric volunteer soldiers of the South were dead. Our soldiers in the field were half starved and half naked, and thousands were languishing and dying in Northern prisons.

The once mighty but now effete, wornout army of Virginia was merely on the defensive in narrow territory, with exhausted resources, facing greatly superior numbers. Sherman's army was marching down through Georgia toward the sea, leaving ruin and desolation in its blood-scathed track, making war "hell."

On the coast of South Carolina the Federal guns were bombarding and battering Fort Sumter, while small mongrel armies were landing at different points. In order to reach and "break the Charleston and Savannah Railroad near Pocotaligo, about December 1," as Gen Sherman had directed, his motive for same being very obvious, his tactics were excellent.

That December morning saw the little army of Gen Foster's 6,000-7,000, infantry, cavalry and artillery, white and negro troops, back at their landing place, Boyd's Landing, re-embarking aboard their boats and barges, whipped back from Honey Hill, a few miles away, the day before by a comparatively very small force of infantry, cavalry and artillery.

On the morning of December 1 my regiment could muster not more than 250 men. These were ready and anxious to fight again and I presumed to suggest to Col Colcock, then in command of forces, that we pursue the enemy and attack them while they were embarking. I suggested also that my regiment would appreciate the privilege of being allowed to lead the attack. I urged that the enemy had been badly whipped and were routed and fleeing; that we had received reinforcements and our troops were flushed with victory.

After a short conference with several officers the commanding officer replied to me that it was "quite possible that the enemy, anticipating attack, have prepared for it and are ready to receive us as we did them yesterday." I then suggested – most respectfully – to be allowed to detach one company of my regiment, advance, deploy and engage them, note developments and act accordingly. The commander replied "That would surely bring on a general engagement. We can afford to rest on our laurels won yesterday."

Perhaps his decision was wise, perhaps his course was best; but, oh, how did this spirit, this disposition and inertia, impede progress, hinder advancement and often arrest success in our mighty struggle for what we deemed the right and for the salvation of our cause.

In the reflection of past events in time's true mirror I sometimes imagine that I can see in the course of conduct of one of our most illustrious leaders, Gen Robert E. Lee, revelation of this disposition of chivalrously rest on laurels in battle won rather than press on, overtake and destroy.

Lee did not, as Thomas, of Virginia, and Farragut, of Tennessee, remain in the United States army, but took his stand gallantly on the soil of his native State in her defence against invasion, ravage and coercion, but I always believed that deep down in his great, tender, sentimental heart Gen Lee loved the old flag of the Stars and Stripes and the blue uniform of his old command.

Lee fought gloriously and with chivalric gallantry in Virginia and in Pennsylvania he made warfare knightly and honorable. HE LOST.

In Tennessee and Georgia Sherman said, "War is hell," and made warfare so. HE WON.

At Gettysburg Gen Lee rested too long on the laurels of the first day's fight. HE LOST.

At Nashville Thomas crushed Hood and rested not, but hotly pursued the shattered, retreating columns of grey and cut them to pieces. HE WON.

Gen Early's troops at Cedar Creek, Va., rested on laurels and revelled in plunder sufficiently long for Sheridan to ride far to his routed and fleeing columns, rally them as they fled when none were pursuing, face "about" and strip Early of laurels and plunder.

Gen Bragg rested too long "on our laurels" won at Chickamauga and subsequently lost at Chattanooga, Lookout Mountain and Missionary Ridge.

We rested on our laurels at Honey Hill and Foster's defeated mongrel horde could well afford to "rest on their oars" in their re-embarkation.

A few days after December 1, I saw my command at Tulifinny, on the line of the Charleston and Savannah Railroad, the next point of anticipated attack by Foster's troops. We found there fairly good, light earthworks, manned by a battery of field artillery, five or six guns, in place and ready for action.

There were several companies of the 3d South Carolina cavalry and of Kirk's squadron under command of Major John Jenkins, of the 3d cavalry, several detachments of Georgia Militia, infantry. These, with my regiment, 47th Georgia, and two companies of Charleston military, Citadel cadets and one regiment of North Carolina "reserves," infantry, comprised our fighting force at that point. Col Edwards, of the 47th, was brevetted brigadier general and given command of the entire force; I was brevetted assistant adjutant general.

I here made the acquaintance and saw much of the genial, modest gentleman and gallant, knightly soldier, Major John Jenkins. When off duty we spent many hours together pleasantly. On one occasion, soon after our meeting, in answer to my inquiries relative to topography, etc, of our locality and surroundings, with which the Major was familiar, after discussing same fully and surmising as to probable time, point and manner of next attack by the enemy, the Major staggered me by suggesting, "It is quite likely that the first attack occurring at this post will be made on your regiment, very soon, and will come from our rear, beyond the line of railroad, and will be, I warrant you, a hot assault."

"Why," I said, "Major, you astonish me. How can any force possibly get in rear of this line of railroad which we are guarding and defending? Of course, an attack from the rear would first strike the encampment of my regiment, but how can an attack come first from the rear?"

"The force to which I have reference is back of us now," said Major Jenkins, "about a mile. Between him and us are many acres, enclosed as a pasture, in which roam herds of cattle, sheep and swine, which he will neither sell nor barter for Confederate shekels. His name is Heyward and he is known in this section as 'Tiger Bill' Heywood because he is as ferocious as a tiger."

"Well," I asked, "what has he to do with the attack to which you refer?"

"As I rode through the camp of the gallant old 47th early this morning on my way to your headquarters," said the Major, "if I didn't smell mutton a-roasting I am the worst fooled man at this post. That mutton was none other than 'Tiger Bill's' sheep and here's my horse, saddle and bridle against your boots that old 'Tiger' will be down on this camp like a summer cyclone in less than twenty-four hours. I KNOW."

(I learned afterwards that Mr. Heyward and Major Jenkins, prior to this time, had had a bitter quarrel on account of trespass and depredation on the aforesaid pasture and stock then therein; that Mr. Heyward had challenged the Major to a duel and that Major Jenkins, claiming the right to choose arms, had mentioned "bombshells with one-inch fuses, and distance between combatants ten feet" – no duel.)

We were lolling on the ground, basking in the genial rays of the December noontide sun, a short distance from headquarters tents. A courier came up at a gallop and Major Jenkins was soon mounting to go forward and strengthen an outer picket post, calling back laughingly to me, "I go to the front, you had better look out in rear."

I was almost dozing into a nap when I was aroused by the tramp of horse's feet near; quickly rising, I was confronted a short distance by an elderly, robust, gentlemanly appearing man on horseback in citizen's dress and a double-barrel shotgun across saddle pommel.

Without salutation or other mark of courtesy, he gruffly and very harshly asked me, "Where is the commanding officer of those Georgia troops?" pointing to the 47th encampment.

"The commanding officer of all troops at this post is in yonder tent," I informed him.

"Well, I wish to speak to him at once."

"Very well, sir, you will have to dismount and enter his tent; he is quite unwell."

"Who is the next officer in command, sir?"

"Major John Jenkins, sir, who is out of camp, but who will soon return."

The old gentleman pulled up so suddenly and so hard on his bridle rein that his horse came near rearing; then urging him closer to me he fairly thundered, "I hold no communication with that man, sir. Who else has authority over those men?"

"I have, sir."

"Well, sir, I demand that you keep those scoundrels out of my pasture. They are a set of thieving scoundrels."

I felt some hot flushes beneath my coat collar, but asked as respectfully as I could, "May I inquire who it is that makes these charges and demands?"

"My name is Heyward, sir, and those men have stolen and butchered a beef and a number of my sheep and hogs."

"Mr. Heyward," I said, "those men you brand as thieving scoundrels are brave and tried Confederate soldiers. They are far from their homes and are standing here in South Carolina, between your home, you and yours, and the threatening and expected United States troops. They are not half fed by the Government and I sincerely regret the necessity of taking food from pastures when they are starving and have got to fight well, here soon. I presume that your pasture and all of yours will be swept clean by less-deserving thieves and scoundrels."

"That, sir, is my business with which you have nothing to do." He said, so harshly and rudely that, forgetting for the moment, all courtesy and respect due his years, I replied hotly, "Then attend to your business, with which I have nothing to do, and damn your business and everything connected with it. Ride into that camp and brand there, those men as thieving scoundrels as you have done here."

"Sir, I will ride my pasture hereafter, myself, and the first man I catch there I will riddle with buckshot." And wheeling his horse he galloped off as unceremoniously as he had ridden up.

I warned the officer in command of the regiment and advised that he keep the men in camp. He replied, "Captain, the 47th is not getting all the meat; there are other hungry men here. Must we starve and fight? I feel like sheathing my sword. Must we pour out blood in defence of this land and people, and if we spill the blood of a sheep or a hog to stay off hunger be riddled with buckshot? By ___ let him try that game."

The following day was "ration day" and slim indeed was the share of each man of my regiment "drawing rations" that morning.

In the late afternoon of that day Mr. Heyward, "Tiger Bill," while riding along a cattle path in his pasture, with his trusty "double-barrel" across his saddle front, suddenly, instantly, found himself confronted by a tall, broad shouldered, swarthy, bearded soldier, who had stepped quickly from behind a tree and held the muzzle of an army Enfield rifle close in Mr. Heyward's face while "Halt" rang out sternly from the bearded lips of the soldier.

"Raise that gun one inch and you are a dead man," said the wire-grass Georgia soldier. "You are my prisoner."

"Who are you, and what business have you here, sir, in my pasture?" asked Mr. Heywood, angrily.

"Too thin, old man, none of your d__d business who I am, but my business is guarding this paster from thieving scoundrels and arrest them, and you are my prisoner. Move that gun and I pull this trigger.

"Boys," he called, and from a nearby clump of bushes there rose up two men – as did Roderick Dhu's clansmen on Benledi's Mountain side – with rifles held at "ready."

"Boys," said Jack Williams, (for it was "Wire-grass Jack," of Appling County, Ga., the most powerful man, physically, of the 47th, the greatest wag and "wit" and one of the most gallant and reckless fighters. The trio of brothers, Jack, Noah and Jim, were as fine soldiers as ever donned a uniform. Jim had fallen in battle out West. Noah had been badly wounded but Jack was still on hand.) "You had as well return to camp and report that I have captured one prisoner, which I will hold till I am relieved of sentinel duty here to-night. And as you are starting now, you had as well take along to camp that shoat that tried to bite us as he trotted along here and which we had to kill and thought we might as well skin, seeing that he was dead. And we won't let him waste. Before starting you might as well relieve the prisoner further fooling with that old double-barrel smooth-bore by takin' it and leaning it up against that big oak. The prisoner can dismount and him and me will chaw tobaccer and pass away the time till I am relieved of guard."

"Now, see here, men," said Mr. Heyward, "this is ridiculous. This is my land and the stock in the pasture is mine. I am Mr. Heyward. As you three men have only killed one hog, that is not so bad. Take it and welcome to it, but you must not and shall not destroy my stock as you have started out to do. Return to your camp and as it is late and threatens rain, I will ride back home."

"Pleased to meet you, Mr. Heyward," said Jack, "and we accept your terms of peace. I wish to God that Jeff Davis and Abe Lincoln could compromise as easy and quick as we have. Move on, boys. I will stand sentinel here, Mr. Heyward, till you have turned the bend of this path at that little branch, then I will come off duty. If you wheel before that time I shall consider our armistice broke and hostility will begin just 'bout immediately." They parted thus.

A drizzling rain began about nightfall and continued during the night. It was cold, damp, foggy and drizzling rain the next morning. Near noon our advanced pickets at one point were driven in, and about noon, a small force of the enemy advancing through a skirt of swampy woodland toward the railroad struck the outpost skirmish line of the 47th Georgia, and there was soon music in the air – the ring of rifles and the scent of battle powder-smoke.

I was hastily mounting to ride to the scene of action when a courier came up and reported that Capt. Sheffield, in command of the skirmish line, was being hard pressed by a large force and asked to be reinforced as quickly as possible. Knowing Sheffield, I knew what such a message portended, and within five minutes I was double-quicking at the head of a detail of thirty men, in charge of a gallant young Lieutenant, to Sheffield's support. Reaching the rear of our lines I found our men hard pressed and fighting gallantly.

We quickly deployed, advanced, closed our intervals and Sheffield pressed forward, and I never saw a finer skirmish fight in my whole experience. I could not resist the temptation to join in, as a private, and hastily catching up the rifle of one of our wounded men and snatching some cartridges from his box, I yelled, loaded, fired and advanced with the men on my right and left – the first time I had fired a gun in action since the battle of Resacca, the spring before. The enemy gave way and Sheffield soon pressed them back, though they were firing stubbornly as they fell back.

I noticed that Capt. Sheffield was exposing himself recklessly, as usual, and before leaving I said to him, "Sheffield, are you trying to get killed here to-day? It looks so. Cease this recklessness. You have them whipped and doggedly retreating; press them, but do not expose yourself so to their aim and fire. Remember, we can't spare you. Do be more careful."

"Thank you, Captain," he said, "we have whipped those devils in here to-day, five to our one and I will spare not one of them that I can get at." Then wheeling to front he commanded loudly, "Forward men, fire quick and straight."

I returned to find the troops under arms and ready. I reported the enemy, a reconnoitering party of perhaps 200 men, repulsed and falling back. I had scarcely made my report and ordered "to quarters" sounded for the troops when a courier came up, almost breathless, and reported Capt. Sheffield killed.

The litter corps hastily went forward, accompanied by the surgeon of the 47th, and returned soon, bearing the lifeless form of the big, brave, dauntless Capt. P. C. Sheffield, Company K, 47th Georgia Volunteers, from Bulloch County, Ga., more 47th blood in South Carolina soil. The surgeon informed me that Capt. Sheffield was shot directly through the heart.

Mr. Heyward, "Tiger Bill" rode up to our headquarters just as the dead captain was borne by to the regimental headquarters. He seemed quite affected and dismounting, approached me in courteous manner and inquired about the dead officer and the recent engagement, random shots of which were still occasionally sounding. He seemed much wrought up in feeling. Noting my bay mare tied nearby with bridle and saddle on, he remarked to me, "That is a fine animal, but rather thin; for want of food, I presume."

"Correct, sir," I replied. "We have had, for some time past, only a small quantity of shelled corn." Conversing pleasantly a few minutes, he inquired my name and rank, extending his hand, shook, bowed, saluted and rode off.

Very early next morning a two-horse wagon, piled high with fodder, stopped near and one of the accompanying negro men came to me and handed a note from Mr. Heyward. It was brief in content: "A load of fodder and ear-corn for use at headquarters, with my compliments. Please accept."

Just at 12 o'clock noon that day a stout negro boy with cap and long white apron on – a la ante-bellum servant – bearing on his head a champagne basket neatly covered with white damask, appeared at our quarters, "With compliments of Mr. Heyward," and one of the finest dinners I had seen in many, many days. Mr. Heyward kept up this kind and hospitable action during the remainder of our stay. He sent beef, mutton and pork to the men of the regiment.

In speaking of Mr. Heyward to me Jack Williams said: "Well, he has just been nacherly converted, and has brought forth meat for repentance; therefore, we must be merciful to him and not take too much and tick the d__d Yankees off when they get here."

The Charleston Sunday News and Courier, Charleston, South Carolina, January 11, 1914

A CONFEDERATE SOLDIER'S MEMOIRS
(By Captain Ben S. Williams, Brunson, S. C.)

On Christmas day, just past, I felt my brain and heart full of memories of old, and teeming sad reflection filled my soul. Somehow I felt as if I wanted to hear again the rolling drum-beat and blasting bugle-call "to arms," to see again the starry Southern Cross floating and waving above those phalanxed lines of grey of old and hear our martial airs – followed by the deathly stillness, the calm before the tempest, that precedes the crashing cannon's road – and clash of din of battle.

Again returned, the scenes of those days of my youth, when a soldier of the army of the Southern Confederacy. Again I saw the forms and faces of comrades by death and parting long estranged.

"They came in dim procession led,
The gallant, faithful, heroic dead;
As firm each step, each brow as gay,
As if we parted Yesterday."

All, only a vision phantoms of reverie – they come no more –

"Like the dew on the mountains, like
the foam on the river,
Like the bubble on the fountain, they
Are gone forever."

And our Cause for which they gave their splendid manhood and precious lives, lost.

By remorseless, irresistible, inevitable fate, destined – though fair and glorious – to death in the hour of its birth.

Wrecked on the frontier of our illusive dreamland on the borderland of fair dreams of victory and future national glory; peace and happiness in lofty, idealistic life and being – against the abutting, abysmal shore of disaster, defeat, destruction of ideals, shattered hopes and stern realization of ruin.

Recollections of our fall and wreck, and "secret woes the world has never known," grow fainter as our lingering footsteps, slow, retire and we are borne down time's ceaseless current, ever toward the fading, vanishing eternal past.

On Christmas Day in my home, amid surroundings pleasing and

gratifying, I wandered from room to room; there were fresh wreaths and garlands in bed room, dining room, sitting room and hall. Turning from these, I went into my little study and library. There I keep, furled, the tattered and rent old battle flag of my old regiment, my old war papers, and a few old war relics. There in my "den" I stood facing and near a good pictured likeness of President Jefferson Davis and near hung the picture of Gens R. E. Lee, Stonewall Jackson, Joseph E. Johnston and others. I looked long and steadily into the pictured face of our martyr-President. God only knows how he battled, and suffered, with foes without and with friends (?) (God save me from such) within. He lost, suffered insult, taunts, indignities, bondage and – oh, shame on dastard officials of the United States Government, inflated with pride of victory and pomp of dominion and burning with rage and thirst for revenge – he was manacled with rude shackles, as a common convicted felon held by canting cowards.

Nearby was a picture of Gen – afterward Governor – Wade Hampton, to whom I owed gratitude for my first office in time of peace, and Gen Johnson Haygood, between whom and myself were strong bonds of friendship broken only by death.

Facing about and going through the yard to a growing laurel tree I cut off a limb and returning, wreathed the pictured brow of our war President with leaves of laurel. Then I crowned with laurel, the pictures of the generals. Then above and around a pictured "head of column" of a marching regiment with a tattered battle flag, up-borne in the ranks, by brave gallant men in dingy uniforms of grey – so like my old command – I bound a large sprig of laurel, and then – if a tear fell upon my cheek I am not ashamed; it was a silent heart-offering sacred to the memory of those who have crossed over that river whose shore sands on this side we, the remaining few, are so nearly pressing.

The last Christmas of the war I spent on the coast of South Carolina. My regiment had been ordered from Honey Hill, just after the battle to Tulifinny – pronounced in Indian vernacular – Tu-le-finne. Relative to same I will copy a few sentences of a letter now before me written forty-nine years ago and dated, "In Bivouac, at Tulifinny, S. C., December, 1864," by my younger brother, who had then been in the army not quite two years and who since went through the Spanish-American war as a surgeon in the United States army – to our mother, refugeeing in the southern part of Georgia.

"We were ordered from James Island to Grahamville, where we arrived November 30, just in time to pitch into the enemy. We drove them back to their landing place. The 47th, some Georgia militia, two or three South Carolina cavalry companies and one or two batteries of artillery were all the troops engaged.

"The 47th lost twenty-odd killed and wounded. Ben was in the hottest of the fight, but as usual was not touched – thank God. The enemy's loss was great. At least 200 dead men were left on the field. They retreated, leaving only their dead and a lot of battlefield plunder of all kinds. I have several little trophies. We were ordered hurriedly to Coosawhatchie and our Regiment skirmished all day long with a force of the enemy. Our loss only three. Ben unhurt. A day or two after in a skirmish fight we charged and drove back the enemy, but lost twelve wounded and two killed. One of the killed was Capt. Sheffield, Company K, shot through the heart. Ben in this fight exposed himself recklessly, unnecessarily, but with his usual good fortune.

"We still hold the road to Hardeeville, but Ben says we will soon evacuate this section and form a line of battle on the Saltkehatchie River, after getting up all this railroad iron. Ben was right sick a few days, but is better. He has got his bay mare back. Capt. Fraser brought her to Savannah and placed her in charge of Major Cunningham, who is now over here. I saw Uncle Asa a short time ago going to Augusta, Ga. He had in charge some six or eight ladies from Savannah. I went to Charleston and spent the night with him. He was in good spirits but says this is a very dark hour but says he still hopes the good Lord will stretch forth His mighty arm and save our country."

The enemy had advanced their line at Tulifinny, intrenched and planted their artillery within three-quarters of a mile of our line on the railway. In our front was an open field, which our guns completely commanded. Their line was back of this opening in a wood, the growth and density of which prevented effective work or damage to our position by their guns. At a point near the left terminus of our line the railway was vulnerable to their fire, within a narrow scope, and – "Yankee like" – they discovered this advantage and – "Yankee like" – availed themselves of it and shelled furiously for a few moments every day the two daily trains as they passed the aforesaid point.

The train crew would try to "fool the Yanks." They would slacken their speed five miles away and approach the danger zone as easily and noiselessly as possible until within a short distance of "the race track," as the soldiers called it, when they would dash by with all the speed they could make. While shot and shell crashed and hurtled as rapidly as they could be fired from the waiting, ready guns of the enemy. Only once did they damage a train. This futile firing was owing to the fact that because of obstacles in their front they had to elevate the muzzles of their guns and depend on descending fragments of exploding shells, but they had accurate knowledge of topography, distance, schedule etc. These "running-shooting matches" afforded these soldiers considerable amusement. Scores of them, off duty, would assemble at the "race track" to see the fun, risking the danger of hurt from shot and shell intended for the fleeting, fleeing trains.

We were soon reinforced by two companies of Charleston military, Citadel cadets, commanded by Major White, Capt. Hugh Thompson commanded one company and – if I mistake not Lieut. Huger commanded the other – a gallant little band of splendidly trained soldier boys, ready for the field, under officers handsome, gallant and accomplished; the entire little corps representative of the chivalry of South Carolina, illustrating in a few hours of their arrival by shedding so gallantly their warm, young blood upon the soil of their State in her defense, the esprit and heroism of their patriotic ancestors.

Another contingent of troops reached us about the same time. This quota, a small regiment of North Carolina "reserves," composed of old and elderly men. "Unique" is apt as a description of that incomparable command. Not one man was clad in grey; the prevailing colors seemed to be butternut – brown pants and dark walnut-colored and blue coats, the material of which, I think, was carded, spun, woven, cut out, fitted and sewn at home. The tails of a majority of these coats hung long beneath the cartridge-box belts and the long-barreled old muskets with which the men were armed were carried on either shoulder. The number "present for duty" was about one hundred. The Lieutenant colonel commanding was very like his men in personal appearance, perhaps a little flatter, leaner and more swarthy, with nose a little more "hooked' and black, grey-streaked hair, and beard somewhat longer. The tail of his coat was longer and came down nearly to the tops of a pair of short-leg brogan boots. He wore a red sash and long sabre, and on his collar were two large stars – one each side – denoting his rank. His assumption of airs and authority convinced me that he was of some importance at home among his class – a kind of "class leader." The train bringing this force had sneaked up very softly and halted in the danger zone alluded to and discharged its load of men and baggage – such quantity of baggage as I had never seen carried onto field or camp by any one command. Pots, ovens, frying-pans, kettles, coffee pots and boxes of plates, cups and saucers, bowls, knives and forks, spoons, etc., big hide bound trunks and great rolls of bedding, mattresses, blankets, quilts and pillows bound round with ropes.

The men, on landing, laid their muskets all about on the ground and began immediately to inspect and separate their baggage. I instructed the Lieutenant colonel to form his men, then detach two to guard the baggage, march his men to their assigned place in camp, stack arms and then detail as many as necessary to convey their baggage into their camp. He drew his sabre and began shouting to his men to "fall in line," after waving, shouting and hustling around for some time he succeeded in getting about one-half of his men to "fall in." The others, in utter disregard of his command, continued to devote their attention and time to the inspection and division of the luggage. I had just ridden close to these men and told them if they did not obey their command and fall into line immediately I would arrest the last man of them, send for a detail of men from the camp and conduct them to where they would be taught to obey orders, when the engineer, who had been oiling the locomotive of the train, sprang into his cab and in starting off made such noise as to attract the attention of the Yankee gunners and instantly draw their fire.

In half a minute shells were whistling through the air and exploding high over head. At the first shell-burst there was a general stampede of the men, getting into line a few steps from the railway for the other side of the slight embankment of the railroad, while the crowd in the baggage were falling over boxes, trunks, bedding and pots in the practice of Gen Forrest's tactics of "getting there first." I turned and looked for the Lieutenant colonel commanding; he was where I last saw him standing, but down on his hands and knees, and as shell after shell exploded he would stare upward with more awful dread, sheer fright and abject fear depleted in every feature and staring from his protruding eyes than I ever saw on human face. I rode close to him, dismounted and said, "Stand up, Colonel, there is little danger, these shells go high over-head and your men see you down here on the ground." He arose and placed one hand on my shoulder and I felt that he was trembling from head to feet. I felt sorry for him, because he seemed to be struggling within to overcome his fear produced by the sudden surprising shock. He was not a coward, but suffered a momentary panic. I hurriedly explained to him the cause and meaning of the fire and said: "Now, Colonel, rally your men and redeem yourself in their sight."

Turning and again waving his sabre, (which he had continued to clutch while on the earth) he shouted to his men: "Feller citizens and feller soldiers, the Cunnel here tells me that them bum-shells come from Yankee cannons in them woods over yander; that they shoot at every train what passes this pint on the railroad, but they can't shoot low enough to do much harm, as they have got to shoot over the tops of them trees in front of them; so fall in men, into line, and les' defend our country. Remember there is them at home what expects to hear some good accounts of us. Fall into line, my men."

The men "came across" and fell into line very slowly. In another moment their commander seemed to receive inspiration and called out; "Men, if we can get into line and form behind our breastworks up thar with the balance of our troops aside of our own cannons we can repulse the Yankees if they advance; but if they advance before we can do that, then all our property here will be taken and confiscated for their own use. Men, think of what we could lose; clothes, bedding, cooking utensils and all. We would be ruined, so fall into line, men, and les' protect our rights" – and they formed rapidly. The Lieutenant colonel commanding gave the order "right face, forward march," and moved off in pursuance of orders and in obedience to instructions.

A few days later the colonel of these North Carolina reserves arrived at camp, and to my surprise he was an educated man of about sixty years of age, a lawyer and a gentleman of refinement and culture, modest and courteous, but with nothing of the soldier about him. He stated to me that he was a personal friend of Governor Vance, of North Carolina, and I conceived the idea that the regiment of reserves was organized and mustered into service to give to the Governor's friend the true rank of "colonel" – about "only this and nothing more."

Our reinforcements came none too soon. The enemy, either hearing that we were being reinforced or ignorant of our strength and wanting to test us, advanced their infantry against us. Their blue lines emerged from the woods into the open field in our front under cover of their hot artillery fire. We were ready to receive them. Our infantry was behind the breastworks on right and left of our field pieces. The breastworks were not sufficiently high enough to protect the men, standing, and it was necessary to remain in a crouching or stooping posture until time to fire – we were holding our infantry fire. In passing down our line from right to left, to see that all was right and ready I was amused at the conduct of many of the Citadel cadets.

With all their training and discipline it was impossible for their officers to prevent their popping up along the line regardless of the whizzing bullets to take a look at "the Yankees," in lines of blue, wreathed in battle smoke, advancing and firing on us. Continuous were the commands of their officers, "Down Mr.____, down Mr.____,' calling the names of the rash offenders, but prefixing the title "Mr."

This amused some of the 47th, who hadn't been called "Mr." In about four years, one of whom said, "Them Charleston people is the damdest politest officers to their men I ever struck up with in the army."

Our fire quickly shattered the enemy's lines and they fell back for shelter to the woods in their rear. After shelling the woods it was decided to throw forward a line of skirmishers and feel the enemy in the woods to which they had retreated. The 47th Georgia would have been advanced, but Major White requested to be allowed to make the reconnaissance with his battalion of cadets. He was ordered to advance and our guns were silenced for the movement in front. The cadets moved out and forward eagerly and beautifully. I accompanied them until they deployed and advanced in skirmish line as evenly as if they had been on their Citadel square parade. Walking rapidly back to the works I passed close to a small basin-like little pond in the field "grown up" in high grass and "cat-tail" reeds, not more than twenty feet across. When right on its edge I was startled by a movement in the tall grass just a few feet away. Drawing my pistol I asked, "Who is there?" No answer. Stepping forward and parting the reeds in front, I beheld two Federal soldiers lying flat, faces downward. My first thought was that wounded, they had crawled in there and died; then I remembered the movement that had attracted my attention, and I commanded, "Get up there." Both raised their faces, and when they saw the pointed pistol, sprang quickly to their feet, and holding their open hands high above their heads, began a chattering, not one word of which did I understand. They seemed awfully frightened until I lowered the pistol and beckoned them to move forward ahead of me. They could not speak English. An Artilleryman – an Englishman – said, "They are Dutchmen from 'Olland and hought to be 'ung." We sent them back to prison.

Big Jim Morgan, of the 47th, asked me, as the cadets were moving out to attack, "Captain, do you reckon them Dandy Jim looking kids will stand square up to the rack when they "strike the Yanks." "Morgan," I said, "that is South Carolina blood. You don't know it." "The ___ I don't," said Morgan, "what was the colonel that made up this regiment? What are you, and half of this regiment? Why, durn it, my daddy and mammy was both born and married in this little old hot fool State and didn't move to Georgy till I was most big enough to wear breeches."

After the engagement I asked Morgan what he thought of those "Dandy Jim boys." His only reply was, "D__d if they don't fight like Hood's Texicans."

Years after the war, when I went up to Columbia a member of the State Legislature, I met Capt. Hugh Thompson – afterward Governor Hugh Thompson – the first time since the war, and we went over the Tulifinny fight. I told him what Morgan, of the 47th, said and in our occasional meetings during the years of our pleasant friendship we had many a laugh over Morgan's "say." Among my old letters on hand are several, written me by Governor Thompson from his home in the north. In several of these is some reference to "Hood's Texicans." God rest the soul of this, another of my departed friends.

After the unsuccessful assault of the enemy at Tulifinny, as in Warsaw, "peace reigned" for a time. The Citadel Cadets were ordered elsewhere.

Col Edwards, of the 47th, brevet brigadier general in command, too sick for duty, had to leave, he felt, never to return. At our parting he begged me in a tearful voice, "If we never meet again, remember me kindly, and may God bless and spare you. I fear that I am done and if you should fall, God help the remnant of the old regiment. For my sake of memory of the past, for my sake, for your sake and the sake of our brave men, preserve our proud record on every field, and may God help you." He never returned. A wreck of splendid, physical manhood he soon "crossed the river."

The colonel of the North Carolina regiment, next highest in rank, was assigned the command of the forces, and moved to headquarters. He was very affable and courteous, modest, sedate and lazy. He had very little experience or knowledge of matters military, and seemed to be quite indifferent as to the acquisition of more. Many years my senior, able, accomplished and experienced in matters of worldly and in civil life – of which I know so little – he entertained and interested me, but he imposed upon me the exercise of most all of his authority, nearly all of the responsibility and just about all the work. All matters, ordinary or emergent, he would quickly settle – as to himself – with one short inquiry of and one shorter mandate to me, to wit: "What would you do in the premises?" "Go ahead." I liked that, was used to it, and we got along splendidly.

Illustrative: Our cavalry outpost pickets had been fired on and we deemed it essential to reinforce our picket line at once. Of the details for that purpose was one on Major Kirk's squadron of fifteen men. I had never met Major Kirk, as he had been absent, and a Captain was in command. I had heard of the major. It was night, the weather a little inclement, and the colonel commanding sat on a camp stool smoking and trying to read near a good fire in front of our headquarters tent. I was busy inside, near a candle on a box, looking over and making up my "report." The different details had reported and moved to the front. Major Kirk's men were due. I heard the quick gallop of a horse abruptly checked near the front of our tent and listening intently for news, heard the following remarks: "Are you the commanding officer here, sir?"

"Yes, sir."

"I am major commanding Kirk's squadron; a call for fifteen of my men has been made for picket duty tonight."

"I presume that is all right, sir."

"No, sir, I am here to protest against this detail. My men and horses are worn and hungry and utterly unfit to go on such duty, and I am surprised that your adjutant general is so ignorant of conditions as to make such an unrighteous demand on my force."

As I stepped from the tent into the circle of firelight I noted at a glance a fine, portly, bearded man in full uniform of a major of cavalry, a typical "rough-rider" trooper; well mounted and plainly discernable in the circle of our campfire light on the opposite side.

"There," said the colonel, who had not risen from his seat, "is the officer you may address your protest."

I saluted and the major returned the salute brusquely, and said to me, "Sir, you have made a detail on my squadron for picket duty tonight."

"Correct, sir," I said.

"Are you aware of the condition of my command, sir?"

"Only by your report this morning," I said.

"Well, sir, if you don't know you ought to know that my men and horses are without food and forage and cannot go on picket."

"I differ with you, sir," I replied. "I neither command your squadron nor issue food or forage to them as commissary or quartermaster."

"Well, sir, I refuse to consent to my men being sent off to the outposts until they are supplied with rations and forage. What are you going to do about it?"

I replied: "Your men are near here: the order for the detail reached you half an hour ago. If your men are not reported here, ready for duty, within the next five minutes, charges against you for insubordination and disobedience of orders, with full specifications, will be preferred and forwarded to division headquarters tomorrow morning."

Without word or salute the sturdy major leaned forward in his saddle and his horse shot from the firelight through the darkness like an arrow from the bow. The colonel laughed heartily and said, "If that Scottish chieftain-looking major don't send those men what will you do in the premises?"

"Quickly make a detail from another command for to-night, arrest the major before sunrise to-morrow, by your orders, and prefer charges against him signed by you as commanding officer of his post," I replied. "Go ahead," said the colonel. In less than five minutes Kirk's detail, in charge of a sergeant, reported at our fire and I noticed that to each trooper's saddle was strapped a bundle of fodder. I said to the sergeant, "You are behind time in reporting, sergeant."

"We were ready and mounted some time ago, sir, but were ordered by Major Kirk to remain ready until he got back to camp."

Afterward the major and I had several good laughs about his attempted "game of bluff," he contending, "all strategy is fair in love and war."

One or two of his squadron are living near me now. They say the major would always try to take care of his men – and the major "went through the war" and met his death a short time after by accident in the machinery of a mill near here.

Christmas at Tulifinny had passed. We were on the threshold of a new year, 1865, awaiting anxiously our next move in the rapidly closing, mighty drama in which we – cavalry, infantry and artillery at Tulifinny – were a few of the actors.

The Charleston Sunday News and Courier, Charleston, South Carolina, February 22, 1914

A CONFEDERATE SOLDIER'S MEMOIRS

(By Captain Ben S. Williams, Brunson, S. C.)

The comparative quiet and inactivity, which mark the period of "in winter quarters" of the armies was over, the winter had about passed and the troops guarding the coast of South Carolina were astir.

Sherman had swept down through Georgia, halting – after being left at Atlanta by Hood – only when there was no more of Georgia to ravage, and the tramp of his despoiling horde was stayed on the shore of the sea at Savannah. The first month of the last year of the war had passed. It was the first of February 1865, and our war was almost over.

Mississippi, Alabama, Tennessee, Virginia, Georgia and Florida were overrun by the armies of the United States. Of all the States of the Southern Confederacy east of the Mississippi River, only North and South Carolina were wholly retained by us. Our "Army of the West," under Hood, had been well-nigh annihilated by Thomas in Tennessee. In Virginia, Sheridan had devastated the Shenandoah. Lee was firmly held in grasp by Grant, while the navy of the North swept our entire coast.

The plan of the campaign of the enemy for 1865 was very apparent. Sherman was to move north from Savannah, Ga., and join his army to Grant's in a final attack on Lee at Richmond. Sheridan, at the head of 10,000 troopers, sweeping down from the Shenandoah, had cut the railroads north of Richmond and was resting within the Union lines before Petersburg. Wilson, with 13,000 cavalry, was campaigning and camping, at will, through Alabama and Georgia, holding and guarding a line of retreat from Virginia westward. Stoneman, with 5,000 cavalry, had ridden through the passes of the Alleghenies and rested in North Carolina, awaiting the issue in Virginia.

Flushed with victory, his troops drunk on rapine and plunder, and thirsting for more spoils and burning with desire for revenge, Sherman gave his troops only a month's rest in Savannah, and early in February 1865, they moved out northward, to scourge South Carolina "with gloves off" on their passage through on their way to Virginia and final victory.

Relative to and descriptive of their forward movement, I read in "history" (?):

"Early in February Sherman's army was put in motion northward. There was no waiting for roads to dry nor for bridges to be built but the troops swept on like a tornado. Rivers were waded and one battle was fought while the water was up to the shoulders of the men."

What distortion of events and falsehood! It takes at least two opposing lines for a battle; both lines could hardly have occupied position in water up to men's shoulders, and if so there could have been only a swimming match. As "Caesar paused upon the banks of the Rubicon," so also in our war, would either side have paused on the banks of any stream, which was in depth "up to the shoulders of the men" before floundering in if the line on the opposite bank was firing. I know whereof I speak. That should – deep wading might have happened after the ball.

Sherman's army was about 100,000 strong and moved out of Savannah, Ga., in four columns, with a breadth of front of about fifty miles. Detachments of thousands of cavalry and foragers swarmed in front of and around the flanks of the army; in its wake were left ashes and ruin. One corps marched along the highway, very near which I am, and have been for the past many years, living. About half a mile from this place is the residence of the father of my wife, a large house, and an enclosed, very large grove of oak, hickory and pine.

Thursday morning February 8, about 10 o'clock, the" head of the column" of one of the four corps, reached that place, where the roads leading from Savannah, the starting point of Sherman, across the Savannah River and on to Augusta, Orangeburg and Columbia. A halt and encampment were made here until the different divisions came up. Gen Sherman accompanied this corps. At once destruction began. Fencing, plantings and everything on the whole plantation convertible into fuel were used for campfires. Cattle and poultry were slain and everything in the way of vegetables that could be found was taken for "rations."

Numbers of soldiers swarmed through the house, from cellar to garret, breaking open trunks, smashing bureau drawers and cutting open feather mattresses and pillows in their search for money, valuables and jewelry. Several of the soldiers hastily applied lighted matches to furniture in the house, but little damage was done by fire.

Later Gen Sherman, accompanied by several officers, went to the house and was met by my wife's father, Mr. Richardson, to whom he made himself known; when Mr. Richardson asked for protection from further damage and trespass, Gen Sherman directed one of the accompanying officers to have, at once, a guard placed at each entrance, with strict orders to allow no trespassing or disorder. In reference to this I have heard Mrs. Richardson, in the presence of Mr. Richardson, allege: "I was present and believe that Mr. Richardson gave Gen Sherman a Masonic 'sign.'" The proud and austere old gentleman would not either plead guilty, or not guilty, to the allegation.

But every morsel of food in kitchen, smoke house, pantry or safe had been taken; every barn and crib emptied, every potato bank leveled, all poultry taken and the family in the "big house up to the yard" were on an enforced fast. Shortly after night "Maum Rece," the cook, and Hagar, the house seamstress, brought up from the "negro quarters" some hominy and fried bacon for "old massa and missus and the chilluns," and were readily admitted by the sentinels.

On the following morning they again brought food for breakfast, but understanding that by that time that they were free, when, in a few hours after the Federal troops filed out into the highway, those house-women, with scores of other slaves "packed up their bags, and followed the drum," not, however, until Dinah, the trusted nurse, who had long lived in the house and been "taught by the white people" and had helped old "missus" bury a lot of good, old wine, had shown some of the blue-coated soldiers where to find it and how to help drink it. Of all the negroes on the place, but one remained at home with her white folks – old Maum Cinda, who, in a short while, was stricken down with Typhoid fever and was nursed through to health, by "old massa and missus and the chillun."

Days after the departure of the troops the only food tasted by Mr. Richardson and his family, and that upon which they subsisted alone, was "hominy" from the corn, raked up and gathered in the trampled ground of the defaced and mutilated lawn, left by the horses of the artillery and cavalry, and sifted in a large sieve to get rid of the sand, and ground in an old fashioned hand mill by Mr. Richardson.

Gen Sherman informed Mr. Richardson, (who had four sons in the Confederate army) that the corps present mustered 22,000 men.

The Confederate troops, long held in Savannah by Gen Hardee, had been moved into South Carolina, and my regiment at Tulifinny, with the other troops guarding the Charleston and Savannah Railway, were moved out in advance of Sherman's movement and we started on the march to the Saltkehatchie River, where in the east side we were to form a line of defense and check Sherman's movements. We moved out in good time and proceeded on our way leisurely. Quite a number of incidents of that short march – not more than sixty miles – occur in my mind.

In the commands moving out from Savannah were a few officers and men of my acquaintance whom I had not seen since 1862. Of these was one Lieut. Col Rockwell, of Savannah, before whom I had on one occasion stood with considerable awe and in some dread, as he was a member of a board of West Point officers before whom I had been ordered for examination for promotion from a sergeantcy to a lieutenantcy. Rigid in dignity, strict as to discipline, scrupulous as to etiquette, proud of military "pomp and circumstance" and merciless to delinquents, this "board of examiners" was dreaded by all aspirants for promotion. I was so fortunate as to "pass," was promoted and later placed in close contact with the members by being appointed by Gen Beauregard – then in command at Savannah – as recorder of said board.

Meeting with Col Rockwell again, on the march above alluded to, the colonel was not marching; he was sitting at the root of a tree fanning himself with his plumed hat. He was very stout and of abnormal abdominal proportion. As my regiment was passing I saw him and recognized him and rode out, dismounted and clasped hands with him. He had apparently "aged" considerably, was stouter and much more protuberant in front. He informed me that he had been marching, afoot, for several miles, but was exhausted and could go no further. After taking some time he stood up by me and I suppose the contrast between my boyish, slender figure and his immense circumference was sufficiently striking to attract the attention of some of the asinine young soldiers, who had been long pent up in Savannah, and in passing they began to inquire loudly of each other for some information concerning "our bass drum." One fellow would say, "Wonder what the devil became of our bass drum last night?" Another would answer, "Why, I saw the man just now who swallowed it", etc.

As soon as the rear of the column had passed I offered the colonel my horse and told him I would walk and could overtake my command, but with our combined efforts he could not mount: the failure he attributed to his exhaustion. I told him to sit and rest. Riding rapidly back I got one of the ambulances to move up quickly until we reached the colonel. I assisted him in getting in, shook hands with him and never met him afterward.

We soon approached the Saltkehatchie River at a point near Patterson's Bridge, close to the coast, and halted late in the evening for detachment of troops to be placed in line on the other side. Here at this junction of commands I saw for the first time Brig Gen B, and his command, comprising, I think, not more than 250 or 300 men, who seemed to be the "last roses of summer" plucked from the stem of a population as a final gleaning of the distant territory whence they had been recruited. This little old bearded brigadier, in full flashing uniform, was an oddity. He was evidently – as I knew him afterward to be – an educated gentleman, a "gentleman by birth and breeding," but his deportment was a combination of dignity, Chesterfieldian courtesy, Quixotic knight errantry and mirth-producing "monkey motions." At a later date, at a point in our march through North Carolina, his men delayed the march of the troops in their rear by refusing to walk through a little branch of water not more than knee-deep and waiting and taking to the "foot-log," one by one, single file, very carefully and slowly. As soon as the cause of the delay was ascertained I was instructed to file forward and "tell Gen B__ to move his command forward through the shallow branch and close up on the line in front." He tried to execute the order. But the men would not wade and stood waiting for room on the foot-log.

During the period of waiting a great strapping Lieutenant of blond complexion, sandy hair and long mustache, tall and of powerful physique, big boots and huge spurs on heels, claiming to be an Austrian and posing as a drill master of sword exercise and aide-de-camp generally (and was an egotistic, bombastic ass especially) all enthusiastically, bombast, fuss-n-feathers, and gas ever-seeking, something ridiculously, notoriety of almost any kind, rode hurriedly up to Gen B, who, with his command, was resting on the roadside, just opposite my regiment, and stated to him in excited manner, that on his way back across the river he had espied a small body of armed Federals, evidently a reconnoitering party and they were now not half a mile away; that if given fifty men he could get between the enemy and the river, cut them off, or attack and capture the whole d___ posse in a glorious coup de etas. I heard all and felt confident that he was feigning and just wanted to stir up a little "tea pot tempest" fuss for personal notoriety. But old Gen B__ was all animation and enthusiasm in a moment. Mounting his horse and cutting off a portion of his command, in the greatest excitement, he rode out in the darkness, guided by the dourly, braggart informant and remarking to some of us who looked on: now is the winter of my discontentment about to be made glorious summer.

The news reaching higher quarters, my regiment and one or two other commands were held at strict "attention," for about two hours during which time we heard not even "a farewell" from the point to which they had hurried. Returned the troops looked mad and angry. The bullying Lieutenant was absolutely sure now at the sight of him the Yankees had hastened to their boats and rapidly retreated down the Saltkehatchie and Combahee rivers. The old Gen B___ stroking his straggling whiskers only said dramatically, in reply to inquiries "Twas there thus from 'childhood's' hour, I have seen my fondest hopes decay; I have loved a tree or flower, but twas first to fade away. And now the joy is like divine, of all I ever dreamed and knew to meet those blue coats; call them mine, oh, misery, I have lost that too."

I wondered how under heaven and on earth this aesthetic old gentleman of the beau-monde ever came to command, at his age, a brigade in our army. But I knew – then – and it is much plainer in my mind now – that politics had crept into our ranks; that policy, to a considerable extent, had supplanted patriotism; that outside parties were prompted by the law of self-promotion and the spirit of self-aggrandizement; that influence of wealth warped need of praise and promotion from true worth and merit into channels of favoritism and nepotism, while the sway of aristocracy shaped many of our affairs and the esprit de corps of the armies of the South was fading.

At the close of the second day following our stop near Patterson's Bridge our brigade, under command of Col E. H. Bacon, of the 32nd regiment, Georgia infantry – a splendid officer – approached the point at which we were to "take our stand and live or die for Dixie" – at least fight again for Dixie. We crossed the river at Broxton's bridge, and as the weather threatened rain, we quickened the march in order to reach a Methodist camp meeting ground, about two or three miles in front. There were a number of small shanties erected for shelter and accommodation of persons who attended these annual meetings. Before crossing the river I had been ordered to take charge of the quartermaster's department of the brigade – owing to the illness of the quartermaster, who requested that I be placed in charge in his stead. Our wagon train, with quartermaster, commissary, and ordnance stores was in advance of the columns.

I rode forward, overtook the train, and on reaching the camp ground, saw to the parking of my train, and then selected the two best cabins on the ground, one for brigade headquarters, brevet Gen Bacon, the other for myself and the regimental quartermasters. I at once took possession of mine, as it began raining, and as Lieut. Finlay, of Bacon's staff, rode up, I pointed out to him "headquarters," and he took possession of that by placing his saddle and himself inside. I was alone, but for one man who was sweeping up, in my cabin – the regimental quartermasters busy with their respective affairs when our brigade surgeon, Dr M., rode up near the door just as I stepped to the open door. We were not on good terms, though once very friendly until he gave warrant – though above me in rank – to call him a liar. Ever afterward he was as insolent in his conduct toward me as he dared to be.

At the door of the cabin he said to me, "Sir, where am I to establish my medical department?" "I do not know, sir," I replied; "I refer you to the colonel commanding." "Well, I refer you to the fact, sir, that you have taken the only house outside the headquarters that does not leak, for yourself." "Good," I said, "but how do you know?" "I have examined and seen and this is the only house fit for the medical department, and I insist that you give this up to me to be used as such." "I decline to do so, sir," I said. "I'll show you that you don't rule this camp," he said, and "I'll show you that you don't rule me," I answered.

The troops had arrived, were stretching "flys" and building fires when the colonel commanding sent for me.

"What's the matter with Surgeon M?" he inquired. "Mad," I said, "because I would not move out of the next best house on this ground and give it to him. There are plenty of other houses here, colonel, good enough, but he just wants the best and if he had not almost ordered me out I would have exchanged for him." "Well, won't you let him have it anyway?" "I'll see him in a hotter climate than this ever is, colonel, first, unless you order it," "No, under the circumstances I will not do that," he said. The old surgeon would not occupy a house, but slept in his ambulance that night. He never spoke to me again.

We moved a few miles further up the river to "Rivers' Bridge," took our stand and began throwing up breastworks and fortifying and preparing to give the enemy a warm reception, on his arrival there, for the last time on the soil of South Carolina.

The Charleston Sunday News and Courier, Charleston, South Carolina, January 10, 1915

A Confederate Soldier's Memoirs

News From Europe's Battlefields and Devastated Regions of Mighty Conflict Reminder of South's Plight During Closing Days of the Confederacy's Struggle, Declares a Veteran

Brunson, S. C.

As each breeze that sweeps over bounding oceans brings tidings from the vast zone of war – of blood and carnage, of battles, of horror, destruction and all of the hell of war – there rises before me the picture – stamped indelibly on my memory in a period of the past – of the trial of the souls and manhood of men and the true womanhood of women here on our own blood-drenched, homeland soil. Our fair fields in their bounteous fruitage were trampled by hostile hordes and in our forests echoed the boom of cannon and the screams of shrapnel.

Ruin replaced the peace and commerce of our cities and our homes were no longer safe under shield of our own civil law. Our foemen, in overwhelming numbers, were on our soil, their "torches at our temple doors." The men of the South were in battle array "against all the world and the rest of mankind," and for four years amid destruction, death, blood, tears and anguish, there was rejoicing in glad acclamation of glorious victory and there was sorrowing in anguish under crushing defeat. Thanks be to God for our present blissful peace and blessing of plenty. Dark, dark, indeed, were the lowering war clouds in the days of my last "New Year" in the army in 1865. No star of hope then glimmered in our paling sky, and shimmered faintly only reflection of the former brilliancy and glory of victory of the arms of the Southern Confederacy, when in February, 1865, the several commands, decimated until mere skeletons of original organizations – forming our little army of resistance – faced about at Rivers' Bridge, on the Saltkehatchie River, and moved rearward away from the last selected line of defence in South Carolina, presenting that most melancholy spectacle, a retreating army. The State of South Carolina was to be given over to the enemy and added to our large scope of abandoned territory. We knew, as we fell back, that our homes and the enemy were in our rear: of our dark abysmal front we knew not. God alone knew of Bentonville, Appomattox, and the near and, I greatly feared that in this dire exigency there would be, to a considerable extent, a dissolving of the commands, companies and regiments nearest the homes of the men comprising the same.

Many Homes, But No Deserters

There were in our ranks, South Carolina troops close to their homes. The distance between the Salkehatchie River, on the banks of which we had stood in line of defence and the Savannah River, dividing line between South Carolina and

Georgia – the two streams running in nearly parallel line is only about twenty-seven miles by highway. Of the two regiments of Georgia veteran troops present – the 32nd and 47th Georgia volunteers – there were several companies, the members of which would have been on the soil of their native counties of Burke, Bullock, Chatham, Effingham and Screven, immediately on reaching at different points the farther shore of the Savannah River. Concealment in the broad, dense swamp of the Salkehatchie in the night of our evacuation would have been in no wise difficult and the return to homes in the rear of the enemy's forces could have been quickly and easily made. But that would have been "desertion," than which nothing was more disgracing or damnable to a soldier of the Southern Confederacy.

Excepting manifestation of grief and regret on account of defeat, the disheartening surrounding conditions had but little apparent effect or influence on the demeanor of our troops. The sullen silence, preservation of close order and firm step in the ranks of our orderly movement to the rear, boded not fear, panic, demoralization or idea of desertion or surrender, and I felt confident then that those men were ready at an instant's notice to face about and fight anything and everything in blue under the heavens to finish. Pretty clearly illustrative of the spirit of the men who were falling back through South Carolina in February, 1865, were the sentiments expressed in characteristic language by two of these "wire grass" men of the 47th Georgia while resting near Branchville soon after the Rivers' Bridge engagement. Tall, broad-shouldered Jim Patterson, of Company F, with several others, lounged around my camp fire, and off duty, smoking and resting, talked freely.

"Patterson," said Bill Morgan, "where do you reckon we are headed for now, anyway, and where in the h__l do you reckon we are going to land finally."

"Well, Bill," said Patterson, "I think we are headed for Richmond, but now as to where in that other place you mention we will land it is pretty hard to say, but judging from all of our past luck and experience from Vicksburg to here, you know whenever there was anything a-doing we generally landed in about the middle of the d__dest hottest place in the whole business and it is not altogether unreasonable to suppose that we might again be likewise accommodated in the future."

"Well," said Morgan, "I reckon there ain't much difference 'twixt hell and Richmond about now, and it ain't very far from one place to another."

"Yes," said Patterson, "Petersburg and Richmond are sort of way stations on the short route."

200 Men Left of 800

"But," said Morgan, "if old McLaws (general commanding our division) will hurry up and get us there soon with Lee's men there'll have to be a few extra trains put on the route to that other place. But, boys, I don't believe the 47th can muster to-night more than 200 men to save our lives – Lord in heaven! Just think, 800 rifles cracking in Jackson, Mississippi, May 1863 – 600 gone! I would give my shoes and hat that I got off that dead Yankee corporal at Honey Hill to know how many Yanks the 47th has put to sleep up to now."

"I have been trying to figure it out," said Patterson, "by taking up fight after fight that we've come through, but it's impossible, for sometimes we could count the dead in our front after the fight and maybe the next time we could only guess at their dead, while they were counting ours in our rear, but I believe if we get anything like a fair show from now on we are good for five hundred more." Yes," said Morgan, "that's only two and a half apiece for us unless they thin us out pretty quick."

Lazy but brave old Ike Collins sat up and taking his short stem clay pipe from his bearded lips said: "By granny, I wish to the Lord they would give us that for task and then let us go home if we made it." "No, Ike," said Morgan, "I'll swear I couldn't go home satisfied at killing two more yanks and wounding another, which would be equal to a half killing. Would you, Jim Patterson?" "No, boys," replied Patterson in sadder tones than usual, "I never expect to go home, but if ever I do of my own free will and accord, it will be when one side or the other is clean licked out, lock, stock and barrel. But I think we are good for five hundred yanks if we can have anything like a fair show and if all the other boys would do likewise; this war ain't near over yet." "No," said Morgan, "if I could get twice two and a half to-night or to-morrow and I was then invited to quit and go home, d___n me if I would go and sit down peaceful at home and let the homes of the people in this State be overrun by Sherman's army. Perish my right arm first. My daddy and mammy were both born and raised in South Carolina." "Right," said Jim Patterson, "we are in it to the end. God knows where and when that will be." "Well, boys," put in Ike Collins, "I fully expect to be along with all that's left of the 47th until my end or the war's end, but I certainly am a-longing to go home, and God knows if I had my way I would land every blasted Yankee in hell before midnight and start for home before day to-morrow morning. But we're here to stay and here to fight."

Plucky to the Last

This was a pretty fair voicing in crude language of the sentiment of the old regiment's remnant of men whose colors had waved, whose rifles had volleyed and whose comrades had fallen on almost every battlefield in the States of Mississippi, Tennessee, Georgia and South Carolina. I was ordered immediately after the beginning of our retreat from Rivers' Bridge to resume charge of the quartermaster's department of our brigade, as Major A. was still absent, sick. We rested near "Four-Hole Swamp," not far from Branchville, for a few days. And the regimental quartermasters and their sergeants foraged for food supplies throughout the neighborhood and found a majority of the citizens very clever and liberal. I was given authority to impress provisions, horses and wagons if necessary, but my instructions to those serving under me were to collect no more than actually required and to use no force or severity where possible to avoid same. We gave a voucher and receipt for collections a "Government slip," which was a promise to pay, equivalent in value to our common currency or "Confederate money."

One day, feeling restless, cheerless, and pretty hungry, too, I concluded to ride out, away from camp, into the country. After riding several miles and passing several farms, I came in sight of a very nice looking place with a large, two-story, painted dwelling. As it was about 11 o'clock A. M., I concluded that here would be a very good place for a stop, a rest and a dinner – (soldiers were always hungry, I can readily prove same by any man who ever really "soldiered" it,)

Riding up to a large gate in front of the house I was met by a negro servant boy, who very politely opened the gate and informed me in answer to my question of who lived there, that Mrs. Rion (or Ryan) did. I mention the name of the family with profoundest respect and have entertained for them the kindest feeling because of the courtesy and kindness shown me, a stranger soldier. I dismounted and, giving my bridle rein to the young darky, I walked up on the high plaza and knocked at the front door: in a few moments this was opened and I stood facing one of the prettiest young ladies I had seen in many a day. I bowed low and informed her, as coherently as I could just then, that I was from the military camp nearby and that I – er – in riding through the neighborhood, in order to obtain information as to our – er – ability to – er – procure food and forage for our stock had concluded to ride by and ask permission to rest for a while, as I was a little tired from quite a long ride. I was invited into a luxurious parlor and – by selection of the young lady, I was seated in a large, comfortable rocking chair, and after one or two casual remarks about "the weather" she excused herself, saying she would ask her mother to see me relative to the matter of which I had spoken.

"Why!"

When the young lady had gone I began to upbraid myself why the h__l should I feel such trepidation and – be so of a tremor at the sight of and in the presence of this gentle, courteous, modest young lady? I, a soldier of many battles, my pride and secret boast that no man in my regiment had ever gone farther to the front in desperate charge or remained longer on the field in strife for victory while facing defeat. I, stammering in confusion in making a simple statement to the soft-eyed, timid, bashful maiden. Ah! That was it. It was her gentle demeanor, her maidenly modesty, her true feminine timidity and loveliness before which I bowed in awed admiration and reverence. She soon returned, accompanying her mother, a lady of mild and gentle manner, reminding me very much of my own mother, whom I had not seen in many months. I felt perfectly at ease, and after conversing for about half an hour very pleasantly rose, very reluctantly, to take my leave: feeling that on them it was not right to impose, even for the sake of a dinner. But I was not allowed to thus depart, and was informed that I was expected to stay for dinner and in anticipation of this my horse had been unsaddled, stabled and fed. This brief and pleasant visit was one of the few pleasing cases alongside the rough pathway of duty in the arid army life of a soldier in the field where he may briefly turn aside and for a moment linger in blissful peace and transient forgetfulness. I never again saw these good ladies but ever afterward whenever the soldiers sang "Annie Laurie," a vision of lovely "Laura Ryan" would appear to my mind's eye.

A "Smart" Sentry

Returning to camp I rode along the public highway, and when within a mile or two of camp I noticed in a small grove in front of a house near the roadside a cavalryman's horse standing hitched. I was riding slowly, and as I came near the horse I noticed, leaning against a tree close to the road, a cavalryman's carbine, (gun,) while about thirty feet away from the gun sat comfortably at the foot of a large tree a cavalryman and an elderly man, citizen and host of the premises, chatting and laughing in a very lively manner. I concluded in a moment that this was a picket post and being very carelessly guarded. I rode slowly opposite and past the sentinel, and wondered why I was not halted. My overcoat was on and buttoned, and no insignia of rank of office visible. I had ridden some paces beyond the post and was about to turn and suggest to the sentinel that he take his post and properly perform his duty, when without rising to his feet he called out to me loudly, rudely and boisterously: "Halt, there, d___n it."

I faced about and moved close to his gun by the tree by the time he had leisurely risen, the elderly citizen rising at the same time. Halting, I asked; "What do you want?" "Want what I'm going to have – a look at your pass, if you've got one. Have you got a pass?" (I saw his egotism and saw that he was trying to "show off" before the elderly citizen.")

"What right have you to demand to see my pass?" I asked. "I am a sentinel and this is my post and my orders are to allow no man to pass here, going or coming, without a pass." "Then, sir," I said, "You have disobeyed orders and neglected your duty. You were off your post, without your gun, saw me pass your post before you halted me. Were you ordered to curse when you halted?" "Show your pass," he said crossly, moving toward me, "or I'll arrest you and that pretty d__d quick."

Moving my horse slightly to the left, I reached down, quickly caught up the carbine and laid it across my saddle front. Suddenly the trooper seemed to "take in" the situation and with true, soldierly instinct, instantly snatched his long cavalry sabre from its scabbard and hissing, "I'll have my gun or die," started toward me. While talking I had quietly unbuttoned my overcoat, and when the advancing trooper was within about three paces of me I quickly threw back the lapel of my overcoat, jerked from the holster my "Colt's army pistol" and turning my horse slightly to left and leveling my weapon, I said "Halt! Another step with that drawn sabre I'll kill you." He stood and gazed in astonishment, glancing rapidly and alternately at the muzzle of the "Colt's army" and at the gilt bars on my inner coat collar.

"Return your sabre," I commanded, and he obeyed instantly, not through fear or cringing or cowardice – for there was nothing of the kind in his "make-up" – his heels went together and with form erect his right hand went to the rim of his hat in salute, mechanically, automatically, instinctively.

Learned His Lesson

Such is the effect of drill and discipline and the force of practice and habit. I returned his salute, "to what command do you belong?" I asked. "Harrison's Tennessee Cavalry." "Where are Col Harrison's headquarters?" He informed me. "All right," I said, "I have the authority to remove you from your post, but I can inform Col Harrison of this affair." For the first time I saw his face pale. "Then God help me! Col Harrison is rigid in his discipline and shows no mercy in punishment for disobedience of orders." "Then why did you not obey orders and act the soldier and gentleman, which under the surface you appear to be?" "I have no excuse," he replied. "I just acted the fool and jackass and will have to take my medicine. I apologize to you and do not blame you. I only ask that you forgive me and return my gun, that I not be thoroughly disgraced." "Take your gun and I will not report you," I said, handing him his gun, "but don't do so again. Be a soldier and a gentleman. Here is my pass, examine it in obedience to orders, your duty. Now, good-by." "God bless you," he said, and there was a quiver in his voice. I never saw him again. But it was not until I turned to go that I noticed the elderly citizen peeping around the tree, behind which he had quickly dodged when I drew upon the trooper (he was exactly within range.) Waving him a farewell I laughed to see how quickly and naturally he had adopted tactics, which I had seen adopted on similar necessary occasions.

Patterson, (J. H.,) above named, returned home of his "own free will and accord" unhurt, when one side had been crushed "lock, stock and barrel," and died about two years ago in the town of Baxley, Appling County, Georgia, where he had held for a number of years the office of ordinary.

The end of the war came for Ike Collins in the heat of our last battle of the war, Bentonville. He never again saw the home for which he was "a-longing."

The right hand and wrist of Bill Morgan were shattered by a ball in the closing fire of the battle of Bentonville. Years ago I met him in Savannah, Ga. When he threw his strong left arm across my shoulders tears trickled down his bronzed, bearded cheeks. Taking the two only remaining fingers of his right hand in mine and raising his sleeve above the shrunken wrist – no larger than an infant's – I said: "Morgan, you stuck to the last, but 'perished your right arm.'"

"Yes," said he, "and perish my body and soul whenever I quit thanking God for letting me fight it out to the last minute of the last fight." And now they sleep where no sound can ever awaken them to battle again.

(By Captain Ben S. Williams, Brunson, S. C.)

The Charleston Sunday News and Courier, Charleston, South Carolina, March 8, 1914

A CONFEDERATE SOLDIER'S MEMOIRS
(By Captain Ben S. Williams, Brunson, S. C.)

From this Point at which I am writing, near the town of Brunson, on the Charleston and Western Carolina Railway, midway between the city of Augusta, Ga., and Port Royal, S. C., the terminus of the railway, on the coast, sixty miles away, distant about thirteen miles northeast we touch the Saltkehatchie River at Rivers' Bridge crossing. In this coast section of South Carolina nearly all streams, large and small, the larger of Indian names, soft and euphonious, such as Saltkehatchie, Coosawhatchie, Tulifinney, etc. are bordered or fringed by belts of alluvial swamp land, increasing in width on approaching the coast and narrowing on nearing the higher clay lands of the up-country, extending often from source to outlet of stream.

On these fertile belts of stream swamp lands, often cut and divided into islets and miniature formations and winding deviously, curving out and in until finding fitting place again to join the mother stream, or met by some rushing tributary current are swept back into the main, all swelling the deepening volume flowing into the nearby vast, engulfing sea, the tidal waves of which lave and kiss our shore.

Nature is lavish in her gifts of beauty and adornment here in the growth and product of these stream border lands. Here grow luxuriantly, in rich profusion blent, beech maple and hickory, juniper, willow and pine, cypress, oak and magnolia, while large folds of "Spanish moss" hang as if in graceful drapery of limb and bough amid the vari-colored foliage. In earliest spring-tide branching hollies and flowering bays are festooned in scarlet bloom of the clinging woodbine and bowed beneath arcade and bower of the fragrant yellow jessamine, verily.

"The land of the cypress and pine.
Where the jessamine blooms and gay woodbine."

On some of my peaceful tramps and hunts through these deeply-shaded morasses, where were waving ferns and beds and borders of violets, I have come suddenly, upon a flowers of rare beauty, either of the richest and most magnificent crimson or of deepest, softest purple or blue, or pure white. Pausing to admire – for I love flowers – I have repeated on these lone wilds "Yea. Many a flower is born to blush unseen." All these, trees, vines, and flowers, are indigenous to our soil.

The main channels of the greater number of our streams do not flow through the centre of the bordering swamp, but flow close along highland and jutting shores on the one side and so pressing and laving continuously as to undermine and form caverns beneath the higher banks, or wash bare, at intervals, massive roots of some forest giant, deeply embedded in the soil close on the resisting shore. So flows the Saltkehatchie, and such is the topography at the approximate crossings, Broxton's and Rivers' bridges – about six miles apart.

To the latter point, my regiment, with other troops, was ordered to proceed, cross over, face about into battle line and – as we had done often and often – impose our inferior and now greatly enfeebled force in front of Sherman's overwhelming, invading hordes and impede their progress and entry onto the narrow strip of territory between Western South Carolina and Virginia – the sole remaining part of the Southern Confederacy east of the Mississippi River within our lines and still our own. "To hinder and impede," 'twas all that we could do, but this, our remnant of brave troops did and did gallantly.

An editorial in the *New York Tribune* of February, 1862, now before me, says:

"Let Unionists everywhere rejoice and take courage. A few days will bring us tidings of heavy blows struck from all sides at the defenses of rebellion. * * * The preponderance of men, arms and resources on the side of loyalty and the nation is so great that within two months – unless all signs fail – the kingdom of Jeff Davis will be a thing of the past and the gigantic treason of 1861 will soon be a hideous, guilty dream."

"All signs" failed and in February 1865, we stood facing in battle that "great preponderance in men and arms of the nation."

Arriving at Rivers' Bridge we took our position on the east shore, near which flowed the main stream. Our force consisted of the 32nd and 47th regiments of Georgia Volunteer infantry, one battery of light artillery, South Carolina troops, and a squadron – three or four companies – of the 3rd regiment, South Carolina cavalry. We were ordered to defend the main crossing at Rivers' Bridge and different points on the line extending on the east toward Broxton's and west toward Buford's bridges, giving us a line of front of about five miles. Our entire force did not number, at the time, more than 700 or 800 men.

Our position was a strong one, as the swamp was on the west side and about half a mile in width, through which the enemy would be forced to pass in his advance. We were ordered in case retreat became necessary to fall back across Lemon Swamp to New Bridge, on the Edisto River. Our guns were planted so as to command and sweep the long, straight, causewayed road in front; rifle pits on either side were manned by the infantry and dismounted cavalry, and thus we awaited the approach of those to many of whom, probably, the two remnants of the old Georgia regiments had extended very warm receptions on quite a number of occasions, and to be treated by our visitors in manner as of yore, to wit, a fierce advance, a recoil and manoeuvering ending in flank movements.

While we waited the citizens of the neighborhood were kind, generous and hospitable and seemed to rejoice in our presence. Numbers for miles around came and witnessed our drill exercises and dress parades. This was inspiring to the troops, but when I saw such manifestation of reliance and implicit faith on the part of these in our ability to defend and protect them, my heart was saddened by my knowledge of our utter inability to hold our position for any considerable length of time against the mighty hosts soon to be hurled upon our slender, unsupported lines. There were some citizens outside our lines, in the zone soon to be occupied by the enemy, who did appear quite independent.

At this time Capt. E. W. Hazzard was the ranking officer present for duty of his regiment – the 47th Georgia infantry – was in command of same. He was a tall, handsome young fellow, a gallant, fearless, splendid soldier, but modest and blushing as a bashful maiden.

Col Bacon, commanding the forces at one point, requested me one afternoon to ride down the line of swamp beyond the river in our front, eastward, and closely inspect for the distance of a mile or two the nature of the ground and get the "lay of the land," etc. (We anticipated a flank movement and dreaded it more than a square face-to-face fight.) He suggested that as Capt. Hazzard had the absent colonel's fine mount I invite him to accompany me. Hazzard accepted with delight, saying: "By George! Let's take along our canteens and see if we can't buy some milk or buttermilk when we leave the swamp and ride back along the highway."

After an unpleasant ride down the swamp for a couple of miles, scanning closely, inspecting and taking notes, we faced to the right and made for the public road, and came out of the woods directly in rear of a horse lot, with barn and stable, near the road. On the opposite side of the road was a neat, painted dwelling house, with nice paled yard in front. We rode around the lot and on reaching the road in front saw several ladies come on to the piazza of the house.

I said: "Hazzard, here is a chance to get our canteens filled."

"All right," he said, "let's try it."

But," I said, "You have got to do the talking."

"By George," he replied, "there are too many women folks there. Suppose we risk striking another house."

"No." I said, "We may not strike another house. Besides, if you notice, those parties are watching us closely, as if wishing to speak to us. Dismount and we'll face the music."

Hazzard, as usual when slightly embarrassed, began laughing. Hitching our horses, we entered the front yard and approached the steps, where stood one or two young ladies and one elderly, all good looking. Removing our hats, we bowed low to the ladies, but received only slight nods in recognition and no word of invitation to enter. Hazzard, with hat still in hand, began very seriously:

"Ladies, we have called up to see if we could buy some milk or buttermilk to take back to camp with us."

"Yes," quickly and sharply replied the eldest of the group. "Called up at the back of my lot for buttermilk? I saw you when you both came sneaking up out of the woods to the back of my lot, and when you saw me come out on the plaza then you came around here and pretend that you are after buttermilk. Why didn't you ride the road and stop at the gate and come in like gentlemen if you are after buttermilk? I had the horses locked up in the stables from just such sharp looking fellers as you two."

I glanced at Hazzard, and his face was crimson with blushes, but he recovered himself sufficiently to say:

"No, madam, you are mistaken." When he was headed off with the rejoinder:

"Oh, yes, of course, you'll deny it but, young man, you are after no good. I can look into your eyes and tell that you are the devil in a rye patch."

That was a telling shot and under it Hazzard went to pieces. He began laughing, and laughed, and could not utter a single word in reply. All laughed and as soon as I could control myself, I said, "My dear madam, you are mistaken. We don't want your horses." "Now just hold on," she said, "you needn't come with any slick lies to me. I see them long boots you've got on and the shiny spurs on your heels, and that gives you away as Wheeler-men, and I hear that they are as big thieves as the Yankees and will steal every horse they can get their hands on."

Hazzard was still laughing, but I replied, "No, madam, neither of us ever belonged to Wheeler's cavalry; we have horses of our own and either of us would shoot any man we saw trying to rob you of your horses. We are stationed at Rivers' Bridge, right on the road across the river, and would be glad to have you ladies come out to our dress parade any afternoon. We bid you good day. I hope our next meeting will be more pleasant than this." "No, hold on," she quickly replied. "Wait! Girls, go get some milk out of the dairy. I'm sorry I said what I did, but I do declare to gracious I thought that you was Wheeler-men."

Hazzard never comprehended or fully recovered from that "devil in the rye patch" allegation. We enjoyed many a good laugh over it afterward. Gallant soldier and true gentleman. We marched, fought, slept and ate together many a day and night. I clasped hands with him at the close of the war and never saw him again. He died in or near Georgetown, this State, a few years ago.

Col Bacon, Lieut. Finlay, of Macon, and I occupied, for sleeping, a little log cabin a short way down the riverside. Finlay placed a pole across one end of the floor and had the space between it and the log walls filled with dry leaves and pine straw, on which we rested quite comfortably, covering with our blankets. We had arranged to use a small plank house near the roadside, about a mile in our rear, as a hospital and to destroy the bridges in our front as soon as our outer line of pickets and videttes came in. And then our little army waited, watched and rested on ground soon to be stained with our blood, and where we well knew some of us would rest throughout all time – "Our warfare o'er" forever.

At length the enemy reached our point in his march and our little band of soldiers braced themselves for the unequal conflict. The enemy's approach was heralded by our returning cavalry pickets, who commenced crossing the river about noon. Maj Gen McLaws, commanding our division, had ordered Col Bacon to destroy the bridges on the approach of the enemy as soon as our forces in front were compelled to fall back upon our main line. The infantry companies forming our picket line in front on the west side of the river held their ground until about 3 o'clock in the afternoon, when they came in, closely followed by the enemy. Indeed, so closely pressed that it was with difficulty that the bridges could be destroyed after our men had crossed, the latter part of the work being done under a galling fire from the enemy.

The enemy swarmed in great numbers to the edge of the swamp, but our field pieces swept the road and our sharpshooters checked the movement through the swamp. They opened a hot fire upon our works and the battle was on. Every effort of the enemy to force a crossing was checked and they were whipped back onto their own side. Sharp-shooting continued throughout the afternoon and picket firing was kept up all night. The next morning repeated efforts were made by the enemy, in strong force, to force a crossing at several points, but our troops fought gallantly and drove them back at every point.

During the day we were reinforced by Findlay's regiment of Georgia troops – 16-year old boys, commanded by Major McGregor – and a brigade of Wheeler's cavalry, numbering only 250 men and commanded by Col Harrison, of Tennessee. Thus our force was increased to about 1,200 men and until afternoon we repulsed the repeated onslaught of the enemy. Many of them during the night before and under smoke of the firing in the day had worked their way far into the swamp, and screening themselves in every way possible, kept up a hot fire upon our lines at the main crossing and upon the guns of our battery. This advanced line the enemy endeavored constantly and persistently to reinforce, but many a blue-coat went down in front as many a brave fellow pressed forward.

The 32nd and 47th Georgia infantry were next to the road close to the battery. The great majority of our casualties occurred in those two regiments, as here the enemy's efforts and fire were centered. We were holding our position and could have held it until now against the force in our front, though 10 to 1 against us, if they had remained in our front and fought it out there.

About 3 o'clock in the afternoon Gen McLaws sent for Col Bacon, who rode rapidly back to near the house used as our hospital and there met

Gen McLaws. Col Bacon reported that he was holding his position, but invited and urged the general to take command in person. This request was prompted, of course, by military courtesy. Col Bacon was a gallant and capable officer, was making a splendid defense and had the situation well in hand, which Gen McLaws knew when he declined and informed the colonel that it was necessary to retire the whole line that night and he had to give his attention to other points. He said: "Keep them at bay until night and save your artillery and I will be perfectly satisfied."

Late in the afternoon the fighting became fierce, and although we were sustaining some loss, our troops were holding our position splendidly, when Col Bacon received notice that the enemy had effected a crossing below and above us at two points, and we could tell by the rapid, heavy fire below, east of us, that they were across. The time had come to save the troops and artillery. Col Bacon ordered that, as quickly as possible, four rounds should be fired from each piece in as rapid succession as possible and that the infantry near the battery should do the same. Under the dense smoke thus created the horses were run rapidly down to the battery, attached to the guns and succeeded in pulling them off with comparatively little loss. The troops to the left and right faced right and left onto the public highway and followed the artillery.

Early on the day of the fight the division surgeon came to Col Bacon for a detail of men from the cavalry to send out to impress wagons and teams to have in readiness to care for our wounded, and took upon himself the responsibility of arranging fully for them. The wounded, or most of them, were left without any special arrangement for their comfort or welfare. This neglect of duty on the part of that medical officer of high rank and the effect consequently on the helpless, wounded men who had so gallantly stood "behind the guns" was a fair sample of much of the conduct affairs in our army by some high, in authority, especially in the latter part of the service.

The Captain of Company C, of my regiment, was a handsome young citizen of Savannah, Ga., Joe C. Thompson, a son of Col Wm T. Thompson, editor of the Savannah Morning News, and author of the well known and widely-read book of ante-bellum popularity, "Major Jones Courtship." On leaving Savannah two years before for our campaign in the West Col Thompson pledged his son, Joe, and me in solemn promise "if either one should fall, the other should, at the earliest opportunity, inform him of the fact without regard to cost, pains or trouble."

At Rivers' Bridge, in the hottest of the fight in the afternoon, Capt. Thompson – Joe – went down, a minie ball striking him on the left cheek under the eye and crushing through, came out neat the angle of the jaw on the right side of his face. The young Captain was left for dead and was so reported in our "report" of the battle. At our first stop near Branchville, S. C., I kept my promise and wrote to my good friend, old Col Thompson, a long letter of condolence and sympathy, informing him of the death of his son, my friend and comrade.

On my first visit to Savannah, after the war, in the fall of 1865, while on my way to call at Col Thompson's home, I met Capt. DeWitt Bruyn, captain of Company E, of my regiment, and told him of my intended visit and expressed my dread of this meeting with the family on account of Joe's death. Bruyn threw his arm around my shoulder and said: "About face and march with me only a block. I want to show you some one and then you can pay your visit to Col, Mrs. and Miss Thompson."

We halted at the open door of an office and Bruyn said, "Go in." I stepped in, a man wheeled about toward me and I stood face to face within five feet of Joe Thompson, ex-captain of Company C, 47th regiment, Georgia volunteers, who had been "killed" at Rivers' Bridge. His face was disfigured and his speech affected, one eye gone, but – there he was. This young captain had, before our retreat, regained consciousness and, one of the favored, had been cared for and removed. He reached Augusta, Ga., and from there, finally, Savannah, and in chaotic condition of all things, was in his home rapidly recovering when my letter describing his death reached his family. He had married his pretty sweetheart, Miss Lizzie Gammon, and years after Joe told me that when at home, if feeling kind of blue and reminiscent, he would get out my letter of condolence to his father and read it aloud to his wife and children. But he too, is now on the other side of the river!

Our dead were buried on the knoll of ground near the battle ground where stood our hospital. They were collected and buried there close together by the good citizens of that community. A handsome stone monument has been raised above them, on which, carved within circling wreaths, are these lines:

"Soldiers rest! Thy warfare o'er.
Sleep the sleep that knows not breaking
Dream of Battlefields no more.
Days of danger, nights of waking."

Annually great numbers of citizens gather from different surrounding communities, and eloquent orations are delivered; patriotic songs sung and flowers are brought in profusion to deck the mound above the gallant men who fought and fell in the last line of defense on the soil of South Carolina.

Again had lives of many true and gallant men been uselessly sacrificed. We had again retreated from our chosen line of defense. Our backs were turned to our pursuing foes, who came with cannon and torch, dire threats and insolent boasting. Our State's Capital was surrendered without a struggle. South Carolina, home of my sires and pride of the South, was abandoned at the mercy of the eager, invading, vassal foe. Under crushing realization of those awful facts, here in our State, the "cradle of secession" was made the grave of my perished, last hope for success of our cause and salvation of our Southern Confederacy.

Through the darkness of the night we marched northward.

The Charleston Sunday News and Courier, Charleston, South Carolina, May 2, 1915

A CONFEDERATE SOLDIER'S MEMOIRS

MARCH, 1865 – NEARING THE END

(By Captain Ben S. Williams, Brunson, S. C.)

The ides of March, A. D. 1865, marked the closing of the fourth year of the bitter war between two sections of the United States, the North and the South, the Federal and the Confederate Governments. In both sections from millions of souls, in cities and hamlets, halls and huts, in churches and homes, in that dark hour of dearth and death, ascended prayer and petition for the blessing of the dawn of peace – prayer, though, in which was incorporated petition for victory, respectively. The men of the armies of Blue and Grey, "tenting on the old camp ground," sang around their camp fires of "many are the hearts longing to-night for the war to cease." The dawn of peace was then very near. At that period the awful drama was nearing its close, when the "war would cease," but many of the actors then upon the gore-drenched stage never hailed the dawn or rejoiced with those rejoicing when the war did cease. There were a few more acts of dire sequence and scenes of carnage before the final fall of the curtain.

In Virginia, the mere wreck of the proud army which, under Lee and Jackson, during the years of bloody strife had dealt the Federal army so many crushing blows, was surrounded by the mighty hosts of Grant and Sheridan like a wounded loin at bay, facing defiantly his advancing foes – and Jackson was not there. The remnants of command of the once splendid Army of the West, reinforced by several small bodies of troops from our coastal region, again under their old commander, Joseph E. Johnston, again faced Sherman's much more powerful and hitherto often met army in North Carolina. Johnston had collected a force of about 22,000 men against which were opposed three armies – Sherman's from South Carolina, Terry's from Wilmington and Schofield's from Kingston, North Carolina, numbering about 120,000, well fed, well equipped troops – with Johnston were not Clebourne and Walker.

Lee, with 35,000 half-starved men, was striving to defend near Petersburg thirty miles of entrenchments. Grant pressed against Lee with 125,000 well equipped troops and was as rapidly as possible concentrating all of the available Federal forces in the South for another and final "On to Richmond." Lee's only hope of continuing the struggle now so vastly unequal lay in abandoning Petersburg and Richmond, the long sought and most often fought for, and uniting his army with Johnston's in North

Carolina – and then – ? Johnston was preparing to resist and impair in every manner possible Sherman's advance through North Carolina to join Grant. Johnston's lean commands in dingy grey were anxious and eager to face again under command of Johnston the hosts of Sherman, as they had done often in Tennessee and Georgia.

This eager, animating spirit more directly from a passionate desire for revenge than from hope of ultimate success or thirst for future glory in victory won. There were no racial prejudices and hatred as between the bearded Slav Cossack and the helmeted Teuton; or as between Briton and Turk. The real issue was between Americans, natives of the soil, acquaintances, schoolmates and often kindred, in many instances close and occasionally of consanguinity of the same degree as between Cain and Able. But there was a burning desire on the part of the few remaining men of the Army of the West to wreak on Sherman's army vengeance in blood for wrongs deep and damnable. The opportunity soon came. On the 17th of March Johnston threw his compacted remnants of commands in Sherman's front at Averysboro and metaphorically, commanded "Halt!" He did not continue with the usual interrogatory of "Who goes there?" We knew in reply to Johnston's "halt" Sherman ordered "forward," and then "things began to happen."

As animating as our thirst for revenge was the enemy's pride of a year of success. Flushed with victory he came proudly, gloriously on, as if naught could check his progress or would dare attempt to stay his advance, yet with that caution in movement and carefulness of formation of rear support and flank protection secured by strength of numbers – that characterized all of Sherman's movements with which Johnston was so familiar and to which formerly so accustomed. Sherman knew, of course, that his force was greatly superior, numerically, to Johnston's, but seemed to realize that he fronted his former able competitor whose removal from command of the Army of the west near Atlanta by President Davis had been hailed with delight by Sherman, and his assaults on our lines were steady, gallant and repeated, but not fierce and reckless. We repulsed assault after assault until the enemy fell back in the dusk of the evening, leaving many dead and wounded in our front.

My regiment was hotly engaged and suffered quite severely. Some of the wounded were brought in and sent to the rear with our own wounded. We were gratified by results, but weary when night came on, and as soon as our line of skirmishers and pickets had been placed in front Major Hazzard – grown from a young lieutenant to captain, then to major – then in command of the regiment and I prepared for rest at the root of quite a large pine tree, its thick-leaved, branching boughs affording us some shelter from the cold drizzle of rain falling. Our preparation was Hazzard's thin rubber blanket on the damp earth, we on that and my thin rubber blanket on us for coverlet. The enemy was still giving us shot and shell from his artillery at a distance in the darkness. As soon as H. and I had nestled closely together on and under our narrow blankets Hazzard said:

"Don't you reckon we'll have the dickens to pay here in the morning?" ("Dickens" was about as vile a word as Hazzard ever uttered.) "No," I said, "only in the way of getting up and skedaddling to right or left to meet Sherman's flank movement." "I wouldn't be surprised," he said, after a moment's silence, "if you are right, but I wish that battery in our front would stop shooting those balls and shells over us and let us rest in peace." "No danger," I said, "they haven't got our range and their missiles go from 15 to 20 feet above us and that is evidence that the batteries firing on us this evening have been withdrawn and Sherman is moving. The constant random shooting is simply to deceive us into the belief that he is there for all night and ready for attack in the morning." "Right," said Hazzard, and the next moment I realized that he was sleeping.

I did not fall suddenly to sleep. I thought of the morrow. Hazzard and I had spent many hours together, pleasantly. Perhaps this was our last night on earth alive. The morrow would bring desperate strife for us somewhere. Hazard was gallant, reckless in action. Tomorrow night might find one or both on the field pale and cold as some of those brave fellows who had charged so gallantly now lying in front of where we had fought. I wondered if Hazzard was dreaming of the girl whose fair hands had fashioned so neatly the beautiful little pocket case of crimson and purple velvet containing a few needles, a few buttons, some thread, a small paper of pins and a pair of slender, silver plated scissors – a little present both beautiful and useful in camp. He had not been the possessor of the tasty little article fifteen minutes before I was admiring it while Hazzard read again, his face suffused with blushes – for he was exceedingly diffident – the letter accompanying the gift.

My own thoughts were gradually drifting into the mystic realms of Morpheus when quickly following the boom of a cannon in front there was a loud crash and jar close to our heads and instantly there rained down upon us what seemed a shower of hail stones, bullets, brickbats or something of that kind. A cannon ball had struck and cut its way through one side of our sheltering pine, raining down a shower of pieces of bark and splinters all over us. Hazzard was on his feet in an instant. In his half-awake state he quickly fell to his knees and catching hold and shaking me, asked hurriedly, "Are you hit?" "Are you hit?" He was under the impression that the enemy had attacked suddenly, had fired a volley and the balls were rattling all over and around us. The solid shot had struck at our heads at a height of about six feet above the earth. I did not rise, for I was not yet asleep, and quickly realized what had happened. Hazzard suggested that we at once change our quarters. "No," I said, "come back to bed. Don't you remember Jack Williams's dictum at Chickamauga – that a d___ cannon ball never strikes twice in the same place?" Before the dawn of day we were aroused under orders to move at once in the direction of Bentonville, Sherman's and Johnston's old tactics and practices – a blow, a side-step and another meeting.

The meeting at Bentonville was fierce and furious – one of the hottest in which I ever engaged. But before reaching that point I became principal in an incident the like hitherto not experienced by me – and I am glad to say never subsequently to date. I submitted without resentment to what Corpl Jack Newman used to term an "all-fired, genuine, teetotal cussing." On our line of march near the road we passed an old frame building, evidently an old church or school house. From the house there issued groans, cries, shouts of defiance, oaths and threats of hanging old __ __ Jeff Davis and every ____ rebel in the South. Seeing the surgeon of our regiment on the inside near the door, I rode apart from the line, dismounted and stepped inside the building, used, as I understood, as a hospital for the wounded Federals fallen into our hands. Listening and looking around I felt as if Dante could not have improved upon it as a picture of one of his compartments of hell.

Our surgeon was exerting himself with all the means at his hands and to the extent of his ability to alleviate the more seriously wounded and suffering. Straightening up from his bending over a poor fellow in blue, who had just breathed his last, he came to me near the door, "Denson," I said, "you seem to have in charge here a tough lot." "A set of the most infernal cusses, with a few exceptions, I ever saw," he said in low tones. "What is the matter with them?" I asked. "They have conceived the idea that we were whipped yesterday and are in full retreat to-day; so they dare, like cowards, to curse and yell at the men who thrashed them yesterday, whom they think are retreating, but who, as you are aware, are just beginning to put a whole lot more of them at the next bout in the same fix, and worse, as these fellows."

We walked down the aisle. The wounded were lying and sitting on the wooden benches, the cursing and yelling at the passing troops continuing, when suddenly a stout, bearded, villainous looking fellow propped up against the wall at end of bench, with shirt and pants dyed with blood pointed his finger, then savagely shook his fist at me and yelled out: "There's the ____ rebel ___ that put two pistol bullets in my side and thigh yesterday. I know you ____ you by the black feather in your hat. I don't know how I missed you. Good G___ don't I wish I had my gun now, you blankety, blankety, blankety, etc. etc. etc.," and yells from half a dozen joined in in cursing and dirty epithets hurled at me. I had turned with contempt from the crowd. Nearing the door, the surgeon walked with me. I was stayed by the upheld hand of a genteel looking corporal.

"Sir," he said, "I regret this low, dirty abuse and insult to which you have been subjected. While too low and contemptible for your notice, I am ashamed. The low blackguard over there, I am pleased to say, does not belong to my company or regiment and is unknown to me, but he disgraces our uniform." "He belongs to my regiment," replied a tall, fine looking Irish sergeant next to the young and gentlemanly corporal; "but he is a dirty devil, and I wish that the first bullet that struck him had cut his devilish tongue from his bloody head. Be jabez, if I was now only in reach of him I would smash his ugly mug to smithereens with one stroke of me fist." "Thank you, corporal!" I said, shaking hands with him, "and may your broken leg soon heal and may you be permitted soon to kiss your folks at home." "And sergeant," I said, "may your wounds heal rapidly and may you be spared to celebrate many a 'St. Patrick's Day in the Morning.'"

Poor, maimed fellows, helpless and suffering, both laughed, and while the corporal said, "Many thanks." The sergeant said "Good luck to ye!" While mounting my horse I heard the blatant blackguard inside cursing me and wishing for his gun.

I spurred forward to overtake and join my regiment: we were nearing Bentonville. Passing files and files of those grey-clad troops, moving steadily, briskly and buoyantly, I experienced a feeling of deep sadness as I thought of the useless sacrifice in front.

"For well I knew that ere the morrow, Some would sleep beneath the sod."

The Charleston Sunday News and Courier, Charleston, South Carolina, April 4, 1915

A CONFEDERATE SOLDIER'S MEMOIRS

MARCH – 1915 AND 1865

(By Captain Ben S. Williams, Brunson, S. C.)

March, 1915, Peace reigns in our United States of America. Thank God! Thundering cannon awaked the echoes of strife around Warsaw. Gathered not, now are beauty and chivalry with happy beating heats to music's "Voluptuous swell" in Belgium's ruined Capital.

The mighty nations of Europe are marshaled in battle's magnificently stern array, millions of civilized, educated, Christianized men are, metaphorically, clutching at the throats of millions of other men and in terrific strife for supremacy and victory are employing arson, rapine and all of the infernal atrocities of hellish war and reveling in bloodshed and death.

For many weeks, morn and midnight, have brought the signal sound of strife and, as if history is nearly repeating what history has said, near Waterloo again:

> "Morn brings the marshalling in arms: the day,
> Battle's magnificently stern array.
> The thunder clouds close o'er it which, when rent.
> The earth is covered thick with clay,
> Which her own clay shall cover, heaped and pent.
> Rider and horse, friend and foe, in one burial bleat.

March, 1915! And to our United States there is no alarm of war, no bugle call, no reveille nor long drum beat "to arms:" no crash of cannon at Vicksburg, Franklin or Chickamauga, Chancellorsville or Gettysburg, nor "By the flow of the inland river, where the fleets of iron have fled."

"All is quiet along the Potomac: and there is not on his outer, long vidette post, even one lone picket as a mark for a rifleman hid in the thicket." Thank God!

In 1865 the nations of Europe bided in peaceful repose while at that time the hitherto "United States" of America were rent asunder and bitterly contending for triumph. The two sections – North and South – had appealed for settlement of differences and contentions to arbitrament of sword and rifle and had ensanguined much of the soil of the south, where contending armies of the sections met in valiant conflict and desperately fought battles, with blood of the best men of both nations.

In March, 1865, the commands of the coast guards of Georgia and South Carolina and some of the fragments of the veteran regiments of the Army of the West were falling back through South Carolina into North Carolina. In my opinion, then and now, we were moving without definite or specific purpose or plan, other than that of eventually consolidating our forces with those of Lee in Virginia, and then (illegible). Councils of war by our leading officers were held frequently, in which were discussed status, possibilities and policy.

Our division under Major Gen McLaws, which had made a last stand in South Carolina, on the line of the Saltkehatchie River, in February, after a hot engagement of almost thirty hours, had been pressed back by Sherman's army and had fallen back and rested briefly, near Branchville, now took up line of march toward Cherhaw, S. C.

The morale of our troops even then was fine. While they could not possibly feel buoyancy in hope of striking "till the last armed foe expires," they seemed braced by determination to strike until the last, for "our altars and our fires."

The rank and file, bone and sinew – of the army were not thoroughly cognizant of existing conditions or the actual status. "Their's not to know or reason why; Their's but to do and die." Hence their cling to hope, their warm zeal, their willingness for service and unfaltering fealty to a "Cause" apparently doomed and already inevitably lost.

We journeyed happily on our pilgrimage toward Cheraw, as pilgrims journey toward a cherished shrine, as we were informed that there were vast stores of provisions in our commissariat for issuing on our arrival. So the burden of thought of the weary, hungry troops was "Oh, when we get there how happy we'll all be." The same old, old story, viz., hungry tired men, tramp, tramp, tramping! News of great stores of provisions at some point on our route – corn, meat, meal, flour, sugar, molasses, tobacco and, perhaps, a little whiskey.

A fat commissary and fat favorites on detailed service in evidence on approach, and if the enemy was not pressing too closely probably there would be issued to the men bacon and meal "rations for twenty-four hours," while to some of the officers might be given better fare, with a few extras as a relish or condimentum. If though the enemy was pressing closely and we were not ready for engagement the order would be, "Forward, men, close up," while quoth our commissary, "The damned Yankees don't fall heir to these goods," and soon huge volumes of smoke, like pillars of cloud by day in our rear would let us know that "the damned Yanks" had been deprived of that of which they stood little in need, but for which we were famishing.

We left Cherhaw, fighting back at the enemy as we departed. Why we tarried so in the near front of a force greatly superior in number, before which we were retreating, without disposition of our force to check or cripple him, thus hazarding capture, I did not then, nor do not now, understand. It appeared to me that the approach of the enemy and his attack was a surprise, or that our commanding officers, in a spirit of sheer daredevil recklessness, lingered close in front of danger and in the face of our formidable foe. It is barely possible that the too free indulgence in some of the aforesaid condimentum intensified the recklessness. (I had witnessed such recklessness on more than one occasion previously.) Well directed fire from a few properly planted batteries of our light artillery might have checked, confused and caused loss to the enemy on his approach, preceding and during which our infantry could have retired leisurely and in perfect order.

    Tarrying with the fragment of my old regiment until all prospect of a battle was past I rode forward to take charge of the quartermaster's train, which had been for some time in my charge. I found the train just going into camp only a few miles from Bennettsville. I was at once informed that we were entirely without forage for our horses and mules. I requested Lieut. Patterson, acting regimental quartermaster, to ride to quite a handsome residence, with large barns in lot, at not a greater distance than 300 yards from our camp, and procure sufficient forage for feed night and morning. The Lieutenant very soon returned and reported to me that "the boss of the mansion – a devilish fine-looking old fellow – on account of the late hour and everything locked up, objects to our going into his lot to his barns on any account, and he means it."

    I mounted and rode to the gate of the front yard and rapped on the gate. A negro serving man quickly approached me and I was informed that "Master says he don't wish to be further disturbed, as he has done sayed all he has to say."

    I dismounted and approached the front steps of the house, where I was met by an elderly, dignified gentlemen in full dress suit of black broad cloth. His manner was austere, but gentlemanly. The following conversation followed: "Sir," I said, "I regret to disturb you, and would not annoy you. I am temporarily in charge of the quartermaster's train and stores of the brigade to which I belong. I am proceeding to North Carolina by direction, and I am under orders to procure along our line of travel food for our stock. I am authorized to give vouchers and receipts for all food taken and payment will be made for same by our Government. To-night I am entirely without food for the stock under my care. We must subsist and I must procure food as ordered." "Yes sir," replied the old gentlemen, "but I object to your going into my lot before morning. It is a rule of mine to permit no fire or lights in my lot after sundown. Therefore, I cannot allow you in my lot until morning. I hope you understand."

    "If you will send a servant or direct me I will secure provisions and will not allow fire or light to be taken anywhere about your lot," I assured him. "No, Sir, I cannot allow you in my lot until morning." "My dear sir," I said to him, "you force me to adoption of very disagreeable measures. I shall go to your barns, as I must have food for our tired and hungry stock, but without fire or lights, and unless you furnish me your keys I shall force your doors open." "You will go without my keys," he said. "I presume you have authority and power and are aware you are in no danger." Stung by his last remark, I said to him: "Danger, sir, would be far preferable to performance of my present unpleasant duty, which you render doubly disagreeable by your unpatriotic obstinacy."

Riding swiftly back to camp I instructed Lieut. R___ to go with two waiting teams and several men and quietly force the locks and doors of barns barring entrance to the needed forage, and secure only enough for feed night and morning. He was met by the negro man servant, who with keys in hand, acted as guide and opened doors. I knew then there was someone behind the old gentleman in the house. The forage laden wagons returned and I had just gone out of a slight drizzling rain into my tent, and was, perforce sniffing the unsavory odor of frying rancid bacon in our camp when a tapping on my front tent pole attracted my attention, and the aforesaid negro servant man stuck his head inside the tent and, with a low duck of his head, handed me a neatly folded piece of paper. Then leaning an umbrella against the tent wall and grinning broadly, said: "They told me to lef this fer you and for me to hurry back." And without further waiting was gone.

I read in delicate handwriting of a lady, but signed in sterner letters by "The Boss of the Mansion" as Lieutenant P. had put it, a cordial invitation to "join us, at your earliest convenience this evening and dine with us. If delayed by any duty inform us at what time you can be here and we will, with pleasure, delay for your coming."

I met a very pleasant and cordial greeting, and was splendidly entertained by the splendid old gentlemen, his daughter, and her cousin, recently arrived from her home in Virginia. The young ladies were refined and beautiful. For me the evening was one of pure delight. Although I was made to feel somewhat jealous and envious because of the extravagant praise of the Virginia beauty given the young officers of the staff formerly of Gen J. E. B. Stuart. "Oh, they were knightly, incomparably, peerless." Etc. etc. When I suggested that we had some knightly and handsome staff, and other officers in our Army of the West, the young lady hostess assured me it would be absolutely fruitless to attempt any comparisons where her cousin presided or acted as judge. That Cupid had, some time since, pinned with his arrow her opinion and made her performance for one blinding as to the glowing and most distinguishing attributes of all others. When I suggested that some "young Lochinyar" might come "out of the West" and reminded her of the capture of the "fair Ellen" on the eve of the bridal, mine host remarked: "I am pleased to note that our young soldier guest is conversant with the writings of my favorite bard." I then instantly remembered that the name to the note of my invitation was "Mac- (something)" I think, McKay. I learned that mine host, Mr. Mc (illegible) was, or had been a banker in the City of Charleston, S. C. They were typical Charlestonians, of antebellum date.

I was invited to remain until morning, as a light rain was still falling, but fearful of contracting cold by sleeping in the warm, plastered room, I returned, at quite a late hour, to camp and moved onward at daybreak the next morning.

Further on our route our force was joined by the remnant of the once Splendid Army of the West. In Hood's ill-fated campaign from Atlanta, Ga., to Nashville, Tenn., the sacrifices of blood and men on the altar of country – and at the base of shrines of personal ambition – was great indeed. Oh, how my heart ached as I met again with those divisions, brigades and regiments with which I had fought through the States of Mississippi, Tennessee and down through Georgia as far as Atlanta, under Bragg, Johnston, and Hood, now mere skeletons of the original commands. Gallant officers once with these marching veterans were missing. Along with many of their commands they had "crossed the river." The gallant, impetuous Major Gen Walker had fallen in battle at Atlanta, Ga. The intrepid, Invincible Major Gen Cleburne commanding one of the best divisions of troops ever mustered on earth had fallen on the captured fortifications of the enemy, at Franklin, Tenn., with many of his men and officers strewn around and near him, among whom was South Carolina's gallant son, Brig Gen Gist. Looking at the awfully decimated command I could not restrain the wail of "Oh, Lord God of Hosts, what sacrifices! How great!" But my heart filled and warmed and every nerve of my being thrilled as these scarred, worn, faithful veterans separated and fighting at different points and localities for a year met again and cheered, and cheered, and cheered for joy at their reunion. I was aroused by the sudden leaping high, of big brave Lieut. Jim Chesser, close by me, and his ringing declaration as he "hit the ground" of "D___d if we can't whip Sherman again."

Soon after our reunion the troops were mustered for inspection and review. Present at the review was North Carolina's Governor, Zebulon Vance. As I saw the phalanxed files of veterans moving proudly and steadily as clockwork and wheeling into line with automatic precision and regularity – our cavalry in front on right, our batteries of light artillery lining several hills on left – approximately 20,000 troops again faint, pale – hope ever lingering to allure, whispering sweetly as echo of notes from midnight-zephyr swept strings of Aeolian harp, "Behold, Faith, abide. There is life in our loved land yet. "Nil Desperandum." Kindled into flickering flames a final glowing spark in my sad, desponding heart; but ere long to glimmer, fade and die. And in my soul I cried in the anguish of forlorn despair "Delusion, delinquent Hope, with these thorns and thistles away, you promised bright laurels and roses to-day." We were on the eve of our last battle at Bentonville, N. C., March 19, 1865.

The Charleston Sunday News and Courier, Charleston, South Carolina, November 19, 1916

Best Sign of Reunited Country

Captain Williams Points to Fraternal Spirit Among Northern and Southern Troops on Border
Relates Some Recent Reminiscences

(By Captain Ben S. Williams, Brunson, S. C.)

To the borderland of our United States of America there have gone thousands of our young men who stand a forbidding wall, a living barricade between a treacherous, threatening foe and our citizens' safety and our country's rights and honor.
The gallant young fellows constituting the commands of our National Guard hail from Maine and Florida, Pennsylvania and Georgia, Massachusetts and South Carolina, throughout the expanse of our whole broad land.

In case of battle the soil of fields of conflicts will be drenched with mingling blood of sons of the North and sons of the South. Of course these are plain facts and are thoroughly realized, yet, notwithstanding, when I read as news that "The Pennsylvania division encamped opposite to the South Carolina brigades, across the railroad," there flashes momently to my mind a picture of columns of blue-clad troops and lines of men in grey in these camps and lines of pickets and videttes respectively, along that line of intervening railroad guarding against surprise the resting troops awaiting the dawning of the morning with light sufficient for an advance, the charge and the carnage.

How plain in my memory are these scenes of my boyhood, as in reminiscence I recall them to view; the march, the encampment, the advance, charge and carnage in the meeting in conflict of the Grey and the Blue.

Instantly, however, vanishes the resting reminiscence, giving place in imagination to the scenes in camp of our khaki-clad soldiers, soldiers of one flag, one army and one country, enlisted to serve side by side and battle shoulder to shoulder, as brothers in defence of their country's rights in one common cause – soldier-sons of veterans of the Blue and soldier-sons of veterans of the Grey.

Prometheus, chained by Jupiter to the rocks of Caucasus, when released by Hercules, son of Jupiter, said: "The sire I hated but the son I love." We of the South, rising from the wreck of our "Lost Cause," in our own invincible might, struck off the chains of despotism that shackle us to the rocks of damnable "reconstruction" policies, and now standing in our pride and independence, can say of the sons of the veterans of the armies of the North phalanxed on the soil of Texas with the sons of the veterans of the armies of the South "their sires I fought but the sons, our soldiers, God bless them and crown them with victory."

Our war is over and all brave, true men have buried wrath and do scorn animosity. We thank God for the halo of glory crowning our part in the past. In the shade of the olive we thank Him for our happy, peaceful present. Under the blue canopy of His heaven, united we stand for any emergency in our country's future.

True, there are dimly smoldering embers deep down in the hearts and memories of a few of the active participants in the events of the "'60s." All then who engaged, on either side, were not saintly gentlemen. Occasionally one of the "old guard" is met who, a Lancelot in valor, in war, a Chesterfield in manners in peace, is no Moses in meekness in discussion of the past. In him a little stirring – the wrong way – of the smoldering embers will quickly kindle a sizzling blaze.

Evidence of these easily kindled flames was very apparent, unfortunately, at the grand reunion of the Blue and the Grey on the battlefield of Gettysburg recently. Knowledge and recognition of this potent fact of the part of thinking, discrete ones prompt now the suggestion of a halt and change of front in the proceeding of preparations for a meeting of the "Blue and Grey" veterans in a grand reunion and parade. In a Washington city, in the near future.

But, verily, "our war is over."

Apropos and in substantiation of this dictum I recall one or two minor facts, unimportant instances, "straws showing the way of the wind," coming within my experience of not long ago.

Two years ago I attended the grand reunion of the Confederate Veterans in the city of Jacksonville, Fla., a beautiful city, splendidly decorated and magnificently arrayed for the reception and entertainment of the various guests. Many were present. They came from every State of the Southern Confederacy. Many were feeble and decrepit; some on crutches, some with an empty sleeve, many showing plainly the marks and scars of war and battle, but – they were "present."

A few were vigorous and quite alive. I witnessed the old Virginia reel, danced according to ante-bellum code and practice by a dozen veterans and a bevy of beautiful young "lady partners." The old "vets" promenaded with amazing vigor and "balanced with partners" with ease, grace and beautiful alacrity. Many were ready for frolic, fun or fight, according to circumstances, as of yore.

During all the years past since our war epoch I have attended but few reunions of Confederate veterans. I have not sought notoriety or rank in post-bellum, quasi-military organizations.

When in '76 at the head of a band of gallant, determined citizens I had given my aid in redeeming my State from the ravenous prey of the white and black buzzards of "reconstruction," fattening on the very vitals of South Carolina and reveling in their iniquity and our ruin, I sheathed my sword forever – perhaps. But I was earnestly urged by many to attend the reunion in Jacksonville. Near and dear kindred whose homes are there insisted.

Of the 49 commissioned officers of my regiment, the only three, besides myself, living were to be there. Of the original one thousand and fifty rank and file of my regiment a majority of the 30 or 40 known to be living were expected there. Our living know and remembered that after Appomattox, on the eve of Johnston's surrender to Sherman in North Carolina, I saved from the wreck of our matter the old bullet-riven, shell-torn battle flag of my regiment. That refusing to surrender, I, with that furled flag and accompanied by four officers all well mounted, turned our backs upon the debris of our last main army of the South and rode westward toward the last lingering faint, lingering ray of hope in an army of twenty-thousand men in our Transmississippi (sic) department toward which our President and his staff went until capture.

My living comrades know that the saved battle flag was presented by my mother and other noble women to our regiment amid scenes of sanguine rejoicing and sparkling splendor; the one under which my father as colonel rendered his service and life; the one that waived in victory in many sanguine fields, waving in the deadly strife over comrades living and dead.

My comrades, aware that the flag was in my possession, appealed to me. "Meet us there with the old regimental colors, so dear to us, that we may once more clasp hands with you and again look upon and touch our dear old flag before we cross over to the "other side of the river."

Great God of our once proud and mighty hosts, could I neglect such a plea? Could such an appeal have reached me from the "other side of the river" I would have stormed its tide in response to the call.

The Jacksonville papers had "caught on" and they published my coming with the old battle flag, and that temporarily unfurled banner of the "Stars and Bars" was the cynosure of thousands and thousands. Often did aged veterans stand still and gaze in silence at its tattered folds, then pass their sleeves across bronzed cheeks that never blanched in fiercest battle fray. Time again did I stand, absolutely voiceless, while gentle women would clasp and fondly fold in loving embrace and moisten with tears the old flag.

Many citizens of the North, in Florida for the winter, delayed their return home in order – as a lady of the State of New York expressed it – "to see the fragmentary remains of the army which had eclipsed the gallantry of the charge at Balaklava and equaled the glory of the stand at Thermopylae."

While at the steps of the beautiful Windsor Hotel, awaiting the car of my brother, who has been for many years a zealous worker and an active factor, holding the rank of general, in the organization of Confederate Veterans, I was holding my flag, not open or flauntingly, but folded and across my arm after hundreds had viewed it. There was a group of a dozen or perhaps twenty standing near me, when an elderly couple came down the steps of the hotel on to the pavement near me. They descended slowly, the man stepping cautiously, aided by a walking-cane, while his companion, much steadier, apparently held on, as if to support more than for support to a part of an arm in a half-empty sleeve. The dress and manner of the handsome old couple indicated wealth and culture.

Arriving in front and near me the man quickly halted and exclaimed with animation, "Wife, as I live there is an old Confederate battle flag; war-torn and time-worn, but still in evidence!" "Sir," he continued, saluting with his cane as an officer salutes with his sword, "was that flag a battle flag of soldiers of the South in the war of the rebellion?"

"Sir," I replied, returning his salute, "this old flag was the battle flag of a regiment of soldiers of the South in the war of repulsion of invaders of the Southern Confederacy."

"Pardon, my dear sir," he said, bowing and smiling, "I meant no offense. That term is commonly used up in Massachusetts, where I dwell."

"Granted, sir," I replied, "but it is a term to which we decidedly object down in South Carolina, where I dwell."

"Shake," said he, placing his cane under his half-arm and extending his right hand, "the war is over and South Carolina and Massachusetts have ere this, disagreed but always got around together, all right."

"Fine, fine," said the lady, her dark eyes beaming, "fine for South Carolina and Massachusetts."

"She is of Virginia," said the soldierly looking old gentleman, "and it was some time after our war and my recovery from the quite severe punishment (and he rapped with his cane upon an artificial leg and shook his half empty sleeve) inflicted for my 'invasion,' that she would consent to terms of peace and our union."

"Will you kindly let me see the flag unfurled," quickly asked the lady. I handed her the corner of the flag to hold. Ungloving her hand first, she caught hold and we let its folds unfurl. Instantly there rang out from a band not far in front the dulcet, soul-inspiring strains of "Dixie." I saw the fair hand on the flag tremble and the instant flush upon her cheek pale as if by death and as she gracefully released to me her gentle hold upon the flag I saw her soulful eyes brimful of tears.

"Wife, wife, come," said the maimed veteran husband, "Let's see the procession. Our war is over and as our Immortal McKinley said, 'We were all brothers anyway.'"

In that tender, trembling hand-clasp, that heart-blood flush and succeeding death-like pallor of cheek, those dimming tears, I imagined evidence of memory of scenes in romance, memory of courses in love, memory of anguish in tragedy and grief in woe.

On the outer edge of the small group around me stood two men, near each other, who had attracted my attention by the strange manner in which they bent forward and gazed at the flag when unfurled at request of the lady. Their look did not express pride or admiration, neither scorn or indignity but was rather of curiosity, interest and surprise.

The line for marching had been formed and at the "head of column" the bugle was sounded "forward." I was listening to the familiar notes which brought back the "light of other days" to me when the two men stepped close to me and gave the military salute. They were of widely different type in physique. One was tall, bent by age, with long gray beard, of dark complexion; the other erect, of smaller stature blond complexion.

"Was that the flag of your command, sir?" asked the elder, bearded man.

"It was," I replied.

"Were you in the army of the West or of Virginia?" he asked.

"Army of the West," I said.

"Well, by George, that flag has been where hot work was going on. Were you at Chickamauga and Lookout Mountain and Missionary Ridge?"

"Yes," I said, "and at Altoona, Dalton, Resacca, New Hope Church, Pine and Kennesaw Mountains, and on down to Atlanta."

"We, sir," said he, "we were in every one of those engagements. My name is Mills, and I was captain of Company K, 84 Illinois infantry, 1st division, 17 corps, and United States army. My friend here is Mr. Ellett, of Company E, 10th Illinois infantry – the bloody tenth – and I wouldn't be surprised to know that we had made some of the holes in that flag. But, by George," he continued before I could reply, "while we were making holes in your flag you were making holes in my men, for at Rivers Bridge, in South Carolina, I lost 16 men of my company in one advance movement to the right of the road as we approached your works. We shot the flagstaff in two and then caught hell as we tried to go forward."

"Well, sir," I said, "I am satisfied. I am pleased to tell you this is the flag that was shot down at the point you designate and the men behind this flag were those who put the gallant 16 poor fellows of your company, along with quite a number of others, out of business at that point in the Rivers' Bridge engagement, for we occupied the position you so exactly describe."

"Well," said he, "our war is over. Let's shake."

My reply to his invitation to "shake" I fear might be considered, under the circumstances, somewhat rude as I demanded to know first if he had allowed his men to indulge in the stealing, house-burning, woman-insulting campaign characterizing Sherman's march through Georgia and South Carolina, but he had warmed my blood, slightly, by his first remark.

When the gallant old captain exonerated himself by a dignified, spurning, spirited denial, we shook hands. Soon after reaching home I received a very courteous and interesting letter from the other man, Mr. Ellett, "of the bloody 10th." He pleaded for a picture of the flag and enclosed a bill of money for payment of expense. My reply letter contained the bill of money and a promise of the picture.

I have received several very interesting letters from Mr. Ellett since. Last spring I received a brief communication from him saying, "I am sending you by today's express a box of oranges from my grove at Fairview, Florida. Hope you will enjoy them. They are from my choicest trees." The following day I received, express prepaid, a box of the most delicious fruit from "the enemy," my friend Ellett, which I greatly enjoyed.

I am glad I did not kill Ellett, while fighting the "bloody 10th Illinois," and I am very glad also that Ellett of the 10th Illinois did not kill me.

More recently, in reply to my invitation to him to come across here and attend with me as my guest the annual ceremony and decoration of the graves of the Confederate soldiers at a monument reared to those who fell in battle at Rivers Bridge, near my home, he wrote:

"It would give me great pleasure to accept your invitation and be with you in the ceremonies of the occasion, but we are in the midst of our packing up and preparation for our move to our summer home. But give my love to your old boys who may be present. I didn't use to love 'em a bit, but I respected them greatly, I had to." Those who truly participated therein. Our war is over. Those who truly participated therein bear no malice.

Our hearts now are with all of our boys on the border and if in a struggle with a foreign foe, which now seems to threaten, inevitably there arose danger of our boys' defeat there are still some of us of the Grey and some of those of the Blue ready and willing to go and give them a sample of "old-time" action.

Ben S. Williams

Hampton County Guardian HAMPTON, S. C., Wednesday, September 19, 1923

CAPTAIN WILLIAMS' BEGINS HIS WAR ARTICLES FOR GUARDIAN

*E*ditor of the Hampton County Guardian:
   I have been earnestly requested by my young friend, the editor if the Hampton County Guardian, to furnish the Guardian for publication, some of my Memoirs as a soldier in the war of the '60s – a period of four years of bitter war, dire carnage and awful destruction between North and South, in our own, our native land.

   At date of 1860, bitterness of feeling on the part of both sections, North and South, of our country was intense. Agitation and heated public discussion of differing interpretation, different construction and conflicting views of provisions of our National Constitution and the adoption of political policies in accordance respectively with said divergent views fanned the flame of war the naturally emotional excitement and bitter prejudice engendered by eager factional contention.

   The ensuing war between the sections, The North and West and the South (the troops from Iowa, Indiana, Illinois and Ohio were the best fighters in the Federal army) was of vastly disproportionate ratio as to men, ammunition, equipment, factories and world credit; also on the part of the United States a small standing regular army of trained troops.

   The South was absolutely unprepared for war; deficient in all essential effects save chivalric spirit of her sons and the heroism and Spartan-like fealty of her daughters.

   The act of greatest wisdom and stupendous importance in the administration of Abraham Lincoln as "war president" of the United States was the forcing of war on the seceding states of the South immediately, before preparation by the South for defense could begin. By overwhelming numbers of Federal troops the states of the South were invaded. "The despot's heel was on our shore; his torch was at our temple door." The men of the South sprang to the defense of their soil, their homes and firesides and all that is dear and sacred on earth to man and woman.

   At some time in the future a true narrative of the causes and events of our war will be recorded and as history, handed down to future generations. All true sons and daughters of the South would hail with pride the emblazoning of such record on the sands of our time.

   The States of the South seceding from the U. S. government formed a Confederacy of States known as the Confederate government, by name of the "Southern Confederacy." All volunteers for resistance to invasion of our soil by troops of the North were with all possible dispatch formed into military companies, squadrons, battalions, regiments, brigades, divisions, corps, these comprising the armies of the Southern Confederacy.

Between the invaders and our troops many hard battles on land were fought in several states west of South Carolina – Kentucky, Mississippi, Tennessee and Georgia. On those battle grounds the life Blood of thousands of brave men on both sides drenched the soil of those states. North of South Carolina, Virginia was invaded by a far greater number of troops than either state of the Southern Confederacy and a greater number of important battles were fought on Virginia's soil, which became the theater of the mighty struggle.

At the battle of Gettysburg, Pa., Lee failed, as did Napoleon at Waterloo and the fate of the Southern Confederacy was sealed. We had fought hard and long for a cause we could not save. At Gettysburg "somebody blundered."

Only a few minor engagements of troops in battles occurred on the land of South Carolina. Heavy bombardments of our forts and batteries on our coasts were made. The first land engagement was on James Island, near Charleston, June 10, 1862. The 47th Ga. Regt. of Infantry, (1,000 in strength) was the only troops on our side engaged. They lost heavily. I was in the engagement. On the same island at Secessionville, June 16th another land engagement in which our troops were victorious. I was in that engagement. Attempts by several detachments of Federal troops were made to cut the Charleston to Savannah R. R. at Pocotaligo and Coosawhatchie. These attacks were met and the Federal troops were driven back by our troops. Our coast was carefully guarded. The most important land engagements in South Carolina were Honey Hill, November 30, 1864, and Rivers Bridge, February, 1865.

Presuming that the readers of the Guardian would be more interested in battles fought in South Carolina than elsewhere and in compliance with request of the Guardian's patriotic editor, I shall endeavor to give an account of one of these battles in the Guardian next week.

BEN S. WILLIAMS

Hampton County Guardian HAMPTON, S. C., Wednesday October 1, 1924

CAPT. B. S. WILLIAMS' WAR REMINISCENSES

Mr. Editor:
In writing my reminiscences as a soldier in the army of our Southern Confederacy for publication in your columns, it is not my intention to write of battles fought, of marches made, of army maneuvers, of my estimate of many of our commanding officers of high rank and my knowledge of the causes of winning and losing victory essential to our ultimate success. In years gone by, I spent considerable time in writing of the matters and events mentioned. They are recorded and may in the future be used. Slight reference to some of the aforesaid events is occasionally by me made.

In these writings of my war reminiscences, I would confine myself in narration to matters of personal interest, experience, events and action.

On the 9th of April, 1861, I, delicate, tenderly reared youth between 17 and 18 years of age, closed my books at school and with several classmates, volunteered for service in the ranks of the Confederate Army. In the rifle company of which I became a member were two of my classmates, John W. McGowan and John H. Smith. They were first cousins and eldest sons of widowed mothers. They were older than I. There came into our company, from a distance, an elder first cousin of the two mentioned, John M. Smith. He left a beautiful young wife and his widowed mother at their home; he, an only son. It would now be and was then, hard to find three as fine and fine appearing young citizens and soldiers as the trio of cousins, all Johns. They were in the company and camp "off duty" known only as "John M.", "John H." and "John W." John the elder was a splendid specimen of manly beauty (if man is ever beautiful.) His form, features, complexion, expression and bearing were faultless. He was proud and reserved in manner, dignified but courteous. The three Johns and I were messmates. We were housed in small picket tents, two only in a tent. John M. insisted in tenting with me and notwithstanding the difference of five or six years in our age, we became close, fond friends.

After drilling six or seven months in the casemates of Fort Pulaski in siege artillery drill and in the court of the fort in infantry drill, our company was sent up the Altamaha River to guard Sansavilla Bluff and prevent the destruction of the railway leading from Savannah to Jacksonville. Soon after reaching that point, I received from our War Department at Richmond, a commission as first lieutenant and orders to proceed at once to Savannah, Ga., for assignment to place. The 47th Regt. of Infantry, in which I was placed, was soon ordered to Mississippi and it was long ere I saw anything of any one of my old rifle company of the 25th Ga. Infantry.

After our battles and campaigning down through Mississippi and Tennessee, we were again in Georgia. We had abandoned much of our inestimably valuable territory in Georgia, but were still in a section of country where ranges of mountains and hills and deep streams of water afforded us positions favorable for resistance and repulsion; positions from which an army properly posted and well commanded can scarcely be driven.

We had withdrawn from our position near New Hope church and were carefully marching and counter marching in counter action of the enemy's very cautious maneuvering in hi advance toward Marietta. We were attacking and driving him at one point, staying his advance at another point, causing him to halt, entrench and flank, sometimes in wide detours.

Halted near the roadside on one of these occasions, to permit the passage of troops down on our left, my command was resting, when the 25th Ga. Infantry filed steadily by us. Recognizing the regiment, I mounted my horse and joined Col Winn, commanding the 25th and Adjt. Lester, both old friends. Their regiment halted, fronted and stacked arms for rest just beyond us. Riding back down the line, I dismounted when I came to Co. F. and shook hands with the men of the company. The ranks had been greatly thinned since I bade good-bye, one year before at Sansavilla. At this, my first meeting with the Company I quickly noticed that John W. and John H. were among those I missed. John M. informed me that both had been killed in battle. He was as handsome and proud in his bearing as ever but I noticed a light, an expression in his eyes, never seen by me before. Bidding all good-bye, I moved toward my horse, near, and John M. walked with me. Preparing to mount, I extended my hand; he clasped it in both of his and said: "Not good-bye, but au revoir, as soon as I can get permission I will walk over there and see you. I have something to impart." "All right," I said, "then au revoir, but hasten your visit as we will remain here not much longer than an hour." He soon came to where I was lying resting in the rear of our line. I well remember his haughty but courteous bearing, his proud and elastic step. Reclining near me in the shade, he confided to me his distress. He began: "I have for some time past been looking, watching and almost praying to meet you, knowing your regiment was here and had been placed in our division, Outside of my company, I know no one in the army and did not wish to confide with Uncle Madison, his captain. I know you and love and trust you and felt assured that you would not let your rank of office bar my approach to our former friendly intercourse and confidence." "No," I said, "speak freely, John M., I am your friend and your trust is safe in my keeping. My rank makes no difference. 'A man's a man for a' that.'" He continued, "Since the falling in battle of the two boys we knew so well, John H. and John W., I have been lonely and restless and at times felt very much like following them to the beyond. In fact in our fight on the 27th, I tried to get hit, but afterward, remembering my dear wife at home, I felt ashamed of my foolhardy conduct. But for the past few days I have lived

and moved in what seems to be a supernatural sphere and God alone knows how I suffer. In bivouac or camp, however worn or fatigued, I cannot sleep. As I close my eyes to sleep, invariably there appears before me, beckoning to me, clearly and plainly outlines as I ever saw she, my wife all white-robed and deathly pale. Sometimes I drop quickly to sleep, only to be awakened by the strange vision and repeatedly the last few nights, I have waked to find myself sitting up, my eyes straining into the darkness and my arms outstretched in an effort to clasp her – not in a loving embrace, but to grasp, support and shield what, so plainly appears to me, her trembling, quivering form. Great God! I cannot much longer stand the strain. I must end it, if in death." And he sprang quickly to his feet. "Sit down, John M." I said, "and calm yourself. When did you last hear from home?" "More than two months ago," he replied, "and I believe my wife is dead." "What do you intend doing?" I asked. "Why I so wished to see you," he replied "was to advise me. I must see my wife in life or in death. I could quit and go home as many are doing, but I would rather die than desert. Tell me what to do, my true and trusted friend and I will abide by your decision and advice, so help me God. I realize my present unfitness to judge as to what is best to do, even had I the privilege of acting in accordance with my judgment. I could easily reach home, but I will stay and sacrifice my life, as I believe we are all now doing in a hopeless cause, before I would cowardly sneak away. If you say so, I will start within this hour; hasten home, spend one day only and return with all dispatch and report immediately to you and rejoin my company. To you I pledge my word as a friend and my scared honor." Reaching across and taking his hand in mine I said to him, "No dear friend, I sympathize with you in the depth of my heart and would risk my life in your relief, but I too, must preserve my honor. I cannot tell you to go. I will, as soon as possible, see your captain and Col. Winn and try to get you off duty for a few days, when you can honorably carry out your program." As he grasped my hand his eyes filled with tears, I heard far down on our left a bugle call of "Forward" then nearer the roll of a drum and another and another. Both we rose. Standing for a moment with hands clasped, he pointed with his left and said: "See, the 25th is falling in to move. I must go. Good bye, Ben and God bless you" and dashed rapidly way to take his place in line.
(Continued next week)

BEN S. WILLIAMS

Hampton County Guardian HAMPTON, S. C., Wednesday, October 8, 1924

CAPT. B. S. WILLIAMS' WAR REMINISCENSES

Brunson, S. C., Oct 6, 1924
Mr. Editor:

As regiment after regiment filed by to take position on our left, the troops appeared in fine spirit. There was no apparent lack of what is known in the military as spirit-de-corps. The trained warriors in gray seemed anxious, eager for the closing in, in the final struggle, the decisive battle between the contending face to face armies of Johnston and Sherman for victory and undisputed possession of our territory in the State of Georgia.

Johnston, with splendid army well "in hand" sought position and opportunity for the finale, the military climax. Sherman, with numerically superior forces, strategically eluded the awful issue. Had these two armies closed there in direful strife for "victory or death," beside historic record of the result, the charge at Balaklava and the stand of the Spartan band at Thermopylae would pale in insignificance. It would have been a "fight to the death"; either victory of annihilation of the last gray column of Johnston's army. The decisive battle was expected daily, hoped for and prayed for by thousands of our side – it never came.

The day following the time of meeting with my friend and fine comrade and his imparting of sad circumstances, there was hot and continuous skirmishing along our entire division front. At times the ringing cheers and yells and rolling volleys of fire denoted fierce, close fighting. The day after was comparatively quiet and my command was withdrawn from the front and moved farther right where we expected to "catch h___ and a whole lot of it in the morning," as Jack Williams expressed it. (Jack generally prophesied truly.) Late that evening I rode to Stephens' brigade and found the 25th Ga. in line but not engaged. Reaching Co. F., Captain Madison Smith met me, grasping my hand tightly, but in perfect silence. I glanced hastily down his company line and missed several of the men I had seen in ranks two days before. I did not see John M. and asked of the Captain, "Where is John M. Smith?" The great broad-shouldered, deep chested, bearded, stern warrior captain for some moments did not, could not reply. Still grasping my hand he said in broken, halting voice, "Poor fellow, the last of my three brave and gallant nephews. He was killed yesterday." "Where and how?" I asked. "We were whipping the Yankees out of the woods; he was in the front of the fight; a mini ball." "Where was he struck Captain?" I inquired. Placing his forefinger in the center of his forehead, he replied, "Just as plumb centrally there as you could have placed your finger. He never knew he was hit."

With no other word I turned and rode sadly back to my own command.

It was night and the troops were soon resting and sleeping. All was comparatively quiet, and as I rested with my back on earth, my saddle for a pillow, I thought, oh that I had detained my dear friend, the gallant, chivalrous young soldier, that I had kept him by some means, out of that last furious engagement.

I looked up at the silent stars in the heavens and wondered was the gallant, chivalrous, spirited young soldier now with his loved young wife? He could not see here "in life" without sacrifice of honor, truth and manhood. He "would rather die than desert." Was he, with her "in death"? He had said "I must see her, in life or in death."

The deep vaulted canopy of the clouds was clear and of azure hue. The stars in their soft light glimmered, and I wondered if beyond "in the infinite meadow of heaven where blossomed the beautiful stars, the forget-me-nots of the angels," there was a Heaven. I wondered if there were angelic hosts there, and if personal recognition was granted. Darkly hung the impenetrable veil which obscures all futurity from mortal vision. I wondered if ere the glow of sunset on the morrow I would know. There would be, in the interim, many other sacrifices of lives upon the altar of our Cause. The soft refreshing air wafted down the mountain-side was cool and soothing and while still gazing upward at the silent stars I was relieved from woe and human cares by "death's deep counterfeit, silent sleep."

BEN S. WILLIAMS

Hampton County Guardian HAMPTON, S. C., Wednesday May 28, 1924

CAPT. B. S. WILLIAMS' WAR REMINISCENSES

$\mathcal{D}$ear Mr. Editor:
When sometime ago, I began writing for publication in your columns my "reminiscences" of our Confederate war, I contemplated confining my pen to transcription of scenes and occurrences transpiring in South Carolina while my command was on duty in this state. The extent of the field of action of the 47th Regiment Georgia Volunteer Infantry to which I was assigned on receiving my commission as first Lieutenant, early in '62 – after serving as a non-commissioned officer in infantry field and siege artillery, beginning April 9th, 1861 – was the Big Black River, near Vicksburg, Miss., to Bentonville, N. C., and yet we were on duty and in action in South Carolina near the beginning and the end.

The 47th Regiment was organized and commanded, until his death Sept 1863, by my father, a South Carolinian with generations of South Carolina ancestors and many of the officers and men of the 47th were of South Carolina stock and ancestry. The names of many in the Regiment denote this fact. Of the officers, Col Williams, Lieut. Col. Edwards, Maj. Cone, Co. A., Capt. Comer, Co. B, Lauren, C. Williams, D. J. Lawton Singleton, E. Capt. Phillips, Lieut. Osteen. F. Capt. Latimer, Lieut. Patterson, G. Capt. Kennedy, H. Capt. Aiken, Lieut. Hazzard, Lieut. Norton, K. Capt. Cone.

The opportune arrival or presence of this command in South Carolina in time of sore need appears to me now as wonderful, and I can conscientiously assert – in no spirit of boastfulness or braggadocio – that the 47th Georgia Regiment took part in a great number of land engagements and lost a far greater number of officers and men on South Carolina soil than any other command of Confederate troops.

Date and place of engagements in South Carolina: James Island, June 10, 1862 (attacked alone and lost heavily.) Secessionville, June 16, 1862. Detached from army at Atlanta and hurried to Johns Island and attacked the enemy before daylight July 1864. Engagement at Honey Hill, Nov. 20, 1864. Rivers Bridge, Feb. 3, 1865, at Tulifinny Dec. 9, 1864. Our causalities were: killed and wounded in S. C., one Major, 4 Captains, 2 Lieutenants: non-commissioned officers and privates 118. Of the officers the Major severely wounded, unfit for further service, Two Lieutenants killed, two severely wounded and unfit for further service.

Several years ago while writing a series of reminiscences of our war, which were published by the *Charleston Sunday News and Courier* and the Richmond Va. "Times Dispatch" a lady of Virginia wrote me concerning subject matter of one of my articles and asked, "How do you retain the incidents related for such a length of time?" The same question was asked me at a Rivers Bridge meeting recently, by a very intelligent lady who reads the *Allendale Citizen*, and says she is "preserving the articles as historic data."

I have a little volume of abbreviated notes kept by me during my service in the war, this is at hand for reference; such reference is necessary only occasionally, as many of the incidents of my soldier life are plainly discernible to me on memory's tablet.

With closed eyes, in my mind's portraiture, I see plainly the form of each of the 49 officers and many of the 1,000 men in the ranks of the companies of my regiment. How plain in my memory are these scenes of my young manhood as in reminiscence I recall them to view, the march, the encampment, the advance charge and the carnage in the meeting in conflict of the Gray and the blue.

As "historical data" I will relate an occurrence unique, unprecedented in all the tactics of our military record during our four years of warfare. This occurrence in South Carolina in the latter part of the year 1864, while we were guarding Charleston from attack by way of Johns and James Islands. (To Be Continued)

BEN S. WILLIAMS

Hampton County Guardian HAMPTON, S. C., WEDNESDAY, JANUARY 23, 1921

CAPT. B. S. WILLIAMS' WAR REMINISCENSES

*E*ditor Guardian:
I am in receipt, from several sources, requests to "write more about our war"; especially about the battles fought in South Carolina. One of the most intelligent ladies in Hampton County, who was a little child in her home in Charleston, S. C., when her father volunteered to help fight the battles of the South says: "give us more of our history which should be one of the most prized assets. Be assured that many read your reminiscences with much interest and pleasure."

Another, dwelling beyond our state's border (Who evidently reads the *Hampton County Guardian*) "I note with regret that for some time past your writings of engagements in our war, in S. C. have failed to appear in your county paper. I am a South Carolinian. Please tell us of other battles. Your account of the battle of Honey Hill was very interesting. My Father knows you and was in that battle.

I am pleased to be understood as writing only of the battles on South Carolina soil, in which I was actively engaged.

That "war is hell" is incontrovertible, an indisputable fact stamped on the mind and implanted on the memory of many living in South Carolina today who experienced "hell on earth" along the line of march of troops of Sherman's invading army. General Sherman was not the originator of the terse phrase quoted above, but the adaptation of his military tactics to his conception of the text was close and unmistakable. Yet Sherman was not "all bad." I could relate an incident occurring in this immediate neighborhood not one mile from where I am now writing illustrative of his personal integrity, benevolence and magnanimity. I, far away at the time of the occurrence, have ever since, felt a spark of admiration and entertained one tender thought of Gen. Wm. Tecumseh Sherman.

From a strictly military standpoint in time of war Sherman's policy though cruel and barbaric was a wise policy, because it was a winning policy. In actual warfare victory is the acme of hope and "all is fair in war," the slogan Sherman used steel and powder to cut and blast the way, crushed as with a sledge hammer opportunity and material for revival of power and continuances of resistance. He blasted, burned, wrecked and ruined in the territory of his enemy. He won.

Gen Robert E. Lee marched his splendid army of Confederate troops, than which no better were ever marshaled over into Pennsylvania. The citizens sought safety in every conceivable place of hiding, but on hearing that orders had been issued to those grey clad soldiers to destroy not, burn not, injure not, insult not, they came forth and vented their spite against the men in grey in hurling epithets, waving flags etc. We marched with dignity and decorum, were tender and chivalric in our enemy's country. Lee lost.

On Christmas day, just passed, I felt my brain and heart full of memories of old, and teeming sad recollection filled my soul. Somehow I felt as I wanted to hear again the rolling drum-beat and blasting bugle call "to arms," to see again the starry Southern Cross floating and waving above those phalanxed lines of grey, of old and hear our martial airs followed by the deathly stillness – the calm before the tempest that precedes the cannon's roar and the clash and din of battle.

Again returned the scenes of those days of my youth, when a soldier of the army of the Southern Confederacy. Again I saw the forms and faces of my comrades by death and parting long estranged.

"They came, in dim procession led
The gallant, faithful, heroic dead;
As firm each step each brow as gay
As if we parted yesterday".
All, only a vision; phantoms of reverie – they come no more
Like the dew on the mountain, like the foam on the river.
Like the bubble on the fountain, they are gone forever".

The last Christmas of the war I spent on the coast of South Carolina. My regiment had been ordered from Honey Hill just after the battle to Tulifinny – pronounced in Indian vernacular Tu-le-finne. Relative to same I will copy a few sentences of a letter now before me written sixty years ago dated "In bivouac at Tulifinny, S. C., Dec. 1864" by my younger brother who had been in the army not quite two years and who since, went through the Spanish-American war as a Surgeon in the U. S. army to our mother refugeeing in the southern part of Georgia. He wrote. "We were ordered from James Island, where we arrived Nov. 30th just in time to pitch into the enemy. We drove them back to their landing place. The 47th (my regiment), some Georgia militia, several South Carolina cavalry companies and one or two batteries of artillery were the troops of our side engaged."

"The 47th lost twenty odd killed and wounded. Ben was in the hottest of the fight, but as usual was not touched – thank God. The enemy's loss was great, at least two hundred men were left dead on the field and a lot of battlefield plunder behind. We were ordered hurriedly to Coosawhatchie and our regiment skirmished all day with a force of the enemy. Our loss only three. Ben unhurt. A day or two after in a skirmish fight with a largely superior force in our front we charged and drove back the enemy, but lost twelve wounded and two killed. One of the killed was brave Captain Sheffield, Co. K., shot through the heart. Ben in this fight exposed himself when Captain Sheffield fell very recklessly, unnecessarily, but with his usual good fortune."

"We still held the road to Hardeeville, but Ben says we will soon evacuate this section and form a line on the Salkehatchie. The enemy had advanced their line at Tulifinny, entrenched and planted their artillery within three quarters of a mile of our line on the Charleston and Savannah Ry. In our front was an open field which our guns completely commanded. Their line was back of this opening in a wood, the growth and density of which prevented effective work or damage to our position by their guns. At a point near the left terminus of our line the railway was vulnerable to their fire, within a narrow scope, and 'Yankee like' they discovered this advantage and 'Yankee like' availed themselves to it and shelled furiously for a few moments every day the two daily trains as they passed the aforesaid point."

"The train crews would try to fool the Yanks. They would slacken their speed five miles away and approach the danger zones easily and noiselessly as possible until within a short distance of the 'race track' as the soldiers called it, when shot and shell crashed and hurtled as rapidly as they could be fired from the waiting ready guns of the enemy. Only once they did damage a train. This futile firing was owing to the fact that because of the obstacles in their front they had to elevate the muzzles of their guns and depend mainly on descending fragments of exploding shells but they had accurate knowledge of the topography, distance, schedule, etc. These running shooting matches afforded our soldiers considerable amusement. Scores of them off duty would assemble at the 'race track' to see the fun, risking the danger of hurt from shot and shell intended for the fleeting, fleeing train."

"We were soon reinforced by two companies of Charleston military Citadel Cadets commanded by Major White. Captain Hugh Thompson, afterward Governor of South Carolina, commanded one company, I do not remember the other Captain commanding. This little battalion was a band of splendid trained soldier boys under officers handsome, gallant and accomplished; the entire little corps representative of the Chivalry of South Carolina, illustrating a few hours after their arrival, by shedding so gallantly their warm young blood upon the soil of their state in her defense, the spirit and heroism of their patriotic ancestors."
(To be continued)

BEN S. WILLIAMS

Hampton County Guardian HAMPTON, S. C., WEDNESDAY, FEBRUARY 6, 1921

CAPT. B. S. WILLIAMS' WAR REMINISCENSES

Years after the war, when I went up to Columbia, a member of our State Legislature, I met Capt. Hugh Thompson – Afterward Governor Hugh Thompson – the first time since the war, and we went over the Tulifinny fight. I told him what Morgan of the 47th said and in our occasional meetings during the years of our pleasant friendship we had many a laugh over Morgan's "say." Among my old letters on hand are several written me by Governor Thompson from his home in the North. In several of those is some reference to "Hood's Texicans." God rest the soul of this, another one of my departed friends.

After the successful assault of the enemy at Tulifinny, as in Warsaw, "peace reigned" for a time. The Citadel Cadets were ordered elsewhere.

Col. Edwards of the 47th, brevet brigadier general in command, too sick for duty, had to leave, he felt never to return. At our parting he begged in a tearful voice "If we never meet again remember me kindly, and may God bless and spare you. I fear that I am done and if you should fall, God help the remnant of the old regiment. For the sake of memory of the past, for my sake, for your sake and for the sake of the brave men, preserve our proud record on every field, and may God help you." He never returned. A wreck of a splendid, physical man he soon "crossed over the river."

The Colonel of a North Carolina regiment, next highest in rank, was assigned to the command of the forces, and moved to headquarters. He was very affable and courteous, modest, sedate and lazy. He had very little experience or knowledge of matters military and seemed quite indifferent as to the acquisition of more. Many years my senior, able, accomplished and experienced in matters worldly and in civil life – of which I knew so little – he entertained and interested me but he imposed upon me the exercise of most all of his authority, nearly all of the responsibility and just about all the work. All matters, ordinary or emergent, he would quickly settle – as to himself – with one short inquiry of and one shorter mandate to me, to wit, "What would you do in the premises?" "Go ahead." I liked that, was used to it, and we got along splendidly.

Illustrative: our cavalry outpost pickets had been fired on and we deemed it essential to reinforce our picket line at once. Of the details for that purpose was one of Major Kirk's squadron of fifteen men. I had never met Major Kirk as he had been absent and a captain was in command. I had never heard of the major. It was night, the weather a little inclement, and the colonel commanding sat on a camp stool smoking and trying to read near a good fire in front of our headquarters' tent. I was busy inside, near a candle on a box, looking over and making up my "report." The different details had reported and moved to the front. Major Kirk's men were due. I heard the quick gallop of a horse abruptly checked near the front of our tent. And listening intently for news heard the following remarks: "Are you the commanding officer here, sir?"

"Yes sir."

"I am major commanding Kirk's squadron; a call for fifteen of my men has been made for picket duty tonight."

"I presume that is all right, sir."

"No, sir, I am here to protest against this detail. My men and horses are worn and hungry and utterly unfit to go on such duty, and I am surprised that your adjutant general is so ignorant of conditions as to make such an unrighteous demand on my force."

As I stepped from the tent into the circle of firelight I noted at a glance a fine, portly, bearded man in full uniform of a major of cavalry, a typical "rough rider" trooper; well mounted and plainly discernable in the circle of our campfire light on the opposite side.

"There," said the colonel, who had not risen from his seat, "is the officer to whom you may address your protest."

I saluted and the major returned the salute brusquely, and said to me, "Sir, you have made a detail on my squadron for picket duty to-night."

"Correct, sir." I said.

"Are you aware of the condition of my command, sir?"

"Only by your report of this morning," I said.

"Well, sir. If you don't know you ought to know that my men and horses are without food and forage and cannot go on picket."

"I differ with you sir." I replied. "I neither command your squadron nor issue food and forage to them as commissary of quartermaster."

"Well, sir. I refuse to consent to my men being sent off to the outposts until they are supplied with rations and forage. What are you going to do about it?"

I replied: "Your men are near here; the order for the detail reached you half an hour ago. If your men are not reported here ready for duty within the next five, charges against you for insubordination and disobedience of orders, with full specifications will be preferred and forwarded to division headquarters to-morrow morning."

Without a word or salute the sturdy major leaned forward in his saddle and his horse shot from the firelight through the darkness like an arrow from a bow. The colonel laughed heartily and said, "If that Scottish chieftain looking major don't send those men what will you do in the premises?"

"Quickly make a detail from another command for to-night, arrest the major before sunrise to-morrow by your orders and prefer charges against him signed by you as commanding officer of this post," I replied. "Go ahead" said the colonel. In less than five minutes Kirk's detail, in charge of a sergeant, reported at our fire and I noticed that to each trooper's saddle was strapped a bundle of fodder. I said to the sergeant. "You are behind time in reporting, sergeant."

"We are ready and mounted some time ago, sir, but were ordered by Major Kirk to remain ready until he got back to camp."

Afterward the major and I had several good laughs about his attempted "game of bluff," he contending "all strategy is fair in love and war."

One or two of his squadron are living now. They say the major would always try to take care of his men – and the major. He "went through the war" and met his death a short time after by accident in the machinery of a mill near here.

Christmas at Tulifinny had passed. We were on the threshold of the new year, 1865, awaiting anxiously our next move in the rapidly closing mighty drama in which we – cavalry, infantry and artillery at Tulifinny were a few of the actors.

BEN S. WILLIAMS

Hampton County Guardian HAMPTON, S. C.

THIRD INSTALLMENT OF CAPTAIN WILLIAMS' STORY OF THE WAR

Other than these engagements on land were James Island, June 10, 1862, near Stono River; Secessionville, James Island, June 16, 1862; Coosawhatchie, 1862; Pocotaligo, 1862; Johns Island, July 1864; Honey Hill, November 3, 1864; Tulifinney, December 9, 1864; Rivers Bridge, February, 1865. Of these Honey Hill though not the greatest in point of number of troops in field was most important because of date, existing conditions and devolving results.

The movement of the United States Forces at that point was a performance of one of the most resourceful tacticians of the United States army of the time, Gen. William T. Sherman. When he had reached Kingston, Ga., on his famous "March to the sea" he telegraphed General Halleck, November 5; "I would like to have Foster break the Charleston & Savannah railroad near Pocotaligo about the first of December."

General Halleck ordered General Foster to make the attack, who replied: "Hilton Head, November 11, 1864: Maj. Gen. Halleck, United States army: General, I have the honor to acknowledge the receipt of your letter. I am preparing to carry out your instructions and shall move on the night of the 28th and make my attack next day."

Attempt to Bottle Up

Sherman's tactics were to break the Charleston & Savannah railway, thus severing the important line of communication and transportation between Savannah, Ga., which he was nearly approaching, and Charleston, bottling up such stores and troops as were in Savannah and preventing reinforcement of the city he was soon to assault.

The point chosen by General Foster for landing his troops was Boyd's landing on Broad river. From this point a broad public highway led through flat pinelands three-fourths of the way to the Charleston & Savannah railway at Grahamville, Foster's chosen point of attack, a distance of about eight miles.

In the early part of 1862 a famous tactician, Gen Robert E. Lee, was in command of this military department and ordered the construction of earthworks about five miles from Boyd's landing on a ridge of highland known then and now as Honey Hill. The earthworks for artillery and infantry were close on both sides of the aforementioned public highway. In strict obedience to orders and true to program General Foster moved with a fleet of five gunboats, carrying a naval brigade composed of 500 sailors, two batteries, under command of Lieut. Col. William Ames, a detachment of the fourth Massachusetts cavalry; two brigades of infantry consisting of the Fifty-sixth, One-hundred and Twenty-seventh, One-hundred and Forty-fifth United States, negro troops, infantry commanded by General Potter, the Fifty-fourth and Fifty-fifth Massachusetts regiments and the Twenty-sixth and One hundred and second regiments United States negro troops commanded by Col. A. S. Hartwell. Total; one company cavalry, three batteries artillery and 12 regiments of infantry, seven white and five negro, about 6,000 troops.

The fleet left Hilton Head before daylight of the morning of November 29, but on account of delays did not reach Boyd's landing until about 8 a. m., then only two advanced naval vessels had arrived. By noon all the craft was up and the place was alive with Federal cavalry, artillery and infantry. General Foster appeared and took command at 2 p. m. One hour later General Potter appeared and the landing of this little army of 6,000 men, 18 field pieces of artillery, horses, stores, etc., began. November 29, was consumed in completely effecting their landing. General Foster made a mistake fatal to his plans and movement. "Somebody blundered."

This part of the military district of South Carolina, where the enemy landed and where he was met, was under the command of Colonel Colcock, Third South Carolina cavalry. The limited forces of his command were in small bodies at wide intervals along the coast. Had General Foster placed his cavalry in his front, supported by his infantry and artillery, immediately on landing and moved vigorously, a la Stonewall Jackson by daylight on the 30th he could have been entrenching with his whole force on the line of the Charleston & Savannah railway. He could have been heavily reinforced. Our force was too weak for his dislodgement and the contiguous communities would have been at his mercy. A mistake like unto some I had witnessed previously and after.

Our cavalry vidette reported the enemy landing as in "Belgium's Capital" there was "mounting in hot haste." In the language of Randall's beautiful poem in pathetic appeal to "Maryland, My Maryland," "The despot's heel was on our shore. His torch was at our temple door."

Word was quickly sent to Grahamville to headquarters. Colonel Colcock was temporally away, about 50 miles distant, at his home with his beautiful and newly wedded wife. A hard night's ride brought the gallant colonel to his headquarters on the morning of the 30th. Major Jenkins, second in command, returned rapidly from Charleston, where he had just gone. Capt. W. B. Peeples, Company K, Third cavalry, was in Grahamville hastily preparing to report with his company to General Wheeler in Georgia, in front of Sherman.

As senior officer present Captain Peeples with his command of about 100 men and some slight detachments of other commands, rode hastily and gallantly forward to meet the enemy's advancing columns.

Small Force to Meet

Captain Peeples was joined by Captain Raysor, Company E, Third cavalry. This little force of about 200 met the advancing, invading columns and by tactful skirmishing, delayed their progress and General Foster bivouacked for the night about two miles from Boyd's landing at Bolan church. The confederates awaited in anxious, sleepless suspense the coming events of another day. The slight force was facing tremendous odds.

Reinforcements were hastily assembling through the darkness at Honey Hill. Guns of he Beaufort artillery of Earle's and Kanapaux's batteries were soon in place and ready for action. Cavalry rode rapidly and took place ready for the fray.

At break of day of the 30th, ready for action according to the most careful estimates were 246 cavalry, 16 pieces of field artillery, 145 men and 560 infantry. The infantry consisted of detachments of the Georgia Militia, Colonels Willis and Wilson and Majors Cook and Jackson. The cavalry and artillery had been "under fire" in several minor engagements on the coast. The infantry commands were untrained state troops.

The Forty-seventh Georgia regiment of infantry, to which I had as an officer been assigned the latter part of 1862, after long and hard service and many battles under Bragg, Johnston, and Hood in the Army of the West, was detached at Atlanta, Ga., and hurried to Charleston to aid in saving that city from assault by way of Johns and James Islands. The regiment had been reduced by service and casualties from 1,000 to 300 in numbers. We aided in driving the United States troops, white and negro, back and we were stationed on James Island for protection to Charleston.

Shortly after dark, November 29, my regiment, the Forty-seventh, received orders to move with all possible dispatch to the railway near Charleston and entrain for reporting at Grahamville, prepared for action.

Hasten to Front

These orders elicited numerous and various remarks and much comment from the men, as knapsacks were hastily strapped, belts buckled and cartridge boxes inspected. "Where the h__l is Grahamville?" "How long do you reckon it will take to reach there?" "What are we going to do for something to eat?" "Our rations were not issued this evening." Prepare for action!" "D—n it, haven't we kept prepared for it for two or three years?" "What other preparing can we do?" "Wonder when this whole d—n business is going to be over anyhow?" etc. etc.

We were soon across the island and clambering into the old box cars of a freight train and off through the darkness destined for something, somewhere. "Ours not to reason why."

Onward in the darkness, o'er bank and brake; through field and forest; our train jogging roughly onward, stopping and waiting sometimes for orders; backing and taking on wood then water. Thus were we spending the night, the last for some of the Forty-seventh. At Honey Hill our comrades in arms were watching and waiting, intently, for the dawning of the morning of a day of direful events.

BEN S. WILLIAMS

Hampton County Guardian HAMPTON, S. C., Wednesday, October 31, 1923

AFTERMATH OF HONEY HILL AS RELATED BY CAPTAIN WILLIAMS

We have lingered somewhat around the battleground of Honey Hill, but that engagement was in my estimation fraught with greater importance than any inland battle fought on South Carolina soil during the entire term of the war. General Foster commanding the Federal troops, so confident of sweeping away the small force interposing between him and his objective point on the C. & S. Ry., was acting strictly under orders of the most adroit tactician of the U. S. Army, Gen. Wm. Tecumseh Sherman. Had Foster passed Honey Hill our main line of communication between Savannah and Charleston would have been destroyed and Gen. Hardee and the troops in his command would have been bottled up in Savannah for capture on Sherman's arrival there or would have had to cross the Savannah river and made their escape by an inland march leaving munitions and military stores behind, and left Savannah open for the triumphant entrance of Sherman without firing a gun, and Sherman could have so stated in his message to Washington when he presented Savannah as a "Christmas present" to the Federal Government. But we said to Foster at Honey Hill "You shall not pass."

Just a little "aftermath" of the battle and we will about face and move away from Honey Hill. My old regiment came out of the wood we had been ordered to clean out, after dark, tired, worn and hungry. We had lost the Major of the regiment, two Captains and 24 enlisted men, a very dear contribution from the 300 who entered the wood.

We were moved to left of our batteries where we expected the next assault if attacked again. The men fell down in line, near the slight earthworks in our front, in exhaustion and slept with their arms at their side. Col. Edwards, quite sick, and I prepared for rest by placing one blanket on earth, our saddles for pillows, and the only other blanket for covering boots and spurs on and belts clasped in front. When I awoke, the stars, like the "forget-me-nots of the angels in the infinite meadows of heaven," greeted my upward gaze. I was suffering intensely with thirst. My lungs seemed filled with the powder smoked air inhaled in the wood. My thirst was excruciating. I had to have water and believed the most accessible was in the canteens of the dead in front. In the small creek in our front were many dead men, white and black. Clasping my belt, easily, I tried to slip from under the cover without disturbing my sick and sleeping comrade; but unluckily one of my spurs caught in the edge of the covering blanked and aroused him. Clasping his belt and raising himself hastily on his elbows he inquired excitedly "Is it a night attack." I lowered him gently and assured him all was quiet, day was near dawning but I was famishing for water and was going in front to get it. He tried to dissuade, saying "the enemy might be near in front" (we had expected a night attack). I told him I believed there was not a live Yankee nearer than their barges at Boyd's landing. Crossing over slight intrenchments I had gone but a short distance toward the road that led across the branch or creek when I was taken by the approach in the darkness of several groups of men coming toward me. I thought of the night attack. Hastily jerking my pistol from scabbard I intended firing rapidly thus arousing our troops, confusing momentarily the enemy and making my escape by a hasty retreat back to my place. But instant action on my part was stayed by a sound of a laugh in the heaviest approaching group and in another moment I recognized the apparent approaching party as men of my own regiment, the old 47th Ga. coming in from the front, in the starlight with loads of overcoats, hats, shoes and blankets. I was recognized instantly and Jack Williams (no relative) but a gallant Georgia "wiregrass soldier" and a splendid fighter saluted and said, "Pardon, Sir, but we just couldn't stand it any longer and as soon as we rested awhile we started out for something to eat and drink as we had to do at Chickamauga, you recollect? And after drinking and eating all we could find and as it is the first day of December, tho' pretty early in the morning, we thought we had better fix for cold weather." "What of the enemy?" I inquired. "You couldn't rake up a live one with a fine tooth cosh betterd." "Many dead in front?" I asked. "Lots of 'em but a heap, the most is damned niggers, that branch out there is chug full of 'em."

"Back to your places, now," I said, "day is breaking." I hurried forward, and stepping over and between dead bodies, crossed the branch not much more than ankle deep in water. Just beyond the branch was an exploded caisson (chest for storing artillery ammunition) shivered to atoms; evidently struck by one of our cannon shot or shell; several dead artillery horses – very fine animals – and many dead men; the men stripped of haversacks and canteens. I turned from the road to the left obliquely, into the open pine woods. When at a distance at approximately 50 yards from the road I saw, somewhat apart from the others a dead soldier who had not been disturbed. He was lying as if only resting; his face upward and his blue eyes open as if gazing at the paling stars. Day plainly dawning in the east. His cap lay near his head, his uniform neat and clean, and the three chevrons on his coat sleeve denoted the rank of sergeant. He was rather under medium height, slender with blonde complexion, light hair and yellow mustache; a handsome face and handsome form. I stopped and unbuckling the narrow canteen strap in front pulled it gently from beneath the reclining body and relieved my scorching thirst and a la the judge to Maude Miller "A sweeter draught was never quaffed." But remembering my thirsty comrade I ceased drinking and turned to go hurriedly back.

Thirst and fatigue had allayed hunger but noticing the clean white cloth haversack on the dead sergeant I clipped with my knife the cloth strap and pulled it as gently as possible from under my fallen foe (I never disturbed a dead body on any battlefield; and never once did I take from the person or clothing of a dead or wounded soldier anything except to relieve pinching hunger or burning thirst. Rifling and pillaging of the dead and wounded were practiced on both sides. Clothing, hats, shoes, money, watches, rings, knives etc. were taken under the plea of "to the victors belong the spoils.")

    Turning to take a last look and uttering – from my heart – "poor fellow," I noticed near his hand at his left side what appeared to me a small bible. I had seen small bibles carried by the soldiers inside their uniforms with name and address on a blank space. I thought this was one and hurriedly pulled it up and thrust it inside my buttoned uniform coat. I hurried back and found my sick comrade sitting up. I extended the canteen and with a courteous bow the sick Colonel drank and drank but soon paused to "beg pardon" and asked "have you had some."

    Our orderly, Sam, was kindling a little fire in front. Rations of food and water were coming in from the rear. Calling Sam I told him to see what the captured haversack contained. I can remember, as well as if it occurred yesterday, the contents. A large piece of fat and lean pickled pork and half a dozen hard tack (crackers), a slice of light bread, a large red onion, a small tin can of yellow butter, and two cloth bags one of salt and one of black pepper. Sam soon had a little "stewpot" on and Col. Edwards and I enjoyed the finest breakfast of many days past. While our breakfast was brewing I saw that all was well along our shortened line and that in very short time we would be ready for action if necessary. Finishing our breakfast I was telling Col. Edwards of my raid for water for our parching throats, of finding the dead Sergeant. I then thought of the book found and taking it from beneath my coat to inspect I found it to be a small daguerreotype case, clasping and opening like a book and containing on one side beneath a glass covering the picture of a slender woman of dark hair and eyes – age apparently about 30 – on the other side a little girl of age 8 or 10 years, resembling in every feature the woman, and beside the girl a boy of perhaps 5 or 6 years a counterpart of the blonde blue eyed sergeant. Evidently the sergeant was wounded and died slowly and looked the last time with fading sight on that which was nearest and dearest on earth. While I now write the picture is within my arms' reach. I have often regretted that I know not where to send it – with a message. There is a shadow of sadness in the soft dark eyes of the woman.

    Breakfast over we were ready again for action. The 47th was extremely anxious to get a "chance" at the negro troops. After conference with Col Edwards, I sought the officer in command who was then Col. Colcock of the 3rd South Carolina Cavalry, as Gen. Smith had left for Savannah as soon as Foster had been whipped out of the wood on the right and began his retreat. I found Col. Colcock on horseback surrounded by a number of mounted officers all unknown to me for we like Lochinvar had recently "come out of the West." I sought information as to our future movements and obtained but little light. Gen. Smith, a "West Pointer," had turned over command without orders as to future action and it appeared to me that the officers had about decided to sit steady "in the saddle," "Only that and nothing more." I informed them that I spoke for Col. Edwards and we were anxious to follow and attack as we believed that owing to demoralization because of defeat and retreat and confusion in their hurrying embarkation we could destroy and capture much of Foster's force and equipment. I gave assurance that the 47th would lead the attack if supported by one of two guns of our artillery. I noticed strong opposition to attack and Col. Colcock soon informed me that "We will rest on our laurels. We have gained ground enough for the time being."

Col Colcock was a fine officer as I came to know him well – and there was perhaps wisdom and valor in his discretion.

Brunson, S. C., Jan 29, 1924

Editor Hampton County Guardian:

Our reinforcements at Tulifinny came none too soon. The troops we had repulsed and driven back at Honey Hill, Nov. 30th, strongly reinforced, were again in our front moving much more cautiously than before upon our slight entrenchments on the Charleston & Savannah Ry., their objective point.

About Dec. 7th their strong skirmish line at some distance left oblique of our position was hotly attacked by a strong line of our regiment, 47th Georgia Infantry, under command of Captain P. C. Sheffield, Captain of Company K of the 47th, a splendid officer, brave as a lion, but reckless in action as I had often witnessed. At headquarters we plainly heard the rapid increasing fire and knew that Sheffield's force was hot pressed by overwhelming numbers. We were soon on Sheffield's lines in a low densely timbered swampy ground and could scarcely distinguish friend from foe on account of the dense settling clouds of powder smoke. We had passed over one dead and several wounded of our men. When our relieving force struck our hard pressed line the "rebel yell" that rang out reverberating and ringing above the rifle fire seemed to startle our enemy. The firing ceased momentarily and they began giving ground. I said to Captain Sheffield "Your worst is over, I must return and report. Hold your ground; they will not again attack. "Sheffield," I said, "I must warn you against your recklessness, you have exposed yourself to the enemy's fire in a most reckless manner. Don't do it. My God we have none such as you to spare." Just then a scattering fire sounded at a greater distance, several bullets whistled by near where Captain Sheffield and I were standing. He said "We will drive them back to where they entered this wood." Returning to our position on the railway I could hear the desultory firing in the wood

I had just left, but by the receding sounds knew that our force was driving the enemy.

Very soon after my arrival at camp a courier from the fight in the swamp, a member of Captain Sheffield's company hastily approached and pale with fatigue and sorrow informed me that "The Yankees have gone back but Captain Sheffield is dead."

Twelve wounded and two dead came back to camp. Our Surgeon informed me that Captain Sheffield was shot directly through the heart. Another officer and thirteen men, another sacrifice of the 47th on South Carolina soil.

About two days after the skirmish fight in the woods our enemy having presumably finished their tactics for assault made their attack on our position. We were ready and waiting to receive them.

In our position behind our slight earthworks the right of the line of Charleston Citadel Cadets rested against the left line of my regiment. After a hot cannonade they advanced their infantry in solid line of battle. Their blue lines emerged beautifully from the woods into the open field in our front. Our breastworks were not sufficiently high to protect our troops standing so it was necessary to remain in a crouching or stooping posture until time to fire while our artillery played upon the advancing lines of battle. In passing down our line from right to left to see that all was right and ready I was amused at the conduct of many of the Citadel Cadets. With all their training and disciplining it was impossible for their officers to prevent their popping up along the line regardless of the whizzing bullets to take a first look at the Yankees in lines of blue wreathed in battle smoke advancing and firing on us. Continuous were the commands of their officers: "Down Mr. ___. Down Mr. _____." Calling the names of the rash offenders but prefixing the title "Mr." This amused some of the old 47th who had not been called "Mr." in about four years, one of whom said "Them Charleston people is the damnedest politest officers to their men I ever struck up with in the army."

The enemy now within reach of our infantry fire, our fire quickly shattered their lines and reeling and broken they fell back in disorder to the shelter of the woods in their rear from which they had come. We continued for some time to shell the woods. As the enemy did not again attack or come within sight it was decided to advance a line of skirmishers enter the woods in our front and endeavor to ascertain the whereabouts and movements of our defeated enemy. The 47th would have been advanced but Major White commanding the battalion of Citadel Cadets earnestly requested to make reconnaissance with his battalion. He was ordered to advance and our guns were silenced for the movement in front. The Cadets moved out and forward eagerly and beautifully. I accompanied them until at the edge of the wood, they deployed in skirmish line as evenly as if they had been on their Citadel Square parade.

Big Jim Morgan of the 47th asked me as the Cadets were moving out to attack "Do you reckon them Dandy Jim looking kids will stand square up to the rack when they strike the Yanks?" "Morgan," I said, "That is South Carolina stock, you don't know it." "The ……….. I don't," said Morgan, "What was the colonel, your father, that made up this regiment and commanded it until his death. What are you and half this regiment? Why durn it my Daddy and Mammy was both born and married somewhere in this little old hot fool state and didn't move to Gerogy till I was most big enough to wear breeches."

After this engagement I asked Morgan what he thought of those "Dandy Jim kids." His only reply was "D____d if they didn't fight like Hood's Texicans."

The casualties of the Cadets in this fight were as follows: Lieut. Amory Coffin, severely wounded in head; Cadet J. B. Patterson, mortally wounded, afterwards died; Cadets Joseph W. Barnwell and M. C. McCarty severely wounded; Cadets S. F. Hollingsworth, A. J. Green, A. R. Heyward and W. A. Pringle slightly wounded.
I give this list as some of that battalion may read this article.

(Continued next week)

BEN. S. WILLIAMS

Hampton County Guardian HAMPTON, S. C., WEDNESDAY, FEBRUARY 27, 1921

CAPT. B. S. WILLIAMS' WAR REMINISCENSES

Col Bacon, Leut. Finlay, on Bacon's Staff, and I occupied, for sleeping, a little log cabin a short way down the riverside. Finlay placed a pole across one end of the floor and had the space between it and the log walls filled with dry leaves and pine straw on which we rested quite comfortably, covering with our blankets. We had arranged to use a small plank house near the roadside, about a mile in our rear, as a hospital and to destroy the bridges in our front as soon as our outer line of pickets and videttes came in. And then our little army waited, watched and rested on ground soon to be stained with our blood, and where we well knew that some of us would rest throughout all time – "Our warfare o'er" forever.

    At length the enemy reached our point in his march and our little band of soldiers braced themselves for the unequal conflict. The enemy's approach was heralded by our returning cavalry pickets, who commenced crossing the river about noon. Major Gen. McLaws, commanding our division, had ordered Col. Bacon to destroy the bridges on the approach of the enemy as soon as our forces in front were compelled to fall back upon our main line. The infantry companies forming our picket line in front on the west side of the river held their ground until about 3:00 o'clock in the afternoon when they came in closely followed by the enemy. Indeed, so closely pressed that it was with difficulty that the bridges could be destroyed after our men had crossed, the latter part of the work being done under galling fire from the enemy.

    The enemy swarmed in great numbers to the edge of the swamp, but our field pieces swept the road and our sharpshooters checked the movement through the swamp. They opened a hot fire on our works and the battle was on. Every effort of the enemy to force a crossing was checked and they were whipped back onto their own side. Sharpshooting continued throughout the afternoon and picket firing was kept up all night. The next morning repeated efforts were made by the enemy, in strong force, to force a crossing at several points, but our troops fought gallantly and drove them back at every point.

    During the day we were reinforced by Finlay's regiment of Georgia troops – 16 year old boys, commanded by Major McGregor – and a brigade of Wheeler's cavalry, numbering only 250 men and commanded by Col. Harrison, of Tennessee. Thus our force was increased to about 1,200 men and until afternoon we repulsed the repeated onslaught of the enemy. Many of them during the night before and under smoke of firing during the day had worked their way far into the swamp, and screening themselves in every way possible, kept up a hot fire upon our lines at the main crossing and upon our guns of our battery. This advanced line the enemy endeavored constantly and persistently to reinforce, but many a blue-coat went down in front as many a brave fellow pressed forward.

The 32nd and 47th Georgia Infantry were next to the road close to the battery. The great majority of our casualties occurred in these two regiments, as here the enemy's efforts and fire were centered. We were holding our position and could have held it until now against the force in front though 10 to 1 against us, if they had remained in our front and fought it out there.

BEN S. WILLIAMS

Hampton County Guardian HAMPTON, S. C., Wednesday, April 2, 1924
CAPT. B. S. WILLIAMS' WAR REMINISCENSES
Brunson, S. C., March 31, 1924

*E*ditor Guardian;

I was ordered immediately after the beginning of our retreat from Rivers Bridge to resume charge of the Quartermaster's department of the brigade, as Major A. was still absent sick. We rested near "Four Hole Swamp" not far from Branchville for a few days, and the regimental quartermasters and their sergeants foraged for food supplies throughout the neighborhood and found a majority of the citizens very clever and liberal. I was given authority to impress provisions, horses and wagons if necessary, but my instructions to those serving under me were to collect no more than actually requisite and to use no force or severity where possible to avoid same. We gave as voucher and receipt for collections, a "Governmental Slip" which was a promise to pay, equivalent in value to our common currency or "Confederate Money."

One day, feeling restless, cheerless and pretty hungry, too, I concluded to ride out, away from camp, into the country. After riding several miles and passing several farms, I came in sight of a very nice looking place, with a large, two-story, painted dwelling. As it was about 11 o'clock A. M. I concluded that here would be a good place for a stop, a rest and a dinner – (soldiers were always hungry. I can prove same by any man who ever really "soldiered" it.)

Riding up to a large gate in front of the house, I was met by a negro servant boy, who very politely opened the gate and informed me, in answer to my question of who lived there that Mr. Rion (or Ryan) did. I mention the name of the family with profoundest respect and ever entertained for them the kindest feeling because of their courtesy and kindness shown to me, a stranger soldier. I dismounted and giving my bridle rein to the young darky, I walked up to the high piazza and knocked on the front door; in a few minutes this was opened by a very pretty young lady. I bowed low and informed her that I was from the military camp nearby and that in riding through the neighborhood, in order to obtain information as to our ability to procure food and forage for our stock, had concluded to ride by and ask permission to rest for a while, as I was tired from quite a long ride. I was invited into a luxurious parlor and after one or two casual remarks about "the weather" she excused herself, saying she would ask her mother to see me relative to the matter of which I had spoken. She soon returned, accompanying her mother, a lady of mild and gentle manner, reminding me of my own mother, whom I had not seen in many months. After conversing about half an hour very pleasantly, I arose very reluctantly to take my leave, feeling that on them it was not right to impose, even for the sake of dinner. But I was not allowed to thus depart, and was informed that I was expected to stay for dinner, and in anticipation of this, my horse had been unsaddled, stabled and fed. This brief and pleasant visit was one of the few pleasing cases alongside the rough pathway of duty in the arid army life of a soldier in the field, where he may briefly turn aside and for a moment linger in blissful peace and transient forgetfulness.

Returning to camp, I rode along the public highway, and when within a mile or two of the camp, I noticed in a small grove in front of a house near the roadside, a cavalryman's horse standing hitched. I was riding slowly, and as I came near the horse I noticed, leaning against a tree close to the road, a cavalryman's carbine (gun), while about thirty feet away from the gun sat comfortably at the foot of a large tree, a cavalryman and an elderly man, citizen and host of the premises, chatting and laughing in a very lively manner. I concluded in a moment that this was a picket post and being carelessly guarded, I rode slowly opposite and past the sentinel and wondering why I was not halted. My overcoat was on and buttoned, and no insignia of rank of office visible. I had ridden some distance beyond the post and was about to turn and suggest to the sentinel that he take his post and properly perform his duty, when without rising to his feet, he called out to me loudly, rudely and boisterously; "Halt there, d___n it."

I faced about and moved close to his gun by the tree, by this time he had leisurely risen, the elderly citizen rising at the same time. Halting, I asked, "What do you want?" "Want what I'm going to have – a look at your pass if you've got one. Have you got a pass?" (I saw his egotism and saw that he was trying to "show off" before the elderly citizen.)

"What right have you to demand to see my pass?" I asked. "I am a sentinel and this is my post and my orders are to allow no man to pass here." "Then, sir," I said, "you have disobeyed orders and neglected your duty. You were off your post, without your gun, saw me pass your post before you halted me. Were your ordered to curse when you halted?" "Show your pass," he said crossly, moving toward me, "or I'll arrest you and that pretty d___n quick."

Moving my horse slightly to the left I reached down quickly caught up the carbine and laid it across my saddle front. Suddenly, the trooper seemed to "take in" the situation and with true soldierly instinct snatched his long cavalry saber from its scabbard and hissing "I'll have my gun or die," started toward me. While talking I had quietly unbuttoned my overcoat, and the advancing trooper was within about three paces of me when I quickly threw back the lapel of my overcoat, jerked from the holster my "Colt's army pistol" and turning my horse slightly to the left and leveling my weapon, I said "Halt! Another step with that drawn saber and I'll kill you." He stood and gazed in astonishment, glancing rapidly and alternately at the muzzle of the "Colt's army" and at the Gilt bars on my inner coat collar. "Return your saber," I commanded, and he obeyed instantly, not through fear or cringing or cowardice for there was nothing of the kind in his "make-up." His heels went together and with form erect his right hand went to the rim of his hat in salute, mechanically, automatically, instinctively.

Such is the effect of drill and discipline and the force of practice and habit. I returned the salute. "To what command do you belong?" I asked. "Harrison's Tennessee Cavalry." "Where are Col. Harrison's headquarters?" He informed me. "All right," I said, "I have not the authority to remove you from your post, but I can inform Col. Harrison of this affair." For the first time I saw his face pale. "Then God help me! Col Harrison is rigid in his discipline and shows no mercy in punishment for disobedience of orders." "Then why did you not obey orders and act the soldier and gentleman, which under the surface you appear to be?" "I have no excuse," he replied, "I just acted the fool and jackass and will have to take my medicine. I apologize to you and do not blame you. I only ask that you forgive me and return my gun, that I not be thoroughly disgraced." "Take your gun and I will not report you," I said handing him his gun, "but don't do so again. Be a soldier and a gentleman. Here is my pass, examine it in obedience to your orders, your duty. Now, good-bye!" "God bless you," he said, and there was a quiver in his voice. I never saw him again.

But it was not until I turned to go that I noticed the elderly citizen peeping around the tree, behind which he had quickly dodged when I drew upon the trooper (he was exactly within range). Waving him a farewell, I laughed to see how quickly and naturally he had adopted tactics which I had seen adopted on similar occasions.

We tarried leisurely, only a few days near Branchville.

BEN S. WILLIAMS

Hampton County Guardian HAMPTON, S. C., Wednesday, April 23, 1924

CAPT. B. S. WILLIAMS' WAR REMINISCENSES

Dear Mr. Editor

The Ides of March A. D., 1865, marked the closing of the fourth year of bitter war between the two sections of the United States, the North and the South, the Federal and the Confederate governments. In both sections from millions of souls, in cities and hamlets, halls and huts, in churches and homes, in that dark hour of death, ascended prayer in petitions for the blessing of the dawn of peace.

The men of the armies of the Blue and Gray, "tenting in the old campground" sang around their camp fires of "many are the hearts longing to-night, longing for the war to cease." The dawn of peace was then very near. At that period the awful drama was then nearing its close. The war would soon cease, but many of the actors then upon the gore-drenched stage never hailed the dawn nor rejoiced with those rejoicing when the war ceased. There were a few more acts and scenes of carnage before the final fall of the curtain.

In Virginia, the mere wreck of the proud army which under Lee and Jackson, during the years of the bloody strife, had dealt the Federal army so many crushing blows, was surrounded by the mighty hosts of Grant and Sheridan like a wounded lion at bay, facing defiantly his advancing foes and Stonewall Jackson was not there. The remnants of the command of the once splendid Army of the West, reinforced by several small bodies of troops from our coastal region, again under their old commander, Joseph E. Johnston, again faced Sherman's much more powerful and hitherto often met army in North Carolina. Johnston had collected a force of about 22,000 men against which were opposed three armies, Sherman's from South Carolina, Terry's from Wilmington and Schofield's from Kingston, North Carolina, numbering in all about 120,000 well fed, well equipped troops – but with Johnston, Cleburne and Walker were not.

Lee, with 35,000 half-starved men was striving to defend thirty miles of intrenchments near Petersburg. Grant pressed against Lee with 125,000 well equipped troops, and was as rapidly as possible, concentrating all of the available Federal forces in the South for another and final "On To Richmond." Lee's only hope of containing the struggle now so vastly unequal, lay in abandoning Petersburg and Richmond, the long sought and mostly often fought for, and uniting his army with Johnston's in North Carolina – and then? Johnston was preparing to resist and impair in every manner possible, Sherman's advance through North Carolina to join Grant.

Johnston's lean commands in dingy gray were anxious and eager to face again under command of Johnston, the hosts of Sherman as they had often done in Tennessee and Georgia. This eager animating spirit appeared to me to spring directly from a passionate desire for revenge than hope of ultimate success or thirst for future glory in victory won. There were no racial prejudices and hatred as between the bearded Slav Cossack and the helmeted Teuton, or as between Briton and Turk. The real issue was between Americans, native of the soil, acquaintances, schoolmates and often kindred; in many instances close and occasionally of consanguinity of the same degree as between Cain and Abel. But there was a burning desire on the part of a few remaining men of the Army of the West to wreak on Sherman's army, vengeance in blood for wrongs deep and damnable. The opportunity soon came. On the 17th day of March, Johnston threw his compacted remnants of command in Sherman's front at Averysboro, N. C., and metaphorically commanded "Halt." He did not continue with the usual interrogatory of "Who comes there?" He knew in reply to Johnston's "Halt" Sherman ordered "Forward" and then "things began to happen."

    As animating as our thirst for revenge was the enemy's pride of a year of success. Flushed with victory he came proudly, gloriously on, as if naught could check his progress or would dare attempt to stay his advance, yet with that caution in movement and carefulness of formation – of rear support and flank protection secured by strength of numbers – that characterized all of Sherman's movements with which Johnston was so familiar and to which formerly so accustomed. Sherman knew, of course, that his force was greatly superior, numerically, to Johnston's, but seemed to realize that he fronted his former able competitor whose removal from command of the Army of the West near Atlanta by President Davis had been hailed with delight by Sherman and his assaults on our lines were steady, gallant and repeated, but not fierce and reckless. We repulsed assault after assault until the enemy fell back in the dusk of evening, leaving many dead and wounded in our front.

    My regiment was hotly engaged and suffered quite severely. Some of their wounded we brought in and sent to the rear with our own wounded. We were gratified by results, but weary when night came on, and as soon as our line of skirmishers and pickets has been placed in front Major Hazzard – grown from a young lieutenant to a captain then to a major – then in command of the regiment – and I prepared for rest at the root of quite a large pine tree. Its thick leaved branching boughs affording us some shelter from the cold drizzle of the rain falling. Our preparation was Hazzard's thin rubber blanket on the damp earth, we on that and my thin rubber blanket on us for covering. The enemy was still giving us shot and shell from his artillery at a distance in the darkness. As soon as Hazzard and I had nestled closely together on and under our narrow blankets Hazzard said:

    "Don't you reckon we'll have the dickens to pay here in the morning?" (Dickens was about as vile a word as Hazzard ever uttered.)

"No," I said, "only in the way of getting up and skedaddling to right or left to meet Sherman's flank movement." "I wouldn't be surprised," he said after a moment's silence, "if you are right, but I wish that battery in our front would stop shooting those balls and shells over us, and let us rest in peace." "No danger," I said, "they haven't got our range and their missiles go from 15 to 20 above us and that is evidence that the batteries firing on us this evening have been withdrawn and Sherman is moving. The constant, random shooting is simply to deceive us into the belief that he is there for all night and ready for attack in the morning." "Right," said Hazzard, and the next moment I realized he was sleeping.

I did not fall suddenly to sleep. I thought of the morrow. Hazzard and I had spent many hours together pleasantly. Perhaps this was our last night on earth alive. The morrow would bring desperate strife for us somewhere. Hazzard was gallant, reckless in action. Tomorrow night might find one or both on the field pale and cold as some brave fellows who had charged so gallantly now lying in front of where we had fought. I wondered if Hazzard was dreaming of the girl whose fair hands had fashioned so neatly the beautiful little pocket case of crimson and purple velvet containing a few needles, a few buttons, some thread, a small paper of pins and a pair of slender silver-plated scissors – a little present both beautiful and useful – in camp. He had not been the happy possessor of the tasty little article fifteen minutes before I was admiring it while Hazzard read again, his face suffused with blushes – for he was exceedingly diffident – the letter accompanying the gift.

My own thoughts were gradually drifting into the mystic realms of Morpheus when quickly following the boom of a cannon in front there was a loud crash and jar close to our heads and instantly there rained down upon us what seemed to be a shower of hail stones, bullets, brickbats or something of that kind. A cannon ball had struck and cut its way through one side of our sheltering pine, raining down a shower of pieces of bark and splinters all over us. Hazzard was on his feet in an instant. In his half awake state he quickly fell to his knees and catching hold and shaking me asked hurriedly, "Are you hit?" "Are you hit?" He was under the impression that the enemy had attacked suddenly, had fired a volley and the balls were rattling all over and around us. The solid shot had struck the tree at our heads at a height of about six feet above the earth. I did not rise for I was not yet asleep, and quickly realized what had happened. Hazzard suggested that we at once change our quarters. "No," I said, "come back to bed. Don't you remember Jack Williams' dictum at Chickamauga – that a d___n cannon ball never strikes twice in the same place?" Before the dawn of day we were aroused under orders to move at once in the direction of Bentonville. Sherman's and Johnston's old tactics and practices – a blow, a side-step and another meeting.

BEN S. WILLIAMS

Hampton County Guardian HAMPTON, S. C., Friday, December 4, 1924

CAPT. B. S. WILLIAMS' WAR REMINISCENSES

Brunson, S. C., Dec. 1, 1924

Dear Mr. Editor:
   Reared in the army, entering before 18 years of age and serving until 22; more than three years of the four years of service as a commissioned officer, the effect of our army regulations, the military courtesy, ethics and etiquette strictly observed by the great majority of our officers, giving exultation and paying honor to rank, an atmosphere of which "I lived and moved and had my being" at a most impressible period of life, is felt by me, somewhat, now. "You may break, you may shatter the vase" etc. Consequently, I sometimes hesitate in expressing my opinion of the conduct of certain officers of high rank in the confederate army in our war between the states. Young and inexperienced as I was I saw, not as plainly as afterward; that politics – the politics that Webster describes as "devoted to a scheme rather than a principal," actuated some of our officers of high rank, the "scheme" an effort for promotion to higher rank and greater power.

   It was the policy of the presidents in America, who were the Commander and Chief of the armies and the navies, to remove the commander of an army who was unsuccessful and lost instead of winning battles. In the Federal Army during our war between the states McClellan, who in Gen Lee's estimation was the best General in the army of the U. S., was removed; so also were Generals Pope and Hooker, principally because of their failure to defeat Stonewall Jackson and crush Lee. In the confederate army Gen Braxton Bragg was relieved from command of the army of the west after loss of battles of Missionary Ridge and Lookout Mountain. Bragg was succeeded by Gen. Joseph E. Johnston.

   Battles were lost at times when the commanding General was not at fault. It was the belief of many army officers and the opinion of many writers that the loss of victory at the great battle of Gettysburg, "the turning point of our war," was not the fault of Gen Lee. Had Gen Longstreet attacked at "daylight" as ordered by Gen Lee, instead of attacking at one o'clock p. m., the victory would have been won by Lee. If Longstreet had "schemed" to have Lee lose and secure for himself promotion, or had Hood in the west "schemed" to have Johnston to continually fall back and give up territory and be removed and himself promoted to supreme command, they would have been only adopting and following the tactics practiced by notorious characters hundreds of years "before Christ."

   Marcus Cato, orator, statesman and military commander in Rome, who flourished 640 years B. C., was "schemed" from command of an army by Scipio, who "wished to have the finishing of the war himself, managed so as to have himself appointed. After which he made all haste to take command of the army from Marcus Cato.

In my last published article after telling of our great joy at the prospect of closing in conflict with the invading hosts of Sherman and then our disappointment and surprise in being ordered to retreat, our suffering etc., I wrote that I would state the cause of the great and sudden change in tactics and action which crushed hope and injured materially the "esprit-de-corps" of the troops of our Army of the West.

For the information of those who may read and are not familiar with military formations and divisions, I would state that formerly five companies made of formed a battalion – ten companies a regiment, two or more regiments a brigade, two or more brigades a division, two or more divisions a corps – any number of corps and army.

Johnston's army facing Sherman at the time of which I write, consisted of three corps, commanded by Lieut. Generals Hardee, Hood and Polk.

The failure in performance of duty in action, or impotence of a unit in either of the divisions or organizations mentioned might destroy possibility of victory for the whole command. Consequently, before the beginning of an important engagement the commanding General would summon his chief officers and in a "council of war" the course and plan of action would be decided on, each assigned his place and part, each expected to "act well his part" for in that all hope of victory depended.

The reason or cause of sudden change of tactics by Gen. Johnston at Cassville, his hasty abandonment of chosen position for action after issuing his "battle order," which thrilled his thousands of gallant troops with joy in expectation of the long looked for, hoped for decisive battle is given by Gen Johnston: "The fire of the enemy's artillery commenced soon after the troops were formed and continued until after dark. Soon after dark Lieut. Generals Polk and Hood together expressed to me, decidedly, the opinion formed upon the observation of the afternoon, that the Federal artillery would render their positions untenable the next day and urged me to abandon the ground immediately and cross the Etowah River. Lieut. Gen Hardee, whose position I thought was weakest, was confident that he could hold it. The other two officers were so earnest, however, and unwilling to depend upon the ability of their corps to defend the ground, that I yielded and the army crossed the Etowah, a step which I have regretted ever since."

Gen. Johnston labored throughout our campaign in Georgia under many difficult and serious disadvantages. There were disloyal citizens in some of the sections of the country through which we passed and in my opinion then and now Gen. Sherman's ability to locate and understand our position before engagement and perform some of his flank movements by devious ways was by reason of information gained from unionist and deserters from our army who were spying our movements and who were familiar with the topography of the country and knew every hill and dale and mountain pass and ford of streams. But for Sherman's knowledge of our position and battle formation he would have immediately attacked at Cassville (our position above alluded to) in which case Sherman's "Marching Through Georgia," to the sea, or "Hood's campaign in Tennessee" would not now be on record in history.

Had Gen. Johnston shot one or two of his lying courier scouts who brought him sensational and misleading reports and cashiered one or two of his self-assertive antagonistic Generals, in my opinion he and his army would have gained by their loss.

On one occasion, and a very important one, Gen. Hood reported to Gen. Johnston a heavy Federal force in line of battle near to his (Hood's) position on the Camden road. This report caused Gen. Johnston to change his lines, formed for battle, and move to the rear, as the Federal force on his (Johnston's) flank was unexpected, and very surprising. Gen Mackall reporting to General Johnston said: "I saw no troops as reported and do not believe there were any there."

Strong influence was exercised on our government at Richmond to have Johnston removed from command. Johnston was relieved of command and Gen Hood placed in command of the Army of the West. Through misunderstanding and irrational proceeding; under existing conditions absolutely irreparable.

BEN S. WILLIAMS

Hampton County Guardian HAMPTON, S. C., Wednesday, May 13, 1924
CAPT. B. S. WILLIAMS' WAR REMINISCENSES
Brunson, S. C., May 13, 1924

Dear Mr. Editor

Recently I wrote of my attendance on occasion of the Memorial ceremonies at the "bivouac of the dead" soldiers, at Rivers Bridge on the Salkehatchie, May 2nd. Soldiers who, like the little Spartan band at Thermopylae, faced a mighty host of foemen, of Sherman's invading army in South Carolina, "with gloves off." They fought bravely and well. Their life blood was their supreme sacrifice upon the altar of their country, 'twas all that they could do.

I wrote of the visit I paid at the Rivers Bridge Memorial several years prior to my visit, on the 2nd inst., being made under circumstances rather peculiar and unique. In explanation, I will go back in time to the surrender of Johnston's army in North Carolina, April 26, 1865, after Lee's surrender at Appomattox, April 9, 1865 (I began my service in the army in Savannah, Ga., April 9, 1861.) I was present for duty with Johnston's army when Johnston had made ready for surrendering but I did not surrender. In the evening of April 25, 1865, I cut the bullet-riven, shell-torn, old battle flag of my regiment from the improvised staff. (The first staff was shot to splinters on the field of Chickamauga) – folded it in my saddle blanket, girthed my saddle tightly upon it and mounting my horse, accompanied by two other young officers – well mounted – started to wind our way to the trans-Mississippi department and join Kirby Smith, who had a small force of fragments of commands and do a little more fighting. (It was the same object in view as to the same objective point that President Jefferson Davis was going when captured). We didn't get there – thanks. But I saved our old battle flag, presented to the regiment by my mother and other noble women of Savannah; under and around which I had seen many comrades fall "like leaves in wintry weather," Flag of my father's regiment, under which he had fought his last battle. These facts were known to every living member of the old 47th Georgia Volunteer Infantry.

A few years ago the General Reunion of Confederate Veterans was held in Jacksonville, Fla. At this time I knew only two of the 49 commissioned officers of my regiment, other than myself, living. They with several others of the ranks were to attend the Reunion. I received notice of this fact with the appeal, "Come and bring our old flag with you that we may clasp hands with you and look once more on our dear old battle flag before we cross over the River." The old flag was sacred in their memory, their appeal was irresistible. I went, and not for the first time carried that flag.

In the crowded city, thousands came or paused to look at the old battle flag and never have I witnessed greater manifestation of sentiment and emotion. Old soldiers, many maimed and decrepit, would touch the old flag and then pass a sleeve across cheeks that never blanched in battle fray. I often stood utterly voiceless while fair women, some aged and weak, would clasp a fold of the old flag to their bosoms, some to their lips, while tears filled their soulful eyes. (This was over ten years ago.) People from every state of the Southern Confederacy came. To the thousands of old veterans, all was heavenly, and could Lee and Jackson and all their comrades of old on the other side of the river have been brought back, they would have been glad to spend the "eternal years of God" fight there.

Many citizens of the North, in Florida for the winter, delayed their return home in order, as a lady of the state of New York expressed it, "to see the fragmentary remains of the army which had eclipsed the gallantry of the charge at Balaklava and equaled the glory of the stand at Thermopylae."

While at the steps of the beautiful Windsor Hotel, awaiting the car of my brother, who had been for many years a zealous worker and an active factor, holding the rank of general in the organization of Confederate Veterans, I was holding my flag, not open nor flauntingly, but folded and across my arm, after hundreds had viewed it. There was a group of a dozen or perhaps twenty standing near me, when an elderly couple came down the steps of the hotel onto the pavement near me. They descended slowly, the man stepped cautiously, aided by a cane, while his companion, much steadier, held on as if to support, rather than for support, to a part of the arm in an empty sleeve. The dress and the manner of the handsome old couple indicated wealth and culture.

Arriving in front and near me, the man quickly halted and exclaimed with animation, "Wife, as I live, there is an old Confederate battle flag; war-torn and time-worn, but still in evidence. Sir," he continued, saluting with his cane as an officer salutes with his sword, "was that flag a battle flag of soldiers in the South in the war of the rebellion?"

"Sir," I replied, returning his salute, "This old flag was the battle flag of a regiment of soldiers of the South in the war of repulsion of invaders of the Southern Confederacy."

"Pardon, my dear sir," he said, bowing and smiling, "I meant no offense. That term is commonly used in Massachusetts, where I dwell."

"Granted, sir," I replied, "but it is a term to which we decidedly object down in South Carolina, where I dwell."

"Shake," said he, placing his cane under his half arm and extending his right hand. "The war is over and South Carolina and Massachusetts have ere this disagreed, but always got around together all right."

"Fine, fine," said the lady, her dark eyes beaming, "fine for South Carolina and Massachusetts."

"She is of Virginia," said the soldierly-looking old gentleman, and it was some time after our war and my recovery from the quite severe punishment (and he rapped with his cane upon an artificial leg and shook his half empty sleeve) inflicted for my invasion, that she would consent to terms of peace and our union."

"Will you kindly let me see the flag unfurled?" quickly asked the lady.

I handed her one corner of the flag to hold. Un-gloving her hand first, she caught hold and let its folds unfurl. Instantly there rang out from a band not far in front the dulcet soul-inspiring strains of "Dixie." I saw the fair hand on the flag tremble and the instant blush upon her cheek pale as if by death and as she gracefully released to me her gentle hold upon the flag, I saw her soulful eyes brimful of tears.

"Wife, wife, come," said the maimed veteran husband, "Let's see the procession. Our war is over and as our immortal McKinley said, 'We are brothers anyway.'"

In that slender trembling hand-clasp, that heart-blood flush and succeeding death-like pallor of cheek, those dimming tears, I imagined evidence of memory of scenes of romance, memory of courses in love, memory of anguish in tragedy and grief in woe.

On the outer edge of the group of men around me stood two men near each other who had attracted my attention by the strange manner in which they bent forward and gazed at the flag when unfurled at the request of the lady. Their look did not express pride or admiration, neither scorn nor dignity, but was rather of curious interest and suspicion.

This line for marching had been formed at the "head of the column" the bugle was sounded "forward." I was listening to the familiar notes which brought back the "light of other days" to me, and gave the military salute. They were widely different in type and in physique. One was tall, bent by age, with long gray beard, of dark complexion; the other erect, of smaller stature, blonde complexion. "Was that the flag of your command, sir?" asked the elder bearded man. "It was," I replied. "Were you in the Army of the West or of Virginia?" he asked. "Army of the West," I said. "Well, by George that flag has been where hot work was going on. Were you at Chickamauga and Lookout Mountain and Missionary Ridge?" "Yes," I said, "and at Altoona, Dalton, Resaca, New Hope Church, Pine and Kennesaw Mountains, and on down in Atlanta." "Well, sir," he said, "we were in every one of those engagements. My name is Mills, and I was Captain of Co. K. 84 Illinois Infantry, 1st division, 17 corps U. S. A. My friend here is Captain Eller of Co. E. 10th Illinois Infantry – "the bloody tenth" – and I wouldn't be surprised to know that we had made some of the holes in that flag. But, by George," he continued before I could reply, "you were making holes in our men at Rivers Bridge, in South Carolina. I lost 16 men of my company in one advance movement to the right of the road as we approached your works. We shot the flagstaff in two and caught hell as we tried to go forward."

"Well, sir," I said, "I am satisfied and I am pleased to tell you this is the flag that was shot down at the point you designate, and the men behind this flag were those who put the gallant 16 poor fellows of your company, along with quite a number of others, out of business at that point in the Rivers Bridge engagement, for we occupied the position you so exactly describe." "Well," said he, "Our war is over. Let's shake."

Hampton County Guardian HAMPTON, S. C., Wednesday, May 21, 1924
CAPT. B. S. WILLIAMS' WAR REMINISCENSES
Brunson, S. C. May 19, 1924

Dear Mr. Editor:
When invited by the old Yankee Captain of a Company in the 84th Illinois regiment of Sherman's army to "shake" as I related in my writing last week – my reply, I fear, might under the circumstances, be considered somewhat rude as I demanded to know first if he had allowed his men to indulge in the stealing, house-burning, woman-insulting campaign characterizing Sherman's march through Georgia and South Carolina, but he had warmed my blood slightly by his first remark. When the gallant old Captain exonerated himself by a dignified, spurning, spirited denial, we shook hands. Soon after reaching home, I received a very courteous and interesting letter from the other man, Captain Ellett, of the "bloody tenth." He pleaded for a picture of the old flag. It contained a bill of money as payment of expense. My reply letter contained the bill of money and a promise of the picture, which I later sent. I received several interesting letters form Captain Ellett, also at regular intervals, boxes of the finest oranges and grapefruit from his Fairview Florida Grove. I am glad I did not kill Ellett while fighting the "bloody tenth" Illinois and I am very glad that Ellet of the 10th Illinois did not kill me. In reply to my invitation to him to come and attend with me, as my guest the annual ceremony and decoration of the graves of the Confederate Soldiers that fell in the battle of Rivers Bridge, he wrote, "It would be with great pleasure to accept your invitation and be with you in the ceremonies of the occasion, but we are in the midst of our packing up and preparation for our moving to our home in Chicago in the summer. But give my love to your old boys who may be present. I didn't use to love them a bit but I respected them greatly. I had to."

The next spring upon my inviting him again to come and be with me at the celebration, he wrote me, "Please tell me how to reach you. I am going to join you and be with you at Rivers Bridge and be present at the memorial ceremonies to which you have so kindly invited me." I forwarded directions and later met him at Fairfax and conveyed him to my home – my former enemy – my welcome guest. This old Captain was a courteous old gentleman and I have no doubt, was a gallant soldier. The following morning we drove over in my car, making an early start in order that we might stop, as I had once long ago aided in compelling him to do, before crossing to our objective point on the other side of the Salkehatchie. But in passing through Brunson a slight occurrence disturbed somewhat my equanimity and "put me to thinking." We stopped near the post office and I stepped in for my mail.

In a few minutes, I stepped from the office door, I saw standing by my car, with elbows resting on the door and head inside of car, talking to my old Yankee Captain friend, an old "Confederate" of the strictest type of "fire-eaters"; a gallant old sergeant of cavalry of the Confederate army, full of pep, utterly unreconstructed, say exactly what he thought, would fight at the "drop of a hat" and go at it as quickly and fervently as when the bugle sound of his Command was "Charge." I thought rapidly and acted quickly. Getting within arms reach I slapped his shoulder and said, "Sergeant, mount up with us and go to Rivers Bridge." He replied, "I was just waiting for you to come out of the post office and invite me." "Mount Sergeant," I replied, "and take that front seat, please, by my driver where I usually ride; you will be in front rank and I, a little hard of hearing can talk to my friend from Florida and hear both of you." I introduced them jocularly and we journeyed in fine spirits. We halted and viewed the place of our first and hostile meeting. The old Captain penciled some notes. As we approached the place for meeting for Memorial exercises, I began considering again. There would come old Confederate Veterans, some with empty sleeves, some with crutches, others maimed otherwise. How would they meet my guest, a Yankee army officer, one who had fought us right here at home? "Too late now," I thought, "for such consideration; he is my guest and I stand by him in all possible occurrence of unpleasant events." But nothing unpleasant occurred; quite the opposite. The old vets shook hands with him and jestingly assured him that "there was a time when he was not welcome around here, but now we're all glad to see you and by the company you are now in, we know you are all right. We would hope rather that Captain Williams capture a Yankee officer than for a Yankee to capture Captain Williams," and were delighted with the guest who was shown every courtesy of the day. Poor old gallant soldier of a proud and victorious army. Returned to my home, while sitting on the porch and reciting to my wife the events of the day, he lost, completely, control of his voice and placing his hands over his face, with bowed head, wept as only a brave man and tender-hearted man could weep.

He spent several days at my home. He declared that his whole visit was the most enjoyable of his life. During about three years of time he wrote to me often. Then came a letter, words sad and pathetic. One who had been his sweetheart in his boyhood days and his wife for fifty years had passed away. Soon his letters ceased coming. The pale courier on the further shore had beckoned him and he crossed the River to rest with his comrades who had gone before him.

The gallant old Cavalry Sergeant of the Confederate army had also crossed over the River to rest with his comrades in gray. The few whose lingering footsteps press close upon the sand shore on this side will attend only a few more Memorial services and then. Farewell.

BEN S. WILLIAMS

Hampton County Guardian HAMPTON, S. C., Wednesday, May 6, 1924

CAPT. B. S. WILLIAMS' WAR REMINISCENSES

Editor Guardian:

On Friday May 2nd, I attended the Memorial exercises held annually near the battle ground at Rivers Bridge on the Salkehatchie River, the last line formed by the depleted commands of the Confederate army in this section of the contracted territory of the Confederacy in opposition to invasion of South Carolina by the overwhelming host of the Union army whose "torches were at our temple doors." I shall not allude to the battle of greatly unequal parts, numerically, as I have done so in former articles in my writing.

A vast concourse of citizens of several counties assembled to honor in memory, the men in grey, whose life blood ensanguined the soil near that in which they now peacefully rest, and:

"Winds of the South blew soft that day;
Whispered the branches overhead;
A mindful people came to pay;
Sweet tribute to their hero dead."

A majority of those resting there are men of my own command, whose forms I saw reel and fall in the dire conflict. To me their "last camp" is holy ground and my heart was touched as never before there when I saw daughters of the Confederate soldiers kneeling and placing wreaths of laurel and roses o'er where, in death's cold embrace, sleep the gallant Sons of the South who died for a Cause they loved but could not save.

By far the greater number of those whose hospitality and kind offices we enjoyed in 1865, while waiting the approach of the invading troops are at rest in heaven, I trust, at peace with their God. We are grateful for and proud of the perpetuation of their loyalty, their patriotism, their fealty on the part of their sons and grandsons, their daughters and granddaughters.

"Lord God of hosts be with us yet, lest we forget, lest we forget."

The preparation and rites of decoration are admirable. Wreaths and bouquets of beautiful flowers completely covered the "bivouac of the dead." "Taps," the saddest of all sounds to a soldier, closed the exercises of the occasion.

The addresses of the several speakers, Judge Henry Tillman, the chief orator of the day, Messrs. B. D. Carter and J. Carl Kearse were fine and appropriate, void of fulsome flattery and verbose oratorical display. Music by the band and choir was fine; the dinner splendid and plentiful.

My attendance at Rivers Bridge, May 2, 1924, was more pleasant by far than on February 3rd and 4th 1865.

    Because of my absence from this section of the state and the transpiring of other events, several years have elapsed since my last attendance at the Rivers Bridge ceremonial prior to the above alluded to. My last attendance of several years ago was under circumstances quite unique.
(To Be Continued)

BEN S. WILLIAMS

Hampton County Guardian HAMPTON, S. C., Wednesday, May 6, 1931
CAPT. WILLIAMS SUFFERS STROKE
Aged Confederate Veteran Remains Unconscious at Home in Brunson

Captain Ben S. Williams, 88, of Brunson, who was stricken with paralysis early Monday morning, remained in a serious condition Late Wednesday. Physicians attending the Confederate veteran said he had not regained consciousness and that little hope was held for his recovery.

Forecasts Political Revolution

Captain Ben S. Williams of Brunson, whose 88 years of life have been lived during many of South Carolina's most strenuous political times, foresees a political campaign as hot as Hades in South Carolina next time unless economy in government becomes the watchword of the office seekers.

Captain Williams sets forth his views in a letter to the Columbia State, which is reproduced here.

To the Editor of The State:
Much of late, prior to and during the session of our legislative body, has been, though, written and talked of existing financial conditions in our state. Heavy bonded indebtedness, state and county deficits, excruciating taxation of tangible property, ruinous to prosperity, happiness and home.

During our last political campaign, much condemnation of the status of our affairs, political and financial, was uttered aloud by candidates for offices of trust and honor; strong new planks of platform declared and pointed out, and hope – which "Springs eternal in the human breast" – was clasped to the bosom of many of the "dear people," who hoped and believed that our next and comparatively new legislative body would materially decrease expenses of government by adoption of more economical measures, and thereby greatly reduce taxes.

Our legislature is still in session but hope in the hearts of the voters is blighted. They conceive that their chosen representatives, framers of our law for government, pilots of our ship of state now lashed by waves, advanced events on our sea of time, have failed to afford the hoped for relief. Careful consideration of our tax problem warrants the conclusion that we have reached a climax when measure must be taken for relief and safety.

There is more real interest manifest in our policies today than I have seen in many years, and not since the dying echoes of the slogan rallying the "one gallus, wool-hat boys" for enlistment in the political revolution in South Carolina years ago, dubbed the "Farmers' Movement," have I seen more earnest agitation, and this agitation is not confined to the "one gallus, wool-hat voters." Many owners of much "visible property," who are deeply interested in our state's affairs, welfare, educational interests, etc., demand relief. What will be the result, the ultimatum?

Among the many matters of importance for consideration by our legislature is the fact that unless by their acts care is shown, proper diagnosis of conditions made, and effective remedy of relief applied, there will be one of the hottest political campaigns on the "stumps" of South Carolina known in our history of campaigns. Some of the issues of "the next time" will be leaner salaries, shorter terms of office, brief legislative sessions, actual practice of economical measures framing of policy of government by the people for all of the people. Our future will depend upon an honest administration of government; upon an honest administration with economy as a basis, a fundamental principal.

In our "multitude of counselors" in Columbia may there be sufficient wisdom to avoid the Scylla of state financial bankruptcy and enable us to escape the Charybdis of a political campaign as hot as Hades in South Carolina next time.

Hampton County Guardian HAMPTON, S. C., Wednesday, May 20, 1931

CAPT. WILLIAMS GOES TO REWARD

Confederate Veteran, Gentleman and Scholar Rests in Beech Branch Cemetery

Capt. Ben S. Williams died at "Woodlawn," his country home near Brunson, on last Wednesday, and was laid to rest by the side of his wife, who preceded him nearly eight years, in the historic Beech Branch Church Cemetery, where for several years before the War Between the Sections, his father, the Rev. G. W. M. Williams, served as pastor.

Funeral services were conducted Friday morning at 11 o'clock by Rev. J. P. Dendy of the Brunson Baptist church, Rev. W. J. Swindell of the Christian church and Rev. M. G. Arant of the Methodist church.

While the flag-draped casket was gently lowered amidst a profusion of beautiful floral offerings, the Boy Scouts of the Brunson School, with Scout master J. B. White, superintendent of the school, stood "at attention," E. M. Peeples, mortician in charge, read the impressive poem, "The velvet curtains softly fall and leave the world outside, that's all."

He is survived by four daughters, misses Josephine, Kate, Etta and Tiny Williams of Brunson, one son, Albert Williams of Ocala Fla., and one brother, Willie Williams of Jacksonville, Fla.

Capt. Williams was born June 25, 1843. When tocsin of war first sounded in the fierce struggle between the states, his father having in the meantime moved to Georgia, he, a lad of seventeen laid down his school books, and aided in forming, uniforming and drilling a rifle company. They tendered their services and were mustered in at Savannah, April 9, 1861. Quoting from his "Memoirs of the War" – "I regret that I did not serve one day as a private in the ranks. I was a non-commissioned officer in the aforesaid company. We became a part of the 25 Georgia Volunteer infantry. About eight months service in said regiment I was commissioned by our war department as a first lieutenant and ordered to report in Savannah, for assignment to duty. I was assigned as adjutant of the 47th regiment, Georgia Volunteer Infantry. To this regiment I belonged till the close of the war, though serving in different stations and holding the rank at the close of brevet major, thus serving throughout the entire four years of the war, the last battle being Bentonville, N. C., March 19, 1865."

"After the surrender of Lee's army at Appomattox, when Johnston surrendered in North Carolina, April 26, 1865, folding the flag of my regiment, which was never to be surrendered – and never was, I laid it under my saddle and rode back to the ruins of a home amid the ashes and desolation of a ruined state."

After the war, during the days of reconstruction, Capt. Williams organized a company of Red Shirts and day or night with his 60-odd true and tried followers rode where-ever danger threatened. On one occasion, near Lawtonville, when a crowd of negroes came from Beaufort to make speeches, prominent among them, Whipper and Bob Smalls, the citizens of the section gathered to divide time, with them in speaking. Several preceding Capt. Williams having apparently wearied the audience, cries of "Williams, Williams, where is Williams." sent searchers to bring the modest Williams to the front. He began addressing the crowd; "ladies, gentlemen and fellow citizens, we are here today to divide time with the speakers for this occasion not for any purpose of contention or striving but merely to see that you hear the truth, the whole truth and nothing but the truth." "So help you, God, eh, Captain," exclaimed Whipper – "Yes, so help me, God." And then followed a stream of oratory, clear, lucid, concise, such as was characteristic of him in these and later years, a gift inherited from his kinsman John C. Calhoun. General Wade Hampton, who was present on this occasion, remarked to a friend of Capt. Williams present; "That was decidedly one of the best speeches I have ever heard throughout the state." And the general was so impressed that later when Hampton County was formed, he appointed Captain Williams the first county auditor.

Several years ago Capt. Williams wrote "Memoirs of the War," published in the Sunday News of Charleston and the articles were copied by leading newspapers of other states, several congratulatory letters reaching him from Virginia, Arkansas and Texas. His timely articles on current events of the day were read with great interest by many, the last appearing a few days before the fatal stroke in the columns of The State and The Hampton County Guardian.

A Gentleman of the old school, a scholar, brave, fearless, generous, loyal to truth, honor and friendship, he led a noble and enviable life, loved and respected by all whose spirits are in accord with the highest Southern Ideals. Charitable and benevolent to a fault, his good deeds and helping hand brought cheer and comfort to many unfortunates.

His presence will be sorely missed but his influence for clean living, character and the beautiful things in life will continue to live throughout the years through the inspiration given to the youth of this section who loved to visit and hear him recount in vivid portrayal, thrilling experiences of bivouac and battle

Captain Benjamin S. Williams with the Flag of the 47th Georgia

Ben Williams and Belle Williams Gautier with the 47th Georgia Flag

Four generations: Esther Williams (maker of the flag), W. M. Williams, R. J. Williams, Magnus Williams

William A. Bowers, Jr.

The Second 47th Georgia Regimental Flag made by the Ladies of Charleston South Carolina

Colonel Gilbert William Martin Williams

The 47th Regiment - Georgia Volunteer Infantry Confederate States Army

1862

27 February 1862: The Mitchell Volunteer Guards elected the following officers and non-commissioned officers:

Michael J. Doyle	Captain
Lawrence Dunn	1st Lieutenant
Alexander Doyle	2nd Lieutenant
Bryan Conner	Jr. 2nd Lieutenant
Michael Reilly	1st Sergeant
John R. Minis	2nd Sergeant
Patrick W. Doyle	3rd Sergeant
Thomas H. McGrath	4th Sergeant
Thomas Kelly	5th Sergeant
John J. Daily	1st Corporal
John Henry	2nd Corporal
John J. Roche	3rd Corporal
Andrew Waters	4th Corporal

4 March 1862: The Randolph Light Guards elected the following officers and non-commissioned officers:

Patrick Gormley	Captain
John J. Harper	1st Lieutenant
Simeon T. Jenkins	2nd Lieutenant
Benjamin A. Graham	Jr. 2nd Lieutenant
Henry O. Beall	1st Sergeant
Walter C. Corley	2nd Sergeant
Seaborn R. Lawrence	3rd Sergeant
Joshua Callaway	4th Sergeant
William B. Oxley	5th Sergeant
Samuel Crapps	1st Corporal
Gabriel Phillips	2nd Corporal
James L. Burney	3rd Corporal
Thomas F Harper	4th Corporal

The Bulloch Guards elected the following officers and non-commissioned officers:

William W. Williams	Captain
W. A. Summerlin	1st Lieutenant
Vin Benjamin Wilson	2nd Lieutenant
David C. Proctor	Jr. 2nd Lieutenant
James E. Burnsides	1st Sergeant
John D. Williams	2nd Sergeant
A. R. Lanier	3rd Sergeant

M. Jones	4th Sergeant
William H. Wise	1st Corporal
M. Mikell	2nd Corporal
T. A. Waters	3rd Corporal
James V. Rowe	4th Corporal

The Screven Guards elected the following officers and non-commissioned officers:

John D. Ashton	Captain
James P. Bazemore	1st Lieutenant
Joseph Lawton	2nd Lieutenant
George M. Thompson	Jr. 2nd Lieutenant
William Alexander Carswell	1st Sergeant
Benjamin C. Buford, Sr.	2nd Sergeant
John G. Thompson	3rd Sergeant
John T. Robbins	4th Sergeant
William H. Mears	1st Corporal
John M. Scott	2nd Corporal
Lovick G. Mock	3rd Corporal
Richard P. Scott	4th Corporal

The Chatham Volunteers elected the following officers and non-commissioned officers:

William S. Phillips	Captain
Clem C. Slater	1st Lieutenant
DeWitt Bruyn	2nd Lieutenant
Thomas J. Osteen	Jr. 2nd Lieutenant
John L. Dukes	1st Sergeant
Harmon L. Davis	2nd Sergeant
Thomas M. Mulryne	3rd Sergeant
Carter W. Futch	4th Sergeant
Juda S. Solomans	5th Sergeant
Frank M. Walls	1st Corporal
Joseph E. Singleton	2nd Corporal
Henry Marsh	3rd Corporal
John H. Ulmer	4th Corporal

The Appling Rangers elected the following officers and non-commissioned officers:

James H. Latimer	Captain
Joseph G. Dedge	1st Lieutenant
James S. Patterson	2nd Lieutenant
Calvin W. Dedge	Jr. 2nd Lieutenant
Nathaniel A. Bell	1st Sergeant
John Cook	2nd Sergeant

John M. Sellers	4th Sergeant
David Rivers Tuten	1st Corporal
William Sellers	2nd Corporal
Abraham J. Crosby	3rd Corporal
Silas Roberson	4th Corporal

The Tattnall Invincibles elected the following officers and non-commissioned officers:

Phillip Glenn Tippins	Captain
Daniel L. Kennedy	1st Lieutenant
Columbus Tootle	2nd Lieutenant
Jeremiah Tootle	Jr. 2nd Lieutenant
Simon W. Brewton	1st Sergeant
James M. Wrenn	2nd Sergeant
John Murphy	3rd Sergeant
Robert J. Coursey	4th Sergeant
Jackson Newborn	1st Corporal
David H. Holland	2nd Corporal
John F. Dubberly	3rd Corporal
Joseph Waters	4th Corporal

The Liberty Rangers elected the following officers and non-commissioned officers:

Isaac M. Aiken	Captain
William M. Moon	1st Lieutenant
Archibald Thompson	2nd Lieutenant
Elliott H. Hazzard	Jr. 2nd Lieutenant
Samuel J. Dean	1st Sergeant
William E. Warnell	2nd Sergeant
Joseph Orlando Dorsey	3rd Sergeant
William F. Moody	4th Sergeant
Richard F. Price	5th Sergeant
John G. Smith	1st Corporal
Flemming B. Terrell	2nd Corporal
Samuel K. Tutty	3rd Corporal
Henry G. Ellerbee	4th Corporal
Andrew J. Pinholster	5th Corporal

The Empire State Guards elected the following officers and non-commissioned officers:

A. C. Edwards	Captain
T. P. Hines	1st Lieutenant
Stephen Alfred Wilson	2nd Lieutenant
Thomas E. Boutquin	Jr. 2nd Lieutenant
Robert Godfred Norton	1st Sergeant

R. T. Bourquin	2nd Sergeant
K. S. Blitch	3rd Sergeant
John A. Tullis	4th Sergeant
Paul R. Duggar	5th Sergeant
Peter F. Broughton	1st Corporal
Lawrence E. Shuptrine	2nd Corporal
R. J. Groover	3rd Corporal
Robert W. Tullis	4th Corporal

10 March 1862: William Allen appointed 5th Corporal, Company A
22 March 1862: The Eleventh Battalion, Georgia Volunteer Infantry was organized on this date at Camp Davis near Guyton, Georgia.
The following Regimental officers were elected:

Gilbert W. M. Williams	Lieutenant Colonel
A. C. Edwards	Major
John R. Minis	Sergeant Major
Thomas McElline	2nd Sergeant, Co. A

William J. Rushing of Company G died at Camp Davis
4 April 1862: The following changes occurred in the Eleventh Battalion:

L. E. M Williams	5th Sergeant, Co. C

8 April 1862: Jabez B. Church of Company D died in Screven Co., Georgia
12 April 1862: Lieutenant Calvin W. Dedge of Company F resigned his commission.
14 April 1862: William F. Hovis elected Jr. 2nd Lieutenant of Company F
19 April 1862: Private Reuben C. Nail of Company F died.
20 April 1862: T. L. Hilton of Company C died at Whitesville, Georgia
21 April 1862: Benjamin S. Williams appointed Adjutant of the Eleventh Battalion
William Watson of Company H died at Camp Davis
23 April 1862: Joseph Hamm of Company C. died at Whitesville, Georgia
27 April 1862: James Kerby of Company C died at Battery Harrison, South Carolina
30 April 1862:
Organization of Troops with the Department of South Carolina and Georgia
    Major General J. C. Pemberton, Commanding
    Brig. General Alexander R. Lawton - Commander, District of Georgia
    Brig. General Hugh W. Mercer - Commander, 2nd Brigade
    Colonel G. M. W. Williams - Commander, 11th Georgia Battalion
    Hugh G. McNeily of Company B died
1 May 1862: Joseph C. Thompson appointed Quartermaster Sergeant of the Eleventh Battalion
2 May 1862: Thomas R. Hines appointed Captain and Assistant

Quartermaster of the Eleventh Battalion.
R. Collins of Company C. died at Whitesville, Georgia
5 May 1862: Company K formed and elected the following officers and non-commissioned officers:

Joseph S. Cone	Captain
James J. Miller	1st Lieutenant
David Beasley	2nd Lieutenant
P. C. Sheffield	Jr. 2nd Lieutenant
Jackson J. Driggers	1st Sergeant
William M. Williams	2nd Sergeant
James Lee	3rd Sergeant
J. W. Proctor	4th Sergeant
John Wise	1st Corporal
Joseph Lee	2nd Corporal
Solomon Hagin	3rd Corporal
Allen Hagin	4th Corporal

10 May 1862: Adolphus S. Canuet elected 2nd Lieutenant of Company C
William Crosby of Company C died in Savannah, Georgia
William Deal of Company C. died in Savannah, Georgia
12 May 1862: The Forty-seventh Regiment, Georgia Volunteer Infantry was formed. The following is the list of officers and non-commissioned officer and the organization of the regiment:

Gilbert W. M. Williams	Colonel
A. C. Edwards	Lieutenant Colonel
James G. Cone	Major
Benjamin S. Williams	Adjutant
H. E. Cassidy	Chaplain
Thomas Hines	Quartermaster (Captain)

Organization of Company A, The Mitchell Volunteer Guards:

Michael J. Doyle	Captain
Alexander Doyle	1st Lieutenant
Bryan Conner	2nd Lieutenant
Patrick W. Doyle	Jr. 2nd Lieutenant
Michael Reilly	1st Sergeant
John R. Minis	2nd Sergeant
Thomas Kelly	3rd Sergeant
John Henry	4th Sergeant
Thomas H. McGrath	5th Sergeant
John J. Daily	1st Corporal
John J. Roche	2nd Corporal
Nicholas Cullen	3rd Corporal
Andrew Waters	4th Corporal

Organization of Company B, The Randolph Light Guards:

Patrick Gormley	Captain
John J. Harper	1st Lieutenant

Simeon T. Jenkins	2nd Lieutenant
Benjamin A. Graham	Jr. 2nd Lieutenant
Henry O. Beall	1st Sergeant
Walter C. Corley	2nd Sergeant
Seaborn R. Lawrence	3rd Sergeant
Joshua Callaway	4th Sergeant
William B. Oxley	5th Sergeant
Samuel Crapps	1st Corporal
Gabriel Phillips	2nd Corporal
James L. Burney	3rd Corporal
Thomas F Harper	4th Corporal

Organization of Company C, The Bulloch Guards:

William W. Williams	Captain
W. A. Summerlin	1st Lieutenant
Vin Benjamin Wilson	2nd Lieutenant
David C. Proctor	Jr. 2nd Lieutenant
James E. Burnsides	1st Sergeant
John D. Williams	2nd Sergeant
A. R. Lanier	3rd Sergeant
M. Jones	4th Sergeant
L. E. M. Williams	5th Sergeant
William H. Wise	1st Corporal
M. Mikell	2nd Corporal
T. A. Waters	3rd Corporal
James V. Rowe	4th Corporal

Organization of Company D, The Screven Guards:

John D. Ashton	Captain
James P. Bazemore	1st Lieutenant
Joseph Lawton	2nd Lieutenant
George M. Thompson	Jr. 2nd Lieutenant
William Alexander Carswell	1st Sergeant
Benjamin C. Buford, Sr.	2nd Sergeant
John G. Thompson	3rd Sergeant
John T. Robbins	4th Sergeant
William H. Mears	1st Corporal
John M. Scott	2nd Corporal
Hiram D. Prescott	3rd Corporal
Richard P. Scott	4th Corporal

Organization of Company E, The Chatham Volunteers:

William S. Phillips	Captain
Clem C. Slater	1st Lieutenant
DeWitt Bruyn	2nd Lieutenant
Thomas J. Osteen	Jr. 2nd Lieutenant
John L. Dukes	1st Sergeant
Harmon L. Davis	2nd Sergeant

Thomas M. Mulryne	3rd Sergeant
Carter W. Futch	4th Sergeant
Juda S. Solomans	5th Sergeant
Frank M. Walls	1st Corporal
Joseph E. Singleton	2nd Corporal
Henry Marsh	3rd Corporal
John H. Ulmer	4th Corporal

Organization of Company F, The Appling Rangers:

James H. Latimer	Captain
Joseph G. Dedge	1st Lieutenant
James S. Patterson	2nd Lieutenant
William F. Hovis	Jr. 2nd Lieutenant
Nathaniel A. Bell	1st Sergeant
John Cook	2nd Sergeant
John M. Sellers	4th Sergeant
Silas Crosby	5th Sergeant
David Rivers Tuten	1st Corporal
William Sellers	2nd Corporal
Abraham J. Crosby	3rd Corporal
Silas Roberson	4th Corporal

Organization of Company G, The Tattnall Invincibles:

Phillip Glenn Tippins	Captain
Danile L. Kennedy	1st Lieutenant
Columbus Tootle	2nd Lieutenant
Jeremiah Tootle	Jr. 2nd Lieutenant
James M. Wrenn	1st Sergeant
Simon W. Brewton	2nd Sergeant
John C. Parker	3rd Sergeant
William E. Southwell	4th Sergeant
John Murphy	5th Sergeant
Robert J. Coursey	5th Sergeant
Jackson Newborn	1st Corporal
David H Holland	2nd Corporal
John F. Dubberly	3rd Corporal
Joseph Waters	4th Corporal

Organization of Company H, The Liberty Rangers;

Isaac M. Aiken	Captain
William M. Moon	1st Lieutenant
Archibald Thompson	2nd Lieutenant
Elliott H. Hazzard	Jr. 2nd Lieutenant
Samuel J. Dean	1st Sergeant
William E. Warnell	2nd Sergeant
Joseph Orlando Dorsey	3rd Sergeant
William F. Moody	4th Sergeant
Richard F. Price	5th Sergeant

John G. Smith	1st Corporal
Flemming B. Terrell	2nd Corporal
Samuel K. Tutty	3rd Corporal
Henry G. Ellerbee	4th Corporal
Andrew J. Pinholster	5th Corporal

Organization of Company I, The Empire State Guards:

T. P. Hines	Captain
Stephen Alfred Wilson	1st Lieutenant
Thomas E. Bourquin	2nd Lieutenant
Robert Godfred Norton	Jr. 2nd Lieutenant
R. T. Bourquin	1st Sergeant
K. S. Blitch	2nd Sergeant
John A. Tullis	3rd Sergeant
Paul R. Duggar	4th Sergeant
Thomas J. Hurst	5th Sergeant
Peter F. Broughton	1st Corporal
Lawrence E. Shuptrine	2nd Corporal
James E. Arnsdorff	3rd Corpora
Robert W. Tullis	4th Corporal

Organization of Company K

Joseph S. Cone	Captain
James J. Miller	1st Lieutenant
David Beasley	2nd Lieutenant
P. C. Sheffield	Jr. 2nd Lieutenant
Jackson J. Driggers	1st Sergeant
William M. Williams	2nd Sergeant
James Lee	3rd Sergeant
J. W. Proctor	4th Sergeant
John Wise	1st Corporal
Joseph Lee	2nd Corporal
Solomon Hagin	3rd Corpora
Allen Hagin	4th Corporal

19 May 1862: Wesley P. Bullard of Company F died of disease
31 May 1862: William H. Coran of Company B died
P. S. S. Ogilvie died at Savannah, Georgia hospital
1 June 1862:
Organization of Troops With the Department of South Carolina and Georgia
    Major General J. C. Pemberton, Commanding
    Brig. General William D. Smith - Commander, 1st Military District
    Brig. General S. R. Gist - Commander, Troops on James Island
    Colonel G. M. W. Williams - Commander, 47th Georgia Regiment
The following changes occurred in the Forty-seventh Regiment:

John Rambo	Surgeon
Stiles Kennedy	Assistant Surgeon

Leonidas McAllister	Assistant Surgeon
James R. Frazier	Assistant Commissary Sergeant
Adolphus S. Canuet	1st Lieutenant - Co. C
L. M. Prime	5th Sergeant - Co. C
Thomas N. Mulrane	1st Sergeant - Co. E
Frank M. Walls	3rd Sergeant - Co. E
Jeremiah Baden	4th Sergeant Co. E
Joseph E. Singleton	5th Sergeant Co. E
John L. Ulmer	2nd Corporal - Co. .E
Archibald Peterdon	5th Sergeant - Co. H
Samuel K. Tutty	1st Corporal - Co. H

2 June 1862: Homer Hamans of Company H died at Savannah, Georgia hospital

3 June 1862: William Alexander of Company E died
Cornelius Carpenter of Company E died

5 June 1862: William W. Dubberly of Company G died of disease at Causton's Bluff, Georgia

6 June 1862: Amos J. Hart of Company B died

8 June 1862: B. J. Lee of Company K died at Causton's Bluff, Georgia

9 June 1862: *James Island, South Carolina*
The Forty-seventh Regiment, Georgia Voluntary Infantry involved in a battle with Federal troops on James Island, South Carolina
"...............We were relieved about half past 10 o'clock A. M. by the Louisiana battalion, commanded by Lieutenant Colonel McHenry. Soon after returning to camp, the Eutaws were again ordered out, and took post behind the breastworks. This was done to be ready for a possible attack, which a movement about to be made by the Forty-seventh Georgia might provoke. This movement was a reconnaissance in force of the woods in front of the enemy's position. Colonel Haygood, with the First regiment, was sent to reinforce the picket. The Georgians pressed forward through the woods on the left of the picket line. The Forty-seventh drove the enemy from their position behind a ditch bank and then fell back themselves, being in turn driven back. The enemy either rallied or were reinforced. The woods were very thick, and the Forty-seventh regiment became separated in marching through. Captain Cone's company, upon getting out of the woods, discovered a body of men near by. An officer beckoned them on. Captain Cone, mistaking them for friends, approached with his company, when fire was opened on him and fifteen of his men were shot down and the Captain wounded. The fighting became very severe. Captain Williams' company and Captain Cone's were almost annihilated. The Forty-seventh then drew off, leaving their dead and many of their wounded in the hands of the enemy.

".....The Forty-seventh Georgia Under Colonel Williams were repulsed in the woods at Grinball's after a gallant onset on the enemy............."
(Battle of Secessionville)

History of the 47th Georgia Volunteer Infantry, CSA

Grinball's on the Stono (near Charleston on Battery Island, South Carolina)

"…….the woods through which the Forty-seventh advanced was so dense that order could not be preserved nor could commands be properly extended

10 June 1862:

Killed	4th Sergeant John Henry - Co. A
	Captain William W. Williams - Co. C
	Private Solomon Brannen - Co. C
	Private E. Helmouth - Co. C
	Private John Kelley - Co. C
	Private A. J. Thompson - Co .C
	Private Allen Wilson - Co. C
	Private Henry T. Neve - Co. E
	Private James L. Coleman - Co. G
	Private John McGinnis - Co. H
	Private John H. Mosley - Co. H
	3rd Sergeant J. E. Gibson - Co. K
	Private John S. Cone Co. K
	Private Wiley A. Martin - Co. K
	Private W. H. Sheffield - Co .K
Wounded	Private John L. Mikell - Co. C
	Private John Williams - Co. F
	Private Richard M. Youmans - Co. F
	Private Simeon Tootle - Co. G
	Private C. C. Fails - Co. H
	Private James J. Rowe - Co. H
	5th Sergeant Leonard W. Kirkland - Co. K
	3rd Corporal Solomon Hagin - Co. K
	Private Paul R. Cone - Co. K
	Private David Daniel DeLoach - Co. K
	Private Thomas Harrison Denmark - Co. K
	Private E. Driggers - Co. K
	Private James J. Johnston - Co. K
	Private John S. Lee - Co. K
	Private J .C. Lee - Co. K
	Private E. H. Martin - Co. K
	Private J. O. Martin - Co. K
	Private Reuben C. Martin - Co. K
	Private Thomas Henry Michael - Co. K
	Private A. J. Proctor - Co. K
	Private P. C. Richardson - Co. K
Captured	Private John J. Mikell - Co. C

Private Seaborn Hall - Co. F
Private David Daniel DeLoach - Co. K
Private J. O. Martin - Co. K

The reported loss of the Forty-seventh Georgia Regiment was sixty-five killed, wounded and missing.

The report of Brigadier General Horatio G. Wright, U. S. Army states that the Forty-seventh Georgia Regiment was in a skirmish with the Sixth Connecticut and the report of captured by Union troops was 16 dead and 4 wounded.

Private James Hearn died of disease.
Private Joseph C. Thompson transferred from Company H to Company C
Leonard W. Kicklighter appointed 5th Sergeant for Company K
11 June 1862: John F. Bacon died of disease in Charleston, South Carolina hospital.
12June 1862: The following change occurred in Company A, Forty-seventh Regiment
  John Daily   5th Sergeant
The following changes occurred in Company K, Forty-seventh Regiment
  John J Roche   1st Corporal
  Nicholas Cullen   2nd Corporal
  Andrew Waters   3rd Corporal
  Patrick S. Campbell 4th Corporal
14 June 1862: Private Simeon Tootle of Company G died of wounds.
Private George W. Spell died of disease.
15 June 1862: One company of the Forty-seventh Regiment on Picket duty at Secessionville, South Carolina.
16 June 1862: *Secessionville, South Carolina.*(Fort Johnson, James Island)
The report of Brigadier General Nathan G. Evans states that Colonel Williams Regiment (47th Georgia) sent in after the second Federal assault on the works at Secessionville.
Killed   Jr. 2nd Lieutenant Benjamin H. Graham - Co. B
18 June 1862: Private James E. Clanton of Company E died at James Island, South Carolina
19 June 1862: Private C. W. Flowers of Company H died in Savannah, Georgia hospital.
Private W. W. Dickerson of Company K died of disease.
23 June 1862: Forty-seventh Georgia Regiment on James Island, South Carolina
25 June 1862: Private Charles Church of Company D died.

Private Austin W. Blount of Company F died of disease.
27 June 1862: Private Austin W. Blount of Company F died in Augusta, Georgia hospital
28 June 1862: Private Madison Ryals of Company G died of disease in Augusta, Georgia hospital
1 July 1862:
Organization of Troops with the Department of South Carolina and Georgia
    Major General J. C. Pemberton, Commanding
    Brig. General Hugh W. Mercer- Commander, District of Georgia
    Colonel G. M. W. Williams - Commander, 47th Georgia Regiment
The following changes occurred in the Forty-seventh Regiment:
    James E. Holmes   Ordinance Sergeant
2 July 1862: Private Reuben Waters on Company D died of Brain Disease at Camp Mackee
3 July 1862: Private Henry Hardin of Company B died in Randolph County, Georgia
   Private William H. McKinney on detached duty at Mission Hospital, Guyton, Georgia.
4 July 1862: The following changes occurred in Company C, Forty-seventh Regiment
    Robert J. Williams   1st Lieutenant
8 July 1862: Private J. C. Lee of Company C died of wounds.
10 July 1862: The following changes occurred in the Forty-seventh Regiment:
Co. C W. A. Summerlin,1st Lieutenant resigned his commission
Co. G Columbus Tootle, 2nd Lieutenant resigned his commission(due to bad health)
    Jeremiah Tootle   2nd Lieutenant
    Thomas Holland   Jr. 2nd Lieutenant

Private H. B. Franklin of Company C died of disease in Savannah, Georgia Hospital.
Private Thomas W. Ward of Company E died of disease.
13 July 1862: Private Calvin C. Cowart of Company E died of disease.
16 July 1862: Private Daniel Nighton of Company H died
17 July 1862: Private Perry J. Miller of Company C. died of disease in Randolph County, Georgia
Private Joshua Arnsdorff of Company I died of disease
18 July 1862: The following changes occurred in Company E, Forty-seventh Regiment
1st Lieutenant Clem C. Slater resigned his commission due to Ill health.
    DeWitt Buryn   1st Lieutenant
    Thomas J. Osteen   2nd Lieutenant
    John J. Dukes   Jr. 2nd Lieutenant

Private Paul R. Cone of Company K died of wounds.
22 July 1862: Private Cornelius Frawley died of Typhoid Fever, Oglethorpe Hospital, Savannah, Georgia.
24 July 1862: The following change occurred in Company B, Forty-seventh Regiment:
    Seaborn R. Lawrence Jr. 2nd Lieutenant
27 July 1862: Private William Gillis of Company H died of disease.
28 July 1862: Private Joseph McCullough died of disease in Savannah, Georgia
30 July 1862: The following change occurred in Company E, Forty-seventh Regiment:

Frank M. Walls	2nd Sergeant
Jeremiah Baden	3rd Sergeant
John H. Ulmer	1st Corporal
John Kuhlman	2nd Corporal
Maximillian D. Osteen	4th Corporal

The following change occurred in Company G, Forty-seventh Regiment:
    Thomas H. Southwell 3rd Sergeant
Private Thomas C. Cowart of Company E. died of disease.
1 August 1862: The following change occurred in the Forty-seventh Regiment:
    John A. Bazemore   Commissary
The following change occurred in Company G, Forty-seventh Regiment:
    John G. Parker   1st Sergeant
2 August 1862: Private Michael Leonard died of disease, Screven's Ferry, Georgia.
3 August 1862: Private Elijah Sapp of Company F died of disease at Camp Williams, Georgia
4 August 1862 : Private Jesse Brown of Company K died of disease
5 August 1862: The following changes occurred in Company F, Forty-seventh Regiment:

Thomas Fletcher	1st Sergeant
John M. Sellers	2nd Sergeant
David Rivers Tuten	3rd Sergeant
Silas Roberson	4th Sergeant
William Sellers	1st Corporal
William S. Holton	3rd Corporal

11 August 1862: Private William Baldwin Davenport of Company B died of disease at Oglethorpe Barracks, Savannah, Georgia.
12 August 1862: 2nd Corporal Nicholas Cullen of Company A died disease in Medical College Hospital, Savannah, Georgia.
The following change occurred in Company F, Forty-seventh Regiment:
    John Aaron Johnson   4th Corporal
16 August 1862: Private Thomas W. Blackburn of Company D died of Brain disease.

Private Phillip Herndon of Company F died of disease at Camp Williams, Georgia.

22 August 1862: The following change occurred in Company E, Forty-seventh Regiment:

    Joseph C. Thompson   2nd Lieutenant

The following change occurred in Company D, Forty-seventh Regiment:

    Adolphus S. Canuet   Captain

1 September 1862: The following change occurred in the Forty-seventh Regiment:

    G. Williams   Quartermaster Sergeant
    John H. Flood   Commissary Sergeant

The following changes occurred in Company A, Forty-seventh Regiment:

    Thomas McElline   1st Sergeant
    Thomas Kelly   2nd Sergeant
    John J. Roche   3nd Sergeant
    Andrew Waters   1st Corporal
    James B. Reed   4th Corporal

Private Patrick Doyle of Company A detached to schooner.

Private Richard M. Youmans of Company F on Picket duty at Proctor's Point, South Carolina

2 September 1862: The following change occurred in the Forty-seventh Regiment:

    John T. McLane   Assistant Surgeon

3 September 1862: Private Christopher C. Coursey of Company G died of disease.

5 September 1862: The following change occurred in Company D, Forty-seventh Regiment:

James P. Bazemore resigned his commission.

15 September 1862: Private James G. Seckinger of Company I died of disease.

16 September 1862: Private James Hamans of Company H accidentally killed at Camp Williams, Georgia.

17 September 1862: John Rambo resigned as Surgeon due to disability.

20 September 1862: Private Richard Williams of Company E died.

21 September 1862: The following change occurred in Company G, Forty-seventh Regiment:

Thomas Holland, Jr. 2nd Lieutenant resigned his commission.

5th Corporal Andrew H. Pinholster of Company H. died of disease in Savannah, Georgia hospital.

24 September 1862: Private William H. Standfield of Company G. died in Whitesville, Georgia hospital.

25 September 1862: 10 companies of the Forty-seventh regiment positioned in Savannah, Georgia; Company B detached with the Savannah River batteries; Company E detached at the Charleston and Savannah Railroad bridge.

26 September 1862: Private John Futrell of Company I died of disease.
28 September 1862: Private John E. Whaley died of disease in Regimental Hospital, Camp Williams, Savannah, Georgia.
The following change occurred in Company A, Forty-seventh Regiment:
    Patrick S. Campbell   2nd Corporal
30 September 1862: The Forty-seventh Regiment is in Oglethorpe Barracks, Savannah, Georgia.
1 October 1862: Private George W. Coxwell of Company B appointed Hospital Steward
Private James M. McNeily of Company B detailed to Gun Boat duty
Private David Yawn of Company F died of disease.
2 October 1862: The records of Company B of the Forty-seventh Regiment show that they left Savannah for Coosawhatchie, South Carolina.
4 October 1862: Private Charles M. Joyce died in Medical Hospital
7 October 1862: Jr. 2nd Lieutenant George M. Thompson of Company D died of disease in camp.
The following change occurred in Company D, Forty-seventh Regiment:
    William Alexander Carswell   Jr. 2nd Lieutenant
8 October 1862: Private Henry Coleman of Company B died in Georgia Hospital, Savannah, Georgia
Private Thomas Crapps of Company F. died of Typhoid Fever at Savannah, Georgia.
10 October 1862: Private Capel Tootle of Company G died of disease.
11 October 1862: Private John Sikes of Company G died of disease in Savannah, Georgia.
14 October 1862: The following changes occurred in Company D, Forty-seventh Regiment:
    Captain John D. Ashton resigned his commission
    Joseph Lawton Singleton   1st Lieutenant
15 October 1862: The following change occurred in Company H, Forty-seventh Regiment:
    James O. Richardson   2nd Sergeant
18 October 1862: Private James R. Johns of Company H was captured at Proctor's Point, Savannah River.
19 October 1862: Private Ambrose H. Ingram of Company B died of disease at Savannah, Georgia.
20 October 1862: Private Benjamin Dawson of Company B died in Regimental Hospital, Camp Williams, Savannah, Georgia.
21 October 1862: The Forty-seventh Regiment is located at Camp Williams, Savannah, Georgia
Private William Lynch of Company I attached to General Hospital, Guyton Georgia as a nurse.
24 October 1862: Company B of the Forty-seventh Regiment is stationed at the Coosawhatchie River in South Carolina. The company leaves Coosawhatchie for Savannah.

Private Hezekiah D. Howard of Company D died of disease in Screven County, Georgia.
25 October 1862: Private Richard Dotson of Company I died of disease at Camp Williams, Georgia.
29 October 1862: The following change occurred in Company D, Forty-seventh Regiment:
    Joseph Lawton Singleton   Captain
31 October 1862: The Forty-seventh Regiment is located at Savannah, Georgia

Privates Jonathan A. Blount and Richard G. Brooker of Company F. on Picket duty at Proctor's Point, Savannah River.

5th Sergeant Silas Crosby of Company F. detailed to assist the Enrolling Officer.

Privates Joseph Henry Comas and Mathias Quinn and Edwards of Company F detailed to gather conscripts.

Private Edward Anderson of Company G detailed to special duty at Proctor's Point, Savannah River

1 November 1862: The following changes occurred in the Forty-seventh Regiment:
    David A. Matthews transferred to the 47th Regiment as Surgeon

The following change occurred in Company A, Forty-seventh Regiment:
    Bryan Conner detailed as Enrolling Officer
    Michael McGuire detailed on Gun Boat

The following changes occurred in Company C, Forty-seventh Regiment:
    Wayne D. Waters   3rd Corporal
    Harmon O. Riggs   4th Corporal

The following change occurred in Company E, Forty-seventh Regiment:
    Private Edward J. Bird detailed with the Engineer Department, Savannah, Georgia

The following changes occurred in Company F, Forty-seventh Regiment:
    Private James M. Hagin assisting Enrolling Officer
    Private Thomas J. Hall assisting Enrolling Officer
    Private Clement T. Latimer detailed to Company Commissary
    Private James Warnock detailed as Wagoner
    Private Daniel R. Varn of Company F died of disease.

6 November 1862: The following change occurred in Company C, Forty-seventh Regiment:
    Jr. 2nd Lieutenant David C. Proctor resigned his commission

The following changes occurred in Company H, Forty-seventh Regiment:
    2nd Lieutenant   Elliott H. Hazzard resigned his commission

8 November 1862: Private John E. Arnsdorff of Company I died of disease at Savannah River Bridge.

10 November 1862: Private James Holton of Company F died of disease at Altamaha River Bridge. Private John Williams of Company F died of wounds

Private James W. Daniel of Company G died of disease in Tattnall County, Georgia.
12 November 1862: Private John W. Tippins of Company G died of disease in Tattnall County, Georgia.
4th Sergeant William F. Moody of Company H died of disease in hospital.
14 November 1862: One company of the Forty-seventh is ordered by General Mercer to report to Colonel E. C. Anderson at the Savannah River batteries located at Proctor's Point to replace the company assigned there.
20 November 1862: The following change occurred in Company I, Forty-seventh Regiment:
    W. T. Copeland   1st Corporal
22 November 1862: The following change occurred in Company C, Forty-seventh Regiment:
    T. A. Waters   1st Corporal
23 November 1862: The following change occurred in Company C, Forty-seventh Regiment:
    S. P. Williams   3rd Sergeant
24 November 1862: The following changes occurred in Company C, Forty-seventh Regiment:
Captain A. S. Canuet Cashiered by Sentence, General Court Martial
Joseph C. Thompson   Captain
1 December 1862: The following change occurred in the Forty-seventh Regiment:
George W. Coxwell   Assistant Surgeon
4 December 1862: The following change occurred in the Forty-seventh Regiment
James B. Wiggins   Assistant Surgeon
5 December 1862: The following change occurred in Company G, Forty-seventh Regiment:
Clement T. Bowen   1st Corporal
8 December 1862: The following change occurred in Company C, Forty-seventh Regiment:
L. E. M. Williams   Jr. 2nd Lieutenant
The following changes occurred in Company G, Forty-seventh Regiment:
John C. Parker   Jr. 2nd lieutenant
Isaac C. Daniel   1st Sergeant
12 December 1862: Private Andrew J. Newman of Company G. died of Typhoid Fever at Camp Anderson.
14 December 1862: The following change occurred in Company I, Forty-seventh Regiment:
    Henry H. Wilson   2nd Corporal
15 December 1862: Private W. B. Williams of Company K died in Savannah, Georgia.
17 December 1862: 3rd Sergeant Joshua Calloway of Company B died in Randolph County, Georgia.

22 December 1862: The following changes occurred in Company H, Forty-seventh Regiment:
1st Lieutenant William B. Moon resigned his commission.
Elliott H. Hazzard   1st Lieutenant
Samuel J. Dean   2nd Lieutenant
J. M. Chesser   Jr. 2nd Lieutenant
Private J. C. Johns died in General Hospital, Augusta, Georgia.
25 December 1862: 3rd Sergeant James Lee died at Wilmington, North Carolina.

1863
1 January 1863: The following changes occurred in Company B, Forty-seventh Regiment:
Joshua Callaway   3rd Sergeant
William B. Oxley   4th Sergeant
Gabriel J. Phillips   5th Sergeant
The following change occurred in Company C, Forty-seventh Regiment:
Jr. 2nd Lieutenant L. E. M. Williams detailed Recruiting Officer
The following change occurred in Company H, Forty-seventh Regiment:
S. M. Ryals   1st Corporal
Private Patrick Tighe of Company A was killed at Savannah by a member of his company.
8 January 1863: The following changes occurred in Company A, Forty-seventh Regiment:
Captain Michael J. Doyle resigned his commission
Bryan Conner   Captain
14 January 1863: Private Thomas A. McWilliams of Company B lost his arm in a railroad accident at Fair Bluff, North Carolina.
Private James Bradley of Company G died of disease at C. S. A. General Military Hospital, Wilmington, North Carolina.
25 January 1863: Private David Groover of Company K died at Top Sail Sound, North Carolina.
28 January 1863: Private Solomon W. Osteen of Company E died in General Hospital #1, Savannah, Georgia.
31 January 1863:
Organization of Troops District of Cape Fear, North Carolina
        Brig. General W..H. Whiting, Commanding
        Colonel Harrison- Commander, Harrison's Brigade
        Colonel G. M. W. Williams - Commander, 47th Georgia Regiment
1 February 1863: The following changes occurred in Company A, Forty-seventh Regiment:
        James B Reed   1st Corporal
        John Frain   3rd Corporal (could have been 2nd Corporal)
        John Knox   3rd Corporal (could have been 2nd Corporal)
        Joseph H. Simpson   4th Corporal

The following changes occurred in Company H, Forty-seventh Regiment:
    Samuel K. Tutty   1st Sergeant
    William W. Hamilton 4th Sergeant
4th Sergeant William W. Hamilton detailed Enrolling Officer for Company H
Private W. R. McVey in Whitesville, Georgia Hospital
8 February 1863: Sunday, the Forty-seventh Georgia Regiment left Wilmington, North Carolina at 12:00 noon.
9 February 1863: Monday, the Forty-seventh Georgia Regiment arrived in Charleston at 10:00 am
Private James Allen Mallett, Sr. of Company I died in Savannah, Georgia Hospital.
Private William W. DeLoach of Company K died at Top Sail Sound, North Carolina.
13 February 1863: The following changes occurred in Company I, Forty-seventh Regiment:
    Captain T. P. Hines resigned his commission
    Stephen Alfred Wilson   Captain
15 February 1863: Private Reuben C. McElveen of Company K died at Savannah, Georgia.
18 February 1863: The following changes occurred in Company I, Forty-seventh Regiment:
    Thomas E. Bourquin   1st Lieutenant
    Robert Godfred Norton   2nd Lieutenant
    R. T. Bourquin   Jr. 2nd Lieutenant
21 February 1863: 4th Sergeant William B. Oxley died in Regimental Hospital, Savannah, Georgia.
22 February 1863: Private Hansford Youmans of Company G died of disease at Wilmington, North Carolina.
23 February 1863: The following change occurred in the Forty-seventh Regiment:
    H. E. Cassidy resigned as Chaplain of the 47th Regiment
25 February 1863: Sylvanius G. Robertson of Company B detailed as Commissary Sergeant in Savannah, Georgia.
28 February 1863: The Forty-seventh Regiment is located in Savannah, Georgia.
4th Sergeant Thomas H. McGrath of Company A on special duty enrolling conscripts.
Private John Nicholson of Company A detailed to Miller's Foundry, Confederate States Government Workshop.
Private James McNeilly of Company B detailed as teamster.
Private Michael C. Parkerson of Company B died.
Private Samuel Wolfe of Company B detailed in Quartermasters Department, Savannah, Georgia.
Private Jacob L. Freeman of Company D died.

1 March 1863: The Forty-seventh Regiment at Red Bluff (near Hardeeville, South Carolina, Colonel Gilbert W. M. Williams, Commanding.
Benjamin S. Williams listed as Adjutant of the Forty-seventh Regiment at Red Bluff.
David A. Matthews listed as Surgeon in charge of the Red Bluff Hospital.
Private Harrison Brannen of Company C died in General Hospital at Wilmington, North Carolina.
2 March 1863: Private G. C. Floyd of Company I died of disease in General Hospital #1, Savannah, Georgia.
6 March 1863: There was a Court Martial in Charleston involving several officers of the Forty-seventh Regiment.
12 March 1863: Private Ransom J. Jarrad of Company H died at Hilton Head, South Carolina.
13 March 1863:
Organization of Troops, Department of South Carolina, Georgia and Florida
    General P. G. T. Beauregard, Commanding
    Brig. General Hugh W. Mercer- Commander, District of Georgia
    Colonel G. M. W. Williams - Commander, 47th Georgia Regiment
March 1863:
Organization of Troops, Department of South Carolina, Georgia and Florida
    General P. G. T. Beauregard, Commanding
    Brig. General Hugh W. Mercer- Commander, District of Georgia
    Colonel G. M. W. Williams - Commander, 47th Georgia Regiment
18 March 1863: Seaborn Hall of Company F appointed Sub-Enrolling Officer, Appling County, Georgia.
20 March 1863: Private Horace Powers of Company B on detached service at the Macon, Georgia Armory.
30 March 1863: The Forty-seventh Regiment is in Oglethorpe Barracks, Savannah, Georgia.
Private Francis Williamson of Company E. died
1 April 1863: The Forty-seventh Georgia Regiment assigned as follows:
Company E detached at the Charleston/Savannah railroad bridge in Georgia.
Company F detailed at the Altamaha River railroad bridge at Doctortown, Georgia
The other eight companies of the regiment were at Red Bluff, South Carolina.
Private J. F. Barbee of Company H deployed as a nurse Removed to Quartermaster Department".
6 April 1863: The following change occurred in Company B, Forty-seventh Regiment:
    Seaborn R. Lawrence   1st Lieutenant
15 April 1863: The following change occurred in Company B, Forty-

seventh Regiment:
    Captain Patrick Gormley   cashiered
    John J. Harper   Captain
    2dn Lieutenant Simeon T. Jenkins resigned due to disability
    Seaborn R. Lawrence   2nd Lieutenant

21 April 1863: The records of Company C of the Forty-seventh Regiment indicates that they left the camp at Red Bluff, South Carolina and marched 5 miles and are now in Camp Allen near Jonesville, South Carolina.

30 April 1863: The Muster Rolls of Company C and Company D of the Forty-seventh Regiment indicate that they are located at Camp Allen, South Carolina on this date.

Remark on the muster Roll of Company D:
 Since last muster this company has been ordered from Mc ..(unintelligible) at Red Bluff, S. C. to Camp Allen near Jonesville and has been engaged in digging rifle pits near the batteries on the road to (unintelligible) bridge landing above Red Bluff."

1 May 1863: The Forty-seventh Georgia Regiment assigned as follows:
Company E detached at the Charleston/Savannah railroad bridge in Georgia.
Company F detailed at the Altamaha River railroad bridge at Doctortown, Georgia
The other eight companies of the regiment at Camp Allen, near Jonesville, South Carolina

2 May 1863: The following change occurred in the Forty-seventh Regiment: Captain Thomas R. Hines, Quartermaster , resigned his commission.
    William Percy Mortimer Ashley   Assistant Quartermaster

6 May 1863: The following change occurred in Company G, Forty-seventh Regiment:
    Captain Phillip Glenn Tippins resigned his commission
Private Albert V. McCrory of Company I died at Jonesville, South Carolina.

8 May 1863:
Organization of Troops, Department of South Carolina, Georgia and Florida
    General P. G. T. Beauregard, Commanding
    Brig. General W. S. Walker- Commander, 3rd Military District
    Colonel G. M. W. Williams - Commander, 47th Georgia Regiment

9 May 1863: The Forty-seventh Georgia Regiment is at New River Battery. Ordinance is transferred on this date.

10 May 1863: Special Order No. 105 ;
Forty-seventh Georgia placed in Hagood's Brigade under Brigadier General Johnson Haygood along with the 11th, 20th and 26th South Carolina Regiments.

13 May 1863: Special Order no. 107;

The Forty-seventh Georgia ordered by General Beauregard to report to Brigadier General W. H. T. Walker at Jackson, Mississippi.
14 May 1863: Major James G. Cone resigned his commission.
18 May 1863: The Forty-seventh Regiment is issued the following new clothing in preparation to ship out:
    300   uniforms
    600   uniform caps
The following change occurred in Company A, Forty-seventh Regiment:
    1st Lieutenant Alexander Doyle resigned his commission
    Patrick W. Doyle   1st Lieutenant
The following change occurred in Company E, Forty-seventh Regiment
    DeWill Bruyn   Captain
19 May 1863: Orders are issued for all absent soldiers to return to Savannah, Georgia.
26 May 1863: Private David Beasley of Company C. Died near Jackson, Mississippi
29 May 1863: The following change occurred in Company K, Forty-seventh Regiment:
    2nd Lieutenant David Beasley resigned his commission
    P. C. Sheffield   2nd Lieutenant
    James S. Hagin   Jr. 2nd Lieutenant
1 June 1863: The following change occurred in Company H, Forty-seventh Regiment:
    Hamilton Clark   3rd Corporal
2 June 1863: Private Calvin Yawn of Company F. died in General Hospital #1, Savannah, Georgia
3 June 1863: The Forty-seventh Georgia Regiment at Jackson Mississippi
Present for duty   27 officers   450 men   455 effective
Aggregate present 532   Total present and absent 778
6 June 1863:
Organization of Forces at Jackson Mississippi
Major General John C. Breckinridge, Commanding
Colonel G. W. M. Williams, Commander, 47th Georgia
Private D. E. Wilson of Company I died in Jackson, Mississippi.
7 June 1863: Private John A. Dale of Company B drowned in the Pearl River, Mississippi
10 June 1863: Private Thomas H. Denmark of Company K attached as guard at General Hospital, Lauderdale Springs, Mississippi.
Private J. C. Morgan of Company I died in Lauderdale Springs, Mississippi Hospital
The following changes occurred in Company H, Forty-seventh Regiment:
    Elliott H. Hazzard   Captain
    Samuel J. Dean   1st Lieutenant
    William R. McDonald   Jr. 2nd Lieutenant

Private J. D. Kehl of Company I died in General Hospital #1, Savannah, Georgia.
17 June 1863: Private Salem Sapp of Company G died of disease.
22 June 1863: The following change occurred in Company B, Forty-seventh Regiment:

    Henry O. Beall   Jr. 2nd Lieutenant

The following changes occurred in Company K, Forty-seventh Regiment:

    P. C. Sheffield   1st Lieutenant
    James S. Hagin   2nd Lieutenant
    James G. Cone   Jr. 2nd Lieutenant

25 June 1863: The following changes occurred in Company G, Forty-seventh Regiment:

    Daniel L. Kennedy   Captain
    John C. Parker   1st Lieutenant
    Francis Dempsey Griffin   2nd Lieutenant

1 July 1863:
Organization of Troops at Jackson, Mississippi
    General Joseph E. Johnston, Commanding
    Major General John C. Breckinridge, Commander - Breckinridge's Division
    Brigadier General Marcus A. Stovall, Commander - Stovall's Brigade
    Colonel G. W. M. Williams, Commander - 47th Georgia

1st Sergeant Jackson J. Driggers of Company K died of disease in Jackson, Mississippi Hospital.
11 July 1863: Private Theodore F. Bazemore of Company D attached to Walker's Division Hospital, Lauderdale Springs, Mississippi.
Private James Allen Mallett, Jr. of Company I detailed as nurse at French's and Forney's Hospital, Enterprise, Mississippi.
Private Henry H. Wilson of Company I detailed as nurse, at Lee Hospital, Lauderdale Springs, Mississippi.
The following change occurred in Company H, Forty-seventh Regiment:
    J. M. Chesser   2nd Lieutenant
12 July 1863: *The Siege of Jackson, Mississippi;*
The Forty-seventh Georgia Regiment engaged in a flanking movement of Union Forces.
In A dispatch from General Joseph E. Johnston he states that the 47th Georgia was engaged this morning and helped to Capture 200 prisoners.
    Wounded: John G. Jackson - Co. D

Jackson, July 12, 1863

Major-General Breckinridge:
    GENERAL: *I have learned with high satisfaction the success of your troops this morning; it increases my confidence in your gallant division. I*

beg you to say so to it for me. Do me the kindness, also, to express to the First and Third Florida, Forty-seventh Georgia, and Fourth Florida Regiments the pride and pleasure with which I have accepted the splendid trophies they have presented me. Assure them that I equally appreciate the soldierly courage and kindly feelings to myself which have gained me these noble complements.
    Respectfully and truly, your obedient servant,
    J. E. JOHNSTON

13 July 1863: Private Felin W. Murdock of Company B died in Mississippi Hospital.
Corporal George W. Hurst of Company I died in Meridian, Mississippi Hospital.
20 July 1863: Private Winfield W. Futch of Company G died of disease in Mississippi Hospital.
26 July 1863: 2nd Corporal John Kuhlman of Company E. detailed to Medical Department at Savannah, Georgia
30 July 1863:
Organization of Troops Near Morton, Mississippi
  Lieutenant General William J. Hardee, Commanding
  Major General John C. Breckinridge, Commander - Breckinridge's Division
  Brigadier General Marcus A. Stovall, Commander - Stovall's Brigade
  Major James S. Cone, Commander - 47th Georgia
1 August 1863: The following changes occurred in Company G, Forty-seventh Regiment
  2nd Lieutenant Jeremiah Tootle resigned his Commission
3 August 1863: Private E. Driggers of Company k died in Breckinridge's Division Hospital, Marion, Mississippi
10 August 1863: Private M. Samuel Sayers of Company B on detached duty as carpenter in Savannah, Georgia.
13 August 1863: Private D. W. Brower of Company C died in Hospital at Meridian, Mississippi.
15 August 1863: Private Sanderson C. Lee of Company I detailed nurse at Walker's Division Hospital, Lauderdale Springs, Mississippi
17 August 1863: Forty-seventh Regiment at Hurricane, Mississippi with Stovall's Brigade.
18 August 1863: Private Benjamin Joiner of Company B died.
20 August 1863:
Organization of Troops Department of Mississippi and East Louisiana
  General Joseph E. Johnston, Commanding
  Major General John C. Breckinridge, Commander - Breckinridge's Division
  Brigadier General Marcus A. Stovall, Commander - Stovall's Brigade
  Major James S. Cone, Commander - 47th Georgia

Private William P. Burney of Company B died in a Mississippi Hospital.
Private Nathaniel C. Cowart of Company K died of disease in Hospital Marion, Mississippi.
Private Nathan R. Purcell of Company H died in Lauderdale Springs Hospital, Mississippi.
25 August 1863: Private Stephen Kirsh of Company E attached to Lauderdale Springs, Mississippi Hospital as nurse.
26 August 1863: Forty-seventh in Hurricane Mississippi with Stovall's Brigade.
30 August 1863: Colonel G. W. M. Williams died
The following changes occurred in the Forty-seventh Regiment::
    A. C. Edwards   Colonel
    William S. Phillips   Lieutenant Colonel
    Joseph S. Cone   Major
1 September 1863: Private N. H. Lightsey of Company I died in Mississippi Hospital.
3 September 1863: Private Howard J. Exley of Company I died in Walker's Division Hospital in Shubuta, Mississippi.
4 September 1863: Private James F. Dale of Company B died in General Hospital at Montgomery, Alabama.
5 September 1863: The following changes occurred in Company D, Forty-seventh Regiment:
    Matthew M. Potter   1st Lieutenant
    William Alexander Carswell   2nd Lieutenant
6 September 1863: Forty Seventh Regiment moving to Chattanooga with Breckinridge's Division.
9 September 1863: *Cumberland Gap, Tennessee;*
Captured.   Private Bartholomew McCarty - Co. A
                    Private A. Nessmith - Co. K
10 September 1863: The following change occurred in the Forty-seventh Regiment
    Leonidas Holt   Surgeon
Private John J. Lightsey of Company I died in Marion Station Hospital, Mississippi.
19 September 1863: *The Battle of Chickamauga*
Organization of Troops Army of Tennessee
    General Braxton Bragg, Commanding
    Lieutenant General Daniel H. Hill, Commander, Hill's Corps
    Major General John C. Breckinridge, Commander - Breckinridge's Division
    Brigadier General Marcus A. Stovall, Commander - Stovall's Brigade
    Captain William S. Phillips and Captain Joseph S. Cone - Commanders - 47th Georgia
The Forty-seventh Georgia Regiment is listed as having the following strength:

178 total   193 aggregate
Stovall's Brigade in the center of Breckinridge's line.

Killed
- Private William Bowie - Co. C
- Private McDaniel Oliver - Co. D
- Private Stephen M. Robbins - Co. D
- Private Richard Simms - Co. D
- Private B. L. Nail - Co. G
- Private C. C. Guest - Co. H
- Private Alexander Pope - Co. H
- Private Thomas Usher - Co. I

Wounded
- Private William Parrish - Co. C
- Private H. H. Touchstone - Co. C
- Captain J. Lawton Singellton - Co. D
- Lieutenant W. A. Carswell - Co. D
- Private William H. Mears - Co. .D
- Private Henry Mobley - Co. D
- Private James J. Peterson - Co. D
- Private Eli Summerlin - Co. D
- Private Seaborn Smith - Co. D
- Private Thomas Wiley - Co. D
- Private William J. G. Hodges – Co. .E
- Private Matthew Johnson - Co. F
- Private Perry Holland - Co. G
- Private Josiah Sikes - Co. G
- Private Ryan T. Ganey - Co. H
- 3rd Corporal Charles C. Beebe - Co. I
- Private Gideon A. Arnsdorff - Co. I
- Private W. W. Gann - Co. I
- Private Shafner E. Sowell - Co. I

Captured.   Private Benjamin Sikes - Co. G

20 September 1863:
"............In the meantime Adams and Stovall advanced steadily, driving back two lines of Skirmishers. Stovall halted at the Chattanooga road.......... Stovall soon encountered the extreme left of the enemy's works .... After a severe and well contested conflict he was checked and was forced to retire."

From Major-General John C. Breckinridge's report of the Battle of Chickamauga.

Stovall had gained a point beyond the angle of the enemy's works.

No. 316

Report of Brig. Gen. Marcellus A. Stovall, C. S. Army, commanding brigade

HEADQUARTERS STOVALL'S BRIGADE
BRECKINRIDGE'S DIVISION, HILL'S CORPS,
Missionary Ridge, October3, 1863.
MAJOR: I have the honor to submit the following report of the part taken by my brigade in the action of Sunday, September 20:

In obedience to the orders from headquarters Breckinridge's division of date September 16, I moved from position on the Alpine road near La Fayette, Ga., on the Catlett's Gap road , at or near the latter place, on the morning of the 17th.

Here I remained in position until the morning of the 18th, when I was ordered to proceed on the Crawfish to the Chattanooga road. I halted at the intersection of the two latter for about thirty minutes, when I marched to Pigeon Ridge, near Glass' Mill (stopping and forming line of battle for a short while in the meantime), and again went into position.

I remained at this place until Saturday, the 19th, when I was again moved down the Chattanooga road to Snow Hill. Skirmishers had scarcely been deployed and the proper dispositions made when I was ordered still farther forward in a northeasterly direction to the battle-field as reenforcements to the right of our line, reported then to be hard pressed by the superior force of the enemy. this move did not commence until 5 p. m., hence I did not get into position until Sunday, the 20th instant.

Saturday night, the 19th instant, we slept upon the edge of the battle-field and moved out into position at 4 a. m., the next (Sunday) morning. We formed a line of battle at sunrise on the extreme right of the army, my brigade being in the center of the division and between the brigades of Brigadier-Generals Adams and Helm, respectively. Skirmishers (25 men from each regiment) were immediately deployed, under command of Lieutenant-Colonel Badger, of the Fourth Florida Regiment. Subsequently, orders were received to advance the line thus deployed, and for a   regiment.

Between 9 and 10 o'clock my brigade to be thrown forward to support them. In obedience thereto I ordered Colonel Bowen, commanding Fourth Florida Regiment, to take out his command as the support required. For the manner in which he maneuvered it while in advance, I respectfully refer to the accompanying report from him was ordered to advance. I moved out in good order parallel to the Chattanooga road about a half mile, not without encountering two distinct lines of the enemy's skirmishers and driving them in. Here the brigade was halted, and by a flank movement formed nearly perpendicular to its former position. Thus reformed I moved forward, and had not gone far before I encountered the enemy in heavy force and strongly entrenched. Here the battle raged fiercely. A concentrated fire of grape and canister, shot and shell of every conceivable character was poured into us from the front, while my left suffered no less from an enflading fire equally galling and severe. Brigadier-General Helm's brigade, having encountered the enemy's breastworks, was unable to keep up the alignment, which taken with the fact that the reserves ordered to our support failed to come up and the further fact that my left was as well as front was thus exposed, the brigade -in fact , the whole line-was forced to retire.

The troops of my command fell back simultaneously, forming in perfect order not exceeding 200 yards in rear of the position for which they had so gallantly contested. From this position I was still farther retired and placed in position on the extreme right of the division, acting as a support to the command of Maj.-Gen. William H. T. Walker. Here I remained at rest for a few hours. During the interval I had my cartridge boxes all replenished, my command remaining quiet until about 4 p. m. About that hour I was ordered to move my brigade to the extreme right of the line; again formed nearly parallel to the Chattanooga road. This latter movement was ordered that we might form the part of a support to the brigades of Brigadier-Generals Liddell and Wathall. They were soon driven in, but were immediately reformed and thrown forward a second time. Just at this juncture I was ordered to advance. Changing my direction by a half wheel, I was brought to the enemy's line. Thus in position I commenced the charge. My brigade pressed through two lines of our own troops, passed over the enemy's breastworks, and with deafening shouts of patriotic enthusiasm pursued the foe to the Chattanooga road, where in obedience to orders, I halted, night putting an end to the conflict.

I respectfully refer to the accompanying statement, *marked__, showing the regiment name, and rank of every officer and soldier killed, wounded, and missing; also the character of the wounds.

I am much indebted to Colonel Dilworth, First and Third Florida; Colonel Bowen, Fourth Florida; Lieutenant-Colonel Ray Smith, Sixtieth North Carolina and Captain Cone, Forty-seventh Georgia, who led their respective commands with skill and judgment. Also Captain Weaver, who succeeded to the command of the Sixtieth North Carolina after its colonel was disabled.

Captain. J. P. C. Whitehead, Jr., my assistant adjutant-general; Lieutenant A. J. Hanson, and Captain. J. H. Hull(who was severely wounded in the shoulder) displayed great coolness and daring during the conflict, and to them I am much indebted for valuable services rendered. Also to Lieut. A. Dunham, ordinance officer, for the promptness manifested in the discharge of the duties of his responsible office.

I have the honor to be, respectfully, your obedient servant,

M. A. STOVALL
Brigadier-General

Maj. James Wilson,
Assistant Adjutant-General

[Inclosure]

The report of Brigadier General M. A. Stovall listed the effective strength of the Forty-seventh Georgia as 178 total; 193 aggregate

No. 319

Report of Captain. Joseph S. Cone,
Forty-seventh Georgia Infantry
HDQRS. BIVOUAC FORTY-SEVENTH GEORGIA VOLS.
September 27, 1863
CAPTAIN: I have the honor to make through you to the brigadier-general commanding a statement of facts which occurred in this regiment during the fight of Chickamauga on Sunday, the 20th instant:

On Sunday [Saturday] night, the 19th instant, we slept in the line of battle very near the edge of the battle-field.

On Sunday morning, about 9 o'clock, our lines being formed and our position assigned us near the right, we were ordered to advance. After advancing in line of battle for a few hundred yards through a piece of woods we emerged from the woods into an open glade, or meadow-like piece of ground, almost entirely free from all undergrowth. Here we encountered the enemy's line of skirmishers or sharpshooters. They commenced a brisk and rapid fire on us as we crossed the open space of ground just referred to. Here the regiment was much exposed to their fire. This piece of meadow land ran nearly parallel with our line of battle. Upon emerging from the woods we discovered that we had obliqued too much to the left, thus leaving quite a space between us and the regiment to our right. As the guide was right, and as we were ordered to dress to that point and conform ourselves to the movements of the regiment on our right, we proceeded to dress and align ourselves while in this open space as directed, thus keeping the regiment for some length of time exposed to the fire coming from the enemy's line of sharpshooters stationed in our front along the piece of woods skirting to open space. While thus engaged we lost 1 man killed and several others wounded. Having obtained our proper distance and dress, all the while advancing, we soon entered the woods on the opposite side. The enemy's line of sharpshooters now gave way, fleeing precipitately through the woods. In a few minutes after, we came to a large, open field, seemingly a corn-field. Here there appears to have been another line of enemy's sharpshooters, as quite a number appeared in the field running in every direction. Several came running up to us and surrendered themselves. Among the number a Captain, commanding Company B, Forty-second Indiana Regiment, came up to Captain Phillips, who was at that time in command of the regiment, and delivered up his sword, saying at the time that he surrendered himself, that his company, which was at the time on picket, was completely surrounded and cut off by our forces. A detail of 2 men was made from the regiment and the prisoners sent to the rear under their charge.

We proceeded across the fields and were halted on the opposite side, where we remained about ten or fifteen minutes. We then recrossed the field in nearly the direction from which we had first marched. While recrossing the field two shells from the enemy's battery passed through our ranks between the files without doing any injury, one exploding at some distance from us, the other exploding very near us just after passing through our ranks. We were now ordered to cross a wood, the undergrowth of which was quite thin and sparse. Beyond this wood in an open old field on quite an elevated piece of ground was stationed a battery of the enemy, which occasionally sent a shell crashing through the piece of woods through which we were now advancing. On nearing the edge of this field we were halted and skirmishers deployed in our front. Company F our left-flank company, armed with rifles, having been sent out the night before on picket, and being still behind, Company E, our right flank company, armed with rifles, and Company D, muskets, were thrown out as skirmishers. After a few shots exchanged the enemy's line retired.

Our companies having again taken their places we again advanced. Their battery now commenced a regular fire with grape, at the same time continuing to throw shells around and above us, cutting down tops of trees, limbs, &c., among us. We advanced steadily, gained the field, and continued on 75 or 100 paces in the field. Seeing that the regiment of our brigade on our left did not advance into the field, we halted, and were ordered by Captain Phillips, commanding, to lie down. We obeyed the order, at the same time directing our fire upon the battery, which continued to send its grape and canister among us killing several and wounding many. We remained thus until we had fired, I presumed, a dozen or more rounds, when Captain Phillips, seeing that our line did not advance, and deeming it prudent to fall back into the edge of the woods and align our regiment on the other regiments of the brigade, gave the order to that effect. Just at that time he received a wound from a ball striking him on the hip. He consequently turned over the command to myself, being the officer next in rank present.

At this time our line here seemed to have been repulsed and was falling back. I, however, on entering the woods, endeavored to rally the regiment, but as all seemed falling back my attempts were vain, as I succeeded in rallying only a part of the regiment. We did not properly rally till we had crossed the woods and reached a small field beyond. We were now withdrawn some distance, stacked our arms, and remained so for several hours. When we were again called it was evening. We were then marched to an old field bordering the Chickamauga Creek, our line being now formed perpendicular to our position of the morning. Here in the edge of the old field farthest from the creek we hastily formed a slight breastwork of rails piled together. In breathless anxiety we now awaited the approach of the enemy, whom we could hear yelling furiously as they drove in our foremost line. The line having fallen back and formed again just in our front, a general movement forward was made. We pressed forward, hopeful and confident of success and victory. They gave way before us and fled in disorder and confusion, leaving us in possession of the entire field and the wounded of both sides. Darkness now closed the scene, and we peacefully slept in bivouac that night within a very short distance of where we had stood before the galling fire of the enemy's battery on the morning of the same day.

The casualties* of the regiment are as follows: Killed 11; wounded 59; missing 6.

I have the honor to be, Captain, your obedient servant.
JOSEPH S. CONE
Captain, Comdg. Forty-seventh Georgia Regiment
Captain WHITEHEAD
Assistant Adjutant-General

No. 320

Report of Captain. James T. Weaver, Sixtieth North Carolina Infantry

HDQRS. SIXTIETH N. C., REGT., STOVALL'S BRIG.
September 28, 1863

CAPTAIN: I have the honor to submit the following report of the part taken by the Sixtieth North Carolina Regiment in the recent battles of Chickamauga, on the 19th and 20th:

On Saturday, the 19th, the regiment was in line of battle all day, but was not engaged until about sundown that evening. Our brigade was moved in a new direction and occupied a position on or near the battle-field of Saturday.

On Sunday morning, the 20th instant, our brigade was formed in the following order: First and Third Florida on the right; Sixtieth North Carolina in the center, and the Forty-seventy Georgia on the left, the Fourth Florida being held in reserve and as a support for the skirmishers. All necessary dispositions having been made, about 9 o'clock we were ordered to move forward until we met the enemy. After advancing about 400 yards we received a fire of musketry from the front, at which time 2 of the lieutenants belonging to this regiment were so severely wounded that they had to be carried from the field. At this juncture we were ordered to charge, which was done in gallant style, and meeting but feeble resistance we crossed the Chattanooga road and advanced beyond that point about 200 yards. Heavy firing being heard to the left, we were ordered to that point. We changed front by filing to the right, and facing by the rear rank were hurriedly marched in the direction of said fire. Having approached to within 400 yards of enemy's line, we received a heavy fire from the front, and from there advanced through a brisk fire to within 200 yards of the enemy's line, where we were halted and returned the enemy's fire. At this place and time Lieutenant-Colonel Ray, commanding regiment , was wounded and left the field. After a sharp engagement for twenty minutes, the Florida regiment on our left was forced back by what I have understood to have been a flank movement of the enemy on their left, of which movement I was ignorant, and held my men firm. However, in a short time the Forty-seventh Georgia, being hotly pressed on my right, was forced to retire, which left me no alternative but to withdraw my men or be captured. I retired out of range, rallied the regiment, and held it steady until relieved by a staff officer, and carried to where the balance of the brigade had formed, still in the rear.

Up to this time my loss was 8 men killed, 6 officers wounded, and 30 enlisted men wounded, 16 enlisted men missing; total loss, 60.

From this time we were comparatively inactive until the last and final charge, which decided the fate of the day, and in which my regiment participated with as much enthusiasm as could be, notwithstanding the regiment had no rations for two days. This last charge was attended with no casualties.

Allow me here to say that the officers and men composing this regiment acted throughout the day in a way entirely satisfactory to their commander, and my thanks are especially due Captain Whitehead for the efficient services rendered me on the field. I would respectfully call attention to his brave and gallant conduct during the whole engagement.

Respectfully submitted.

J. T. WEAVER,
Captain, Commanding Regiment
[Captain. J. P. C. Whitehead, Jr. Assistant Adjutant-General.]

Killed.
- Private N. N. Collins of Co. C
- Private James W. Green - Co. C
- 2nd Lieutenant William Alexander Carswell - Co. D
- Private David A. Metzger - Co. I
- Private M. A. Metzger - Co. I
- Private Thomas E. Martin - Co. K

Wounded.
- Private Moses Faircloth - Co. B
- 1st Corporal William H. Mears - Co. D
- Private Jackson Newborn - Co. G
- Private Neil Gillis - Co. H

William A. Bowers, Jr.

                    Private R. C. Haralson - Co. I
                    Private William B. Nungazer - Co. I

Captured.   Private Patrick Creaghan - Co. A
                    Private S. W. Smith - Co. D
                    Sergeant James M. Wrenn - Co. G

Roll of Honor
Battle of Chickamauga
47th Georgia
Sergeant John Frain (Color Bearer - Co. A
Sergeant S. S. Wacasar - Co. B
Private William Hart - Co. C
Private William Hardin - Co. F
Private P. G. Dickerson - Co. G
Private Alexander Pope (killed in action) - Co. H
Corporal J. S. Lee - Co. K

Private Jacob Riggs of Company C. died in Atlanta, Georgia
23 September 1863: Private Hope Farmer of Company I attached to Lee Hospital, Lauderdale Springs, Mississippi as nurse.
24 September 1863: Private Cuthbert Joiner of Company D captured at Chattanooga, Tennessee.
Private Asberry R. Taylor of Company F died of Typhoid in Lauderdale Springs, Hospital, Mississippi.
Private Henry Quinn of Company A captured at Chattanooga, Tennessee.
29 September 1863: Private John Paul Thompson of Company B died at home.
30 September 1863: The following change occurred in Company D, Forty-seventh Regiment:
        John Z. Lowther   Jr. 2nd Lieutenant
1 October 1863: 2nd Sergeant Thomas Kelly of Company A in Fortney's Division Hospital, Enterprise, Mississippi.
5 October 1863: Private J. P. Edwards of Company K died.
7 October 1863: Private Rogers Folliard of Company F died.
8 October 1863: Private J. F. Darley of Company H died in Atlanta, Georgia.
13 October 1863: Private William Joiner of Company B died in Sumter County, Georgia.
17 October 1863: Private Jesse M. Woodman of Company B died at Atlanta, Georgia.
Private C. Brown of Company H died in Acadamy Hospital, Marietta, Georgia.
18 October 1863: 2nd Sergeant John M. Sellers of Company F died of

disease at University Hospital, Cassville, Georgia.
20 October 1863: Private Benjamin F. Bullard of Company F died in Institute Hospital, Atlanta, Georgia.
Private S. W. Smith of Company B died POW
21 October 1863: Private Bartholomew McCarty died POW.
Private E. L. Lard of Company I died in Atlanta, Georgia
24 October 1863: Private A. Nessmith of Company K died POW
26 October 1863: The following change occurred in Company F, Forty-seventh Regiment.
Captain James H. Latimer resigned his commission due to ill health.

Joseph G. Dedge	Captain
James S. Patterson	1st Lieutenant
William F. Hovis	2nd Lieutenant
Thomas Fletcher Barnett	Jr. 2nd Lieutenant

29 October 1863: Private Patrick Walsh of Company A died of disease in Medical College Hospital, Atlanta, Georgia.
Private E. L. Nessmith of Company K died at Atlanta, Georgia.
30 October 1863: Private Shafner E. Sowell of Company I died of wounds.
31 October 1863:
Organization of Troops Army of Tennessee
    General Braxton Bragg, Commanding
    Major General John C. Breckinridge, Commander, Hill's Corps
    (No Division Commander) - Breckinridge's Division
    Brigadier General Marcus A. Stovall, Commander - Stovall's Brigade
    Captain J. J. Harper, Commander - 47th Georgia
1 November 1863: Private W. R. McVey of Company C. in Jackson's Cavalry Hospital, Marion, Mississippi.
Private Watson Leggett of Company F died of disease in General Hospital #1, Savannah, Georgia.
2 November 1863: Private John M. Brown of Company K died in Oliver Hospital, LaGrange, Georgia.
3 November 1863: Private Jackson Gill of Company E died POW.
8 November 1863: Private Jesse S. Taylor of Company F died at Atlanta, Georgia.
11 November 1863: Private James H. Mobley of Company D died at Atlanta, Georgia.
12 November 1863: Forty-seventh Regiment transferred to Jackson's Brigade, Cheatham's Division.
13 November 1863: The Forty-seventh Georgia Regiment is transferred from Breckinridge's Division, Stovall's Brigade to Cheatham's Division, Jackson's Brigade.
20 November 1863:
Organization of Troops Army of Tennessee
    General Braxton Bragg, Commanding

Lieutenant General William J Hardee, Commander, Hardee's Corps
Major General Benjamin F. Cheatham, Commander- Cheatham's Division
Brigadier John K. Jackson, Commander - Jackson's Brigade
Captain J. J. Harper, Commander - 47th Georgia

22 November 1863: Private Gideon Arnsdorff of Company I died of wounds.

23 November 1863: Private Perry Sapp of Company G died of Disease.

25 November 1863: *The Battle of Missionary Ridge, Tennessee*

Killed	Private John B. George - Co. B
	Private F. S. Sinquefield - Co. B
	Private W. R. McVey - Co. C
	Private John Dickerson - Co. G
	Private Charles C. Elkins - Co. I
	Private Samuel F. Futch - Co. K
Wounded:	Captain William S. Phillips
	1st Corporal T. A. Waters - Co. C
	Private Wiley Bird - Co. C
	Private James Riggs - Co. C
	Private Simon Waters - Co. C
	Private William S. Westberry - Co. C
	Private John Barbour - Co. D
	Private Henry C. Wells - Co. D
	Private Jordan Cribbs - Co. E
	Private Paul A. Colson - Co. G
	Private Jackson Newborn - Co. G
Captured	Private Michael Dillon - Co. A
	Private Michael Drury - Co. A
	Private John Powers - Co. A
	Private Lemuel Sanderlin - Co. B
	Private Edwin R. Slaughter - Co. B
	Private Hezekiah J. Parrish - Co. C
	Private James Pridgen - Co. C
	Private Matthew Rushing - Co. C
	Private Joe Newsom - Co. C
	Private Dedrick Hildebrand - Co. E
	Private James W. Shuman - Co. E
	Private Francis M. Goodin - Co. F
	Private David Hester - Co. F
	Private Henry N. Howard - Co. F
	Private Samuel Hughes - Co. F
	Private Thomas W. Shumans - Co. F
	Private James K. Johnson - Co. F

Private Daniel Lynn - Co. G
Private Dennis E. Lynn - Co. G
1st Sergeant Samuel K. Tutty - Co. H
Private William T. Gibson - Co. H
Private Martin Mosley - Co. H
Private Ranson C. Ganey - Co. H
Private S. C. Elkins - Co. I
Private William H. Knight - Co. K
Private Eli C. Proctor - Co. K

Surgeon Leonidas Holt transferred.
27 November 1863: Private J. Boyswon of Company I died in Atlanta, Georgia.
28 November 1863: 2nd Sergeant John J. Roche of Company A admitted to Floyd House and Ocmulgee Hospital, Macon, Georgia.
30 November 1863: Private Archibald Johnson of Company F died of disease in General Hospital #1, Savannah, Georgia.
1 December 1863: Private John Barker of Company D attached as cook to lee Cavalry Division Hospital, Montgomery, Alabama.
2 December 1863: Private A. Turner of Company C died in Gilmer Hospital, Marietta, Georgia.
3 December 1863: 2nd Sergeant John D. Williams of Company C. died at Fair Grounds Hospital #2, Atlanta, Georgia.
4 December 1863: Private D. Dugger of Company K died in Atlanta, Georgia.
Corporal J. H. Martin of Company K died at Atlanta, Georgia.
5 December 1863: Private John Hilton of Company C. died in Empire Hospital, Atlanta, Georgia.
9 December 1863: Private Jesse Phillips of Company K died in Polk Hospital, Rome, Georgia.
10 December 1863:
Organization of Troops Army of Tennessee
    Lieutenant General William J Hardee, , Commanding
    Major General Benjamin F. Cheatham, Commander, Hardee's Corps
    Brigadier John K. Jackson, Commander- Cheatham's Division
    Colonel John C. Wilkinson, Commander - Jackson's Brigade
    Captain Joseph S. Cone, Commander - 47th Georgia

Private George W. Hicks of Company B died in Randolph County, Georgia.
11 December 1863: Private Jackson Newborn of Company G died of wounds.
12 December 1863: Private T. M. Hodges of Company C in Institute Hospital, Atlanta, Georgia.
3rd Sergeant S. P. Williams of Company C. died in Newsom Hospital,

Cassville, Georgia.
Private William G. Wiley of Company F died.
Private James Peevy of Company I died in Griffin, Georgia Hospital.
14 December 1863:
The strength of the Forty-seventh Regiment is as follows:

Effective total	188
Total present	291
Aggregate present and absent	556
Number of Arms	226
Rounds of ammo per man	40

Private Aaron B. Varn of Company F died at Atlanta, Georgia.
18 December 1863: Private William M. Futch of Company E died in Fair Grounds Hospital, Atlanta, Georgia.
20 December 1863: Private David Hester of Company F died of disease POW
25 December 1863: Private Hezekiah J. Parrish of Company C captured at Chattanooga, Tennessee.
26 December 1863: Private Lewis A. Joiner of Company B died in Randolph, County, Georgia.
Private R. G. Southwell of Company K died in Hood Hospital, Covington, Georgia.
Private James Pridgen of Company C died POW
27 December 1863: Private Thomas W. Shuman of Company F died POW
31 December 1863:
Organization of Troops Army of Tennessee
    General Joseph E. Johnston, Commanding
    Lieutenant General William J Hardee, Commander, Hardee's Corps
    Major General Benjamin F. Cheatham, Commander- Cheatham's Division
    Brigadier John K. Jackson, Commander - Jackson's Brigade
    Lieutenant Colonel A. C. Edwards, Commander - 47th Georgia

1864
4 January 1864: Private Joseph W. Crosby of Company I died in Atlanta, Georgia Hospital.
8 January 1864: 4th Corporal Joseph Waters of Company G died of disease in Dalton, Georgia Hospital.
10 January 1864: Private Hezekiah J. Parrish of Company C died POW
11 January 1864: 3rd Corporal Thomas F. Harper of Company B died
Private William Farmer of Company I died of disease in Griffin, Georgia Hospital.
20 January 1864:
Organization of Troops Army of Tennessee

General Joseph E. Johnston, Commanding
Major General Benjamin F. Cheatham, Commander, Hardee's Corps
Brigadier General Marcus J. Wright, Commander- Cheatham's Division
Brigadier John K. Jackson, Commander - Jackson's Brigade
Lieutenant Colonel A. C. Edwards, Commander - 47th Georgia

25 January 1864: Private John L. Brown of Company B died in Randolph County, Georgia.
Private Wiley Bird of Company C died of wounds in Hospital #3, Nashville, Tennessee
3 February 1864: Private Macklin Wildes of Company I died in camp near Dalton, Georgia
4 February 1864: The following change occurred in Company A:
    John Joseph Purtill   Jr. 2nd Lieutenant
15 February 1864: Private Lemuel Sanderlin of Company B died POW
27 February 1864: Private Michael Dillon of Company A died POW
1 March 1864: Private James M. Waters of Company G died of disease in Dalton, Georgia.
7 March 1864: The following change occurred in Company C:
1st Lieutenant Robert J. Williams resigned his commission die to disability
10 March 1864: Private John Green
12 March 1864: The following change occurred in Company F:
    2nd Lieutenant William F. Hovis resigned his commission
19 March 1864: Private Eli C. Proctor of Company K died POW
22 March 1864: Private John L. Youmans of Company G died.
26 March 1864: Private Edwin R. Slaughter of Company B died POW
30 March 1864: The following change occurred in Company F:
    Thomas Fletcher Barnett   1st Lieutenant
6 April 1864: The following changes occurred in Company B:
    Captain John J. Harper resigned his commission
    Seaborn R. Lawrence   Captain
    Henry O. Beall   1st Lieutenant
The Forty-seventh Georgia, Fifth Georgia and the Fifty-fifth Georgia under Brigadier General John K. Jackson are relieved at Dalton by Mercer's Brigade, the First Georgia, Fifty-fourth Georgia and the Fifty-seventh Georgia Under Brigadier General Hugh W. Mercer. Jackson's Brigade to proceed to Savannah.
9 April 1864: Private Jasper Caile of Company D died in Atlanta, Georgia.
11 April 1864: 1st Sergeant Samuel K. Tutty of Company h died POW
Private Claibourne C. Bevil of Company I died at Savannah River Bridge.
Private Paul Bevil of Company I died at Savannah River Bridge.
22 April 1864: Private James S. Shuman of company E died in Atlanta, Georgia.

30 April 1864:
Organization of Troops Army of Tennessee
    General Joseph E. Johnston, Commanding
    Lieutenant General William J. Hardee, Commander, Hardee's Corps
    Major General William H. T. Walker, Commander- Walker's Division
    Brigadier John K. Jackson, Commander - Jackson's Brigade
    Lieutenant Colonel A. C. Edwards, Commander - 47th Georgia

5 May 1864: Private William Parker of Company B died of disease in Fair Ground Hospital #2, Atlanta, Georgia.

12 May 1864: Private Joseph Sikes of Company G died of disease at Academy Hospital, Marietta, Georgia.

13 May 1864:

14 May 1864: *The Battle at Resaca, Georgia:*
Oostanaula:

Killed:	Private Christian J. Cryder - Co. B
Wounded:	Private Thomas Wiley - Co. D
Captured	Private William Devine - Co. A

The following change occurred in Company E:
Thomas J. Osteen   1st Lieutenant

15 May 1864: *The Battle at Oostanaula (Lay's Ferry)*

Lay's Ferry was about five miles downstream of Resaca on the Oostanaula River. Originally Sherman had planned to utilize two pontoon bridges there to follow the Confederate force if General Johnston chose not to fight and retreat. Originally the crossing was protected by a detachment of confederate Cavalry and a battery of artillery.

Walkers Division of Confederate infantry was called out of the reserve at Resaca and deployed at Lay's Ferry but was recalled to Resaca leaving Jackson's Brigade in the area. After several movements of the opposing forces and the deployment of the pontoon bridges Sweeny's Division crossed the river during the night. Jackson's Brigade which included the 47th Georgia attacked the federal Division there on the afternoon of May 15th and was repulsed.

Correspondence from Brigadier General Corse U. S. Army at Lay's Ferry to General William T. Sherman indicates that Jackson's Brigade (which included the Forty-seventh Georgia) attacked Second Division, Second Corps, U. S. Army and drove them toward the river until Federal batteries opened on Jackson's Brigade driving them back.

Killed:	Private C. J. Suyder - Co. B
Wounded:	Private Laurence Callaghan - Co. A
	Corporal Jacob Matthews - Co. B

Private M. Blackwell - Co. B
Private Isham Roberts - Co. D
Private Benjamin Summerlin - Co. D
Private Henry Kangter - Co. E
Private John Khulman - Co. E
Private Henry Marsh - Co. E
Private John Newman - Co. E
Private G. W. Tillman - Co. E
Sergeant Archibald Johnson - Co. F
Corporal Noah Williams - Co. F
Private J. T. Milton - Co. F
Private Dennis Smith - Co. F
Lieutenant T. H. Southwell - Co. G
Sergeant John Murphy - Co. G
Corporal Brady Harralson - Co. H
Private J. F. Barbee - Co. H
Lieutenant T. E. Bourquin - Co. I
Private Daniel W. Edwards, Sr. - Co. I
Private W. W. Gnann - Co. I
Private Robert W. Tullis - Co. I

Captured:
Private Patrick Callahan - Co. A
Private Joseph H. Simpson - Co. A
Private James Willis - Co. A
Private Barrack Stark - Co. A
Corporal A. R. Pomeroy - Co. E

Missing:
Private Patrick Campbell - Co. A
Private Martin E. Jones - Co. G
Private Jacob Oliver - Co. G
Private Elam Sapp - Co. G
Private Abner Pomeroy - Co. I

20 May 1864: The following change occurred in the Forty-seventh Regiment.
    Thomas E. Wakefield   Ensign
21 May 1864: Private Newton C. Southwell of Company G died of disease in General Hospital #1, Savannah, Georgia.
23 May 1864: Private Archibald McClelland of Company F died of disease in Dawson Hospital, Greensboro, Georgia.
26 May 1864: Jr. 2nd Lieutenant Thomas H. Southwell of Company G died at Atlanta, Georgia.
4 June 1864: The following change occurred in Company B:
    Walter B. Corely   2nd Lieutenant
12 June 1864: Private Jacob Matthews of Company B died of wounds in

General Field Hospital.

19 June 1864: Private Jeremiah Cremmin of Company A captured at Marietta, Georgia.

22 June 1864: Private Jeremiah Cremmin of Company A died of disease POW

27 June 1864: *The Battle at Kennesaw Mountain, Georgia*
Wounded: Sergeant David Rivers Tuten Co. F
1st Lieutenant John C. Parker - Co. G
Private John W. DeLoach –Co. G
Captain Stephen Alfred Wilson – Co. I

30 June 1864:
Organization of Troops Army of Tennessee
General Joseph E. Johnston, Commanding
Lieutenant General William J. Hardee, Commander, Hardee's Corps
Major General William H. T. Walker, Commander- Walker's Division
Brigadier John K. Jackson, Commander - Jackson's Brigade
Lieutenant Colonel A. C. Edwards, Commander - 47th Georgia

3 July 1864: Private William B. Devine of Company A captured at Chattahoochee, Georgia.

5 July 1864:

HEADQUARTERS,
Chattahoochee Bridge, July 5, 1864 8:30 a. m.
Maj. Gen. SAMUEL JONES, Charleston, S. C.
　I sent Brigadier General Jackson, with the Fifth and Forty-seventh Georgia Regiments. It is not possible to send more. *

J. E. JOHNSTON

7 July 1864: Forty-seventh Georgia ordered to John's Island, South Carolina.

8 July 1864: The Forty-seventh Georgia Regiment Reported to John's Island, South Carolina.

9 July 1864: *Action at John's Island, South Carolina:*
The Forty-seventh Georgia Regiment was in the advance Column and drove the enemy off one line of defensive works.

Wounded: Private Jonathan A. Blount - Co. F
Private James Williams - Co. F

10 July 1864: *Action at John's and James Island, South Carolina:*

No. 39

Report of Col. George P. Harrison, Jr., Thirty-second Georgia Infantry, commanding brigade, of action at Burden's Causeway, John's Island.

HEADQUARTERS ADVANCED FORCES,
John's Island, S. C., July 10, 1864

CAPTAIN: I have the honor to submit the following report of the assault upon the enemy's works on the morning of the 9th instant;

Having been ordered by Brigadier-General Robertson to assault the enemy in his intrenchments at daylight with my brigade, consisting of the Thirty-second Georgia Regiment, Lieutenant-Colonel Bacon commanding; the Forty-seventh Georgia Regiment, Colonel Edwards commanding; and Bonaud's battalion, Major Bonaud commanding. I moved it forward at 2 a. m. about 1 1/4 miles from its bivouac of the night before, and formed line of battle immediately in front of a hedge held by our troops, and about 700 or 800 yards from the enemy's works across an open field. Having thrown forward a line of skirmishers covering my entire front, at the dawn of day I ordered the whole line to advance to the assault, the Thirty-second Georgia being on the right, the Forty-seventh on the left, and Bonaud's battalion in the center, the Thirty-second and Bonaud's being separated by a hedge road running perpendicularly to our line and toward the works of the enemy.

Having advanced about 350 yards, my skirmishers came upon the pickets of the enemy, who fired upon us and hastily retreated. With a loud cheer from the whole line my skirmishers dashed off in pursuit, closely followed by the main body. A rapid fire was at once opened upon us by the enemy behind his works, and as we moved onward it became more accurate and deadly until within about 250 yards of their intrenchments, when it became plainly visible that the enemy were in strong force and ready for us. Volley after volley, linked as it were by scattering reports, were poured into our advancing ranks, and musket-balls swept the field in reckless profusion, mowing down many of our brave and gallant men; but my line pressed steadily on, never at any time showing the least sign of wavering. Our advance was bloodily contested along the whole line until within a few paces of the enemy's works, and in some places till our men mounted the parapet, when he gave way, leaving his works in our possession. Our loss would have been much greater up to this time but for the dense smoke from the enemy's fire, which from the peculiar state of the atmosphere did not rise, but hid us from the sight of the foe. It was so thick that in places a man could not be seen at five paces.

Feeling satisfied that the enemy was much stronger in numbers than ourselves, and having been informed of the strength of the ground immediately in our front, I halted my line upon the captured works and opened a rapid fire upon the retreating foe, with considerable effect, the exact amount of which it is difficult to estimate, as the enemy carried off his wounded with him, and probably a portion of his dead, the dense woods affording him this facility with little risk. having gained the entire front line of the enemy's works and Major Jenkins having come to my assistance with the First Georgia Regulars, a detachment of the Thirty-second Georgia Regiment, a portion of the Fourth Georgia Cavalry (dismounted) which had been held in reserve, I immediately threw forward two companies of the Thirty-second Georgia, under Major Holland, of the same regiment, and three companies of Forty-seventh Georgia and Bonaud's battalion together, under Major Cone, of Forty-seventh Georgia with instructions to press the enemy closely and discover his next position, which was found to be behind another line of works, just beyond a creek, passable for artillery only by a narrow bridge, which the enemy tore up as he fell back.

About this time I received instructions from Brigadier-General Robertson not to assault the enemy further, but to hold the ground already taken. This I did, keeping my skirmishers well up to the enemy and exchanging a rapid fire with him during the morning and at intervals during the afternoon. Toward evening the firing ceased, and under the cover of night the enemy withdrew from our front and fell back to his gun-boats, leaving considerable quartermaster, commissary, and ordnance stores in our possession.

My whole brigade displayed great coolness and bravery, and too much cannot be said in commendation of both officers and men.

Inclosed find list of casualties. *

Very respectfully,
GEO. P. HARRISON, JR.
Colonel Thirty-second Georgia Infy. Regt. ,Comdg., &c
Captain. T. Henry Johnston,
Assistant Adjutant-General.

Killed: Private Martin M. Deen - Co. F
Private Samuel Deen - Co. F
Private John Green - Co. F
Private John E. Googe - Co. F
Private John A. Tullis - Co. I
Wounded: Sergeant Lovick G. Mock
Private Adam W. Rigdon - Co. F

Report of Casualties John's and James Island, South Carolina from July 1 to July 10, 1864.
The Forty-seventh Georgia Regiment sent To General Taliaferro at James Island, South Carolina.
Forty-seventh Georgia   7 men killed   9 men wounded
16 total

13 July 1864: 4th Sergeant Paul A. Duggar of Company I died of disease in Guyton, Georgia Hospital

28 July 1864: The Forty-seventh Regiment is headquartered at Secessionville, James Island, South Carolina

The following changes occurred in Company D, Forty-seventh Regiment:
Benjamin C. Buford	1st Sergeant
John P. Mock	2nd Sergeant
John R. Sellers	5th Sergeant
Henry C. Wells	3rd Corporal
John Baptist Mock	4th Corporal

31 July 1864:
Organization of Troops Department of South Carolina, Georgia and Florida
    Major General Samuel Jones, Commanding
    Colonel J. L. Black, Commander - Taliaferro's Brigade
    Major A. G. Cone, Commander - 47th Georgia

1 August 1864: 4th Corporal Henry G. Ellerbee of Company H detached as laborer and boatman in Charleston, South Carolina.

6 August 1864: Private Berry S. Taylor of Company F died in Newsome Hospital, Thomasville, Georgia.

16 August 1864: Forty-seventh Georgia Regiment on John's and James Island, South Carolina (notation shows that they have been there since the beginning of July 1864).

2 September 1864: The Forty-seventh Georgia Regiment at Secessionville, South Carolina.

21 September 1864: The Forty-seventh Regiment is headquartered at Secessionville, James Island, South Carolina.

27 September 1864: The Forty-seventh Regiment is headquartered at Secessionville, James Island, South Carolina.

3 October 1864: The Forty-seventh Regiment is headquartered at Secessionville, James Island, South Carolina.

The following changes occurred in Company I:
J. G. Morgan	4th Sergeant
O. G. Watt	5th Sergeant
D. L. Smith	3rd Corporal
John A. Elkins	4th Corporal

9 September 1864: Private T. J. Everett of Company I died in General Hospital at Guyton, Georgia.

17 October 1864: Private Abel W. Thompson of Company H died of disease.

24 October 1864: The Forty-seventh Regiment is headquartered at Secessionville, James Island, South Carolina.

31 October 1864:
Organization of Troops Department of South Carolina, Georgia and Florida
    Lieutenant General William J. Hardee, Commanding
    Brigadier General William H. Taliaferro, Commander - Taliaferro's Brigade
    Major A. G. Cone, Commander - 47th Georgia

1 November 1864: The Forty-seventh Regiment is headquartered at Secessionville, James Island, South Carolina.

3 November 1864: Private Ephraim E. Kessler of Company I died of disease POW

5 November 1864: The following change occurred in the Forty-seventh Regiment:

    Lieutenant Colonel William S. Phillips retired to Invalid Corps
    Joseph S. Cone   Lieutenant Colonel

6 November 1864: The following change occurred in Company C:

    J. R. Miller   Jr. 2nd Lieutenant

14 November 1864: The following change occurred in Company D:

    Captain Joseph Lawton Singleton dropped from the rolls by Special Order.

18 November 1864: The Forty-seventh Regiment is headquartered at Secessionville, James Island, South Carolina.

20 November 1864:
Organization of Troops Department of South Carolina, Georgia and Florida

    Lieutenant General William J. Hardee, Commanding
    Major General LaFayette McLaws, Commander - McLaws' Division
    Brigadier General William H. Taliaferro, Commander - Taliaferro's Brigade
    Colonel Aaron C. Edwards, Commander - 47th Georgia

26 November 1864: The Forty-seventh Regiment is headquartered at Secessionville, James Island, South Carolina.

29 November 1864: Correspondence from H. W. Feilden in Charleston, South Carolina to Co. T. B. Ray in Savannah, Georgia indicates that the Forty-seventh Georgia Regiment at the rail depot in Charleston, South Carolina. The regiment, some 400 men strong have been ordered to the Grahamville area. They are delayed by a train coming from Savannah, Georgia. They depart without being issued rations.

30 November 1864: *Action at Honey Hill, South Carolina*
The "Veteran troops" of the Forty-seventh Georgia Regiment have been delayed and are expected at Grahamville, South Carolina. They arrive at Grahamville and march toward where the Confederate position is located. The Confederate forces consist of dismounted cavalry and Militia. The 47th arrives an hour after the battle had started. They were in position when General Smith directed the "Battle Hardened" 47th into action in the right of the attack where the enemy was attempting to flank. After a tough fight were able to drive the Union forces, though badly outnumbered, sending them back to Boyd's Landing where they had landed. Since they had been without rations they foraged the rations that were in the possession of the enemy left on the field in order to eat.

Killed: Private Thomas H. Hall - Co. F

Wounded: Private William P. Owens - Co. D
Private Thomas J. Wells - Co. D
Captain Joseph G. Dedge - Co. F
Private Arthur Ray - Co. F
Private Dennis Smith - Co. F

4 December 1864:
Private Jacob W. Scott of Company D wounded at Bee's Creek, South Carolina

5 December 1864: The Forty-seventh Georgia Regiment between Pocotaligo, South Carolina and the Savannah River.

6 December 1864:

Coosawhatchie, December 6, 1864 - 10 a. m.
GENERAL SAM JONES,
Twelve barges are landing at Gregory's on the Tulifinney about three miles distant. Send Forty-seventh and a section of artillery.
L.J. GARTRELL
Brigadier-General, Commanding

COOSAWHATCHIE,
December 6, 1864.

Major STRINGFELLOW:
The Forty-seventh Georgia just arrived. Section of Artillery will come by next train. Send 40,000 rounds of ammunition, caliber .69. Some of the boxes have no caps. We have only 35 wounded, most of them slightly.

L. G. GARTRELL.

HEADQUARTERS,

December 6, 1864
2:40 o'clock.

Maj. Gen. S. Jones,
    Commanding:
GENERAL: The enemy advanced in heavy force from Gregory's Point. They are now on the road from Old Pocotaligo to this place (Coosawhatchie), and on both sides. We fought them two hours and a half, but had to fall back to our works. If you send a force in their rear, on the road from Old Pocotaligo, it will not only assist us, but probably cut off the enemy. Some provision had better be made to prevent their getting between you and us. I would have communicated with you by telegraph,

but the operator says the wires are cut, I must have some old troops; the new ones won't stand.

 Very respectfully, your obedient servant,
L. J. GARTRELL,
Brigadier-General, Commanding

COOSAWHATCHIE,
December 6, 1864.

General Jones:

 The enemy advanced in large force on the road from Gregory's. We met them and drove them back. They were re-enforced, and, Portion [of] the troops becoming demoralized, I ordered them to fall back to this side of the river. Enemy not pursuing. The engagement lasted two hours and a half. Lost slight. Send Forty-seventh Georgia Volunteers and any other troops you can spare. The main attack seems to be intended for this point. I would have dispatched you sooner, but being at the front and informed by operator that the line would not work, I sent a courier some time since. We can hold this place. Ammunition is getting short.

L. J. GARTRELL.

POCOTALIGO,
December 6, 1864.

Col. A. C. Edwards,

 Commanding Forty-seventh Georgia Regiment:

COLONEL: Brigadier-General Gartrell has been ordered to send your regiment to the position now occupied by the State Cadets, at Tullifinney trestle, on the railroad, where other troops, under Lieutenant-Colonel Bacon, will be collected before morning. You will be the ranking officer, and will therefore take command. Colonel Bacon's command, with the cadets, will number about 550 men, with two pieces artillery. At the earliest dawn of day you will move down by a plantation road, which crossed the railroad near Tullifiney trestle and nearly parallel to Tullifinney Creek, until it intersects the road from Old Poco to Coosaw, about 150 yards on the Coosaw side. Lieutenant-Colonel Bacon has a guide with him who knows the road, and you will therefore confer with him. Attack the enemy vigorously at that point and drive him off if possible. The Fifth Georgia will attack in front of Coosawhatchie when your fire is heard. Carry out these instructions promptly and with spirit.

 Very respectfully,

C. S. STRINGFELLOW,
Assistant Adjutant-General.

December 6, 1864.

Major Stringfellow,
    Assistant Adjutant-General:

    COLONEL: The major-general commanding has ordered Colonel Edwards, of the Forty-seventh Georgia, to the position near the trestle-work on the railroad now occupied by the State Cadets. Leave the cavalry company (Captain Peeples') to picket the road to Coosawhatchie and watch the position at Tullifinny Bridge, and proceed with the rest of your command to report to Colonel Edwards at the place designated. That officer has been ordered to move at the earliest dawn of day to attack the enemy in flank and rear. The guide Craddock left with you knows the road. Inform major Jackson that the baggage of his command will be at the crossing of the country road over the railroad by the time you reach that point. Move promptly. If you have or can procure any axes carry them with you to clear out the [sic] should the enemy blockade it; Captain Bachman has perhaps some with his battery. Direct Captain Peeples to keep the major-general commanding fully informed of any movement on the road to Pocotaligo.
    Your obedient servant,
C. S. STRINGFELLOW,
Assistant Adjutant-General.

The Forty-seventh Georgia Regiment sent to The Tullifinney trestle.
Colonel Edwards of the Forty-seventh Georgia Regiment ordered to "........ attack the enemy with force at daydawn the next morning (December 7, 1864)
7 December 1864: *The Forty-seventh Georgia Regiment engaged the federal troops at Tullifinny, South Carolina*

GRAHAMVILLE, December 7, 1864.
Maj. Gen. S. Jones:
    Have the Forty-seventh [Georgia] on the march to you. I am left with the militia only, yet unorganized, and many of them are sick. My reserves relieved the forces at Bee's Creek, who have been sent to Coosawhatchie this afternoon.
JAS. CHESNUT, Jr.,

Brigadier-General.

COOSAWHATCHIE, December 7, 1864--11:30.

General Jones:
Colonel Daniel has returned with the Fifth Georgia Regiment and reports four regiments of the enemy on both sides of the main road in 400 yards of these works. I have put his regiment on the railroad to protect it, and will open upon the enemy with my guns as soon as position can be ascertained. It is impossible to get re-enforcements to Colonel Edwards.
L. G. GARTRELL.

COOSAWHATCHIE, December 7, 1864--12:30 o'clock.

General Jones:
This place is seriously threatened by force of four regiments, and several pieces of artillery. I am making disposition to repel the enemy and save the railroad and works. Send re-enforcements if possible. They are said to be planting batteries to shell us.
L. J. GARTRELL,
Brigadier-General.

Private John A. Lee of Company I died in Bucknor hospital, Newnan, Georgia.
9 December 1864:
HEADQUARTERS ADAMS RUN, SOUTH CAROLINA, January 5, 1865.
Major CHARLES. STRINGFELLOW,
Assistant Adjutant General, Charleston, South Carolina:
Major-- I have the (not legible) to report that in obedience to instructions from Major-General Jones, I assumed command of all the troops between Bee's Creek and Tulifinny trestle on the 8th of December, ultimo.

About 9 o'clock on the morning of the 9th, the enemy opened on the left of my line a very rapid and continuous fire, from some eight guns. His line of skirmishers advanced about 10 o'clock, and immediately after the entire left became hotly engaged, our men fighting behind temporary earth works. Several attempts were made to carry our lines, but all were hansomely repulsed. The troops fought with great spirit. Foiled in his undertaking, the enemy moved to his left, in the direction of Coosawhatchie. The engagement was renewed most vigorously on our right at 3 o'clock P. M., and after an obstinate resistance by the enemy, lasting some two hours, he was driven eight hundred yards from his original line.

The Thirty-second and Forty-seventh Georgia regiments, the Seventh North Carolina battalion, and the battalion of South Carolina cadets, all under the immediate command of Colonel Edwards, occupied the left; the Fifth Georgia regiment, the First and Third Georgia reserves, under Colonel Daniel, the right. It was reported that General Gantrell was slightly wounded, by a fragment of a shell, before he reached the field.

The German artillery, Captain Bachman, rendered very efficient service on the left, as was proved by the number of dead found in their front. Major Jenkins, commanding the cadets, was particularly conspicuous during the morning fight.

Colonel Edwards deserves especial credit for the admirable disposition of his troops

The enemy's loss, though not accurately ascertained, must have been heavy, as quite a number of his dead were left on the field.

Our casualties during the day were fifty-two killed and wounded. A tabulated list is herewith enclosed.

Both officers and men of my command behaved well. Captains Haxall and Worthington and Lieutenants Johnston and Stoney rendered most valuable assistance in the execution of orders while the fight was progressing.

I am, major, most respectfully, your obedient servant,
B. H. ROBERTSON, Brigadier-General.

HEADQUARTERS,
Tullifinny Works, S. C.,
December 19, 1864

MAJOR: In obedience to instructions from Major General Jones, dated Pocotaligo, December 6, 1864, directing me to attack the enemy early on the 7th in his position near this point, I made the following disposition of the force under my command -- consisting of about 200 men of the Forty-seventh Regiment Georgia Volunteers, commanded by Captain J. C. Thompson, two companies of the Thirty-second Georgia, with the Augusta battalion (local troops), on company of the First South Carolina Infantry [Regulars}, (Captain King), and 130 South Carolina militia, commanded by Maj. J. B. White, making in all 700 or 800 men. Early in the morning four companies were thrown forward as skirmishers, under the command of Major White. The line--composed of the Forty-seventh Georgia, on the right, and the troops under the command of Lieutenant-Colonel Bacon, on the left--moved just in rear of the skirmishers. In a thick wood near a bend in the old Pocotaligo road the right of my skirmish line struck the enemy. The front was then changed gradually to the right until the line crossed the said road at nearly right angles, when it confronted the enemy, and became engaged throughout its entire length. At this stage of the action the command of Lieutenant-Colonel Nesbett arrived, and was posted on the left of my line of battle. Our skirmishers drove the enemy vigorously until the right of the line became engaged with the enemy's line of battle, our left at the same time overlapping his right. This position was maintained until after Colonel Daniel's demonstration on my right, when the enemy made new dispositions on and extending beyond my left. It becoming apparent that the enemy's force considerably outnumbered mine, which consisted largely of raw troops, it was deemed impracticable to attack him in force, without which it was impossible to drive him from his position. I therefore withdrew in good order, unpursued by the enemy, to my present position. The troops engaged, which were my skirmishers only, behaved with great gallantry.

By permission of the major-general, commanding, we began on the morning of the 8th to fortify our position. The work was continued uninterruptedly until the morning of the 9th, when the enemy drove in our pickets and advanced in force to within 250 yards of our position. We opened upon him with artillery and musketry, and in a very short time drove him back, with considerable loss. On the afternoon of the same day, in the attempt to re-establish our picket-line, the enemy was found in the wood on our right within 100 yards of the railroad. After severe fighting for about two hours, he was driven off and our line re-established.

On the next morning it was ascertained that he had fallen back to his original position, and our picket-line was advanced 400 or 500 yards beyond its former position.

The casualties amounted in all to 4 killed, 1 commissioned officer and 31 men wounded, many of them very slightly. Judging from the unburied dead, the graves, and other evidence found upon the field, the enemy must have suffered a loss of not less than 250 in the fighting of the 9th, and not less than 50 in that of the 7th, making in all a loss of not less than 300.

Respectfully submitted,

A. C. EDWARDS
Colonel, Commanding

Maj. CHARLES S. STRINGFELLOW,
    Assistant Adjutant-General, Charleston, S. C.

P. S. --I omitted to mention, in enumerating the force under my command on the 7th instant, the three pieces of Captain Bachman's battery, which, owing to the character of the country, it was found impracticable to

use in action.
   Respectfully,

A. C. EDWARDS,
Colonel, Commanding.

Wounded: Private James M Richardson - Co. B
                         Private Jacob W. Scott
                         Private Henry C. Wells - Co. D

The loss for the Forty-seventh was 2 men killed; 6 men wounded for a total of 8.

17 December 1864: The following change occurred in Company B:
     Horace Hicks   2nd Lieutenant

18 December 1864: Private Dennis Smith of Company F died in Hospital, Charleston, South Carolina.

21 December 1864:
captured in Savannah, Georgia   5th Sergeant L. M. Prine - Co. C
                                      Private Arthur Ray- - Co. F
                                      3rd Corporal James E. Arnsdorff - Co. I   (in hospital)

22 December 1864:
Wounded and captured in Savannah, Georgia   Private Ellis Woodson - Co. F

24 December 1864: The following change occurred in Company A:
2nd Lieutenant John Joseph Purtill resigned his commission

26 December 1864: Forty-seventh Georgia Regiment under Captain Thompson (282 men) at Tulifinny works.
Private Isham Roberts of Company D died POW

28 December 1864: Pocotaligo, South Carolina:
Field returns of effective total of troops between Grahamville and the Combahee River;
Forty-seventh Georgia Regiment stationed at Coosawhatchie River (Harrison's Bridge)

effective total	266
total present	304
aggregate present	328

1865

9 January 1865: Private Ellis Woodson of Company F died of wounds (POW)

17 January 1865: Colonel George P. Harrison reports that "Lieutenant Colonel Bacon with the Thirty-second and Forty-seventh Georgia Regiments hold Rivers' Bridge.
The Forty-seventh is commanded by Captain J. C. Thompson.

The effective Strength of the Forty-seventh Georgia Regiment is:

Effective total   241
Effective aggregate   259

18 January 1865: Private Clinton Sapp of Company D died in Savannah, Georgia Hospital (POW)
31 January 1865:
Organization of Troops Department of South Carolina, Georgia and Florida
    Lieutenant General William J. Hardee, Commanding
    Major General LaFayette McLaws, Commander - McLaws' Division
    Colonel George P. Harrison, Jr., Commander - Harrison's Brigade
    Captain J. C. Thompson, Commander - 47th Georgia

2 February 1865: The Forty-seventh Georgia Regiment positioned at River' Bridge on the Salkehatchie River. They are under the command of Captain Joseph C. Thompson. The Forty Seventh Regiment is an element of Harrison's Brigade, under the command of Lieutenant Colonel Edwin H. Bacon, Jr.
3 February 1865: *The Battle of River's Bridge, South Carolina*
General William T. Sherman, United States Army had intended to cut a path through South Carolina, which both he and his men considered the cause of all their troubles, toward the capital, Columbia. He had configured his force in two large wings. The purpose was to direct one wing via Beaufort and Pocotaligo and the other wing via Hardeeville and Robertsville. The Goal was to reach Columbia by the first of February.

    The Salkehatchie River was the main line of the Confederate defense. There were three major bridges, spaced about six miles apart, over the Salkehatchie River. They were Buford's Bridge, Rivers' Bridge and Braxton's Bridge. The 47th Georgia Regiment was positioned at Rivers' Bridge. The small Confederate force had prepared earthworks along the ridge that overlooked the causeway and bridge. There were four cannon of the Palmetto Battalion deployed to defend the position. Two of these cannon defended the approach to Rivers' bridge.
    After the Confederates defending Braxton's Bridge had burned the bridge across the river the Union Army attempted to cross the Salkehatchie at Rivers' Bridge on February the 2nd. Although the Confederates were heavily outnumbered they put up stout resistance and the Union attack faltered. The Confederates had planned well and inflicted heavy losses upon the leading elements of the attack.
    The morning of February 3rd the Union Army abandoned their plan to cross over Rivers' Bridge and began to build a corduroyed road the right of the confederate line in order to flank the confederates and avoid another

costly frontal assault The fighting was described as being "quite sharp" and lasted several hours. The Confederates reinforced early that morning held the flanking movement until dark, withdrawing from their positions that night

The following is an incomplete report of casualties of the Forty-seventh Regiment at the Battle of Rivers' Bridge:

Killed: Private John Barbour - Co. D

Wounded: Captain Joseph C. Thompson
                            (acting regiment commander)
                            Private Thomas J Ferguson - Co. B
                            Private Britton G. Smith - Co. D
                            Private Willis Miles – Co. F
                            Private J. D. Seckinger - Co. I

Captured: 5th Sergeant John J. Daily - Co. A
                            Private James Larkin - Co. A
                            Private Dennis Quiggley - Co. A
                            Private Michael Wells - Co. A
                            Private John M. F. Newman - Co. E
                            1st Corporal John H Ulmer - Co. E
                            Private Aaron Meadows - Co. F
                            Private Perry Holland - Co. G
                            3rd Corporal John F. Dubberly - Co. G
                            Private Wesley T. Clements - Co. G
                            Private James Conner - G
                            Private Thomas Standfield - Co. G
                            Private Martin Sullivan - Co. G
                            Private E. H. Martin - Co. K

The casualty report for the Forty-seventh Georgia Regiment is:
1 killed; 8 wounded; 34 missing; 43 total
After Captain Joseph C. Thompson was wounded, Captain Elliott W. Hazzard took command of the Forty-seventh Regiment
5 February 1865: The Forty-seventh Georgia Regiment is stationed at Rivers' Bridge, South Carolina
10 February 1865:
Organization of McLaw's Division
Major General LaFayette McLaws, Commander - McLaws' Division
Colonel George P. Harrison, Jr., Commander - Harrison's Brigade
Captain J. C. Thompson, Commander - 47th Georgia
16 February 1865:
The morning report of Harrison's Brigade [2 1/2 miles from Dean's Bridge] shows the Forty-seventh Georgia Regiment with Captain Bryan Comer (or

_____Conner), commanding:

Total present for duty   155
Aggregate present for duty   169
Total present   191
Aggregate present   206

Private Thomas Wiley of Company D died of wounds at Post Hospital, Savannah, Georgia (POW)
18 February 1865: Private D. A. Bennett of Company K died of disease in General Hospital #1 at Columbia, South Carolina.
1 March 1865: 2nd Lieutenant John Z Lowther of Company D died.
19 March 1865: *The Battle of Bentonville, North Carolina:*
General Joseph E. Johnston decided to attack General Slocum's Federals at Bentonville, North Carolina because they were separated from the rest of General Sherman's army.

Killed: Private James Bennett - Co. C
                   Private J. T. Lee - Co. C
                   4th Sergeant John T. Robbins - Co. D
                   Private Benjamin Taylor - Co. F
                   Private Elisha Taylor - Co. F

Wounded: Private Jesse L. Wilkerson Co. B
                   Sergeant Benjamin C. Buford, Jr. - Co. D
Captured: Private William M. Fudge Co. E

23 March 1865:
The Report of Harrison's Brigade this date shows the Forty-seventh Georgia Regiment with Captain Elliott W. Hazzard, commanding:
Total present for duty   120
Aggregate present for duty   138
Total present   160
Aggregate present   177

24 March 1865: Private William Parrish of Company C died of disease in General Hospital #3 in High Point, North Carolina.
25 March 1865:
Organization of McLaw's Division
Major General LaFayette McLaws, Commander - McLaws' Division
Colonel George P. Harrison, Commander - Harrison's Brigade
Captain Elliott W. Hazzard, Commander - 47th Georgia
31 March 1865:
Organization of Troops Confederate States Army at Smithville, North

Carolina
> General Joseph E. Johnston, Commanding
> Lieutenant General William J. Hardee, Commander - Hardee's Corps
> Major General LaFayette McLaws, Commander - McLaws' Division
> Colonel George P. Harrison, Commander - Harrison's Brigade
> Captain Elliott W. Hazzard, Commander - 47th Georgia

1 April 1865: Corporal John T. Smith of Company B captured.

4 April 1865: Privates James M. Hall and Daniel Miles of Company F wounded at Coleman's Creek in Appling County, Georgia chasing deserters.

9 April 1865:
Organization of Troops Confederate States Army at Smithville, North Carolina
> General Joseph E. Johnston, Commanding
> Lieutenant General William J. Hardee, Commander - Hardee's Corps
> Major General Edward C. Wathall, Commander - Wathalls' Division
> Colonel George P. Harrison, Commander - Harrison's Brigade
> _____, Commander - 47th Georgia and Bonaud's Battalion

10 April 1865:
Organization of McLaw's Division
Major General LaFayette McLaws, Commander - McLaws' Division
Colonel George P. Harrison, Commander - Harrison's Brigade, Commander - 47th Georgia

16 April 1865: John M. F. Newman of Company E died POW

20 April 1865: The following change occurred in Company C, Forty-seventh Regiment:

E. O. Miller   2nd Lieutenant

26 April 1865: *Surrender - Greensboro, North Carolina:* On This day General Joseph E. Johnston signed the final papers surrendering the remainder of the army of the Confederate States of America. Surrendering with him was the Forty-seventh Regiment, Georgia Volunteer Infantry. They were as follows:

Organization of Troops Confederate States Army at the surrender, Greensboro, North Carolina
> General Joseph E. Johnston, Commanding
> Lieutenant General William J. Hardee, Commander - Hardee's Corps
> Major General Edward C. Wathall, Commander - Wathalls' Division
> Colonel George P. Harrison, Commander - Harrison's Brigade
> _____, Commander - 47th Georgia and Bonaud's Battalion

Company A:
Privates;
John P. Dill

Company B:
1st Lieutenant Henry O. Beall
Privates:
Madison W. Bell   William J. M. Gardne   George P. Hart
James P. Hay   Charles A. Crawford   Enoch L. Hudson
J. D. Irwin   A. J. Martin   Jesse J. Stewart
John P. Stuart   Christopher Columbus Taylor Marion Taylor

Company C;

Corporal Mitchell Dixon   3rd Corporal Wayne D. Waters
Privates:
Mitchell A. Alderman   James Bland   Mitchell Collins, Jr.
Michael Dixon, Jr.   J. J. Driggers   Eli Lee
Simon Waters   John Turner

Company D:

Lieutenant James Alexander Carswell
Privates:
A. E. Hodges   William H. McKinney   Joseph M. Minton
John Baptist Mock, Jr. William P. Owens   Demas F. Robbins
Robert M. Shadron   George W. Blackston   Martin V. Blackston
Miles Smith

Company E:

Privates:
James P. Hay   Lorenzo H. Williams
Company F:

Corporal William M. Stone   3rd Corporal William S. Holton
Privates:
Elias Altaman   John Buchan   John F. Hutto
Absalom S. Stone   Isaac Taylor   William Taylor

Company G:

Privates:
Jesse D. Collins   Isaac C Daniel   Isham Clayton
William DeLoach   Jackson Griffin   Daniel E. Lynn
John L. Lynn   Arthur Sikes   Daniel Sikes
Joseph Sikes   Altamond Williams

Company H:

1st Lieutenant Samuel J. Dean
Privates:
Henry Cooper	John H. Flood	James J. Moody
C. C. Parsons	George W. Peterson	Elisha Thornton
Samuel W. Brown	George W. McIntyre	A. M. F. Peterson

Company I:

1st Lieutenant Thomas E. Bourquin   Sergeant F. S. Exley
4th Corporal Robert W. Tullis
Privates:
Charles C. Beebe	Christopher Conaway	James R. Crosby
William J. Wheler	James M. Edwards	Obediah I Edwards
William H Hodges		

Company K:

2nd Lieutenant James S. Hagin
Privates:
Reuben H. Johnston   M. W. Woodcock

Surgeon Stiles Kennedy

Sergeant David Rivers Tuten Company F

William A. Bowers, Jr.

**Private Samuel Deen, Company F, Appling Rangers
Killed at John's Island South Carolina**

Lt. Jeremiah Tootle Company G.

William A. Bowers, Jr.

Private Jacob Oliver Company G

**Sergeant Simon Brewton Co. G Tattnall Invincibles
and his wife Susannah Hagan Brewton**

Private Sherrod Willis Company H

Private Matthew Mathis Quinn Co F Appling Rangers

Private James A. Williams Company F

History of the 47th Georgia Volunteer Infantry, CSA

CONFEDERATE VETERANS IDENTIFIED—All of the above Confederate veterans were identified by R. S. Wolfe and H. G. (Cap) Branch. The picture was taken at the site of the old Spring Branch Baptist Church in 1908. Several readers recognized some of them. They are, front row, left to right, Ben B. Milikin, Henry V. Beecher, John Gardner, Mathew (Luck) Johnson, Absalon Stone, Duncan Campbell, Tom Knight, Daniel W. Long, Jacob White and Lovett Baxley; back row, Jim Hall, Berry White, W Lumpkin Beecher, Joe Baxley, W. Alfred Beecher, Nat A. Thomas, Clem Byrd, Noah Altman, W. D. Simmons, Mitchell Stone, E. T. Kennedy and Thomas H. Willoughby.

UCV Reunion at Spring Branch Church, Appling County

William A. Bowers, Jr.

REUNION OF THE UNITED CONFEDERATE VETERANS
OF TATTNALL COUNTY -- JULY 3, 1909

UCV Reunion at Reidsville, Tattnall County

History of the 47th Georgia Volunteer Infantry, CSA

ROSTER OF FIELD, STAFF AND BAND OF THE 11th BATTALION GA. INFANTRY AND 47th REGT. GA. VOLUNTEER INFANTRY
ARMY OF TENNESSEE
C.S.A.

Name	Highest Rank Attained	Remarks
Gilbert W. M. Williams	Colonel	
A. C. Edwards	Colonel	
William S. Phillips	Lieutenant Col.	
Joseph S. Cone	Lieutenant Col	
James Cone	Major	
Thomas R. Hines	Captain	Also Quartermaster
Benjamin S. Williams	Adjutant	
H. E. Cassidy	Chaplin	
John R. Minis	Sergeant. Major	
Edward W. Wilson	Sergeant. Major	
William Percy Mortimer Ashley	Assistant Quartermaster	
Joseph C. Thompson	Quartermaster Sergeant	
G. Williams	Quartermaster Sergeant	
James E. Holmes	Ordinance Sergeant	
Leonidas Holt	Surgeon	
David A. Matthews	Surgeon	
John Rambo	Surgeon	
C. A. W. Bostick	Assistant Surgeon	
George W. Coxwell	Assistant Surgeon	
Calley Adrian Denson	Assistant Surgeon	
Stiles Kennedy	Assistant Surgeon	
Albert Thaddeus Lipfort	Assistant Surgeon	
John T. McLain	Assistant Surgeon	
Leonidas McLester	Assistant Surgeon	
James B. Wiggins	Asst Surgeon	
George W. Coxwell	Hospital Steward	
O. P. Matthews	Hospital Steward	
James E. Burnsides	Comm. Sergeant.	
James R. Frazier	Assistant Comm. Sergeant.	
Thomas Wakefield	Ensign	
Robert Low	Leading Musician	
Robert Burke	Musician	
Francis DeVersur	Musician	
Brave Golphin	Musician	
John Jellinan	Musician	
Charles Jones	Musician	

George Jones	Musician
James Larkin	Musician
Joseph Millen	Musician
Robert Oliver	Musician
Eugene Touchelet	Musician
Robert Woodhouse	Musician
William Woodhouse	Musician

COMPANY COMMANDERS

Co. "A" Mitchell Volunteer Guards (Chatham County)	Captain. Michael J. Doyle(Captain. Bryan Comer
Co. "B" Randolph Light Guards (Randolph County)	Captain. Patrick Gormley Captain. John J Harper Captain. Seaborn R. Lawrence
Co. "C" Bulloch Guards (Bulloch County)	Captain. William W. Williams Captain. Joseph C. Thompson
Co. "D" Screven Guards (Screven County)	Captain. John D. Ashton Captain. Joseph Lawton Singleton
Co. "E" Chatham Volunteers (Bryan, Chatham &Effingham Counties)	Captain. William S. Phillips Captain. DeWitt Bruyn
Co. "F" Appling Rangers (Appling County)	Captain. James H. Latimer Captain. Joseph G. Dedge
Co. "G" Tattnall Invincibles (Tattnall County)	Captain. Phillip Glenn Tippins Captain. Daniel L. Kennedy
Co. "H" Liberty Rangers (Glynn County)	Captain. Isaac M. Aiaken Captain. Elliott W. Hazzard
Co. "I" Empire State Guards (Effingham County)	Captain. A. C. Edwards Captain. T. P. Hines Captain. Stephen A. Wilson
Co. "K" (Bulloch County)	Captain. Joseph S. Cone Captain. James G. Cone Captain. Peter C. Sheffield

The following lists contain the names of the men that comprised the Companies of the Eleven Battalion and Forty-seventh Regiment of the Georgia Volunteer Infantry. The Names in **Bold were wounded** and the names in **Bold/Underlined died** while in service.

COMPANY A - CHATHAM COUNTY, GEORGIA
MITCHELL VOLUNTEER GUARDS

James Adams	Patrick Doyle	Thomas McElline
William Allen	Patrick W. Doyle	Thomas McGinnis
Henry Brenner	Michael Drury	Patrick McGough
J. D. Bud	James Dunigan	Thomas H. McGrath
William Butler	Lawrence Dunn	Michael McGuire
Laurence Callaghan	James S. Eden	J. Mclaughlin
Patrick Callahan	Cornelius Flournoy	Hugh Martin
Patrick S. Campbell	John Folliard	William Martin
William Carroll	Rogers Folliard	John Masterson
William Civil	A. Frazier	Henry Meinhart
Hugh Clancey	John Frain	Henry Miller
Matthew Clancey	John Gallagher	John R. Minis
A. Coffin	Lawrence Gallagher	James Morrison
Bryan Conner	Francis Garraghy	J. S. Neely
Richard Cotter	James Garrity	Patrick Newby
John Cox	Michael Garrity	John Nicholson
Partick Creaghan	August Gerber	James O'Brien
Jeremiah Cremmin	A. Graves	Michael O'Callaghan
Nicholas Cullen	R. H. Harris	B. C. O'Kelley
John J. Daly	Patrick Hays	Patrick O'Learcy
John Davis	**John Henry**	Antionio Piper
Patrick Davis	James Holland	Thomas J. Ponder
William Delaney	George H. Jones	John Powers
William B. Devine	Andrew Keating	John Joseph Purtill
John P. Dill	Thomas H. Kelly	Dennis Quigley
Michael Dillon	John Knox	Henry Quinn
Phillip F. Dillon	Amos Larkin	James B. Reed
Benard Dolan	James Larkin	John Reilly,#1
John Downey	Michael Leonard	John Reilly,#2
Alexander Doyle	Francis McCann	John Reilly,#3
James M. Doyle	James H. McCann	Michael Reilly
Matthew J. Doyle	Thomas McCann	James Reynolds
Michael J. Doyle	**Bartholomew McCarty**	John J. Roche
Owen Rock	John Simon	James F. Torrell
Matt Rooney	M. Smith	John Walsh
William R. Ross	J. Spears	**Patrick Walsh**
Marcus Selig	Barrack Starkke	James Walton

William A. Bowers, Jr.

John Sheils	Thomas Stone	Andrew Waters
James Shine	W. Strickland	Michael Well
Richard Simms	Michael Sullivan	Partick White
John Simpson	William G. Thomas	Peter Whitty
Joseph H. Simpson	**Patrick Tighe**	James Willis

COMPANY B - RANDOLPH COUNTY, GEORGIA
RANDOLPH LIGHT GUARDS

William T. Amoss
William Arnett
John Arthur
Zachariah Bailey
George William Beall
Henry O. Beall
Elijah C. Belcher
Thomas M. P. Belcher
George W. Bell
Madison W. Bell
M. Blackwell
M. Bridges
John M. K. Britt
Absalom Brown
John L. Brown
Needham R. Brown
William H. Buchanan
James L. Burney
William P. Burney
Joshua Callaway
Edwin S. Cheshire
C. Clark
James Clem
John S. Cobb
Henry Coleman
G. W. Cooper
William H Coram
Walter C. Corely
George W. Coxwell
Samuel Crapps
Charles A. Crawford
Christain J. Cryder
James F. Dale
John A. Dale
Wm. Baldwin Davenport
Benjamin Dawson
Morris Dixon
R. T. Duke
A. Elliott
Moses Cook Faircloth
John Farrell
Isaac R. Ferguson

James M. Ferguson
Partick Henry Ferguson
Thomas J. Ferguson
John Freeman
William M. Fudge
William J. M. Gardner
J. M. Garnett
John H. George
John T. George
Hugh A. Gilmore
J. M. Gordon
Patrick Gormley
William P. Gormley
Z. F. Goza
Benjamin A. Graham
William Graham
John A. Green
Henry Harden
John J. Harper
Thomas F. Harper
William O. Harper
Amos J. Hart
George P. Hart
Henry L. Hart
Jesse R. Harvey
Isaac P. Hay
James P. Hay
George W. Hicks
R. D. Nelson
Horace Hicks
George W. Hobbs
James W. Holman
Enoch L. Hudson
Ambrose H. Ingram
J. D. Irwin
Simeon T. Jenkins
Benjamin Joiner
Lewis A. Joiner
Shade G. Joiner
William Joiner
J. W. Jones
Joseph Jones

Henry M. Kaigler
William Kersey
Seaborn R. Lawrence
Thomas J. Lee
James C. Lilly
Henry LaFayette Long
Marshall Mainor
A. J. Martin
Jacob Mathews
James C. McCann
J. G. McCann
Leonidas McLester
Benjamin McMillan
Borgum McMillan
Richard F. McMillian
William W. McNeil
Hugh G. McNeily
James M. McNeily
Thomas A. McWilliams
Elbert G. Melton
Henry C. Melton
S. B. Melton
William P. Melton
Finney J. Miller
Lewis B. Miller
John Moore
Robert J. Morris
William Morris
Jonathan A. Mullins
Felin W. Murdock
John F. Murdock
Thomas J. Murdock
William M. Murray
H. T. Oakley
Henry Q. Odom
John C. Oliver
Hardy F. Oxle
William B. Oxley
Robert G. Ozier
William Parker
Michael C. Parkerson
John K. Patterson

James G. Ferguson **Charles M. Joyce** Gabriell J. Phillips
Horace Powers **Edwin R. Slaughter** H. J. Walker
Thomas Prather John T. Smith William A. Ward
Thomas A. Ragan W. C. Spears W. W. Way
James M. Richardson Jesse J. Stewart Lewis Webb
Sylvanus G. Robertson John P. Stuart Charles P. West
Lewis M. Rozier **C. J. Suyder** Charles Weston
Lemuel Sanderlin Christopher Columbus Taylor **John E. Whaley**
George W. Sanders Marion Taylor **Jesse L. Wilkerson**
E. Murrell Satterwhite **John Paul Thompson** J. W. Williams
LaFayette Satterwhite Seborn J. Thornton Samuel W. Williams
J Saunderton William Thurman Samuel Wolfe
Samuel M. Sayers James W. Toombs Harry G. Woodman
S. Scraps J. W. Tumlin **Jesse M. Woodman**
Frank S. Sinquefield J. A. Tuttle John C. Young
A. Bradley Slaughter Sidney S. Wacasar Noah Zane

COMPANY C - BULLOCH COUNTY, GEORGIA
BULLOCH GUARDS

James Ailand
Malachi Akins
T. Y. Akins
Mitchell A. Alderman
A. J. Baughn
James Bennett
Wiley Bird
James Bland
William Bowie
P. Bracmin
Harrison Brannen
M. S. Brannen
P. U. Brannen
Solomon Brannen
William Alexander Brannen
D. W. Brower
Neil Buie
August Burin
James E. Burnside
Ambrose Campbell
A. S. Canuet
James Carroll
B. Collins
Mitchell Collins, Jr.
Mitchell Collins, Sr.
N. N. Collins
R. Collins
William Crosby
James Deal
William Deal
Michael Dixon, Jr.
Mitchell Dixon
J. J. Driggers
John Farr
C. E. Fletcher
H. B. Franklin
James Gould
James W. Green
Joseph Hamm
William B. Hart
E. Helmouth
John Hilton
T. L. Hilton

J. Hodges
T. M. Hodges
James Hollaway
M. Jones
John Kelley
James Kerby
James A. Kerby
Seaborn Kicklighter
A. R. Lanier
Eli Lee
George W. Lee, Jr.
George W. Lee, Sr.
Henry C. Lee, Sr.
J. T. Lee
J. V. Lee
Thomas L. Lee
J. T. Lindsey
W. H. Lofton
J. H. Martins
George W. McFarland
W. R. McVey
Malachi Mercer
Alexander Mikell
John L. Mikell
M. Mickell
B. O. Miller
Joseph Miller
J. R. Miller
Robert Miller
James W. Mincey
William W. Mincey
___ Mitchell
Joel Newsom
Owen Oliff
Hezekiah J. Parrish
William Parrish
James Pridgen
L. M. Prine
James Pritchet
David C. Proctor
Harmon O. Riggs
Jacob Riggs
James Riggs

Jasper Riggs
John W. Riggs
J. W. Rowe
James V. Rowe
Matthew Rushing
W. Ryan
Fredrick Schultz
James W. Schuman
D. Sheffield
Leaston C. Slator
W. Thomas Smith
W. A. Summerlin
A. J. Thompson
Joseph C. Thompson
J. Timmerlin
Thoedore Todd
T. Toler
H. H. Touchston
Timothy Towler
A. Turner
John Turner
H. Irwin Waters
H. J. Waters
M. Waters
Millington Waters, Jr.
Millington Waters, Sr.
Simon Waters
T. A. Waters
Wayne D. Waters
William S. Westberry
B. Williams
John D. Williams
Josiah G. Williams
J. L. Williams
L. E. M. Williams
Matthew Williams
Robert J. Williams
Robert M. Williams
S. P. Williams
William W. Williams
Allen Wilson
Vin Benjamin Wilson
William H. Wise

COMPANY D - SCREVEN COUNTY, GEORGIA
SCREVEN GUARDS

Amos Andrews
John D. Ashton
John Barbour
John Barker
B. Bartlett
A. J. Bazemore
James P. Bazemore
James R. Bazemore
John A. Bazemore
Robert R. Bazemore
Theodore F. Bazemore
Thomas W. Blackburn
George W. Blackston
Martin V. Blackston
Henry Brigdon
Robert Brinson
Thomas S. Brown
Benjamin C. Buford, Jr.
Benjamin C. Buford, Sr.
Francis M. Buford
John G. Buford
William J. L. Buford
A. H. Caile
D. A. Caile
Jasper Caile
Thomas Call
A. Hilliard Call
James N. Carlisle
James Alexander Carswell
William A. Carswell
S. A. Chapman
Charles Church
Jabez B. Church
Moses Church
Alfred B. Clayton
Dennison Clayton
Marion V. Clayton
John E. Coleman
John R. Evans, Jr.
James D. Ferguson
Cornelius Frawley
Benning Freeman
David Freeman
Jacob L. Freemen
Thomas C. B. Freeman
Sampson Griffin
Daniel D. Gross
Henry H. Hines
Isham Hisely
A. E. Hodges
Hezekiah D. Howard
William Howard
Benjamin Humphries
Samuel Humphries
David Jacobson
J. J. Jeans
William A. Johnson
Cuthbert Joyner
H. M. Joyner
Joseph B. Lee
Nathan W. Lee
Washington N. Lee
Stephen Lewis
John Z. Lowther
Samuel H. Lowther
O. P. Matthews
George McDuffie
Orin D. McFadden
William H. McKinney
James Henry Mears
William H. Mears
A. B. Mincey
Joseph M. Minton
Daniel W. Mitchell
James H. Mobley
George H. Mock
John Baptist Mock, Jr.
John Henry Mock
John P Mock
Josiah M. Mock
Lovick G. Mock
Wells J. Mock
Wilson Mock
Thomas J. Moore
C. T. Mosley
John C. Odom
P. S. S. Ogilvie
Elijah Oliver
Jack Oliver
John H. Oliver
McDaniel Oliver
William P. Owens
Boy Peterson
James J. Peterson
M. M. Potter
Lewis K. Powell
John M. Poythress
E. J. W. Prescott
Hiram D. Prescott
J. P. Prescott
Matthew Potter
Edward Reynolds
Delmus F. Robbins
Dennis F. Robbins
John D. Robbins
John T. Robbins
Stephen M. Robbins
Arthur Roberts
Isham Roberts
Hoke B. Scott
Jacob W. Scott
John M. Scott
Philetus B. Scott
Richard P. Scott
John R. Sellers
Eli Sellers
Robert Shadrack
Robert M. Shadron
Richard Simms
Joseph Lawton Singleton
Thomas W. Smiley
Britton G. Smith
James A. Smith
James H. Smith

Miles Smith
Seaborn W. Smith
Daniel J. Stewart
Thomas G. Stewart
Benjamin Summerlin
Berrien Summerlin
Eli Summerlin
George M. Thompson

Hardee C. Thompson
Jesse M. Thompson
John A. Thompson
John G. Thompson
Paul C. Thompson
Robert F. Thompson
Samuel C. Umphries
John R. Wade

Leroy Wade
Reuben Waters
Henry C. Wells
Thomas J. Wells
Robert Wiley
Thomas Wiley
William Williams
Robert Wooward

COMPANY E - BRYAN, CHATHAM & EFFINGHAM COUNTY, GEORGIA CHATHAM VOLUNTEERS

William Alexander
Thomas Ard
William Arkwright
Alfred Bacon
Jeremiah Baden
Alfred C. Baker(Bacon)
George Baker
William Barrett
W. H. H. Bartley
Granville Bevill
Stephen B. Bevill
Solomon Bingham
Thomas W. Bingham
Edward J. Bird
John Bonner
W. H. Brooks
George Brown
DeWitt Bruyn
J. M. Bryant
Charles R. Carpenter
Cornelius Carperter
Sayers Christerson
James E. Clanton
William H. Cope
G. Corbitt
Calvin C. Cowart
Thomas C. Cowart
Zachariah Cowart
Jordan Cribbs
Sheppard Cribbs
Cosmo R. Davis
Harmon L. Davis
William Derrance
William J. Dotson
George Douglas
Jordan Driggers
J. Thomas Dukes
John L. Dukes
Henry R. Eastmead
Stephen Ellenton(Ellington)
William Ennis
Albert A. Fudge
Carter W. Futch
Hampton J. Futch
James H. Futch, Jr.
James H. Futch, Sr.
Jesse Futch
William M. Futch
Jackson Gill
James Gill
G. W. Grace
George Grace
Richard Grant
Jefferson Hart
James Oliver Harvey
James P. Hay
James Hearn(Harn)
Thomas Hearn(Harn)
Joshua Helmsley
Dedrick Hildebrand
William J. G. Hodges
John Hogan
H. Holiday
Henry Holiday
Josiah E. Horning
George O. Jenkins
John Johnson
Henry Kangter
Robert W. King
Stephen Kirsh(Kirsch)
William H. Kirsh(Kirsch)
John Kuhlman
Calvin J. Marsh
Henry Marsh
C. T. McCorkle
Robert R. McCorkle
William B. Moore
Thomas N. Mulryne
Henry T. Neve
Ebenezer Newman
Ira J. Newman
Jesse Newman
John M. F. Newman
John Noonan
H. W. Osteen
Maximilian D. Osteen
Solomon W. Osteen
John H. Plate
William S. Phillips
Albert R. Pomeroy
John Powers
Andrew Purvis
Thomas Raye
S. R. Savilley
Thomas C. Scott
James S. Shuman
James W. Shuman
Joseph E. Singleton
William J. Singleton
John H. Slate
Clement C. Slater
William Thomas Smith
Juda S. Soloman
Robert W. Stokes
S. A. Swilly(Snelling)
James Tapper
Henry Thompson
John A. Thompson
Malachi Thompson
Francis M. Tillman
George W. Tillman
John H. Ulmer
Adolph Vesting
Hiram Waller
Frank M. Walls
Francis M. Walls
J. Walls
Thomas W. Walls
Thomas W. Ward
H Warnock
John V. Whitaker
James White
Peter Whity
Athur Williams
Henry Williams
Lorenzo H. Williams
Richard Williams
Francis Williamson
Petty Witle

COMPANY F - APPLING COUNTY, GEORGIA
APPLING RANGERS

Berry H. Aldridge	Richard D. Foster	John Aaron Johnson
Elias Altman	J. A. George	**John W. Johnson**
Sampson Altman	John A. George	**Matthew Johnson**
J. M. Askin	Francis M. Goodin	Francis Marion Jones
Thomas Fletcher Barnett	James W. Googe	Henry W. Jordan
Doctor Barrentine	William Googe	H. H. King
William Lumpkin Beecher	**John E. Googe**	J. K. King
Nathaniel A. Bell	Henry W. Gordon	Clement T. Latimer
Austin W. Blount	James H. Graham	James H. Latimer
Jonathan A. Blount	Henry P. Graham	Thomas P. Lee
Joseph Bowers	**John Green**	Abraham Eason Leggett
William Brantley	J. Grelold	**Watson Leggett**
Richard G. Brooker	James M. Hagin	**Richard G. Long**
John Buchan	**James M. Hall**	Alpheas D. McClelland
Benjamin F. Bullard	Instance Hall	**Archibald McClelland**
Wesley P. Bullard	Seaborn Hall	John McClelland
Josiah Cannon	**Thomas J. Hall**	Hector McEachin
David Carter	Elbert Hand	Eli McCauley
William Carter	W. Hansell	Henry McGauley
Joseph Henry Comas	James Hardin	M. McGauley
John Cook	Thomas Harrison	H McGeaghan
Jehu Cook	**Phillip Herndon**	**Charles W. Meeks**
Allen Cooper	**David Hesters**	**Redding G. Meeks**
Andrew B. Courson	R. M. Hodges	John T. Melton
James R Courson	Gideon J. Holton	Daniel Miles
Thomas Crapps	**James Holton**	**Willis Miles**
Abraham J. Crosby	John R. Holton	**J. T. Milton**
Berry Thomas Crosby	William S. Holton	Isaac Moody
Benjamin Crosby	William F. Hovis	**Reuben C. Nail**
Riley Crosby	H. W. Howard	James S. Patterson
Silas Crosby	Henry N. Howard	J. S. Paylor
Calvin W. Dedge	Samuel Hughes	George W. Pitts
Joseph G. Dedge	John F. Hutto	Jesse Prescott
Martin M. Deen	Aaron Johnson	Mathias Quinn
Samuel Deen	**Archibald Johnson**	**Arthur Ray**
Michael W. Douglas	James K. Johnson	**William Ray**
Calvin Q. Ellis	James W. Johnson	Aaron Meadows Rentz
Woodson Ellis	G. W. Rentz	George Rentz
Isiah Tanner	James Warnock	Joseph M. (W) Rentz
Asberry R. Taylor	Benjamin Warren	**Adam W. Rigdon**
Benjamin Taylor	Oscar Weatherly	Green Berry Rigdon
Berry S. Taylor	Charles M. Wheeler	Henry H. Rigdon

Burwell W. Taylor
Eli Taylor
Elisha Taylor
Henry Taylor
Isaac Taylor
James B. Taylor
Jesse S. Taylor
William Taylor
William D. Taylor
Willis F. Taylor
Andrew H Thomas
Edward Thomas
David Rivers Tuten
James C. Tuten
C. Tuten
Aaron B. Varn
Daniel R. Varn
George Walker

John L. Wheeler
William Wheeler
John F. White
James Wiley
William G. Wiley
Jackson Williams
James Williams
John Williams
Joseph J. Williams
L. Williams
Noah Williams
Calvin Yawn
David Yawn
Lewis Yawn
Uriah N. Yawn
R. N. Yeoman
Richard M. Youmans

Silas Roberson
Richard M Romans
Clinton Sapp
Elijah Sapp
James M. Sellers
Jimpsey M. Sellers
John M. Sellers
William H. Sellers
Thomas W. Shumans
Dennis Smith
E. Stacy
George W. Spell
Absalom S. Stone
William M. Stone
Asberry C. Tanner
Asberry D. Tanner
Green Tanner

COMPANY G - TATTNALL COUNTY, GEORGIA
TATTNALL INVINCIBLES

Aaron Anderson	John F. Dubberly	William H. H. O'Neal
Edward Anderson	**William W. Dubberly**	Jacob Owens
John G. Anderson	Daniel Ferry	**John C. Parker**
John S. Anderson	**Winfield W. Futch**	Solomon Rewis
William J. Anderson	**John Green**	**William J. Rushing**
John F. Bacon	Francis Dempsey Griffin	Henry Ryals
William H. Bazemore	William Jackson Griffin	**Madison Ryals**
Joseph J. Bell	John E. Hammock	Benjamin Sapp
Clement T. Bowen	W. S. Hartsfield	Elam Sapp
James Bradley	David H. Holland	Luke L. Sapp
W. Brasey	David Holland, Sr.	**Perry Sapp**
Simon W. Brewton	J. Holland	**Salem Sapp**
T. W. Carlton	J. B. Holland	Stephen Screws
Wesley T. Clements	**Perry Holland**	Lewis Shenoch(Shenock)
Harrison Clifton	Thomas Holland, Jr.	Arthur Sikes
John H. Clifton	J. H. Huff	Benjamin Sikes
James L. Coleman	Martin Jones	Daniel Sikes
Bryant Collins	William Jones	Dyer C. Sikes
C. Collins	Daniel L. Kennedy	**John Sikes**
George W. Collins	W. L. Kennedy	Joseph Sikes
Jesse D. Collins	J. M. F. King	**Josiah Sikes**
James Collins	William T. Lightfoot	William W. Sikes
Lewis Collins	Daniel C. Lynn	**James H. Smith**
Mitchell Collins	Dennis E. Lynn	**Newton C. Southwell**
Newton Collins	John L. Lynn	**Thomas H. Southwell**
Robert Henry Collins	Josiah J. Lynn	William E. Southwell
Robert R. Collins	Isham Martin	Andrew Standfield
Rufus Collins	James Martin	Jesse Standfield
Thomas C. Collins	James S. Mayfield	**John Standfield**
Paul J. A. Colson	**Joseph McCullough**	Thomas Standfield
Z. G. Colson	Samuel McCullough	**William H. Standfield**
James Conner	**Elliott E. Mimbs**	Benjamin Stripling
Christopher C. Coursey	Alfred C. Moore	G. W. Sullivan
Robert J. Coursey	**John Murphy**	Martin Sullivan
James Cowart	William H. Murray	John F. Tatum
John Cowart	**B. L. Nail**	D. Terry
Leonard Jackson Cowart	**Jackson Newborn**	B. F. Thompson
William M. Crosby	**Andrew J. Newman**	**John W. Tippins**
Isaac C. Daniel	Jacob Oliver	Lucius A. H. Tippins
James W. Daniel	Daniel C. O'Neal	Phillip Glenn Tippins
William W. Daniel	**John Dickerson**	**B. F. Thompson**
Isham C. DeLoach	Peter G. Dickerson	**Capel Tootle**

William A. Bowers, Jr.

John W. DeLoach	A. J. Dubberly	Columbus Tootle
Enoch Tootle	**Joseph Waters**	Edward W. Wilson
Jeremiah Tootle	Stephen Weidencamp	James M. Wrenn
Simeon Tootle	James G. Wilds(Wiles)	**Hansford Yeomans**
James H. Warren	George B. Wilkes	John H. Yeomans
James M. Warren	George E. Wilkes	**John L. Yeomans**
James M. Waters	Altamond Williams	Redding Yeomans
James Morris Waters	Benjamin S. Williams	

History of the 47th Georgia Volunteer Infantry, CSA

COMPANY H - GLYNN COUNTY, GEORGIA
LIBERTY RANGERS

Matthias C. Adams	Jackson W. Grimes	W. H Newby
Isaac M. Aiken	William Grouse	**Daniel Nighton**
J. F. Barbee	Benjamin Guess	James Jackson O'Neal
J. F. Barrett(Bartlett)	**C. C. Guest**	C. C. Parsons
Caraway. Brown	**Homer Hamans**	Archibald Peterson
James R. Brown	**James Hamans**	A. M. F. Peterson
Lovett Brown	**William W. Hamilton**	George W. Peterson
Samuel W. Brown	John A. Hampton	Henry W. Piles
W. J. B. Buchanan	**Wiley M. Harnage**	**Andrew J .Pinholster**
J. A. Carmichael	**Brady Harralson**	**Alexander Pope**
J. M. Chesser	Elliott H. Hazzard	George W. Price
C. M. Clark	T. A. Hillier	**Richard F. Price**
Hamilton Clark	W. G. Holland	**Nathan R. Purcell**
John M. Clark, Jr.	James E. Holmes	**Nathan Robert Purcell**
John M. Clark, Sr.	Jacob Horch	James O. Richardson
Matthew Clark	Willis Horch	**James J. Rowe**
Daniel F. Clements	Henry Hutto	Jesse J. Rowe
Wesley T. Clements	John Jackson	T. J. Russ
M. Green Conley	**Ransom J. Jarrad**	S. M. Ryals
Henry Cooper	**J. C. Johns**	Jenkins Salens
John Corbett	James R. Johns	George Scarlett
John A. Cribb	David Knowles	Richard Simmons
J. F. Darley	James L. Lanier	Robert Simmons
James Darley	James Lowe	Edmund Smith
John A. Darley	Joseph Martin	Edward T.Smith
Thomas C. Darley	William R. McConnell	John G. Smith
Joseph O. Darsey	**John McGinnis**	J. L. Sommersall
B. L. Dean	George W. McIntyre	William Spell
Samuel J. Dean	James J. Moody	John F. Stanley
Lewis Dempsey	**William F. Moody**	Thomas M. Stuart
Joseph Orlando Dorsey	William M. Moon	W. A. Tennell
William Driggers	J. J. Morrell	Flemming B. Terrell
Henry G. Ellerbee	Jesse Morris	James F. Terrell
C. C. Fails	D. M. Morton	T. B. Terell
John H. Flood	Dennis Mosley	**Able W. Thompson**
C. W. Flowers	J. R. Mosley	**Archibald Thompson**
Ransom C. Ganey	J. S. Mosley	Barney Thompson
Ryan T. Ganey	**John H. Mosley**	Berry Thompson
William T. Gibson	Martin Mosley	Henry Thompson
Neil Gillis	Charles Myers	John A. Thompson
William Gillis	Timmons Myers	Joseph C. Thompson
Alexander Graham	J. A. Nash	L. J. Thompson

Thomas Thompson	**William Watson**	Reuben Willis
Elisha Thornton	**George Wilkes**	Seaborn D. Willis
Samuel K. Tutty	J. J. Williams	Sherrod Willis
H. Wamock	Ephraim Green Willis	George W. Wilson
William E. Warnell	Jacob E. Willis	G. Ziffroury
Daniel Watson	L. Willis	

History of the 47th Georgia Volunteer Infantry, CSA

COMPANY I - EFFINGHAM COUNTY, GEORGIA
EMPIRE STATE GUARDS

Joseph Adams
Daniel A. Arnsdorff
Gideon A. Arnsdorff
James E. Arnsdorff
John E. Arnsdorff
Joshua Arnsdorff
Charles C. Beebe
George W. Berry
Claibourne C. Bevil
Paul Bevil
K. S. Blitch
Robert T. Bourquin
Thomas E. Bourquin
J. Boyswon
L. P. Broughton
Peter F. Broughton
E. J. Brown
George W. Burns
James T. Burns
R. M. Chitwood
David Coddington
Christopher C. Conaway
W. T. Copeland
H. J. Crosby
James R. Crosby
W. Joseph Crosby
W. W. Cussey
Burgman .B. Dasher
Thomas M. Dasher
Richard Dotson
Paul R. Duggar
A. C. Edwards
Daniel W. Edwards, Sr.
James M. Edwards
Obediah I. Edwards
William H. Edwards
Charles C. Elkins
John A. Elkins
S. C. Elkins
Thomas J. Everett
Francis S. Exley
Howard J. Exley

William Farmer
Benjamin Flood
Jesse Floyd
G. C. Floyd
John Futrell
John I. Geiger
J. Gilder
Benjamin Robert Gnann
David E. Gnann
William W. Gnann
Robert I. Groover
R. J. Groover
Robert C. Harrison
Allen P. Heidt
Thadeus P. Hines
S. A. Hodges
William H. Hodges
William H. Honaley
John J. Howell
Allen J. Hurst
George W. Hurst
Thomas J. Hurst
John J. Jackson
James D. Kehl
George Kendrick
Ephraim E. Kessler
E. L. Lard
William M. Lard
John A. Lee
John H. Lee
Sanderson C. Lee
John J. Lightsey
N. H. Lightsey
Samuel H. Lightsey
William Lynch
James Allen Mallett, Jr.
James Allen Mallett, Sr.
Joseph A. Mallette
Albert V. McRory
J. W. McRory
Samuel Mercer
David A. Metzger

John C. Morgan
William H. Morgan
Isaiah G. Morgan
J. Irwin Morrell
David M. Morton
C. W. Narris
J. J. Nease
Robert Godfred Norton
William B. Nungazer
Lewis Parker
Gulliford Peavy
Henry Peavy
James Peavy
Milton Peavy
Thomas M. Peavy
A. Phillis
John D. Pitts
Abner R. Pomeroy
J. F. Powers
James R. Rahn
Thaddeus M. Rahn
George W. Seckinger
J. D. Seckinger
Jackson G. Seckinger
L. A. Seckinger
Thomas C. Seckinger
Benjamin Sennell
Washington E. Shearhouse
Lawrence E. Shuptine
A. L. Smith
D. L. Smith
Henry J. Smith
Lamar A. Smith
E. Shafner Sowell
Thomas T. Sowell
George W. Spell
Martin Sullivan
Robert Trout
John A. Tullis
Robert W. Tullis
Thomas Usher
Thomas C. Wakefield

Hope Farmer
H. P. Watt
Octavus G. Watt
Hiram Wheeler
Thomas Wheeler
William J. Wheeler
J. J. Whiting

<u>M. A. Metzger</u>
<u>Macklin Wiles</u>
Abraham Williams
G. Williams
Andrew J. Wilson
<u>David E. Wilson</u>
Henry H. Wilson

William H. Warnock
John Winburn Wilson
Stephen Alfred Wilson
W. W. Wilson
William Wright

COMPANY K - BULLOCH COUNTY, GEORGIA

David Beasley
Barnabas J. Bennett
D. A. Bennett
James W. Bennett
Jesse Bradley
Jesse Brown
John M. Brown
William A. Cannon
Adolphus S. Canuet
Hiram Collins
Aaron D. Cone
James G. Cone
John S. Cone
Joseph S. Cone
Paul R. Cone
Nathaniel C. Cowart
Berry Davis
L. A. Davis
Miles Davis
S. S. Davis
W. B. Davis
William D. Davis
Calvin Deal
David Daniel DeLoach
Eli DeLoach
William W. DeLoach
Thomas H. Denmark
W. W. Dickerson
E. Driggers
Jackson J. Driggers
M. Driggers
D. Dugger
J. P. Edwards
J. W. Flemming
Frederick H. Futch
Isaac Futch

J. Futch
J. O. Futch
Solomon F. Futch
Cornelius Geiger
J. E. Gibson
Charles A. Groover
David Groover
Allen Hagin
James S. Hagin
Solomon Hagin
Adam Jones Ihler
James J. Johnston
Reuben H. Johnston
A. Kicklighter
Leonard W. Kicklighter
William H. Knight
J. A. Lastinger
B. J. Lee
Hampton Lee
J. C. Lee
Charles J. Lee
James Lee
John S. Lee
Joseph Lee
William N. Lee
General Lewis
E. H. Martin
J. H. Martin
J. O. Martin
Reuben C. Martin
Thomas E. Martin
Wyley A. Martin
Reuben C. McElveen
Thomas Henry Michael
James J. Miller

W. Mitchell
A. Nessmith
E. L. Nessmith
James Nessmith
Sovereigh Nessmith
J. Nesbit
J. Nevil
Thomas Nicholson
Jesse Phillips
Onesimus Phillips
A. J. Proctor
Eli C. Proctor
J. W. Proctor
W. J. Proctor
Alexander Richardson
Henry Richardson
P. C. Richardson
Stephen Richardson
J. C. Rogers
Charles W. Ryals
E. Sheffield
P. C. Sheffield
W. A. Sheffield
W. H. Sheffield
R. G. Southwell
H. Turner
J Warren
Gilbert W. M. Williams
J. M. Williams
William B. Williams
William M. Williams
John Wise
William H. Wise
N. W. Woodcock
R. Woodcock

The following is an alphabetical listing of the soldiers of the 47th Georgia Volunteer Infantry Regiment extracted from the data contained in the National Archives.

ADAMS, JAMES: Company A, private.

ADAMS, MATTHIAS C.: Company H, private, March 4, 1862 enlisted in Mount Vernon as a private in Co. H, 11th Battalion. May 12, 1862 transferred to Co. H, 47th Regiment. June 1, 1862 discharged, furnished Alexander Graham as a substitute. August 4, 1863 elected 2nd Lieutenant of Co. B, 22nd Battalion, Georgia State Guards. May 1864 according to pension records he enlisted as a private in Co. B, 7th Regiment, Georgia Militia. September 1864 sent home on sick furlough. (Born in Montgomery County, Georgia March 1828).

ADAMS, JOSEPH: Company I, private, March 4, 1862 enlisted as a private in Co. I, 11th Battalion. discharged, disability.

AIKEN, ISAAC M.: Company H, Captain, March 4, 1862 enlisted in Darien and elected Captain Co. H, 11th Battalion. May 12, 1862 transferred to Co. H, 47th Regiment as Captain June 11, 1863 resigned his commission due to ill health.

AKINS, MALACHI: Company C, private, March 4, 1862 enlisted as a private in Co. C, 11th Battalion. May 12, 1862 transferred to Co. C, 47th Regiment. August 31,1863 in French's Division Hospital at Lockhart, Mississippi.

AKINS, T. Y.: Company C, private, March 4, 1862 enlisted as a private in Co. C, 11th Battalion. May 12, 1862 transferred to Co. C, 47th Regiment. February 28, 1863 roll, last on record, shows him present.

ALDERMAN, MITCHELL A.: Company C, private March 4, 1862 enlisted as a private in Co. C, 11th Battalion. May 12, 1862 transferred to Co. C, 47th Regiment. June 25, 1864 admitted to St. Mary's Hospital at LaGrange, Georgia. July 11, 1864 returned to duty. April 26, 1865 surrendered at Greensboro, North Carolina according to pension records.

ALDRIDGE, BERRY H.: Company F, private, November 24, 1862 enlisted as a private in Co. F, 47th Regiment, Georgia Infantry.

ALEXANDER, WILLIAM: Company E, private, March 4, 1862 enlisted as a private in Co. E, 11th Battalion. May 12, 1862 transferred to Co. E, 47th Regiment. June 3, 1862 died.

ALLEN, WILLIAM: Company A, 5th corporal, March 10, 1862 appointed 5th corporal of Co. A, 11th Battalion. May 12, 1862 transferred to Co. A, 47th Regiment as a private. May 12, 1862 discharged due to disability.

ALTMAN, ELIAS: Company F. private. May 18, 1862 enlisted as a private (substitute for Sampson Altman) in Co. F, 47th Regiment, Georgia Infantry. September 24, 1863 admitted to Floyd House and Ocmulgee Hospitals at Macon, Georgia, with chronic diarrhea. October 3, 1863 furloughed for

30 days. April 26, 1865 according to pension records he surrendered at Greensboro, North Carolina. (born in Georgia about 1846)

ALTMAN, SAMPSON: Company F, private, March 4, 1862 enlisted as a private in Co. F, 11th Battalion. May 12, 1862 transferred to Co. F, 47th Regiment. May 8, 1862 discharged, furnished Elias Altman as substitute.

AMOSS, WILLIAM T.: Company B, private, May 16, 1862 enlisted as a private in Co. B, 47th Regiment, Georgia Infantry. December 11, 1862 discharged, furnished Samuel Wolfe as substitute.

ANDREWS, AMOS: Company D, private, March 4, 1862 enlisted as a private in Co. D, 11th Battalion. May 12, 1862 transferred to Co. D, 47th Regiment. October 19, 1862 (May 19, 1863) discharged due to disability.

ARKWRIGHT, WILLIAM: Company E, private, March 4, 1862 enlisted as a private in Co. E, 11th Battalion. Never reported.

ARNETT, WILLIAM: Company B, private, March 4, 1862 enlisted as a private in Co. B, 11th Battalion. May 12, 1862 transferred to Co. B, 47th Regiment. February 28, 1863 roll, last on record, shows him present.

ANDERSON, AARON: Company G, private, March 4, 1862 enlisted as a private in Co. G, 11th Battalion. May 12, 1862 transferred to Co. G, 47th Regiment. August 1863 in Breckinridge's Division Hospital at Marion, Mississippi. January 6, 1865 pension records show he was furloughed home. (Born in Tattnall County, Georgia September 16, 1837)

ANDERSON EDWARD: Company G. private. April 29, 1862 enlisted as a private in Co. G, 11th Battalion. May 12, 1862 transferred to Co. G, 47th Regiment. October 31, 1862 detailed on special duty at Proctor's Point, Savannah, Georgia. December 1, 1862 discharged, furnished Martin Sullivan as substitute.

ANDERSON, JOHN G.: Company G, private, April 29, 1862 enlisted as a private in Co. G, 11th Battalion. May 12, 1862 transferred to Co. G, 47th Regiment. 1862 or 1863 died.

ANDERSON, JOHN S.: Company G, private, April 29, 1862 enlisted as a private in Co. G, 11th Battalion. May 12, 1862 transferred to Co. G, 47th Regiment. November 6, 1863 admitted to Floyd House and Ocmulgee Hospitals at Macon, Georgia. November 7, 1863 returned to duty. December 20, 1864 to close of the war pension records show he was at home on sick furlough. (Born in Tattnall County, Georgia May 28, 1840)

ANDERSON, WILLIAM J.: Company G, private, March 4, 1862 enlisted as a private in Co. G, 11th Battalion. May 12, 1862 transferred to Co. G, 47th Regiment. August 1, 1862 transferred to Co. A. 1st Battalion, Georgia Sharpshooters. January 4, 1865 wounded in right arm and captured at Murfreesboro, Tennessee. January 4, 1865 admitted to Division #1 U. S. A. General Hospital in Murfreesboro, Tennessee. February 15, 1865 transferred to U. S. A. General Hospital at Nashville, Tennessee. February 25, 1865 sent to military Prison at Louisville, Kentucky. March 26, 1865 transferred from Camp Chase, Ohio to Point Lookout, Maryland. June 5, 1865 Released from Point Lookout, Maryland.

ARNSDORFF, D. A: Company I, private, February 13, 1863 enlisted as a private in Co. I, 47th Regiment, Georgia Infantry. January 1864 - February 1864 roll of General Hospital at Guyton, Georgia shows him present. No later record.

ARNSDORFF, GIDEON A.: Company I, private, March 4, 1862 enlisted as a private in Co. I, 11th Battalion. May 12, 1862 transferred to Co. I, 47th Regiment. September 19, 1863 wounded at Chickamauga, Georgia. November 2, 1863 died of wounds.

ARNSDORFF, JAMES E.: Company I, 3rd corporal, March 4, 1862 enlisted as a private in Co. I, 11th Battalion. May 12, 1862 transferred as 3rd corporal to Co. I, 47th Regiment. July 8, 1864 in Cannon Hospital at Union Springs, Alabama. December 1864 according to pension records, captured in Savannah, Georgia Hospital. December 1864 admitted to 1st Division Hospital, 20th Army Corporals, with chronic dysentery. 1865 released at Hilton Head, South Carolina. Died in Effingham County, Georgia in 1914.

ARNSDORFF, JOHN E.: Company I, private, March 4, 1862 enlisted as a private in Co. I, 11th Battalion. May 12, 1862 transferred to Co. I, 47th Regiment. November 8, 1862 died of disease at Savannah River Bridge.

ARNSDORFF, JOSHUA: Company I, private, March 4, 1862 enlisted as a private in Co. I, 11th Battalion. May 12, 1862 transferred to Co. I, 47th Regiment. July 17, 1862 died of disease.

ARTHUR, JOHN: Company B, private, March 4, 1862 enlisted as a private in Co. B, 11th Battalion. Absent without leave.

ASHLEY, WILLIAM PERCY MORTIMER: Field Staff, Assistant Quartermaster, September 2, 1861 elected Lieutenant Colonel of the 25th Georgia Regiment. May 11, 1862 Relieved from duty. May 12, 1862 appointed. Assistant Quartermaster 47th Regiment. January 21, 1865 by Special Order granted leave of absence for 15 days.

ASHTON JOHN D.: Company D, Captain, April 19, 1861 enlisted as a private in Co. D, 2nd Regiment, Georgia Infantry. March 4, 1862 elected Captain of Co. D, 11th Battalion. May 12, 1965 transferred to Co. D., 47th Regiment as Captain. October 14, 1862 resigned Commission. Elected Captain of Co. M, 4th Regiment Georgia Cavalry (Avery's). September 19, 1863 captured at Chickamauga, Georgia (also shown as Summerville, Georgia September 10, 1863 and Lawrenceville, Georgia September 20, 1863). October 10, 1863 received at Military Prison, Louisville, Kentucky. October 13, 1863 forwarded to Johnson's Island, Ohio. June 25, 1864 sent from Point lookout, Maryland to Fort Delaware, Delaware. August 20, 1864 forwarded to Hilton Head, South Carolina. December 15, 1864 paroled at Charleston Harbor, South Carolina. May 10, 1865 surrendered. May 17, 1865 paroled, Albany, Georgia.

BACON, JOHN F.: Company G, private, March 4, 1862 enlisted as a private in Co. G, 11th Battalion. May 12, 1862 transferred to Co. G, 47th Regiment. June 11, 1862 died of disease in Charleston, South Carolina

Hospital.

BADEN, JEREMIAH: Company E, 4th sergeant, March 4, 1862 enlisted as a private in Co. E, 11th Battalion. May 12, 1862 transferred to Co. E, 47th Regiment. June 1862 appointed 4th sergeant Co. E, 47th regiment. July 1862 appointed 3rd sergeant Co. E, 47th Regiment. October 31, 1862 roll, last on record, shows him present.

BAILEY, ZACHARIAH: Company B, private, March 4, 1862 enlisted as a private in Co. B, 11th Battalion. May 12, 1862 transferred to Co. B, 47th Regiment. October 6, 1862 discharged under age and disability. June 10, 1864 enlisted as a private in Co. H, 51st. Regiment Georgia Infantry. April 6, 1865 captured at High Bridge, Virginia. June 24, 1865 released at Point Lookout, Maryland.

BAKER (BACON), ALFRED C.: Company E, private, March 4, 1862 enlisted as a private in Co. E, 11th Battalion. May 12, 1862 transferred to Co. E, 47th Regiment. August 25, 1862 discharged by civil authority.

BAKER, GEORGE: Company E, private, March 4, 1862 enlisted as a private in Co. E, 11th Battalion. Never reported.

BARBEE, J. F.: Company H, private, March 4, 1862 enlisted as a private in Co. H, 11th Battalion. May 12, 1862 transferred to Co. H, 47th Regiment. March - April 1863 roll shows him present. March 1, 1863 deployed as nurse. April 1, 1863 "Removed to Quartermaster Department".

BARKER, JOHN: Company D, private, March 4, 1862 enlisted as a private in Co. D, 11th Battalion. May 12, 1862 transferred to Co. D, 47th Regiment. February 29, 1864 roll for Lee Cavalry Division Hospital Montgomery, Alabama attached to the hospital as a cook since December 1, 1863.

BARNETT, THOMAS FLETCHER: Company F, 1st Lieutenant, enlisted as a private in Co. I, 27th Regiment, Georgia Infantry. 1861 appointed 5th sergeant. December 10, 1861 discharged due to disability at Camp Pickens, Virginia. March 4, 1862 appointed 2nd sergeant in Co. F, 11th Battalion. May 12, 1862 transferred to Co. F, 47th Regiment. August 5, 1862 appointed 1st sergeant Co. F, 47th. Regiment. October 26, 1863 elected Jr. 2nd lieutenant Co. F, 47th Regiment March 30, 1864 elected 2nd lieutenant, Co. F, 47th Regiment. (Born in Madison, Florida in 1845)

BARRENTINE, DOCTOR: Company F, private, March 4, 1862 enlisted as a private in Co. F, 11th Battalion. May 12, 1862 transferred to Co. F, 47th Regiment. August 30, 1862 transferred to Co. A. 1st Battalion, Georgia Sharpshooters. August 1864 in Forsyth, Georgia Hospital. November 4, 1864 admitted to Ocmulgee Hospital at Macon, Georgia with pneumonia, ascites and general debility.

BARRETT, J. B.: Company H, private, March 4, 1862 enlisted as a private in Co. H, 11th Battalion. May 12, 1862 transferred to Co. H, 47th Regiment. August 18, 1864 received pay for services from January 1 to April 30, 1864.

BARRETT, WILLIAM: Company E, private, March 4, 1862 enlisted as

a private in Co. E, 11th Battalion. May 12, 1862 transferred to Co. E, 47th Regiment. November 1, 1863 died in Jackson Cavalry Division Hospital at Old Mansion, Mississippi.
BAUGH, A. J.: Company C, private, July 22, 1862 enlisted as a private in Co. C, 47th Regiment, Georgia Infantry. February 28, 1863 roll, last on file, shows him home on sick furlough.
BAZEMORE, JAMES F.: Company D, 1st Lieutenant, May 12, 1862 transferred to Co. D, 47th Regiment as 1st Lieutenant.
BAZEMORE, JAMES P.: Company D, 1st Lieutenant, March 4, 1862 appointed 1st lieutenant Co. D, 11th Battalion. May 12, 1862 transferred to Co. C, 47th Regiment as 1st lieutenant. September 5, 1862 resigned Commission. February 11, 1864 died at home in Screven County, Georgia
BAZEMORE, JAMES R.: Company D, private, March 4, 1862 enlisted as a private in Co. D, 11th Battalion. May 12, 1862 transferred to Co. D, 47th Regiment. February 28, 1863 roll, last on record, shows him present. April 26, 1865 according to pension records he surrendered at Greensboro, North Carolina. Died in Screven County, Georgia in 1928.
BAZEMORE, JOHN A.: Company D, private, March 4, 1862 enlisted as a private in Co. D, 11th Battalion. May 12, 1862 transferred to Co. D, 47th Regiment. August 1862 appointed Commissary. February 28, 1863 roll, last on record, shows him present.
BAZEMORE, ROBERT R.: Company D, private, May 18, 1865 surrendered Augusta, Georgia.
BAZEMORE, THEODORE F.: Company D, private, March 4, 1862 enlisted as a private in Co. D, 11th Battalion. May 12, 1862 transferred to Co. D, 47th Regiment. July 11, 1863 attached to Walker's Division Hospital, Lauderdale, Mississippi. August 31, 1863 roll for Walker's Division Hospital, Lauderdale, Mississippi shows him present.
BAZEMORE, WILLIAM H.: Company G, private, March 4, 1862 enlisted as a private in Co. G, 11th Battalion. May 12, 1862 transferred to Co. G, 47th Regiment. February 28, 1863 roll, last on record, shows him present.
BEALL(BELL), GEORGE WILLIAM: Company B, private, March 4, 1862 enlisted as a private in Co. B, 11th Battalion. May 12, 1862 transferred to Co. B, 47th Regiment. February 28, 1863 roll, last on record, shows him present.
BEALL, HENRY O.: Company B, 1st Lieutenant, March 4, 1862 appointed 1st sergeant Co. B, 11th Battalion. May 13, 1862 transferred to Co. B, 47th Regiment as 1st. sergeant. June 22, 1863 elected Jr. 2nd Lieutenant Co. B, 47th Regt, April 6, 1864 elected 1st Lieutenant Co. B, 47th Regiment. April 26, 1865 surrendered, Greensboro, North Carolina.
BEASLEY, DAVID: Company K, 2nd Lieutenant, October 15, 1861 elected Jr. 2nd Lieutenant of Co. G, 5th Regiment, Georgia State Troops. December 21, 1861 elected Captain of Co. G, 5th Regiment, Georgia State

Troops. April 1862 mustered out. May 6, 1862 elected 2nd lieutenant Co. K, 47th Regiment. December,1862 detailed Enrolling Officer. May 29, 1863 resigned his commission

BEEBE, CHARLES C.: Company I, private, March 4, 1862 enlisted as a private in Co. I, 11th Battalion. May 12, 1862 transferred to Co. I, 47th Regiment. Appointed 3rd corporal. September 19, 1863 wounded at Chickamauga, Georgia. April 26, 1865 pension records show he surrendered at Greensboro, North Carolina.

BELCHER, ELIJAH C.: Company B, private, October 6, 1862 enlisted as a private in Co. B, 47th Regiment, Georgia Infantry. Substitute for Isaac Hay. February 28, 1863 roll, last on file, shows him present.

BELCHER, THOMAS M. F.: Company B, private, March 4, 1862 enlisted as a private in Co. B, 11th Battalion. May 12, 1862 transferred to Co. B, 47th Regiment. December 1, 1862 discharged due to disability.

BELL, JOSEPH J.: Company G, 1st. sergeant, March 4, 1862 enlisted as a private in Co. G, 11th Battalion. May 12, 1862 transferred to Co. G, 47th Regiment and appointed 1st sergeant, Co. G, 47th Regiment, Georgia Infantry.

BELL, MADISON W.: Company B, private, Company B, private, March 4, 1862 enlisted as a private in Co. B, 11th Battalion. May 12, 1862 transferred to Co. B, 47th Regiment. February 28, 1863 roll, last on record, shows him present. April 26, 1865 pension records show he surrendered, Greensboro, North Carolina. (Born in Stewart County, Georgia August 7, 1841)

BELL, NATHANIEL A.: Company F, 1st. sergeant, March 4, 1862 elected 1st sergeant Co. F, 11th Battalion. May 12, 1862 transferred to Co. F, 47th Regiment as 1st sergeant. August 5, 1862 discharged, furnished substitute.

BENNETT, BARNABUS J.: Company K, private, October 15, 1861 enlisted as a private of Co. G, 5th Regiment, Georgia State Troops. April 1862 mustered out. May 6, 1862 enlisted as a private in Co. K, 47th Regiment. February 1863 died in Macon, Georgia hospital before this date.

BENNETT, D. A.: Company K, private, May 6, 1862 enlisted as a private in Co. K, 47th Regiment. February 18, 1865 died of disease General Hospital. #1 at Columbia, South Carolina.

BENNETT, JAMES: Company C, private, March 4, 1862 enlisted as a private in Co. C, 11th Battalion. May 12, 1862 transferred to Co. C, 47th Regiment. April 7, 1865 killed Bentonville, North Carolina.

BENNETT, JAMES W.: Company K, private, October 15, 1861 enlisted as a private of Co. G, 5th Regiment, Georgia State Troops. April 1862 mustered out. May 6, 1862 enlisted as a private in Co. K, 47th Regiment. February 28, 1863 roll, last on record, shows him present.

BERRY, GEORGE W.: Company I, private, August 27, enlisted as a private in Co. I, 47th Regiment, Georgia Infantry. February 28, 1863 roll, last on record, shows him present.

BETCHER (BEECHER, WILLIAM LUMPKIN: Company F, private, March 4, 1862 enlisted as a private in Co. F, 11th Battalion. May 12, 1862 transferred to Co. F, 47th Regiment. August 1, 1862 transferred to Co. A. 1st Battalion, Georgia Sharpshooters. September 1862 sick at Springfield in this company. September 10, 1863 enlisted as a private in Co. I, 27th Regiment, Georgia Infantry. April 26, 1865 surrendered at Greensboro, North Carolina. (Born in Georgia in 1845)

BEVIL, CLAIBOURNE C.: Company I, private, March 4, 1862 enlisted as a private in Co. I, 11th Battalion. May 12, 1862 transferred to Co. I, 47th Regiment. April 11, 1864 died at Savannah River Bridge.

BEVIL, PAUL: Company I, private, March 4, 1862 enlisted as a private in Co. I, 11th Battalion. May 12, 1862 transferred to Co. I, 47th Regiment. April 11, 1864 died at Savannah River Bridge, Georgia. Death claim field April 11, 1864.

BEVILL (BEVIL), GRANVILLE: Company E, private, April 8, 1862 enlisted as a private in Co. E, 11th Battalion. May 12, 1862 transferred to Co. E, 47th Regiment. October 31, 1862 roll, last on file, shows him present. (Born in Georgia September 12, 1845. Died October 8, 1902)

BEVILL (BEVIL), STEPHEN B.: Company E, private, April 24, 1862 enlisted as a private in Co. E, 11th Battalion. May 12, 1862 transferred to Co. E, 47th Regiment. October 31, 1862 roll, last on file, shows him present.

BIRD, EDWARD J: Company E, private, August 9, 1861 enlisted as a private in 1st Co. I, 25th Regiment, Georgia Infantry. September 1861 detached as acting hospital Steward. January 5, 1862 discharged on account of a hernia. September 3, 1862 enlisted as a private in Co. E, 47th Regiment, Georgia Infantry. November 1862 detailed with the Engineer Department, Savannah, Georgia. December 8, 1863 appears on receipt roll given at Savannah, Georgia for expenses for board and lodging for November 1862, while detailed with the engineer Department.

BIRD, WILEY: Company C, private, March 4, 1862 enlisted as a private in Co. C, 11th Battalion. May 12, 1862 transferred to Co. C, 47th Regiment. November 25, 1863 wounded at Missionary Ridge, Tennessee. January 1864 died of wounds in Hospital. No.3 Nashville, Tennessee.

BINGHAM, SOLOMON: Company E, private, March 4, 1862 enlisted as a private in Co. E, 11th Battalion. May 12, 1862 transferred to Co. E, 47th Regiment. October 31, 1863 roll, last on record, shows him present.

BINGHAM, THOMAS W.: Company E, private, March 4, 1862 enlisted as a private in Co. E, 11th Battalion. May 12, 1862 transferred to Co. E, 47th Regiment. June 11, 1862 discharged, furnished John Johnson as substitute.

BLACKBURN, THOMAS W.: Company D, private, March 4, 1862 enlisted as a private in Co. D, 11th Battalion. May 12, 1862 transferred to Co. D, 47th Regiment. August 16, 1862 died of brain disease while home on furlough.

BLACKSTON, GEORGE W.: Company D, private, September 1864 enlisted in Company D, 47th Regiment, Georgia infantry (according to pension records). April 26, 1865 pension records show he surrendered at Greensboro, North Carolina. (Born in Georgia July 4, 1841)

BLACKSTON, MARTIN V.: Company D, private, September 1864 enlisted in Company D, 47th Regiment, Georgia infantry (according to pension records). April 26, 1865 pension records show he surrendered at Greensboro, North Carolina. (Resident of Georgia since 1838)

BLAND, JAMES: Company C, private, April 26, 1865 surrendered at Greensboro, North Carolina.

BLITCH, K: Company I, 3rd sergeant, March 4, 1862 elected 3rd sergeant, Co. I, 11th Battalion. May 12, 1862 transferred to Co. I, 47th Regiment as 2nd sergeant. June 15, 1862 discharged, disability.

BLOUNT, AUSTIN W.: Company F, private, March 4, 1862 enlisted as a private in Co. F, 11th Battalion. May 12, 1862 transferred to Co. F, 47th Regiment. June 25, 1862 died of disease.

BLOUNT, JONATHAN A.: Company F, private, April 25, 1862 enlisted as a private in Co. F, 11th Battalion. May 12, 1862 transferred to Co. F, 47th Regiment. October 31, 1862 roll, last on file, shows him on picket duty at Proctor's Point. July 9, 1864 (according to pension records) wounded in left arm at John's Island, South Carolina. (Resident of Georgia since January 15, 1845)

BONNER (BONER), JOHN: Company E, private, March 4, 1862 enlisted as a private in Co. E, 11th Battalion. never reported.

BOURQUIN, R. T. : Company I, 2nd Lieutenant, March 4, 1862 elected 2nd sergeant, Co. I, 11th Battalion. May 12, 1862 transferred to Co. I, 47th Regiment as 1st sergeant. February 18, 1863 elected Jr. 2nd Lieutenant, Co. I, 47th Regiment.

BOURQUIN, THOMAS E.: Company I, 2nd Lieutenant, March 4, 1862 elected Jr. 2nd lieutenant Co. I, 11th Battalion, May 12, 1862 transferred to Co. I, 47th Regiment as 2nd Lieutenant, February 18, 1863 elected 1st. lieutenant Co. I, 47th regiment. April 26, 1865, pension records show he surrendered at Greensboro, North Carolina. (Born in Georgia)

BOWEN, CLEMENT T.: Company G, corporal, March 4, 1862 enlisted as a private in Co. G, 11th Battalion. May 12, 1862 transferred to Co. G, 47th Regiment. December 5, 1862 appointed 1st corporal Co. G, 47th regiment. February 28, 1863 roll, last on record, shows him absent without leave.

BOWIE, WILLIAM: Company C, private, November 29, 1862 enlisted as a private in Co. C, 47th Regiment, Georgia Infantry. September 19, 1863 killed Chickamauga, Georgia.

BOYSWON (BOSYNON), J.: Company I, private, March 4, 1862 enlisted as a private in Co. I, 11th Battalion. May 12, 1862 transferred to Co. I, 47th

Regiment. November 27, 1863 died in Atlanta, Georgia. Buried there in Oakland Cemetery (this name has not been identified there)

BRADLEY, JAMES: Company G, private, March 4, 1862 enlisted as a private in Co. G, 11th Battalion. May 12, 1862 transferred to Co. G, 47th Regiment. January 14, 1863 died of pneumonia, CSA General Military Hospital, Wilmington, North Carolina.

BRADLEY, JESSE: Company K, private, October 15, 1861 enlisted as a private of Co. G, 5th Regiment, Georgia State Troops. April 1862 mustered out. May15, 1862 enlisted as a private in Co. K, 47th Regiment. August 1862 appears last on this roll.

BRANNEN, HARRISON (HAMPTON): Company C, private, March 4, 1862 enlisted as a private in Co. C, 11th Battalion. May 12, 1862 transferred to Co. C, 47th Regiment. March 1, 1863 died in CSA General Hospital at Wilmington, North Carolina.

BRANNEN, P. U.: Company C, private, March 4, 1862 enlisted as a private in Co. C, 11th Battalion. May 12, 1862 transferred to Co. C, 47th Regiment. February 1863 sick in Wilmington, North Carolina hospital. December 7, 1863 in General Hospital, Guyton, Georgia.

BRANNEN, SOLOMON: Company C, private, March 4, 1862 enlisted as a private in Co. C, 11th Battalion. May 12, 1862 transferred to Co. C, 47th Regiment. June 10, 1862 killed James Island, South Carolina.

BRANNEN, WILLIAM ALEANDER: Company C, private, March 4, 1862 enlisted as a private in Co. C, 11th Battalion. May 12, 1862 transferred to Co. C, 47th Regiment. March 7, 1864 admitted to Floyd House and Ocmulgee Hospitals at Macon, Georgia. Furloughed for 30 days date not stated.

BANTLEY, WILLIAM: Company F, private, April 29, 1862 enlisted as a private in Co. F, 11th Battalion. May 12, 1862 transferred to Co. F, 47th Regiment. October 31, 1863 roll, last on record, shows him present.

BRENNER, HENRY: Company A, private, February 27, 1862 Co. A, 11th Battalion. May 12, 1862 transferred to Co. A, 47th Regiment as private. November 1862 discharged.

BREWTON, SIMON W.: Company G, 1st sergeant, March 4, 1862 elected 1st sergeant, Co. G, 11th Battalion. May 12, 1862 transferred to Co. G, 47th Regiment as 2nd sergeant. September 30, 1862 discharged, furnished Martin E. Jones as a substitute. Reenlisted, command not given. Wounded, date and place not given. Died in service.

BRITT, JOHN M. K.: Company B, private, March 4, 1862 enlisted as a private in Co. B, 11th Battalion. May 12, 1862 transferred to Co. B, 47th Regiment. October 20, 1862 discharged under age and disability at Camp Williams. (Appears as John N. K and John R. Britt)

BROOKER, RICHARD G.: Company F, private, Company F, private, October 1862 enlisted as a private in Co. F, 11th Battalion. May 12, 1862 transferred to Co. F, 47th Regiment. October 31, 1862 on Picket duty at Proctor's Point.

BROOKS, W. H.: Company E, private, March 4, 1862 enlisted as a private in Co. E, 11th Battalion. Never reported.

BROUGHTON, PETER F: Company I, 1st corporal, March 4, 1862 elected 1st corporal, Co. I, 11th Battalion. May 12, 1862 transferred to Co. I, 47th Regiment as 1st corporal. February 28, 1863 roll, last on record, shows him present.

BROWN C.: Company H, private, May 12, 1862 enlisted as a private in Co. H, 47th Regiment. October 17, 1863 died in Academy Hospital, Marietta, Georgia.

BROWN, E. J.: Company I, private, March 4, 1862 enlisted as a private in Co. I, 11th Battalion. May 12, 1862 transferred to Co. I, 47th Regiment. July 30, 1863 transferred to Co. A. 1st Battalion, Georgia Sharpshooters. August 1864 roll shows him sick in General Hospital.

BROWN, GEORGE: Company E, private, March 4, 1862 enlisted as a private in Co. E, 11th Battalion. Never reported.

BROWN, JAMES R.: Company H, private, May 12, 1862 enlisted as a private in Co. H, 47th Regiment. December 21, 1863 in Catoosa Hospital at Griffin, Georgia. (Born in Montgomery County, Georgia December 25, 1842)

BROWN, JESSE: Company K, private, May 6, 1862 enlisted as a private in Co. K, 47th Regiment. August 4, 1862 Jesse Brown died of disease at home.

BROWN, JOHN L.: Company B, private, May 16, 1862 enlisted as a private in Co. B, 47th Regiment, Georgia Infantry. January 25, 1864 died in Randolph, County, Georgia.

BROWN, JOHN M.: Company K, private, October 15, 1861 enlisted as a private of Co. G, 5th Regiment, Georgia State Troops. April 1862 mustered out. May 6, 1862 enlisted as a private in Co. K, 47th Regiment. November 2, 1863 died in Oliver Hospital, La Grange, Georgia.

BROWN, LOVETT: Company H, private, May 12, 1862 enlisted as a private in Co. H, 47th Regiment. February 28, 1863 roll, last on record, shows absent, sick. Pension records show him at home on furlough at the close of the war.

BROWN, NEEDHAM R.: Company B, private, April 23, 1862 enlisted as a private in Co. B, 11th Battalion. May 12, 1862 transferred to Co. B, 47th Regiment. February 28, 1863 roll, last on record, shows him present.

BROWN, SAMUEL W.: Company H, private, May 12, 1862 enlisted as a private in Co. H, 47th Regiment. December 21, 1863 in Catoosa Hospital at Griffin, Georgia. April 26, 1865 pension records show he surrendered at Greensboro, North Carolina. (Born in Montgomery County, Georgia in 1839)

BROWN, THOMAS S.: Company D, private, March 4, 1862 enlisted as a private in Co. D, 11th Battalion. May 12, 1862 transferred to Co. D, 47th Regiment. March 11, 1863 transferred to Co. C, 21st Battalion, Georgia Cavalry. February 29, 1864 received pay.

BROWNER, D. W.: Company C, private, March 4, 1862 enlisted as a private in Co. C, 11th Battalion. May 12, 1862 transferred to Co. C, 47th Regiment. August 13, 1863 died in hospital in Meridian Mississippi.

BRUYN, DEWITT: Company E, Captain, March 4, 1862 appointed 2nd Lieutenant Co. E, 11th Battalion, March 4, 1862 transferred to Co. E, 47th Regiment as 2nd Lieutenant, July 18, 1862 elected 1st Lieutenant, Co. E. 47th Georgia. May 14, 1863 elected Captain Co. E, 47th regiment. January 17, 1865 dropped from rolls for prolonged absence without leave. (Born in Ithaca, New York, December 30, 1830). Died at Confederate Soldier's home, Atlanta, Georgia July 27, 1909.

BUCHAN, JOHN: Company F, private, March 4, 1862 enlisted as a private in Co. F, 11th Battalion. May 12, 1862 transferred to Co. F, 47th Regiment. October 31, 1863 roll, last on record, shows him present. April 26, 1865 pension records show he surrendered at Greensboro, North Carolina. (Born in Tattnall County, Georgia in 1832)

BUCHANAN, W. J. B.: Company H, private, May 12, 1862 enlisted as a private in Co. H, 47th Regiment. February 28, 1863 roll, last on record, shows him present.

BUCHANAN, WILLIAM H.: Company B, private, March 4, 1862 enlisted as a private in Co. B, 11th Battalion. May 12, 1862 transferred to Co. B, 47th Regiment. February 6, 1864 discharged disability. (Born in Cuthbert, Georgia in 1843)

BUIE (BOUIE), NEIL: Company C, private, March 4, 1862 enlisted as a private in Co. C, 11th Battalion. May 12, 1862 transferred to Co. C, 47th Regiment. April 18, 1862 discharged disability.

BUFORD, BENJAMIN C., JR.: Company D, private, March 4, 1862 enlisted as a private in Co. D, 11th Battalion. May 12, 1862 transferred to Co. D, 47th Regiment. August 12, 1862 discharged, furnished Robert Bronson (Brunson) as substitute.

BUFORD, BENJAMIN C., Sr.: Company D, 2nd sergeant, March 4, 1862 appointed 2nd sergeant Co. D, 11th Battalion. May 12, 1862 transferred to Co. D, 47th Regiment as 2nd sergeant. February 28, 1863 roll shows him present.

BUFORD, FRANCIS M.: Company D, private, March 4, 1862 enlisted as a private in Co. D, 11th Battalion. May 12, 1862 transferred to Co. D, 47th Regiment. June 27, 1862 discharged due to disability.

BUFORD, JOHN G.: Company D, private, March 4, 1862 enlisted as a private in Co. D, 11th Battalion. May 12, 1862 transferred to Co. D, 47th Regiment. June 11, 1862 discharged. January 9, 1863 reenlisted. February 28, 1863 roll shows him present.

BUFORD, WILLIAM J. L.: Company D, private, March 4, 1862 enlisted as a private in Co. D, 11th Battalion. May 12, 1862 transferred to Co. D, 47th Regiment. January 21, 1864 discharged at Dalton, Georgia. (Born in Screven County, Georgia. Died at Confederate Soldiers Home, Atlanta, Georgia May 9, 1915).

BULLARD, BENJAMIN F.: Company F, private, March 4, 1862 enlisted as a private in Co. F, 11th Battalion. May 12, 1862 transferred to Co. F, 47th Regiment. October 20, 1863 died in Institute Hospital Atlanta, Georgia. Buried there in Oakland Cemetery.

BULLARD, WESLEY P.: Company F, private, March 4, 1862 enlisted as a private in Co. F, 11th Battalion. May 12, 1862 transferred to Co. F, 47th Regiment. May 19, 1862 died of disease.

BURKE, ROBERT: Field Staff, Musician, May 31, 1862 appointed Musician. December 1872 shows him present.

BURNEY, JAMES L.: Company B, 3rd corporal, March 4, 1862 appointed 3rd corporal Co. B, 11th Battalion. May 12, 1862 transferred to Co. B, 47th Regiment as 3rd corporal. February 28, 1863 roll, last on file, shows him present.

BURNEY, WILLIAM P.: Company B, private, April 25, 1862 enlisted as a private in Co. B, 11th Battalion. May 12, 1862 transferred to Co. B, 47th Regiment. August 20, 1863 died in Mississippi hospital.

BURNS, GEORGE W.: Company I, private, March 4, 1862 enlisted as a private in Co. I, 11th Battalion. May 12, 1862 transferred to Co. I, 47th Regiment. July 1863 - August 1863 in Loring's Division Hospital at Lauderdale Springs, Mississippi.

BURNS, JAMES: Company I, private, enlisted as a private in Co. I, 47th Regiment, Georgia Infantry.

BURNSIDES, JAMES E.: Company C., 1st sergeant. March 4, 1862 appointed 1st sergeant Co. C, 11th Battalion. May 12, 1862 transferred to Co. C 47th Regiment. as 1st sergeant. September 1862, appointed Commissary Sergeant. February 28, 1863 roll, last on file, shows him sick in Wilmington, North Carolina Hospital.

BUTLER, WILLIAM: Company A, private, March 4, 1862 enlisted as a private in Co. A, 11th Battalion. May 12, 1862 transferred to Co. A, 47th Regiment as a private. January 1, 1865 appears on a list of deserters which shows he "came into lines December 10, 1864, at Devereaux Neck, South Carolina, at work in Q. M. Department"

CAILE, A. H.: Company D, private, March 4, 1862 enlisted as a private in Co. D, 11th Battalion. May 12, 1862 transferred to Co. D, 47th Regiment. October 9, 1863 discharged, disability caused by tuberculosis. (Appears as Cail, Cayle, Coile and Coyle)

CAILE, JASPER: Company D, private, March 4, 1862 enlisted as a private in Co. D, 11th Battalion. May 12, 1862 transferred to Co. D, 47th Regiment. August 31, 1863 in French's Division Hospital at Lockhart, Mississippi. April 9, 1864 died Atlanta, Georgia. Buried there at Oakland Cemetery. (Appears as Cail, Cayle, Coile and Coyle)

CALLAGHAN, LAURENCE: Company A, private, enlisted February 27, 1862 in Co. A, 11th Battalion as a private. May 12, 1862 transferred to Co. A, 47th Regiment as a private. December 5, 1864 deserted at Honey Hill, South Carolina. December 8, 1865 went North.

CALLAHAN, PATRICK: Company A, private, enlisted March 12, 1862 as a private in Co. A, 11th Battalion. May 12, 1862 transferred to Co. A, 47th Regiment as a private. May 18, 1864 captured at Calhoun Ferry, Georgia. May 18, 1865 released at Camp Morton, Indiana.

CALLAWAY, JOSHUA: Company B, 3rd sergeant, March 4, 1862 in Randolph County appointed. 4th sergeant, Co. B, 11th Battalion. May 12, 1862 transferred to Co. B, 47th Regiment as 4th sergeant. Appointed 3rd sergeant Co. B, 47th Regiment. December 17, 1863 died in Randolph County.

CAMPBELL, AMBROSE: Company C, private, October 1, 1862 enlisted as a private in Co. C, 47th Regiment, Georgia Infantry. 1865 died of pneumonia at Kingstree, South Carolina.

CAMPBELL, PATRICK S.: Company A, 2nd corporal, Enlisted May 4, 1862 Co. A, 11th Battalion as private, May 12, 1862 transferred to Co. A, 47th regiment Georgia Infantry. June 12, 1862 appointed 4th corporal Co. A, 47th Regiment. September 1862 appointed 2nd corporal Co. A, 47th Regiment. May 18, 1864 .captured at Calhoun Ferry, Georgia. May18, 1865 released at Camp Morton, Indiana.

CANNON, JOSIAH: Company F, private, March 4, 1862 enlisted as a private in Co. F, 11th Battalion. May 12, 1862 transferred to Co. F, 47th Regiment. August 1, 1862 transferred to Co. A. 1st Battalion, Georgia Sharpshooters.

CANNON, W. A.: Company K, private, May 6, 1862 enlisted as a private in Co. K, 47th Regiment. February 28, 1863 roll, last on record, shows him present.

CANUET, ALDOLPHUS S.: Company C, Captain, May 6, 1862 enlisted as a private in Co. K, 47th Regiment. May 10, 1862 elect 2nd Lieutenant Co. C, 47th Regiment. June 1862 elect 1st Lt Co. C, 47th Regiment. August 25, 1862 elect Captain Co. C, 47th Regiment. November 24, 1862 cashiered by sentence Gen. Court Martial. (Died Savannah, Georgia December 21, 1909)

CARMICHAEL, J. A.: Company H, private, March 2, 1862 enlisted as a private in Co. H, 11th Battalion. May 12, 1862 transferred to Co. H, 47th Regiment. February 28, 1863 roll, last on record, shows him present. Pension records show he was sick in hospital at the close of the war. (Born in Telfair County, Georgia in 1844)

CARPENTER, CHARLES: Company E, private, March 4, 1862 enlisted as a private in Co. E, 11th Battalion. May 12, 1862 transferred to Co. E, 47th Regiment. August 25, 1862 discharged by civil authority.

CARPENTER, CORNELIUS: Company E, private, March 4, 1862 enlisted as a private in Co. E, 11th Battalion. May 12, 1862 transferred to Co. E, 47th Regiment. June 3, 1862 died

CARROL, WILLIAM: Company A, private, May 14, 1862 enlisted as a private in Co. A, 47th Regiment. February 28, 1863 roll, last on record, shows him present.

CARLISLE, JAMES N.: Company D, private, March 4, 1862 enlisted as a private in Co. D, 11th Battalion. May 12, 1862 transferred to Co. D, 47th Regiment. Died 1864 or 1865.

CARSWELL, JAMES ALEXANDER: Company D, Lieutenant, September 11, 1862 enlisted as a private in Co. D, 47th Regiment, Georgia Infantry. 1864 elected Lieutenant. April 26, 1865 surrendered at Greensboro, North Carolina.

CARSWELL, WILLIAM ALEXANDER: Company D, 2nd Lieutenant, March 4, 1862 appointed 1st sergeant Co. D, 11th Battalion. May 12, 1862 transferred to Co. D, 47th Regiment as 1st sergeant. October 7, 1862 elected Jr. 2nd Lt Co. D, 47th Regiment. September 5, 1863 elected 2nd lieutenant Co. D, 47th Georgia. September 20, 1863 killed at Chickamauga, Georgia.

CARTER, DAVID: Company F, private, March 4, 1862 enlisted as a private in Co. F, 11th Battalion. May 12, 1862 transferred to Co. F, 47th Regiment. August 31, 1863 in Breckenridge's Division Hospital at Lauderdale Springs, Mississippi.

CARTER, WILLIAM: Company F, private, March 4, 1862 enlisted as a private in Co. F, 11th Battalion. May 12, 1862 transferred to Co. F, 47th Regiment. August 1864 in First Louisiana Hospital at Charleston, South Carolina.

CASSIDY, H. E.: Company H, Chaplin, May 12, 1862 appointed Chaplin of 47th Regiment. February 23, 1863 resigned as Chaplin of the 47th Regiment.

CHESHIRE, EDWIN S.: Company B, private, March 4, 1862 enlisted as a private in Co. B, 11th Battalion. May 12, 1862 transferred to Co. B, 47th Regiment. May 25, 1864 admitted to Ocmulgee Hospital at Macon, Georgia. May 29, 1864 returned to service. April 26, 1865 pension records show he surrendered at Greensboro, North Carolina. (Born in Stewart County, Georgia April 20, 1843)

CHESSER, J. M.: Company H, 2nd Lieutenant, March 4, 1862 enlisted as a private in Co. H, 11th Battalion. May 12, 1862 transferred to Co. H, 47th Regiment. December 22, 1862 elected Jr. 2nd Lt Co. H, 47th Regiment. July 11, 1863 elected 2nd Lt Co. H, 47th Regiment. (Born March 20, 1833)

CHRISTERSON (CHRISTENSON), SAYERS: Company E, private, March 4, 1862 enlisted as a private in Co. E, 11th Battalion. Never reported.

CHURCH, CHARLES: Company D, private, Company D, private, March 4, 1862 enlisted as a private in Co. D, 11th Battalion. May 12, 1862 transferred to Co. D, 47th Regiment. June 25, 1862 died.

CHURCH, JABEZ: Company D, private, March 4, 1862 enlisted as a private in Co. D, 11th Battalion. April 8, 1862 died in Screven County, Georgia.

CIVIL, WILLIAM: Company A, private, March 13, 1862 enlisted as a private in Co. A, 11th Battalion. May 12, 1862 transferred to Co. D, 47th Regiment. November 1862 discharged by order of General Beauregard.

CLANCEY, HUGH: Company A, private,

CLANCEY (CLANCY), MATTHEW: Company A, private, July 25, 1861 enlisted as a private in Captain J. B. Read's Independent Company Georgia Infantry. January 25, 1862 mustered out. March 3, 1862 enlisted in Co. A, 11th Battalion as a private. May 12, 1862 transferred to Co. A, 47th Regiment as a private. August 30, 1864 deserted at Secessionville, South Carolina. August 31, 1864 took oath of allegiance to the United States Government at Morris Island, South Carolina. September 1, 1864 received at Hilton Head, South Carolina.

CLANTON, JAMES E.: Company E., private, April 28, 1862 enlisted as a private in Co. E, 11th Battalion. May 12, 1862 transferred to Co. E, 47th Regiment. June 18, 1862 died at James Island South Carolina.

CLARK, C. M.: Company H, private, May 12, 1862 enlisted as a private in Co. H, 47th Regiment. June 8, 1862 discharged due to disability.

CLARK, HAMILTON: Company H, 3rd corporal, March 4, 1862 enlisted as a private in Co. H, 11th Battalion. May 12, 1862 transferred to Co. H, 47th Regiment. June 1863 Appointed 3rd corporal Co. H, 47th regiment. August 25 - September 13, 1863 paid for commutation of rations while on sick furlough.

CLARK, JOHN M., JR.: Company H, private, May 12, 1862 enlisted as a private in Co. H, 47th Regiment. February 28, 1863 roll, last on record, shows him present.

CLARK, JOHN M., SR.: Company H, private, May 12, 1862 enlisted as a private in Co. H, 47th Regiment. February 28, 1863 roll, last on record, shows him present.

CLAYTON, A. B.: Company D, private, March 4, 1862 enlisted as a private in Co. D, 11th Battalion. May 12, 1862 transferred to Co. D, 47th Regiment. October 29, 1862 discharged, under age.

CLAYTON, ISHAM: Company G, private, April 26, 1865 surrendered at Greensboro, North Carolina.

CLAYTON, MANDOSA V.: Company D, private, March 4, 1862 enlisted as a private in Co. D, 11th Battalion. May 12, 1862 transferred to Co. D, 47th Regiment. February 28, 1863 roll, last on record, shows him present.

CLEMENTS, DANIEL F.: Company H, private, March 4, 1862 enlisted as a private in Co. H, 11th Battalion. May 12, 1862 transferred to Co. H, 47th Regiment. August 1863 in Breckinridge's Division Hospital #2 at Lauderdale Springs, Mississippi. May 1865 pension records show he was sick in North Carolina Hospital from then to the close of the war. (Born in Montgomery County, Georgia October 27, 1841)

CLEMENTS, WESLEY T.: Company G, private, August 1, 1862 enlisted as a private in Co. G, 47th Regiment, Georgia Infantry. February 28, 1863 absent without leave. February 9, 1865 captured at Edisto River, South

Carolina. April 2, 1865 sent from Fortress Monroe, Virginia to Washington, D. C. where he took the oath of allegiance to the United States Government and was furnished transportation to New York City, New York. (Born in Georgia in 1844)

CLIFTON, HARRISON: Company G, private, March 4, 1862 enlisted as a private in Co. G, 11th Battalion. May 12, 1862 transferred to Co. G, 47th Regiment. August 12, 1862 transferred to Captain Abial Winn's Company, 1st Battalion, Georgia Cavalry. January 23, 1863 transferred to Co. G, 5th Regiment, Georgia Cavalry. Pension records show he was on detail at the close of the war.

CLIFTON, JOHN H.: March 4, 1862 enlisted as a private in Co. G, 11th Battalion. May 12, 1862 transferred to Co. G, 47th Regiment. 1862 detailed Hospital Steward. July 31, 1862 discharged, furnished John L. Yeomans as substitute.

COBB, JOHN S.: Company B, private, March 4, 1862 enlisted as a private in Co. B, 11th Battalion. May 12, 1862 transferred to Co. B, 47th Regiment. February 28, 1863 roll, last on record, shows him present.

CODDINGTON, DAVID: Company I, Sergeant, March 4, 1862 enlisted as a private in Co. I, 11th Battalion. May 12, 1862 transferred to Co. I, 47th Regiment. Appointed Sergeant January 26, 1864 furloughed for 15 days. March 24, 1865 took oath of allegiance to the United States Government in Savannah, Georgia "and was to remain in that city".

COLEMAN, HENRY: Company B, private, April 28, 1862 enlisted as a private in Co. B, 11th Battalion. May 12, 1862 transferred to Co. B, 47th Regiment. October 8, 1862 died in Georgia Hospital, Savannah, Georgia.

COLEMAN, JAMES L.: Company G, private, March 4, 1862 enlisted and appointed 5th sergeant in Co. F, 11th Battalion. May 12, 1862 transferred to Co. F, 47th Regiment. June 10, 1862 killed at James Island, South Carolina.

COLEMAN JOHN: Company D, private, September 1, 1862 enlisted as a private (substitute for Hiram D. Prescott) in Co. D, 47th Regiment, Georgia Infantry. August 1863 in Breckenridge's Division Hospital #2 at Lauderdale Springs, Mississippi. September 13, 1863 discharged, disability

COLLINS, B.: Company C, private, July 22, 1862 enlisted as a private in Co. C, 47th Regiment, Georgia infantry. Died in Tennessee.

COLLINS, BRYANT: Company G, private, May 12, 1862 transferred to Co. G, 47th Regiment, Georgia Infantry. 1864 pension records show he was furloughed home on account of dropsy to close of the war. (Born in Bulloch County, Georgia April 6, 1830)

COLLINS, GEORGE W.: Company G, private, March 4, 1862 enlisted as a private in Co. G, 11th Battalion. May 12, 1862 transferred to Co. G, 47th Regiment. August 27, 1862 discharged, under age.

COLLINS, JAMES: Company G, private, 1863 enlisted as a private in Co. G, 47th Regiment, Georgia Infantry. Discharged on account of blindness. (Born in Tattnall County, Georgia November 23, 1836)

COLLINS, JESSE D.: Company G, private, March 4, 1862 enlisted as a private in Co. G, 11th Battalion. May 12, 1862 transferred to Co. G, 47th Regiment. February 28, 1863 roll, last on record, shows him present. April 26, 1865 pension records show he surrendered at Greensboro, North Carolina. (Born in Tattnall County, Georgia November 20, 1838)

COLLINS, LEWIS: Company G, private, March 4, 1862 enlisted in Reidsville, Georgia in Co. G, 11th Battalion. May 12, 1862 transferred to Co. G, 47th Regiment. May-June 1862 shows him absent sick on furlough. July, August, September, October 1862 roll shows him present. November-December 1862 rolls show him absent sick. January-Fbruary 1863 roll shows him at home absent sick. Roll dated August 31, 1863 shows him present in Walker's Division Hospital, Lauderdale, Mississippi. November 1864 died at James Island, South Carolina.

COLLINS, MITCHELL, JR.: Company C, private, March 4, 1862 enlisted as a private in Co. C, 11th Battalion. May 12, 1862 transferred to Co. C, 47th Regiment. February 28, 1863 roll, last on record, shows him present. April 26, 1865 surrendered Greensboro, North Carolina according to pension records. (Born in Ware County, Georgia in 1841).

COLLINS, MITCHELL, SR.: Company C, private, March 4, 1862 enlisted as a private in Co. C, 11th Battalion. May 12, 1862 transferred to Co. C, 47th Regiment. February 28, 1863 roll, last on record, shows him absent without leave.

COLLINS, N. N.: Company C, private, July 22, 1862 enlisted as a private in Co. C, 47th Regiment, Georgia infantry. September 20, 1863 killed at Chickamauga, Georgia.

COLLINS, NEWTON: Company G, private, March 4, 1862 enlisted as a private in Co. G, 11th Battalion. May 12, 1862 transferred to Co. G, 47th Regiment. February 28, 1863 roll, last on record, shows him absent without leave.

COLLINS, R.: Company C, private, March 4, 1862 enlisted as a private in Co. C, 11th Battalion. May 2, 1862 died at Whitesville, Georgia.

COLLINS, ROBERT HENRY: Company G, private, March 4, 1862 enlisted as a private in Co. G, 11th Battalion. May 12, 1862 transferred to Co. G, 47th Regiment. September 1, 1862 discharged, furnished Elam Sapp as a substitute. March 2, 1864 enlisted as a private in Co. D, 61st Regiment, Georgia Infantry. March 25, 1865 captured near Petersburg, Virginia. June 26, 1865 released at Point Lookout, Maryland. (Born in Georgia about 1840)

COLLINS, ROBERT R.: Company G, private, March 4, 1862 enlisted as a private in Co. G, 11th Battalion. May 12, 1862 transferred to Co. G, 47th Regiment. May 12, 1864 clothing was issued to him.

COLLINS, RUFUS: Company G, private, March 4, 1862 enlisted as a private in Co. G, 11th Battalion. May 12, 1862 transferred to Co. G, 47th Regiment. July 1 - October 31, 1863 in Flewellen Hospital at Cassville, Georgia. Pension records show that he was at home on sick furlough from winter of 1864 to the close of the war. (Born in Tattnall County, Georgia in 1842 or 1843)

COLLINS, THOMAS C.: Company G, private, March 4, 1862 enlisted as a private in Co. G, 11th Battalion. May 12, 1862 transferred to Co. G, 47th Regiment. February 28, 1863 roll, last on record, shows him present.

COLSON, PAUL J. A.: Company G, private, March 4, 1862 enlisted as a private in Co. G, 11th Battalion. May 12, 1862 transferred to Co. G, 47th Regiment. February 28, 1863 roll, last on record, shows him present. November 25, 1863 pension records show he was wounded at Missionary Ridge, Tennessee. December 2, 1863 was at home on wounded furlough to the close of the war. (Born in Tattnall County, Georgia in 1831. Died in Toombs County, Georgia February 9, 1928)

COMAS, JOSEPH HENRY: Company F, private, March 4, 1862 enlisted as a private in Co. F, 11th Battalion. May 12, 1862 transferred to Co. F, 47th Regiment. October 31, 1863 roll, last on record, shows him detailed to gather conscripts.

CONAWAY CHRISTOPHER C.: Company I, private, March 4, 1862 enlisted as a private in Co. I, 11th Battalion. May 12, 1862 transferred to Co. I, 47th Regiment. February 28, 1863 roll, last on record, shows him present. April 26, 1865 pension records show he surrendered at Greensboro, North Carolina. (Born in Georgia about 1837)

CONE, AARON D.: Company K, private, May 6, 1862 enlisted as a private in Co. K, 47th Regiment. August 23, 1862 discharged, furnished N C. Cowart as a substitute.

CONE, JAMES G.: Field Staff, Major, Company K, Jr. 2nd. Lieutenant, October 15, 1861 elected 2nd Lieutenant of Co. G, 5th Regiment, Georgia State Troops. December 21, 1861 elected Captain of Co. G, 5th Regiment, Georgia State Troops. April 1862 mustered out. May 12, 1862 elected Major of the 47th Regiment, Georgia Infantry. May 13, 1863 resigned his commission. June 22, 1863 elected Jr. 2nd Lieutenant, Co. K, 47th Regiment. August 25,1864 appears on inspection Report this date James Island, South Carolina.

CONE, JOHN S.: Company K, private, May 6, 1862 enlisted as a private in Co. K, 47th Regiment. June 10, 1862 killed at James Island, South Carolina.

CONE, JOSEPH S.: Field Staff, Lieutenant Colonel, October 15, 1861 elected 1st lieutenant of Co. G, 5th Regiment, Georgia State Troops. April 1862 mustered out. May 6, 1862 elect Captain Co. K, 47th Regiment. August 30, 1863 elected major 47th regiment. November 5, 1864 elected Lieutenant Col. 47th Regiment.

CONE, PAUL R.: Company K, private, October 15, 1861 enlisted as a private of Co. G, 5th Regiment, Georgia State Troops. April 1862 mustered out. May 6, 1862 enlisted as a private in Co. K, 47th Regiment. June 10, 1862 wounded at James Island, South Carolina. July 18, 1862 died of wounds.

CONLEY, M. G.: Company H, private, May 12, 1862 enlisted as a private in Co. H, 47th Regiment. February 28, 1863 roll, last on record, shows him present. March 9, 1905 pension records show he was sick in Charlotte, North Carolina Hospital to the close of the war. (Born in Wilkinson County, Georgia in 1830)

CONNER, BRYAN: Company A, Captain, May 30, 1861 enlisted as a private in Co. C, 1st Regiment Georgia Infantry (Olmstead's). February 27, 1862 elected Jr. 2 Lt, Co. A, 11th Battalion. May 12, 1862 transferred to 47th as 2nd Lt, Co. A. November 1862 detailed as enrolling officer of Co. A., 47th Regiment. January 8, 1863 elected Captain Co. A, 47th regiment. Roll for February 28, 1863 shows him present.

CONNER, JAMES: Company G, private, March 4, 1862 enlisted as a private in Co. G, 11th Battalion. May 12, 1862 transferred to Co. G, 47th Regiment. February 6, 1865 captured in South Carolina. June 15, 1865 released at Hart's Island, New York Harbor. (Born in Tattnall County, Georgia in 1831. Died in Cobbtown, Tattnall County, Georgia February 28, 1920)

COOK, JEHU: Company F, private, April 29, 1862 enlisted as a private in Co. F, 11th Battalion. May 12, 1862 transferred to Co. F, 47th Regiment. March 2, 1864 received pay.

COOK, JOHN: Company F, 2nd Sergeant, March 4, 1862 elect 2nd sergeant Co. F, 11th Battalion. May 12, 1862 transferred to Co. F, 47th regiment as 3rd sergeant. July 1, 1862 discharged, furnished Louis Yawn as substitute.

COOPER, HENRY: Company H, private, May 5, 1862 enlisted as a private in Co. H, 11th Battalion. May 12, 1862 transferred to Co. H, 47th Regiment. February 28, 1863 roll, last on record, shows him present. April 26, 1865 pension records show he surrendered at Greensboro, North Carolina. (Born in Montgomery County, Georgia March 16, 1833)

COPE, WILLIAM H.: Company E, private, March 4, 1862 enlisted as a private in Co. E, 11th Battalion. Never reported.

COPELAND, W. T.: Company I, 1st. corporal, March 4, 1862 enlisted as a private in Co. I, 11th Battalion. May 12, 1862 transferred to Co. I, 47th Regiment. February 28, 1863, roll, last on record, shows him present. November 20, 1862 appointed 1st corporal Co. I, 47th Regiment. May 19, 1865 paroled at Thomasville, Georgia.

CORAM, WILLIAM H.: Company B, private, March 4, 1862 enlisted as a private in Co. B, 11th Battalion. May 12, 1862 transferred to Co. B, 47th Regiment. May 31, 1862 died

CORBETT, JOHN: Company H, private, March 4, 1862 enlisted as a private in Co. H, 11th Battalion. Never reported for duty.

CORLEY, WALTER C.: Company B, 2nd sergeant, May 10, 1861 enlisted as a private in Co. F, 5th Regiment, Georgia infantry. June 30, 1861 roll shows him present. March 4, 1862 appointed 2nd sergeant Co. B, 11th Battalion. May 12, 1862 transferred to Co. B, 47th Regiment as

2nd sergeant elected 2nd lieutenant Co. B, 47th regiment March, 1865 on Company B, roll.

COTTER, RICHARD: Company A, private, May 14, 1862 enlisted as a private in Co. A, 47th Regiment. December 1862 roll shows him as being detailed on Gun Boat.

COURSEY, CHRISTOPHER C.: Company G, private, March 4, 1862 enlisted as a private in Co. G, 11th Battalion. May 12, 1862 transferred to Co. G, 47th Regiment. September 3, 1862 died of disease at home.

COURSEY, ROBERT J.: Company G, 4th sergeant, March 4, 1862 elected 4th sergeant Co. G, 11th Battalion. May 12, 1862 transferred to Co. G, 47th Regiment, Georgia Infantry as 5th sergeant. January 17, 1863 died of disease at home.

COURSON, ANDREW B.: Company F, private, March 4, 1862 enlisted as a private in Co. F, 11th Battalion. May 12, 1862 transferred to Co. F, 47th Regiment. October 31, 1863 roll, last on record, shows him present. (Appears as Coursan and Coursen)

COURSON, JAMES R.: Company F, private, enlisted as a private in Co. F, 47th Regiment, Georgia Infantry. October 13, 1863 admitted to Floyd House and Ocmulgee Hospitals at Macon, Georgia. October 27, 1863 furloughed for 30 days.

COWART, CALVIN C.: Company E, private, March 4, 1862 enlisted as a private in Co. E, 11th Battalion. May 12, 1862 transferred to Co. E, 47th Regiment. July 13, 1862 died of disease in hospital.

COWART, JAMES: Company G, private, November 20, 1862 enlisted as a private in Co. G, 47th Regiment, Georgia Infantry. February 28, 1863 roll, last on record, shows him present.

COWART, JOHN: Company G, private, November 20, 1862 enlisted as a private in Co. G, 47th Regiment, Georgia Infantry. February 28, 1863 roll, last on record, shows him present.

COWART, LEONARD JACKSON: Company G, private, enlisted as a private in Co. G, 47th Regiment, Georgia Infantry. Discharged on account of crippled foot. December 21, 1863 enlisted as a private in Co. C, 3rd. Regiment, Georgia Infantry. April. 9, 1865 surrendered at Appomattox Courthouse, Virginia.

COWART, NATHANIEL C.: Company K, private, May 6, 1862 enlisted (substitute for A. D. Cone) as a private in Co. K, 47th Regiment. August 20, 1863 died of typhoid dysentery at Marion Hospital Mississippi.

COWART, THOMAS C.: Company E, private, Company E, private, March 4, 1862 enlisted as a private in Co. E, 11th Battalion. May 12, 1862 transferred to Co. E, 47th Regiment. July 30, 1862 died of disease.

COWART, ZECHARIAH: Company E, private, March 4, 1862 enlisted as a private in Co. E, 11th Battalion. May 12, 1862 transferred to Co. E, 47th Regiment. Appointed corporal. October 31, 1863 roll, last on record, shows him present.

COXWELL, GEORGE W.: Company B, Hospital Staff, April 25, 1862 enlisted as a private in Co. B, 11th Battalion. May 12, 1862 transferred to Co. B, 47th Regiment. October 1, 1862 appointed hospital steward. December 1, 1862 appointed Assistant Surgeon. December 22 1862 transferred to 18th Battalion Georgia Infantry as Assistant Surgeon. February 24, 1865 cut off from command by Federal Army. (Died July 10, 1880. Buried at Shellman, Georgia)

CRAPPS (CRAPS), SAMUEL: Company B, 1st corporal, March 4, 1862 appointed 1st corporal. Co. B, 11th Battalion. May 12, 1862 transferred to Co. B, 47th Regiment. as 1st. corporal. Transferred to the 32nd Regiment. December 31, 1864 roll, last on file, shows him in Cuthbert, Georgia hospital.

CRAPPS, THOMAS: Company F, private, March 4, 1862 enlisted as a private in Co. F, 11th Battalion. May 12, 1862 transferred to Co. F, 47th Regiment. October 8, 1862 died of Typhoid fever at Savannah, Georgia

CRAWFORD, CHARLES A.: Company B, private, July 31, 1863 enlisted as a private in Co. H, 1st Regiment, Local Defense Troops (Augusta, Georgia). June 1864 roll, last on file, shows him present. November 1864 Pension records show he enlisted as a private in Co. B, 47th Regiment, Georgia Infantry. April 26, 1865 surrendered Greensboro, North Carolina. (Born in Columbia, County, Georgia June 14, 1823)

CREAGHAM, PATRICK: Company A, private, March 3, 1862 enlisted in Co. A, 11th Battalion as a private. May 12, 1862 transferred to Co. A, 47th Regiment as a private. September 20, 1863 captured at Chickamauga, Georgia. April 20, 1865 took oath of allegiance at Camp Morton, Indiana and released.

CREMMIN, JEREMIAH: Company A, private. March 10, 1862 enlisted in Co. A, 11th Battalion as a private. May 12, 1862 transferred to Co. A, 47th Regiment as a private. June 19, 1864 captured at Marietta, Georgia. July 22, 1864 died of typho-malarial fever Camp. Morton, Indiana. (Also appears as Cramer, Cremer and Crimmon)

CRIBB, JOHN A.: Company H, private, March 4, 1862 enlisted as a private in Co. H, 11th Battalion. May 12, 1862 transferred to Co. H, 47th Regiment. July - August 1863 in Breckinridge's Division Hospital at Marion, Mississippi.

CRIBBS, JORDAN: Company E, private, March 20, 1862 enlisted as a private in Co. E, 11th Battalion. May 12, 1862 transferred to Co. E, 47th Regiment. October 31, 1863 roll, last on record, shows him present. Pension records indicate November 25, 1863 wounded in shoulder at Missionary Ridge, Tennessee. February 1865 left command on sick furlough, unable to return. (Born in Bryan County, Georgia in 1843)

CRIBBS, SHEPPARD: Company E, private, March 4, 1862 enlisted as a private in Co. E, 11th Battalion. May 12, 1862 transferred to Co. E, 47th Regiment. October 31, 1863 roll, last on record, shows him present.

CROSBY, ABRAHAM J.: Company F, 3rd corporal, March 4, 1862 elected 3rd corporal, Co. F, 11th Battalion. May 12, 1862 transferred to Co.

F, 47th Regiment as 3rd corporal. August 5, 1862 appointed 2nd corporal. November 1862 Regimental return shows that he was "Assisting the Enrolling officer." March 1865 pension records show he was furloughed on account of sickness. (Born in Appling County, Georgia December 20, 1829)

CROSBY, BERRY THOMAS: Company F, private, March 4, 1862 enlisted as a private in Co. F, 11th Battalion. May 12, 1862 transferred to Co. F, 47th Regiment. October 14, 1863 admitted to Floyd House and Ocmulgee Hospitals at Macon, Georgia, with typhoid fever. October 20, 1863 furloughed for 30 days.

CROSBY, JAMES R.: Company I, private, March 4, 1862 enlisted as a private in Co. I, 11th Battalion. May 12, 1862 transferred to Co. I, 47th Regiment. February 28, 1863, roll, last on record, shows him present. April 26, 1865 pension records show he surrendered at Greensboro, North Carolina.

CROSBY, JOSEPH W.: Company I, private, March 4, 1862 enlisted as a private in Co. I, 11th Battalion. May 12, 1862 transferred to Co. I, 47th Regiment. February 28, 1863, roll, last on record, shows him present. January 4, 1864 died in Atlanta, Georgia Hospital. Buried there in Oakland Cemetery.

CROSBY, RILEY: Company F, private, March 4, 1862 enlisted as a private in Co. F, 11th Battalion. May 12, 1862 transferred to Co. F, 47th Regiment. August 1862 appears last on roll.

CROSBY, SILAS. Company F, 5th sergeant, March 4, 1862 enlisted as a private in Co. F, 11th Battalion. May 12, 1862 transferred to Co. F, 47th Regiment and appointed 5th sergeant Co. F, 47th regiment. October 31, 1862 detailed to assisting Enrolling Officer.

CROSBY, WILLIAM: Company C, private, March 4, 1862 enlisted as a private in Co. C, 11th Battalion. May 12, 1862 transferred to Co. C, 47th Regiment. May 10, 1862 died Savannah, Georgia.

CRYDER (CRIDER), CHRISTIAN J: Company B, private, March 4, 1862 enlisted as a private in Co. B, 11th Battalion. May 12, 1862 transferred to Co. B, 47th Regiment. May 1864 killed at Oostanaula, Georgia.

CULLEN, NICHOLAS: Company A, 2nd corporal, July 25, 1861 enlisted as a private in Captain J. B. Read's Independent Company Georgia Infantry. January 25, 1862 mustered out. March 3, 1862 enlisted in Co. A, 11th Battalion as a private. May 12, 1862 transferred to Co. A, 47th Regiment as 3rd corporal. June 12, 1862 appointed 2nd corporal of Co. A, 47th Regiment. August 12, 1862 died of disease in Medical College Hospital at Savannah, Georgia.

DALE, JAMES F.: Company B, private, April 25, 1862 enlisted as a private in Co. B, 11th Battalion. May 12, 1862 transferred to Co. B, 47th Regiment. September 4, 1863 died in General Hospital at Montgomery, Alabama.

DALE JOHN A.: Company B, private, March 4, 1862 enlisted as a private in Co. B, 11th Battalion. May 12, 1862 transferred to Co. B, 47th Regiment.

June 7, 1863 drowned in Pearl River, Mississippi.

DALY, JOHN J.: Company A, 5th sergeant, February 27, 1862 appointed. 1st Corporal. Co. A., 11th Battalion. May 12, 1862 transferred to Co. A, 47th Regiment as 1st Corporal. May 12, 1862 Appointed 5th sergeant, Co. A, 47th Regt. February 3, 1865 captured at Rivers Bridge, South Carolina (Remarks "Claims to have given himself up, was not bearing arms at time of capture." April 5, 1865 Transferred to Washington, D. C., took oath, Transportation furnished to Savannah, Georgia.

DANIEL, ISAAC C.: Company G, 1st. sergeant, March 4, 1862 enlisted as a private in Co. G, 11th Battalion. May 12, 1862 transferred to Co. G, 47th Regiment. May 12, 1862 Daniel transferred to Co. G, 47th regiment as 1st corporal. December 8, 1862 appointed 1st sergeant Co. G, 47th Georgia. February 28, 1863 roll, last on record, shows him present. April 26 1865 pension records show he surrendered at Greensboro, North Carolina.

DANIEL, JAMES W.: Company G, private, May 13, 1862 enlisted as a private in Co. G, 47th Regiment, Georgia Infantry. November 10, 1862 died of disease in Tattnall County, Georgia.

DANIELM WILLIAM W.: Company G, private, September 1, 1862 enlisted as a private in Co. G, 47th Regiment, Georgia Infantry. February 28, 1863 roll, last on record, shows him present.

DARLEY, J. F.: Company H, private, March 4, 1862 enlisted as a private in Co. H, 11th Battalion. May 12, 1862 transferred to Co. H, 47th Regiment. October 8, 1863 died in Atlanta, Georgia and is buried there in Oakland Cemetery.

DARLEY, JAMES: Company H, private, January 8, 1863 enlisted as a private in Co. H, 47th Regiment. Died in service.

DARLEY, THOMAS C.: Company H, private, March 4, 1862 enlisted as a private in Co. H, 11th Battalion. May 12, 1862 transferred to Co. H, 47th Regiment. February 28, 1863 roll, last on record, shows him present. (Born in Montgomery County, Georgia in 1827)

DASHER, B. B.: Company I, 2nd corporal, March 4, 1862 enlisted as a private in Co. I, 11th Battalion. May 12, 1862 transferred to Co. I, 47th Regiment. Appointed 2nd corporal. February 28, 1863 roll, last on record, shows him present.

DASHER, THOMAS M.: Company I, private, March 4, 1862 enlisted as a private in Co. I, 11th Battalion. May 12, 1862 transferred to Co. I, 47th Regiment. February 28, 1863 roll, last on record, shows him present.

DAVENPORT, WILLIAM BALDWIN: Company B, private, April 25, 1862 enlisted as a private in Co. B, 11th Battalion. May 12, 1862 transferred to Co. B, 47th Regiment. August 11, 1862 died of disease, Oglethorpe Barracks, Savannah, Georgia.

DAVIS, BERRY: Company K, private, May 6, 1862 enlisted as a private in Co. K, 47th Regiment. 1863 died in Mississippi.

DAVIS, COSMO: Company E, private, March 4, 1862 enlisted as a private in Co. E, 11th Battalion. May 12, 1862 transferred to Co. E, 47th

Regiment. July 14, 1862 discharged at Savannah, Georgia.

DAVIS, HARMON L.: Company E, 2nd sergeant, March 4, 1862 appointed 2nd sergeant Co. E, 11th Battalion. May 12, 1862 transferred to Co. E, 47th regiment as 2nd sergeant. August 22, 1862 discharged.

DAVIS, JOHN: Company A, private, August 18, 1861 enlisted as a private in Captain J. B. Read's Independent Company Georgia Infantry. January 25, 1862 mustered out. March 3, 1862 enlisted in Co. A, 11th Battalion as a private. February 27, 1862 transferred to Co. D, 2nd Battalion, Georgia Cavalry.

DAVIS, M.: Company K, private, May 6, 1862 enlisted as a private in Co. K, 47th Regiment. February 28, 1863 roll, last on record, shows him absent with leave on Surgeon's certificate for 60 days.

DAVIS, PATRICK: Company A, private. March 5, 1862 enlisted in Co. A, 11th Battalion as a private. May 12, 1862 transferred to Co. A, 47th Regiment as a private. December 27, 1862 discharged on account of chronic rheumatism, at Savannah, Georgia.

DAVIS, S. S.: Company K, private, May 6, 1862 enlisted as a private in Co. K, 47th Regiment. March - April 1864 sick in Empire Hotel Hospital at Atlanta, Georgia.

DAVIS, WILLIAM: Company K, private, May 15, 1862 enlisted as a private in Co. K, 47th Regiment. February 28, 1863 roll, last on record, shows him absent with leave on Surgeon's certificate.

DAVIS, WILLIAM D.: Company K, private, May 15, 1862 enlisted as a private in Co. K, 47th Regiment. February 28, 1863 roll, last on record, shows him absent with leave on Surgeon's certificate, 30 days from February 13, 1863.

DAVIS, W. B.: Company K, private, December 5, 1862 enlisted as a private in Co. K, 47th Regiment. February 28, 1863 roll, last on record, shows him present.

DAWSON, BENJAMIN: Company B, private, October 9, 1861 enlisted as a private in Co. F, 1st. Regiment, 1st Brigade, Georgia State Troops. April 9, 1862 roll, last on file, shows him present. April 1862 mustered out. April 25, 1862 enlisted as a private in Co. B, 11th Battalion. May 12, 1862 transferred to Co. B, 47th Regiment. October 20, 1862 died Regt. Hosp., Camp. Williams, Savannah, Georgia.

DEAL, CALVIN: Company K, private, May 6, 1862 enlisted as a private in Co. K, 47th Regiment. February 28, 1863 roll, last on record, shows him present.

DEAL, JAMES: Company C, private, March 4, 1862 enlisted as a private in Co. C, 11th Battalion. May 12, 1862 transferred to Co. C, 47th Regiment. October 7, 1862 discharged, under age.

DEAL, WILLIAM: Company C, private, March 4, 1862 enlisted as a private in Co. C, 11th Battalion. May 10, 1862 died Savannah, Georgia.

DEAN, B. L.: Company H, private, March 4, 1862 enlisted as a private in Co. H, 11th Battalion. May 12, 1862 transferred to Co. H, 47th Regiment.

September 26, 1862 discharged at Camp Williams, Georgia by civil authority.

DEAN, SAMUEL J.: Company H, 1st. Lieutenant, March 4, 1862 elected 1st sergeant Co. H, 11th Battalion. May 12, 1862 transferred to Co. H, 47th Regiment as 1st sergeant. December 22, 1862 elected 2nd Lieutenant Co. H, 47th Regiment. June 11, 1863 elected 1st Lieutenant Co. H., 47th Regiment. April 26, 1865 surrendered at Greensboro, North Carolina. December 5, 1873 died of disease contracted in service.

DEDGE, CALVIN W.: Company F, Jr. 2nd Lieutenant, March 4, 1862 elected Jr. 2nd Lt Co. F. 11th Battalion. April 12, 1862 resigned his commission.

DEDGE, JOSEPH G.: Company F, Captain, March 4, 1862 elected 1st Lt Co F, 11th Battalion. May 12, 1862 transferred to Co. F, 47th regiment as 1st Lieutenant. October 26, 1863 elected Captain Co F, 47th regiment. November 30, 1864 wounded and permanently disabled at Honey Hill, South Carolina and was at home wounded at the close of the war. (Born in Appling County, Georgia September 23, 1834).

DEEN, MARTIN M.: Company F, private, March 4, 1862 enlisted as a private in Co. F, 11th Battalion. May 12, 1862 transferred to Co. F, 47th Regiment. March 2, 1864 received pay. July 10, 1864 killed at John's Island, South Carolina.

DEEN, SAMUEL: Company F, private, March 4, 1862 enlisted as a private in Co. F, 11th Battalion. May 12, 1862 transferred to Co. F, 47th Regiment. October 1863 in Breckenridge's Division Hospital at Marion, Mississippi. July 10, 1864 killed at John's Island, South Carolina.

DELANEY, WILLIAM: Company A, private, May 15, 1862 enlisted in Co. A, 47th Regiment. December 1862 roll shows he was detailed on Gun Boat.

DELOACH, DAVID DANIEL: Company K, private, May 15, 1862 enlisted as a private in Co. K, 47th Regiment June 10, 1862 wounded and captured at James, Island, South Carolina. November 10, 1862 Exchanged at Aiken's Landing, Virginia. August 13, 1864 admitted to 1st Division, 15th Corporals Hospital near Atlanta, Georgia.

DELOACH, ELI: Company K, private, October 15, 1861 enlisted as a private of Co. G, 5th Regiment, Georgia State Troops. April 1862 mustered out. May 6, 1862 enlisted as a private in Co. K, 47th Regiment. February 28, 1863 roll, last on record, shows him absent sick, in Georgia.

DELOACH, ISHAM CLAYTON: Company G, private, March 4, 1862 enlisted as a private in Co. G, 11th Battalion. May 12, 1862 transferred to Co. G, 47th Regiment. February 28, 1863 roll, last on record, shows him present. August - September 1864 on furlough. April 26, 1865 pension records show he surrendered at Greensboro, North Carolina.

DELOACH, JOHN WASHINGTON: Company G, private, March 4, 1862 enlisted as a private in Co. G, 11th Battalion. May 12, 1862 transferred to Co. G, 47th Regiment. June 27, 1864 wounded (bone fractured in left leg above the ankle, resulting in permanent disability) at Kennesaw Mt., Georgia. Furloughed home on account of wounds in 1864, and was on wounded furlough until the close of the war. (Born in Georgia in 1843)

DELOACH, WILLIAM W.: Company K, private, October 15, 1861 enlisted as a private of Co. G, 5th Regiment, Georgia State Troops. October 18, 1861 appointed 3rd sergeant. April 1862 mustered out. May 6, 1862 enlisted as a private in Co. K, 47th Regiment. February 8, 1863 died at Top Sail Sound, North Carolina.

DEMPSEY, LEWIS (LOUIS): Company H, private, March 4, 1862 enlisted as a private in Co. H, 11th Battalion. May 12, 1862 transferred to Co. H, 47th Regiment. February 28, 1863 roll, last on record, shows him absent, sick. June 25, 1864 admitted to St. Mary's Hospital at LaGrange, Georgia. July 11, 1864 returned to duty.

DENMARK, THOMAS HARRISON: Company K, private, October 15, 1861 Enlisted as a private in Company G. 5th Regiment, Georgia State Troops. April 1862 mustered out. May 6, 1862 Enlisted as a private in Co. K, 47th Regiment, Georgia Infantry. June 10, 1862 wounded at James Island, South Carolina. June 10, 1863 attached as guard, General Hospital at Lauderdale Springs, Mississippi. September 1, 1863 Discharged.

DERRENCE, WILLIAM: Company E, private, September 13, 1862 enlisted as a private in Co. E, 47th Regiment, Georgia Infantry. October 31, 1863 roll, last on record, shows him present.

DEVERSUR, FRANCIS: Field Staff, Musician, May 31, 1862 appointed Musician. December 1872 shows him present.

DEVINE, WILLIAM B.: Company A, private, April 15, 1862 enlisted as private in Co. A, 11th Battalion. May 12, 1862 transferred to Co. A, 47th Regiment, Georgia Infantry. May 13, 1864 captured at Marietta (Chattahoochee), Georgia. May 20, 1865 released Camp Morton, Indiana.

DICKERSON, JOHN: Company G, private, March 4, 1862 enlisted as a private in Co. G, 11th Battalion. May 12, 1862 transferred to Co. G, 47th Regiment. November 25, 1863 killed at Missionary Ridge, Tennessee.

DICKERSON, PETER G.: Company G, private, March 4, 1862 enlisted as a private in Co. G, 11th Battalion. May 12, 1862 transferred to Co. G, 47th Regiment. February 28, 1863 roll, last on record, shows him present.

DICKERSON, W. W.: Company K, private, May 6, 1862 enlisted as a private in Co. K, 47th Regiment. June 19, 1862 died of disease.

DILL, JOHN P.: Company A, private, July 1862 enlisted in Co. A, 47th Regiment. April 26, 1865 pension records show he surrendered at Greensboro, North Carolina. (born in Lincoln County, Georgia July 22, 1845)

DILLON, MICHAEL: Company A, private, February 27, 1862 enlisted Co. A, 11th Battalion as a private. May 12, 1862 transferred to Company A, 47th Regiment as a private. November 26, 1863 captured at Ringgold,

Georgia. February 27, 1864 died of chronic diarrhea, Nashville Tennessee as a POW.

DILLON, PHILLIP: Company A, private, February 27, 1862 enlisted Co. A, 11th Battalion as a private. May 12, 1862 transferred to Company A, 47th Regiment as a private. December 1862 roll shows he was discharged by Judge Harden, C. C.

DIXON, MICHAEL, JR.: Company C, private, March 4, 1862 enlisted as a private in Co. C, 11th Battalion. May 12, 1862 transferred to Co. C, 47th Regiment. February 28, 1863 roll, last on record, shows him present. April 26, 1865 pension records show he surrendered Greensboro, North Carolina.

DIXON, MITCHELL: Company C, corporal, July 22, 1862 enlisted as a private in Co. C, 47th Regiment, Georgia infantry. Appointed corporal. April 26, 1865 surrendered at Greensboro, North Carolina.

DIXON (DICKSON), MORRIS: Company B, private, April 25, 1862 enlisted as a private in Co. B, 11th Battalion. March, 1862 transferred to Co. A, 2nd Regiment, Georgia Cavalry. May 3, 1865 surrendered at Charlotte, North Carolina (born in Georgia March 6, 1836.)

DOLAN, BERNARD: Company A, private, December 1, 1862 enlisted in Co. A, 47th Regiment. March 4, 1865 deserted in Savannah, Georgia where he took the oath of allegiance to the United States Government Remarks "wishes to go north"

DORSEY (DARSEY), JOSEPH ORLANDO: Company H, 3rd. sergeant, March 4, 1862 elect 3rd sergeant Co. H, 11 Battalion. May 12, 1862 transferred to Co. H, 47th Regiment as 3rd sergeant. February 28, 1863 roll, last on record, shows him present. (Died July 19, 1876)

DOTSON, RICHARD: Company I, private, March 4, 1862 enlisted as a private in Co. I, 11th Battalion. May 12, 1862 transferred to Co. I, 47th Regiment. October, 25, 1862 died of disease at Camp Williams, Georgia.

DOTSON, WILLIAM J.: Company E, private, March 4, 1862 enlisted as a private in Co. E, 11th Battalion. May 12, 1862 transferred to Co. E, 47th Regiment. July 14, 1862 discharged.

DOUGLAS, GEORGE: Company E, private, March 4, 1862 enlisted as a private in Co. E, 11th Battalion. May 12, 1862 transferred to Co. E, 47th Regiment. October 31, 1863 roll, last on record, shows him present.

DOUGLAS, MICHAEL: Company F, private, March 4, 1862 enlisted as a private in Co. F, 11th Battalion. May 12, 1862 transferred to Co. F, 47th Regiment. July 30, 1862 transferred to Co. A. 1st Battalion, Georgia Sharpshooters. August 31, 1864 roll, last on file, shows him present.

DOWNEY, JOHN: Company A, private, March 3, 1862 enlisted Co. A, 11th Battalion as a private. May 12, 1862 transferred to Company A, 47th Regiment as a private. February 28, 1863 roll (last on file) shows him present.

DOYLE, ALEXANDER: Company A, 2nd Lieutenant, February 27, 1862 elected 2nd Lieutenant Co. A, 11th Battalion. May 12, 1862 transferred to 47th Regiment as 2nd Lieutenant Co. A. May 18, 1863 resigned commission.

DOYLE, JAMES M.: Company A, private, April 16, 1862 enlisted Co. A, 11th Battalion as a private. May 12, 1862 transferred to Company A, 47th Regiment as a private. November 1862 discharged by order of General Beauregard.

DOYLE, MICHAEL J.: Company A, Captain, February 27, 1862 elected Captain of Co. A. 11th Battalion. May 12, 1862 transferred to Co. A, 47th Regiment as Captain. January 8, 1863 resigned commission.

DOYLE, MATTHEW J.: Company A, private, April 30, 1862 (substitute for Henry Meinhard) enlisted Co. A, 11th Battalion as a private. May 12, 1862 transferred to Company A, 47th Regiment as a private. December 1862 detailed to gun boat.

DOYLE, PATRICK W.: Company A, 1st Lieutenant, February 27, 1862 Appointed 3rd sergeant of Co. A, 11th Battalion. May 12, 1862 transferred to Co. A., 47th Regiment as Jr. 2nd. Lieutenant. May 18, 1863 elected 1st Lieutenant Co. A, 47th Regiment. Appears last on regimental roster for March 1865.

DOYLE, PATRICK: Company A, private, April 15, 1862 enlisted Co. A, 11th Battalion as a private. May 12, 1862 transferred to Company A, 47th Regiment as a private. September 1862 detached to Command Schooner. November 1862 discharged by Examining Board at Savannah, Georgia.

DRIGGERS, E.: Company K, private, May 6, 1862 enlisted as a private in Co. K, 47th Regiment. June 10, 1862 wounded at James Island, South Carolina. August 3, 1863 died in Breckinridge's Division Hospital at Marion, Mississippi.

DRIGGERS, J. J.: Company C, March 4, 1862 enlisted as a private in Co. C, 11th Battalion. May 12, 1862 transferred to Co. C, 47th Regiment. September 23, 1863 admitted to Floyd House and Ocmulgee Hospitals at Macon, Georgia. October 6, 1863 furloughed for 30 days. April 26, 1865 pension records show he surrendered at Greensboro, North Carolina. (Born in Effingham County, Georgia September 8. 1837)

DRIGGERS, JACKSON J.: Company K, 1st sergeant, May 6, 1862 elected 1st sergeant, Co. K, 47th Regiment. February 28, 1863 roll, last on record, shows him present. July 1863 died of chronic diarrhea in Jackson, Mississippi Hospital.

DRIGGERS, JORDAN: Company E, private, March 4, 1862 enlisted as a private in Co. E, 11th Battalion. Joined another company. March 21, 1862 enlisted as a private in Co. K, 5th Regiment, Georgia Cavalry. Transferred to Co. B. May 17, 1863 deserted near Darien, Georgia. June 4, 1863 apprehended and returned to his command. October 21, 1863 deserted. May 27, 1864 deserted. December 31, 1864 roll, last on file, shows him absent without leave from October 1, 1864.

DRIGGERS, WILLIAM: Company H, private, March 4, 1862 enlisted as a private in Co. H, 11th Battalion. May 12, 1862 transferred to Co. H, 47th

Regiment. February 28, 1863 roll, last on record, shows him present.

DRURY, MICHAEL: Company A, private, February 27, 1862 enlisted Co. A, 11th Battalion as a private. May 12, 1862 transferred to Company A, 47th Regiment as a private November 25, 1863 captured at Missionary Ridge, Tennessee. January 25, 1864 enlisted in the United States Navy at Rock Island, Illinois.

DUBBERLY, JOHN F. (A. JOHN): Company G, 3rd corporal, Mach 4, 1862 elected 3rd Corporal Co. G, 11th Battalion. May 12, 1862 transferred to Co. G., 47th Regiment as 3rd corporal. February 6, 1865 captured in Barnwell District, South Carolina. June 15, 1865 released at Hart's Island, New York Harbor.

DUBBERLY, WILLIAM W.: Company G, private, March 4, 1862 enlisted as a private in Co. G, 11th Battalion. May 12, 1862 transferred to Co. G, 47th Regiment. June 5, 1862 died of disease at Causton's Bluff, Georgia.

DUGGAR, PAUL R.: Company I, 4th sergeant, March 4, 1862 elected 5th sergeant Co. I, 11th Battalion. May 12, 1862 transferred to Co. I, 47th Regiment as 4th sergeant. July 13, 1864 died of disease in Guyton, Georgia Hospital. Buried at Little Ogeechee Church.

DUGGAR, D.: Company K, private, May 6, 1862 enlisted as a private in Co. K, 47th Regiment. December 4, 1863 died in Atlanta, Georgia. Buried there in Oakland Cemetery (not in original rolls).

DUIGNAN (DINGNAN), JAMES: Company A, private, February 27, 1862 enlisted Co. A, 11th Battalion as a private. May 12, 1862 transferred to Company A, 47th Regiment as a private. February 1864 in Hospital.

DUKE, R. T.: Company B, private, July 1864 enlisted as a private in Co. B, 47th Regiment, Georgia Infantry. 1864 Sent to hospital in James Island, South Carolina. March 30, 1864 furloughed from James Island, South Carolina Hospital for 60 days. (Born in Morgan County, Georgia in 1821)

DUKES, J. THOMAS: Company E, private, March 4, 1862 enlisted as a private in Co. E, 11th Battalion. May 12, 1862 transferred to Co. E, 47th Regiment. October 31, 1863 roll, last on record, shows him present.

DUKES, JOHN L.: Company E, Jr. 2nd. Lieutenant, March 4, 1862 appointed 1st sergeant Co. E. 11th Battalion. May 12, 1862 transferred to Co. E, 47th regiment as 1st sergeant. July 18, 1862 elected Jr. 2nd Lt Co. E, 47th regiment. December 1863 in General Hospital #2 at Savannah, Georgia. March 1865 appears on roster dated this date.

DUNN, LAWRENCE: Company A, 1st.lieutenant, February 27, 1862 elected 1st Lieutenant of Co. A, 11th Battalion.

EASTMEAD, HENRY R.: Company E, private, March 4, 1862 enlisted as a private in Co. E, 11th Battalion. May 12, 1862 transferred to Co. E, 47th Regiment. April 5, 1865 received by Provost Marshal General at Washington, D. C., a Confederate refugee. April 5, 1865 admitted to Douglas U. S. A. General Hospital at Washington, D. C. May 9, 1865 discharged from there and furnished transportation to Savannah, Georgia.

EDEN, JAMES S.: Company A, private, March 4, 1862 enlisted Co. A, 11th Battalion as a private. May 12, 1862 transferred to Company A, 47th Regiment as a private. February 28, 1863 roll (last on file) shows him present.

EDWARDS, A. C.: Field Staff, Colonel, March 4, 1862 Edwards elected Captain Co. I., 11th Battalion. March 22, 1862 elected Major 11th Battalion. May 12, 1862 elected Lieutenant Col 47th Regiment. August 30, 1863 elected Colonel 47th regiment. July 11, 1864 August 25, 1864 in hospital. September 12, 1864 application on this date from Guyton Hospital for 30 day's furlough, based on Surgeon's certificate of disability appears to have been approved.

EDWARDS, DANIEL W., SR.: Company I, private, May 16, 1862 enlisted as a private in Co. I, 47th Regiment, Georgia Infantry. May 15, 1864 wounded, right thigh and permanently disabled and captured at Resaca, Georgia. March 14, 1865 paroled at Camp Douglas, Illinois and transferred to City Point, Virginia for exchange. Pension records show he was at home on furlough at the close of the war. (born in Georgia in 1842)

EDWARDS, JAMES M.: Company I, private, September 18, 1862 enlisted as a private in Co. I, 47th Regiment, Georgia Infantry. February 28, 1863 roll, last on record, shows him present. April 26, 1865 pension records show he surrendered at Greensboro, North Carolina. Born in Effingham County, Georgia in 1836. Died in Johnson County, Georgia in 1903)

EDWARDS, J. P.: Company K, private, December 10, 1862 enlisted as a private in Co. K, 47th Regiment. October 5, 1863 died.

EDWARDS, OBEIDAH I.: Company I, private, 1863 enlisted as a private in Co. I, 47th Regiment, Georgia Infantry. April 26, 1865 pension records show he surrendered at Greensboro, North Carolina. (Born in Effingham County, Georgia in 1845)

EDWARDS, WILLIAM H.: Company I, private, May 16, 1862 enlisted as a private in Co. I, 47th Regiment. 1863 discharged at Savannah, Georgia.

ELKINS, CHARLES C.: Company I, private, June 17, 1862 enlisted as a private in Co. I, 47th Regiment November 25, 1863, killed at Missionary Ridge, Tennessee.

ELKINS, JOHN A.: Company I, private, May 13, 1862 enlisted as a private in Co. I, 47th Regiment. February 28, 1863 roll, last on record, shows him present. (Born in Effingham County, Georgia in 1833)

ELKINS, S. C.: Company I, private, March 4, 1862 enlisted as a private in Co. I, 11th Battalion. May 12, 1862 transferred to Co. I, 47th Regiment. November 24, 1863 captured at Lookout Mountain, Tennessee. December 2, 1863 admitted to General Field Hospital at Bridgeport, Alabama, with pneumonia. December 3, 1863 transferred to Nashville, Tennessee.

ELLENTON (ELLINGTON), STEPHEN: Company E, private, March 4, 1862 enlisted as a private in Co. E, 11th Battalion. May 12, 1862 transferred to Co. E, 47th Regiment. October 31, 1863 roll, last on record, shows him present.

ELLERBEE, HENRY G.: Company H, 4th corporal, March 4, 1862 elected 4th corporal Co. H, 11th Battalion. May 12, 1862 transferred to Co. H, 47th regiment as 4th corporal. August 1864 detached as laborer and boatman in Charleston, South Carolina. Pension records show he was on detached duty in torpedo department at close of the war.

ELLIS, CALVIN O.: Company F, private, April 26, 1862 enlisted as a private in Co. F, 11th Battalion. May 12, 1862 transferred to Co. F, 47th Regiment. November 29, 1863 admitted to Floyd House and Ocmulgee Hospitals at Macon, Georgia. may 2, 1864 admitted to Floyd House and Ocmulgee Hospitals at Macon, Georgia. Pension records show he was at home on wounded furlough at the close of the war. (Born in Georgia)

ELLIS, WOODSON: Company F, private, March 4, 1862 enlisted as a private in Co. F, 11th Battalion. May 12, 1862 transferred to Co. F, 47th Regiment. December 22, 1864 wounded in both legs and captured at Savannah, Georgia. January 9, 1865 died of wounds.

ENNIS, WILLIAM: Company E, private, March 4, 1862 enlisted as a private in Co. E, 11th Battalion. May 12, 1862 transferred to Co. E, 47th Regiment. October 31, 1863 roll, last on record, shows him present.

EVANS, JOHN R., JR.: Company D, private, March 4, 1862 enlisted as a private in Co. D, 11th Battalion. May 12, 1862 transferred to Co. D, 47th Regiment. August 30, 1862 discharged, under age.

EVERETT, T. J.: Company I, private, March 4, 1862 enlisted as a private in Co. I, 11th Battalion. May 12, 1862 transferred to Co. I, 47th Regiment. September 9, 1864 died in Gen. Hospital at Guyton, Georgia.

EXLEY, F. S.: Company I, sergeant, March 4, 1862 enlisted as a private in Co. I, 11th Battalion. May 12, 1862 transferred to Co. I, 47th Regiment. Appointed sergeant. June 17, 1864 admitted to Ocmulgee Hospital at Macon, Georgia. June 18, 1864 transferred. April 26, 1865 pension records show he surrendered at Greensboro, North Carolina.

EXLEY, HOWARD J.: Company I, private, August 24, 1862 enlisted as a private in Co. I, 47th Regiment. September 3, 1863 died in Walkers Division Hospital, Shubuta, Mississippi.

FAILS, C. C.: Company H, private, March 4, 1862 enlisted as a private in Co. H, 11th Battalion. May 12, 1862 transferred to Co. H, 47th Regiment. June 10, 1862 wounded at James Island, South Carolina. February 28, 1863 roll, last on record, shows him absent, sick. May 15, 1865 paroled at Tallahassee, Florida.

FAIRCLOUTH, MOSES: Company B, private, March 4, 1862 enlisted as a private in Co. B, 11th Battalion. May 12, 1862 transferred to Co. B, 47th Regiment. September 20, 1863 wounded, through thigh and hand, Chickamauga, Georgia. October 14, 1864 retired to Invalid corps P. A. C. S. November 17, 1864 "Sent to Post". February 14 1875 (1876) died from disease contracted in service.

FARMER, HOPE: Company I, private, August 17, 1862 enlisted as a private in Co. I, 11th Battalion. May 12, 1862 transferred to Co. I, 47th

Regiment. September 23, 1863 - August 1864 attached to Lee Hospital, Lauderdale Springs Mississippi, as nurse.

FARMER, WILLIAM: Company I, private, Company I, private, September 29, 1862 enlisted as a private in Co. I, 47th Regiment. January 11, 1864 died of Typhoid- pneumonia in Griffin, Georgia Hospital.

FARR, JOHN: Company C, private, March 4, 1862 enlisted as a private in Co. C, 11th Battalion. May 12, 1862 transferred to Co. C, 47th Regiment. February 28, 1863 roll, last on record, shows him present.

FARRELL, JOHN: Company B, private, February 19, 1863 enlisted as a private in Co. B, 47th Regiment, Georgia Infantry as a substitute for Robert J. Morris. February 20, 1863 deserted.

FERGUSON, ISAAC R.: Company B, private, April 25, 1862 enlisted as a private in Co. B, 11th Battalion. May 12, 1862 transferred to Co. B, 47th Regiment. February 28, 1863 roll, last on record, shows him present.

FERGUSON, JAMES G.: Company B, private, October 9, 1861 enlisted as a private in Co. F, 1st. Regiment, 1st Brigade, Georgia State Troops. April 9, 1862 roll, last on file, shows him present. April 1862 mustered out. May 12, 1862 transferred to Co. B, 47th Regiment. February 28, 1863 roll, last on record, shows him present.

FERGUSON, JAMES M.: Company B, private, April 25, 1862 enlisted as a private in Co. B, 11th Battalion. May 12, 1862 transferred to Co. B, 47th Regiment. February 28, 1863 roll, last on record, shows him present.

FERGUSON, PATRICK HENRY: Company B, private, April 25, 1862 enlisted as a private in Co. B, 11th Battalion. May 12, 1862 transferred to Co. B, 47th Regiment. June 1, 1862 discharged furnished Frank S. Sinquefield as substitute.

FERGUSON, THOMAS J.: Company B, private. October 9, 1861 enlisted as a private in Co. F, 1st. Regiment, 1st Brigade, Georgia State Troops. April 9, 1862 roll, last on file, shows him present. April 1862 mustered out. April 25, 1862 enlisted as a private in Co. B, 11th Battalion. May 12, 1862 transferred to Co. B, 47th Regiment. February 28, 1863 roll, last on record, shows him present. February 9, 1865 wounded at Salkehatchie, South Carolina. Was at home wounded at the close of the war. Died in Randolph County, Georgia November 1, 1896.

FERRY, DANIEL: Company G, private, January 9, 1863 enlisted as a private in Co. G, 47th Regiment, Georgia Infantry. February 28, 1863 absent without leave. April 5, 1865 received in Washington, D. C. took oath and furnished transportation to New York City, New York.

FLETCHER, C. E.: Company C, private, March 4, 1862 enlisted as a private in Co. C, 11th Battalion. May 12, 1862 transferred to Co. C, 47th Regiment. 1862 appointed commissary. November 13, 1863 discharged due to disability.

FLOOD, BENJAMIN: Company I, private. March 4, 1862 enlisted as a private in Co. I, 11th Battalion. May 12, 1862 transferred to Co. I, 47th Regiment. February 28, 1863 roll, last on record, shows him present.

FLOOD, JOHN H.: Company H, private. March 4, 1862 enlisted as a private in Co. H, 11th Battalion. May 12, 1862 transferred to Co. H, 47th Regiment. September 1862 appointed Company Commissary. April 26, 1865 surrendered at Greensboro, North Carolina.

FLOURNOY, CORNELIUS: Company A, private, March 21, 1861 enlisted as a private in Co. I, 1st Regiment, Georgia Regulars: Transferred to Co. D in 1861. October 1, 1862 transferred to Co. A, 47th Regiment. February 28, 1863 roll, last on file, shows him present.

FLOWERS, C. W.: Company H, private, March 4, 1862 enlisted as a private in Co. H, 11th Battalion. May 12, 1862 transferred to Co. H, 47th Regiment. June 19, 1862 died in Savannah, Georgia Hospital.

FLOYD, BENJAMIN: Company I, private, March 4, 1862 enlisted as a private in Co. I, 11th Battalion. May 12, 1862 transferred to Co. I, 47th Regiment. February 28, 1863 roll, last on record, shows him present.

FLOYD, G. C.: Company I, private, April 10, 1862 enlisted as a private in Co. I, 11th Battalion. May 12, 1862 transferred to Co. I, 47th Regiment. March 2, 1863 died of disease in Gen. Hospital #1, Savannah, Georgia.

FLOYD, JESSE: Company I, private, March 4, 1862 enlisted as a private in Co. I, 11th Battalion. May 12, 1862 transferred to Co. I, 47th Regiment. August, 1863 discharged due to disability.

FOLLARD, A. ROGERS: Company A, private, September 6, 1862 enlisted in Co. A, 47th Regiment as a private. October 7, 1863 died.

FOLLARD, JOHN: Company A, private, February 28, 1862 enlisted Co. A, 11th Battalion as a private. May 12, 1862 transferred to Company A, 47th Regiment as a private. February 28, 1863 roll, last on record, shows him present.

FRAIN (FAIN), JOHN: Company A, 3rd. corporal, July 25, 1861 enlisted as a private in Captain J. B. Read's Independent Company Georgia Infantry. January 25, 1862 mustered out. February 28, 1862 enlisted in Co. A, 11th Battalion as a private. May 12, 1862 transferred to Co. A, 47th Regiment. February 1863 appointed. 3rd corporal Co. A, 47th Georgia Regiment. February 28, 1863 roll, last on record, shows him present.

FRANKLIN, H. B.: Company C, private, March 4, 1862 enlisted as a private in Co. C, 11th Battalion. May 12, 1862 transferred to Co. C, 47th Regiment. July 10, 1862 died of disease in Savannah, Georgia.

FRAWLEY, CORNELIUS: Company D, private, July 22, 1862 died of Typhoid Fever, Oglethorpe Hospital Savannah, Georgia.

FRAZIER, JAMES R.: Field Staff, sergeant, June 1, 1862, appointed assistant commissary sergeant. August 1, 1863 office was abolished.

FREEMAN, JACOB L.: (JACOB S.): Company D, private, March 4, 1862 enlisted as a private in Co. D, 11th Battalion. May 12, 1862 transferred to Co. D, 47th Regiment. February 28, 1863 died subsequent to this date.

FREEMEN, JOHN: Company B, private, March 4, 1862 enlisted as a private in Co. B, 11th Battalion. Absent without leave.

FREEMAN, THOMAS C. B.: Company D, private, March 4, 1862 enlisted as a private in Co. D, 11th Battalion. May 12, 1862 transferred to Co. D, 47th Regiment. February 28, 1863 roll, last on record, shows him home sick.

FUDGE, WILLIAM M.: Company B, private, March 4, 1862 enlisted as a private in Co. B, 11th Battalion. May 12, 1862 transferred to Co. B, 47th Regiment. March 20, 1865 captured at Bentonville, North Carolina. June 15, 1865 released at Hart's Island, New York Harbor, New York.

FUTCH, CARTER W.: Company E, 4th sergeant, March 4, 1862 appointed 4th sergeant Co. E, 11th Battalion. May 12, 1862 transferred to Co. E, 47th regiment as 4th sergeant. October 31, 1862 roll shows him present.

FUTCH, FREDERICK H.: Company K, private, October 15, 1861 appointed 2nd corporal of Co. G, 5th Regiment, Georgia State Troops. April 1862 mustered out. May 6, 1862 enlisted as a private in Co. K, 47th Regiment. September - October 1863 in Jackson's Cavalry Division Hospital at Old Marion, Mississippi.

FUTCH, HAMPTON J.: Company E, private, March 4, 1862 enlisted as a private in Co. E, 11th Battalion. May 12, 1862 transferred to Co. E, 47th Regiment. October 31, 1863 roll, last on record, shows him present.

FUTCH, ISAAC: Company K, private, October 15, 1861 enlisted and appointed 3rd corporal of Co. G, 5th Regiment, Georgia State Troops. April 1862 mustered out. May 15, 1862 enlisted as a private in Co. K, 47th Regiment. September - October 1863 in Jackson's Cavalry Division Hospital at Old Marion, Mississippi.

FUTCJ, J. O.: Company K, private, May 6, 1862 enlisted as a private in Co. K, 47th Regiment. February 8, 1864 furloughed from Floyd House and Ocmulgee Hospitals at Macon, Georgia.

FUTCH, JAMES H., JR.: Company E, private, March 4, 1862 enlisted as a private in Co. E, 11th Battalion. May 12, 1862 transferred to Co. E, 47th Regiment. October 31, 1863 roll, last on record, shows him present.

FUTCH, JAMES H., SR.: Company E, private, March 4, 1862 enlisted as a private in Co. E, 11th Battalion. May 12, 1862 transferred to Co. E, 47th Regiment. October 31, 1863 roll, last on record, shows him present.

FUTCH, JESSE: Company E, private, March 4, 1862 enlisted as a private in Co. E, 11th Battalion. May 12, 1862 transferred to Co. E, 47th Regiment. October 31, 1863 roll, last on record, shows him present.

FUTCH, SOLOMON F.: Company K, private, October 15, 1861 enlisted as a private of Co. G, 5th Regiment, Georgia State Troops. March 22, 1862 discharged. July 10, 1862 enlisted as a private in Co. K, 47th Regiment. October 12, 1863 appears on a voucher for pay. November 25, 1863 killed at Missionary Ridge, Tennessee.

FUTCH, WINFIELD W.: Company G, private, March 4, 1862 enlisted as a private in Co. G, 11th Battalion. May 12, 1862 transferred to Co. G, 47th Regiment as corporal. Appointed sergeant. July 20, 1863 died of disease in Mississippi Hospital.

FUTCH, WILLIAM M.: Company E, private, March 4, 1862 enlisted as a private in Co. E, 11th Battalion. May 12, 1862 transferred to Co. E, 47th Regiment. December 18, 1863 died in Fair Grounds Hospital in Atlanta, Georgia. Buried there in Oakland Cemetery.

FUTRELL, JOHN: Company I, private, March 4, 1862 enlisted as a private in Co. I, 11th Battalion. May 12, 1862 transferred to Co. I, 47th Regiment. September 26, 1862 died of disease.

GALLAGHER, JOHN J.: Company A, private, April 15, 1862 enlisted in Co. A, 11th Battalion as a private. May 12, 1862 transferred to Co. A, 47th Regiment. February 28, 1863 roll shows him present.

GANEY, RYAN T.: Company H, private, March 4, 1862 enlisted as a private in Co. H, 11th Battalion. May 12, 1862 transferred to Co. H, 47th Regiment. February 28, 1863 roll, last on record, shows him absent, sick. March 3, 1863 transferred to General Hospital at Macon, Georgia. September 19, 1863 pension records show he was wounded in the right arm which was permanently disabled at Chickamauga, Georgia. At home wounded at the close of the war. (Born in Georgia October 27, 1838)

GANEY, RANSON C.: Company H, private. January 16, 1863 enlisted as a private in Co. H, 47th Regiment. November 25, 1863 captured at Missionary Ridge, Tennessee. February 15, 1865 transferred for exchange. February 26, 1865 admitted to General Hospital at Howard's Grove Farm, Richmond, Virginia. March 29, 1865 furloughed for 30 days.

GARDNER, WILLIAM J. M.: Company B, private, March 4, 1862 enlisted in Co. B, 11th Battalion as a private. May 12, 1862 transferred to Co. B, 47th Regiment. February 28, 1863 roll ,last on record, shows him present. April 26, 1865 pension records show he surrendered at Greensboro, North Carolina. (Born in Decatur County, Georgia July 1843)

GARRAGHY, FRANCIS: Company A, private, April 15, 1862 enlisted in Co. A, 11th Battalion as a private. May 12, 1862 transferred to Co. A, 47th Regiment. June 23, 1862 Deserted from James Island, South Carolina.

GARRITY, JAMES: Company A, private, March 4, 1862 enlisted in Co. A, 11th Battalion as a private. May 12, 1862 transferred to Co. A, 47th Regiment. November 1862 discharged by Judge Harden C. C.

GARRITY, MICHAEL: Company A, private, March 4, 1862 enlisted in Co. A, 11th Battalion as a private. May 12, 1862 transferred to Co. A, 47th Regiment. December 26, 1864 deserted.

GEIGER, CORNELIUS: Company K, private, October 29, 1862 enlisted (substitute for Hampton Lee) as a private in Co. K, 47th Regiment. August 20, 1863 died in Lauderdale Springs, Mississippi hospital with diarrhea.

GEORGE, JOHN H.: Company B, private, March 1, 1862 enlisted in Co. B, 11th Battalion as a private. May 12, 1862 transferred to Co. B, 47th Regiment. November 25, 1863 killed at Missionary Ridge, Tennessee.

GEORGE, JOHN T.: Company B, private, March 1, 1862 enlisted in Co. B, 11th Battalion as a private. May 12, 1862 transferred to Co. B, 47th Regiment. November 27, 1862 discharged furnished Noah Zane as a substitute. June 1864 Pension records show he enlisted as a private in

Company K, 10th Regiment, Georgia Militia. March 1865 at home with typhoid fever to close of war. (Born in Georgia)

GERBER, AUGUST: Company A, private, March 4, 1862 enlisted in Co. A, 11th Battalion as a private. May 12, 1862 transferred to Co. A, 47th Regiment. November 6, 1863 in General Hospital, Savannah, Georgia.

GIBSON, J. E.: Company K, 3rd sergeant, June 10, 1862 killed at James Island, South Carolina

GIBSON, WILLIAM T.: Company H, private, March 4, 1862 enlisted as a private in Co. H, 11th Battalion. May 12, 1862 transferred to Co. H, 47th Regiment. November 25, 1863 captured at Missionary Ridge, Tennessee. February 25, 1865 transferred for exchange. March 5, 1865 received at Boulware & Cox's Wharves, James River, Virginia.

GILDER, J.: Company I, private, March 4, 1862 enlisted as a private in Co. I, 11th Battalion. May 12, 1862 transferred to Co. I, 47th Regiment. May 12, 1863 died in Richmond, Virginia and is buried in Hollywood Cemetery.

GILL, JACKSON: Company E, March 4, 1862 enlisted as a private in Co. E, 11th Battalion. May 12, 1862 transferred to Co. E, 47th Regiment. July 3, 1863 captured at Gettysburg, Pennsylvania. November 4, 1863 died of small pox at Fort Delaware, Delaware as a POW.

GILL, JAMES: Company E, private, March 4, 1862 enlisted as a private in Co. E, 11th Battalion. May 12, 1862 transferred to Co. E, 47th Regiment. October 31, 1863 roll, last on record, shows him present.

GILLIS, NEIL: Company H, private, March 4, 1862 enlisted as a private in Co. H, 11th Battalion. May 12, 1862 transferred to Co. H, 47th Regiment. September 20, 1863, wounded in the thigh at Chickamauga, Georgia. October 1, 1863 admitted to Floyd House and Ocmulgee Hospitals at Macon, Georgia. Pension records show he was at home on furlough at the close of the war. (Born in Georgia February 15, 1840)

GILLIS, WILLIAM: Company H, private, March 4, 1862 enlisted as a private in Co. H, 11th Battalion. May 12, 1862 transferred to Co. H, 47th Regiment. July 27, 1862 died of disease in hospital.

GILMORE, HUGH A.: Company B, private, March 1, 1862 enlisted in Co. B, 11th Battalion as a private. Absent without leave.

GNANN, BENJAMIN ROBERT: Company I, private, March 1862 enlisted as a private in Co. I, 47th Regiment. August 18, 1864 - August 31, 1864 on extra duty at Charleston, South Carolina. September 12, 1864 and September 27, 1864 clothing was issued to him. Pension records show he was at Fayetteville, North Carolina at the close of the war. (Died in Savannah, Georgia May 10, 1907)

GNANN, DAVID E.: Company I, private, March 4, 1862 enlisted as a private in Co. I, 11th Battalion. May 12, 1862 transferred to Co. I, 47th Regiment. November 1863 - December 1863 in Breckinridge's Division Hospital at Lauderdale Springs, Mississippi.

GNANN, W. W.: Company I, private, March 4, 1862 enlisted as a private in Co. I, 11th Battalion. May 12, 1862 transferred to Co. I, 47th Regiment. February 28, 1863 roll, last on record, shows him present. September 19, 1863 wounded at Chickamauga, Georgia.

GOLPHIN, BRAVE: Field Staff, Musician, May 31, 1862 appointed Musician. December 1872 shows him present.

GOODIN, FRANCIS M.: Company F, private, March 4, 1862 enlisted as a private in Co. F, 11th Battalion. May 12, 1862 transferred to Co. F, 47th Regiment. November 25, 1863 captured at Missionary Ridge, Tennessee. January 25, 1864 enlisted in the United States Navy at Rock Island, Illinois and transferred to Naval Rendezvous at Camp Douglas, Illinois.

GOOGE, JAMES W.: Company F, private, April 26, 1862 enlisted as a private in Co. F, 11th Battalion. May 12, 1862 transferred to Co. F, 47th Regiment. October 1, 1862 returned to company from hospital. Pension records show he was at home on furlough at the close of the war.

GOOGE, JOHN E.: Company F, private, November 27, 1862 enlisted as a private in Co. F, 47th Regiment, Georgia Infantry. July 10, 1864 killed at John's Island, South Carolina.

GOOGE, WILLIAM: Company F, private, March 4, 1862 enlisted as a private in Co. F, 11th Battalion. May 12, 1862 transferred to Co. F, 47th Regiment. October 31, 1863 roll, last on record, shows him present. April 10, 1865 pension records show that he was cut off from his command.

GORDON (JORDAN), HENRY W.: Company F, private, April 29, 1862 enlisted as a private in Co. F, 11th Battalion. May 12, 1862 transferred to Co. F, 47th Regiment. August 1, 1862 transferred to Co. A. 1st Battalion, Georgia Sharpshooters. June 14, 1864 deserted.

GORMLEY, PATRICK: Company B, Captain, March 4, 1862 elected Captain Co. B. 11th Battalion. December 1862, transferred to Co. B, 47th Regiment as Captain. April 15, 1863 cashiered.

GORMLEY, WILLIAM P.: Company B, private, March 4, 1862 enlisted in Co. B, 11th Battalion as a private. May 12, 1862 transferred to Co. B, 47th Regiment. June 1, 1862 transferred to Co. B, 13th Regiment (but name does not appear on rolls of that company)

GOULD, JAMES: Company C, private, March 4, 1862 enlisted as a private in Co. C, 11th Battalion. May 12, 1862 transferred to Co. C, 47th Regiment. September 30, 1862 discharged, under age.

GRACE, GEORGE: Company E, private, March 4, 1862 enlisted as a private in Co. E, 11th Battalion. May 12, 1862 transferred to Co. E, 47th Regiment. July 2 - August 1, 1863 on sick furlough.

GRAHAM, AQUILLA: Company F, private, 1863 enlisted as a private in Co. F, 47th Regiment, Georgia Infantry. He was sent home due to extreme youth. Re-enlisted in 1864. April 1865 at home on furlough die to being wounded. He was serving in Captain Silas Crosby's Militia Company chasing deserters in Appling County, Georgia at the close of the war.

GRAHAM, ALEXANDER: Company H, private, June 1, 1862 enlisted as a private in Co. H, 47th Regiment. July 26, 1864 appears on a register dated 1864, of St. Mary's Hospital, LaGrange, Georgia with remark: "returned to duty July 26, 1864".

GRAHAM, BENJAMIN A.: Company B, Jr. 2nd Lieutenant, March 4, 1862 appointed Jr. 2nd Lieutenant Co. B, 11th Battalion. May 12, 1862 transferred to Co. B, 47th Regt. as Jr. 2nd Lieutenant. June 16, 1862 killed at Secessionville, South Carolina.

GRAHAM, JAMES: Company F, private, June 2, 1862 enlisted as a private in Co. F, 47th Regiment, Georgia Infantry. October 31, 1863 roll, last on record, shows him present. Pension records show that he was at home on sick furlough at the close of the war.

GRAHAM, WILLIAM: Company B, private, 1862 enlisted as a private in Co. B, 47th Regiment, Georgia Infantry. 1862 died in Cuthbert, Georgia in 1862 and buried there.

GRANT, RICHARD: Company E, private, March 4, 1862 enlisted as a private in Co. E, 11th Battalion. Never reported.

GREEN, JAMES W.: Company C, private, July 22, 1862 enlisted as a private in Co. C, 47th Regiment, Georgia Infantry. September 20, 1863 killed at Chickamauga, Georgia.

GREEN, JOHN: Company G, private, September 1, 1862 enlisted as a private in Co. G, 47th Regiment, Georgia Infantry. March 10, 1864 died of pneumonia in Newsome Hospital, Cassville, Georgia.

GREEN, JOHN: Company F, private, March 4, 1862 enlisted as a private in Co. F, 11th Battalion. May 12, 1862 transferred to Co. F, 47th Regiment. July 10, 1864 killed at John's Island, South Carolina.

GREEN, JOHN A.: Company B, private, May 10, 1861 enlisted in Co. F, 5th Regiment, Georgia Infantry as a private. September 11, 1861 discharged. March 4, 1862 enlisted in Co. B, 11th Battalion as a private. May 12, 1862 transferred to Co. B, 47th Regiment.

GRIFFIN, FRANCIS DEMPSEY: Company G, 2nd. Lieutenant, March 4, 1862 enlisted as a private Co G, 11th Battalion. May 12, 1862 transferred to Co. G, 47th Regiment. December 1862 appointed 2nd sergeant Co. G, 47th Regiment. June 25, 1863 elected 2nd lieutenant in Co. G, 47th regiment. March 1865 appears on roster.

GRIFFIN, SAMSON: Company D, private, April 25, 1862 enlisted as a private in Co. D, 25th Regiment, Georgia Infantry. 1862 discharged disability. December 1, 1862 enlisted (substitute for T. J. Moore) as a private in Co. D, 47th Regiment, Georgia Infantry. November 30, 1863 discharged disability at Marion Station, Mississippi. (Born in Burke County, Georgia in 1827)

GRIFFIN, WILLIAM JACKSON: Company G, private, March 4, 1862 enlisted as a private in Co. G, 11th Battalion. May 12, 1862 transferred to Co. G, 47th Regiment. February 28, 1863 roll, last on record, shows him present. April 26, 1865 pension records show he surrendered Greensboro, North Carolina. (Born in Georgia). Died June 3, 1835. Buried in Ebenezer Cemetery at Glennville, Georgia)

GRIMES, JACKSON W.: Company H, private, May 12, 1862 enlisted as a private in Co. H, 47th Regiment. February 1864 in Blackie Hospital at Madison, Georgia. (Born in Montgomery County, Georgia May 14, 1834)

GROOVER, CHARLES A.: Company K, private, May 6, 1862 enlisted as a private in Co. K, 47th Regiment. December 1862 discharged due to disability.

GROOVER, DAVID: Company K, private, May 6, 1862 enlisted as a private in Co. K, 47th Regiment. January 25, 1863 died at Top Sail Sound, North Carolina.

GROOVER, R. J.: Company I, 3rd corporal, March 4, 1862 elected 3rd corporal Co. I, 11th Battalion. 1862 died at the Savannah River Bridge.

GROSS, DANIEL D.: Company D, private. March 4, 1862 enlisted as a private in Co. D, 11th Battalion. May 12, 1862 transferred to Co. D, 47th Regiment. June 27, 1862 discharged, disability.

GROUSE, WILLIAM: Company H, private, March 4, 1862 enlisted as a private in Co. H, 11th Battalion. Never reported for duty.

GUEST, C. C.: Company H, private, March 4, 1862 enlisted as a private in Co. H, 11th Battalion. May 12, 1862 transferred to Co. H, 47th Regiment. September 19, 1863 killed at Chickamauga, Georgia.

HAGIN, ALLEN: Company K, 4th corporal. October 15, 1861 enlisted as a private of Co. G, 5th Regiment, Georgia State Troops. April 1862 mustered out. May 6, 1862 appointed 4th corporal Co. K, 47th Regiment. February 28, 1863 roll, last on record, shows him present.

HAGIN, JAMES S.: Company K, 2nd Lieutenant, October 15, 1861 enlisted and appointed 2nd sergeant of Co. G, 5th Regiment, Georgia State Troops. April 1862 mustered out. May 6, 1862 enlisted as a private in Co. K, 47th Regiment December 12 1862 appointed 3rd sergeant Co. K, 47th Regiment. May 29, 1863 elected Jr. 2nd lieutenant, Co. K, 47th Regiment. June 22, 1863 elected 2nd Lieutenant Co. K, 47th Regiment. April 26, 1865 surrendered at Greensboro, North Carolina. (Born in Georgia)

HAGIN, JAMES M.: Company F, private, March 4, 1862 enlisted as a private in Co. F, 11th Battalion. May 12, 1862 transferred to Co. F, 47th Regiment. November 1862 appointed assistant Enrolling Officer.

HAGIN, SOLOMON: Company I, 3rd corporal, May 6, 1862 appointed 3rd Corporal Co. K, 47th Regimen. June 10, 1862 wounded at James Island, South Carolina.

HAGIN, SOLOMON: Company K, 3rd. corporal, October 15, 1861 enlisted as a private of Co. G, 5th Regiment, Georgia State Troops. April 1862 mustered out. May 6, 1862 enlisted as a 3rd corporal in Co. K, 47th Regiment. June 10, 1862 wounded at James Island, South Carolina. April 6, 1865 pension records show that he was sent to Camden, South Carolina Hospital and remained there until after the close of the war. (Born in Bulloch County, Georgia in 1840 or 1842. Died in Bulloch County, Georgia about 1905)

HALL, JAMES M.: Company F, private, June 1863 enlisted as a private in Co. F, 47th Regiment, Georgia Infantry. April 4, 1865 wounded at Coleman's Creek, Appling County, Georgia chasing deserters. at home, wounded, at the close of the war.

HALL, SEABORN: Company F, Senior Enlisting Officer, March 4, 1862 enlisted as a private in Co. F, 11th Battalion. May 12, 1862 transferred to Co. F, 47th Regiment. June 10, 1862 captured at James Island, South Carolina. December 15, 1862 paroled at Fort Delaware, Delaware and sent to Fortress Monroe, Virginia for exchange. December 18, 1862 received at City point, Virginia. March 18, 1863 appointed Sub-Enrolling Officer-Appling County, Georgia. March 3, 1864 received pay at Savannah, Georgia.

HALL, THOMAS J,: Company F, private, March 4, 1862 enlisted as a private in Co. F, 11th Battalion. May 12, 1862 transferred to Co. F, 47th Regiment. November 1862 Assistant Enrolling Officer. November 30, 1864 killed at Honey Hill, South Carolina.

HAMANS, HOMER: Company H, private, April 25, 1862 enlisted as a private in Co. H, 47th Regiment, Georgia Infantry. June 2, 1862 died in Savannah, Georgia Hospital.

HAMANS, JAMES: Company H, private, March 4, 1862 enlisted as a private in Co. H, 11th Battalion. May 12, 1862 transferred to Co. H, 47th Regiment. September 16, 1862 accidentally killed at Camp Williams, Georgia.

HAMILTON, WILLIAM W.: Company H, 4th sergeant, March 4, 1862 enlisted as a private in Co. H, 11th Battalion. May 12, 1862 transferred to Co. H, 47th Regiment. February 1863 appointed 4th sergeant Co. H, 47th regiment and detailed Enrolling Officer. Died in service.

HAMM, JOSEPH: Company C, private, March 4, 1862 enlisted as a private in Co. C, 11th Battalion. April 23, 1862 died at Whitesville, Georgia.

HAMPTON, JOHN A.: Company H, private. March 4, 1862 enlisted as a private in Co. H, 11th Battalion. May 12, 1862 transferred to Co. H, 47th Regiment. October 21, 1863 Admitted to Floyd House and Ocmulgee Hospitals at Macon, Georgia.

HAND, ELBERT: Company F, private, March 4, 1862 enlisted as a private in Co. F, 11th Battalion. May 12, 1862 transferred to Co. F, 47th Regiment. December 11, 1863 received pay.

HARALSON, R. C.: Company I, private, March 4, 1862 enlisted as a private in Co. I, 11th Battalion. May 12, 1862 transferred to Co. I, 47th Regiment. September 20, 1863 wounded at Chickamauga, Georgia.

HARDIN, JAMES: Company F, private, April 29, 1862 enlisted as a private in Co. F, 11th Battalion. May 12, 1862 transferred to Co. F, 47th Regiment. November 29, 1863 admitted to Floyd House and Ocmulgee Hospitals at Macon, Georgia.

HARDIN (HARDEN), HENRY: Company B, private, April 25, 1862 enlisted in Co. B, 11th Battalion as a private. May 12, 1862 transferred to Co. B, 47th Regiment. July 3, 1862 died in Randolph County, Georgia.

HARNAGE, WILEY M.: Company H, private, March 4, 1862 enlisted as a private in Co. H, 11th Battalion. May 12, 1862 transferred to Co. H, 47th Regiment. Died in 1864.

HARPER, JOHN J.: Company B, Captain, March 4, 1862 appointed 1st Lieutenant Co. B, 11th Battalion. May 12, 1862 transferred to Co. B, 47th Regiment as 1st Lieutenant. April 15, 1863 elected Captain Co. B, 47th Regiment. April 6, 1864 resigned due to disability.

HARPER, THOMAS F.: Company B, 3rd. corporal, March 4, 1862 appointed 4th corporal Co. B, 11th Battalion. May 12, 1862 transferred to Co. B, 47th Regiment as 3rd corporal. January 11, 1864 died.

HARPER, WILLIAM O.: Company B, private, April 25, 1862 enlisted as a private in Co. B, 11th Battalion. May 12, 1862 transferred to Co. B, 47th Regiment. February 28, 1863 roll, last on record, shows him present.

HARRALSON (HARRELSON), B.: Company H, private, March 4, 1862 enlisted as a private in Co. H, 11th Battalion. May 12, 1862 transferred to Co. H, 47th Regiment. February 28, 1863 roll, last on record, shows him present.

HARRISON, THOMAS: Company F, private, November 16, 1862 enlisted as a private in Co. F, 47th Regiment, Georgia Infantry. November 23, 1862 received pay. Pension records show he was at home, on furlough, at the close of the war.

HART, AMOS J.: Company B, private, March 4, 1862 enlisted as a private in Co. B, 11th Battalion. May 12, 1862 transferred to Co. B, 47th Regiment. June 6, 1862 died.

HART, GEORGE P.: Company B, private, October 9, 1861 enlisted as a private in Co. F, 1st. Regiment, 1st Brigade, Georgia State Troops. April 9, 1862 roll, last on file, shows him present. April 1862 mustered out. April 25, 1862 enlisted as a private in Co. B, 11th Battalion. May 12, 1862 transferred to Co. B, 47th Regiment. April 26, 1869 surrendered, Greensboro, North Carolina. 1825 (Died in Randolph County, Georgia)

HART, HENRY L.: Company B, private, March 4, 1862 enlisted as a private in Co. B, 11th Battalion. May 12, 1862 transferred to Co. B, 47th Regiment. February 28, 1863 roll, last on record, shows him present.

HART, WILLIAM: Company C, private, August 25, 1862 enlisted as a private in Co. C, 47th Regiment, Georgia infantry. February 28, 1863 roll, last on file, shows him present. March 1865 pension records show that he was at home on sick furlough at the close of the war. (Born in Georgia)

HARVEY, JESSE R.: Company B, private, March 4, 1862 enlisted as a private in Co. B, 11th Battalion. May 12, 1862 transferred to Co. B, 47th Regiment. October 1862 Transferred to company I, 56th Regiment Virginia infantry. November 5, 1863 died.

HARVEY, OLIVER JAMES: Company E, private, September 7, 1862 enlisted as a private in Co. E, 47th Regiment, Georgia Infantry. October

31, 1863 roll, last on record, shows him present.

HAY, ISAAC P.: Company B, private, April 25, 1862 enlisted as a private in Co. B, 11th Battalion. May 12, 1862 transferred to Co. B, 47th Regiment. October 6, 1862 discharged, furnished Elijah C. Belcher as substitute.

HAY, JAMES P.: Company B, private, October 21, 1861 enlisted as a private in Co. K, 7th. Regiment, Georgia State Troops. April 9, 1862 roll, last on file, shows him present. April 1862 mustered out. April 25, 1862 enlisted as a private in Co. B, 11th Battalion. May 12, 1862 transferred to Co. B, 47th Regiment. April 26, 1869 Pension records show that he surrendered, Greensboro, North Carolina. (Born in Sumter County, Georgia, May 9, 1842)

HAY, JAMES P.: Company E, private, enlisted as a private in Co. E, 47th Regiment, Georgia Infantry. April 26, 1865 surrendered at Greensboro, North Carolina.

HAYS, PATRICK P.: Company A, private, March 4, 1862 enlisted in Co. A, 11th Battalion as a private. May 12, 1862 transferred to Co. A, 47th Regiment. 1864 captured in Marietta, Georgia. June 19, 1864 took oath of allegiance to United States Government at Camp Morton, Indiana and was released.

HAZZARD, ELLIOTT H.: Company H, Captain, March 4, 1862 elected Jr. 2nd Lt Co. H, 11th Battalion. May 12, 1862 transferred to Co. H, 47th Regiment as Jr. 2nd Lieutenant. November 6, 1862 elected 2nd Lt Co. H, 47th Regiment. December 22, 1862 elected 1st Lt Co. H, 47th regiment. June 11, 1863 elected Captain Co. H, 47th Regiment.

HEARN (HARN), JAMES: Company E, private, May 15, 1862 enlisted as a private in Co. E, 47th Regiment, Georgia Infantry. June or July 10, 1862 died of disease.

HEARN (HARN), THOMAS: Company E, private, March 4, 1862 enlisted as a private in Co. E, 11th Battalion. May 12, 1862 transferred to Co. E, 47th Regiment. October 31, 1863 roll, last on record, shows him present. (Died at LaGrange, Georgia. Buried there at Stonewall Cemetery)

HEIDT, ALLEN P.: Company I, private, March 4, 1862 enlisted as a private in Co. I, 11th Battalion. May 12, 1862 transferred to Co. I, 47th Regiment. September - October 1862 appears on roll.

HELMSLEY, JOSHUA: Company E, private, September 12, 1862 enlisted as a private in Co. E, 47th Regiment, Georgia Infantry. October 31, 1863 roll, last on record, shows him absent without leave.

HELMOUTH, E.: Company C, private, March 4, 1862 enlisted as a private in Co. C, 11th Battalion. May 12, 1862 transferred to Co. C, 47th Regiment. June 10, 1862 killed James Island, South Carolina.

HENRY, JOHN: Company A, 4th sergeant, July 25, 1861 Appointed 1st. Corporal of Captain J. B. Read's Independent Company Georgia Infantry. January 25, 1862 mustered out. February 27, 1862 appointed 2nd corporal Co. A, 11th Battalion. May 12, 1862 transferred To, Co. A, 47th Regiment as 4th sergeant. June 10, 1862 killed at James Island, South Carolina.

HERNDON, PHILLIP: Company F, private, March 4, 1862 enlisted as a private in Co. F, 11th Battalion. May 12, 1862 transferred to Co. F, 47th Regiment. August 16, 1862 died of disease at Camp Williams, Georgia.

HESTER, DAVID: Company F, private, September 10, 1861 enlisted as a private in Co. I, 27th Regiment, Georgia Infantry. December 10, 1861 discharged on account of hernia at Camp Pickens, Virginia. May 10, 1862 enlisted as a private in Co. F, 47th Regiment, Georgia Infantry. November 25, 1863 captured at Missionary Ridge, Tennessee. December 20, 1863 died of diarrhea and pneumonia at Rock Island, Illinois in prison as POW.

HICKS, GEORGE W.: Company B, private, April 25, 1862 enlisted as a private in Co. B, 11th Battalion. May 12, 1862 transferred to Co. B, 47th Regiment. December 10, 1863 died in Randolph County, Georgia.

HICKS, HORACE: Company B, 2nd Lieutenant, March 4, 1862 enlisted as a private in Co. B, 11th Battalion. May 12, 1862 transferred to Co. B, 47th Regiment, appointed sergeant. November 17, 1864 elected 2nd Lieutenant Co. B, 47th Regiment. January 2, 1865 election approved.

HILDEBRAND, DEDRICK: Company E, private, March 4, 1862 enlisted as a private in Co. E, 11th Battalion. May 12, 1862 transferred to Co. E, 47th Regiment. November 27, 1863 captured at Ringgold, Georgia. December 11, 1863 forwarded to Louisville, Kentucky for exchange. January 25, 1864 enlisted in the United States Navy at Rock Island, Illinois and transferred to Naval Rendezvous at Camp Douglas, Illinois.

HILLIER, T. A.: Company H, private, March 4, 1862 enlisted as a private in Co. H, 11th Battalion. never reported to camp.

HILTON, JOHN: Company C, private, March 4, 1862 enlisted as a private in Co. C, 11th Battalion. May 12, 1862 transferred to Co. C, 47th Regiment. December 5, 1863 died in Empire Hospital, Atlanta, Georgia. Buried there at Oakland Cemetery.

HILTON, T. L.: Company C, private, March 4, 1862 enlisted as a private in Co. C, 11th Battalion. April, 20, 1862 died at Whitesville, Georgia.

HINES, HENRY H.: Company D, private, March 4, 1862 enlisted as a private in Co. D, 11th Battalion. May 12, 1862 transferred to Co. D, 47th Regiment. February 28, 1863 roll, last on record, shows him present. May 20, 1865 paroled in Augusta, Georgia.

HINES T. P.: Company I, Captain, March 4, 1862 elected 1st Lieutenant Co. I, 11th Battalion. May 2, 1862 appointed Captain and Assistant Quartermaster 47th Regiment. May 12, 1862 transferred to Co. I, 47th Regiment as Captain. May 2, 1863 resigned his commission.

HINES, THOMAS R.: Field Staff, Captain, May 12, 1862 Appointed Quartermaster 47th Regiment. May 12, 1863 resigned his commission.

HISELY, ISHAM: Company D, private, enlisted as a private in Co. D, 47th Regiment, Georgia Infantry. February 28, 1863 roll, last on record, shows him present.

HOBBS, GEORGE W.: Company B, private, March 4, 1862 enlisted as a private in Co. B, 11th Battalion. May 12, 1862 transferred to Co. B, 47th

Regiment. February 28, 1863 roll, last on record, shows him present.

HODGES, A. E.: Company D, private, March 4, 1862 enlisted as a private in Co. D, 11th Battalion. May 12, 1862 transferred to Co. D, 47th Regiment. March 5, 1864 clothing was issued to him. April 26, 1865 according to pension records he surrendered Greensboro, North Carolina. (Born in Effingham County, Georgia December 20, 1833)

HODGES, T. M.: Company C, private, March 4, 1862 enlisted as a private in Co. C, 11th Battalion. May 12, 1862 transferred to Co. C, 47th Regiment. December 12, 1863 died in Institute Hospital, Atlanta, Georgia. Buried there at Oakland Cemetery.

HODGES, WILLIAM H.: Company I, private, July 20, 1862 enlisted as a private in Co. I, 47th Regiment. February 28, 1863 roll, last on record, shows him present. April 26, 1865 pension records show he surrendered Greensboro, North Carolina.

HODGES, WILLIAM J. G.: Company E, private, September 9, 1862 enlisted as a private in Co. E, 47th Regiment, Georgia Infantry at Camp Berrien. October 31, 1862 roll, last on record, shows him "absent under orders". September 19, 1863 according to pension records he was wounded at Chickamauga, Georgia. He was in Augusta, Georgia Hospital at close of the war.

HODGES, S. A.: Company I, private, March 4, 1862 Enlisted. May 12, 1862 transferred to Company I, 47th Regiment, Georgia Infantry. October 7, 1862 discharged by civil authority Camp Williams, Georgia.

HODGES, T. M.: Company C, private, March 4, 1862 enlisted as a private in Co. C, 11th Battalion. May 12, 1862 transferred to Co. C, 47th Regiment. December 12, 1863 died in Institute Hospital at Atlanta, Georgia and is buried in Oakland Cemetery.

HOGAN, JOHN: Company E, private, March 4, 1862 enlisted as a private in Co. E, 11th Battalion. May 12, 1862 transferred to Co. E, 47th Regiment. September 24, 1863 admitted to Floyd House and Ocmulgee Hospitals at Macon, Georgia with chronic diarrhea. October 14, 1863 returned to duty.

HOLLAND, DAVID H.: Company G, 2nd corporal. March 4, 1862 Enlisted in Reidsville, Georgia and elected. 2nd corporal Co. G, 11th Battalion. May 12, 1862 transferred to Co. G, 47th Regiment as a private. February 28, 1863 roll, last on record, shows him absent sick. January 1865 pension records show he was at home on account of spinal infection to the close of the war. (Born in Tattnall County, Georgia March 3, 1837)

HOLLAND, J. B.: Company G, private, September 1, 1862 enlisted as a private in Co. G, 47th Regiment, Georgia Infantry. August 31, 1863 in Walker Division Hospital at Lauderdale Springs, Mississippi.

HOLLAND, JAMES: Company A, private, November 1, 1862 enlisted in Co. A, 47th Regiment. February 28, 1863 roll, last on record shows him "Absent without leave". He left company in Charleston, South Carolina.

HOLLAND, PERRY: Company G, private, March 4, 1862 enlisted as a private in Co. G, 11th Battalion. May 12, 1862 transferred to Co. G, 47th Regiment. September 19, 1863 wounded in left shoulder at Chickamauga, Georgia. February 3, 1865 captured at River's Bridge, South Carolina. April 5, 1865 received at Washington, D. C. Name appears on a register of refugees and rebel deserters, Provost Marshal General, Washington, D. C., which shows he took oath and was furnished transportation to Savannah, Georgia. (Born in Tattnall County, Georgia about 1838)

HOLLAND, THOMAS: Company G, Jr. 2nd Lieutenant, April 21, 1862 enlisted as a private in Co. G, 11th Battalion. May 12, 1862 transferred to Co. G, 47th Regiment. July 10, 1862 elected Jr. 2nd lieutenant Co. G, 47th regiment. September 21, 1862 resigned his commission and as a private was transferred to Co. E, 5th Regiment, Georgia Cavalry. December 31, 1864 roll, last on file, shows him present.

HOLLIDAY, HENRY: Company E, private, March 4, 1862 enlisted as a private in Co. E, 11th Battalion. May 12, 1862 transferred to Co. E, 47th Regiment. November 12, 1862 discharged by civil authority.

HOLLIDAY, HENRY: Company E, private, November 12, 1862 enlisted as a private in Co. E, 47th Regiment, Georgia Infantry. December 26, 1862 discharged due to disability.

HOLLOWAY, JAMES: Company C, private, March 4, 1862 enlisted as a private in Co. C, 11th Battalion. May 12, 1862 transferred to Co. C, 47th Regiment. May 26, 1863 died near Jackson, Mississippi. (Born in Bulloch County, Georgia)

HOLMES, JAMES E.: Field Staff, Ordinance Sergeant, May 14, 1862 enlisted as a private in Co. H, 47th Regiment. July 1, 1862 appointed Ordinance Sergeant of 47th Regiment. August 18, 1864 received pay at Charleston, South Carolina.

HOLT, LEONIDAS: Field Staff, Surgeon, August 29, 1862 appointed Surgeon P. A. C. S. and ordered to report to General Beauregard. May 18, 1863 Resigned. May 28, 1863 resignation accepted. September 10, 1863 appointed Surgeon of the 47th Regiment. November 25, 1863 transferred.

HOLTON, GIDEON: Company F, private, April 29, 1862 enlisted as a private in Co. F, 11th Battalion. May 12, 1862 transferred to Co. F, 47th Regiment. October 1862 discharged, furnished Richard G. Brooker as a substitute.

HOLTON, JAMES: Company F, private, April 26, 1862 enlisted as a private in Co. F, 11th Battalion. May 12, 1862 transferred to Co. F, 47th Regiment. November 10, 1862 died of disease at Altamaha Bridge (Doctortown), Georgia.

HOLTON, JOHN R.: Company F, private, April 26, 1862 enlisted as a private in Co. F, 11th Battalion. May 12, 1862 transferred to Co. F, 47th Regiment. October 31, 1863 roll, last on record, shows him present.

HOLTON, WILLIAM S.: Company F, 3rd corporal, March 4, 1862 enlisted as a private in Co. F, 11th Battalion. May 12, 1862 transferred to Co. F, 47th Regiment. August 5, 1862 appointed 3rd corporal Co. F, 47th Regiment. April 26, 1865 pension records show he surrendered Greensboro, North Carolina.

HORCH, JACOB: Company H, private, March 4, 1862 enlisted as a private in Co. H, 11th Battalion. Never reported to camp.

HORCH, WILLIS: Company H, private, March 4, 1862 enlisted as a private in Co. H, 11th Battalion. Never reported to camp.

HORNING, JOSIAH E.: Company E, private, August 4, 1862 enlisted as a private in Co. E, 47th Regiment, Georgia Infantry. November 1862 Regimental returns show him absent without leave.

HOVIS (HAVIS), WILLIAM F.: Company F, 2nd Lieutenant, April 14, 1862 elected Jr. 2nd lieutenant Co. F, 11th Battalion. May 12, 1862 transferred to Co. F, 47th Regiment as Jr. 2nd Lieutenant. October 26, 1863 elected 2nd Lieutenant Co. F, 47th regiment. March 12, 1864 resigned his commission.

HOWARD, HEZEKIAH D.: Company D, private, March 4, 1862 enlisted as a private in Co. D, 11th Battalion. May 12, 1862 transferred to Co. D, 47th Regiment. October 24, 1862 died of disease in Screven County, Georgia.

HOWARD, HENRY N.: Company F, private, March 4, 1862 enlisted as a private in Co. F, 11th Battalion. May 12, 1862 transferred to Co. F, 47th Regiment. November 25, 1863 captured at Missionary Ridge, Tennessee. March 5, 1865 received at Boulware & Cox's Wharves, James River, Virginia for exchange.

HOWARD, WILLIAM: Company D, private, March 4, 1862 enlisted as a private in Co. D, 11th Battalion. May 12, 1862 transferred to Co. D, 47th Regiment. February 28, 1863 roll, last on record, shows him present. May 8, 1865 paroled at Augusta, Georgia.

HOWELL, JOHN J.: Company I, private, March 4, 1862 enlisted as a private in Co. I, 11th Battalion. May 12, 1862 transferred to Co. I, 47th Regiment. January 1865 pension records show he was cut off from command while on picket duty. (Born in Georgia)

HUDSON, ENOCH L.: Company B, private, September 14, 1862 enlisted as a private in Co. B, 47th Regiment, Georgia Infantry. February 28, 1863 roll, last on record, shows him present. April 26, 1865 Pension records show he surrendered Greensboro, North Carolina.

HUGHES, SAMUEL: Company F, private, March 4, 1862 enlisted as a private in Co. F, 11th Battalion. May 12, 1862 transferred to Co. F, 47th Regiment. November 25, 1863 captured at Missionary Ridge, Tennessee. October 31, 1864 enlisted in the United States Army for frontier service at Rock Island, Illinois.

HURST, ALLEN J.: Company I, private, March 4, 1862 enlisted as a private in Co. I, 11th Battalion. May 12, 1862 transferred to Co. I, 47th Regiment. October 7, 1862 discharged at Camp Williams, Georgia by civil authority.

HURST, GEORGE W.: Company I, corporal, March 4, 1862 enlisted as a private in Co. I, 11th Battalion. May 12, 1862 transferred to Co. I, 47th Regiment. Appointed Corporal. July 13, 1863 died in Meridian, Mississippi hospital.

HURST, THOMAS J.: Company I, 5th sergeant, March 4, 1862 enlisted as a private in Co. I, 11th Battalion. May 12, 1862 transferred as 5th sergeant to Co. I, 47th Regiment. November 28, 1863 admitted to Macon, Georgia hospital.

HUTTO, JOHN F.: Company F, private, May 1, 1862 enlisted as a private in Co. F, 11th Battalion. May 12, 1862 transferred to Co. F, 47th Regiment. October 31, 1863 roll, last on record, shows him absent sick. April 26, 1865 pension records show he surrendered Greensboro, North Carolina. (Born in Appling County, Georgia September 27, 1843)

HUTTO, HENRY: Company H, private, March, 1862 pension records show he enlisted as a private in Co. H, 47th Regiment. March 1865 sent to Columbus, North Carolina Hospital with typhoid pneumonia. June 1865 left hospital. (Born in Pulaski County, Georgia in 1839)

IHLER, ADAM JONES: Company K, private, October 15, 1861 enlisted as a private of Co. G, 5th Regiment, Georgia State Troops. April 1862 mustered out. May 6, 1862 enlisted as a private in Co. K, 47th Regiment. May 29, 1862 discharged, furnished R. C. Martin as substitute.

INGRAM, AMBROSE H.: Company B, private, September 14, 1862 enlisted as a private in Co. B, 47th Regiment, Georgia Infantry. October 19, 1862 died of disease in Savannah, Georgia.

IRWIN, J. D.: Company B, private, 1864 (according to pension records) enlisted as a private in Co. B, 47th Regiment, Georgia Infantry. April 26, 1865 (according to pension records) Holton surrendered Greensboro, North Carolina.

JACKSON, JOHN J.: Company I, private, March 4, 1862 enlisted as a private in Co. I, 11th Battalion. May 12, 1862 transferred to Co. I, 47th Regiment. August 1, 1862 transferred to Co. A. 1st Battalion, Georgia Sharpshooters. January 10, 1864 died in Marietta, Georgia hospital.

JACKSON, NEWBORN: Company G, private, September 20, 1863, wounded at Chickamauga, Georgia.

JACOBSON, DAVID: Company D, private, March 4, 1862 enlisted as a private in Co. D, 11th Battalion. May 12, 1862 transferred to Co. D, 47th Regiment. February 28, 1863 roll, last on record, shows him present.

JARRAD, RANSOM J.: Company H, private, March 4, 1862 enlisted as a private in Co. H, 11th Battalion. May 12, 1862 transferred to Co. H, 47th Regiment. March 12, 1863 died at Hilton Head, South Carolina.

JENKINS, GEORGE O.: Company E, private, March 4, 1862 enlisted as a private in Co. E, 11th Battalion. May 12, 1862 transferred to Co. E, 47th Regiment. October 31, 1863 roll, last on record, shows him present.

JENKINS, SIMEON T.: Company B, 2nd Lieutenant, March 4, 1862 appointed 1st Lieutenant Co. B, 11th. Battalion. May 12, 1862 transferred to Co. B, 47th regiment as 2nd Lieutenant. April 24, 1863 resigned, disability.

JOHNS, JAMES R.: Company H, private, March 4, 1862 enlisted as a private in Co. H, 11th Battalion. May 12, 1862 transferred to Co. H, 47th Regiment. October 18, 1862 captured at Proctor's Point, Savannah. River, Georgia. June 16, 1865 released at Fort Delaware, Delaware. (Born in Liberty County, Georgia July 30, 1838)

JOHNS, J. C.: Company H, private, March 4, 1862 enlisted as a private in Co. H, 11th Battalion. May 12, 1862 transferred to Co. H, 47th Regiment. December 22, 1862 died in General Hospital, Augusta, Georgia.

JOHNSON, JAMES K.: Company F, private, September 2, 1862 enlisted as a private in Co. F, 47th Regiment, Georgia Infantry. November 25, 1863 captured at Missionary Ridge, Tennessee. February 1865 paroled at Fort Delaware, Delaware. Entry cancelled. March 1, 1865 to close of the war pension records show he was sick in Augusta, Georgia Hospital. (Born in Appling County, Georgia in 1846)

JOHNSON, ARCHIBALD: Company F, private, March 4, 1862 enlisted as a private in Co. F, 11th Battalion. May 12, 1862 transferred to Co. F, 47th Regiment. November 30, 1863 died of disease in General Hospital #1, Savannah, Georgia.

JOHNSON, JOHN: Company E, private, June 11, 1862 enlisted as a private (substitute for T. W. Bingham) in Co. E, 47th Regiment, Georgia Infantry. October 31, 1863 roll, last on record, shows him under arrest at Savannah, Georgia.

JOHNSON, JOHN AARON: Company F, 4th corporal, March 4, 1862 enlisted as a private in Co. F, 11th Battalion. May 12, 1862 transferred to Co. F, 47th Regiment. August 12, 1862 appointed 4th corporal Co. F, 47th Regiment. November 15, 1862 pension records show he was discharged, disability. (Born in Georgia)

JOHNSON, JOHN W.: Company F, private, March 4, 1862 enlisted as a private in Co. F, 11th Battalion. May 12, 1862 transferred to Co. F, 47th Regiment. December 1864 killed at Morris Island, South Carolina.

JOHNSON, MATTHEW: Company F, private, April 29, 1862 enlisted as a private in Co. F, 11th Battalion. May 12, 1862 transferred to Co. F, 47th Regiment. September 19, 1863 wounded in left leg necessitating amputation below knee, at Chickamauga, Georgia. At home at close of the war. (Resident of Georgia since August 3, 1833)

JOHNSON, WILLIAM A.: Company D, private, July 25, 1862 enlisted as a private in Co. D, 47th Regiment, Georgia Infantry. December 3, 1863 received pay.

JOHNSTON, JAMES J.: Company K, private, October 15, 1861 enlisted as a private of Co. G, 5th Regiment, Georgia State Troops. April 1862 mustered out. May 6, 1862 enlisted as a private in Co. K, 47th Regiment. June 10, 1862 wounded at James Island, South Carolina. October 1863 in Breckinridge's Division Hospital at Marion, Mississippi.

JOHNSTON, REUBEN H.: Company K, private, May 12, 1864 enlisted as a private in Co. K, 47th Regiment. Transferred to the 1st. Georgia Regulars. April 26, 1865 surrendered at Greensboro, North Carolina. (Born March 6, 1846. Died in Waycross, Georgia November 15, 1939)

JOINER, BENJAMIN: Company B, private, March 4, 1862 enlisted as a private in Co. B, 11th Battalion. May 12, 1862 transferred to Co. B, 47th Regiment. August 18, 1863 died.

JOINER, LEWIS A.: Company B, private, April 25, 1862 enlisted as a private in Co. B, 11th Battalion. May 12, 1862 transferred to Co. B, 47th Regiment. December 26, 1863 died in Randolph County, Georgia.

JOINER, SHADE G.: Company B, private, March 4, 1862 enlisted as a private in Co. B, 11th Battalion. May 12, 1862 transferred to Co. B, 47th Regiment. October 31, 1863 in Marion, Mississippi hospital. Pension records show that he was sick in hospital until close of the war. (Born in Georgia in 1841)

JOINER, WILLIAM: Company B, private, March 4, 1862 enlisted as a private in Co. B, 11th Battalion. May 12, 1862 transferred to Co. B, 47th Regiment. October 13, 1863 died in Sumter County, Georgia.

JONES, CHARLES: Field Staff, Musician, May 31, 1862 appointed Musician. December 1872 shows him present.

JONES, FRANCIS MARION: Company F, private, March 4, 1862 enlisted as a private in Co. F, 11th Battalion. May 12, 1862 transferred to Co. F, 47th Regiment. February 28, 1863 received pay. 1864 pension records show he was detailed to drive a wagon in Engineer Corps. April 1865 paroled at Broad River, North Carolina. (Born in Laurens County, Georgia March 23, 1841)

JONES, GEORGE: Field Staff, Musician, May 31, 1862 appointed Musician. December 1872 shows him present.

JONES, JOSEPH: Company B, private, March 4, 1862 enlisted as a private in Co. B, 11th Battalion.

JONES, M.: Company C. 4th Sergeant, March 4, 1862 appointed 4th sergeant Co. C, 11th Battalion. May 12, 1862 transferred to Co. C, 47th Regiment as 4th sergeant. February 28, 1863 roll, last on record, shows him present. Discharged, furnished substitute.

JONES, MARTIN E.: Company G, private, September 30, 1862 enlisted (substitute for Simon W. Brewton) as a private in Co. G, 47th Regiment, Georgia Infantry. May 16, 1864 captured at Resaca, Georgia. February 21, 1865 sent form Alton, Illinois to James River, Virginia for exchange. March 6 or 9, 1865 received at Boulware & Cox's Wharves, James River, Virginia. (Born in Georgia)

JOYCE (JOICE), CHARLES M.: Company B, private, March 4, 1862 enlisted as a private in Co. B, 11th Battalion. May 12, 1862 transferred to Co. B, 47th Regiment. October 4, 1862 died in Medical Hospital.

JOYCE, CUTHBERT: Company D, private, September 24, 1863 captured at Chattanooga, Tennessee.

JOYNER, CUTHBERT: Company D, private, March 4, 1862 enlisted as a private in Co. D, 11th Battalion. May 12, 1862 transferred to Co. D, 47th Regiment. September 24, 1863 captured at Chattanooga, Tennessee. September 14, 1864 paroled at Fort Delaware, Delaware. September 18, 1864 received at Aiken's landing, Virginia for exchange. September 23, 1864 admitted to Jackson Hospital at Richmond, Virginia. September 26, 1864 furloughed for 30 days. Pension records show that he was at home on sick furlough at close of war. (Born in Screven County, Georgia March 1842)

KAIGLER, HENRY M.: Company B, private, March 4, 1862 enlisted as a private in Co. B, 11th Battalion. Absent without leave.

KANGTER, HENRY: Company E, private, March 4, 1862 enlisted as a private in Co. E, 11th Battalion. May 12, 1862 transferred to Co. E, 47th Regiment. May 17, 1864 captured at Calhoun, Georgia. May 22, 1865 released at Rock Island, Illinois.

KEATING, ANDREW: Company A, private, March 4, 1862 enlisted in Co. A, 11th Battalion as a private. May 12, 1862 transferred to Co. A, 47th Regiment. February 28, 1863 roll, last on record, shows him present.

KEHL, J. D.: Company I, private, March 27, 1862 enlisted as a private in Co. I, 11th Battalion. May 12, 1862 transferred to Co. I, 47th Regiment. June 10, 1863 died in General Hospital #1, Savannah, Georgia.

KELLEY, JOHN: Company C, private, March 4, 1862 enlisted as a private in Co. C, 11th Battalion. May 12, 1862 transferred to Co. C, 47th Regiment. June 10, 1862 killed James Island, South Carolina.

KELLY, THOMAS: Company A, 2nd sergeant, July 25, 1861 enlisted as a private in Captain J. B. Read's Independent Company Georgia Infantry. February 27, 1862 appointed 3rd sergeant Co. A. 11th Battalion. May 12, 1862 transferred to Co. A, 47th Regiment. and appointed 3rd sergeant. September 1, 1862 appointed 2nd sergeant. October 1863 in Fortney's Division Hospital, Enterprise Mississippi. September 5, 1864 retired at Richmond, Virginia. December 21, 1864 deserted at Savannah, Georgia. February 11, 1865 detailed for light duty and ordered to report to Commandant of Post at Richmond, Virginia. February 1865 appears on list of deserters turned over to Provost Marshall General, Department of the South, to be furnished transportation to New York City, New York, per Steamer Fulton.

KENNEDY, DANIEL L.: Company G, Captain, September 17, 1861 enlisted as a private in Co. A, 2nd Battalion, Georgia Cavalry. March 4, 1862 elected 1st Lieutenant Co. G, 11th Battalion. May 12, 1862 transferred to Co. G, 47th Georgia Regiment as 1st Lieutenant. June 25, 1863 elected Captain, Co. G, 47th Georgia.

KENNEDY, STILES: Field Staff, Assistant Surgeon, June 1, 1862 appointed assistant surgeon 47th Regiment. May 1, 1863 appears on a list of Medical Officers of the Department of South Carolina, Georgia and Florida which shows him at Hardeeville, South Carolina. July 1,

1863 requested 15 days leave of absence. September 19, 1863 appointed Surgeon from the State of Maryland and sent to the 8th Regiment, North Carolina Infantry. March 8, 1865 captured at Southwest Creek. March 17, 1865 transferred to Washington, D. C. March 4, 1865 sent to Fortress Monroe, Virginia. March 30, 1865 Paroled at point Lookout, Maryland and received at Boulware's Warf, James River, Virginia for exchange.

KERBY, JAMES: Company C, private, March 4, 1862 enlisted as a private in Co. C, 11th Battalion. April 27, 1862 died at Battery Harrison, South Carolina.

KERBY, JAMES A.: Company C, private, March 4, 1862 enlisted as a private in Co. C, 11th Battalion. May 12, 1862 transferred to Co. C, 47th Regiment. February 28, 1863 roll, last on record, shows him present. Discharged, furnished substitute. Company C, private,

KERSEY, WILLIAM: Company B, 1st sergeant, October 21, 1861 appointed 3rd corporal of Co. K, 7th Regiment, Georgia State Troops. April 20, 1862 mustered out at Camp Brown. April 25, 1862 enlisted as a private in Co. B, 11th Battalion. May 12, 1862 transferred to Co. B, 47th Regiment. August 1, 1862 transferred to Co. A, 1st Battalion Georgia Sharpshooters. Wounded in 1863. Appointed 1st sergeant. April 1864 roll, last on file, shows him sick in General Hospital. January 23, 1865 furloughed for sixty days by medical Examining board.

KESSLER, EPHRAIM E.: Company I, private, March 4, 1862 enlisted as a private in Co. I, 11th Battalion. May 12, 1862 transferred to Co. I, 47th Regiment. March 11, 1964 died of Typhoid in Gilmer Hospital, Michigan as a P. O .W

KICKLIGHTER, A.: Company K, private, February 25, 1863 enlisted as a private in Co. K, 47th Regiment. February 28, 1863 roll, last on record, shows him present.

KICKLIGHTER, LEONARD W.: Company K, 5th sergeant, October 15, 1861 enlisted as a private of Co. G, 5th Regiment, Georgia State Troops. April 1862 mustered out. May 15, 1862 enlisted as a private in Co. K, 47th Regiment. June 10, 1862 appointed 5th sergeant, Co. K, 47th Regiment. June 10, 1862 wounded at James Island, South Carolina. February 28, 1863 roll, last on record, shows him present. (Born in Bulloch County, Georgia November 29, 1845)

KICKLIGHTER, SEABORN: Company C, private, March 4, 1862 enlisted as a private in Co. C, 11th Battalion. May 12, 1862 transferred to Co. C, 47th Regiment. September 23, 1863 admitted to Floyd House and Ocmulgee Hospitals at Macon, Georgia. October 6, 1863 furloughed for 30 days. (Born February 8, 1836)

KING, ROBERT W.: Company E, private, March 4, 1862 enlisted as a private in Co. E, 11th Battalion. May 12, 1862 transferred to Co. E, 47th Regiment. October 31, 1863 roll, last on record, shows him present.

KIRSH (KIRSCH), STEPHEN: Company E, private, March 4, 1862 enlisted as a private in Co. E, 11th Battalion. May 12, 1862 transferred to Co. E, 47th Regiment. August 25, 1863 attached to Lauderdale Springs Hospital, Mississippi as nurse. December 29, 1863 examined for furlough, on account of chronic diarrhea.

KIRSH (KIRSCH), WILLIAM H.: Company E, private, March 4, 1862 enlisted as a private in Co. E, 11th Battalion. May 12, 1862 transferred to Co. E, 47th Regiment. November 15, 1864 in Ladies Hospital at Montgomery, Alabama.

KNIGHT, WILLIAM H.: Company K, private, December 10, 1862 enlisted as a private in Co. K, 47th Regiment November 25, 1863 captured at Graysville, Georgia. December 18, 1863 sent from Louisville, Kentucky to Rock Island, Illinois.

KNOX, JOHN: Company A, 3rd corporal, May 14, 1862 enlisted in Co. A, 47th Regiment as private. February 1863 appointed 3rd corporal Co. A, 47th Regiment. April 7, 1865 appears on roll of deserters "to be delivered to Provost Marshal General, New York City, New York."

KUHLMAN, JOHN: Company E, 2nd corporal, March 4, 1862 enlisted as a private in Co. E, 11th Battalion. May 12, 1862 transferred to Co. E, 47th Regiment. June 1862 appointed 3rd corporal Co. E. 47th Regiment. July 1862 appointed 2nd corporal Co. E, 47th Regiment. July 26, 1863 detailed to Medical Department at Savannah, Georgia.

LANIER, A. R.: Company C, 3rd. sergeant, March 4, 1862 appointed. 3rd Sergeant Co. C, 11th Battalion. May 12, 1862 transferred to Co. C, 47th Regiment as 3rd Sergeant. October 1862 appears last on roll. Discharged, furnished substitute.

LANIER, JAMES L.: Company H, private, March 4, 1862 enlisted as a private in Co. H, 11th Battalion. May 12, 1862 transferred to Co. H, 47th Regiment. February 28, 1863 roll, last on record, shows him present.

LARD, E. L.: Company I, private, March 4, 1862 enlisted as a private in Co. I, 11th Battalion. May 12, 1862 transferred to Co. I, 47th Regiment. October 23, 1863 died in Atlanta, Georgia. Buried there in Oakland Cemetery.

LARD, WILLIAM M.: Company I, private, enlisted as a private in Co. I, 47th Regiment. March 29, 1864 transferred to Co. G, 50th Regiment, Alabama Infantry.

LARKIN, JAMES: Company A, private, March 9, 1862 enlisted in Co. A, 11th Battalion as a private. May 12, 1862 transferred to Co. A, 47th Regiment as a Musician. February 3, 1865 captured at River's Bridge, South Carolina. April 2, 1865 forwarded from Fort Monroe, Virginia to Washington, D. C.

LASTINGER, J. A.: Company K, private, May 6, 1862 enlisted as a private in Co. K, 47th Regiment. January 12, 1864 furloughed from Floyd House and Ocmulgee Hospitals at Macon, Georgia.

LATIMER, CLEMENT T. (W): Company F, private, April 26, 1862 enlisted as a private in Co. F, 11th Battalion. May 12, 1862 transferred to Co. F, 47th Regiment. November 1862 detailed to Company Commissary.

LATIMER, JAMES H.: Company F, Captain, March 4, 1862 elected Captain Co F, 11th Battalion. May 12, 1862 transferred to Co. F, 47th Regiment as Captain in. October 26, 1863 resigned his commission due to ill health.

LAWRENCE, SEABORN R.: Company B, Captain, May 10, 1861 enlisted as a private in Co. F, 5th Regiment Georgia Infantry. January 26, 1862 shows him discharged, disability in Pensacola, Florida. March 4, 1862 appointed 3rd sergeant Co. B, 11 Battalion. May 12, 1862 transferred to Co. B 47th Regiment as 3rd sergeant. July 24, 1862 elected Jr. 2nd Lieutenant Co. B., 47th Regiment. April 6, 1863 elected 1st Lieutenant Co. B, 47th Regiment. April 15, 1863 elected 2nd lieutenant Co. B, 47th Regiment. April 6, 1864 elected Captain Co. B, 47th Regiment.

LEE, B. J.: Company K, private, May 6, 1862 enlisted as a private in Co. K, 47th Regiment. June 8, 1862 died at Causton's Bluff, Georgia.

LEE, ELI: Company C, private, March 4, 1862 enlisted as a private in Co. C, 11th Battalion. May 12, 1862 transferred to Co. C, 47th Regiment. February 28, 1863 roll, last on record, shows him present. April 26, 1865 pension records show he surrendered Greensboro, North Carolina.

LEE, GEORGE W., SR.: Company C, private, March 4, 1862 enlisted as a private in Co. C, 11th Battalion. May 12, 1862 transferred to Co. C, 47th Regiment. 1862 discharged, furnished substitute. Enlisted in Georgia Militia. (Born in Georgia)

LEE, HAMPTON: Company K, private, May 6, 1862 enlisted as a private in Co. K, 47th Regiment. October 29, 1862 discharged, furnished C. Geiger as a substitute.

LEE, HENRY C, SR.: Company C, private, March 4, 1862 enlisted as a private in Co. C, 11th Battalion. May 12, 1862 transferred to Co. C, 47th Regiment. June 30, 1862 appears on roll.

LEE, J. C.: Company K, private, May 6, 1862 enlisted as a private in Co. K, 47th Regiment. June 10, 1862 wounded at James Island, South Carolina. July 8, 1862 died of wounds.

LEE, J. T.: Company C, private, March 4, 1862 enlisted as a private in Co. C, 11th Battalion. May 12, 1862 transferred to Co. C, 47th Regiment. February 15, 1864 in General Hospital in Guyton, Georgia. March 18, 1865 killed Bentonville, North Carolina.

LEE, J. V.: Company C, private, September 10, 1862 enlisted as a private in Co. C, 47th Regiment, Georgia Infantry. 1864 wounded in the leg. December 22, 1864 admitted to 2nd Division, 20th Army Corps Hospital. January 16, 1865 sent to General hospital.

LEE, JAMES: Company K, 3rd, sergeant, October 15, 1861 enlisted as a private of Co. G, 5th Regiment, Georgia State Troops. April 1862 mustered out. May 6, 1862 appointed 3rd sergeant, Co. K, 47th Regiment. December 25, 1862 died at Wilmington, North Carolina.

LEE, JOHN A.: Company I, private, March 4, 1862 enlisted as a private in Co. I, 11th Battalion. May 12, 1862 transferred to Co. I, 47th Regiment.

December 7, 1864 died of disease in Buckner Hospital Newnan, Georgia and is buried there.

LEE, JOHN S.: Company K, private, May 6, 1862 enlisted as a private in Co. K, 47th Regiment. June 10, 1862 wounded at James Island, South Carolina. February 28, 1863 roll, last on record, shows him present.

LEE, JOSEPH: Company K, 2nd corporal, October 15, 1861 enlisted as a private of Co. G, 5th Regiment, Georgia State Troops. April 1862 mustered out. May 6, 1862 appointed 2nd Corporal Co. K, 47th Regiment.

LEE, JOSEPH B.: Company D, private, March 4, 1862 enlisted as a private in Co. D, 11th Battalion. May 12, 1862 transferred to Co. D, 47th Regiment. August 1, 1862 transferred to Co. A. 1st Battalion, Georgia Sharpshooters. May 18, 1864 captured at Adairsville, Georgia. June 17, 1865 at Rock Island, Illinois.

LEE, NATHAN: Company D, private, May 12, 1862 enlisted as a private in Co. D, 47th Regiment, Georgia Infantry. July 30, 1862 transferred to Co. A. 1st Battalion, Georgia Sharpshooters. August 31, 1864 captured at Jonesboro, Georgia. May 12, 1865 released at Camp Douglas, Illinois.

LEE, SANDERSON C.: Company I, sergeant, September 18, 1861 enlisted as a private in Co. C, 1st Regiment, Georgia State Troops. March 13, 1862 mustered out. April 17, 1862 enlisted as a private in Co. I, 11th Battalion. May 12, 1862 transferred to Co. I, 47th Regiment. April; 1 1863 assignment was color sergeant. July 11, 1863 through August 31, 1863 detailed nurse, Walker Division Hospital, Lauderdale Springs, Mississippi.

LEE, THOMAS J.: Company B, private, October 9, 1861 enlisted as a private in Co. F, 1st. Regiment, 1st Brigade, Georgia State Troops. April 9, 1862 roll, last on file, shows him present. April 1862 mustered out. April 25, 1862 enlisted as a private in Co. B, 11th Battalion. May 12, 1862 transferred to Co. B, 47th Regiment. August 1, 1862 transferred to Co. S, 1st Battalion Georgia Sharpshooters. September 19, 1863 wounded at Chickamauga, Georgia. December 15, 1863 died of wounds in Atlanta, Georgia hospital.

LEE, THOMAS P.: Company F, private, March 4, 1862 enlisted as a private in Co. F, 11th Battalion. May 12, 1862 transferred to Co. F, 47th Regiment. October 31, 1863 roll, last on record, shows him present.

LEE, WILLIAM N.: Company K, private, May 6, 1862 enlisted as a private in Co. K, 47th Regiment. February 28, 1863 roll, last on record, shows him present.

LEGGETT, ABRAHAM EASON: Company F, private, November 11, 1862 enlisted as a private in Co. F, 47th Regiment, Georgia Infantry. May 16, 1864 enlisted as a private in Co. I, 6th Regiment, Georgia Militia.

LEGGETT, WATSON: Company F, private, November 20, 1862 enlisted as a private in Co. F, 47th Regiment, Georgia Infantry. November 1, 1863 died of chronic dysentery in General Hospital #1, Savannah, Georgia.

LEONARD, MICHAEL: Company A, private. May 14, 1862 enlisted in Company A, 47th Regiment (substitute for Michael Selig). August 2, 1862 died of disease, Screven's Ferry, Georgia.

LEWIS, GENERAL: Company K, private, February 21, 1863 enlisted as a private in Co. K, 47th Regiment. February 28, 1863 roll, last on record, shows him present. October 1864 pension records show he was in Whiteville, South Carolina hospital with typhoid fever. Unfit for further service.

LIGHTFOOT, WILLIAM T.: Company G, private, March 4, 1862 enlisted as a private in Co. G, 11th Battalion. May 12, 1862 transferred to Co. G, 47th Regiment. August 1, 1862 transferred to Co. A. 1st Battalion, Georgia Sharpshooters. June 30, 1864 deserted.

LIGHTSEY, JOHN J.: Company I, private, March 4, 1862 enlisted as a private in Co. I, 11th Battalion. May 12, 1862 transferred to Co. I, 47th Regiment. September 10, 1863 died in Marion Station Hospital, Mississippi.

LIGHTSEY, N. H.: Company I, private, March 4, 1862 enlisted as a private in Co. I, 11th Battalion. May 12, 1862 transferred to Co. I, 47th Regiment. September 1, 1863 died in Mississippi Hospital.

LIGHTSEY, SAMUEL: Company I, private, March 4, 1862 enlisted as a private in Co. I, 11th Battalion. May 12, 1862 transferred to Co. I, 47th Regiment. October 7, 1862 discharged by civil authority at Camp Williams, Georgia. December 7, 1863 enlisted as a private in Co. H, 4th Regiment. Georgia Cavalry (Clinch's). August 15, 1864 captured near Atlanta, Georgia, June 11, 1865 released from Camp Chase, Ohio.

LILLY, JAMES C.: Company B, private, March 4, 1862 enlisted as a private in Co. B, 11th Battalion. May 12, 1862 transferred to Co. B, 47th Regiment. March 1 - July 30, 1864 in Summerville, South Carolina hospital.

LOFTON, W. H.: Company C, private, March 4, 1862 enlisted as a private in Co. C, 11th Battalion. May 12, 1862 transferred to Co. C, 47th Regiment. Killed in South Carolina.

LONG, HENRY LAFAYETTE: Company B, private, March 4, 1862 enlisted as a private in Co. B, 11th Battalion. June 1862 appears last on roll. Pension records show he was disabled by measles contracted in service. May 26, 1865 paroled in Albany, Georgia.

LONG, RICHARD G.: Company F, private, March 4, 1862 enlisted as a private in Co. F, 11th Battalion. May 12, 1862 transferred to Co. F, 47th Regiment. July 30, 1862 transferred to Co. A. 1st Battalion, Georgia Sharpshooters. September 19, 1863 killed at Chickamauga, Georgia.

LOW, JAMES: Company H, private, March 4, 1862 enlisted as a private in Co. H, 11th Battalion. never reported to camp.

LOW, ROBERT: Field Staff, Leading Musician, May 31, 1862 appointed Leading Musician. December 1872 shows him present.

LOWTHER, JOHN Z.: Company D, Jr. 2nd Lieutenant. October 14, 1861 enlisted as a private in Co. I, 5th. Regiment, 1st Brigade, Georgia State Troops. April 1862 mustered out. April 28, 1862 enlisted as a private in

Co. D, 11th Battalion. May 12, 1862 transferred to Co. D, 47th Regiment. September 30, 1863 elected Jr. 2nd Lt Co. D, 47th Regiment. 1863 elected 2nd lieutenant. March 1, 1865 died.

LOWTHER, SAMUEL H.: Company D, private, March 4, 1862 enlisted as a private in Co. D, 11th Battalion. May 12, 1862 transferred to Co. D, 47th Regiment. October 31, 1863 appears on roll of 1st Georgia Hospital at Charleston, South Carolina as being paid to that date.

LYNCH, WILLIAM: Company I, private, March 20, 1862 enlisted as a private in Co. I, 11th Battalion. May 12, 1862 transferred to Co. I, 47th Regiment. October 21, 1862 - January 1864 attached to General Hospital, Guyton, Georgia as nurse.

LYNN, DANIEL C.: Company G, private, March 4, 1862 enlisted as a private in Co. G, 11th Battalion. May 12, 1862 transferred to Co. G, 47th Regiment. November 25, 1863 captured at Missionary Ridge, Tennessee. October 11, 1864 released at Rock Island, Illinois.

LYNN, DANIEL E.: Company G, private, September 10, 1861 enlisted as a private in Co. I, 27th Regiment, Georgia Infantry. June 30, 1864 received pay. March 1865 Pension records show he transferred to Co. G, 47th Regiment, Georgia Infantry. April 26, 1865 pension records show he surrendered at Greensboro, North Carolina. (Born in Georgia December 16, 1832)

LYNN, DENNIS E.: Company G, private, March 4, 1862 enlisted as a private in Co. G, 11th Battalion. May 12, 1862 transferred to Co. G, 47th Regiment. November 25, 1863 captured at Missionary Ridge, Tennessee. January 7, 1864 took oath of allegiance to the United States Government at Nashville, Tennessee.

LYNN, JOHN L.: Company G, private, November 20, 1862 enlisted as a private in Co. G, 47th Regiment, Georgia Infantry. April 26, 1865 surrendered at Greensboro, North Carolina. (Born in Tattnall County, Georgia June 5, 1825)

LYNN, JOSIAH J.: Company G, private, March 4, 1862 enlisted as a private in Co. G, 11th Battalion. May 12, 1862 transferred to Co. G, 47th Regiment. August 1, 1862 discharged, under age. February 1864 pension records show he enlisted in Captain Silas Crosby's Company, Georgia Militia. (born in Georgia in 1845)

MAINOR, MARSHALL.: Company B, private, March 4, 1862 enlisted as a private in Co. B, 11th Battalion. May 12, 1862 transferred to Co. B, 47th Regiment. December 15, 1863 admitted to Floyd House and Ocmulgee Hospital at Macon, Georgia, on account of debility.

MALLETT, JAMES ALLEN, JR.: Company I, private, August 27, 1862 enlisted as a private in Co. I, 47th Regiment. February 28, 1863 December 1863 rolls show him as nurse at Frenchs' and Forney's Hospital at Enterprise, Mississippi. (Born in Georgia June 17, 1832)

MALLETT, JAMES ALLEN, SR.: Company I, private, August 27, 1862 enlisted as a private in Co. I, 47th Regiment. February 8, 1863 died in

Savannah, Georgia Hospital.

MARSH, HENRY: Company E, 3rd corporal. March 4, 1862 appointed 3rd corporal, Co. E, 11th Battalion. May 12, 1862 transferred to Co. E, 47th Regiment as 3rd corporal. November 29, 1863 admitted to Floyd House and Ocmulgee Hospitals at Macon, Georgia with chronic diarrhea.

MARSH, J. CALVIN: Company E, private, October 9, 1862 enlisted as a private in Co. E, 47th Regiment, Georgia Infantry. October 31, 1863 roll, last on record, shows him present.

MARTIN, A. J.: Company B, private, October 1, 1864 (according to pension records) enlisted as a private in Co. B, 47th Regiment, Georgia Infantry. April 26, 1865 surrendered Greensboro, North Carolina. (Born in Monroe County, Georgia in 1842)

MARTIN, E. H.: Company K, private, May 6, 1862 enlisted as a private in Co. K, 47th Regiment. June 10, 1862 wounded at James Island, South Carolina. February 3, 1865 captured At River's Bridge, South Carolina. April 5, 1865 took oath of allegiance to the United States Government at Washington, D. C., and furnished transportation to Savannah, Georgia.

MARTIN, HUGH: Company A, private, March 1, 1862 enlisted in Co. A, 11th Battalion as a private. May 12, 1862 transferred to Co. A, 47th Regiment. December 26, 1864 deserted at Savannah, Georgia remark "at work in Quartermasters Department" (Born in Ireland)

MARTIN, ISHAM: Company G, private, March 4, 1862 enlisted as a private in Co. G, 11th Battalion. May 12, 1862 transferred to Co. G, 47th Regiment. February 28, 1863 roll, last on record, shows him present.

MARTIN, J. H.: Company K, corporal, May 6, 1862 enlisted as a private in Co. K, 47th Regiment. November 28, 1862 appointed corporal at hospital in camp at Savannah, Georgia. December 4, 1863 died at Fairground Hospital No.1 at Atlanta, Georgia.

MARTIN, J. O.: Company K, private, May 6, 1862 enlisted as a private in Co. K, 47th Regiment. June 10, 1862 wounded and captured at James Island, South Carolina. November 10, 1862 exchanged at Aiken's Landing, Virginia.

MARTIN, RUEBEN C.: Company K, private, October 15, 1861 enlisted as a private of Co. G, 5th Regiment, Georgia State Troops. April 1862 mustered out. May 20, 1862 enlisted as a private in Co. K, 47th Regiment. June 10, 1862 wounded at James Island, South Carolina. November 18, 1862 discharged at Camp Williams, Georgia by civil authority.

MARTIN, THOMAS E.: Company K, private, May 6, 1862 enlisted as a private in Co. K, 47th Regiment Georgia Infantry as a private. February 28, 1863 roll, last on record, shows him present. September 20, 1863 killed at Chickamauga,

MARTIN, WILEY A.: Company K, private, October 15, 1861 enlisted as a private of Co. G, 5th Regiment, Georgia State Troops. April 1862 mustered out. May 6, 1862 enlisted as a private in Co. K, 47th Regiment Georgia Infantry as a private. June 10, 1862 killed at James Island, South

Carolina.

MARTIN, WILLIAM: Company A, private, May 15, 1862 enlisted in Co. A, 47th Regiment as private. February 28, 1863 roll, last on file, shows him present.

MASTERSON, JOHN: Company A, private, March 3, 1862 enlisted in Co. A, 11th Battalion as a private. May 12, 1862 transferred to Co. A, 47th Regiment. December 5, 1863 admitted to Floyd House & Ocmulgee Hospitals at Macon, Georgia.

MATTHEWS, DAVID A.: Field Staff, Surgeon, August 16, 1862 appointed Surgeon of the 30th Regiment. November 1, 1862 transferred to the 47th Regiment as surgeon. March 1, 1863 listed as Surgeon in charge of Red Bluff Hospital. March- April 1863, last roll on file, signed hospital muster roll for the 47th Regiment as Surgeon in charge of the Hospital.

MATTHEWS, JACOB: Company B, private, March 4, 1862 enlisted as a private in Co. B, 11th Battalion. May 12, 1862 transferred to Co. B, 47th Regiment. May 15, 1864 wounded near Resaca, Georgia. June 12, 1864 died as a result of amputation of left leg, General Field Hospital near Resaca, Georgia.

MATTHEWS, O. P.: Field Staff, Hospital Steward, May 18, 1861 enlisted as a private in Co. D, 8th a Regiment Georgia Infantry, 1862 and 1863 appointed sergeant. Acting as Hospital Steward for the 47th Georgia Regiment. October 31, 1864 roll for the 8th Regiment Georgia Infantry reports him "Absent, detailed as Hospital Steward."

MCCANN, FRANCIS: Company A, private, March 3, 1862 enlisted in Co. A, 11th Battalion as a private. May 12, 1862 transferred to Co. A, 47th Regiment. November 1, 1862 detailed on Gun Boat.

MCCANN, JAMES C.: Company B, private, April 25, 1862 enlisted as a private in Co. B, 11th Battalion. May 12, 1862 transferred to Co. B, 47th Regiment. December 21, 1863 in Catoosa Hospital at Griffin, Georgia.

MCCANN, JAMES H.: Company A, private, March 4, 1862 enlisted in Co. A, 11th Battalion as a private. May 12, 1862 transferred to Co. A, 47th Regiment. October 26, 1862 deserted to enemy at Savannah, Georgia.

MCCANN, THOMAS: Company A, private, April 15, 1862 enlisted in Co. A, 11th Battalion as a private. May 12, 1862 transferred to Co. A, 47th Regiment. October 26, 1862 deserted to enemy at Savannah, Georgia.

MCCARTHY, BARTHOLOMEW: Company A, private, March 3, 1862 enlisted in Co. A, 11th Battalion as a private. May 12, 1862 transferred to Co. A, 47th Regiment. September 9, 1863 captured at Cumberland Gap, Tennessee. October 21, 1863 died, inflammation of lungs, Camp Douglas, Illinois as a POW. Buried in Chicago City Cemetery, Grave #755, Block 2.

MCCLELLAND (MCLELLAN), ALPHEAS D.: Company F, private, March 4, 1862 enlisted as a private in Co. F, 11th Battalion. May 12, 1862 transferred to Co. F, 47th Regiment. October 31, 1863 roll, last on record, shows him present.

MCCLELLAND, ARCHIBALD.: Company F, private, November 24, 1862 enlisted as a private in Co. F, 47th Regiment, Georgia Infantry. May 23, 1864 died of chronic diarrhea in Dawson Hospital Greensboro, Georgia.

MCCLELLAND (MCLELLAN) JOHN: Company F, private, May 3, 1862 enlisted as a private in Co. F, 11th Battalion. May 12, 1862 transferred to Co. F, 47th Regiment. October 31, 1863 roll, last on record, shows him absent sick. March 1865 pension records show he was separated from his command at Sautee River, North Carolina.

MCCOLLOUGH, JOSEPH: Company G, private, March 4, 1862 enlisted as a private in Co. G, 11th Battalion. May 12, 1862 transferred to Co. G, 47th Regiment. July 28, 1862 died of disease in Savannah, Georgia.

MCCOLLOUGH, SAMUEL: Company G, private, March 4, 1862 enlisted as a private in Co. G, 11th Battalion. May 12, 1862 transferred to Co. G, 47th Regiment. February 28, 1863 roll, last on record, shows him present. (Died at Cobbtown, Tattnall County, Georgia November 18, 1906).

MCCONNELL, WILLIAM R.: Company H, Jr. 2nd Lieutenant, March 4, 1862 enlisted as a private in Co. H, 11th Battalion. May 12, 1862 transferred to Co. H, 47th Regiment. June 11, 1863 elected Jr. 2nd lieutenant Co. H, 47th Regiment. March 1865 appears on roster.

MCCORKLE, C. T.: Company E, private, enlisted as a private in Co. E, 47th Regiment, Georgia Infantry. August 8, 1863 discharged on account of chronic asthma at Gainesville, Alabama.

MCCORKLE, ROBERT R.: Company E, private, enlisted as a private in Co. E, 47th Regiment, Georgia Infantry. October 31, 1863 roll, last on record, shows him present.

MCCROY, ALBERT V.: Company I, private, March 4, 1862 enlisted as a private in Co. I, 11th Battalion. May 12, 1862 transferred to Co. I, 47th Regiment. May 6, 1863 died at Jonesville, South Carolina.

MCCRORY, J. W. S.: Company I, private, April 20, 1862 enlisted as a private in Co. I, 11th Battalion. May 12, 1862 transferred to Co. I, 47th Regiment. September - October 1863 in Breckinridge's Division Hospital at Marion, Mississippi.

MCEACHIN, HECTOR: Company F, private, November 19, 1862 enlisted as a private in Co. F, 47th Regiment, Georgia Infantry. November 29, 1863 admitted to Floyd House and Ocmulgee Hospitals at Macon, Georgia with chronic rheumatism.

MCELLINE, THOMAS: Company A, 1st sergeant, March 1, 1862 Enlisted. May 12, 1862 transferred to Co. A, 47th Regiment. April 1, 1862 appointed 2nd sergeant, Co. A, 47th Regiment. September 1, 1862 appointed 1st sergeant, Co. A, 47th Regiment. August 31, 1864 deserted at Secessionville, James Island, South Carolina and took oath of allegiance to the United States Government on Morris Island, South Carolina. September 1, 1864 received at Hilton Head, South Carolina. (Also appears as McEllinne, McEllynn and McElynn)

MCELVEEN, REUBEN C.: Company K, private, October 15, 1861 enlisted as a private of Co. G, 5th Regiment, Georgia State Troops. April 1862 mustered out. May 6, 1862 enlisted as a private in Co. K, 47th Regiment Georgia Infantry. February 15, 1863 died at Savannah, Georgia.

MCFADDEN, ORIN: Company D, private, July 25, 1862 enlisted as a private in Co. D, 47th Regiment, Georgia Infantry. October 13, 1862 deserted at Camp Williams, Georgia and went to Blockading Squadron at Fort Pulaski. Georgia.

MCGAULEY, HENRY: Company F, private, November 12, 1862 enlisted as a private in Co. F, 47th Regiment, Georgia Infantry. Sent to Hospital. Did not return.

MCGAULEY, M: Company F, private, November 12, 1862 enlisted as a private in Co. F, 47th Regiment, Georgia Infantry.

MCGINNIS, JOHN: Company H, private, March 4, 1862 enlisted as a private in Co. H, 11th Battalion. May 12, 1862 transferred to Co. H, 47th Regiment. June 10, 1862 killed at James Island, South Carolina.

MCGINNIS, THOMAS: Company A, private, March 3, 1862 enlisted in Co. A, 11th Battalion as a private. May 12, 1862 transferred to Co. A, 47th Regiment. February 4, 1864 admitted to Floyd House and Ocmulgee Hospitals at Macon, Georgia with phthisis. Disposition from hospital is not shown. Remarks "sick seven or eight months."

MCGOUGH, PATRICK: Company A, private, March 3, 1862 enlisted in Co. A, 11th Battalion as a private. May 12, 1862 transferred to Co. A, 47th Regiment. December 1862 roll shows him absent sick. February 28, 1863 roll shows him absent without leave since January 30, 1863.

MCGRATH, THOMAS H.: Company A, 4th sergeant, February 27, 1862 appointed. 4th sergeant Co. A., 11th Battalion. May 12, 1862 transferred to Co. A, 47th Regiment. as 5th sergeant. June 12, 1862 appointed 4th sergeant Co. A, 47th Regiment. February 28, 1863 on special duty enrolling conscripts. May 1, 1863 received pay.

MCGUIRE, MICHAEL: Company A, private, April 15, 1862 enlisted in Co. A, 11th Battalion as a private. May 12, 1862 transferred to Co. A, 47th Regiment. November 1862 detailed on Gun Boat.

MCINTYRE, GEORGE W.: Company H, private, July 1864 enlisted as a private in Co. H, 47th Regiment. April 26, 1865 surrendered at Greensboro, North Carolina.

MCKINNEY, WILLIAM H.: Company D, private, March 4, 1862 enlisted as a private in Co. D, 11th Battalion. May 12, 1862 transferred to Co. D, 47th Regiment. July 3, 1862 to December 31, 1863 on detached duty Mission Hospital, Guyton, Georgia. April 26, 1865 according to pension records surrendered Greensboro, North Carolina.

MCLAIN, JOHN T.: Field Staff, Assistant Surgeon, September 2, 1862 appointed assistant surgeon of 47th Regiment. July 26, 1863 recommended for duty in hospitals, by reason of rheumatism which rendered him unfit for field duty. February 1865 in Prison Hospital at Macon, Georgia.

MCLESTER, LEONIDAS: Field Staff, Assistant Surgeon, March 4, 1862 enlisted as a private in Co. B, 11th Battalion. June 1, 1862 Assistant Surgeon and transferred to 47th Regiment Georgia Infantry. December 8, 1862 received pay.

MCMILLAN, BENJAMIN: Company B, private, March 4, 1862 enlisted as a private in Co. B, 11th Battalion. Absent without leave.

MCMILLAN, RICHARD F.: Company B, private, March 4, 1862 enlisted as a private in Co. B, 11th Battalion. Absent without leave.

MCNEIL, WILLIAM W.: Company B, private, March 4, 1862 enlisted as a private in Co. B, 11th Battalion. May 12, 1862 transferred to Co. B, 47th Regiment. February 28, 1863 roll, last on record, shows him present.

MCNEILY, HUGH G.: Company B, private, .March 4, 1862 enlisted as a private in Co. B, 11th Battalion. April 30, 1862 died.

MCNEILY, JAMES M.: Company B, private, March 4, 1862 enlisted as a private in Co. B, 11th Battalion. May 12, 1862 transferred to Co. B, 47th Regiment. October 1862 detailed to Gun Boat Duty. February 28, 1863 roll, last on record, shows him detailed as teamster. May 11, 1863 detached to Camp Allen, South Carolina.

MCVEY (MCVAY), W. R.: Company C, private, July 22, 1862 enlisted as private. February 1863 in Whitesville, Georgia. Hospital. November 1, 1863 in Jackson's Cavalry Hospital, Old Marion Mississippi. November 25, 1863 killed Missionary Ridge, Tennessee.

MCWILLIAMS, THOMAS A.: Company B, private, May 10, 1861 enlisted as a private in Co. F, 5th. Regiment Georgia Infantry. November 8, 1861 discharged due to disability. May 7, 1862 enlisted as a private in Co. F, 32nd Regiment. November 1, 1862 transferred to Co. B, 47th Regiment. January 14, 1863 left arm crushed in railroad accident near Fair Bluff, North Carolina resulting in amputation below the elbow. January - February 1863 in Wilmington, North Carolina Hospital. (Born in Georgia June 15, 1838)

MEARS, JAMES HENRY: Company D, private, March 4, 1862 enlisted as a private in Co. D, 11th Battalion. May 12, 1862 transferred to Co. D, 47th Regiment. September 6, 1862 discharged, furnished Edward Reynolds as a substitute. (Born in Screven County, Georgia November 13, 1840)

MEARS, WILLIAM H.: Company D, 1st. corporal, March 4, 1862 appointed 1st corporal. Co. D, 11th Battalion. May 12, 1862 transferred to Co. D, 47th Regiment as 1st corporal.. September 20, 1863 wounded at Chickamauga, Georgia. Pension records show that he was at home wounded, close of war. (Born in Screven County, Georgia November 13, 1840)

MEEKS, CHARLES: Company F, private, May 15, 1862 enlisted as a private in Co. F, 47th Regiment, Georgia Infantry. April 1864 pension records show he was discharged, furnished substitute.

MEEKS, REDDING G.: Company F, private, May 1, 1862 enlisted as a private in Co. F, 11th Battalion. May 12, 1862 transferred to Co. F, 47th Regiment. Pension records show he was wounded, date and place not given, and was home, on wounded furlough, at the close of the war.

MIENHART, HENRY: Company A, private, March 4, 1862 enlisted in Co. A, 11th Battalion as a private. April 30, 1862 discharged, furnished Matthew J. Doyle as substitute.

MELTON, ELBERT G: Company B, private, October 21, 1861 enlisted as a private in Co. K, 7th. Regiment, 1st Brigade, Georgia State Troops. April 20, 1862 mustered out at Camp Brown, Georgia. April 25, 1862 enlisted as a private in Co. B, 11th Battalion. May 12, 1862 transferred to Co. B, 47th Regiment. August 1, 1862 transferred to Co. A. 1st Battalion, Georgia Sharpshooters.

MELTON, HENRY C.: Company B, private, October 21, 1861 enlisted as a private in Co. K, 7th. Regiment, 1st Brigade, Georgia State Troops. April 20, 1862 mustered out at Camp Brown, Georgia. May 16, 1862 enlisted as a private in Co. B, 47th Regiment. July 30, 1862 transferred to Co. A. 1st Battalion, Georgia Sharpshooters. August 1964 roll, last on file shows him sick in hospital.

MELTON, WILLIAM P.: Company B, private, October 21, 1861 enlisted as a private in Co. F, 1st. Regiment, 1st Brigade, Georgia State Troops. April 20, 1862 mustered out at Camp Brown. May 16, 1862 enlisted as a private in Co. B, 47th Regiment. June 30, 1862 transferred to Co. A, 1st Battalion, Georgia Sharpshooters. August 1964 roll, last on record, shows him present.

MERCER, MALACHI: Company C, private, March 4, 1862 enlisted as a private in Co. C, 11th Battalion.

MERECR SAMUEL: Company I, 1st.corporal. March 4, 1862 enlisted as a private in Co. I, 11th Battalion. May 12, 1862 transferred to Co. I, 47th Regiment. Appointed 1st corporal. February 28, 1863 roll, last on record, shows him present.

METZGER, DAVID A.: Company I, private, March 4, 1862 enlisted as a private in Co. I, 11th Battalion. May 12, 1862 transferred to Co. I, 47th Regiment. September 20, 1863 killed at Chickamauga, Georgia.

METZGER, M. A.: Company I, private, March 4, 1862 enlisted as a private in Co. I, 11th Battalion. May 12, 1862 transferred to Co. I, 47th Regiment. September 20, 1863 killed at Chickamauga, Georgia.

MICHAEL, THOMAS HENRY: Company K, private, May 6, 1862 enlisted as a private in Co. K, 47th Regiment. June 10, 1862 severely wounded at James, Island, South Carolina. September 9, 1862 discharged at Savannah, Georgia.

MIKELL, ALEXANDER: Company C, private, March 4, 1862 enlisted as a private in Co. C, 11th Battalion. May 12, 1862 transferred to Co. C, 47th Regiment. October 21, 1862 discharged, under age. July 24, 1863 enlisted as a private in Co. E, 5th Regiment, Georgia Cavalry. December 31, 1864 roll, last on file, shows him absent without leave since December

1, 1864.

MIKELL, JOHN L.: Company C, private, March 4, 1862 enlisted as a private in Co. C, 11th Battalion. May 12, 1862 transferred to Co. C, 47th Regiment. June 10 1862 wounded in arm, necessitating amputation and captured James, Island, South Carolina. Sent from Fort Delaware, Delaware to Fortress Monroe, Virginia for exchange. December 18, 1862 received at City Point, Virginia. At home wounded at close of the war. Died in 1900.

MIKELL, M.: Company C, 2nd corporal, March 4, 1862 appointed 2nd corporal. Co. C, 11th Battalion. May 12, 1862 transferred to Co. C, 47th regiment as 2nd corporal. October 7, 1862 discharged, under age,

MILES, DANIEL: Company F, private, March 4, 1862 enlisted as a private in Co. F, 11th Battalion. May 12, 1862 transferred to Co. F, 47th Regiment. April 1865 pension records show he was wounded, shot through right arm and lung, while on detail hunting deserters at Coleman Creek, Appling County, Georgia. Was at home wounded at the close of the war. (Born in Georgia August 14, 1833 died in Appling County, Georgia August 1912)

MILES, WILLIS: Company F, private, April 29, 1862 enlisted as a private in Co. F, 11th Battalion. May 12, 1862 transferred to Co. F, 47th Regiment. August 1863 in Breckenridge's Division Hospital at Marion, Mississippi. Died of disease in South Carolina (near Augusta, Georgia. Buried near Waynesboro, Georgia) (Born in Georgia February 19, 1839 died circa 1864-1865)

MILLEM, JOSEPH: Field Staff, Musician, May 31, 1862 appointed Musician. December 1872 shows him present.

MILLER, LEWIS B.: Company B, private, April 25, 1862 enlisted as a private in Co. B, 11th Battalion. May 12, 1862 transferred to Co. B, 47th Regiment. November 1, 1862 transferred to Co. F, 32nd Regiment Georgia Infantry (name does not appear on the record of that company).

MILLER, E. O. (BURT O.): Company C, 2nd. Lieutenant, March18, 1861 enlisted as a private in Co. D, 1st Regiment, Georgia Infantry (Ramsey's). April 10, 1862 appointed 10th corporal of 1st. Co. A, 12th Battalion, Georgia Light Artillery. October 1862 transferred to Co. A, 63rd Regiment, Georgia infantry. February 1863 appointed 9th corporal. August 1863 appointed 2nd corporal. February 1864 appointed 1st corporal. (According to pension records) April 20, 1865 elected 2nd lieutenant Co. C, 47th Regiment. April 1865 was at home on furlough. May 9, 1865 paroled at Augusta, Georgia. (Resident of Georgia since 1841)

MILLER, HENRY: Company A, private, March 4, 1862 enlisted in Co. A, 11th Battalion as a private. May 12, 1862 transferred to Co. A, 47th Regiment. February 28, 1863 roll, last on file, shows him present.

MILLER, JAMES J.: Company K, 1st. Lieutenant, May 6, 1862 elected 1st Lieutenant Co. K, 47th Regiment. February 28, 1863 roll, last on record, shows him sick at Savannah, Georgia. June 22, 1863 "Dropped by General Stovall".

MILLER, J. R.: Company C, Jr. 2nd. Lieutenant, March 4, 1862 enlisted as a private in Co. C, 11th Battalion. May 12, 1862 transferred to Co. C, 47th Regiment. Appointed 1st sergeant. November 6, 1864 elected Jr. 2nd Lieutenant Co. C, 47th regiment. March 6, 1865 admitted to C. S. A. General Hospital #11 at Charlotte, North Carolina. April 18, 1865 furloughed.

MILLER, PENNY J.: Company B, private, October 9, 1861 enlisted as a private in Co. F, 1st. Regiment, 1st Brigade, Georgia State Troops. April 9, 1862 roll, last on file, shows him present. April 1862 mustered out. April 25, 1862 enlisted as a private in Co. B, 11th Battalion. May 12, 1862 transferred to Co. B, 47th Regiment. July 17, 1862 died of disease in Randolph County, Georgia.

MIMS, ELLIOTT E.: Company G, private, May 26, 1862 enlisted as a private in Co. G, 47th Regiment, Georgia Infantry. February 15, 1863 transferred to Co. F, 47th Regiment. Pension records show he was wounded, date and place not given, and was home wounded at the close of the war.

MINCEY, JAMES W.: Company C, private, March 4, 1862 enlisted as a private in Co. C, 11th Battalion. May 12, 1862 transferred to Co. C, 47th Regiment. September 17, 1862 discharged, under age.

MINCEY, WILLIAM W.: Company C, private, March 4, 1862 enlisted as a private in Co. C, 11th Battalion. May 12, 1862 transferred to Co. C, 47th Regiment. August 16, 1862(3) to January 10, 1864 on detached duty as a nurse in Breckenridge's Division Hospital at Marion, Mississippi.

MINIS, JOHN R.: Company A, sergeant major, July 25, 1861 elected Jr. 2nd Lieutenant of Captain J. B. Read's Independent Company, Georgia infantry. January 25, 1862 mustered out. February 27, 1862 appointed 2nd sergeant of Co A, 11th Battalion. April 1, 1862 appointed sergeant major of 11th Battalion. May 12, 1862 transferred to Co A., 47th Regiment as sergeant. July 1864 report shows he was detailed by order of General Johnston as "Pkg. and County Stores. Retained on sick furlough".

MINTON, JOSEPH M.: Company D, private, March 4, 1862 enlisted as a private in Co. D, 11th Battalion. May 12, 1862 transferred to Co. D, 47th Regiment. February 28, 1863 roll, last on record, shows him present. April 26, 1865 pension records show that he surrendered at Greensboro, North Carolina. (Born in Copiah County, Mississippi October 12, 1835. Died in Echols County, Georgia in 1910)

MITCHELL, DANIEL W.: Company D, private, March 4, 1862 enlisted as a private in Co. D, 11th Battalion. May 12, 1862 transferred to Co. D, 47th Regiment. February 28, 1863 roll, last on record, shows him present.

MITCHELL, W.: Company K, private, December 9, 1862 enlisted as a private in Co. K, 47th Regiment. February 28, 1863 roll, last on record, shows he deserted.

MOBLEY JAMES H.: Company D, private, March 4, 1862 enlisted as a private in Co. D, 11th Battalion. May 12, 1862 transferred to Co. D, 47th

Regiment. November 11, 1863 died at Atlanta, Georgia.

MOCK, GEORGE H.: Company D, private, March 4, 1862 enlisted as a private in Co. D, 11th Battalion. May 12, 1862 transferred to Co. D, 47th Regiment. February 28, 1863 roll, last on record, shows him present.

MOCK, JOHN BAPTIST, JR.: Company D, private, March 4, 1862 enlisted as a private in Co. D, 11th Battalion. May 12, 1862 transferred to Co. D, 47th Regiment. February 28, 1863 roll, last on record, shows him present. April 26, 1865 pension records show he surrendered Greensboro, North Carolina. (Born in Screven County, Georgia August 3, 1846)

MOCK, JOHN P.: Company D, private, March 4, 1862 enlisted as a private in Co. D, 11th Battalion. May 12, 1862 transferred to Co. D, 47th Regiment. May 18, 1865 paroled at Augusta, Georgia.

MOCK, JOSIAH M.: Company D, private, March 4, 1862 enlisted as a private in Co. D, 11th Battalion. May 12, 1862 transferred to Co. D, 47th Regiment. August 1863 in Kingston, Georgia Hospital.

MOCK, LOVICK G.: Company D, 3rd corporal, March 4, 1862 appointed 3rd Corporal Co. D, 11th Battalion. May 12, 1862 transferred to Co. C, 47th Regiment. February 28, 1863 roll, last on record, shows him present. April 12, 1865 to April 26, 1865 pension records show he was at home, disabled by rheumatism.

MOCK, WELLS J.: Company D, private. March 4, 1862 enlisted as a private in Co. D, 11th Battalion. May 12, 1862 transferred to Co. D, 47th Regiment. May 18, 1865 captured and paroled at Augusta, Georgia. Pension records show that on April 26, 1865 he surrendered at Greensboro, North Carolina. (Born in Georgia May 23, 1843)

MOODY, JAMES J.: Company H, private, March 4, 1862 enlisted as a private in Co. H, 11th Battalion. May 12, 1862 transferred to Co. H, 47th Regiment. February 28, 1863 roll, last on record, shows him present. April 26, 1865 pension records show he surrendered at Greensboro, North Carolina.

MOODY, WILLIAM F.: Company H, 4th sergeant, March 4, 1862 elected 4th sergeant Co. H, 11th Battalion. May 12, 1862 transferred to Co. H, 47th Regiment as 4th sergeant. November 12, 1862 died of disease in hospital.

MOON, WILLIAM M.: Company H, 1st Lieutenant, March 4, 1862 elected 1st Lieutenant Co. H, 11th Battalion. May 12, 1862 transferred to Co. H, 47th regiment as 1st Lieutenant. December 22, 1862 resigned his commission.

MOORE, ALFRED C.: Company G, private, October 1, 1862 enlisted as a private in Co. G, 47th Regiment, Georgia Infantry. Transferred to Co. H, 1st Georgia Regulars. April 26, 1865 surrendered at Greensboro, North Carolina. (Resident of Georgia since 1833).

MOORE, JOHN: Company B, private. October 1864 enlisted as a private in Co. B, 47th Regiment, Georgia Infantry. April 26, 1865 surrendered at Greensboro, North Carolina. (Born in Richmond County, Georgia September 12, 1823)

MOORE, THOMAS J.: Company D, private, March 4, 1862 enlisted as a private in Co. D, 11th Battalion. May 12, 1862 transferred to Co. D, 47th Regiment. November 1862 transferred to Co. D, 25th Regiment, Georgia Infantry. December 1, 1862 discharged, furnished Solomon Griffin as substitute.

MOORE, WILLIAM B.: Company E, private, April 1, 1862 enlisted as a private in Co. E, 11th Battalion. May 12, 1862 transferred to Co. E, 47th Regiment. June 1, 1862 discharged.

MORGAN, J. C.: Company I, private, March 4, 1862 enlisted as a private in Co. I, 11th Battalion. May 12, 1862 transferred to Co. I, 47th Regiment. June 10, 1863 died in Lauderdale Springs, Mississippi Hospital.

MORGAN, J. G.: Company I, sergeant, March 4, 1862 enlisted as a private in Co. I, 11th Battalion. May 12, 1862 transferred to Co. I, 47th Regiment. Appointed sergeant. September - October 1863 in Breckinridge's Division Hospital at Marion, Mississippi.

MORGAN, W. H.: Company I, private, March 4, 1862 enlisted as a private in Co. I, 11th Battalion. May 12, 1862 transferred to Co. I, 47th Regiment. February 28, 1863 roll, last on record, shows him present.

MORRELL, J. IRWIN: Company I, private, March 4, 1862 enlisted as a private in Co. I, 11th Battalion. May 12, 1862 transferred to Co. I, 47th Regiment. August 1, 1862 transferred to Co. A. 1st Battalion, Georgia Sharpshooters. (Died in Effingham County, Georgia March 20, 1864)

MORRIS, JESSE: Company H, private, January 8, 1863 enlisted as a private in Co. H, 47th Regiment. February 28, 1863 roll, last on record, shows him absent without leave.

MORRIS, ROBERT J.: Company B, private, May 7, 1862 enlisted as a private in Co. F, 32nd Regiment, Georgia Infantry. November 1, 1862 transferred to Co. B, 47th Regiment. February 19, 1863 discharged, furnished John Farrell as substitute.

MORRIS, WILLIAM: Company B, private, September 19, 1862 enlisted as a private in Co. B, 47th Regiment, Georgia Infantry. (Substitute for John R. Patterson). September 14, 1863 discharged, disability, at Lauderdale Springs, Mississippi. Died prior to March 21, 1864.

MORRISON, JAMES: Company A, private, March 1, 1862 enlisted in Co. A, 11th Battalion as a private. May 12, 1862 transferred to Co. A, 47th Regiment. October 31, 1862 discharged due to disability.

MORTON, D. M.: Company I, private, March 4, 1862 enlisted as a private in Co. I, 11th Battalion. May 12, 1862 transferred to Co. I, 47th Regiment. July 30, 1862 transferred to Co. A. 1st Battalion, Georgia Sharpshooters.

MOSELEY, C. T.: Company D, private, 1862 enlisted as a private in Co. D, 47th Regiment, Georgia Infantry. August 12, 1862 discharged furnished Hardee C. Thompson as substitute.

MOSELEY (MOSLEY), DENNIS: Company H, private, March 4, 1862 enlisted as a private in Co. H, 11th Battalion. May 12, 1862 transferred to Co. H, 47th Regiment. August 29, 1864 received pay.

MOSELEY (MOSLEY), JOHN H.: Company H, private, March 4, 1862 enlisted as a private in Co. H, 11th Battalion. May 12, 1862 transferred to Co. H, 47th Regiment. June 10, 1862 killed at James Island, South Carolina.

MOSELEY (MOSLEY), J. R.: Company H, private, March 4, 1862 enlisted as a private in Co. H, 11th Battalion. May 12, 1862 transferred to Co. H, 47th Regiment. February 28, 1863 roll, last on record, shows him " deserted , supposed to be at home". (Born in Montgomery County, Georgia in 1840)

MOSLEY (MOSLEY), MARTIN: Company H, private, March 4, 1862 enlisted as a private in Co. H, 11th Battalion. May 12, 1862 transferred to Co. H, 47th Regiment. November 25, 1863 captured at Missionary Ridge, Tennessee. February 1865 transferred from Rock Island, Illinois to Point Lookout, Maryland. February 15, 1865 transferred to James River, Virginia. Escaped. April 3, 1865 captured at Richmond, Virginia. May 28, 1865 in Jackson Hospital at Richmond, Virginia.

MULLINS, JONATHAN A.: Company B, private, March 4, 1862 enlisted as a private in Co. B, 11th Battalion. May 12, 1862 transferred to Co. B, 47th Regiment. August 1, 1862 transferred to Co. A. 1st Battalion, Georgia Sharpshooters. December 7, 1892 deserted from Camp Anderson, Georgia.

MULRYNE, THOMAS N.: Company E, 1st sergeant, March 4, 1862 appointed 3rd sergeant Co. E, 11th Battalion. May 12, 1862 transferred to Co. E, 47th Regiment as 3rd Sergeant. August 22, 1862 appointed 2nd sergeant Co. E, 47th Regiment. June 1863 appointed 1st sergeant Co. E, 47th Regiment. September 23, 1863 admitted to Floyd House and Ocmulgee Hospitals at Macon, Georgia. September 24, 1863 furloughed for 30 days.

MURDOCK, FELIN W.: Company B, private, April 25, 1862 enlisted as a private in Co. B, 11th Battalion. May 12, 1862 transferred to Co. B, 47th Regiment. July 13, 1863 died in a Mississippi Hospital.

MURDOCK, JOHN F.: Company B, private, April 25, 1862 enlisted as a private in Co. B, 11th Battalion. May 12, 1862 transferred to Co. B, 47th Regiment. August 1, 1862 transferred to Co. A. 1st Battalion, Georgia Sharpshooters. February 28, 1863 roll, last on record, shows him present.

MURDOCK, THOMAS J.: Company B, private, March 4, 1862 enlisted as a private in Co. B, 11th Battalion. May 12, 1862 transferred to Co. B, 47th Regiment. August 1, 1862 transferred to Co. A. 1st Battalion, Georgia Sharpshooters. June 5, 1863 died of Typhoid pneumonia at Savannah, Georgia.

MURPHEY (MURPHY), JOHN: Company G, 3rd sergeant, March 4, 1862 elected 3rd sergeant Co. G, 11th Battalion. May 12, 1862 transferred to Co. G, 47th Regiment as 5th sergeant. December 2, 1863 received pay.

MURPHEY, WILLIAM M.: Company B, private, April 25, 1862 enlisted as a private in Co. B, 11th Battalion. Absent without leave.

MYERS, CHARLES: Company H, private, March 4, 1862 enlisted as a private in Co. H, 11th Battalion. April 9, 1862 transferred to Co. A, 4th Regiment Georgia Cavalry (Clinch's). April 1863 Co. K, 4th Regiment, Georgia Cavalry (Clinch's), roll shows him present.

MYERS, TIMMONS: Company H, private, March 4, 1862 enlisted as a private in Co. H, 11th Battalion. Never reported.

NAIL, B. L.: Company G, private, December 5, 1862 enlisted in Savannah, Georgia as a private Co. G, 47th Regiment. January and February roll (last on record) shows him present: September 19, 1863 killed at Chickamauga, Georgia.

NAIL, REUBEN C.: Company F, private, March 4, 1862 enlisted as private in Appling County, Georgia in Company F, 11th Georgia Battalion. April 19, 1862 died at Camp Davis, Effingham County, Georgia.

NEELY, J. S.: Company A, private, May 1, 1862 enlisted in Co. A, 11th Battalion as a private. May 12, 1862 transferred to Co. A, 47th Regiment. June 1, 1862 discharged, furnished Patrick White as substitute.

NELSON, R. D.: Company B, private, 1864 enlisted as a private in Co. B, 47th Regiment, Georgia Infantry (according to pension records). April 1865 paroled at Bentonville, North Carolina.

NESSMITH, A.: Company K, private, May 6, 1862 enlisted as a private in Co. K, 47th Regiment. September 9, 1863 captured at Cumberland Gap, Tennessee. October 24, 1863 died of inflammation of lungs at Camp Douglas, Illinois as a POW.

NESSMITH, E. L.: Company K, private, May 6, 1862 enlisted as a private in Co. K, 47th Regiment. October 29, 1863 died at Atlanta, Georgia. Buried there in Oakland Cemetery.

NESSMITH, JAMES: Company K, private, October 15, 1861 enlisted as a private of Co. G, 5th Regiment, Georgia State Troops. April 1862 mustered out. May 6, 1862 enlisted as a private in Co. K, 47th Regiment. October 2, 1863 examined by Medical Board at Dalton, Georgia for furlough on account of tuberculosis. (Born in Bulloch, County, Georgia in 1836)

NESSMITH, SOVEREIGN: Company K, private, May 15, 1862 enlisted as a private in Co. K, 47th Regiment. February 23, 1863 transferred to Co. H, 7th Regiment, Georgia Cavalry. April 9, 1865 surrendered at Appomattox Courthouse, Virginia. (Died in Bulloch County, Georgia March 13, 1911)

NESBIT, J.: Company K, private, June 3, 1862 enlisted (as substitute for W. A. Sheffield) as a private in Co. K, 47th Regiment.

NEVE, HENRY T.: Company E, private, April 3, 1862 enlisted as a private in Co. E, 11th Battalion. May 12, 1862 transferred to Co. E, 47th Regiment. June 10, 1862 killed at James Island, South Carolina.

NEWBORN, JACKSON: Company G, private, March 4, 1862 elected 1st Corporal Co. G, 11th Battalion. May 12, 1862 transferred to Co. F, 47th Regiment, Georgia Infantry. September 20, 1863 wounded at Chickamauga, Georgia. December 11, 1863 died of wounds. (Also appears as Newbern and Newburn)

NEWBY, W. H.: Company H, private, March 4, 1862 enlisted as a private in Co. H, 11th Battalion. May 12, 1862 transferred to Co. H, 47th Regiment. August 1862 discharged, furnished substitute.

NEWMAN (NEWMANS), ANDREW J.: Company G, private, March 4, 1862 enlisted as a private in Co. G, 11th Battalion. May 12, 1862 transferred to Co. G, 47th Regiment. August 1, 1862 transferred to Co. A. 1st Battalion, Georgia Sharpshooters. December 12, 1862 died of Typhoid Pneumonia at Camp Anderson, Georgia.

NEWMAN, EBENEZER: Company E, private, April 20, 1862 enlisted as a private in Co. E, 11th Battalion. May 12, 1862 transferred to Co. E, 47th Regiment. October 31, 1863 roll, last on record, shows him present.

NEWMAN, IRA J.: Company E, private, March 4, 1862 enlisted as a private in Co. E, 11th Battalion. April 30, 1862 shows he reported with certificate of 3 months inability from Dr. B. W. Hardee.

NEWMAN, JESSE: Company E, private, March 4, 1862 enlisted as a private in Co. E, 11th Battalion. May 12, 1862 transferred to Co. E, 47th Regiment. October 31, 1863 roll, last on record, shows him present.

NEWMAN, JOHN M. F.: Company E, private, April 24, 1862 enlisted as a private in Co. E, 11th Battalion. May 12, 1862 transferred to Co. E, 47th Regiment. February 3, 1865 captured at Rivers Bridge, South Carolina. April 16, 1865 died of chronic diarrhea in Douglas U. S. A. General Hospital at Washington, D. C as a POW.

NEWSON, JOEL: Company C, private, July 22, 1862 enlisted as a private in Co. C, 47th Regiment, Georgia Infantry. November 25, 1863 captured at Missionary Ridge, Tennessee. June 22, 1865 released at Rock Island, Illinois.

NICHOLSON, JOHN: Company A, private, March 4, 1862 enlisted in Co. A, 11th Battalion as a private. May 12, 1862 transferred to Co. A, 47th Regiment. February 28, 1863 shows he was detailed to Miller's Foundry, Confederate States Government Workshop. May 11, 1863 on detail as blacksmith at Camp Allen, South Carolina.

NIGHTON, DANIEL: Company H, private, March 4, 1862 enlisted as a private in Co. H, 11th Battalion. May 12, 1862 transferred to Co. H, 47th Regiment. July 16, 1862 died.

NORTON, ROBERT GODFRED: Company I, 2nd Lieutenant, March 4, 1862 elected 1st sergeant Co. I, 11th Battalion. May 12, 1862 transferred to Co. I, 47th regiment as Jr. 2nd Lieutenant. October 1862 on General Harrison's Staff. February 18, 1863 elected 2nd Lieutenant Co. I, 47th Regiment. February 28, 1863 roll, last on record, shows him on special service. August 25, 1865 paroled in Augusta, Georgia.

NUNGAZER, WILLIAM B.: Company I, private, November 19, 1862 enlisted as private in the 47th Regiment at Camp Williams, Georgia. January-February 1863 roll, last on record, shows him present. September 20, 1863 wounded at Chickamauga, Georgia.

O'BRIEN, JAMES: Company A, private, March 3, 1862 enlisted in Co.

A, 11th Battalion as a private. May 12, 1862 transferred to Co. A, 47th Regiment. July 22-October 1863 in Breckenridge's Division Hospital #1, at Lauderdale Springs, Mississippi.

O'CALLAGHAN, MICHAEL: Company A, private, March 10, 1862 enlisted in Co. A, 11th Battalion as a private. May 12, 1862 transferred to Co. A, 47th Regiment. December 17, 1862 discharged, disability by asthma.

ODAM, HENRY Q.: Company B, private, March 4, 1862 enlisted as a private in Co. B, 11th Battalion. Absent without leave.

ODOM, JOHN C.: Company D, private, March 4, 1862 enlisted as a private in Co. D, 11th Battalion. May 12, 1862 transferred to Co. D, 47th Regiment. February 28, 1863 roll, last on record, shows him present. (Born in Screven County, Georgia February 6, 1828)

OGILVIE, P. S. S.: Company D, private, March 4, 1862 enlisted as a private in Co. D, 11th Battalion. May 12, 1862 transferred to Co. D, 47th Regiment. May 31, 1862 died at Savannah, Georgia Hospital.

O'LEARY, PATRICK: Company A, private, March 3, 1862 enlisted in Co. A, 11th Battalion as a private. May 12, 1862 transferred to Co. A, 47th Regiment. February 28, 1863 roll, last on record, shows he was left sick in Regimental Hospital at Savannah, Georgia.

OLIFF, OWEN: Company C, private, March 4, 1862 enlisted as a private in Co. C, 11th Battalion. May 12, 1862 transferred to Co. C, 47th Regiment. February 28, 1863 roll, last on record, shows him present.

OLIVER, ELIJAH: Company D, private, March 4, 1862 enlisted as a private in Co. D, 11th Battalion. May 12, 1862 transferred to Co. D, 47th Regiment. May 12, 1862 died in Savannah, Georgia Hospital.

OLIVER, JACOB: Company G, private, March 4, 1862 enlisted as a private in Co. G, 11th Battalion. May 12, 1862 transferred to Co. G, 47th Regiment. May 16, 1864 captured at Tanner's Ferry, Georgia. February 1864 Paroled for exchange. March 6 or 9, 1865 received at Boulware & Cox's Wharves, James River, Virginia. March 10, 1865 sick in 3rd Division General Hospital at Camp Winder, Richmond, Virginia. (Born in Emanuel County, Georgia, May 5, 1838)

OLIVER, JOHN C.: Company B, private, March 4, 1862 enlisted as a private in Co. B, 11th Battalion. Absent without leave.

OLIVER, JOHN H.: Company D, private, March 6, 1862 enlisted as a private in Co. D, 11th Battalion. May 12, 1862 transferred to Co. D, 47th Regiment. August 31, 1863 roll for Breckenridge's Division Hospital #2 at Lauderdale Springs, Mississippi shows him present.

OLIVER, MCDANIEL: Company D, private, March 4, 1862 enlisted as a private in Co. D, 11th Battalion. May 12, 1862 transferred to Co. D, 47th Regiment. February 28, 1863 roll, last on record, shows him present. (Born in Screven County, Georgia April 11, 1820)

OLIVER, ROBERT: Field Staff, Musician, May 31, 1862 appointed Musician. December 1862 shows him present.

O'NEAL, DANIEL C.: Company G, private, March 4, 1862 enlisted as a private in Co. G, 11th Battalion. May 12, 1862 transferred to Co. G, 47th Regiment. February 28, 1863 roll, last on record, shows him present.

O'NEAL, JAMES JACKSON: Company H, private, March 4, 1862 enlisted as a private in Co. H, 11th Battalion. May 12, 1862 transferred to Co. H, 47th Regiment. February 28, 1863 roll, last on record, shows him present. (Born in North Carolina in 1839)

O'NEAL, WILLIAM H. H.: Company G, private, March 4, 1862 enlisted as a private in Co. G, 11th Battalion. May 12, 1862 transferred to Co. G, 47th Regiment. November 29, 1863 admitted to Floyd House and Ocmulgee Hospitals at Macon, Georgia with intermittent fever.

OSTEEN, MAXIMILLIAN D.: Company E, 4th corporal, March 4, 1862 enlisted as a private in Co. E, 11th Battalion. May 12, 1862 transferred to Co. E, 47th Regiment. July 1862 appointed 4th Corporal Co. E, 47th Georgia Regiment.

OSTEEN, SOLOMON W. (T.): Company E, private, March 4, 1862 enlisted as a private in Co. E, 11th Battalion. May 12, 1862 transferred to Co. E, 47th Regiment. January 28, 1863 died in General Hospital #1, Savannah, Georgia.

OSTEEN, THOMAS J.: Company E, 1st. Lieutenant, March 4, 1862 appointed Jr. 2nd Lieutenant, Co. E, 11th Battalion. May 12, 1862 transferred to Co. E, 47th Regiment as Jr. 2nd Lieutenant. July 18, 1862 elected 2nd Lieutenant Co. E, 47th Regiment. May 14, 1864 elected 1st Lieutenant Co. E, 47th Regiment. April 9, 1865 pension records show he was granted 60 days leave of absence.

OWENS, WILLIAM P.: Company D, private, March 4, 1862 enlisted as a private in Co. D, 11th Battalion. May 12, 1862 transferred to Co. D, 47th Regiment. February 28, 1863 roll, last on record, shows him present. April 26, 1865 pension records show he surrendered at Greensboro, North Carolina. (Born in Screven County, Georgia December 1844)

OXLEY, HARDY F.: Company B, private, April 25, 1862 enlisted as a private in Co. B, 11th Battalion. May 12, 1862 transferred to Co. B, 47th Regiment. February 18, 1864 discharged on account of heart trouble. (Born in Kinston, North Carolina April 21, 1832 - Died in Worth County, Georgia May 19, 1899)

OXLEY, WILLIAM B.: Company B, 4th sergeant, March 4, 1862 appointed 5th sergeant Co. B. 11 Battalion. May 12, 1862 transferred to Co. B, 47th Regiment as 5th sergeant. January 1, 1863 appointed 4th sergeant Co. B, 47th Regiment. February 21, 1863 died Regiment Hospital, Savannah, Georgia.

OZIER, ROBERT G.: Company B, private, April 25, 1862 enlisted as a private in Co. B, 11th Battalion. November 21, 1863 admitted to Floyd House and Ocmulgee Hospital with diarrhea. February 18, 1864 discharged from hospital. November 1864 pension records show he was discharged on account of heart disease. (Born in Kinston, North Carolina

April 21, 1862)

PARKER, JOHN C.: Company G, 1st Lieutenant, March 4, 1862 enlisted as a private in Co. G, 11th Battalion. May 12, 1862 transferred to Co. G, 47th Regiment as 3rd sergeant. August 1, 1862 appointed 1st sergeant Co. G, 47th Regiment. December 8, 1862 elected Jr. 2nd Lieutenant Co. G, 47th Regiment. June 25, 1863 elected 1st Lieutenant Co. G, 47th Regiment. June 20, 1864 Parker wounded at Kennesaw Mountain, Georgia. March 1865 appears on roster dated this date. (Born in Georgia)

PARKER, WILLIAM: Company B, private, March 4, 1862 enlisted as a private in Co. B, 11th Battalion. May 12, 1862 transferred to Co. B, 47th Regiment. May 5, 1864 died of pneumonia, Fair Ground Hospital #2, Atlanta. Buried there in Oakland Cemetery.

PARKERSON, MICHAEL C.: Company B, private, March 4, 1862 enlisted as a private in Co. B, 11th Battalion. May 12, 1862 transferred to Co. B, 47th Regiment. Subsequent to February 28, 1863 died.

PARRISH, HEZEKIAH J.: Company C, private, March 4, 1862 enlisted as a private in Co. C, 11th Battalion. May 12, 1862 transferred to Co. C, 47th Regiment. November 25, 1863 captured Missionary Ridge, Tennessee (also shown as Chattanooga, Tennessee December 25, 1863). January 10, 1864 died of Typhoid Malarial Fever in Military Prison Hospital at Louisville, Kentucky as a POW. Grave # 69, Range #2, Cave Hill Cemetery.

PARRISH, WILLIAM: Company C, private, March 4, 1862 enlisted as a private in Co. C, 11th Battalion. May 12, 1862 transferred to Co. C, 47th Regiment. September 19, 1863 wounded Chickamauga, Georgia. March 19, 1865 admitted to C. S. A. General Hospital at Greensboro, North Carolina. March 24, 1865 died of pneumonia General Hospital #3, High Point, North Carolina.

PARSONS, C. C.: Company H, private, March 4, 1862 enlisted as a private in Co. H, 11th Battalion. May 12, 1862 transferred to Co. H, 47th Regiment. February 28, 1863 roll, last on record, shows him present. April 26, 1865 surrendered at Greensboro, North Carolina.

PATTERSON, JAMES S.: Company F, 1st. Lt, March 4, 1862 elected 2nd Lt Co. F, 11th Battalion. May 12, 1862 transferred to Co. F, 47th Regiment as 2nd Lieutenant. October 23, 1863 elected 1st Lieutenant Co. F, 47th Regiment. Pension records show he was on furlough at close of the war.

PATTERSON, JOHN K.: Company B, private, April 25, 1862 enlisted as a private in Co. B, 11th Battalion. May 12, 1862 transferred to Co. B, 47th Regiment. September 19, 1862 discharged furnished William Morris as substitute.

PEEVY (PEAVY), GUILFORD: Company I, private, March 10, 1862 enlisted as a private in Co. I, 11th Battalion. May 12, 1862 transferred to Co. I, 47th Regiment. October 15, 1862 discharged, under age and disability at Montgomery, Alabama.

PEEVY (PEAVY), HENRY: Company I, private, November 28, 1862 enlisted as a private in Co. I, 47th Regiment. February 1863 roll, last on record, shows him present.

PEEVY (PEAVY), JAMES: Company I, private, March 4, 1862 enlisted as a private in Co. I, 11th Battalion. May 12, 1862 transferred to Co. I, 47th Regiment. December 12, 1863 died in Griffin, Georgia Hospital.

PEEVY (PEAVY), MILTON: Company I, private, March 4, 1862 enlisted as a private in Co. I, 11th Battalion. May 12, 1862 transferred to Co. I, 47th Regiment. February 28, 1863 roll, last on record, shows him present.

PEEVY (PEAVY), THOMAS: Company I, private, 1862 enlisted as a private in Co. I, 47th Regiment, Georgia Infantry. September 8, 1864 paid for services from March 1, 1863 to August 31, 1863. Pension records show he was on detached duty caring for horses at the close of the war. (Born in Screven County, Georgia 1832. Died in Effingham County, Georgia in 1910)

PETERSON, A. M. F.: Company H, private, pension records show he enlisted as a private in Co. H, 47th Regiment and April 26, 1865 surrendered at Greensboro, North Carolina. (Born in Montgomery County, Georgia January 13, 1833)

PETERSON, ARCHIBALD: Company H, 5th sergeant, May 16, 1862 enlisted as a private in Co. H, 47th Regiment. June 1862 appointed 5th sergeant Co. H, 47th Regiment. May 23, 1864 admitted to Ocmulgee Hospital at Macon, Georgia. May 28, 1864 transferred.

PETERSON, JAMES J.: Company D, private, March 4, 1862 enlisted as a private in Co. D, 11th Battalion. May 12, 1862 transferred to Co. D, 47th Regiment. September 19, 1863 wounded at Chickamauga, Georgia. October 31, 1863 in Kingston, Georgia Hospital. Pension records show he was totally disabled by wounds. (Born in Georgia July 14, 1845)

PETERSON, GEORGE W.: Company H, private, March 4, 1862 enlisted as a private in Co. H, 11th Battalion. May 12, 1862 transferred to Co. H, 47th Regiment. February 28, 1863 roll, last on record, shows him present. April 26, 1865 pension records show he surrendered at Greensboro, North Carolina. (Born in Montgomery County, Georgia March 22, 1840)

PHILLIPS, GABRIEL J.: Company B, 5th sergeant, March 4, 1862 appointed 2nd corporal Co. B, 11th Battalion. May 12, 1862 transferred to Co. B, 47th Regiment as 2nd Corporal. January 1, 1863 appointed 5th sergeant Co. B, 47th Regiment. October 31, 1863 received pay.

PHILLIPS, JESSE: Company K, private, October 15, 1861 enlisted as a private of Co. G, 5th Regiment, Georgia State Troops. April 1862 mustered out. May 6, 1862 enlisted as a private in Co. K, 47th Regiment. December 9, 1863 died in Polk Hospital., Rome Georgia.

PHILLIPS, ONESIMUS: Company K, private, May 6, 1862 enlisted as a private in Co. K, 47th Regiment. March 25, 1864 admitted to Ocmulgee Hospital at Macon, Georgia with epilepsy. June 5, 1864 transferred, place not stated. (Born in Bryan County, Georgia June 1, 1835)

PHILLIPS, WILLIAM S.: Field Staff, Lieutenant Colonel, March 4, 1862 appointed Captain Co. E, 11th Battalion. May 12, 1862 transferred to Co. E, 47th Regiment as Captain. May 14, 1863 elected Major 47th Regiment. August 30, 1863 elected Lieutenant Colonel 47th Regiment. November 5, 1864 retired to Invalid Corps. February 7, 1865 assigned to duty.

PILES, HENRY W.: Company H, private, March 4, 1862 enlisted as a private in Co. H, 11th Battalion. Never reported to camp.

PINHOLSTER, ANDREW J.: Company H, 5th corporal, March 4, 1862 elected 5th corporal Co. H, 11th Battalion. May 12, 1862 transferred to Co. H, 47th Regiment as 5th Corporal. September 21, 1862 died of disease in Savannah, Georgia Hospital.

PIPER, ANTONIO: Company A, private, February 27, 1862 enlisted in Co. A, 11th Battalion as a private. May 12, 1862 transferred to Co. A, 47th Regiment. March 1, 1865 reported to the Provost Marshall General, District of Savannah, Georgia. March 8, 1865 took oath of allegiance to the United States Government at Savannah, Georgia.

PITTS, JOHN D.: Company I, private, September 18, 1862 enlisted as a private in Co. I, 47th Regiment, Georgia Infantry. February 1863 roll, last on record, shows him absent without leave.

PLATE, JOHN H.: Company E, private, March 4, 1862 enlisted as a private in Co. E, 11th Battalion. March 27, 1862 absent without leave.

POMEROY, ABNER R.: Company I, private, March 4, 1862 enlisted as a private in Co. I, 11th Battalion. May 12, 1862 transferred to Co. I, 47th Regiment. February 25, 1863 transferred to Company E, 47th Regiment, Georgia Infantry. May 17, 1864 captured at Calhoun, Georgia. October 25, 1864 took oath of allegiance to the United States Government at Rock Island Illinois and was released.

POPE, ALEXANDER: Company H, private, May 1, 1862 enlisted as a private in Co. H, 11th Battalion. May 12, 1862 transferred to Co. H, 47th Regiment. September 19, 1863 killed at Chickamauga, Georgia.

POTTER, MATTHEW M.: Company D, 1st Lieutenant, August 28, 1861 enlisted as a private in Co. D, 25th Regiment, Georgia infantry. September 5, 1863 elected 1st Lieutenant of Co. D, 47th Georgia. March 1865 appears on roll.

POWELL, LEWIS (LOUIS) K.: Company D, private, March 4, 1862 enlisted as a private in Co. D, 11th Battalion. May 12, 1862 transferred to Co. D, 47th Regiment. July 2, 1862 discharged due to disability. July 26, 1863 enlisted as a private in Co. F, 5th Regiment, Georgia Cavalry. (Died February 9, 1934. Buried at Sylvania, Georgia)

POWERS, HORACE: Company B, private, March 4, 1862 enlisted as a private in Co. B, 11th Battalion. May 12, 1862 transferred to Co. B, 47th Regiment. March 20, 1863 on detached service, Macon Georgia Armory.

POWERS, JOHN: Company A, private, April 15, 1862 enlisted in Co. A, 11th Battalion as a private. May 12, 1862 transferred to Co. A, 47th Regiment. November 26, 1863 captured at Chattanooga, Tennessee. January 25, 1864 enlisted in the United States Navy at Rock Island, Illinois and transferred to naval Rendezvous at Camp Douglas, Illinois.

POYTHRESS, JOHN M.: Company D, private, March 4, 1862 enlisted as a private in Co. D, 11th Battalion. May 12, 1862 transferred to Co. D, 47th Regiment. February 28, 1863 roll, last on record, shows him present.

PRATHER, THOMAS: Company B, private, March 4, 1862 enlisted as a private in Co. B, 11th Battalion.

PRESCOTT, E. J. W.: Company D, private, March 4, 1862 enlisted as a private in Co. D, 11th Battalion. May 12, 1862 transferred to Co. D, 47th Regiment. September - October 1862 roll bears remark "Isham Hisely substituted for month of September".

PRESCOTT, HIRAM D.: Company D, 3rd. corporal, March 4, 1862 enlisted as a private in Co. D, 11th Battalion. May 12, 1862 transferred to Co. D, 47th Regiment as 3rd corporal. September 1, 1862 discharged, furnished John Coleman as substitute.

PRESCOTT, JESSE: Company F, private, March 4, 1862 enlisted as a private in Co. F, 11th Battalion. May 12, 1862 transferred to Co. F, 47th Regiment. Returns for 1862 show him absent, assisting Enrolling officer.

PRICE, GEORGE W.: Company H, private, March 4, 1862 enlisted as a private in Co. H, 11th Battalion. May 12, 1862 transferred to Co. H, 47th Regiment. December 15, 1863 received pay at Marietta, Georgia.

PRICE, RICHARD F.: Company H, 5th sergeant, March 4, 1862 elected 5th sergeant Co. H, 11th Battalion. May 12, 1862 transferred to Co. H, 47th Regiment as 5th sergeant. Appears on Register of General Hospital #1, at Savannah, Georgia with remarks "chronic bronchitis and anemia". February 9, 1863 transferred to Macon, Georgia hospital. Died in service.

PRIDGEN, JAMES: Company C, private, March 4, 1862 enlisted as a private in Co. C, 11th Battalion. May 12, 1862 transferred to Co. C, 47th Regiment. November 25, 1863 captured Missionary Ridge, Tennessee. December 26, 1863 died at Rock Island, Illinois as a POW.

PRINE, L. M.: Company C, 5th sergeant, March 4, 1862 enlisted as a private in Co. C, 11th Battalion. May 12, 1862 transferred to Co. C, 47th Regiment. June 1862 appointed 5th sergeant. Wounded date and time not specified. December 21, 1864 captured Savannah, Georgia. June 10, 1865 released from Fort Delaware, Delaware.

PROCTOR, A. J.: Company K, private, May 6, 1862 enlisted as a private in Co. K, 47th Regiment. June 10, 1862 wounded at James Island, South Carolina. March 4, 1864 in Blackie Hospital at Madison, Georgia.

PROCTOR, DAVID C.: Company C, Jr. 2nd Lieutenant, August 15, 1861 enlisted as a private in Co. I, 9th Regiment, Georgia Infantry. October 5, 1861 sent to Richmond, Virginia Hospital. December 1861 discharged in Virginia. March 4, 1862 elected Jr. 2nd Lieutenant Co. C, 11th Battalion. May 12, 1862 transferred to Co. C, 47th Regiment as Jr. 2nd Lieutenant. November 6, 1862 resigned Commission.

PROCTOR, ELI C.: Company K, private, May 6, 1862 enlisted as a private in Co. K, 47th Regiment. November 23, 1863 captured at Missionary

Ridge, Tennessee. March 19, 1864 died of typhoid fever at Fort Delaware, Delaware as a POW.

PROCTOR, J. W.: Company K, 4th sergeant, May 6, 1862 appointed 4th sergeant Co. K, 47th Regiment. February 28, 1863 roll, last on record, shows him present.

PURCELL, NATHAN R.: Company H, private, June 1862 enlisted as a private in Co. H, 47th Regiment. August 23, 1863 died in Lauderdale Springs Hospital, Mississippi.

PURCELL, NATHAN ROBERT: Company H, private, March 4, 1862 enlisted as a private in Co. H, 11th Battalion. May 12, 1862 transferred to Co. H, 47th Regiment. February 28, 1863 roll, last on record, shows him absent, sick. 1863 died of chronic dysentery at Jackson, Mississippi.

PURVIS, ANDREW: Company E, private, March 4, 1862 enlisted as a private in Co. E, 11th Battalion. May 12, 1862 transferred to Co. E, 47th Regiment. October 31, 1863 roll, last on record, shows him present.

PUTRILL, JOHN JOSEPH: Company A, 2nd. Lieutenant. August 27, 1861 enlisted as a private in Captain J. B. Read's Independent Company, Georgia Infantry. January 25, 1862 mustered out. February 27, 1862 enlisted in Co. A, 11th Battalion as a private. May 12, 1862 transferred to Co. A, 47th Regiment. February 4, 1864 elected Jr. 2nd Lieutenant Co. A, 47th Regiment. December 24, 1864 resigned commission. January 27, 1865 resignation accepted. March 1, 1865 reported to the office of Provost Marshall General, District of Savannah, Georgia. March 8, 1865 took oath of allegiance to the United States Government, at Savannah, Georgia.

QUIGLEY, DENNIS.: Company A, private, March 1, 1862 enlisted in Co. A, 11th Battalion as a private. May 12, 1862 transferred to Co. A, 47th Regiment. February 3, 1865 captured at River's Bridge, South Carolina. Remarks. "Claims to have given himself up. Was not bearing arms at time of capture." April 5, 1865 received by provost Marshal General, Washington, D. C. Took oath of allegiance and furnished transportation to Savannah, Georgia.

QUINN, HENRY: Company A, private, March 27, 1862 enlisted in Co. A, 11th Battalion as a private. May 12, 1862 transferred to Co. A, 47th Regiment. September 25, 1863 deserted. Captured at Chattanooga, Tennessee. October 17, 1863 took oath of allegiance to the United States Government, and released to go north of Ohio River.

QUINN, MATHIAS: Company F, private, March 4, 1862 enlisted as a private in Co. F, 11th Battalion. May 12, 1862 transferred to Co. F, 47th Regiment. October 31, 1862 detailed to gather conscripts.

RAGAN, THOMAS A.: Company B, private, October 9, 1861 enlisted as a private in Co. K, 7th. Regiment, 1st Brigade, Georgia State Troops. April 9, 1862 roll, last on file, shows him present. April 20, 1862 mustered out at Camp Brown, Georgia. April 25, 1862 enlisted as a private in Co. B, 11th Battalion. May 12, 1862 transferred to Co. B, 47th Regiment. August 1, 1862 transferred to Co. A. 1st Battalion, Georgia Sharpshooters. August

1864 Roll, last on record, shows him absent without leave. (Also appears as Reagan and Reagin)

RAHN, J. R.: Company I, private, June 1864 enlisted as a private in Co. I, 47th Regiment, Georgia Infantry. February 12, 1865 "went home on furlough." (Born in Effingham County, Georgia in 1829)

RAHN, T. M.: Company I, private, March 4, 1862 enlisted as a private in Co. I, 11th Battalion. May 12, 1862 transferred to Co. I, 47th Regiment. February 28, 1863 roll, last on record, shows him present.

RAMBO, JOHN: Field Staff, Surgeon, June 1, 1862 appointed. Surgeon P. A. C. S. of 47th Regiment. September 17, 1862 dropped as surgeon of 47th Regiment due to physical disability.

RAY, ARTHUR: Company F, private, March 4, 1862 enlisted as a private in Co. F, 11th Battalion. May 12, 1862 transferred to Co. F, 47th Regiment. November 30, 1864 wounded at Honey Hill, South Carolina. December 21, 1864 captured at Savannah, Georgia. June 10, 1865 released at Fort Delaware, Delaware. (Born in Telfair County, Georgia October 25, 1832)

RAY, WILLIAM: Company F, private, March 4, 1862 enlisted as a private in Co. F, 11th Battalion. May 12, 1862 transferred to Co. F, 47th Regiment. October 17, 1863 died in Atlanta, Georgia and buried in Oakland Cemetery.

RAYE, THOMAS: Company E, private, September 10, 1862 enlisted as a private in Co. E, 47th Regiment, Georgia Infantry. Deserted same day.

REED, JAMES B.: Company A, 1st corporal, March 4, 1862 enlisted in Co. A, 11th Battalion as a private. May 12, 1862 transferred to Co. A, 47th Regiment. September 1, 1862 appointed. 4th corporal. Co. A, 47th Regiment. February 1863 appointed 1st corporal. Co. A, 47th Regiment. February 1863 in Breckenridge's Division Hospital at Marion, Mississippi.

REILLY, JOHN: Company A, private, March 3, 1862 enlisted in Co. A, 11th Battalion as a private. May 12, 1862 transferred to Co. A, 47th Regiment. December 1862 detailed to Gun Boat. October 1863 in hospital.

REILLY, MICHAEL: Company A, 1st. sergeant, August 10, 1861 enlisted as a private in Co. A, 1st Regiment, Georgia Infantry (Olmstead's). February 27, 1862 appointed. 1st sergeant Co. A, 11th Battalion. May 12, 1862 transferred, to 47th Regiment as 1st sergeant Co. A, October 1, 1862 transferred to Captain Jacob Read's Company, Georgia Light Artillery. October 1864 Maxwell's Battery, Georgia Light Artillery roll shows him present.

RENTZ, AARON MEADOWS: Company F, private, March 4, 1862 enlisted as a private in Co. F, 11th Battalion. May 12, 1862 transferred to Co. F, 47th Regiment. February 3, 1865 captured at River's Bridge, South Carolina. June 17, 1865 released at Point Lookout, Maryland.

RENTZ, GEORGE: Company F, private, 1862 enlisted as a private in Co. F, 47th Regiment, Georgia Infantry. Died at Macon, Georgia in 1863 or 1864 buried in Rose Hill Cemetery, Macon, Georgia

RENTZ, JOSEPH M. (W.): Company F, private, April 1863 enlisted as a private in Co. F, 47th Regiment, Georgia Infantry. Was at home on furlough at the close of the war. (Born in South Carolina. Died in Appling County, Georgia January 13, 1934.)

REWIS, SOLOMON: Company G, private, pension records show April 1864 he enlisted as a private in Co. G, 47th Regiment, Georgia Infantry. February 8, 1865 captured at Rivers' Bridge, South Carolina. April 1865 paroled at Fayetteville, North Carolina. (Born in Georgia. Died in Colquitt County, Georgia in 1923)

REYNOLDS, EDWARD: Company D, private, September 6, 1862 enlisted as a private (substitute for John H, Mears) in Co. D, 47th Regiment, Georgia Infantry. October 24, 1862 deserted from camp near Savannah, Georgia.

REYNOLDS, JAMES: Company A, private. September 4, 1862 enlisted in Co. A, 47th Regiment as a private. December 26, 1864 deserted at Savannah, Georgia.

RICHARDSON, ALEXANDER: Company K, private, October 15, 1861 enlisted as a private of Co. G, 5th Regiment, Georgia State Troops. April 1862 mustered out. May 6, 1862 enlisted as a private in Co. K, 47th Regiment. February 28, 1863 roll shows him sick in Savannah, Georgia hospital.

RICHARDSON, HENRY: Company K, private, May 6, 1862 enlisted as a private in Co. K, 47th Regiment. February 1863 sick in Macon, Georgia Hospital. Pension records show he was on sick furlough at the close of the war.

RICHARDSON, JAMES O.: Company H, 2nd sergeant, March 4, 1862 enlisted as a private in Co. H, 11th Battalion. May 12, 1862 transferred to Co. H, 47th Regiment. October 15, 1862 appointed 2nd sergeant Co. H, 47th Regiment. February 28, 1863 roll, last on record, shows him present. 1865 pension records show he surrendered at Charlotte, North Carolina. (Born in New York in 1835)

RICHARDSON, JAMES M.: Company B, private, enlisted as a private in Co. B, 47th Regiment, Georgia Infantry. December 1864 according to pension records he was wounded Pocotaligo, South Carolina (wounded in the leg necessitating amputation above the knee)

RICHARDSON, P. C.: Company K, private, May 6, 1862 enlisted as a private in Co. K, 47th Regiment. June 10, 1862 wounded at James Island, South Carolina. February 28, 1863 roll, last on record, shows him present.

RICHARDSON, STEPHEN: Company K, private, May 6, 1862 enlisted as a private in Co. K, 47th Regiment. December 31, 1862 discharged due to disability prior to this date.

RIGDON, ADAM W.: Company F, private, March 4, 1862 enlisted as a private in Co. F, 11th Battalion. May 12, 1862 transferred to Co. F, 47th Regiment. October 13, 1863 admitted to Floyd House and Ocmulgee

Hospitals at Macon, Georgia. October 24, 1863 furloughed for 30 days. July 1864 pension records show he was wounded in finger, resulting in amputation. (Born in Appling County, Georgia December 26, 1830)

RIGDON, GREEN BERRY: Company F, private, March 4, 1862 enlisted as a private in Co. F, 11th Battalion. May 12, 1862 transferred to Co. F, 47th Regiment. May 8, 1865 paroled, Charlotte, North Carolina.

RIGGS, HARMON O.: Company C, 4th corporal, March 4, 1862 enlisted as a private in Co. C, 11th Battalion. May 12, 1862 transferred to Co. C, 47th Regiment. November 1862 appointed 4th corporal Co. C. 47th Regiment. June 25, 1964 admitted to St. Mary's Hospital at LaGrange, Georgia. July 11, 1864 returned for duty. December 1, 1864 pension records show back was injured while unloading ammunition. He was in Augusta, Georgia Hospital at close of the war. (Born in Georgia. Died in Bulloch County, Georgia in 1928)

RIGGS, JACOB: Company C, private, March 4, 1862 enlisted as a private in Co. C, 11th Battalion. May 12, 1862 transferred to Co. C, 47th Regiment. September 20, 1863 died in Atlanta, Georgia. Buried there in Oakland Cemetery.

RIGGS, JAMES: Company C, private, March 4, 1862 enlisted as a private in Co. C, 11th Battalion. May 12, 1862 transferred to Co. C, 47th Regiment. November 25, 1863 wounded at Missionary Ridge, Tennessee. At home wounded at the close of the war. (Born in Georgia in 1844. Died in Bulloch County, Georgia in 1928)

RIGGS, JOHN W.: Company C, private, March 4, 1862 enlisted as a private in Co. C, 11th Battalion. May 12, 1862 transferred to Co. C, 47th Regiment. (March 29, 1864 died in Bulloch County, Georgia)

ROBBINS, DEMAS (DEMUS) F.: Company D, private, October 7 1861 enlisted as a private in Co. I, 5th. Regiment, 1st Brigade, Georgia State Troops. April 1862 mustered out. April 28, 1862 enlisted as a private in Co. D, 11th Battalion. May 12, 1862 transferred to Co. D, 47th Regiment. July 22, 1864 received pay. April 26, 1865 pension records show he surrendered at Greensboro, North Carolina.

ROBBINS, JOHN T.: Company D, 4th sergeant, March 4, 1862 appointed 4th sergeant, Co. D, 11th Battalion. May 12, 1862 transferred to Co. D, 47th Regiment as 4th sergeant. March 25, 1865 killed at Bentonville, North Carolina.

ROBBINS, STEPHEN M.: Company D, private, March 4, 1862 enlisted as a private in Co. D, 11th Battalion. May 12, 1862 transferred to Co. D, 47th Regiment. September 19, 1863 wounded at Chickamauga, Georgia. Died of wounds at Newnan, Georgia hospital and is buried there.

ROBERSON, SILAS: Company F, 4th sergeant, March 4, 1862 elected 4th corporal, Co. F, 11th Battalion. May 12, 1862 transferred to Co. F, 47th Regiment as 4th corporal. August 5, 1862 appointed 4th sergeant, Co. F, 47th Regiment. May 23, 1865 paroled, Thomasville, Georgia. (Born in Appling County, Georgia December 20, 1836)

ROBERTS, ISHAM: Company D, private, March 4, 1862 enlisted as a private in Co. D, 11th Battalion. May 12, 1862 transferred to Co. D, 47th Regiment. May 16, 1864 captured at Resaca, Georgia. December 26, 1864 died of small pox at Camp Douglas, Illinois as a POW.

ROBERTSON, SYLVANUS G.: Company B, private, March 4, 1862 enlisted as a private in Co. B, 11th Battalion. May 12, 1862 transferred to Co. B, 47th Regiment. February 28, 1863 roll, last on record, shows him "detailed Commissary Sergeant, left at Savannah, Georgia February 25."

ROCK, OWEN: Company A, private, March 10, 1862 enlisted in Co. A, 11th Battalion as a private. May 12, 1862 transferred to Co. A, 47th Regiment. February 28, 1863 roll, last on file, shows him present.

ROCHE, JOHN J.: Company A, 2nd sergeant, February 27, 1862 appointed. 3rd corporal, Co., A, 11th Battalion. May 12, 1862 transferred to Co. A, 47th Regiment as 2nd Corporal. June 12, 1862 appointed 1st corporal. Co. A, 47th Regiment. September 1, 1862, appointed 2nd sergeant Co. A, 47th Regiment. November 28, 1863 admitted to Floyd House & Ocmulgee Hospital at Macon, Georgia, with chronic diarrhea. December 26, 1864 deserted at Savannah, Georgia Remark "At work in Q. M. Department." (Born in Ireland)

ROGERS, J. C.: Company K, private, May 6, 1862 enlisted as a private in Co. K, 47th Regiment. February 28, 1863 roll, last on record, shows him sick in Savannah, Georgia hospital.

ROSS, WILLIAM R.: Company A, private, March 3, 1862 enlisted in Co. A, 11th Battalion as a private. March 25, 1862 sent to Confederate Hospital at Macon, Georgia.

ROWE, JAMES J.: Company H, private, March 4, 1862 enlisted as a private in Co. H, 11th Battalion. May 12, 1862 transferred to Co. H, 47th Regiment. June 10, 1862 wounded at James Island, South Carolina. February 28, 1863 roll, last on record, shows him present.

ROWE, JAMES J.: Company H, private. March 4, 1862 enlisted as a private in Co. H, 11th Battalion. May 12, 1862 transferred to Co. H, 47th Regiment. February 28, 1863 roll, last on record, shows him present.

ROWE, JAMES V.: Company C, 4th corporal. March 4, 1862 appointed 4th corporal Co. C, 11th Battalion. May 12, 1862 transferred to Co. C, 47th Regiment as 4th corporal. October 31, 1863 signed receipt for pay at Savannah, Georgia while on furlough.

ROZIER, LEWIS M.: Company B, private, March 4, 1862 enlisted as a private in Co. B, 11th Battalion. May 12, 1862 transferred to Co. B, 47th Regiment. February 28, 1863 roll, last on record, shows him present.

RUSHING, MATTHEW: Company C, private, March 4, 1862 enlisted as a private in Co. C, 11th Battalion. May 12, 1862 transferred to Co. C, 47th Regiment. November 25, 1863 captured Missionary Ridge, Tennessee. December 7, 1863 sent to Louisville, Kentucky for exchange. March 6, 1865 admitted to General Hospital #9 at Richmond, Virginia. March 7, 1865 furloughed.

RUSHING, WILLIAM J.: Company G, private, March 4, 1862 enlisted as a private in Co. G, 47th Regiment, Georgia Infantry. April 1, 1862 died at Camp Davis.

RYALS, HENRY: Company G, private, March 4, 1862 enlisted as a private in Co. G, 11th Battalion. May 12, 1862 transferred to Co. G, 47th Regiment. February 28, 1863 roll, last on record, shows him present. Pension records show he was at home sick at the close of the war.

RYALS, MADISON: Company G, private, March 4, 1862 enlisted as a private in Co. G, 11th Battalion. May 12, 1862 transferred to Co. G, 47th Regiment. June 27, 1862 died of disease at Augusta, Georgia.

RYALS, S. M.: Company H, 1st corporal, March 4, 1862 enlisted as a private in Co. H, 11th Battalion. May 12, 1862 transferred to Co. H, 47th Regiment. January 1, 1863 appointed 1st corporal Co. H. 47th Regiment. February 28, 1863 roll, last on record, shows him present.

SALENS, JENKINS: Company H, private, March 4, 1862 enlisted as a private in Co. H, 11th Battalion. Never reported to camp.

SANDERLIN, LEMUEL: Company B, private, October 21, 1861 enlisted as a private in Co. K, 7th. Regiment, 1st Brigade, Georgia State Troops. November 27, 1861 discharged. March 4, 1862 enlisted as a private in Co. B, 11th Battalion. May 12, 1862 transferred to Co. B, 47th Regiment. November 25, 1863 captured at Ringgold, Georgia. February 25, 1864 died POW of diarrhea at Rock Island, Illinois. Buried there in grave #602.

SANDERS, GEORGE W. (OR GEORGE F.): Company B, private, April 25, 1862 enlisted as a private in Co. B, 11th Battalion. May 12, 1862 transferred to Co. B, 47th Regiment. December 1, 1862 transferred to Co._, 32nd Regiment, Georgia Infantry.

SAPP, CLINTON: Company F, private, November 16, 1862 enlisted as a private in Co. F, 47th Regiment, Georgia Infantry. November 30, 1864 wounded and lost both eyes at Honey Hill, South Carolina. January 18, 1865 died in Savannah, Georgia hospital.

SAPP, ELAM: Company G, private, September 1, 1862 enlisted as a private in Co. G, 47th Regiment, Georgia Infantry. May 16, 1864 captured at Calhoun, Georgia. February 1865 sent to Alton, Illinois. March 6, 1865 received at Boulware & Cox's Wharves, James River, Virginia for exchange.

SAPP, ELIJAH: Company F, private, March 4, 1862 enlisted as a private in Co. F, 11th Battalion. May 12, 1862 transferred to Co. F, 47th Regiment. August 3, 1862 died of disease at Camp Williams. Georgia.

SAPP, LUKE L.: Company G, private, March 4, 1862 enlisted as a private in Co. G, 11th Battalion. May 12, 1862 transferred to Co. G, 47th Regiment. February 28, 1863 roll, last on record, shows him present.

SAPP, PERRY: Company G, private, March 4, 1862 enlisted as a private in Co. G, 11th Battalion. May 12, 1862 transferred to Co. G, 47th Regiment. November 23, 1863 died of disease.

SAPP, SALEM: Company G, private, March 4, 1862 enlisted as a private in Co. G, 11th Battalion. May 12, 1862 transferred to Co. G, 47th Regiment June 17, 1863 died of disease at home.

SATTERWHITE, E. MURRELL: Company B, private, March 4, 1862 enlisted as a private in Co. B, 11th Battalion. Absent without leave.

SATTERWHITE, LAFAYETTE: Company B, private, March 4, 1862 enlisted as a private in Co. B, 11th Battalion. Absent without leave

SAYERS, M. SAMUEL: Company B, private, May 1, 1862 enlisted as a private in Co. B, 11th Battalion. May 12, 1862 transferred to Co. B, 47th Regiment. August 10, 1863 - May 11, 1863 on detached duty as carpenter in Savannah, Georgia. Pension records indicate that he transferred to Engineering Corps. (Born in Virginia, October 22, 1824)

SECKINGER, GEORGE W.: Company I, private, March 4, 1862 enlisted as a private in Co. I, 11th Battalion. May 12, 1862 transferred to Co. I, 47th Regiment. August 1862 appears last in this roll. Died at Savannah, Georgia.

SECKINGER, J. D.: Company I, private, July 1864 enlisted as a private in Co. I, 47th Regiment, Georgia Infantry. February 4, 1865 pension records show he was wounded in right hand, resulting in amputation of fingers, at Rivers' Bridge, South Carolina. March 4, 1865 furloughed for 30 days. Unable to return to his command. (Born in Georgia October 1847)

SECKINGER, JACKSON G.: Company I, private, March 4, 1862 enlisted as a private in Co. I, 11th Battalion. May 12, 1862 transferred to Co. I, 47th Regiment. September 15, 1862 died of disease.

SECKINGER, THOMAS C.: Company I, private, August 27, 1862 enlisted as a private in Co. I, 47th Regiment, Georgia Infantry. February 1863 sick in Guyton, Georgia Hospital.

SCARLETT, GEORGE: Company H, private, March 4, 1862 enlisted as a private in Co. H, 11th Battalion. Never reported to camp.

SCOTT, JOHN M.: Company D, 2nd corporal. March 4, 1862 appointed 2nd corporal. Co. D. 11th Battalion. May 12, 1862 transferred to Co. D, 47th Regiment as 2nd corporal. February 28, 1863 roll, last on record, shows him present.

SCOTT, JACOB W.: Company D, private, March 4, 1862 enlisted as a private in Co. D, 11th Battalion. May 12, 1862 transferred to Co. D, 47th Regiment. February 28, 1863 roll, last on record, shows him present. December 4, 1864 pension records indicate he was wounded in the head, right foot and leg and totally disabled at Bee's Creek, South Carolina.

SCOTT, PHILETUS P.: Company D, private, March 4, 1862 enlisted as a private in Co. D, 11th Battalion. May 12, 1862 transferred to Co. D, 47th Regiment. February 28, 1863 roll, last on record, shows him present. (Born in 1834)

SCOTT, RICHARD P.: Company D, 4th corporal, March 4, 1862 appointed 4th corporal. Co. D, 11th Battalion May 12, 1862 transferred to Co. D, 47th regiment as 4th Corporal. February 28, 1863 roll, last on record, shows him present.

SCOTT, THOMAS: Company E, private, March 4, 1862 enlisted as a private in Co. E, 11th Battalion. May 12, 1862 transferred to Co. E, 47th Regiment. April 4, 1865 appears on list of deserters and refugees to be delivered to Provost Marshal General, New York City (Dated headquarters Department of the South, Office Provost Marshal General, Hilton Head, South Carolina - April 4, 1865) which shows he came into the line February 1, 1865, at Savannah, Georgia. (Born in North Carolina)

SCREWS, STEPHEN: Company G, private, March 4, 1862 enlisted as a private in Co. G, 11th Battalion. May 12, 1862 transferred to Co. G, 47th Regiment. February 28, 1863 roll, last on record, shows him present.

SECKINGER, J. D.: Company I, private, February 4, 1865 wounded at River's Bridge, South Carolina.

SECKINGER, JACKSON G.: Company I, private, September 15, 1862 died of disease

SELIG, MARCUS: Company A, private, February 28, 1862 enlisted in Co. A, 11th Battalion as a private. May 12, 1862 transferred to Co. A, 47th Regiment. May 13, 1862 discharged, furnished Michael Leonard as substitute.

SELLERS, JAMES M.: Company F, private, March 4, 1862 enlisted as a private in Co. F, 11th Battalion. May 12, 1862 transferred to Co. F, 47th Regiment. October 31, 1863 roll, last on record, shows him present.

SELLERS, JIMPSEY M.: Company F, private, July 13, 1862 enlisted as a private in Co. F, 47th Regiment, Georgia Infantry. October 31, 1863 roll, last on record, shows him present. Pension records show that he was at home at the close of the war.

SELLERS (SELLARS), JOHN M.: Company F, 2nd sergeant, March 4, 1862 elected 4th sergeant Co. F, 11th Battalion. May 12, 1862 transferred to Co. F, 47th Regiment as 4th sergeant. August 5, 1862, appointed 2nd sergeant Co. F, 47th Regiment. October 18, 1863 died of disease at University Hospital, Cassville, Georgia.

SELLERS, JOHN R.: Company D, private, March 4, 1862 enlisted as a private in Co. D, 11th Battalion. May 12, 1862 transferred to Co. D, 47th Regiment. February 28, 1863 roll, last on record, shows him present. May 16, 1865 paroled at Thomasville, Georgia.

SELLERS, WILLIAM: Company F, 1st. corporal, March 4, 1862 elected 2nd corporal Co. F, 11th Battalion. May 12, 1862 transferred to Co. F, 47th Regiment as 2nd corporal. August 5, 1862 appointed 1st corporal Co. F, 47th Regiment. Died of disease in service.

SHADRON, ROBERT M.: Company D, private, March 4, 1862 enlisted as a private in Co. D, 11th Battalion. May 12, 1862 transferred to Co. D, 47th Regiment. November 18, 1863 received pay. April 26, 1865 pension records show he surrendered Greensboro, North Carolina. (Born in Burke County, Georgia April 6, 1845)

SHEFFIELD, D.: Company C, private, March 4, 1862 enlisted as a private in Co. C, 11th Battalion. May 16, 1862 died Savannah Georgia (or Bulloch

County, Georgia)
SHEFFIELD, E.: Company K, private, May 6, 1862 enlisted as a private in Co. K, 47th Regiment. February 28, 1863 roll, last on record, shows him sick in Guyton, Georgia hospital.
SHEFFIELD, P. C.: Company K, 1st Lieutenant, May 6, 1862 elected Jr. 2nd Lieutenant, Co. K, 47th Regiment. May 29, 1863 elected 2nd Lieutenant Co. K, 47th Regiment. June 22, 1863 elected 1st. Lieutenant Co. K, 47th regiment. March 1865 appears on the roster.
SHEFFIELD, W. A.: Company K, private, May 6, 1862 enlisted as a private in Co. K, 47th Regiment. July 3, 1862 discharged, furnished J. Nesbit as substitute.
SHEFFIELD, W. H.: Company K, private, May 6, 1862 enlisted as a private in Co. K, 47th Regiment. June 10, 1862 killed at James Island, South Carolina.
SHEILS, JOHN: Company A, private, February 27, 1862 enlisted in Co. A, 11th Battalion as a private. Not on subsequent rolls.
SHENOCH (SHENOCK), LEWIS: Company G, private, March 4, 1862 enlisted as a private in Co. G, 11th Battalion. May 12, 1862 transferred to Co. G, 47th Regiment. November 29, 1863 admitted to Floyd House and Ocmulgee Hospitals at Macon, Georgia.
SHINE, JAMES: Company A, private, February 27, 1862 enlisted in Co. A, 11th Battalion as a private. May 12, 1862 transferred to Co. A, 47th Regiment. November 26, 1862 discharged by civil authority.
SHUMAN, JAMES S.: Company E, private, March 4, 1862 enlisted as a private in Co. E, 11th Battalion. May 12, 1862 transferred to Co. E, 47th Regiment. August 31, 1863 in French's Division Hospital at Lockhart, Mississippi. April 22, 1864 died in Atlanta Georgia. Buried there in Oakland Cemetery.
SHUMAN, JAMES W.: Company E, private, March 4, 1862 enlisted as a private in Co. E, 11th Battalion. May 12, 1862 transferred to Co. E, 47th Regiment. November 25, 1863 captured at Missionary Ridge, Tennessee. February 1865 paroled at Fort Delaware, Delaware. March 11, 1865 received at Boulware & Cox's Wharves, James River, Virginia.
SHUMANS, THOMAS W.: Company F, private, April 26, 1862 enlisted as a private in Co. F, 11th Battalion. May 12, 1862 transferred to Co. F, 47th Regiment. November 25, 1863 captured at Missionary Ridge, Tennessee. December 27, 1863 died at Rock Island, Illinois prison as POW.
SHUPTRINE, LAWRENCE E (S.): Company I. 2nd corporal, March 4, 1862 elected 2nd corporal, Co. I, 11th Battalion. 12, 1862 transferred to Co. H, 47th Regiment. 1864 transferred to the Confederates States Navy.
SIKES, ARTHUR: Company G, private, Pension records show June 1863 he enlisted as a private in Co. G, 47th Regiment, Georgia Infantry. April 26, 1865 surrendered at Greensboro, North Carolina. (Born in Tattnall County, Georgia in 1846)
SIKES, BENJAMIN: Company G, private, March 4, 1862 enlisted as a

private in Co. G, 11th Battalion. May 12, 1862 transferred to Co. G, 47th Regiment. September 19, 1863 captured at Chickamauga, Georgia. June 15, 1865 released at Camp Douglas, Illinois.

SIKES, DANIEL: Company G, private. March 4, 1862 enlisted as a private in Co. G, 11th Battalion. May 12, 1862 transferred to Co. G, 47th Regiment. February 28, 1863 roll, last on record, shows him absent without leave. April 26, 1865 pension records show he surrendered at Greensboro, North Carolina. (Born in Tattnall County, Georgia in 1846 or 1847)

SIKES, DYER (DYRE) C.: Company G, private, March 4, 1862 enlisted as a private in Co. G, 11th Battalion. May 12, 1862 transferred to Co. G, 47th Regiment. February 28, 1863 roll, last on record, shows him present. Pension records show he was at home on sick furlough November 1864 to the close of the war. (Born in Tattnall County, Georgia February 1, 1830)

SIKES, JOHN: Company G, private. March 4, 1862 enlisted as a private in Co. G, 11th Battalion. May 12, 1862 transferred to Co. G, 47th Regiment. October 11, 1862 died of disease in Savannah, Georgia.

SIKES, JOSEPH: Company G, private, 1863 enlisted as a private in Co. G, 47th Regiment, Georgia Infantry. April 26, 1865 surrendered at Greensboro, North Carolina.

SIKES, JOSIAH: Company G, private. March 4, 1862 enlisted as a private in Co. G, 11th Battalion. May 12, 1862 transferred to Co. G, 47th Regiment. September 19, 1863 wounded at Chickamauga, Georgia. May 12, 1864 died of disease Academy Hospital, Marietta, Georgia.

SIKES, WILLIAM W.: Company G, private, March 4, 1862 enlisted as a private in Co. G, 11th Battalion. May 12, 1862 transferred to Co. G, 47th Regiment.

SIMMONS, ROBERT: Company H, private, May 9, 1862 enlisted as a private in Co. H, 11th Battalion. May 12, 1862 transferred to Co. H, 47th Regiment. June 17, 1864 admitted to Ocmulgee Hospital at Macon, Georgia. June 18, 1864 transferred.

SIMMS, RICHARD: Company A, private, March 4, 1862 enlisted in Co. A, 11th Battalion as a private. May 12, 1862 transferred to Co. A, 47th Regiment. December 1862 detailed to Gun Boat.

SIMPSON, JOSEPH H.: Company A, 4th corporal. February 27, 1862 enlisted in Co. A, 11th Battalion as a private. May 12, 1862 transferred to Co. A, 47th Regiment. February 1863 appointed. 4th corporal Co. A, 47th Regiment. May 18, 1864 captured at Kingston, Georgia. May 24, 1864 sent to military Prison at Louisville, Kentucky. May 25, 1864 transferred to Rock island, Illinois where he enlisted in the United States Navy. June 10, 1864 transferred.

SIMON (SINON), JOHN: Company A, private, February 28, 1862 enlisted in Co. A, 11th Battalion as a private. May 12, 1862 transferred to Co. A, 47th Regiment. November-December 1862 deserted at Savannah, Georgia.

SINGLETON, JOSEPH E.: Company E, 5th sergeant, March 4, 1862 appointed 2nd corporal Co. E, 11th Battalion. May 12, 1862 transferred to Co. E, 47th Regiment, Georgia Infantry as 2nd corporal. July 1862 appointed 5th sergeant Co. E, 47th Regiment. October 31, 1862 roll, last on file, shows him present.

SINGLETON, JOSEPH LAWTON: Company D, Captain, March 4, 1862 appointed 2nd Lieutenant Co. D, 11th Battalion. May 12, 1862 transferred to Co. D, 47th Regiment as 2nd Lieutenant. October 14, 1862 elect 1st Lieutenant Co. D, 47th Regiment. October 29, 1862 elected Captain Co. D, 47th Regiment. November 14, 1864, dropped from rolls by Spec. Order, by reason of prolonged absence without leave.

SINGLETON, WILLIAM J.: Company E, private, March 4, 1862 enlisted as a private in Co. E, 11th Battalion. Never reported.

SINQUEIELD, FRANK S.: Company B, private, June 1, 1862 enlisted as a private in Co. B, 47th Regiment, Georgia Infantry. (Substitute for Patrick H. Ferguson) November 25, 1863 killed at Missionary Ridge, Tennessee.

SLATER, CLEM C.: Company E, 1st Lieutenant, March 4, 1862 appointed 1st Lieutenant Co. E, 11th Battalion. May 12,. 1862 transferred to Co. E, 47th Regiment as 1st Lieutenant. July 18, 1862 resigned his commission due to ill health.

SLATOR, LEASTON C.: Company C, private, July 1864 enlisted as a private in Co. C, 47th Regiment, Georgia infantry. November 1864 pension records show that he left command at Savannah, Georgia, sick with Typhoid Fever. 1864 furloughed for 60 days from Guyton, Georgia hospital. (Born in Georgia)

SLAUGHTER, A. BRADLEY: Company B, private, April 25, 1862 enlisted as a private in Co. B, 11th Battalion. May 12, 1862 transferred to Co. B, 47th Regiment. February 28, 1863 roll, last on record, shows him present.

SLAUGHTER, EDWIN R.: Company B, 4th corporal, March 4, 1862 enlisted as a private in Co. B, 11th Battalion. May 12, 1862 transferred to Co. B, 47th Regiment as 4th corporal. November 25, 1863 captured at Missionary Ridge, Tennessee. March 26, 1864 died POW of variola at Rock Island, Illinois.

SMILIE (SMILEY), THOMAS W.: Company D, private, March 4, 1862 enlisted as a private in Co. D, 11th Battalion. May 12, 1862 transferred to Co. D, 47th Regiment. November 16, 1863 admitted to Floyd House and Ocmulgee Hospitals at Macon, Georgia.

SMITH, A. L.: Company I, private, March 4, 1862 enlisted as a private in Co. I, 11th Battalion. May 12, 1862 transferred to Co. I, 47th Regiment. February 28, 1863 roll, last on record, shows him sick in Guyton, Georgia hospital. (Born in Screven county, Georgia July 18, 1843)

SMITH, B. G.: Company D, private, March 4, 1862 enlisted as a private in Co. D, 11th Battalion. May 12, 1862 transferred to Co. D, 47th Regiment. August 1863 in Breckenridge's Division Hospital, Lauderdale Springs, Mississippi.

SMITH, D. L.: Company I, private, March 4, 1862 enlisted as a private in Co. I, 11th Battalion. May 12, 1862 transferred to Co. I, 47th Regiment. February 28, 1863 roll, last on record, shows him present.

SMITH, DENNIS: Company F, private, April 26, 1862 enlisted as a private in Co. F, 11th Battalion. May 12, 1862 transferred to Co. F, 47th Regiment. November 30, 1864 wounded at Honey Hill, South Carolina. December 18, 1864 died in hospital at Charleston, South Carolina.

SMITH, EDWARD T.: Company H, private, March 4, 1862 enlisted as a private in Co. H, 11th Battalion. May 12, 1862 transferred to Co. H, 47th Regiment. February 28, 1863 roll, last on record, shows him present.

SMITH, HENRY J.: Company I, private, March 4, 1862 enlisted as a private in Co. I, 11th Battalion. May 12, 1862 transferred to Co. I, 47th Regiment. October 26, 1862 discharged at Camp Williams, Georgia by civil authority. (Born in Effingham County, Georgia in 1846)

SMITH, JAMES H.: Company G, private, March 4, 1862 enlisted as a private in Co. G, 11th Battalion. May 12, 1862 transferred to Co. G, 47th Regiment. September - October 1863 in Walker Division Hospital at Newton, Mississippi with broken leg. Died at home during the war.

SMITH, JOHN G.: Company H, 1st corporal, March 4, 1862 elected 1st corporal. Co. H, 11th Battalion. May 12, 1862 transferred to Co. H, 47th Regiment as 1st corporal. February 28, 1863 roll, last on record, shows him present. April 1865 according to pension records he was in Columbia, South Carolina Hospital. (Born in Bulloch County, Georgia in 1840)

SMITH, JOHN T.: Company B, color corporal, March 4, 1862 enlisted as a private in Co. B, 11th Battalion. May 12, 1862 transferred to Co. B, 47th Regiment. December 1862 appointed Color Corporal. February 15, 1863 sent to Randolph County, Georgia on recruiting duty. May 16, 1864 Admitted to Ocmulgee Hospital at Macon, Georgia. May 23, 1864 returned to duty. April 1865 captured by 1st Brigade, 2nd Cavalry Division.

SMITH, LAMAR A.: Company I, private, March 4, 1862 enlisted as a private in Co. I, 11th Battalion. May 12, 1862 transferred to Co. I, 47th Regiment. October 7, 1862 discharged at Camp Williams, Georgia by civil authority.

SMITH, MILES: Company D, private, October 7, 1861 enlisted as a private in Co. I, 5th Regiment, 1st Brigade, Georgia State Troops. April 1862 mustered out. 1862 enlisted as a private in Co. D, 47th Regiment, Georgia Infantry. April 26, 1865 pension records show he surrendered at Greensboro, North Carolina. May 18, 1865 paroled at Augusta, Georgia.

SMITH, S. W. (SEABORN): Company D, private, March 4, 1862 enlisted as a private in Co. D, 11th Battalion. May 12, 1862 transferred to Co. D, 47th Regiment. September 20, 1863 captured at Chickamauga, Georgia. October 20, 1863 died of inflammation of lungs at Camp Douglas, Illinois as a POW.

SMITH, WILLIAM THOMAS: Company E, private, March 4, 1862 enlisted as a private in Co. E, 11th Battalion. May 12, 1862 transferred to

Co. E, 47th Regiment. October 9, 1862 discharged, disability.

SOLOMONS, JUDA S.: Company E, 5th sergeant, March 4, 1862 appointed 5th sergeant Co. E, 11th Battalion. May 12, 1862 transferred to Co. E, 47th Regiment as 5th sergeant. October 21, 1862 discharged, disability.

SOMMERSALL (SUMMERSALL), J. L.: Company H, private, March 4, 1862 enlisted as a private in Co. H, 11th Battalion. May 12, 1862 transferred to Co. H, 47th Regiment. October 13, 1863 admitted to Floyd House and Ocmulgee Hospitals at Macon, Georgia. November 6, 1863 returned to duty.

SOUTHWELL, NEWTON C.: Company G, private, December 5, 1862 enlisted as a private in Co. G, 47th Regiment, Georgia Infantry. Wounded, date and place nor given, May 21, 1864 died of pyemia in General Hospital #1, Savannah, Georgia.

SOUTHWELL, R. G.: Company K, private, May 6, 1862 enlisted as a private in Co. K, 47th Regiment. December 26, 1863 died in Hood Hospital, Covington, Georgia.

SOUTHWELL, THOMAS H.: Company G, Jr. 2nd Lieutenant, April 15, 1862 enlisted as a private in Co. G, 11th Battalion. May 12, 1862 transferred to Co. G, 47th Regiment. July 1862 appointed 3rd sergeant Co. G, 47th Regiment. June 25, 1863 elected Jr. 2nd Lieutenant Co. G, 47th Regiment. May 26, 18641 died at Atlanta, Georgia and is buried in Oakland Cemetery:

SOUTHWELL, WILLIAM E.: Company G, 4th sergeant, March 4, 1862 enlisted as a private in Co. G, 11th Battalion. May 12, 1862 transferred to Co. G, 47th Regiment, Georgia Infantry as 4th sergeant. February 28, 1863 roll, last on record, shows him present.

SOWELL, SHAFNER W.: Company I, private, March 4, 1862 enlisted as a private in Co. I, 11th Battalion. May 12, 1862 transferred to Co. I, 47th Regiment. September 19, 1863 wounded at Chickamauga, Georgia. October 30, 1863 died of wounds

SOWELL, T. T.: Company I, private, March 4, 1862 enlisted as a private in Co. I, 11th Battalion. May 12, 1862 transferred to Co. I, 47th Regiment. February 28, 1863 roll, last on record, shows him absent without leave. May 17, 1865 paroled at Madison, Florida.

SPELL, GEORGE W.: Company F, private, April 26, 1862 enlisted as a private in Co. F, 11th Battalion. May 12, 1862 transferred to Co. F, 47th Regiment. June 14, 1862 died of Typhoid Fever. in Chimborazo, Hospital #3, Richmond, Virginia.

SPELL, WILLIAM: Company H, private, October 12, 1862 enlisted as a private (substitute for W. E. Warnell (Wornell) in Co. H, 47th Regiment, Georgia Infantry. February 28, 1863 roll, last on record, shows him present.

STANDFIELD, ANDREW: Company G, private, March 4, 1862 enlisted as a private in Co. G, 11th Battalion. May 12, 1862 transferred to Co. G,

47th Regiment. August 1, 1862 discharged, under age.

STANDFIELD, JESSE: Company G, private, March 4, 1862 enlisted as a private in Co. G, 11th Battalion. May 12, 1862 transferred to Co. G, 47th Regiment. October 6, 1862 discharged by civil authority at Camp Williams, Georgia.

STANDFIELD, THOMAS: Company G, private, March 4, 1862 enlisted as a private in Co. G, 11th Battalion. May 12, 1862 transferred to Co. G, 47th Regiment. February 3, 1865 captured at River's Bridge, South Carolina. June 5, 1865 released at Point Lookout, Maryland. (Born in Tattnall County, Georgia February 4, 1843)

STANDFIELD, WILLIAM H.: Company G, private, March 4, 1862 enlisted as a private in Co. G, 11th Battalion. May 12, 1862 transferred to Co. G, 47th Regiment. September 24, 1862 died in Whitesville, Georgia Hospital.

STANLEY, JOHN F.: Company H, private, March 4, 1862 enlisted as a private in Co. H, 11th Battalion. May 12, 1862 transferred to Co. H, 47th Regiment. February 28, 1863 roll, last on record, shows him present.

STARKE, BARRAK: Company A, private, February 27, 1862 enlisted in Co. A, 11th Battalion as a private. May 12, 1862 transferred to Co. A, 47th Regiment. May 17, 1864 captured at Calhoun, Georgia. June 10, 1864 sent to Rock Island, Illinois where he enlisted in the United States Navy and was transferred.

STEWART, JESSE J.: Company B, private, July 1, 1864 enlisted as a private in Co. B, 47th Regiment, Georgia Infantry. April 26, 1865 surrendered Greensboro, North Carolina

STEWART, DANIEL J.: Company D, private, March 4, 1862 enlisted as a private in Co. D, 11th Battalion. May 12, 1862 transferred to Co. D, 47th Regiment. August 13, 1863 sent to Breckenridge's Division Hospital #2 at Lauderdale Springs, Mississippi. 1865 discharged at Florence, South Carolina. (Born in Screven County, Georgia November 29, 1825)

STEWART, THOMAS G.: Company D, private, March 4, 1862 enlisted as a private in Co. D, 11th Battalion. May 12, 1862 transferred to Co. D, 47th Regiment as 5th sergeant. September 29, 1862 discharged, under age.

STOKES, ROBERT: Company E, private, March 4, 1862 enlisted as a private in Co. E, 11th Battalion. May 12, 1862 transferred to Co. E, 47th Regiment. November 29, 1862 admitted to Floyd House and Ocmulgee Hospitals at Macon, Georgia.

STONE, ABSALOM S.: Company F, private, April 26, 1862 enlisted as a private in Co. F, 11th Battalion. May 12, 1862 transferred to Co. F, 47th Regiment. June 17, 1864 admitted to Ocmulgee Hospital at Macon, Georgia. June 27, 1864 furloughed. April 26, 1865 pension records show he surrendered at Greensboro, North Carolina.

STONE, THOMAS: Company A, private, March 4, 1862 enlisted in Co. A, 11th Battalion as a private. May 12, 1862 transferred to Co. A,

47th Regiment. February 28, 1863 roll, last on record, shows him sick in Wilmington, North Carolina hospital.

STONE, WILLIAM M.: Company F, corporal, March 4, 1862 enlisted as a private in Co. F, 11th Battalion. May 12, 1862 transferred to Co. F, 47th Regiment. Appointed corporal. July 19, 1864 received pay at Charleston, South Carolina. April 26, 1865 pension records show he surrendered at Greensboro, North Carolina.

STRIPLING, BENJAMIN: Company G, private, 1863 enlisted as a private in Co. G, 47th Regiment, Georgia Infantry.

STUART, JOHN P.: Company B, private, October 1, 1863 enlisted as a private (according to pension records) Born in Monroe County, Georgia October 10, 1844. April 26, 1865 surrendered at Greensboro, North Carolina.

STUART, THOMAS M.: Company H, private, March 4, 1862 enlisted as a private in Co. H, 11th Battalion. Appears only on an updated bounty receipt roll for 1862, which bears the remark: "Transferred."

SULLIVAN, G. W.: Company G, private, November 1, 1862 enlisted (substitute for Columbus Tootle) as a private in Co. G, 47th Regiment, Georgia Infantry. June 17, 1864 transferred to Invalid Corps.

SULLIVAN, MARTIN: Company G, private, December 1, 1862 enlisted (substitute for Edward Anderson) as a private in Co. G, 47th Regiment, Georgia Infantry. February 3, 1865 captured at River's Bridge, South Carolina. June 13, 1865 released at Point Lookout, Maryland.

SULLIVAN, MICHAEL: Company A, private, March 4, 1862 enlisted in Co. A, 11th Battalion as a private. May 12, 1862 transferred to Co. A, 47th Regiment. February 28, 1863 roll, last on record, shows him "Absent without leave, left company at Charleston, South Carolina."

SUMMERLIN, BENJAMIN: Company D, 5th sergeant. March 4, 1862 enlisted as a private in Co. D, 11th Battalion. May 12, 1862 transferred to Co. D, 47th Regiment. February 28, 1863 treated for fever in General hospital #1 at Savannah, Georgia and transferred to General Hospital at Macon, Georgia. Died 1863 or 1864.

SUMMERLIN, BERRIEN: Company D, 5th sergeant, March 4, 1862 enlisted as a private in Co. D, 11th Battalion. May 12, 1862 transferred to Co. D, 47th Regiment. July 1862 appointed 5th Sergeant. February 28, 1863 roll, last on record, shows him absent sick.

SUMMERLIN, ELI: Company D, private, March 4, 1862 enlisted as a private in Co. D, 11th Battalion. May 12, 1862 transferred to Co. D, 47th Regiment. 1862 wounded. September 19, 1863 wounded at Chickamauga, Georgia. Pension records show that he was totally disabled by wounds. (Born in Georgia February 12, 1841)

SUMMERLIN W. A.: Company C, 1st Lieutenant, March 4, 1862 appointed 1st Lieutenant Co. C, 11th Battalion. May 12, 1862 transferred to Co. C, 47th Regiment as 1st Lieutenant. July 10, 1862 resigned Commission.

SWILLY (SNELLING), S. A.: Company E, private, August 16, 1862 enlisted as a private in Co. E, 47th Regiment, Georgia Infantry. Discharged furnished F. Williamson as substitute.

TANNER, ASBERRY C.: Company F, private, March 4, 1862 enlisted as a private in Co. F, 11th Battalion. May 12, 1862 transferred to Co. F, 47th Regiment. July 30, 1862 transferred to Co. A. 1st Battalion, Georgia Sharpshooters. August 31, 1864 roll, last on file, shows him sick in General Hospital.

TANNER, GREEN: Company F, private, March 4, 1862 enlisted as a private in Co. F, 11th Battalion. May 12, 1862 transferred to Co. F, 47th Regiment. July 30, 1862 transferred to Co. A. 1st Battalion, Georgia Sharpshooters. August 1864 furloughed by Medical Board.

TANNER, ISAIAH: Company F, private, March 4, 1862 enlisted as a private in Co. F, 11th Battalion. May 12, 1862 transferred to Co. F, 47th Regiment. July 30, 1862 transferred to Co. A. 1st Battalion, Georgia Sharpshooters. April 8, 1863 deserted at Savannah, Georgia.

TAPPER, JAMES: Company E, private, March 4, 1862 enlisted as a private in Co. E, 11th Battalion. Never reported.

TATUM, JOHN F.: Company G, private, March 4, 1862 enlisted as a private in Co. G, 11th Battalion. May 12, 1862 transferred to Co. G, 47th Regiment. February 28, 1863 roll, last on record, shows him present. Transferred to 25th Regiment, Georgia infantry (not on the rolls of the 25th Regiment, Georgia infantry). May 21, 1865 captured and paroled at Thomasville, Georgia. (Born in Tattnall County, Georgia in 1844)

TAYLOR, ASBERRY: Company F, private, March 4, 1862 enlisted as a private in Co. F, 11th Battalion. May 12, 1862 transferred to Co. F, 47th Regiment. August 1863 in Breckinridge's Division Hospital #2 at Lauderdale Springs, Mississippi. September 24, 1863 died of Typhoid fever in Lauderdale Springs Hospital, Mississippi.

TAYLOR, BENJAMIN: Company F, private, May 1, 1862 enlisted as a private in Co. F, 11th Battalion. May 12, 1862 transferred to Co. F, 47th Regiment. April 18, 1865 killed at Bentonville, North Carolina.

TAYLOR, BERRY S.: Company F, private, March 4, 1862 enlisted as a private in Co. F, 11th Battalion. May 12, 1862 transferred to Co. F, 47th Regiment. August 6, 1864 died in Newsome Hospital, Thomasville, Georgia.

TAYLOR, BURRELL: Company F, private, May 1, 1862 enlisted as a private in Co. F, 11th Battalion. May 12, 1862 transferred to Co. F, 47th Regiment. October 31, 1863 roll, last on record, shows him present. October 10, 1863 according to disapproved pension records he left command on 60 days sick furlough and did not return to the command. (Born in Appling County, Georgia in 1839)

TAYLOR, CHRISTOPHER COLUMBUS: Company B, private, November 9, 1862 enlisted as a private in Co. B, 47th Regiment, Georgia Infantry. November 21, 1863 admitted to Floyd House and Ocmulgee Hospitals at Macon, Georgia with diarrhea (disposition not shown). April

26, 1865 surrendered Greensboro, North Carolina (according to Pension records)

TAYLOR, ELISHA: Company F, private, May 1, 1862 enlisted as a private in Co. F, 11th Battalion. May 12, 1862 transferred to Co. F, 47th Regiment. April 18, 1865 killed at Bentonville, North Carolina.

TAYLOR, ISAAC: Company F, private, March 4, 1862 enlisted as a private in Co. F, 11th Battalion. May 12, 1862 transferred to Co. F, 47th Regiment. April 26, 1865 according to pension records he surrendered at Greensboro, North Carolina.

TAYLOR, JAMES B.: Company F, private, March 4, 1862 enlisted as a private in Co. F, 11th Battalion. Discharged due to disability.

TAYLOR, JESSE S.: Company F, private, April 29, 1862 enlisted as a private in Co. F, 11th Battalion. May 12, 1862 transferred to Co. F, 47th Regiment. November 8, 1863 died at Atlanta, Georgia and is buried there in Oakland Cemetery.

TAYLOR, MARION: Company B, private, pension records show that in the winter of 1863 he enlisted as a private in Co. B, 47th Regiment, Georgia Infantry. April 26, 1865 surrendered at Greensboro, North Carolina.

TAYLOR, WILLIAM: Company F, private, March 4, 1862 enlisted as a private in Co. F, 11th Battalion. May 12, 1862 transferred to Co. F, 47th Regiment. February 21, 1864 on furlough. April 26, 1865 according to pension records he surrendered at Greensboro, North Carolina.

TAYLOR, WILLIAM D.: Company F, private, April 29, 1862 enlisted as a private in Co. F, 11th Battalion. May 12, 1862 transferred to Co. F, 47th Regiment. October 31, 1863 roll, last on record, shows him present. February 1865 according to disapproved pension records he was cut off from command while on picket duty in South Carolina. (Born in Appling County, Georgia May 10, 1862 or 1864)

TAYLOR, WILLIS F.: Company F, private, March 4, 1862 enlisted as a private in Co. F, 11th Battalion. May 12, 1862 transferred to Co. F, 47th Regiment. August 1863 in Breckinridge's Division Hospital #2 at Lauderdale Springs, Mississippi.

TERRELL, FLEMMING B.: Company H, 2nd corporal. March 4, 1862 elected 2nd corporal. Co. H, 11th Battalion. May 12, 1862 transferred to Co. H, 47th Regiment as 2nd corporal. February 28, 1863 roll, last on record, shows him present.

TERRELL, JAMES F.: Company H, private, November 29, 1862 enlisted as a private in Co. H, 47th Regiment. August 19, 1864 clothing issued to him.

THOMAS, ANDREW H.: Company F, private, March 4, 1862 enlisted as a private in Co. F, 11th Battalion. May 12, 1862 transferred to Co. F, 47th Regiment. June 22, 1862 discharged, furnished Jackson Williams as a substitute. Enlisted as a private in Co. I, 27th Regiment, Georgia Infantry. April 26, 1865 surrendered at Greensboro, North Carolina.

THOMAS, EDWARD: Company F, private, March 4, 1862 enlisted as a private in Co. F, 11th Battalion. May 12, 1862 transferred to Co. F, 47th Regiment. August 10, 1863 discharged on account of epilepsy. (Born in Ware County, Georgia December 1824)

THOMPSON, A. J.: Company C, private, March 4, 1862 enlisted as a private in Co. C, 11th Battalion. May 12, 1862 transferred to Co. C, 47th Regiment. June 10, 1862 killed at James Island, South Carolina.

THOMPSON, ABEL W.: Company H, private, March 4, 1862 enlisted as a private in Co. H, 11th Battalion. May 12, 1862 transferred to Co. H, 47th Regiment. August 31, 1863 in Breckinridge's Division Hospital #1 at Lauderdale Springs, Mississippi. September 1864 pension records show he was discharged from Richmond, Virginia Hospital. October 17, 1864 died of typhoid dysentery at home.

THOMPSON, ARCHIBALD: Company H, 2nd Lieutenant, March 4, 1862 elected 2nd Lieutenant Co. H, 11th Battalion. May 12, 1862 Thompson transferred to Co. H, 47th Regiment as 2nd Lieutenant. November 6, 1862 resigned his commission. Pension records show he enlisted on Co. F, 25th Regiment, Georgia Infantry. December 16, 1864 wounded at Franklin, Tennessee. Was at home, wounded at the close of the war. (Born in Bryan County, Georgia October 11, 1824)

THOMPSON, B. F.: Company G, private, March 4, 1862 enlisted as a private in Co. G, 11th Battalion. May 12, 1862 transferred to Co. G, 47th Regiment. Died in LaGrange, Georgia and is buried there in Stonewall Cemetery.

THOMPSON, BARNEY: Company H, private. May 1, 1862 enlisted as a private in Co. H, 47th Regiment. February 28, 1863 roll, last on record, shows him present.

THOMPSON, GEORGE M.: Company D, Jr. 2nd. Lieutenant, March 4, 1862 appointed Jr. 2nd Lt Co. D, 11th Battalion. May 12, 1862 transferred to Co. D, 47th Regiment as Jr. 2nd Lieutenant. October 7, 1862 died of disease in camp.

THOMPSON, HARDEE C.: Company D, private, August 12, 1862 enlisted (substitute for C. T. Moseley) as a private in Co. D, 47th Regiment, Georgia Infantry. February 28, 1863 roll shows him absent without leave.

THOMPSON, HENRY: Company E, private, March 4, 1862 enlisted as a private in Co. E, 11th Battalion. May 12, 1862 transferred to Co. E, 47th Regiment. November 30, 1862 shown as sick.

THOMPSON, HENRY: Company H, private, March 4, 1862 enlisted as a private in Co. H, 11th Battalion. May 12, 1862 transferred to Co. H, 47th Regiment. June 30, 1863 in General Hospital at Marion, Mississippi.

THOMPSON, JOHN A.: Company E, private, March 4, 1862 enlisted as a private in Co. E, 11th Battalion. May 12, 1862 transferred to Co. E, 47th Regiment. October 31, 1863 roll, last on record, shows him present. Pension records show that he was wounded, date and place not stated, and was at home wounded at close of the war.

THOMPSON, JOHN A.: Company H, private, August 25, 1862 enlisted as a private in Co. H, 47th Regiment. February 28, 1863 roll, last on record, shows him present. May 26, 1865 paroled in Augusta, Georgia.

THOMPSON, JOHN G.: Company D, 3rd sergeant, March 4, 1862 Appointed 3rd sergeant Co. D, 11th Battalion.. May 12, 1862 transferred to Co. D, 47th Regiment as 3rd Sergeant. July 12, 1863 wounded in arm, necessitating amputation at Jackson, Mississippi. September 10, 1863 received pay. (Born in Georgia September 28, 1826)

THOMPSON, JOHN PAUL: Company B, private, April 25, 1862 enlisted as a private in Co. B, 11th Battalion. May 12, 1862 transferred to Co. B, 47th Regiment. September 29, 1863 died at home of diarrhea.

THOMPSON JOSEPH C.: Company C, Captain, May 31, 1861 enlisted as a private in Captain Screven's Company, 1st Regiment, Georgia infantry (Olmstead's). April 11, 1862 transferred to Co. A, 11th Battalion, Georgia Infantry. May 1, 1862 appointed Quartermaster Sergeant. May 12, 1862 transferred to Co. C, 47th Regiment, Georgia Infantry. August 25, 1862 elected 2nd Lieutenant. November 24, 1862 elected Captain of Company C, 47th Regiment, Georgia Infantry. January 24, 1863 in C. S. A. General Military Hospital #4 at Wilmington, North Carolina. March 4, 1863 furloughed. May 30, 1865 paroled at Augusta, Georgia.

THOMPSON, L. J.: Company H, private, March 4, 1862 enlisted as a private in Co. H, 11th Battalion. May 12, 1862 transferred to Co. H, 47th Regiment. February 28, 1863 roll, last on record, shows him "taken out by writ of habeas corpus."

THOMPSON, MALACHI: Company E, private, March 4, 1862 enlisted as a private in Co. E, 11th Battalion. May 12, 1862 transferred to Co. E, 47th Regiment. October 31, 1863 roll, last on record, shows him present.

THOMPSON, ROBERT F.: Company D, sergeant. March 4, 1862 enlisted as a private in Co. D, 11th Battalion. May 12, 1862 transferred to Co. D, 47th Regiment. Appointed 2nd sergeant. September 6, 1863 appears on list of sick transferred from St. Mary's Hospital at Dalton, Georgia.

THOMPSON, THOMAS: Company H, private, March 4, 1862 enlisted as a private in Co. H, 11th Battalion. May 12, 1862 transferred to Co. H, 47th Regiment. November 29, 1863 admitted to Floyd House and Ocmulgee Hospitals at Macon, Georgia. July 1864 left command on account of typhoid dysentery and was in Montgomery, Alabama hospital at the close of the war. (According to pension application in Toombs County, Georgia, 1919).

THORNTON, ELISHA: Company H, private, March 4, 1862 enlisted as a private in Co. H, 48th Regiment. March 1862 transferred to Co. H, 11th Battalion. May 12, 1862 transferred to Co. H, 47th Regiment. February 28, 1863 roll, last on record, shows him present. April 26, 1865 pension records show he surrendered at Greensboro, North Carolina. (Born in Wayne County, Georgia January 5, 1841)

THORNTON, SEABORN: Company B, private, March 4, 1862 enlisted as a private in Co. B, 11th Battalion. May 12, 1862 transferred to Co. B, 47th Regiment.

THURMAN, WILLIAM: Company B, private, March 1, 1862 enlisted as a private in Co. B, 11th Battalion. Absent without leave.

TIGHE, PARTICK: Company A, private, July 25, 1861 enlisted as a private in Captain J. B. Read's Independent Company, Georgia Infantry. January 25, 1862 mustered out. March 1, 1862 enlisted in Co. A, 11th Battalion as a private. May 12, 1862 transferred to Co. A, 47th Regiment. January 1, 1863 killed at Savannah (by member of Company)

TILLMAN, FRANCIS M.: Company E, private, March 4, 1862 enlisted as private in Co. E, 11th Battalion. (Born in Chatham County, Georgia in 1841). May 12, 1862 transferred to Co. E, 47th Regiment. Roll for October 31, 1862 shows him present (last on file). Pension records show that he was sick in Hospital at close of the war.

TILLMAN, GEORGE W.: Company E, private, March 4, 1862 enlisted as private. May 12, 1862 transferred to Co. E, 47th Regiment. March 21, 1865 captured at Bentonville, North Carolina. June 15, 1865 released at Hart's Island, New York Harbor.

TIMMERMAN, J.: Company C, private, March 4, 1862 enlisted as a private in Co. C, 11th Battalion. May 12, 1862 transferred to Co. C, 47th Regiment. 1864 discharged.

TIPPENS, JOHN W.: Company G, private, September 1, 1862 enlisted as a private in Co. G, 47th Regiment, Georgia Infantry. November 12, 1862 died of disease at home in Tattnall Co.

TIPPENS, PHILLIP GLENN: Company G, Captain, March 4, 1862 elected Captain Co. G, 11th Battalion. May 12, 1862 transferred to Co. G, 47th Georgia Regiment as Captain. May 6, 1863 resigned his commission.

TIPPINS, LUCIUS A. H.: Company G, private, April 29, 1862 enlisted as a private in Co. G, 11th Battalion. May 12, 1862 transferred to Co. G, 47th Regiment. February 28, 1863 roll, last on record, shows him present.

TODD, THEODORE: Company C, private, July 25, 1862 enlisted as a private in Co. C, 47th Regiment, Georgia Infantry. February 28, 1863 roll, last on record, shows him present. Pension records show that he was at home on sick furlough at the close of the war. (Born in South Carolina in 1844)

TOLER, T.: Company C, private, March 4, 1862 enlisted as a private in Co. C, 11th Battalion. May 12, 1862 transferred to Co. C, 47th Regiment. February 1863 in Savannah, Georgia Hospital. Died in service.

TOOTLE, COLUMBUS: Company G, March 4, 1862 elected 2nd Lt Co. G, 11th Battalion. May 12, 1862 transferred to Co. G, 47th Georgia as 2nd Lieutenant. July 10, 1862 resigned his commission due to bad health.

TOOTLE, COLUMBUS: Company G, 3nd Lieutenant, September 15, 1862 enlisted as a private in Co. G, 47th Regiment, Georgia Infantry. November 1, 1862 discharged, furnished G. W. Sullivan as a substitute.

TOOTLE, CAPEL: Company G, private, April 15, 1862 enlisted as a private in Co. G, 11th Battalion. May 12, 1862 transferred to Co. G, 47th

Regiment. October 10, 1862 died of disease at home.

TOOTLE, ENOCH: Company G, private, September 1, 1862 enlisted as a private in Co. G, 47th Regiment, Georgia Infantry. December 10, 1862 discharged due to disability.

TOOTLE, JEREMIAH: Company G, 2nd Lieutenant, March 4, 1862 elected Jr. 2nd Lieutenant Co. G, 11th Battalion. May 12, 1862 transferred to Co. G., 47th Regiment, Georgia Infantry as Jr. 2nd Lieutenant. July 10, 1862 elected 2nd Lieutenant, Co. G, 47th Regiment. August 1, 1863 resigned his commission.

TOOTLE, SIMEON: Company G, private, April 18, 1862 enlisted as a private in Co. G, 11th Battalion. May 12, 1862 transferred to Co. G, 47th Regiment. June 10, 1862 wounded at James Island, South Carolina. June 14, 1862 died of wounds.

TOUCHELET, EUGENE: Field Staff, Musician, May 31, 1862 appointed Musician. December 1862 shows him present.

TOUCHSTONE, H. H.: Company C, private, March 4, 1862 enlisted as a private in Co. C, 11th Battalion. May 12, 1862 transferred to Co. C, 47th Regiment. September 19, 1863 wounded at Chickamauga, Georgia. May 10, 1865 surrendered Tallahassee, Florida. May 18, 1865 paroled at Thomasville, Georgia. (Born in South Carolina about 1830)

TROUT, ROBERT: Company I, private, March 4, 1862 enlisted as a private in Co. I, 11th Battalion. April 20, 1862 last appears on roll.

TULLIS, JOHN A.: Company I, 3rd sergeant, March 4, 1862 elected 4th sergeant, Co. I, 11th Battalion. May 12, 1862 transferred to Co. I, 47th regiment as 3rd sergeant. July 1864 killed at John's Island, South Carolina.

TULLIS, ROBERT W.: Company I, 4th corporal, March 4, 1862 elected 4th corporal Co. I, 11th Battalion. May 12, 1862 transferred to Co. I, 47th Regiment as 4th corporal. February 28, 1863 roll, last on record, shows him present. April 26, 1865 pension records show he surrendered at Greensboro, North Carolina. (Born in Effingham County, Georgia September 13, 1844)

TURNER, A.: Company C, private, March 4, 1862 enlisted as a private in Co. C, 11th Battalion. May 12, 1862 transferred to Co. C, 47th Regiment. November 1863 left sick on retreat from Missionary Ridge, Tennessee. December 2, 1863 died Gilmer Hospital, Marietta, Georgia.

TURNER, JOHN: Company C, private, July 1, 1862 enlisted as a private in Co. C, 47th Regiment, Georgia Infantry. April 26, 1865 surrendered at Greensboro, North Carolina.

TUTEN, DAVID RIVERS: Company F, 3rd sergeant, March 4, 1862 elected 1st corporal Co. F, 11th Battalion. May 12, 1862 transferred to Co. F, 47th Regiment as 1st corporal, August 5, 1862 appointed 3rd sergeant Co. F, 47th Regiment. October 31, 1862 roll, last on file, shows him absent sick. Wounded and lost arm in Atlanta Campaign. Born in Beaufort District, South Carolina February 17, 1842. Died in Appling County, Georgia March

16, 1880. (Shot off his horse while in route to Holmesville, Georgia to testify in a hog stealing case.)

TUTTY, SAMUEL K.: Company H, 1st. sergeant, March 4, 1862 elect 3rd corporal Co. H, 11th Battalion. May 12, 1862 transferred to Co. H, 47th Regiment as 3rd corporal. June 1862 appointed 1st Corporal Co. H, 47th regiment. February 1863 appointed 1st sergeant Co. H, 47th Regiment. November 25, 1863 captured at Missionary Ridge, Tennessee. April 11, 1864 died in U. S. A. Hospital #1 at Nashville, Tennessee.

ULMER, JOHN H.: Company E, 1st. corporal, March 4, 1862 appointed 4th corporal Co. E, 11th Battalion. May 12, 1862 transferred to Co. E, 47th Regiment as 4th corporal. June 1862 appointed 2nd corporal Co. E, 47th Regiment July 1862 appointed 1st corporal Co. E, 47th regiment. November 28, 1863 admitted to Floyd House and Ocmulgee Hospitals at Macon, Georgia with diabetes. April 1865 pension records show he was captured at Coosawhatchie, South Carolina and released at Hilton Head, South Carolina.

UMPHRIES, SAMUEL C.: Company D, private, March 4, 1862 enlisted as a private in Co. D, 11th Battalion. May 12, 1862 transferred to Co. D, 47th Regiment. February 28, 1863 roll, last on record, shows him sick in hospital.

USHER, THOMAS: Company I, private, March 4, 1862 enlisted as a private in Co. I, 11th Battalion. May 12, 1862 transferred to Co. I, 47th Regiment. September 19, 1863 killed at Chickamauga, Georgia.

VARN, AARON B.: Company F, private, March 4, 1862 enlisted as a private in Co. F, 11th Battalion. May 12, 1862 transferred to Co. F, 47th Regiment. December 14, 1863 died at Atlanta, Georgia and is buried there in Oakland Cemetery.

VARN, DANIEL R.: Company F, private, March 4, 1862 enlisted as a private in Co. F, 11th Battalion. May 12, 1862 transferred to Co. F, 47th Regiment. November 1, 1862 died of disease

VESTING, ADOLPH: Company E, private, March 4, 1862 enlisted as a private in Co. E, 11th Battalion. May 12, 1862 transferred to Co. E, 47th Regiment. October 31, 1863 roll, last on record, shows absent without leave.

WACASAR, SIDNEY B.: Company B, sergeant, March 4, 1862 enlisted as a private in Co. B, 11th Battalion. May 12, 1862 transferred to Co. B, 47th Regiment. December 1862 detailed company commissary. Appointed sergeant. October 12, 1863 signed receipt for commutation of rations at Camp Chickamauga, Georgia.

WADE, JOHN R.: Company D, corporal, March 4, 1862 enlisted as a private in Co. D, 11th Battalion. May 12, 1862 transferred to Co. D, 47th Regiment. Appointed 3rd corporal. February 28, 1863 roll, last on record, shows him present.

WADE, LEROY: Company D, private, May 13, 1862 enlisted as a private in Co. D, 47th Regiment, Georgia Infantry. February 28, 1863 roll, last on record, shows him present.

WAKEFIELD, THOMAS E.: Company I, Ensign, March 4, 1862 enlisted as a private in Co. I, 11th Battalion. May 12, 1862 transferred to Co. I, 47th Regiment. May 20, 1864 Appointed Ensign. July 10, 1864 inspection Report dated August 25, 1864, report him in hospital since July 10, 1864. April 10, 1865 pension records show he was on furlough at Augusta, Georgia. (Born in England in 1836)

WALLER, HIRAM: Company E, private, March 4, 1862 enlisted as a private in Co. E, 11th Battalion. May 12, 1862 transferred to Co. E, 47th Regiment. October 31, 1863 roll, last on record, shows him present.

WALLS, FRANK (FRANCIS) M.: Company E, 2nd sergeant. March 4, 1862 appointed 4th corporal Co. E, 11th Battalion. May 12, 1862 transferred to Co. E, 47th Regiment as 1st corporal. June 1862 appointed 3rd sergeant Co. E, 47th Regiment. July 1862 appointed 2nd sergeant Co. E, 47th Regiment. November 29, 1863 admitted to Floyd House and Ocmulgee Hospitals at Macon, Georgia with fever.

WALLS, THOMAS W.: Company E, private, March 4, 1862 enlisted as a private in Co. E, 11th Battalion. May 12, 1862 transferred to Co. E, 47th Regiment. October 31, 1863 roll, last on record, shows him present.

WALSH, JOHN: Company A, private, April 25, 1862 enlisted in Co. A, 11th Battalion. April 30, 1862 deserted (Supposed to be on Gun Boat.)

WALSH, PARTICK: Company A, private, July 25, 1861 enlisted as a private in Captain J. B. Read's Independent Company, Georgia Infantry. January 25, 1862 mustered out. March 1, 1862 enlisted in Co. A, 11th Battalion as a private. May 12, 1862 transferred to Co. A, 47th Regiment. October 29, 1863 died of disease in Medical College Hospital, Atlanta, Georgia.

WALTON, JAMES: Company A, private, April 22, 1862 enlisted as private in Co. A, 11th Battalion. April 30, 1862 deserted at Savannah, Georgia.

WARD, THOMAS W.: Company E, private, March 4, 1862 enlisted as a private in Co. E, 11th Battalion. May 12, 1862 transferred to Co. E, 47th Regiment. July 10, 1862 died of disease.

WARD, WILLIAM A.: Company B, private, April 25, 1862 enlisted as a private in Co. B, 11th Battalion. May 12, 1862 transferred to Co. B, 47th Regiment. August 27, 1862 discharged furnished substitute.

WARNELL WILLIAM E: Company H, 2nd sergeant, March 4, 1862 elected. 2nd sergeant Company H, 11th Battalion. May 12, 1862 transferred to Co. H, 47th Regiment as 2nd sergeant. October 12, 1862 discharged furnished William Spell, as substitute.

WARNOCK, JAMES: Company F, private, April 29, 1862 enlisted as a private in Co. F, 11th Battalion. May 12, 1862 transferred to Co. F, 47th Regiment. November 1862 detailed as a Wagoner.

WARNOCK, W. H.: Company I, private, March 4, 1862 enlisted as a private in Co. I, 11th Battalion. May 12, 1862 transferred to Co. I, 47th

Regiment. December 10, 1863 captured in Effingham County, Georgia. September 14, 1863 took oath of allegiance to the United States Government and was sent north.

WARREN, JAMES M.: Company G, private, 1862 enlisted as a private in Co. G, 11th Battalion. May 12, 1862 transferred to Co. G, 47th Regiment. February 28, 1863 sick in Savannah, Georgia Hospital. November 1864 pension records show he was furloughed due to sickness and was unable to return to command before the close of the war. (Born in Tattnall County, Georgia February 1, 1830)

WATERS, ANDREW: Company A, 1st corporal. February 28, 1862 appointed 4th corporal., Co. A, 11th Battalion. May 12, 1862 transferred to Co. A, 47th Regiment as 4th corporal. June 12, 1862 Appointed 3rd corporal, Co. A. 47th Regiment. September 1, 1862 appointed 1st corporal Co. A, 47th Regiment. February 28, 1863, last on file, shows him present.

WATERS, JAMES M.: Company G, private, 1862 enlisted as a private in Co. G, 11th Battalion. May 12, 1862 transferred to Co. G, 47th Regiment. March 1, 1864 died of chronic diarrhoea in Dalton, Georgia (place and date of death also given as Jackson, Mississippi Hospital August 1, 1863)

WATERS, JOSEPH: Company G, 4th corporal. March 4, 1862 elected 4th corporal Co. G, 11th Battalion. May 12, 1862 transferred to Co. G, 47th regiment as 4th corporal. January 8, 1864 died of disease in Dalton, Georgia Hospital.

WATERS, MILLINTON, JR.: Company C, private, March 4, 1862 enlisted as a private in Co. C, 11th Battalion. May 12, 1862 transferred to Co. C, 47th Regiment. September -December 1862 absent without leave.

WATERS, MILLINNTO, SR.: Company C, private, March 4, 1862 enlisted as a private in Co. C, 11th Battalion. May 12, 1862 transferred to Co. C, 47th Regiment. February 28, 1863 roll, last on record, shows him present.

WATERS, REUBEN: Company D, private, March 4, 1862 enlisted as a private in Co. D, 11th Battalion. May 12, 1862 transferred to Co. D, 47th Regiment. July 2, 1862 died of brain disease at Camp Mackee.

WATERS, SIMON: Company C, private, March 4, 1862 enlisted as a private in Co. C, 11th Battalion. May 12, 1862 transferred to Co. C, 47th Regiment. November 25, 1863 wounded at Missionary Ridge, Tennessee. April 26, 1865 pension records indicate that he surrendered Greensboro, North Carolina.

WATERS, T. A.: Company C, 1st. corporal, March 4, 1862 appointed 3rd Corporal Co. C, 11th Battalion. May 12, 1862 transferred to Co. C, 47th Regiment. as 3rd corporal. November 22, 1862 appointed 1st corporal Co. C, 47th Regiment. November 25, 1863 wounded Missionary Ridge, Tennessee. At home, wounded at close of the war.

WATERS WAYNE D.: Company C, 3rd corporal, October 15, 1861 enlisted as a private in Co. G, 5th Regiment, Georgia State Troops. April 1862 mustered out. September 1, 1862 enlisted as a private in Co. C,

47th Regiment, Georgia Infantry. November 1862 appointed 3rd corporal Co. C, 47th Regiment. April 26, 1865 pension records show that he was wounded and in Greensboro, North Carolina Hospital. (Born in Bulloch County, Georgia, June 16, 1843)

WATSON, DANIEL: Company H, private, May 1, 1862 enlisted as a private in Co. H, 11th Battalion. May 12, 1862 transferred to Co. H, 47th Regiment. February 28, 1863 roll, last on record, shows him present.

WATSON, WILLIAM: Company H, private, March 4, 1862 enlisted as a private in Co. H, 11th Battalion. April 21, 1862 died at Camp Davis.

WATT, H. P.: Company I, private, March 4, 1862 enlisted as a private in Co. I, 11th Battalion. May 12, 1862 transferred to Co. I, 47th Regiment. January 2, 1864 in St. Mary's Hospital at LaGrange, Georgia. January 11, 1864 returned to duty.

WEATHERLY, OSCAR: Company F, private, March 4, 1862 enlisted as a private in Co. F, 11th Battalion. May 12, 1862 transferred to Co. F, 47th Regiment. October 31, 1863 roll, last on record, shows him present.

WEIDENCAMP, STEPHEN: Company G, private, March 4, 1862 enlisted as a private in Co. G, 11th Battalion. May 12, 1862 transferred to Co. G, 47th Regiment. February 28, 1863 roll, last on record, shows him present.

WELLS, HENRY C.: Company D, private, March 4, 1862 enlisted as a private in Co. D, 11th Battalion. May 12, 1862 transferred to Co. D, 47th Regiment. February 28, 1863 roll, last on record, shows him present. July 1863 detailed courier for Brigadier General Stovall. May 18, 1865 paroled at Augusta, Georgia. (Born in Georgia)

WELLS, MICHAEL: Company A, private, 1862 enlisted as a private in Co. C, 13th Regiment, Georgia Infantry in. (Listed as a substitute for W. A. Manes). May 30, 1862 Transferred to Co. A, 47th Regiment February 3, 1865 captured at River's Bridge, South Carolina (Union records show him as a deserter.) April 5, 1865 furnished transportation to Savannah, Georgia.

WELLS, THOMAS J.: Company D, private. March 4, 1862 enlisted as a private in Co. D, 11th Battalion. May 12, 1862 transferred to Co. D, 47th Regiment. November 18, 1862 discharged by civil authority.

WEST, CHARLES P.: Company B, private, April 25, 1862 enlisted as a private in Co. B, 11th Battalion. May 12, 1862 transferred to Co. B, 47th Regiment. July 15, 1862 discharged furnished Samuel W. Williams as substitute,

WESTBERRY, WILLIAM S.: Company C, private, March 4, 1862 enlisted as a private in Co. C, 11th Battalion. May 12, 1862 transferred to Co. C, 47th Regiment. November 25, 1863 wounded at Missionary Ridge, Tennessee. October 1864 furloughed for 60 days and sent to his home in Hamilton County, Florida. Records indicate that he was trying to reach his command at the close of the war. (Died in Hamilton County, Florida on October 4, 1873)

WHATLEY, JOHN E.: Company B, private, March 4, 1862 enlisted as a private in Co. B, 11th Battalion. May 12, 1862 transferred to Co. B, 47th Regiment. September 28, 1862 died of disease in Regimental Hospital, Camp Williams, Savannah, Georgia.

WHEELER, CHARLES M: Company F, private, April 27, 1862 enlisted as a private in Co. F, 11th Battalion. May 12, 1862 transferred to Co. F, 47th Regiment. August 1, 1862 transferred to Co. A. 1st Battalion, Georgia Sharpshooters. June 14, 1864 deserted.

WHEELER, HIRAM: Company I, private, March 4, 1862 enlisted as a private in Co. I, 11th Battalion. May 12, 1862 transferred to Co. I, 47th Regiment. November 29, 1863 admitted to Floyd House and Ocmulgee Hospitals at Macon, Georgia with chronic diarrhoea. (Born in Effingham County, Georgia October 25, 1838)

WHEELER, JOHN L.: Company F, private, March 4, 1862 enlisted as a private in Co. F, 11th Battalion.

WHEELER, THOMAS: Company I, private, March 4, 1862 enlisted as a private in Co. I, 11th Battalion. May 12, 1862 transferred to Co. I, 47th Regiment. February 5, 1865 admitted to C. S. A. General Hospital #11 at Charlotte, North Carolina. 1865 paroled at Charlotte, North Carolina. (Born in Effingham County, Georgia in 1831)

WHEELER, WILLIAM: Company F, private, April 22, 1862 enlisted as a private in Co. F, 11th Battalion. May 12, 1862 transferred to Co. F, 47th Regiment. July 30, 1862 transferred to Co. A. 1st Battalion, Georgia Sharpshooters. August 1864 roll, last on file, shows him detailed as Brigade Provost Guard Hospital.

WHEELER, WILLIAM J.: Company I, private, March 4, 1862 enlisted as a private in Co. I, 11th Battalion. May 12, 1862 transferred to Co. I, 47th Regiment. June 30, 1864 received pay. April 26, 1865 pension records show he surrendered at Greensboro, North Carolina. (Born in Effingham County, Georgia about 1821)

WHITAKER, JOHN V.: Company E, private, March 4, 1862 enlisted as a private in Co. E, 11th Battalion. May 12, 1862 transferred to Co. E, 47th Regiment. October 31, 1863 roll, last on record, shows him present. (Born in Surry County, North Carolina in 1824).

WHITE, JAMES: Company E, private, March 4, 1862 enlisted as a private in Co. E, 11th Battalion. May 12, 1862 transferred to Co. E, 47th Regiment. October 31, 1863 roll, last on record, shows him present.

WHITE, JOHN F.: Company F, private, April 26, 1862 enlisted as a private in Co. F, 11th Battalion. May 12, 1862 transferred to Co. F, 47th Regiment. November 7, 1862 absent without leave. (Born in Georgia)

WHITE, PATRICK: Company A, private, June 1, 1862 enlisted in Company A, 47th Regiment as a private. (Substitute for J. S. Neely. December 1862 appears on last roll with remark "Detailed on Gun Boat)

WHITTY, PETER: Company A, private, March 3, 1862 enlisted in Co. A, 11th Battalion as a private. May 12, 1862 transferred to Co. A, 47th

Regiment. June 30, 1863 in French's Division Hospital at Enterprise, Mississippi.

WIGGINS, JAMES: Hospital Staff, Assistant Surgeon. December 4, 1862 Appointed assistant surgeon 47th Regiment, to rank from August 29, 1862. September 24, 1863 serving as Assistant Surgeon at Fort McAllister, Georgia. December 13, 1864 captured at Fort McAllister, Georgia. January 1, 1865 sent across line with "Flag of Truce", at Devereaux Neck, South Carolina.

WILES, MACKLIN: Company I, private, March 4, 1862 enlisted as a private in Co. I, 11th Battalion. May 12, 1862 transferred to Co. I, 47th Regiment. February 3, 1864 died in camp near Dalton, Georgia.

WILES, JAMES C.: Company G, private, November 20, 1862 enlisted as a private in Co. G, 47th Regiment, Georgia Infantry. February 28, 1863 roll, last on record, shows him present. Pension records show he was at home on furlough at the close of the war.

WILEY, JAMES: Company F, private, March 4, 1862 enlisted as a private in Co. F, 11th Battalion. May 12, 1862 transferred to Co. F, 47th Regiment. October 31, 1863 roll, last on record, shows him present.

WILEY (WYLEY), ROBERT: Company D, private. March 4, 1862 enlisted as a private in Co. D, 11th Battalion. May 12, 1862 transferred to Co. D, 47th Regiment. February 28, 1863 roll, last on record, shows him present. May 29, 1865 paroled at Augusta, Georgia. February 1865 pension records show he was sent to Columbia, South Carolina Hospital with pneumonia. (Born in Screven County, Georgia)

WILEY (WYLEY), THOMAS: Company D, private, March 4, 1862 enlisted as a private in Co. D, 11th Battalion. May 12, 1862 transferred to Co. D, 47th Regiment. Wounded in the right lung. February 16, 1865 died of wounds at Post Hospital, Savannah, Georgia.

WILEY, WILLIAM G.: Company F, private, March 4, 1862 enlisted as a private in Co. F, 11th Battalion. May 12, 1862 transferred to Co. F, 47th Regiment. December 12, 1863 died.

WILKERSON, JESSE L.: Company B, private, July 1864 according to his pension records he enlisted as a private in Co. B, 47th Regiment, Georgia Infantry. March 21, 1865 wounded at Bentonville, North Carolina and was in the hospital in Thomasville, North Carolina at the close of the war. (Born in Baker County, Georgia in 1839.)

WILKES, GEORGE B.: Company G, private, March 4, 1862 enlisted as a private in Co. G, 11th Battalion. May 12, 1862 transferred to Co. G, 47th Regiment.

WILLIAMS, ALTAMOND: Company G, private, March 4, 1862 enlisted as a private in Co. G, 11th Battalion. May 12, 1862 transferred to Co. G, 47th Regiment. February 28, 1863 roll, last on record, shows him present. April 26, 1865 pension records show he surrendered at Greensboro, North Carolina

WILLIAMS, ARTHUR: Company E, private, March 4, 1862 enlisted as a private in Co. E, 11th Battalion. May 12, 1862 transferred to Co. E, 47th Regiment. October 31, 1863 roll, last on record, shows him present.

WILLIAMS, B.: Company C, private, March 4, 1862 enlisted as a private in Co. C, 11th Battalion. May 12, 1862 transferred to Co. C, 47th Regiment. June 28, 1862 died of disease in Augusta, Georgia Hospital.

WILLIAMS, BENJAMIN S.: Field Staff, Captain. August 14, 1861 appointed 1st corporal Co. F, 25th Regiment, October 22, 1861, 5th sergeant. April 21, 1862 appointed Adjutant 11th Battalion as lieutenant. May 12, 1862 transferred to 47th Regiment as private. May 12, 1862 appointed Adjutant 47th Regiment. Promoted to captain. March 1, 1863 Adjutant of the Post at Red Bluff. Appears without remark on roster for March 1865

WILLIAMS, EDWARD W.: Company G, Sergeant Major., March 4, 1862 enlisted as a private in Co. G, 11th Battalion. May 12, 1862 transferred to Co. G, 47th Regiment. Appointed Sergeant Major. February 28, 1863 roll, last on record, shows him present. May 23, 1865 paroled at Augusta, Georgia.

WILLIAMS, FRANCIS: Company E, private, August 17, 1862 enlisted as a private (substitute for S. A. Swilly) in Co. E, 47th Regiment, Georgia Infantry. Died prior to March 30, 1863.

WILLIAMS, G: Company I, Quartermaster sergeant, September 1, 1862 enlisted as a private in Co. I, 47th Regiment, Georgia Infantry. September 1, 1862 Appointed Quartermaster Sergeant.

WILLIAMS, GILBERT W. M.: Field Staff, Colonel, October 6, 1861 elected Captain of Company K, 6th Regiment, Georgia State Troops. October 25, 1861 elect major of 11th Battalion. March 22, 1862 elected Lieutenant Col. 11th Battalion. May 12, 1862 elected Col. 47th Regiment March 1, 1863 roll for March April 1863 commanding 47th Regiment at Red Bluff. August 30, 1863 Col. Gilbert W. M. Williams died in Mississippi.

WILLIAMS, HENRY: Company E, private, March 4, 1862 enlisted as a private in Co. E, 11th Battalion. May 12, 1862 transferred to Co. E, 47th Regiment. October 31, 1863 roll, last on record, shows him present.

WILLIAMS, J. G.: Company C, private, March 4, 1862 enlisted as a private in Co. C, 11th Battalion. May 12, 1862 transferred to Co. C, 47th Regiment. February 28, 1863 roll, last on record, shows him present.

WILLIAMS, J. J.: Company H, private. March 4, 1862 enlisted in Co. H, 11th Battalion. May 12, 1862 transferred to Co. H, 47th Regiment Georgia Infantry. May 17, 1862 discharged due to disability.

WILLIAMS, J. M.: Company K, private, May 6, 1862 enlisted as a private in Co. K, 47th Regiment. February 28, 1863 roll, last on record, shows him absent for 30 days on Surgeons Certificate.

WILLIAMS, JACKSON: Company F, private, July 22, 1862 enlisted as a private (substitute for Andrew H. Thomas) in Co. F, 47th Regiment, Georgia Infantry.

WILLIAMS, JAMES: Company F, private, March 4, 1862 enlisted as a private in Co. F, 11th Battalion. May 12, 1862 transferred to Co. F,

47th Regiment. October 31, 1863 roll, last on record, shows him present. July 9, 1864 pension records show he was wounded in the left shoulder at John's Island South Carolina. December 1864 pension records show he was wounded in the right arm at Coosawhatchie, South Carolina sent to Augusta, Georgia Hospital. At home on wounded furlough at the close of the war. (Born in Georgia)

WILLIAMS, JOHN: Company F, private, March 4, 1862 enlisted as a private in Co. F, 11th Battalion. May 12, 1862 transferred to Co. F, 47th Regiment. June 10, 1862 wounded at James Island South Carolina. November 10, 1862 died of wounds in Appling County, Georgia.

WILLIAMS, JOHN D.: Company C, 2nd sergeant. March 4, 1862 2nd sergeant Co. C, 11th Battalion. May 12, 1862 transferred to Co. C, 47th Regiment.as 2nd sergeant. December 3, 1863. Died in Fair Grounds Hospital #2, Atlanta, Georgia. Buried there at Oakland Cemetery.

WILLIAMS, JOSEPH J.: Company F, private, March 4, 1862 enlisted as a private in Co. F, 11th Battalion. May 12, 1862 transferred to Co. F, 47th Regiment. October 31, 1863 roll, last on record, shows him present.

WILLIAMS, L. E. M.: Company C, 2nd Lieutenant. April 4, 1862 appointed sergeant Co. C. 11th Battalion. May 12, 1862 transferred to Co. C. 47th Regiment as sergeant. December 8, 1862 elected Jr. 2nd Lieutenant Co. C, 47th Regiment. January 1863 detailed Recruiting Officer Co. C, 47th Regiment.

WILLIAMS, LORENZO H.: Company E, private, March 4, 1862 enlisted as a private in Co. E, 11th Battalion. May 12, 1862 transferred to Co. E, 47th Regiment. October 31, 1863 roll, last on record, shows him present. Pension records show April 26, 1865 he surrendered at Greensboro, North Carolina. (Born in South Carolina in 1833)

WILLIAMS, MATTHEW: Company C, private, March 4, 1862 enlisted as a private in Co. C, 11th Battalion. May 12, 1862 transferred to Co. C, 47th Regiment. September 17, 18962 discharged, under age.

WILLIAMS, NOAH: Company F, private, March 4, 1862 enlisted as a private in Co. F, 11th Battalion. May 12, 1862 transferred to Co. F, 47th Regiment. November 1862 shown on extra duty. February 10, 1865 pension records show he left command, at Rivers' Bridge, South Carolina, on 30 days furlough to go home to marry, and could not reach the command due to intervention of Sherman's Army. (Born in Georgia in 1838)

WILLIAMS, RICHARD: Company E, private, March 4, 1862 enlisted as a private in Co. E, 11th Battalion. May 12, 1862 transferred to Co. E, 47th Regiment. September 20, 1862 died.

WILLIAMS, ROBERT J.: Company C, 1st Lieutenant, September 9, 1861 enlisted as a private in Co. D, 61st Regiment, Georgia Infantry. June 27, 1862 wounded at Cold Harbor, Virginia. July 4, 1862 elected 1st Lieutenant Co. C, 47th Regiment. March 7, 1864 Williams resigned due to disability. April 19, 1864 resignation accepted. (Born in Georgia in 1838)

WILLIAMS, ROBERT M.: Company C, private, March 4, 1862 enlisted as a private in Co. C, 11th Battalion. May 12, 1862 transferred to Co. C, 47th Regiment. September 17, 1862 discharged, under age.

WILLIAMS, S. P.: Company C, 3rd sergeant, March 4, 1862 enlisted as a private in Co. C, 11th Battalion. May 12, 1862 transferred to Co. C, 47th Regiment. November 23, 1862 appointed 3rd Sergeant Co. C., 47th Regiment. December 12, 1863 died in Newsom Hospital, Cassville, Georgia.

WILLIAMS, SAMUEL W.: Company B, private. July 15, 1862 enlisted as a private in Co. B, 47th Regiment, Georgia Infantry as a substitute for Charles P. West. August 1863 in Breckenridge's Division Hospital at Marion, Mississippi.

WILLIAMS, W. B.: Company K, private. May 6, 1862 enlisted as a private in Co. K, 47th Regiment. December 15, 1862 died in Savannah, Georgia.

WILLIAMS, WILLIAM: Company D, private. March 4, 1862 enlisted as a private in Co. D, 11th Battalion. May 12, 1862 transferred to Co. D, 47th Regiment. February 28, 1863 roll, last on record, shows him present.

WILLIAMS, WILLIAM M.: Company K, 2nd sergeant, October 15, 1861 enlisted as a private of Co. G, 5th Regiment, Georgia State Troops. April 1862 mustered out. May 6, 1862 appointed 2nd sergeant Co. K, 47th Regiment. February 28, 1863 roll, last on record, shows him present.

WILLIAMS, WILLIAM W.: Company C, Captain, March 4, 1862 appointed Captain Co. C, 11th Battalion. May 12, 1862 transferred to Co. C, 47th Regiment, as Captain. June 10, 1862 killed at James Island, South Carolina. (Born December 27, 1823)

WILLIAMSON FRANCIS: Company E, private, March 30, 1863 died.

WILLIS, JAMES: Company A. private, March 4, 1862 enlisted in Co. A, 11th Battalion as a private. May 12, 1862 transferred to Co. A, 47th Regiment. May 20, 1864 captured at Cassville, Georgia. May 29, 1864 received at Military Prison at Louisville, Kentucky, from Nashville, Tennessee. July 1, 1864 received at Rock Island, Illinois prison. July 15, 1865 escaped from prison at Rock Island, Illinois.

WILLIS, JACOB E.: Company H, Private, May 1, 1862 in 11th Battalion. May 12, 1862 transferred to Co. H, 47th Regiment. Roll for February 1863 roll, last on file, shows him present. Pension records show he was at home on sick furlough December 1864, to close of war. (Born in Emanuel County, Georgia in 1834)

WILLIS, REUBEN: Company H, private, March 4, 1862. May 12, 1862 transferred to Company H, 47th Regiment, Georgia Infantry. November 28, 1863 admitted to Floyd House and Ocmulgee Hospitals at Macon, Georgia with intermittent fever.

WILLIS, (SEEB) SEBRON D.: Company H, private, May 1, 1862 enlisted as a private in Co. H, 11th Battalion. May 12, 1862 transferred to Co. H, 47th Regiment Georgia infantry. Roll for February 1863, last on file shows him present.

WILLIS SHERROD: Company H, private, May 1, 1863 enlisted as a private in Co. H, 11th Battalion. May 12, 1862 transferred to Co. H, 47th Regiment, Georgia Infantry. Roll for February 1863 Last on file, shows him absent in arrest. Salt book for Montgomery County, Georgia indicates that his wife (he married in 1864 after returning from the Atlanta Campaign) received a salt ration as the wife of a soldier in 1864.

WILSON, A. J.: Company I, private, July 25, 1864 enlisted as a private in Co. I, 47th Regiment. September 26, 1864 discharged, disabled by heart disease, at Charleston, South Carolina. (Born in Effingham County, Georgia in 1840)

WILSON, ALLEN: Company C., private, March 4, 1862 enlisted as a private in Co. C, 11th Battalion. May 12, 1862 transferred to Co. C, 47th Regiment. June 10, 1862 killed James Island, South Carolina.

WILSON, D. E.: Company I, private, March 4, 1862 enlisted as a private in Co. I, 11th Battalion. May 12, 1862 transferred to Co. I, 47th Regiment. June 6, 1863 died in Jackson Mississippi Hospital

WILSON, GEORGE W.: Company H, private, March 4, 1862 enlisted Co. H, 11th Battalion. Never reported at camp.

WILSON, HENRY H.: Company I, 2nd corporal. March 4, 1862 enlisted as a private in Co. I, 11th Battalion. May 12, 1862 transferred to Co. I, 47th Regiment. December 14, 1862 appointed 2nd corporal, Co. I, 47th Regiment. March, 1863 - April 1864 detailed as nurse, Lee Hospital at Lauderdale Springs, Mississippi.

WILSON, J. W.: Company I, private, March 4, 1862 enlisted as a private in Co. I, 11th Battalion. May 12, 1862 transferred to Co. I, 47th Regiment. October 24, 1862 discharged at Camp Williams, Georgia by civil authority.

WILSON, STEPHEN ALFRED: Company I, Captain March 4, 1862 elected 2nd Lieutenant Co. I, 11th Battalion May 12, 1862, transferred to Co. I, 47th Regiment as 1st Lieutenant. February 13, 1863 Wilson elected Captain Co. I. June 27, 1864, wounded at Kennesaw Mt., Georgia. September 25, 1864 report dated this date from James Island, South Carolina shows him absent, sick in hospital since June 16, 1864.

WILSON VIN BENJAMIN: Company C, 2nd Lieutenant, March 4, 1862 enlisted as a private in Co. B, 11th Battalion. April 4, 1862 appointed 2nd Lt Co. C, 11th Battalion.

WISE, JOHN: Company K, 1st corporal. May, 6, 1862 Appointed 1st Corporal, Co. K, 47th Regiment. February 28, 1863 roll, last on record, shows him "Absent as Enrolling Officer for 20 days beginning the 15th instant. "

WISE, WILLIAM H.: Company C, 1st. corporal, March 4, 1862 appointed 1st corporal Co. C, 11th Battalion. May 12, 1862 transferred to Co. C, 47th Regiment as 1st corporal. November 22, 1862 transferred to Co. K, 47th Regiment. November 30, 1864 wounded in left arm, resulting in amputation at Honey Hill, South Carolina. December 22, 1864 admitted in 2nd. Division, 20th Army Corps Hospital. January 16, 1865 sent to General Hospital. (Born in Georgia November 9, 1823)

WOLFE, SAMUEL: Company B, private, December 11, 1862 enlisted as a private in Co. B, 47th Regiment, Georgia Infantry as a substitute for William T. Amoss. February 28, 1863 detailed in Quartermaster Department, Savannah, Georgia. May 11, 1863 detailed as harness maker, Camp. Allen, South Carolina.

WOODCOCK, N. W.: Company K, private, May 6, 1862 enlisted as a private in Co. K, 47th Regiment. April 26, 1865 surrendered at Greensboro, North Carolina.

WOODCOCK, R.: Company K, private, May 6, 1862 enlisted as a private in Co. K, 47th Regiment. February 28, 1863 roll, last on record, shows him present.

WOODHOUSE, ROBERT: Field Staff, Musician, May 31, 1862 appointed Musician. December 1872 shows him present.

WOODHOUSE, WILLIAM: Field Staff, Musician, May 31, 1862 appointed Musician. December 1872 shows him present.

WOODMAN, HARRY G.: Company B, private, March 4, 1862 enlisted as a private in Co. B, 11th Battalion.

WOODMAN, JESSE M.: Company B, private, March 4, 1862 enlisted as a private in Co. B, 11th Battalion. May 12, 1862 transferred to Co. B, 47th Regiment. October 17, 1863 died at Atlanta, Georgia. (Buried there in Oakland Cemetery)

WOODSON, ELIAS: Company F, private, December 22, 1864 wounded and captured at Savannah, Georgia. January 9, 1865 died of wounds.

WOODWARD, ROBERT: Company B, private. March 4, 1862 enlisted as a private in Co. D, 11th Battalion. May 12, 1862 transferred to Co. D, 47th Regiment. February 28, 1863 roll, last on record, shows him present.

WRENN, JAMES M.: Company G, 2nd sergeant, March 4, 1862 elected 2nd sergeant, Co. G, 11th Battalion, May 12, 1862 transferred to Co. F, 47th Regiment. September 20, 1863 captured at Chickamauga, Georgia. June 15, 1865 released.

YAWN, CALVIN: Company F, private, April 29, 1862 enlisted as a private in Co. F, 11th Battalion. May 12, 1862 transferred to Co. F, 47th Regiment. June 2, 1863 died in General Hospital #1, Savannah Georgia.

YAWN, DAVID: Company F, private, March 4, 1862 enlisted as a private in Co. F, 11th Battalion. May 12, 1862 transferred to Co. F, 47th Regiment. October, 1862 died of disease subsequent to this date.

YAWN, LEWIS: Company F, private. July 31, 1862 enlisted as a private (substitute for John Cook) in Co. F, 47th Regiment, Georgia Infantry. October 31, 1863 roll, last on record, shows him present.

YAWN, URIAH N.: Company F, private, 1863 enlisted as a private in Co. F, 47th Regiment, Georgia Infantry. Pension records show he was on detail duty in Virginia at the close of the war.

YEOMANS, JOHN L.: Company G, private, August 1, 1862 enlisted (substitute for John H. Clifton) as a private in Co. G, 47th Regiment, Georgia Infantry. September 2, 1863 furloughed from Breckinridge's Division Hospital #1 at Lauderdale Springs, Mississippi. Died prior to March 22, 1864.

YOUMANS, HASFORD: Company G, private. February 22, 1863 died of disease at Wilmington, North Carolina.

YOUMANS, JOHN L.: Company G, private. March 22, 1864 died.

YOUMANS, HANSFORD: Company G, private, March 4, 1862 enlisted as a private in Co. G, 11th Battalion. May 12, 1862 transferred to Co. G, 47th Regiment. February 22, 1863 died of disease at Wilmington, North Carolina.

YOUMANS, JOHN R.: Company G, private, March 4, 1862 enlisted as a private in Co. G, 11th Battalion. May 12, 1862 transferred to Co. G, 47th Regiment. November 29, 1863 admitted to Floyd House and Ocmulgee Hospitals at Macon, Georgia.

YOUMANS, REDDING: Company G, private, April 21, 1862 enlisted as a private in Co. G, 11th Battalion. April 27, 1862 rejected by Surgeon. October 9, 1862 discharged at Camp Williams, Georgia.

YOUMANS RICHARD M.: Company F, sergeant major. March 4, 1862 enlisted as a private in Co. F, 11th Battalion. May 12, 1862 transferred to Co. F, 47th Regiment. June 10, 1862, wounded at James Island, South Carolina. September 1862 shown as a private on picket duty at Proctor's Point, South Carolina.

YOUNG, JOHN C.: Company B, private, March 1862 enlisted as a private in Co. B, 11th Battalion. Absent without leave.

ZANE, NOAH: Company B, private, November 27, 1862 enlisted as a private in Co. B, 47th Regiment, Georgia Infantry as a substitute for John T. George. February 28, 1863 roll, last on record, shows him present,

References

Roster of the confederate Soldiers of Georgia 1861 - 1865, Volume III, by Lillian Henderson

Pioneers of Wiregrass Georgia, Volume 1-7, by Judge Folks Huxford. Volumes 8-9, by the Huxford Genealogical Society.

The War of the Rebellion: A Compilation of the Official Records of the Union and the Confederate Armies.

Historical Times - Illustrated Encyclopedia of the Civil War, Patricia L. Faust, Editor

The Civil War - the American Iliad, by Otto Eisenschiml and Ralph Newman

Our Heritage, Volumes I - IV, by Mary Ketus Holland

The Tuten Family, by Mary Ketus Holland and Allen Vernon Tuten

Footprints in Appling County, by Ruth T. Barron

Historical Society Papers, edited by Rev J. William Jones, D. D., Secretery - Southern Historical Society

Confederate Military History, edited by General Clement A. Evans of Georgia

Battles and Leaders of the Civil War, Castle

Units of the Confederate States Army, by Joseph H. Crute, Jr.

United Daughters of the Confederacy, bound typescripts

Those Gallant Georgians who Served in The War Between the States, by Jimmy E. Arnsdorff

Historical Sketch and Roster, Ga 47th Infantry Regiment, by John Rigdon

The Barefoot Confederate, by Dixon Hollingsworth

THANKS TO:

Charlotte Ray, Georgia Department of Archives and History - Atlanta, Ga.

Dan Bell, South Carolina State Park Service, Rivers Bridge State Park, Rivers Bridge, South Carolina

Emory University Rare Book Collection, Emory University, Atlanta, Georgia

Duke University, Perkins Rare Manuscript Collection

Kathy Shoemaker, Associate Reference Archivist, Special Collections, Woodruff Library, Emory University, Atlanta, GA

THANKS ALSO TO THE STAFF AT THE FOLLOWING STATE AND NATIONAL BATTLEFIELDS:

Chickamauga Battlefield

Kennesaw Mountain Battlefield

Rivers Bridge Battlefield

Bibliography

Dan Bell, South Carolina State Park Service, Rivers Bridge State Park, Rivers Bridge, South Carolina

Emory University Rare Book Collection, Emory University, Atlanta, Georgia

Duke University, Perkins Rare Manuscript Collection

Kathy Shoemaker, Associate Reference Archivist, Special Collections, Woodruff Library, Emory University, Atlanta, GA 30322-2870

Charleston County Public Library, Charleston, South Carolina

The 47th Georgia Flag returned to the State of Georgia

Appendix

The Return of the 47th Georgia Volunteer Infantry Flag to its Home After 135 years

Early in 1998 as I researched the 47th Georgia Volunteer Infantry for available information I came across an interesting piece of news. I learned the Adjutant of the Regiment, Captain Benjamin S. Williams, had hidden the flag under his saddle at the surrender in North Carolina on April 26, 1865 and had brought it back to his home in Savannah, Georgia. I further learned that his mother had made the flag.

I had also learned that his last living, unmarried daughter had given the flag to the Rivers Bridge State Park in South Carolina, the site of a battle where the 47th Georgia was prominent in the center as Sherman's forces attacked around the bridge and were first repulsed greatly in part by the galling fire from the 47th. The flag had been on display but had been recently stolen in a break in. The culprit was caught and the flag recovered along with an 1865 South Carolina State flag. After the recovery the flags were transported to Columbia for safe keeping.

Derwood, my cousin, who was in our SCV camp and was descended from 47th Georgians checked on a trip to Columbia and not only found the location but was able to touch and photograph it.

I then got in touch with one of Captain Ben's brothers grandchildren and was in communication with her in Utah along with another of her cousins. We all agreed that the flag should reside in Georgia which it had not since Captain Ben moved to Brunson South Carolina not long after the war.

The Williams descendants asked if I could check on how to get it to Georgia, to find the best place for the flag to be located and who would be the contact person. My inclination was that the flag should be in the Georgia Historical Society collection in Savannah or in the Capital Flag Collection in Atlanta.

When I found that the Capital Collection had means to preserve and protect the flags better I then contacted Mrs. Dorothy Olson who was in charge of the capital collection. We had many emails between the three of us and the man in South Carolina in charge of the flag.

It was finally decided that the flag would be given over to the State of Georgia and a reproduction be made by the Williams Family and presented to the Rivers Bridge State Park to be on permanent display.

On May 5, 2000 (South Carolina's Confederate Memorial Day) The Lt. Governor of the State of South Carolina presented the flag to an Honor Guard of descendants of 47th Georgians who were dressed out in their Confederate Uniforms. I had the privilege of being a part of that Honor Guard along with Derwood, the cousin who had made the trip to Columbia.

The flag now resides in the Capital Collection in the Georgia Capital in Atlanta. The flag has been completely restored and is rotated as are all the flags to protect them from being damaged by the light. It can be viewed on the Georgia Secretary of State's website along with all the other flags in the collection including all the flags returned to Georgia by the Federal government.

This event and result ranks as one of the top accomplishments of my life.

William A. Bowers, Jr.

Index of Captain Ben Williams Letters and Articles

Letter About 47th Flag and Brief Account of 47th's Involvement March 27, 1907	1
The Charleston Sunday News and Courier, Charleston, South Carolina, August 31, 1913 The Battle at Secessionville, South Carolina – June 16, 1862	6
The Sunday News, Charleston South Carolina – October 15, 1911 March 1863	12
The Sunday News, Charleston South Carolina – October 1, 1911 Savannah Georgia to Jackson Mississippi April 1863	15
The Sunday News, Charleston South Carolina – October 29, 1911 The Battle at Chickamauga, – September 20, 1863	20
The Sunday News, Charleston South Carolina – November 12, 1911 The Battle at Chattanooga	24
The Sunday News, Charleston South Carolina – December 10, 1911 Missionary Ridge and Lookout Mountain	32
The Sunday News, Charleston South Carolina – January 28, 1912 Cassville	38
The Sunday News, Charleston South Carolina – March 16, 1912 Beginning of 1864 Campaign	47
The Sunday News, Charleston South Carolina - April 14, 1912 Resacca	50
The Sunday News, Charleston South Carolina – October 12, 1913 Kennesaw Mountain	58
The Sunday News, Charleston South Carolina – September 17, 1911	64
The Sunday News, Charleston South Carolina – May 12, 1912	71
The Sunday News, Charleston South Carolina – June 9, 1912 Marietta. Georgia	76
The Sunday News, Charleston South Carolina – August 17, 1913 Death of Polk	84
The Sunday News, Charleston South Carolina – July 14, 1912 Camp of Invalid – Macon, Georgia	89
The Sunday News, Charleston South Carolina – August 18, 1912 Stoneman's Raid	100
The Charleston Sunday News and Courier, Charleston, South Carolina, October 26, 1913 September and October 1864	109
Charleston Sunday News and Courier, September 21, 1913	113

James Island August 1864

The Sunday News, Charleston South Carolina – November 9, 1913 Grahamville ... 120

The State: Columbia S. C., Sunday Morning, September 4, 1921 ... 124

The Sunday News and Courier, Charleston, South Carolina, September 5, 1897 ... 131

The Sunday News and Courier, Charleston, South Carolina, November 23, 1913 ... 139

The News and Courier, Monday Morning, Charleston South Carolina July 26, 1897 Honey Hill ... 148

The Sunday News, Charleston South Carolina – January 25, 1914 ... 152

The Sunday News, Charleston South Carolina – February 1, 1914 Tulifinney ... 157

The Sunday News, Charleston South Carolina – December 21, 1913 Before Rivers Bridge ... 159

The Charleston Sunday News and Courier, Charleston, South Carolina, January 11, 1914 Rivers Bridge ... 167

The Charleston Sunday News and Courier, Charleston, South Carolina, February 22, 1914 Avreysboro ... 176

The Charleston Sunday News and Courier, Charleston, South Carolina, January 10, 1915 Before Bentonville ... 182

The Charleston Sunday News and Courier, Charleston, South Carolina, March 8, 1914 ... 188

The Charleston Sunday News and Courier, Charleston, South Carolina, May 2, 1915 ... 195

The Charleston Sunday News and Courier, Charleston, South Carolina, April 4, 1915 ... 200

The Charleston Sunday News and Courier, Charleston, South Carolina, November 19, 1916 ... 205

The Flag Returned to Georgia

About the Author

William A. Bowers, Jr. was born August 5, 1947 in Saint Augustine, Florida to William Alfred Bowers, Sr. and Lora Elizabeth Tuten. When he was young his family returned to Baxley, Appling County, Georgia where he lived, was raised and educated. He is a 1965 graduate of Appling County High School, an Eagle Scout and is retired from the Georgia Department of Transportation as an Area Engineer in South Georgia. He is married to Anna Deloris Willis of Toombs County. He is a member of the First United Methodist Church in Baxley, Georgia.

For the last 20 years he has been involved in researching Confederate Units, battles and genealogy. Bill has been to almost all the places that the 47th fought and has stood where they stood in his research of this unit. He has given speeches across South Georgia concerning those Confederate units and their part in the War for Southern Independence. He resides still in Appling County and has served as a scout leader for 30 years, an officer in the Appling Grays Camp #918 Sons of Confederate Veterans, the Appling County Board of Education, the First United Methodist Church Administrative Board and the Appling County Heritage Center Board of Directors.

www.ingramcontent.com/pod-product-compliance
Lightning Source LLC
Chambersburg PA
CBHW071952290426
44109CB00018B/1992